WIDE ACCLAIM FOR MIRIAM WEINSTEIN'S

# MAKING A DIFFERENCE
# COLLEGE & GRADUATE GUIDE

"Buy this book. It's the bible for students who seek higher education for higher purposes — one of the most practical and insightful college selection resources today."

Marcy Hamilton, College Counselor, CA

"Profiles hidden gem colleges that most students should know about but rarely do. It is *the* college guide for idealistic students, and fills a tremendous need"

Marty Nemko, College Counselor; *Cool Careers for Dummies*

"Commitment to community and caring about both our human and physical environments should be critical components of a student's educational experience. We feel fortunate to be considered with other colleges that emphasize consciousness about and responsibility for the future of our world."

Richard H. Shaw Jr., Dean of Admissions, Yale University

"Our nation is fortunate that so many of its youth seek to contribute to a more just and sustainable future. And fortunate, as well, are the students, parents, and college counselors who get this book. The institutions profiled within offer academic preparation that enables students to promote social justice and environmental protection. And the guide is not only idealistic, but also pragmatically career-oriented so that students can go on to make a difference in the context of a decent job."

Richard Clugston, Exec. Director, Center for Respect of Life & Environment

"Until the emergence of *Making A Difference College Guide*, high school students who care about the world blindly faced a bewildering array of questionable college options, but not anymore. Even thumbing through this book, you'll wonder how any intelligent student, parent, or guidance counselor could do without it." *Green Teacher Magazine*

"So many students are being directed into corporate and business life which is soulless and will not serve their future. This extremely important book, however, could help them assist in saving the Planet." Dr. Helen Caldicott

"What an amazing feat this guide has accomplished! First it harnesses the idealism of today's college bound youth, next it points them to relevant, value-based education, often filled with service programs — whether in local communities or abroad, and then tops it off with practical yet meaningful career-oriented studies!"

Youth Service America

"Weinstein targets those students who are dissatisfied with the prospects of a traditional, passive, and one-dimensional approach to higher education. Interesting, informative and well-written, this book can make a difference for us all."

*Journal of College Admission*

MORE. . . .

WIDE ACCLAIM FOR MIRIAM WEINSTEIN'S
# MAKING A DIFFERENCE
# COLLEGE & GRADUATE GUIDE

"*Making A Difference College Guide* is distinctive in that its criteria focus on what should be the fundamental purpose of our campuses: launching students, with heart and mind, to enhance life for present and future generations. The Guide's value-centered approach to college selection fulfills a much needed demand."
Doug Orr, President, Warren Wilson College

"Deserves to be on the shelf of every career counselor in the country."
*Career Planning & Adult Development Network Newsletter*

"Lights the path to a values-based education." *College Bound*

"Through I*EARN Global Telecommunications Network, high school students collaborate internationally on projects that make a meaningful difference in the health and welfare of the planet and its people. Afterwards, students are hungry to build on their experience and commitment in both college and career. Ms. Weinstein's book is the first resource to which we point them."
Edwin Gragert, Ph.D. Executive Director, I*EARN

"Thanks for making this book available. It is exactly like the kind of information I've been killing myself trying to track down in the library." Ed Lawson, VA

"The Exxon oil spill, the vanishing rain forests, and the starving children in Rwanda all made you want to throw out your homework and pitch in. But first you had to finish high school. Now it's time for college, and with this guide's help in finding socially aware colleges, you may actually get that chance to help save the world."
*Detroit Free Press*

"Three of our children have found wonderful colleges through this guide that we would have never known about otherwise. Our children are inspired, and as parents, we are most grateful." Richard & Marie Mermin, CA

"Most college students attend massive state universities because their peers and elders consider it the only option. This guide allowed me to find a smaller, more alternative college with a friendly atmosphere, a family-like structure and wonderful professors who enjoy their occupation. Ms. Weinstein's book led me to the path of a higher education."
Amy Mermin, CA

"Recommended. In spirit the Guide resembles the *Whole Earth Catalog*."
*American Library Association Booklist*

"How wonderful it is that nobody need wait a single
moment before starting to improve the world."
— Anne Frank

"Anyone can be great, because anyone can serve."
— Martin Luther King Jr.

"It's better to light a candle than to curse the darkness."
— Eleanor Roosevelt

"When I was young, I was quite idealistic. We had the freedom in those days to
be idealistic and not necessarily to have to produce immediate results....
But the reality is, you don't have the time, the world doesn't have the time,
for the sort of idealism my generation enjoyed. You have to be so much
more practical than we had to be at your age. You must look at your idealism
and not compromise it. And yet, you must also be wise enough and
smart enough and patient enough to know how to go by steps...."
— Theresa Heinz, Heinz Family Fdn.
Campus Earth Summit remarks

"To be free is to be able to enjoy the fruits of life in
a just, caring, and compassionate community."
— Abraham Heschel

"If we really want the next millennium to be happier, more peaceful and more
harmonious for humankind we will have to make the effort to make it so.
This is in our hands, but especially in the hands of the younger generation.
Along with education, which generally deals only with academic accomplishments,
we need to develop more altruism and a sense of caring and responsibility
for others in the minds of the younger generation studying in various educational
institutions. One could therefore call this 'secular ethics', as it in fact consists
of basic human qualities such as kindness, compassion, sincerity and honesty.
We need to address the issue of the gap between the rich and the poor,
both globally and nationally. For the sake of our future generations,
we need to take care of our earth and of our environment."
— The 13th Dalai Lama
Millenium Address

"Religions are too pious, the corporations too plundering, the
government too subservient to provide any adequate remedy. In
this situation, the university has a special role... to reorient
the human community toward a greater awareness that the human
exists with the single great community of the planet Earth."
— Thomas Berry

SEVENTH EDITION

# MAKING A DIFFERENCE

# COLLEGE & GRADUATE GUIDE

## MIRIAM WEINSTEIN

NEW SOCIETY PUBLISHERS

**Cataloguing in Publication Data:**
A catalog record for this publication is available from the National Library of Canada.

Cover design by Miriam MacPhail, with Miriam Weinstein.

Printed in Canada on acid-free, partially recycled (20 percent post-consumer) paper using soy-based inks by Transcontinental/Best Book Manufacturers.

New Society Publishers acknowledges the support of the Government of Canada through the Book Publishing Industry Development Program (BPIDP) for our publishing activities, and the assistance of the Province of British Columbia through the British Columbia Arts Council.

BRITISH
COLUMBIA
ARTS COUNCIL
Supported by the Province of British Columbia

Paperback ISBN: 0-86571-412-6

Inquiries regarding requests to reprint all or part of *Making A Difference College & Graduate Guide* should be addressed to New Society Publishers at the address below.

Published in cooperation with Sageworks Press: www.making-a-difference.com
sageworks@igc.org

To order directly from the publishers, please add $4.00 shipping to the price of the first copy, and $1.00 for each additional copy (plus GST in Canada). Send check or money order to:

New Society Publishers
P.O. Box 189, Gabriola Island, BC V0R 1X0, Canada

New Society Publishers aims to publish books for fundamental social change through nonviolent action. We focus especially on sustainable living, progressive leadership, and educational and parenting resources. Our full list of books can be browsed on the worldwide web at: http://www.newsociety.com

NEW SOCIETY PUBLISHERS
Gabriola Island BC, Canada

*For my children,*
*Radha, Elam, Pascal, and Mira*
*and to native peoples struggling to maintain*
*their cultures and their lands.*

# CONTENTS

## MAKING A DIFFERENCE COLLEGES

## MAKING A DIFFERENCE GRADUATE PROGRAMS

## RESOURCES & INDEXES

# ACKNOWLEDGMENTS

I'D LIKE TO GIVE MY SINCEREST APPRECIATION to Marty Nemko, who was a gracious mentor in many arenas. Thanks to my childhood neighborhood - The Amalgamated — a hotbed of social consciousness, and to my beloved friend Joanne Lukomnik who dragged me along on so many picket lines and demonstrations. Helen Gibbs, thank you and Bob for your friendship and listening to my many complaints! Thanks to Aftab Choudhary for his calm generosity. I am indebted to the gracious thinkers and organizations for contributing essays and, in particular, I am honored to have thoughts from Matthew Fox , Jeremy Rifkin, and David Orr.

I appreciate the permission from the Peace Corps to include their Master's Internationalist and Fellows Programs. I am especially grateful for the enthusiastic reception, cooperation, and faith I've received from the colleges and programs profiled in the guide, and for the valuable service they render.

I'm very pleased that this edition is being co-published by New Society Publishers — what a gift to have an association with people of like vision and wonderful integrity — thank you Chris Plant for sharing my belief in the value of this guide, and for your remarkable decency.

I've received valuable feedback from a superlative board of advisors: Anthony Cortese of Second Nature; Rick Clugston of University Leaders for a Sustainable Future; Robert Hackett of the Bonner Foundation; Professor David Orr of Oberlin; Professor Milly Henry of the New College of California; author and career counselor Marty Nemko; Pam Boylan of Campus Compact, and Stephen Antonoff, author and career counselor.

Thanks to my children for being my inspiration, and lastly, heartfelt gratitude to Mother Earth who sustains us all.

# PREFACE

## WALTER H. CORSON

### GLOBAL TOMORROW COALITION

DAILY WE SEE MOUNTING SOCIAL AND ENVIRONMENTAL PROBLEMS that threaten our communities and the survival of our global life-support systems. These problems underscore the need for an education that sheds light on the underlying causes of issues such as poverty, unemployment, and crime; and ecological concerns such as environmental pollution and natural resource depletion.

Miriam Weinstein's *Making A Difference College & Graduate Guide* moves well beyond the traditional guides and highlights a wide range of innovative, programs and courses that provide practical, problem-solving approaches to some of the great issues of our time — issues that may ultimately imperil our future survival.

The book features colleges and universities that, through their development of programs and selection of faculty, demonstrate a concern for social responsibility, the quality of life, and the future of humankind. Most entries contain a description of the institution's philosophy and its approach to social and environmental concerns, and provide summaries of key programs designed to "make a difference."

The *Guide* highlights innovative programs at more traditional universities such as Tufts, Michigan, and Oregon; at well-known colleges such as Oberlin, St. Olaf, and Swarthmore, at less-known but valuable institutions such as Warren Wilson, Earlham and Prescott, and tiny but unique programs such as the Institute for Social Ecology, and the School for International Training.

A wide range of practical programs leading to good employment opportunities are covered in areas such as forestry, applied environmental technology, environmental engineering, natural resource management, community health, and social work.

The publication is obviously a labor of love; Miriam Weinstein is committed to promoting critical values needed for the twenty-first century such as environmental protection, conflict resolution, and social equity. *Making A Difference College & Graduate Guide* reveals educational programs that will help students make the planet a better place for themselves and for future generations.

*Walter Corson is a Senior Associate at Global Tomorrow Coalition, a not-for-profit alliance of nearly 100 U.S. organizations, institutions, corporations, and individuals committed to acting today to assure a more sustainable, equitable, and humane global future.*

# INTRODUCTION

## MIRIAM WEINSTEIN

YOU KNOW WHY YOU CHOSE THIS COLLEGE GUIDE, now let me tell you how I got to write it. I didn't decide to write this book, this book picked me. It picked me because I was committed to healing the Earth, to healing people. I'm not an expert on education. I'm not a college counselor. I'm a mother of four, armed with an "empowering" education from one of the colleges in this guide, which, like you, cares deeply about life on earth. Back in 1988, while doing a college search with my eldest child, I scoured the college guides and the viewbooks, and wondered if we were living on the same troubled planet! I figured there had to be more out there. The good news is the answer is yes, there are colleges committed to the environment, social change and service. Some of the colleges which offer a relevant, values-based education are true hidden treasures; others are among the nation's most prestigious.

This edition is graced with essays by three seminal, inspirational thinkers and doers: Matthew Fox on *From Wisdom to Knowledge*, Jeremy Rifkin on *Rethinking the Mission of American Education* and David Orr on *What Is Education For?* I urge you all, particularly parents, to read their thought provoking words. There is much to chew on in all the introductory essays — from national student and college organizations, from activist groups, and more.

And you, college seekers, do you feel your life has a purpose; do you have a desire to make a difference? Do you ask yourself what kind of meaningful work awaits you? Maybe you want to become a lawyer working to prevent logging of the last ancient forests in North America, or a policy planner helping to decide how to best protect the water supply and still meet the needs of farmers and wildlife. Maybe you'd like to help inner city kids make it through college. Perhaps you'll do that by becoming a wealthy dot-commer and giving money through philanthropy. Maybe you'll write about indigenous cultures and help protect them and their knowledge. Maybe you don't have a clue, you just know you want to make a difference. But you correctly sense that the right college education can be a significant factor.

For you then, choosing a college involves very different questions than the standard "Will I get a good name education?" "How's the football?" "Will I get a high paying job?" Your questions are also: "Will this college help me discover my calling?" "Will this college provide me with the tools to make a better world?" and "Does this college support my values?" Use this book to find a college where you're not strange because you want to make a better world, where one-third or even 100% of the students are actively involved in community service. You'll also discover that most colleges in this guide are committed to and actively engaged in helping solve our world's complex and pressing needs, both in and out of the classroom.

When considering a college, of course you'll look at academic caliber, location, majors and courses, and accessibility of professors. But also learn if it has an ethic of service, concerns for peace and social justice, an environmental focus, and how these concerns are brought into the classroom and the world. Then ask yourself — will this college give me what I need in order to fulfill my purpose? The nearly 100 profiled herein can give you the skills, tools, self-trust, and connections you'll need. Read the profiles and find which colleges are most consistent with your values and goals. Pick out several that pique your interest. Then seriously start checking the colleges out to see if they are really a good fit for you. Use Martin Nemko's *College Report Card* to evaluate a college's fit. Take advantage of *How To Test Drive A College* to learn how to conduct an educated armchair tour that can be as valuable as a real tour.

The spectrum of colleges profiled in this guide is truly unique. There are colleges dedicated to peace and social justice (i.e. Quaker and Mennonite,) strongly environmental colleges (i.e., Northland, Green Mountain, Unity,) and a Buddhist college (Naropa.) There are work colleges (i.e. Goddard and Warren Wilson,) international colleges (Friends World) and travel programs (i.e. Audubon, Living Routes and International Honors.) You'll find colleges on islands at opposite ends of the country (College of the Atlantic and Sheldon Jackson.) At "60's colleges" such as Evergreen or Hampshire you can take courses taught by teams of teachers from different disciplines, or design you own major incorporating your own interests in your own particular way, or take service-learning courses. Many offer a holistic approach to education.

What else is different? At these distinctive campuses you'll find opportunities to learn while doing service. Imagine working in a health clinic in a remote part of Nepal, assisting migrant laborers in the South, teaching sustainable agriculture in Central America, or building water cisterns at a school in the African countryside. You might help monitor a local river for pollution, save a threatened species such as the peregrine falcon, or sail on a clipper ship to study marine mammals. You might design affordable housing or erect an ecological straw bale building. You can spend study in rainforests, student-teach at Native American reservations, tutor inner city kids, or have a say in local development plans.

This is the kind of education your parents would likely have died for! But if your parents are worried that this doesn't sound sufficiently academic, put their fears to rest. Many educators consider this the most effective kind of learning, and it's blossoming in schools, colleges and universities nationwide. While the potential for awakening students to the value of social change is tremendous, in many cases, such service becomes a "feel good" experience. And while valuable for the student in terms of moral development, and valuable for the recipient in terms of help received, often these programs amount to no more than a bandaid approach. The intent of this guide is to take the next step — from feel good service to deep-rooted pervasive social change and environmental stewardship. Finally, college students who are out of the ivory tower get experience, the opportunity to try out their career interests, and valuable contacts which often turn into a job offer upon graduation.

From the smallest hidden-gem college to the prestigious Ivy Leagues, every school in this guide has something valuable to offer you. Many socially committed colleges are small, undergraduate-centered, and have approachable faculty who care more about teaching than research. They generally have fewer students per class, resulting in more personal attention. Universities, on the other hand, offer a mind-boggling array of majors, star professors, greater opportunities to participate in advanced research, vast resources, and often a more diverse student body.

While some schools in this guide characterize themselves as only moderately, or even non-selective in their admissions process, be aware that selectivity is a function of the number of applications received as well as academic difficulty. It is not always a direct reflection of a quality undergraduate education. It doesn't matter how prestigious or selective a college is, what matters is if it is the *right* college for *you*. This is why selectivity classifications are no longer listed herein.

As you read this guide, you'll notice its emphasis on meaningful career-oriented studies. The more specialized your area of study, the easier it is to initially find work. Experts are quick to note, however, liberal arts students often find greater flexibility in career opportunities over the years. And although studies such as social work, peace, urban planning, and natural resources are the ones listed herein, students who major in traditional liberal arts such as literature gain critical thinking skills beneficial in many careers, and often specialize further in graduate school.

Many parents fear that making a difference means a life of poverty, but these fears are unfounded. The *Making A Difference Careers* section lists hundreds of pathways corresponding to the myriad studies noted in this guide, some of which have both good pay and tremendous demand for graduates. Job opportunities in the non-profit sector continue to expand rapidly. This is a practical career-oriented college guide.

However, we all also know that a college degree doesn't guarantee a secure, interesting, or high paying job. It's also true that if you're looking to make a better world, there is a meaningful career waiting for you. Even if you won't be able to measure your wealth in dollars, you will have the immeasurable gains that come from a life of integrity, the joy of improving lives and of caring for the earth.

Then of course, there's finances. College costs are no longer listed, please don't base your decisions on cost. If you are interested in a school, contact it. Talk with them about the financial aid picture. If you are low or even moderate income, take the time to learn the ins and outs of financial aid; the benefits might be more substantial than you realize. If you need aid, apply early. While the largest aid is government and college based, learn to seek out scholarships which aren't need based. Many of the colleges in this guide offer scholarships for students engaged in community service. You can learn about these scholarships in the *Making A Difference Scholarship Guide*. If at the end, finances don't add up, one possible strategy is to attend a community college for the first two years, and then transfer into the college of your choice as a junior. If graduate school is in your plans, another way to shave expenses is to look for a 3/2 program, where you can obtain a master's degree after your fifth year. Whatever your family's income, don't give up on attending a particular college based on its sticker price. With school grants, even an expensive private college education may be much more affordable than you realize. So, once again, even if your income is upper middle-class, depending upon your age, income, asset level, and number of children, your family may be eligible for grant aid.

As for the profiles and course listings, a few notes. The colleges were evaluated according to the criteria: historic concerns for peace, social justice and the environment; an ethic of service; a holistic educational perspective; high participation in community service; and practical, meaningful making-a-difference majors (particularly environmental, peace and women's studies). Furthermore, catalogs were scoured to ascertain the courses offered in the various majors, and colleges were queried about the percentage of graduates going into 'make-a-difference' professions, whether teaching, social work, urban planning or marine biology. In the case of public universities, I mostly looked for a lot of making-a-difference studies, a reputation as a liberal/progressive institution, and a fairly activist student body. The *Making A Difference Studies* listed after the profiles are a small selection of those studies offered at any individual institution. Likewise, the courses listed are only a sample. Most often the studies listed are majors, but an occasional interesting minor makes an appearance here and there. Also, the courses listed may not be currently offered. The vegetarian meals designation means the college *claims* to have nutritious vegetarian meals available *in addition* to the regular fare. I make no promises, however, about the caliber of the cooking!

Also eliminated was an attempt to note schools with a gender balanced faculty. In those few, rare institutions where anything like gender balance exists, I've noted it. Otherwise, assume you are still looking, as a rule, at a faculty that is at least 65-75% male. There are signs of change as faculty hired in the 1950's are starting to retire, but it's profoundly slow.

Lastly, I have chosen to let the schools speak for themselves. Also, I have neither the expertise nor the desire to rank or judge them beyond their fitness for inclusion in this guide. The absence of a school you are interested in could be due to several things: 1) I'm unfamiliar with it; 2) they didn't meet enough of the criteria; or 3) they didn't respond to requests for information. The profiles have been written by the colleges, and the colleges profiled graciously pay a small fee for their listings to cover part of the cost of producing the book. An outstanding a terrific board of advisors has helped evaluate the colleges, and I am sincerely grateful for their input. Feedback received from students I've met at environmental and youth-service conferences have also influenced decisions about including or removing colleges.

Both for you and the world, the choices before you are pivotal. I applaud your wish to stand up and be counted. Use this book to choose a college as an important step on your way to contributing to a better world. My sincere gratitude is extended to you for joining with the many caring and often courageous people across the planet (the original world wide web) who are working to make a difference.

# RETHINKING THE MISSION OF AMERICAN EDUCATION

## JEREMY RIFKIN

THE SHIFT FROM THE INDUSTRIAL AGE TO THE INFORMATION AGE is transforming our civilization. Vast economic, social, and political changes are already underway. Preparing students for a radically different world in the 21st century requires a reaffirmation of the principles of democracy and community that have served as a beacon in the first two centuries of the American experience. Our schools, colleges and universities can play a key role in fostering a more civil society.

Corporate downsizing, the increasing automation of the manufacturing and service sectors, the shift from mass to elite workforces, growing job insecurity, the widening gap between rich and poor, continued racial tensions, escalating crime, new patterns of immigration, an aging population, and the globalization of the economy are creating a host of new uncertainties and challenges for the American economy.

At the same time, government, at every level, is being fundamentally transformed. The "welfare state" is being pared down and entitlement programs are shrinking. The social net is being streamlined and overhauled and government subsidies of various kinds are being reduced or eliminated.

The new economic and political realities stir us to look once again to America's civil society for help and guidance as we have on so many occasions in the past when our country found itself in the midst of profound change. While historians are quick to credit the market economy and democratic form of government with America's greatness, the civil society — the Third Sector — has played an equally significant role in defining the American way of life.

The nation's hospitals, social service organizations, religious institutions, fraternal orders, women's clubs, youth organizations, civil rights groups, animal welfare organizations, theaters, orchestras, art galleries, libraries, museums, civic associations, community development organizations, neighborhood advisory councils, volunteer fire departments and civilian security patrols are all institutions of the Third Sector.

Today, more than 1,400,000 nonprofit organizations are serving the needs and helping fulfill the dreams of millions of Americans. The civil society is the bonding force, the social glue that unites the many diverse interests of the American people into a cohesive social identity. If there is a single defining characteristic that sums up the unique qualities of being an American, it would be our capacity to join together in civic associations to serve one another.

5

America's Third Sector will need to play a far more expansive role in the coming century as an arena for job creation and social service provider. The civic sector must also become a more organized social and cultural force in every community, working with, and, at times, pressuring the market and government sectors to meet the needs of workers, families and neighborhoods. Thinking of society as three sectors that work together to create a productive and caring society opens up new possibilities for reconceptualizing the social contract and the kind of education we give our young people.

### Broadening The Mission Of American Education

Weaving a seamless web between school and community needs to be made an urgent priority if we are to meet the growing challenges of the coming century. A quiet revolution, to bring school and community closer together, has been spreading through the nation's schools and colleges over the past ten years. The effort is designed to create that seamless web. "Civil education" is based on the premise that a primary purpose of schooling is to help young people develop the skills and acquire the values necessary for civic life. Advancing the goals of a civil education requires that educators look to the non-profit sector in addition to the marketplace and government, to inform curriculum development, pedagogy, and the organization of schooling.

Civil education is gaining ground in schools around the country. Many school systems have established service learning activities which integrate service within the curriculum and/or enable students to earn credit for their involvement in neighborhood non-profit organizations, service oriented businesses, and other Third Sector enterprises. Some schools have established character education and citizen education programs to promote civic values. A growing number of schools have begun to recognize the power of connecting civil society and course curriculum. The civil society furnishes ample material for broadening and deepening the school experience across a range of academic studies. All of these initiatives are designed to create a seamless web between school and community.

At a time when teachers, parents, and communities are becoming more concerned about the growing sense of alienation, detachment, and aimlessness of the nation's students, civil education is an important development. Civil education engenders a sense of personal responsibility and accountability, fosters self esteem and leadership, and most of all, allows the feeling of empathy to grow and flourish.

Civil education can give a student a sense of place and belonging, as well as add personal meaning to his or her life. Civil education also provides a much needed alternative frame of reference for a generation increasingly immersed in the simulated worlds of the new telecommunications revolution. Television, computers, and now cyberspace, are becoming an ever more pervasive force in the lives of our students. The new Information Age media technologies offer an array of innovative teaching tools and learning environments for American students. Still, a growing number of educators worry that children growing up in front of the computer screen and TV set are at risk of being less exposed to the kind of authentic real world experiences that are such a necessary part of normal social education and youth development. Civil education, combined with the appropriate use of the new Information Age technologies, can act as an antidote to the increasingly isolated world of simulation and virtual reality young people experience.

We believe that civil education needs to be incorporated into the heart of the school experience. Learning that occurs through active student participation in service and other aspects of civil life benefits the student, as well as the community. Students learn best by doing. At the same time, weaving the rich 200-year historical legacy and values of the Third Sector into a broad range of curricula, provides a context and framework for youth to understand the importance of service learning in the community and the central role that the civil society plays in the life of the country. Learning about the heroes and heroines and the many organizations, movements and causes that have helped forge America's civil society, offers historical role models for young people to emulate and a positive vision to help guide their personal journeys in life. Weaving a seamless web between school and community can enhance academic performance and provide a more meaningful educational experience for American students. A civil education also benefits the community itself. Millions of young people reaching out with helping hands to friends and neighbors can enrich the civic life of communities across the country.

As we enter the Information Age, we face the very real challenge of redirecting the course of American education so that our young people will be ready to wrestle with both the demands of the new global economy and the austere new realities facing government. We need to bear in mind that the strength of the market and the effectiveness of our democratic form of government have always depended, in the final analysis, on the vitality of America's civil sector. It is the wellspring of our spirit as a people. Shifting the social paradigm from a two sector to a three sector focus and strengthening the role of the civil society, making it once again the center of American life, is essential if we are to renew our social covenant in the new century. Preparing the next generation for a life-long commitment to the civil society is, perhaps, the single most important challenge facing educators and the American K-12 and collegiate systems as we make the transition into a new era and a new economic epoch in history.

*Jeremy Rifkin is the author of* The End of Work: The Decline of the Global Labor Force and the Dawn of the Post Market Era *(Tarcher/Putnam). He is also co-chair of The Partnering Initiative on Education and Civil Society, whose mission is to prepare students for a lifelong commitment to the values of the civil society.*

# BRINGING WISDOM BACK
# TO THE NEW WORLD

## MATTHEW FOX

THE THEME THAT I'VE BEEN ASKED TO SPEAK TO IS WISDOM. E.F. Schumacher, the great British economist, says "We are far too clever today to survive without wisdom." There is so much evidence at our fingertips, especially around the ecological crisis and the youth crisis that points to how we have lost touch with wisdom. I think we have essentially lost touch with wisdom because our educational systems and our political, economic, and even religious systems during this modern era, ran from wisdom into the lap of knowledge.

A number of years ago I was invited to give a series of talks at a university and I was told "You can give four talks... we'll give you the title for the first, the others you make up your own titles." I said "Okay, what's the first title?" They said, "Wisdom and the University." Well, I have to tell you, I sweated and sweated over that talk. I couldn't create a talk. So an hour before I was to speak I took a hot bath. I said, "Maybe a revelation will come to me in the bath tub." And the revelation came, and it said, "Tell the truth." I thought "That's pretty simple." So there I was in front of an audience of about 300 faculty and  students and this was my opening line. I said, "Frankly, talking about wisdom in the university today is a bit like talking about chastity in a brothel." I tell you, the audience moved.

I wish I could say that things have changed a lot since then. But I don't feel they have. I've worked in academia for 25 years; I've kept a foot in there and a foot in the church, a pretty masochistic vocation I have chosen — because I believe essentially in both. I believe in the spiritual experience that learning is, and the power when it connects to wisdom, and I also believe in the potential of religion to recover its real task which is to teach spirituality.

The university was invented in the 12th Century. At that time there was a big influx of cosmology. The West was rediscovering the cosmos. What "university" meant was this: "A place to find your place in the universe." That's what it meant to go to the university, to find your place in the UNIVERSE. Today you go to university and you find your place in sociology, or art, or economics, or business, or history, or science; that's due to the Newtonian Revolution. That's due to the modern world set where we've been taught that the universe itself is really built on little pieces. The university today is far more indebted to the mistaken and disproved Newtonian physics of the modern era than it is to its original inspiration which was embedded in wisdom. Because wisdom is always about the universe — that's the first element of wisdom.

Lester Brown, of the World Watch Institute, who collects data on the state of the earth says that today every living system on Earth is in decline. Every living system on Earth is in decline. We're destroying 27,000 species a year. This is the greatest rate of destruction on this planet in 60 million years; the greatest destruction of species since the dinosaurs. At the rate that we are going, in 50 years... that means when you young students are grandparents there will be no species. That is the direction in which we are headed.

Now remember that the opposite of wisdom is folly, and we are headed in a direction of folly. No being would want to foul its nest in the ways in which we are fouling ours or to bring down the other species with which we are so interdependent, not only for food and clothing and shelter and shade and energy, but we are also interdependent with those species for their beauty. They feed our hearts and our souls and our music and our poetry and our dance and our ritual. To think that the path we are on in 50 years will leave us utterly lonely and indeed incapable of survival is really something to meditate on because it is a question of wisdom.

We have been developing powers around knowledge for three-hundred years. Unfortunately, our universities are still essentially knowledge directed. I call them "knowledge factories." What we need today are wisdom schools, especially for the young who, of course, will bear the burden and are bearing the burden of the ecological destruction that is all around us. In California alone one out of three children are living in poverty, the highest percentage of anyplace in the nation. There is not less money in this country; it is being hoarded by fewer and fewer people. Fewer and fewer people are making decisions.

Today, even as we speak, people in China and peasants in India are getting reruns of Dallas on their television sets. This is very destructive. This is what destroys ancient cultures and rooted people. These are some of the realities of the time in which we live; the facts of life of our time. It is a time for not taking for granted. We cannot take health for granted anymore. We can't take healthy soil, forest air, water, ozone, for granted anymore. The reason we can't is that our civilization, so addicted to knowledge, has fled from wisdom. Knowledge is very, very powerful. If it is not tempered and contoured by greater visions, like justice, compassion, beauty, grace and thinking of the next generation and the seven generations to come — then indeed, it is dangerous. Unfortunately, many of our educational systems in the West are still very dangerous places.

So what are some of the elements of wisdom that can help us to redeem not only education but our professions as well? When you look at our work world today — when you look at law, religion, economics, and education, what you realize is we separated learning from education, we separated justice from law, we separated stewardship from commerce. And where does this separation begin? It begins at the university. What do lawyers, bankers, business people, theologians and so forth, all have in common? Most of them pass through the university. The university is like a funnel that unfortunately has damaged the heart and the conscience of our people, because it has sought knowledge at the expense of wisdom.

So, I want to talk about bringing wisdom back and what are the signs of wisdom, what are the elements of wisdom. The physicist Eric Yansh wrote in his very provocative book, The Self-Organizing Universe, "God is the mind of the universe." He defines mind as self-organization dynamics at many levels. A dynamics which itself evolves. In this respect he writes, "All natural history is also history of mind." Self-transcendence, the evolution of evolutionary process is this evolution of the mind. In other words, there has been mind in the universe from the very first millisecond of the fireball 15 billion years ago.

In the West we don't believe something until science puts its stamp of approval on it as a rule. Yansh was one of the first scientists to come out of the closet as a mystic, as so many are doing today. He was saying, "What I am talking about from my scientific research, that there's mind in the universe, is what the mystics have understood for centuries — eons. Now we can bring it together and it will enter our everyday life."

One word for recovering wisdom is "cosmology." The word "cosmos" is a Greek word for "whole." We need to recover cosmology because during the Newtonian era, the era that gave us all this knowledge with so little wisdom, we were told we lived in a machine. We were told our bodies were machines. That's exactly what Descartes said, "The nearest thing to your body is a clock."

Our souls have shrunk during this modern era. Education and religion have often gone along with the shrinking. In the seventeenth century scientists concluded these believer types can be dangerous. In fact they said, "We better work out some kind of truce. We'll take the universe. You religious people, you take the soul." And, that's what happened. Scientists set out and discovered the power of the universe — atomic power and other powers. But without a conscience, without wisdom. That's why we've had the destruction and the wars — including the war against nature that we've had, right up through today. Religion meanwhile, took the soul and became more and more introspective, rendered it punier and punier. The good news of the time in which we live is that scientists themselves are bringing the psyche and cosmos together again. When mysticism and science come together you have an explosion of cosmology and you have new energy. And wisdom can happen again.

Wisdom is not just about knowledge, it's about love. That's what science is rediscovering, what the mystics have been telling us. We have been loved from before the beginning. This is what I call "Original Blessing." There have been so many blessings, that preceded our coming. Reconnecting with this blessing that is the origin of wisdom. In the 12th Century when the university was invented, when cosmology and the goddess came roaring into European civilization, a theologian called Adelard of Bath wrote "Were we to neglect coming to know the admirable, rational beauty of the universe in which we live, we would deserve to be cast out from it, like guests incapable of appreciating a home in which hospitality is offered to them." That is the juncture at which our species finds itself at this moment. Because knowledge alone does not teach you gratitude, reverence, a sense of the sacred — only wisdom teaches those things. Hildegard de Bingen of the twelfth century wrote that, "If humanity breaks the web of justice, of creation, the web of justice that is all creation, then God's justice is to punish humanity." God is not up in the sky punishing us, but because we have part of a web of justice, if we break that relationship with the rest of creation, creation itself will wreak its havoc on our species, which is what is happening.

When you fall in love, everything is affected. Your whole way of seeing the world is affected. Falling in love is not just about falling in love with another two-legged one. We need to fall in love with the forest and the soil and the water and the animals and the birds and poetry and music and the children that are to come and are to come and are to come. We have to make broader this experience of falling in love. According to biblical teaching the shortcut to wisdom is eros, is falling in love with life itself. And what a moment to do this because life itself is so jeopardized. Antoine Artaud, a French playwright who wrote in the 30's said, "It is right that from time to time, cataclysms occur that compel us to return to nature. That is to rediscover life." A very prophetic sentence. I can't imagine a sentence that applies more to the moment in which we live. A cataclysm is all around us; it's in the ecological disaster; it's in the despair among the young. It's in the despair among inner city people and other unemployed. It's in despair in the developing countries. It's in our prisons.

We're still clinging to models of education from Europe of the modern era, that are not working for young people today and certainly not for inner-city people. I'll tell you how to reinvent education. You reinvent it with ceremony, with ritual, with art and creativity. This is the ancient way to teach people. This is how indigenous people all over the world taught their young people, for tens of thousands of years. Why? Because you can't tell cosmology through books alone and lectures alone. The heart has to be opened up.

It's a hell of a lot cheaper to build schools based on creativity and what's powerful in the human spirit than it is to send people to prison at $30,000 a year. We need ways of learning that — open the heart up, because the heart can relate to the cosmos. Johnny Moses, a Native American from the northwest tribes feels very called as many young people do today, to spiritual leadership. He says "the essence of our teaching is very simple — of medicine teaching, healing, it is this, that we must relate to everything as sacred." He also said, "You cannot relate to everything as sacred until first you relate to yourself as sacred." Compassion is the moral attribute of God, and if we can be compassionate, we're on a Godly path.

One of the great sins of our time and culture is that of couch potato-itis. It is being forced upon us by an economic system that wants to render us passive consumers, not only consumers of goods, but consumers of our time. People drag themselves home from work that is too small for their souls; they have no energy but to turn on a dial to watch other people live for them and play for them. The Dallas Cowboys spent 33 million dollars on a football player. They tell us we don't have money for schools and for a decent police department and what else? Nonsense. We're living vicariously. People who live vicariously are not living. Spirituality is about living in depth, being alive. So getting back to our own creativity is the path of empowerment. Who is going to birth the God in you, the wisdom in you, if not you?

Thomas Aquinas in the thirteenth century said, "The spirit, the same spirit that hovered over the waters of the beginning of creation, hovers over the mind of the artist giving birth." That's so beautiful — that the great spirit, the birth of creation continues to work and continues to birth us, to birth our creativity.

The modern age began in the fifteenth century with the invention of the printing press. That's why the modern age, including academia, has been so textually bound. Now that's not all negative of course, but we paid a price for it. I'm not saying we're to throw out all books, not at all. I'm saying we have to open our hearts up.

The scripture says wisdom is prophetic, she walks the streets. She's not elitist. This is why we have to take it back and pass it through hearts of compassion and values of justice. Because one of the lies of the modern era, and you still get it in academia, is that knowledge is value free. Don't tell me that building a nuclear bomb is value free. Don't tell me that creating machines that can tear down rain forests in a day that it takes nature 10,000 years to create is value free. Nothing humans do is value free. Nothing we give birth to is value free. We have to critique what we give birth to with a mirror of justice and of compassion. That's the test to put to our work and to our creativity.

During the modern age beauty was tossed out as a philosophical and theological category. Descartes, who is still the father of Western academia, has a whole philosophy with no philosophy of esthetics. That's why we have an ecological crisis. In the Middle Ages, when we had a cosmology, God was called Beauty.

Part of post-modernism is to incorporate what's true and good from the past, including the modern era. I'm glad we have a microphone that works and a light that works. From the pre-modern we read too of the aboriginal people, the wisdom of the pre-moderns. The modern era was intensely elitist and arrogant, as if the only way to learn was through text and books. So in the post-modern era we want to welcome knowledge and wisdom from the past, from our ancestors, including the modern era.

Lester Brown, of the World Watch Institute, says that what we need is an environment revolution, comparable to the industrial revolution of 200 years ago or the agricultural revolution of 10,000 years ago. Eight years ago he said "We have only 20 years to pull it off." Meaning today, we have 12 years left, as a species. This is why, my friends, this is not a time for business as usual, religion as usual, education as usual, politics as usual. We have 12 years left. His data suggests that after 12 more years on the path we're on, we will not be able to undo the damage we are doing as a species to this planet and therefore to ourselves. He said, "I'm convinced the number one obstacle to bringing about the environmental revolution is human inertia." Human inertia is a sin of the spirit. Aquinas analyzed that, "What's the medicine for inertia?" What's the medicine for being couch potatoes? Aquinas says "Zeal." Zeal comes, he says, from an intense experience of the beauty of things.

I think that is so insightful. Your energy is going to come from your awareness of beauty. It is when you fall in love with the rain forests that you will dedicate your life to defending them. Or when you fall in love with young people who are hurting that you will commit to them, to that work of compassion.

Nothing is more natural than wanting to celebrate together, wanting to laugh and to sing, because when our hearts are purified we see the world this way, we are blessed by everything and everything we look upon is blessed. It is that experience of blessing that is at the heart of all wisdom. That is what is needed at this moment in history, in which we have 12 years left to do something. So I invite all of you to mediate on this: ask what can you do, given your gift, your talent, your know how, your connections, your role in life. What can you do to contribute to the environmental revolution to move our species from folly to wisdom?

The Celtic poet, W. B. Yeats says that "education is not about filling a pail, but about lighting a fire." It is the fire that each of you is here to set on the earth. Wherever you are destined to study, to work, to relate, to be citizens, to return, to infiltrate.

Relate with persons different from yourself. Whites with blacks, blacks with whites and Asians, young with older and vice versa; women with men and men with women, gays with straights; Christian with other-than-Christian; all of us with beings more than human. In this way community happens of a wider sort — the tribal impulse that is in all is tamed somewhat. Tribalism is both a strength and a weakness. Pluralism is a moral imperative of our time and places. Diversity is our richness.

The only proof of good teaching, good education will be the news that three years from now and five years from now you will have not grown cynical in the struggle, but strong, that you have not let sadness overtake you; that you keep your heart and your mind green and moist and juicy; and that you are always learning; and continually in trouble. May the Spirit accompany you on your journey. Keep your passion for learning alive. May you be lit fires wherever you are, wherever you find yourselves studying and working, may the conflagration accompany you!

*This essay is edited from a speech given by Matthew Fox at UCLA. Fox, a former Dominican priest, is the founder and director of the University of Creation Spirituality (see profile in graduate section) and the author of* Reinventing Work, *among other books.*

# WHAT IS EDUCATION FOR?

## DAVID W. ORR

*If humans are to flourish on this planet, education, whose dominant focus has been human culture, must clearly place culture within the larger context of nature. Here, David Orr, Professor of Environmental Studies at Oberlin College in Ohio, speaks to the myths that drive modern education and suggests a set of principles that might replace them.*

IF TODAY IS A TYPICAL DAY ON PLANET EARTH, we will lose 116 square miles of rainforest or about an acre a second. We will lose another 72 square miles to encroaching deserts, the results of human mismanagement and overpopulation. We will lose 40 - 100 species, and no one knows whether the number is 40 or 100. Today the human population will increase by 250,000. And today we will add 2,700 tons of chlorofluorocarbons to the atmosphere and 15 million tons of carbon. Tonight the Earth will be a little hotter, its waters more acidic, and the fabric of life more threadbare. By the year's end the numbers are staggering: the total loss of rainforest will equal an area the size of the state of Washington; expanding deserts will equal an area the size of the state of West Virginia; and the global population will have risen by more than 90,000,000. By the year 2000 perhaps as many as 20% of the life forms on the planet in the year 1900 will be extinct.

The truth is that many things on which our future health and prosperity depend are in dire jeopardy; climate stability, the resilience and productivity of natural systems, the beauty of the natural world, and  biological diversity.

It is worth noting that this is not the work of ignorant people. It is rather largely the results of work by people with B.A.s, B.S.s, M.B.A.s and Ph.D.s. Elie Wiesel recently made the same point in a speech to the Global Forum in Moscow, saying that the designers and perpetrators of Auschwitz, Dachau, and the Buchenwald were the heirs of Kant and Goethe. In most respects the Germans were the best educated people on Earth, but their education did not serve as an adequate barrier to barbarity. What was wrong with their education? In Wiesel's words: "It emphasized theories instead of values, concepts rather than human beings, abstraction rather than consciousness, answers instead of questions, ideology and efficiency rather than conscience."

I believe that the same could be said for our education. Toward the natural world it too emphasizes theories, not values, abstraction rather than consciousness, neat answers instead of questions, and technical efficiency over conscience. It is a matter of no small consequence that the only people who have lived sustainably on the planet for any length of time could not read or, like the Amish, do not make a fetish of reading. My point is simply that education is no guarantee of decency, prudence, or wisdom. This is not an argument for ignorance, but rather a statement that the world of education must now be measured against the standards of decency and human survival — the issues now looming so large before us in the decade of the 1990's and beyond. It is not education that will save us, but education of a certain kind.

What went wrong with contemporary culture and with education? We can find insight in literature including Christopher Marlowe's Faust who trades his soul for knowledge and power, Mary Shelley's Dr. Frankenstein who refuses to take responsibility for his creation, and Herman Melville's Captain Ahab who says "All my means are sane, my motive and my object mad." In these characters we encounter the essence of the modern drive to dominate nature.

Historically, Francis Bacon's proposed union between knowledge and power foreshadowed the contemporary alliance between government, business, and knowledge that has wrought so much mischief. Galileo's separation of the intellect foreshadowed the dominance of the analytical mind over that part given to creativity, humor, and wholeness. And in Descartes' epistemology one finds the roots of the radical separation of self and object. Together these three laid the foundations for modern education, foundations that now are enshrined in myths that we have come to accept without question. Let me suggest six.

First there is the myth that ignorance is a solvable problem. Ignorance is not a solvable problem; it is rather an inescapable part of the human condition. We cannot comprehend the world in its entirety. The advance of knowledge always carries with it the advance of some form of ignorance. For example, in 1929, ignorance of what chlorofluorocarbons would do to the stratospheric ozone and climate stability was of no importance, since they had not been invented. But after Thomas Midgley, Jr. discovered CFCs in 1930, what had been trivial ignorance became a life-threatening gap in human understanding of the biosphere. Not until the early 1970s did anyone think to ask "what does this substance do to what?" In 1986 we discovered that CFCs had created a hole in the ozone over the South Pole the size of the lower 48 states, and by 1990 a serious general thinning of ozone worldwide. With the discovery of CFC's, knowledge increased, but like the circumference of an expanding circle, ignorance grew as well.

A second myth is that, with enough knowledge and technology, we can manage planet Earth. Higher education has been largely shaped by the drive to extend human domination to its fullest. In this mission human intelligence may have taken the wrong road. Nonetheless, managing the planet has a nice ring to it. It appeals to our fascination with digital readouts, computers, buttons, and dials. But the complexity of Earth and its life systems can never be safely managed. The ecology of the top inch of topsoil is still largely unknown, as is its relationship to the large systems of the biosphere. What might be managed, however, is us: human desires, economies, politics, and communities. But our attention is caught by those things that avoid the hard choices implied by politics, morality, ethics, and common sense. It makes far better sense to reshape ourselves to fit a finite planet than to attempt to reshape the planet to fit our infinite wants.

A third myth is that knowledge is increasing and, by implication, so is human goodness. There is an information explosion going on, by which I mean a rapid increase in data, words, and paper. But this explosion should not be mistaken for an increase in knowledge and wisdom, which cannot be measured so easily. What can be said truthfully is that some knowledge is increasing, while other kinds of knowledge are being lost. For example, David Ehrenfeld has pointed out that biology departments no longer hire faculty in such areas as systematics, taxonomy, or ornithology. In other words, important knowledge is being lost because of the recent overemphasis on molecular biology and genetic engineering, which are more lucrative but not more important areas of inquiry. Despite all of our advances in some areas, we still do not have anything like the science of land health that Aldo Leopold called for half a century ago.

It is not just knowledge in certain areas that we're losing, but vernacular knowledge as well, by which I mean the knowledge that people have of their places. In Barry Lopez's words: "It is the chilling nature of modern society to find an ignorance of geography, local or national, as excusable as an ignorance of hand tools, and to find the commitment of people to their home places only momentarily entertaining, and finally naive.... (I am) forced to the realization that something strange, if not dangerous, is afoot. Year by year the number of people with firsthand experience in the land dwindles. Rural populations continue to shift to the cities. In the wake of this loss of personal and local knowledge, the knowledge from which a real geography is derived, the knowledge on which a country must ultimately stand, has come something hard to define but I think sinister and unsettling."

The modern university does not consider this kind of knowledge worth knowing except to record it as an oddity of "'folk culture." Instead it conceived its mission as that of adding to what is called the "fund of human knowledge" through research. And what can be said of research? Historian Page Smith offers one answer: "The vast majority of so-called research turned out in the modern university is essentially worthless. It does not in the main result in greater health or happiness among the general populace or any particular segment of it. It is busywork on a vast, almost incomprehensible scale. It is dispiriting, it depresses the whole scholarly enterprise, and most important of all, it deprives the student of what he or she deserves — the thoughtful and considered attention of a teacher deeply and unequivocally committed to teaching."

In the confusion of data with knowledge is a deeper mistake that learning will make us better people. But learning, as Loren Eiseley once said, "is endless and in itself it will never make us ethical men." Ultimately, it may be the knowledge of the good that is most threatened by all of our other advances. All things considered, it is possible that we are becoming more ignorant of the things we must know to live well and sustainably on the Earth.

In thinking about the kinds of knowledge and the kinds of research that we will need to build a sustainable society, there is a distinction to be made between intelligence and cleverness. Intelligence is long term and aims toward wholeness. Cleverness is mostly short term and tends to break reality into bits and pieces. Cleverness is personified by the functionally rational technician armed with know-how and methods, but without a clue about the higher ends to which technique should be subservient. The goal of education should be to connect intelligence, with its emphasis on whole systems and the long term, with cleverness, which is being smart about details.

A fourth myth of higher education is that we can adequately restore that which we have dismantled. I am referring to the modern curriculum. We have fragmented the world into bits and pieces called disciplines, hermetically sealed from other disciplines. As a result most students graduate without any broad, integrated sense of the unity of things. The consequences for their personhood and for the planet are large. For example, we routinely produce economists who lack the most rudimentary knowledge of ecology. This explains why our national accounting systems do not subtract the costs of biotic impoverishment, soil erosion, and poisons in our air and water from gross national product. We add the price of the sale of a bushel of wheat to GNP while forgetting to subtract the three bushels of topsoil lost in its production. As a result of incomplete education, we've fooled ourselves into thinking that we're much richer than we are. The same point could be made about other hermetically sealed disciplines.

Fifth, there is a myth that the purpose of education is that of giving you the means for upward mobility and success. Thomas Merton once identified this as the "mass production of people literally unfit for anything except to take part in an elaborate and completely artificial charade." The plain fact is that the planet does not need more successful people. But it does desperately need more peacemakers, healers, restorers, storytellers, and lovers. It needs people who live well in their places. It needs people of moral courage willing to join the fight to make the world habitable and humane. These have little to do with success as our culture has defined it.

Finally, there is a myth that our culture represents the pinnacle of human achievement. This myth represents cultural arrogance of the worst sort, and a gross misreading of history and anthropology. Recently this view has taken the form that we won the cold war. Communism failed because it produced too little at too high a cost. But capitalism has also failed because it produces too much, shares too little, at too high a cost to our children and grandchildren. Communism failed as an aesthetic morality. Capitalism has failed because it destroys morality altogether. This is not the happy world that advertisers and politicians describe. We have built a world of sybaritic wealth for a few and Calcutta poverty for a growing underclass. At its worst it is a world of crack on the streets, insensate violence, and desperate poverty. The fact is that we live in a disintegrating culture. In the words of Ron Miller, editor of *Holistic Review*: "Our culture does not nourish that which is best or noblest in the human spirit. It does not cultivate vision, imagination, or aesthetic or spiritual sensitivity. It does not encourage gentleness, generosity, caring, or compassion. Increasingly in the last twentieth century, the economic-technocratic-statist world view has become a monstrous destroyer of what is loving and life-affirming in the human soul."

Measured against the agenda of human survival, how might we rethink education? Let me suggest six principles.

First, all education is environmental education. By what is included or excluded we teach students that they are part of or apart from the natural world. To teach economics, for example, without relevance to the laws of thermodynamics or those of ecology is to teach a fundamentally important ecological lesson: that physics and ecology have nothing to do with the economy. It just happens to be dead wrong. The same is true throughout all of the curriculum.

A second principle comes from the Greek concept of Paideia: the goal of education is not a mastery of subject matter, but mastery of one's person. Subject matter is simply the tool. Much as one would use a hammer and chisel to carve a block of marble, one uses ideas and knowledge to forge one's own personhood. For the most part we labor under a confusion of ends and means, that the goal of education is to stuff all kind of facts, techniques, methods, and information into the student's mind, regardless of how and with what effect it will be used. The Greeks knew better.

Third, I would like to propose that knowledge carries with it the responsibility to see that it is well used in the world. The results of a great deal of contemporary research bear resemblance to those foreshadowed by Mary Shelley: monsters of technology and its byproducts for which no one takes responsibility or is even expected to take responsibility. Whose responsibility is Love Canal? Chernobyl? Ozone depletion? The Valdez oil spill? Each of these tragedies was possible because of knowledge created for which no one was ultimately responsible. This may finally come to be seen for what I think it is: a problem of scale. Knowledge of how to do vast and risky things has far outrun our ability to responsibly use it. Some of it cannot be used responsibly, which is to say safely and to consistently good purposes.

Fourth, we cannot say that we know something until we understand the effects of this knowledge on real people and their communities. I grew up near Youngstown, Ohio, which was largely destroyed by corporate decisions to "dis-invest" in the economy of the region. In this case M.B.A.s, educated in the tools of leveraged buyouts, tax breaks, and capital mobility have done what no invading army could do — they destroyed an American city with total impunity on behalf of something called the "bottom line." But the bottom line for society includes other costs, those of unemployment, crime, alcoholism, child abuse, lost savings, and wrecked lives. In this instance what was taught in the business schools and economics departments did not include the value of good communities, or the human costs of a narrow destructive economic rationality that valued efficiency and economic abstractions above people and community.

My fifth principle has to do with the power of example over words. Students hear about global responsibility while being educated in institutions that often spend their budgets and invest their endowments in the most irresponsible things. The lessons being taught are those of hypocrisy and ultimately despair. Students learn, without anyone ever saying it, that they are helpless to overcome the frightening gap between ideals and reality. What is desperately needed are faculty and administrators who provide role models of integrity, care, thoughtfulness, and institutions capable of embodying ideals wholly and completely in all of their operations.

Finally, I would like to propose that the way learning occurs is as important as the content of particular courses. Process is important for learning. Lecture courses tend to induce passivity. Indoor classes create the illusion that learning only occurs inside four walls isolated from what students call, without apparent irony, the "real world." Dissecting frogs in biology teaches lessons about nature that no one would verbally profess. Campus architecture is crystallized pedagogy that often reinforces passivity, monologue, and artificiality. My point is simply that students that are being taught in various and subtle ways beyond the content of courses (the tacit curriculum).

If education is to be measured against the standard of sustainability, what can be done? I would like to propose four things. First, I would like to propose a dialogue in every educational institution about the substance and process of education. Are graduates better planetary citizens or are they, in Wendell Berry's words, "itinerant professional vandals?" Does the institution contribute to the development of sustainable regional economy, or in the name of efficiency, to the processes of destruction?

My second suggestion is to use campus resource flows (food, energy, water, materials, and waste) as part of curriculum. Faculty and students together might study the wells, mines, farms, feed-lots, and forests that supply the campus, as well as the dumps, smokestacks, and outfall pipes at the other end. The purpose is both pedagogic, using real things to teach stewardship, and practical, to change the way the particular institution spends its operational budget. One result would be to engage the creative energy of students in finding ways to shift the institutional buying power to support better alternatives that do less environmental damage, reduce use of toxic substances, promote energy efficiency and of solar energy, help to build a sustainable regional economy, cut long-term costs, and provide an example to other institutions. Study results should be woven into the curriculum as interdisciplinary courses, seminars, lectures, and research.

My third suggestion is to examine institutional investments. Is the endowment invested according to the Valdez Principles? Is it invested in companies doing things that the world needs done and in a responsible manner? Can some part of it be invested locally to help leverage energy efficiency and the evolution of a sustainable economy in the surrounding region? The research necessary to answer such questions might also form the basis of courses that focus on the development of sustainable local and regional economies.

Finally, every educational institution should set a goal of ecological literacy for all of its students. No student should graduate from any educational institution without a basic comprehension of: (1) the laws of thermodynamics; (2) the basic principles of ecology; (3) carrying capacity; (4) energetics; (5) least-cost, end-use analysis; (6) how to live well in a place; (7) limits of technology; (8) sustainable agriculture and forestry; (9) appropriate scale; (10) steady-state economics and (11) environmental philosophy and ethics. Collectively these imply the capacity to distinguish between health and disease, development and growth, sufficient and efficient, optimum and maximum, and "should do" from "can do."

As Aldo Leopold asked in a similar context: "If education does not teach us these things, then what is education for?"

*David Orr, Professor of Environmental Studies at Oberlin College is the co-founder of the Meadowcreek Project, a nonprofit environmental organization in Arkansas and author of* Ecological Literacy: Education and the Transition to a Postmodern World. *This essay is from his book* Earth in Mind *published by Island Press. The Campus Blueprint for a Sustainable Future crafted by delegates from 111 U.S. colleges and universities at the Campus Earth Summit in 1995 included many of the principles advocated here by Professor Orr.*

# AMERICORPS:

## GOOD FOR YOUR COUNTRY, GOOD FOR YOUR CAREER

### CORPORATION FOR NATIONAL SERVICE

IF YOU'RE READING THIS BOOK, chances are you want more than a quality college education. You also want to change the world — or at least make a difference. What if there was a way you could earn money for college, gain real life skills and get a leg up in the admissions process — all while solving problems and making a difference in your community?

Well, now there is. It's called AmeriCorps, the domestic Peace Corps. Created by Congress and President Clinton in 1993, AmeriCorps has already offered more than 100,000 Americans this simple bargain: if you give a hand to your country, you'll get a hand up for your education. Just like the G.I. Bill for military service, those who serve in AmeriCorps earn money for college in exchange for serving their country. This year 40,000 men and women will take AmeriCorps' pledge to "get things done for America — to make our people safer, smarter and healthier." Working through national and local nonprofits, members will tutor and mentor children, build Habitat for Humanity homes, fight crime, run afterschool programs, restore parks and streams, help the Red Cross rebuild after floods and hurricanes, and do countless other things to improve our lives and bring people together.

As an AmeriCorps member, you will receive a living allowance and health insurance. After completing a year of full-time service, you'll receive an education award worth $4,725. This award can be used to pay off student loans or to finance college, graduate school or vocational training.

At a time of rising college costs, AmeriCorps' education award is helping thousands of young Americans achieve their dream of a college degree. Equally important, AmeriCorps is helping communities across America solve their toughest social problems. We live in a time of great prosperity, but our country continues to face profound challenges that need our attention — from hunger and homelessness and environmental degradation, to city streets plagued by crime and children who can't read. At a time of shrinking government, we need citizens to do more and young people have the time, energy and talents to lead the way.

### A Life-Changing Experience

You know that a college education will help you make a difference later in life. But do you want to wait? What about starting right now, before college, by giving a year of service in AmeriCorps? Not only will you learn new skills and feel the satisfaction of helping others, you will gain valuable insights to help decide what college to attend and what career to pursue.

Beyond the skills and real life experience, AmeriCorps can change your life in another more subtle way — by raising your self-confidence and aspirations. Consider the path of Marilyn Concepcion of Providence, RI. In 1993, Marilyn was a high school dropout working on an assembly line. Then she joined the City Year AmeriCorps program, where she helped renovate a community center and taught English to elementary students. AmeriCorps helped Marilyn discover gifts she didn't know she had, and boosted her self-esteem. She applied to Brown University, where she's now studying to be a pediatrician.

At age 19, Kristen Woolf didn't know what she wanted to study in college — or how to pay for it. For Kristen, AmeriCorps was just the answer. She joined AmeriCorps and worked with young people in an afterschool program in Austin, Texas. She enjoyed the experience so much that she signed up for another year as an AmeriCorps Leader. With nearly $10,000 in college money and two years of real-world experience, Kristen was ready to go to school. She's now a sophomore at Southwest Texas State University pursuing a degree in social work.

After four years of high school, some students want to take a break before plunging into full-time academics. Beyond helping others, they want an adventure, the chance to meet new people, experience new things and visit parts of the country they've never been before. All AmeriCorps programs offer this, but one in particular, the National Civilian Community Corps (NCCC) is ideally suited to this type of student.

The NCCC is a 10-month residential service program for men and women ages 18-24. It takes its inspiration from the Depression-era Civilian Conservation Corps, which put millions of young people to work restoring our natural environment. AmeriCorps NCCC retains this focus on the environment, but recognizes that our nation's challenges today are more diverse. NCCC members work in teams on a variety of projects — building trails, restoring streams and parks, building low-income housing, tutoring children, and providing disaster relief. Members live together on closed military bases and are often sent on 'spikes' to other parts of the country to work on special projects.

With no required skills necessary, AmeriCorps NCCC teaches members what they need to get the job done. Just ask NCCC member Lisa Melkert. After renovating a Denver inner-city school and repairing a school for the deaf in Indianapolis, Lisa attended an AmeriCorps crash course on the IRS tax system. Trained and armed with a lap top, she visited local senior centers providing free tax services for low-income senior citizens. Several NCCC teams are trained by the U.S. Forest Service in forest fire suppression. One member said, "My favorite part of the NCCC so far was the time we got called out to Idaho to put out forest fires. Who ever thought I could do that?"

For parents worried about paying for college, the AmeriCorps education award can be a big help. And a growing number of colleges and universities are offering to match the $4,725 education award with their own scholarship aid. But AmeriCorps can offer more than financial help. The qualities AmeriCorps promotes — creativity, teamwork, initiative, problem-solving — are just what college admissions officers are looking for in a prospective student. Of course GPA and SAT scores are the first thing any college will look at. But increasingly colleges are looking for well-rounded students who have volunteer experience. Nearly every college and university considers preparing students to be responsible citizens as part of their mission. What better way to fulfill that mission than by selecting those who've already given a year of their life to serve their country?

### A Year Off — Or On?

AmeriCorps helps thousands of young people make a difference and figure out what they want to do before college. But it's also a very popular option for students already in college. About one-third of AmeriCorps members have a year or two of college under their belt, and are taking time off to serve their communities and explore different career paths.

Sara Potts had just finished her sophomore year at Truman State University in Missouri and had no idea what to major in. "I was involved in everything, but I just couldn't make up my mind." She heard about AmeriCorps and within months was tutoring in an elementary school. Potts believes this experience has changed her life. Not only has she changed majors, she even transferred colleges. Because of AmeriCorps, she now knows she wants to spend her life working with children.

There are increasing opportunities for college students to serve in AmeriCorps while they are in college. More and more universities are sponsoring AmeriCorps programs, often with part-time positions that allow students to continue taking classes while they serve. Most of these are in the area of education and childhood literacy.

AmeriCorps is in the forefront of America Reads, a national campaign launched by President Clinton in 1996 to ensure that every American child learns to read independently and well by the end of the third grade. AmeriCorps members are helping meet this goal by tutoring elementary students one-on-one and recruiting and mobilizing other volunteer tutors. In many cases, AmeriCorps members recruit college work-study students, who serve ten hours a week tutoring children instead of working on campus shelving books or washing dishes in the dining hall. In one program called JumpStart, college work- study students in Boston, New Haven and Washington, DC serve as AmeriCorps members tutoring children in Head Start centers.

History and common sense tells us the best way to make a lasting difference is to empower people to improve the conditions of their own lives. That's the key idea behind Volunteers in Service to America (VISTA), the national service program started in the 1960s which is now part of AmeriCorps. As an AmeriCorps' VISTA member, you might help start a youth center, establish a job bank, set up a literacy program or organize a domestic violence program. Whatever you do, you'll be be helping low-income communities help themselves to create long-term sustainable change. VISTA members must be at least 18 years old and usually have a bachelor's degree or three years of related work experience.

Many AmeriCorps VISTA assignments are in cutting-edge fields such as microenterprise credit, business development and computer technology. For example, AmeriCorps members in the IBM Team Tech program help nonprofit organizations effectively use technology to increase the impact of their work.

In eleven cities, AmeriCorps VISTA Team Tech members offer computer hardware and software assistance, design websites and provide Internet training to nonprofit agencies. Members learn extremely valuable computer and training skills that can be transferred to other work in the nonprofit, government or private sectors.

In addition to AmeriCorps NCCC and VISTA, there are literally hundreds of national and local nonprofits that sponsor AmeriCorps members. They range from America's largest and most respected groups — Habitat for Humanity, American Red Cross, Boys and Girls Clubs, Big Brothers Big Sisters — to local homeless shelters, food banks and conservation corps. You can serve in your hometown or across the country; in a large city or rural hamlet; in teams or individually; whatever your interests and background, there's likely to be an AmeriCorps position right for you.

So whether you are in high school, have a few years of college, or are a college graduate, you can be a part of this national movement to get things done and bring communities together. The spirit of service runs deep in America. You can be part of that proud tradition. Call AmeriCorps today. You'd be surprised what a year of service could do for your community, your country, and your future.

> *I will get things done for America — to make our people safer,*
> *smarter and healthier.*
> *I will bring Americans together to strengthen our communities.*
> *Faced with apathy, I will take action.*
> *Faced with conflict, I will seek common ground.*
> *I will carry this commitment with me this year and beyond.*
> *I am an AmeriCorps member, and I will get things done.*
> — AmeriCorps Pledge

To learn more about AmeriCorps, please call 1(800) 942-2677
(TDD 1-800-833-3722)
www.americorps.org

Editor's note: For a list of colleges offering AmeriCorps Matching Grants, get a copy of *Making A Difference Scholarships*, available from New Society Publishers.

# CAMPUS COMMUNITY SERVICE:
# THE EXPERIENCE OF A REAL CITIZEN

## ELIZABETH L. HOLLANDER

### CAMPUS COMPACT

AS AN UNDERGRADUATE IN THE 1960S so much was going on in the country — anti-war rallies, civil rights protests, the war on poverty — that my friends and I felt compelled to call attention to issues of neglect and injustice, and make a difference. In Philadelphia it was easy to become part of the action around campus. Some of us picketed stores with no minority employees; others started a soup kitchen; still others fought to integrate public housing. We called exercising our rights as citizens "activism"; today student community service is more prevalent on campuses.

Sadly, these civic problems are still with us, and college students continue to use their citizenship rights to try and make a difference. What's new is that campuses are now full participants in the action. An incredible array of community service opportunities await the student who wants to feel like a citizen. Whatever issue motivates you, whatever level of commitment you bring, whatever your style and talents, the campus is a place to contribute, develop yourself, and benefit others.

The community service movement is breaking down walls between campuses and communities, from rural towns to urban centers; and by working to strengthen communities, is breathing new life into the concept of student as citizen. My organization, Campus Compact, is a leader in this effort, helping schools develop service programs that challenge, enlighten, and even inspire.

You can get involved through classroom work and through activities you pursue on your own time. Faculty are adding community service-learning to the curriculum because they see that when service is linked to course content, students become engaged in their own education. The American college classroom has become a powerful springboard to citizenship. I believe that students enrolled in service learning courses today are able to access the highest quality campus community service work available.

This kind of "engaged citizenship" increases a student's sense of self. First, it's an opportunity for personal development, so whatever community service you undertake can add to your sense of competence and self-confidence. Second, engaging with others through community service can grab you in satisfying ways, and become a "habit of the heart." Students often find that in selecting a community service setting that matches their interests or skills, the involvement becomes part of their identity. If you're not sure of your skills and interests, community service can teach you about yourself in surprising and satisfying ways. If you have already encountered service opportunities, you understand what this means. If community service will be new to you, an eye-opening experience awaits you. In the last academic year alone, 374,000 undergraduates were involved in ongoing community service activities, totalling an estimated 32 million hours.

Another attraction of community service is that it offers students the chance for leadership experiences. Every day new programs are developed to address local needs, and students are behind much of the creativity and planning. Indeed, they are accomplishing great things, and the nation has taken notice and is following their lead. Campus Compact was founded by college and university presidents in 1985 to support the community service movement. The founding group saw how service activities springing up on their campuses were igniting students' passions while also promoting good will in town. The presidents also understood that when students get connected to service and community, they take on the habits of authentic citizenship. By involving themselves in projects like AmeriCorps, Learn and Serve America, National Service Scholars and VISTA, and by voting in elections, students' lives, and the lives they touch, take on new meaning. These students know they are contributing something tangible to the fabric of citizenship — more than just lip service about what's right for America. And this enhanced self-awareness lasts a lifetime.

As you consider what colleges best fit who you are, and who you want to become, I encourage you to look closely at the service programs available at the schools you consider. Often admissions materials include project descriptions, and the admissions staff can give you keen insights about them. Your campus visit will help in this regard, and asking questions of current students is another good strategy before you make final choices. Some schools provide specialized service scholarships, so if you already have service experience, find out if you are eligible.

Identify schools that present an interesting array of activities. If you have a passion for a particular issue like mentoring, the environment or literacy, you might want to look for schools with service programs that address them. And if a school you like does not, you'd be surprised how easy it is to find faculty allies to help you create one. Next, find out who on the faculty offer service-learning courses. Colleges and universities that combine service with learning will expose you to the subtle relationships between your coursework, the social and economic problems we face together, and the institutions working to address them. Some provide for student-directed programs which will develop your leadership and organizational skills but may take time away from direct service. Others offer more time for direct service, but you will probably have less influence over the project as a whole. You will need to decide which types of activities best match the level of responsibility you seek.

Student community service will change the way you look at the world, and give you experiences within a context you will not find anywhere else. Good luck!

*Elizabeth Hollander is the Executive Director of Campus Compact, Higher Education in Service to the Nation. Campus Compact is headquartered at Brown University.*

Elizabeth Hollander
Campus Compact
Box 1975, Brown University
Providence, RI 02912

401.863.1119
ehollander@compact.org
www.compact.org

# WELCOME TO THE MOVEMENT

## LLOYD JACOBSON

### CAMPUS OPPORTUNITY OUTREACH LEAGUE (COOL)

WELCOME TO THE MOVEMENT. The fact that you are reading this book suggests that you are interested in joining a movement of people and ideas that is making college more about producing citizens, than just producing workers. This movement has many facets; some concentrating on issues of poverty and social disadvantage, some focusing on environmental issues, and some concerned primarily with peace and justice. What these facets all have in common though is a need for committed individuals dedicated to learning how to produce substantive and positive change in the world.

The schools you will find profiled in this book are true leaders in their field. They are taking on the challenge of expanding academic programs, or even creating new areas of study, that allow students to explore the real world. Students attending these schools are involved first-hand in work that makes learning come alive through service-learning, a teaching concept that encourages the gaining of knowledge not solely from books and lecture, but also through personal experience and observation in the community.

But just what has led these schools to become so different from all the others? In many cases these schools have distinguished themselves because of the initial efforts of an organized mass of students, just like you, who banded together to help create these programs. Starting in the mid-1980s, thousands of students across the country started to challenge themselves and their colleges to become involved in addressing our most pressing social and environmental problems through service and social action. Working with national organizations such as the Campus Outreach Opportunity League (COOL), the National Student Campaign Against Hunger and Homelessness, and the Student Environmental Action Committee, among many others, these students forged connections with the communities just outside their campus walls that in many cases never existed before. These connections took the form of community service partnerships with people in need, or involved getting students working directly to help save our threatened environment. Based on the ever expanding numbers of participants in these programs, and given the noticeable difference in these students' learning levels, faculty on many campuses started to take an interest in promoting this kind of activity with even more students by integrating it into the curriculum. Thus these student service leaders had not merely helped change the face of their communities, but they were also helping change the face of higher education.

As you read this book and research campuses you should keep the importance of that student leadership role in mind. As someone interested in making a difference, you should not merely be considering a college based on its offering of degree programs, but also how you might be able to contribute to the on-going expansion of the movement on that campus. If you are lucky you will discover a campus with many of the same types of student groups that helped introduce service-learning in the first place. Many of these groups continue to be the source of the most innovative ideas for addressing community problems on today's college campuses, and they continue to influence the direction of their campuses own academic programs. Also these groups will many times offer you the best opportunity to practice and develop essential leadership, organizing, and advocacy skills which often can not be taught within the curriculum. In short, they will help you round out your interests in social change as well as help you supplement the skills you will learn in the classroom.

Even if you should end up not attending one of the schools profiled in this book, understanding the importance of this student role will be of tremendous help to you. If you are truly committed to making a difference, recognize that you can still create, innovate and organize at that school for the benefit of yourself, the school, and the community it shares. Even so, the book you hold in your hands will still be an excellent guide. The profiles enclosed can serve as a source of inspiration for you as well as a kind of road map to discover those schools, student groups, and national organizations that you can contact for helpful ideas in creating the kind of experience you want to bring to your own campus.

Over the past few years the number of students seeking a meaningful education has increased significantly. Over that same time the number of schools profiled in this book has grown steadfastly. Wherever you may end up choosing to attend college, I hope you take on the responsibility of helping to continue this growth. Once again, welcome to the movement.

*Lloyd Jacobson was the former National Programs Director for COOL - Campus Outreach Opportunity League - the national student-led organization founded in 1984 to encourage, support and improve campus-based service programs.*

# ENVIRONMENTAL LITERACY: A GUIDE TO CONSTRUCTING AN UNDERGRADUATE EDUCATION

## THOMAS H. KELLY

### UNIVERSITY OF NEW HAMPSHIRE

BECAUSE ALL HUMAN ACTIVITIES are dependent upon and have repercussions within the environment, you have an opportunity to make a difference no matter what your interests. Whether you major in marketing, biology, mathematics or music and you spend your professional life in industry, government or journalism, your actions will have an environmental impact. So, remember whatever your major is, in a certain sense, it is an environmental one.

Ask yourself then, what kind of impact do you want to make? Where do you want to make it? How do you want to make it? These questions have important implications for deciding on the kind of college education you want. If you are concerned about the environment and want your education to reflect that concern and strengthen your capacity to assess, evaluate and judge where you fit into the environment, think about these questions. Independent of your ultimate career choice, what knowledge, skills and experiences do you want from your undergraduate education? If you are concerned about the Earth, yet do not wish to choose an environmental career, consider the notion of "environmental literacy."

An environmentally literate person understands the nature of the interdependence between human activities and the non-human world. With a modern education, so often career-oriented, if we are to graduate environmentally literate citizens, environmental concerns must be incorporated across the curriculum and even beyond the classroom. The prominence of the environment and an ecological perspective emphasizing systems such as the biosphere within the liberal arts education is relatively new. Many educators now seek to connect a broad range of disciplines in an effort to grasp complex, large-scale ecological problems. This is a tall order because there is a fundamental tension between the broad inclusive character of environment, and the practical significance of specialization to the job market or graduate school.

Moreover, recognition of the need to understand the social aspects of ecological problems has introduced questions of racism, equity, human rights, national sovereignty and national security into the environmental debate. These aspects of ecological problems are now widely acknowledged to be part and parcel of these issues.

Internationally, the scientific, educational, and governmental communities agree that segregation of the so-called "natural sciences" from "social sciences" is a significant obstacle to environmental education. Accordingly, calls for interdisciplinary and multidisciplinary educational programs are being heard from many quarters. Prospective undergraduates should be aware that while intuitively appealing, interdisciplinary and multidisciplinary education are interpreted differently by different schools. It is one thing to take a collection of courses from different disciplines; it is another to integrate and internalize their contents so that you can apply them to your personal and professional life.

When you are evaluating schools and deciding what kind of education you want, one consideration is the degree of disciplinary integration. Does a given program simply offer varying menus of courses from different disciplines? Or, does it offer an integrating mechanism such as a core curriculum or a culminating course or project specifically designed to aid your incorporation of the material into thinking and action? Is there a sufficient range of sciences in the curriculum to provide a graduate with a basic understanding of the materials, energy, and processes within which human activity occurs? But beware of a scientific bias in course requirements; make sure adequate study of cultural, political and economic aspects of the environment are included. How integrated are environmental perspectives with the curriculum of other majors such as international relations, chemical engineering or theater? In addition to these types of general questions, you should also frame questions specific to your interests. For example, does the university offer semester abroad programs in developing countries? To what degree does the curriculum employ field work or problem-based learning?

While a general awareness of environmental issues has been prominent since the late 1960's, colleges and universities often change slowly. Therefore you should get the most specific information you can about the school you are considering before making a choice. The institutions in this book are among the nations strongest in environmental curricula.

But of equal importance, you will be well served in your search for the best education for you, if you begin by asking questions of yourself.

*Thomas H. Kelly, Ph.D. is with the Environmental Studies Department and director of the Sustainability Program at the University of New Hampshire.*

# MAKING A DIFFERENCE IN THE WORLD

## HOWARD BERRY

### INTERNATIONAL PARTNERSHIP FOR SERVICE LEARNING

YOU WANT TO HELP PEOPLE. You want to go abroad, or at least experience another culture in depth. You don't want to do the usual tourist thing. You want to be challenged. You want to see for yourself what this "globalization" is all about. In short, you want something different, and you want to make a difference.

One experience that responds to these concerns is service-learning. Service-learning joins study and learning with substantive community service. It has been achieving much popularity and acceptance in US colleges and universities.

When held in international/intercultural settings its value is deepened. It allows students to encounter levels of the other culture not usually possible with more traditional programs. In addition to the enhanced learning, it encourages personal development and allows students to challenge and test themselves in accomplishing tasks for the common good.

Even further, service-learning develops what Robert Bellah termed the "habits of the heart." Through the service experience students are introduced to the realities of globalization and what it means to be a citizen of their nation and of the world.

A service-learning program can be a summer, a semester, or a year, serving the needs of the hungry, the homeless, the ill or handicapped, the very young or very old. It can be teaching literacy; caring for the sick, supervising recreation for troubled teens, working in micro-economic projects. The needs and possibilities are endless.

Interestingly, the intellectual and cultural learning through the experience of responding to these issues is as equally valuable in a developed nation as in a developing country. A service-learning experience is not easy, and shouldn't be. But if you approach it with flexibility, openness, and a willingness to learn and to suspend judgment — you too will encounter the host culture in a way not possible as a tourist or a traditional study-abroad student.

Students come to international service-learning programs from a wide variety of social and religious backgrounds, academic majors, abilities, skills and goals. But there is a consistency to their choice of a service-learning experience. They want to encounter the world directly, and they want to do it in a meaningful way.

One student participated as a sophomore from a private college in New York. A Jewish-American, he worked in a Christian Jamaican church-based community center providing holistic (physical, mental and spiritual) services to people from low income neighborhoods. At first he felt uneasy, but he soon realized "...our religious tenets shared the common principle that one who asks shall receive, and we were to assist in this process. Never before have I encountered a place where people were willing to give so much and expect nothing in return."

Students often find that their ideas about what constitutes service are challenged by the values of their host culture. Another student from a public university spent a semester in Ecuador and learned to face the differences between his notions of service and those of the community and the service agency. "The feelings and help of gringos come second in this organization. I realize now that that is how it should be."

Service learning addresses many of the complaints about higher education in this country. Concerns about its efficacy and value, doubts about the teachability of students coming into college who are alienated from the passive classroom educational process, frustration about inability to find jobs upon graduation, and lack of educational preparation for increasing globalization beset education. Educators find it difficult to teach community in a world where the traditional ideas of community no longer work.

It is here that the concept of service-learning enters. Service learning involves far more than opportunities to work while pursuing studies. It is an integrating volunteer experience, often in another culture, designed to improve one's sense of values, to provide new knowledge, and to assist in the relief of human needs.

Service-learning is based on some simple but effective and proven educational premises. That learning is easier when rooted in practical experience. Service learning programs enrich both learning and experience by providing them with meaning. By linking formal study, formal evaluation, and formal expectation with service, it becomes not an interlude in formal education but a part of it.

Volunteer work requires a willingness to put others before self, a willingness to give up something material in order to receive something spiritual in return. The right way to learn self-worth is by observing one's ability to better the self-worth of others. Living in another culture is the best way to prepare young people for the multicultural and globalized world of today and tomorrow. Programs take place in other cultures to broaden students' horizons to the maximum, to teach them what is relative about their cultures, and to teach them to view their sense of self and their acquisition of knowledge through the values of another culture.

Students who have been through such experiences are better able to deal with the world of work, more employable, more mature, and more knowledgable about and sensitive to the changing global world.

Lastly, when all of this has gone on, there is something left behind and that something is good. A student who participates leaves a measurable improvement in the lives of others and hence in society. International service-learning puts new life and vigor into liberal education for the 21st century, fights valuelessness and materialism, and helps students go on to live more useful lives in the new multicultural, fragile, yet infinitely absorbing world that is before us.

*Professor Howard A. Berry is the President of The International Partnership for Service Learning. For more information about IPSL's graduate program in service learning see their listing under the heading "International Service." For information about IPSL service learning programs, visit their website at www.ipsl.org.*

# I'M CHANGING THE WORLD, I'M HAPPY, AND LOOK MOM, I'M EVEN EARNING A GOOD LIVING!

## ANGELA CURTES

### EDUCATION DIRECTOR, PACIFIC ENVIRONMENT AND RESOURCES CENTER

IT WAS VERY DIFFICULT FOR ME TO DECIDE what path to take after high school. I had received a basketball scholarship from the University of Wisconsin, Parkside and that seemed to get my feet moving into a collegiate setting. I focused on the career of education — maybe physical education, maybe science or English. But to my dismay I never found passion nor extreme interest in any of the topics a typical professor taught. Eventually, I transferred, left sports, left my identity in some ways and, most of all, was left with very little hope for my future. The University of Wisconsin at Madison which has a student population of over 55,000 was my next stop. In neither of these places did I feel I had made the contribution to the greater community of life that I was seeking to make.

The more I talked with teachers, and the more student teaching I did, the more disillusioned I gradually became about public school education. I wanted to choose a career that would sustain my aspirations for a life time. But the more I pondered this direction, the more I realized that I wanted to make a bigger difference in life than just teaching kids to read, write or dissect earthworms!

My love for the outdoors since childhood was really my only true passion. Fortunately, three and half months in the wilderness with the National Outdoor Leadership School introduced me to environmental education. During my youth the act of passionately caring for something outside of the self had been forever instilled in me through my encounters with nature. Until NOLS, I never imagined this love for the natural environment could be a career choice.

After 3 years of attending various colleges I finally enrolled at Prescott College in Arizona. It was here I discovered the beauty of experiential education, self-directed learning, and in-depth self exploration. My dedication to studying the natural world and human relationships to it became my main focus, and has shaped my present reality. In my second year at Prescott, I signed up for its first community service course ever offered. I felt the class was long overdue. The students at this alternative, progressive college had no interaction with the conservative townspeople. I felt our knowledge needed to be shared with the greater community, and this class helped to bridge the gap. I served the Prescott community by organizing the town Earth Day Celebration. This event took about four months to organize and became a central task in my life, in addition to being Co-president of the Student Union.

The many service oriented experiences throughout my years at Prescott College were in some ways like a profound spiritual ritual. Each of them challenged my perception of self and each of them dynamically contributed to the empowerment of the self. Every endeavor I've begun since graduating has been successful and valuable for both myself and the endeavor.

Building strong relationships with others as well as the Earth is central to shaping a more positive and hopeful future. Overall, my experiences have reassured me of the resilience of the Earth and the pockets of true support and empathy that are woven through our communities. Until individuals learn to care for things outside of themselves, society will remain ignorant in its own temporary bliss. Shedding blinders enables others to be considered, respected, and even honored, but blindness only allows suffering to prevail. Service towards any moral cause is the beginning!

Presently, I work for a non-profit organization in the San Francisco Bay Area which strives for the protection of the natural environment through law advocacy, grassroots activism, and eduction. As the Environmental Education Director, I work to establish environmental awareness in youth, grades K-12, through interactive and experiential programs. Six program topics generate increased knowledge about global environmental issues as well as an understanding of the reverence for all life. Topics allow students to become aware of the impacts to the natural environment and how they are dynamically connected to the problems and the solutions.

Throughout the summer and fall I also co-direct a wilderness education program for women called Common Earth. As the co-founder of this program I strive to incorporate natural and cultural history, wilderness skills and safety, and empowerment of women from various cultural and socioeconomic backgrounds.

*In addition to her work in environmental education, Angela Curtes leads wilderness trips for women.*

# JUDD WALSON

## PRE-MEDICAL STUDENT

GRADUATING FROM HIGH SCHOOL with a 2.70 GPA did not, as my parents put it, leave me many options. I remember the college application process well. While many of my friends were praying to get into this Ivy league or that Top 10 school, I was hoping to get accepted... well... anywhere.

Coming from the background that I did, I was expected to go to college. I was going for that reason alone. The worries and anxieties of my peers when they discussed futures in law, medicine or business seemed distant and foreign. I had no idea what I wished to do, but I did know that these options sounded far removed from what I wanted as my future.

I first heard about Pitzer College from my cousin, while I was looking for a school that might be suckered into admitting me. At my interview, learning that I had been a professional magician since age 12, the Pitzer admissions staff demanded a magic show, just like that, on the spur of the moment. They liked my show, and I was accepted.

At Pitzer the professors actually cared about what you thought, as long as you had a reason and were ready to discuss it. This was all part of the community awareness and service philosophy that Pitzer strives to impart to all of it's students. By the time I graduated, I had volunteered in a homeless shelter, helped serve food in a soup kitchen, worked with the Pomona Police Department, did research in an emergency room, and flown half-way around the world to Nepal.

The events that led to my decision to attend a post-baccalaureate pre-medical program, however, are all tied to my experiences in the last five years. One particular experience had a profound impact on my choice of careers.

The two women in front of me are wrinkled and look old, though they are probably only in their mid-thirties. I am in the middle of the Himalayas, the Kingdom of Nepal, seven days from the nearest road, light bulb, running water, or hospital. I know the women, they are friends of a Sherpa acquaintance of mine who is off trekking on an expedition in another part of Nepal. I have been living in Nepal for about a year and a half at this point, and my Nepali is good enough to communicate well with the women. They know that I am managing a small "health project" as an intern for Pitzer College. The women tell me that my friend's wife has been gored by a bull, she's not doing well, and that she is still a good two days walk from where I am. As if this were not enough, she is also eight months pregnant.

I was overcome by a tremendous feeling of helplessness. I was isolated from anyone who could be of help. I also had a tremendous feeling of inexcusable ignorance. Even if I could get to the woman, I was unsure of what I could do. For two days I trudged up the trail towards the woman's village. I had been told my friend's wife had been gored in the lower back, not reassuring, especially since she was pregnant. If the woman died, was I supposed to somehow try to save the baby? If there was an infection would the pregnancy prove more dangerous to the mother? As these thoughts ran through my mind, I began to contemplate the possibility of becoming a doctor.

When I finally did reach the woman, I discovered her wound was superficial, not in her back, but instead passing between her legs and tearing the skin of her buttocks and genitals. A health worker had already sutured her up, and I had only to clean her wound and give her antibiotics. Eventually she went to a hospital and had a healthy baby boy. The experience was an incredible lesson in the value of a medical education.

After finishing my internship I was hired as Marketing Manager by a Hong Kong pharmaceutical company to conduct various studies concerning Nepalese health care issues specifically related to pharmaceutical use. The position was offered to me because of my fluency in Nepali, my experiences in Nepal, and because I had worked to develop the trust of many people there.

Now I find myself back in the USA. I am currently working for the University of California, Office of the President, Division of Agriculture and Natural Resources. In a few months I will be entering medical school at Tufts University.

My college experiences in community service have made such a difference in everything about me including my future. They are undoubtedly the reason that I was admitted into the medical program that I will be attending. To say that I did these things unselfishly would be a lie, yet this is perhaps the most important lesson I learned. I see so many people working so hard for personal achievement and status. So many people who base their happiness on material wealth. I wish that I could say that I am not driven by the same motivations, but I am. We are all striving to be happy and feel successful. I work in community service because by doing so I feel successful and worthwhile. I can go home at night and sleep comfortably, secure in the knowledge that I am doing what I need to be doing. Through community service I learned how wonderful it is to help others and to be helped by others. There is no one way street. In Nepal I took back far more than I could ever give. I have uncovered a wonderful secret, that the more I give of myself, the more I can receive, enabling me to gain far more than would by possible if I was working for myself alone.

*During his semester in Nepal, Judd Walson found time to make friends while working at a health project.*

# WORKING FOR A BETTER WORLD WHERE SCIENCE AND TECHNOLOGY ARE USED IN SOCIALLY RESPONSIBLE WAYS

## DAVID ANDERSEN

### STUDENT PUGWASH USA

SCIENCE MAJORS SPEND COUNTLESS HOURS IN LABORATORIES, peering into microscopes, designing experiments, and cleaning petri dishes. In the midst of endless assignments and tests it is easy to lose sight of the uses of the science we are doing. Rarely do we find time to think about how science and technology should be used in socially responsible ways. With the rapid pace of scientific and technological development, however, it is important to step back, examine the work that is being done, and ask tough questions about its applications. On college, university, and high school campuses across the United States, students are thinking critically about science, technology, global affairs, and social responsibility at Student Pugwash campus chapters.

Founded in 1979, Student Pugwash USA is the US student affiliate of the Pugwash Conferences on Science and World Affairs, recipients of the 1995 Nobel Peace Prize. With the advent of the hydrogen bomb as a humbling and frightening backdrop, Albert Einstein and Bertrand Russell co-authored a manifesto urging scientists to consider the social, moral, and ethical implications of weapons of mass destruction. This manifesto led to the first Pugwash Conference, held in Pugwash, Nova Scotia in 1957. The Pugwash spirit has always implied the need for scientists to broadly consider the ethical implications of their work, beyond the challenges raised by nuclear weapons.

The mission of Student Pugwash USA is to promote the socially responsible application of science and technology in the 21st century. As a student organization, Student Pugwash USA encourages young people to examine the ethical, social, and global implications of science and technology, and to make these concerns a guiding focus of their academic and professional endeavors. Student Pugwash USA offers educational programs that are interdisciplinary, intergenerational, and international in scope, reflecting a belief that all citizens share a responsibility to ensure that science and technology are utilized for the benefit of humankind. Student Pugwash is guided by respect for diverse perspectives and, as such, does not adopt advocacy positions.

Student Pugwash USA chapters are always asking the tough questions, such as: What are the effects of science and technology on society and individuals? How can we responsibly manage science and technology? What is the role of the individual in examining these issues? What ethical questions should be considered when doing scientific research? In a given year, a single chapter of Student Pugwash USA might address issues ranging from the future of nuclear energy to the emerging trends in communications technology and from the international arms trade to the social consequences of the Human Genome Project. They do this by organizing events such as roundtable discussions, lectures, movie nights, and panels on their campus. In addition, the national office organizes national and international conferences, and regional events. Students from all over the country pile into cars, trains, and planes to travel to these events where they are able to listen to important leaders, learn valuable leadership skills, and meet like-minded "Puggers." Often conversations last late into the night and friendships are formed that last a life time.

Student Pugwash USA's national office also has resources to help you and your chapter. This includes a Chapter Organizing Guide which explains the A to Z of starting and running a chapter; Pugwatch, the monthly chapter newsletter; and mind•full: a brainsnack for future leaders with ethical appetites, a series of issue briefs.

Asking tough questions and organizing events that address those questions adds a new level to a student's education. Instead of passively taking classes, someone involved in a Student Pugwash USA chapter takes control of his or her education. A member of Student Pugwash USA is able to influence debate on campus and encourage discussions about critical issues that otherwise might never be addressed.

In addition to the chapter program, Student Pugwash USA encourages young people to take a pledge that commits them to work for a better world. On December 10, 1995, the Pugwash Conferences on Science and World Affairs and its then-president, Professor Joseph Rotblat, received the Nobel Peace Prize. In honor of the Nobel Peace Prize and inspired by Professor Rotblat's idea of a Hippocratic Oath for young scientists, Student Pugwash USA developed a pledge that advocates the responsible use of science and technology. The pledge campaign celebrates the work of the Pugwash Conferences and encourages students and young professionals to commit themselves to the high standards of Pugwash.

*I promise to work for a better world, where science and technology are used in socially responsible ways. I will not use my education for any purpose intended to harm human beings or the environment. Throughout my career, I will consider the ethical implications of my work before I take action. While the demands placed upon me may be great, I sign this declaration because I recognize that individual responsibility is the first step on the path to peace.*

The pledge embodies the ideals we promote at Student Pugwash USA, and is our way of saying that the time has come for young people to actively promote the kind of world in which they want to live. You can take the pledge at: www.spusa.org/pugwash/.

To get involved in Student Pugwash USA contact the national office in Washington, DC. The national chapter coordinator can send you a Chapter Organizing Guide and talk with you about what you can do to start a chapter on your campus. The pledge coordinator can help you initiate a pledge campaign on your campus or in your community.

*David Andersen is National Chapter Coordinator for Student Pugwash.*

*For more information:*

Student Pugwash USA
1 (800) WOW-A-PUG

spusa@spusa.org
www.spusa.org/pugwash/

# GRADUATION PLEDGE OF ENVIRONMENTAL AND SOCIAL RESPONSIBILITY

**I, _____ PLEDGE TO EXPLORE AND TAKE INTO ACCOUNT THE SOCIAL AND ENVIRONMENTAL CONSEQUENCES OF ANY JOB OPPORTUNITY I CONSIDER AND WILL TRY TO IMPROVE THESE ASPECTS OF ANY ORGANIZATIONS FOR WHICH I WORK.**

BEGUN IN 1987, the Graduation Pledge is intended to be taken by students and celebrated as a part of commencement ceremonies. Since its founding, dozens of schools around the country have instituted such an effort, and the Pledge has now gone international. The commitment is voluntary and allows students to determine for themselves what they consider to be socially and environmentally responsible.

Instituting the pledge gets at the heart of a good education and can benefit society as a whole. Not only does it remind students of the ethical implications of the knowledge and training they received, but it can help lead to a socially-conscious citizenry and a better world. The pledge can also serve as a focal point for further consciousness-raising around campus.

Each year more than one million American students enter the work force who might potentially influence the shape of corporate America, as well as other segments of society. Think of the impact if even a significant minority of applicants and job holders inquired about or questioned the ethical practices of their potential or current employers. And shouldn't a job represent more than just a paycheck — a place where one can feel good about his/her own assignments and the general practice of the company?

We have learned of inspiring examples concerning student commitment to the pledge after graduation. "I told my boss of the pledge and my concerns. He understood and agreed, and the company did not pursue the (chemical warfare) project." Another supporter, "Now I make an effort to teach and think about social and environmental responsibility on a daily basis." Others have turned down potential jobs they did not feel comfortable with morally.

The pledge was founded at California's Humboldt State University and has been headquartered at Manchester College since 1996.

*For more information:*

Graduation Pledge Alliance
MC Box 135
Manchester College
604 E. College Ave.,
North Manchester, IN 46962

NJWollman@Manchester.edu
//www.manchester.edu.
Select "Graduation Pledge Alliance."

# THE TALLOIRES DECLARATION

ASSOCIATION OF UNIVERSITY LEADERS FOR A SUSTAINABLE FUTURE

THE ASSOCIATION OF UNIVERSITY LEADERS FOR A SUSTAINABLE FUTURE (ULSF) is an international membership organization of academic leaders and institutions committed to the advancement of global environmental literacy and sustainability. ULSF supports members in their efforts to unite administration, faculty, staff, and students in a collaborative effort to create sustainable institutions. ULSF promotes the Talloires Declaration and maintains an international network, facilitating information exchange, providing technical support, and operating educational programs that build organizational and individual capacity to develop sustainable policies and practices.

The Talloires Declaration is an international consensus document created by a gathering of university leaders in 1990 in Talloires, France. This Declaration is a commitment to specific actions to realize higher education leadership for global environmental literacy and sustainable development. It is founded on the belief that institutions of higher learning must exercise leadership to promote and reinforce environmental responsibility by integrating the ethical, social, economic, and ecological values of environmentally sustainable development into institutional policies and practices. This leadership begins with each university's mission and expands into the community, the region, and the national and international spheres. As a signatory to the Talloires, an institution is making a commitment to providing this essential leadership and uniting with other institutions around the world in forwarding this agenda.

## Talloires Declaration 10 Point Action Plan

We, the presidents, rectors, and vice chancellors of universities from all regions of the world are deeply concerned about the unprecedented scale and speed of environmental pollution and degradation, and the depletion of natural resources.

Local, regional, and global air and water pollution; accumulation and distribution of toxic wastes; destruction and depletion of forests, soil, and water; depletion of the ozone layer and emission of "green house" gases threaten the survival of humans and thousands of other living species, the integrity of the earth and its biodiversity, the security of nations, and the heritage of future generations. These environmental changes are caused by inequitable and unsustainable production and consumption patterns that aggravate poverty in many regions of the world.

We believe that urgent actions are needed to address these fundamental problems and reverse the trends. Stabilization of human population, adoption of environmentally sound industrial and agricultural technologies, reforestation, and ecological restoration are crucial elements in creating an equitable and sustainable future for all humankind in harmony with nature.

Universities have a major role in the education, research, policy formation, and information exchange necessary to make these goals possible. Thus, university leaders must initiate and support mobilization of internal and external resources so that their institutions respond to this urgent challenge.

**We, therefore, agree to take the following actions:**

### Increase Awareness of Environmentally Sustainable Development

Use every opportunity to raise public, government, industry, foundation, and university awareness by openly addressing the urgent need to move toward an environmentally sustainable future.

### Create an Institutional Culture of Sustainability

Encourage all universities to engage in education, research, policy formation, and information exchange on population, environment, and development to move toward global sustainability.

### Educate for Environmentally Responsible Citizenship

Establish programs to produce expertise in environmental management, sustainable economic development, population, and related fields to ensure that all university graduates are environmentally literate and have the awareness and understanding to be ecologically responsible citizens.

### Foster Environmental Literacy For All

Create programs to develop the capability of university faculty to teach environmental literacy to all undergraduate, graduate, and professional students.

### Practice Institutional Ecology

Set an example of environmental responsibility by establishing institutional ecology policies and practices of resource conservation, recycling, waste reduction, and environmentally sound operations.

### Involve All Stakeholders

Encourage involvement of government, foundations, and industry in supporting interdisciplinary research, education, policy formation, and information exchange in environmentally sustainable development. Expand work with community and nongovernmental organizations to assist in finding solutions to environmental problems.

### Collaborate for Interdisciplinary Approaches

Convene groups of university faculty and administrators with environmental practitioners to develop interdisciplinary approaches to curricula, research initiatives, operations, and outreach activities that support an environmentally sustainable future.

### Enhance Capacity of Primary and Secondary Schools

Establish partnerships with primary and secondary schools to help develop the capacity for interdisciplinary teaching about population, environment, and sustainable development.

### Broaden Service and Outreach Nationally and Internationally

Work with national and international organizations to promote a worldwide university effort toward a sustainable future.

### Maintain the Movement

Establish a Secretariat and a steering committee to continue this momentum, and to inform and support each other's efforts in carrying out this declaration.

*For more information:*
*University Leaders for a Sustainable Future*          *www.ulsf.org*

# THE COLLEGE REPORT CARD: A TOOL FOR CHOOSING FROM AMONG YOUR TOP-CHOICE COLLEGES

## MARTIN NEMKO

### DIRECTIONS

THERE ARE 47 ITEMS ON THE REPORT CARD. They are the major factors that affect students' success and happiness at college. Put a checkmark next to the 5-15 factors you consider most likely to affect your success and happiness.

Make a copy of the Report Card for each college you're considering.

Over the coming months, you'll have the chance to learn how each college measures up on your 5-15 factors: by reading college guides and materials from the colleges, talking with your counselor and college students home for vacation, asking questions at college nights, phoning college personnel and students, and making a campus visit. (See "How to Test Drive a College"). A primary source of information for each item is listed alongside it. Write what you learn in the margins of each college's Report Card.

*Important!!!* You can get information on most of the items by phone. For example, to talk with students, call the college's switchboard (the phone numbers are available from directory assistance and have the call transferred to a residence hall front desk, the student newspaper office, or the student government office.

By spring of your senior year, you'll have a wonderful basis for choosing your college. After you've finished recording what you learned, compare the report cards, then choose your college based on your gut feeling as to which one will best promote your intellectual, social, emotional, and ethical development.

# THE COLLEGE REPORT CARD
## FOR_____ COLLEGE/UNIVERSITY

### The Students

1. To what extent are you comfortable with the student body: intellectually, values, role of alcohol, work/play balance, etc.

### In the Classroom

2. What percentage of the typical first years' class time is spent in classes of 30 or fewer students? (*Ask students.*)

3. What percentage of class time is spent in lecture versus active learning? (*Ask students.*)

   Most educators agree that learning is often enhanced when students are active; for example, participating in discussions, case studies, field studies, hands-on activities. It's tough to achieve active learning in an auditorium. It's particularly important that first year classes be small because frosh are just getting used to college-level work. Students who might be tempted to space out or even play hooky in a large lecture class, should pay special attention to class size.

   Many colleges report a misleading statistic about class size: the faculty/student ratio. This statistic typically ranges from 1:10 to 1:25, even at mega state universities, evoking images of classes of 10-25 students. The faculty/student ratio is deceptive because it often includes faculty that do research but never teach, or at least never teach undergraduates. The faculty/student ratio also includes courses that you're unlikely to take. What good is it that Medieval Horticulture has three students if Intro to Anything has 300? Hence, the previous two questions are important.

4. How easy is it to register for the classes you want; e.g., do students register by telephone? Are enough sections of classes offered? (*Ask students*)

5. If you are attending a large school, are there special programs that enable you to get into smaller classes: e.g., honors programs, college within-a-college, living-learning centers? How are students selected for these programs? (*Read college guides and admissions material.*)

6. What percentage of your instructors would you describe as inspirational? (*Ask students.*)

7. What letter grade would you give to the average instructor? (*Ask students.*)

8. Does the college make available to students a booklet summarizing student evaluations of faculty? (*Ask students.*)

   Such a booklet makes it much easier to find good instructors. Also, its presence suggests that the college is more concerned about student rights as a consumer than it is about covering up professors' failings.

9. In a typical introductory social science or humanities course, how many pages of writing are typically assigned? In an advanced class? (*Ask students.*)

10. Does feedback on written work typically include detailed suggestions for improvement or just a letter grade with a few words of feedback? (*Ask students.*)

11. Must all assignments be done individually, or are there sufficient opportunities to do team projects? (*Ask students.*)

12. Is the institution strong in your major area of interest?

13. If you might want a self-designed major, is this a strong point at the school or an infrequently made exception. (*See catalog, ask students*)

14. Are there mechanisms for integrating different disciplines: interdisciplinary seminars, team teaching, internships, capstone classes? (*See catalog, ask admissions*)

**Intellectual life outside the classroom**

15. Describe and evaluate the advising you've received. (*Ask students.*)

16. How easy is it to get to work on a faculty member's research project? (*Ask students and faculty in your prospective major.*)

    Working under a professor's wing is an excellent opportunity for active learning, also when students become part of the research effort, they feel more like a member of the campus community.

17. To what extent do the viewpoints expressed on campus represent a true diversity of perspectives rather than, for example, just the liberal view or just the conservative stance? (*Ask students and faculty.*)

18. How frequently do faculty invite students to share a meal? (*Ask students.*)

19. How much does the typical student study between Friday dinner and Sunday dinner? (*Read college guides, ask students*)

20. Do faculty live in student residence halls? Does it encourage good faculty-student interaction? (*Call a residence hall front desk.*)

**The remaining questions in this section can probably best be answered via a phone call or a visit to the academic affairs office.**

21. How does the institution assess a prospective faculty member's ability to teach?

    Ideally, undergraduate institutions should require prospective undergraduate faculty members to submit a teaching portfolio consisting of videotapes of undergraduate classes, student evaluations, syllabi, and conduct a demonstration class at the freshman level. Many colleges only require prospective faculty to do a demonstration of a graduate level seminar in their research area. That says little about their ability to teach undergraduates.

22. Recognizing that this will vary from department to department, how likely is it that a good teacher who publishes little will get tenure?

23. On your most recent student satisfaction survey, what was the average rating for academic life? For out-of-classroom life?

This is the equivalent of asking hundreds of students how they like their college. If they say that the institution doesn't conduct student satisfaction surveys, you've learned that the institution doesn't care enough to assess student satisfaction.

24. How much money per student is spent annually on helping faculty to improve their teaching? (not to include money for research-related sabbaticals and conventions.)

Colleges frequently espouse the importance of good teaching. The answer to this question lets you know if a college puts its money where its mouth is.

25. What is done to ensure that students receive high quality advising?

For example, does faculty get special training in how to advise students? Does advising count in faculty promotion decisions? Can students and advisors, via computer, see what courses the student has taken and yet must take?

## Co-Curricular Life

26. Does the new-student orientation program extend beyond the traditional 1-3 days? (*Ask students, consult admissions brochure, and/or catalog.*)

27. What percentage of freshmen, sophomores, juniors, and seniors can obtain on-campus housing? This affects campus community. (*Consult admissions material, ask admissions or housing office.*)

28. Describe residence hall life. How close is it to the living-learning environment described in admission brochures? (*Ask students.*)

29. How attractive is student housing? (*Ask students. Tour facilities.*)

30. How well did you like your freshman roommate? This item assesses the quality of the college's roommate-matching procedure. (*Ask students.*)

31. Is the school's location a plus or minus. Why? (*Read college guides, ask students.*)

32. How many crimes were committed on or near campus last year? Ask admissions reps for the "crime pamphlet." (*Each school is required to provide one.*)

33. What is the quality of life for special constituencies; e.g., gay, adult, minority, or handicapped students? (*Read admission materials, ask students, phone the office that serves that constituency.*)

34. How strong is the sense of community and school spirit among the students? (*Read college guides, ask students.*)

35. In the dining hall, do students primarily eat in homogeneous groups: for example international, racial groups, etc. (*Ask students, observe first-hand.*)

36. How extensive are the opportunities for community service? What percentage of students participate in it? (*Ask students, the career center, service office.*)

## The "Real" World

37. How extensive are the internship opportunities?

    Internships embody active learning, allow students to bridge theory and practice, try out a career without penalty, and make job connections. (*Ask students, contact the career center.*)

38. How good are the career planning and placement services? (*Ask upperclass students*)

    Most colleges offer some career planning and placement, but the best ones offer critiques of videotaped mock interviews, the SIGI or Discover computer career guidance systems, video-interviewing with distant employees, extensive counseling, many job listings, on-campus employee interviews, and connections with alumni. (*Ask students and personnel at the career center.*)

39. In your field, what percentage of students get jobs or into graduate school? What percentage go into service-oriented careers? (*Ask students, faculty in your prospective major, ask at the career center.*)

## Overall Indicators of the Institution's Quality

40. What percentage of incoming freshmen return for the sophomore year? (*Consult college guides, ask admissions rep or call the office of institutional research.*)

41. What percentage of students graduate within four years? Five years? (*Consult college guides, ask admissions rep, or call the office of institutional research.*)

    Graduation rate depends in part on student quality: the better the students, the higher the college's graduation rate. But take note if two institutions with similar S.A.T. averages have very different graduation rates. The one with a higher graduation rate will generally have more satisfied students.

42. What should I know about the college that wouldn't appear in print? (*Ask everyone.*)

43. What's the best and worst thing about this college? (*Ask everyone.*)

44. In what ways is this college different from_____College? Ask about a similar institution that you're considering. (*Ask admissions rep, students, perhaps faculty.*)

45. What sorts of students are the perfect fit for this school? A poor fit? (*Read college guides, ask everyone.*)

46. What is the total cost of attending this college, taking into account your likely financial aid package? (*Ask the financial aid office.*)

47. What other information about the school could affect your decision? E.g., beauty of campus, food, a graduation requirement you object to, percent of students of your religious or ethnic group. (*Consult catalog, college guides, ask admissions rep.*)

# HOW TO TEST-DRIVE A COLLEGE

## MARTIN NEMKO

COLLEGE A OR COLLEGE B? A visit is the best key to deciding. You wouldn't even buy a jalopy without popping the hood and test-driving it. With a college, you're spending thousands of dollars and four or even six years of your life, so better take it for a good spin.

Trouble is, many students make a worse decision after a visit than they would have made without one. A college can feel so overwhelming that many students come away with little more than, "The campus was beautiful and the tour guide was nice."

Here's how to put a college through its paces.

### Preparing

Plan to visit when school is in session. Visiting a college when it isn't in session is like test-driving a car with the engine off.

Call ahead. Ask the admissions office if you can spend the night in a residence hall, perhaps with a student in your prospective major. If you think it might help, make an appointment for an interview. Get directions to campus, a campus map, and where to park. Also find out when and from where tours are given.

Reread the college guides. If you're just about to visit, that seemingly boring profile of Sonoma State may become fascinating. It can also raise questions, like, "The book describes Sonoma's Hutchins School of Liberal Studies as excellent. Is it?"

Review the questions on the College Report Card.

### The Visit

Write what you learn on the College Report Card. Especially if you're visiting more than one college, the differences between them can blur.

Here are the stops on my campus tour. If you're with parents, split up, at least for part of the time. Not only can you see more, but it's easier to ask questions like, "What's the social life like?"

### The Official Tour

Take the tour mainly to orient you to campus geography, not to help you pick your college. Tour guides are almost always enthusiastic unless, of course, they're in a bad mood. The tour guide, however, is usually a knowledgeable student, so while walking to the next point of interest, you may want to ask some questions.

## Grab Students

I know it's scary, but grab approachable students in the plaza or student union and ask a question. Most love to talk about their school. You might start with, "Hi, I'm considering coming to this school. Are you happy here? What would you change about the school? What should I know about it that might not appear in print?"

In addition to students at random, consider dropping by a residence hall and talking with the student at the front desk. Or pay a visit to the student government or student newspaper office. Folks there know a lot about life on campus. While you're at the newspaper office, pick up a few copies of the student newspaper. What sorts of stories make the front page? What's in the letters to the editor? Athletes should query players on the team, oboeists should quiz orchestra members.

The key is: never leave a campus without talking with at least five people that the admissions director did not put in front of you. Don't just speak with who's paid by the school, speak with who's paying the school. Like at high school, some people love the school and others hate it, but talk with ten people, and you'll get the picture.

## A Dining Hall and/or the Student Union

Sample the food. Tasty nuggets or chicken tetrachloride? Are you a vegetarian? See if there's more than salad bar and cheese-drenched veggies.

While you're in the dining hall (or in the student union), eavesdrop on discussions. Can you see yourself happily involved in such conversations?

Most colleges claim to celebrate diversity. The dining hall is a great place to assess the reality because, there, integration is voluntary. Do people of different races break bread together?

Bulletin boards are windows to the soul of a college. Is the most frequent flyer, "Noted scholar speaks," "Political action rally," or "Semi-formal ball"?

## Sit In On A Class

Best choices are a class in your prospective major, a required class, or in a special class you're planning to enroll in, for example, an honors class.

At the break, or at the end of the class, stop a group of students and ask them questions. If it's a class in your prospective major, ask students how they like the major and what you should know about the major that might not appear in the catalog.

## How to Visit 10 Classes in Half an Hour

Rather than following the standard advice to "sit in on a class" which only lets you know about one class, ask a student for the name of a building with many undergraduate classes.

Walk down its halls and peek into open doors. What percentage of classes are alive and interactive? In what percentage is the professor droning on like a high schooler reciting the pledge of allegiance with the students looking as bored as career bureaucrats two days from retirement?

Some students say that they are too shy to peek into or sit in on classes, but it's worth conquering the shyness. Shouldn't you look at a sample of classes before committing to four years worth?

### A Night in the Dorm

It's an uncomfortable thought. "I'm a dippy high school kid. I'll feel weird spending a whole night with college students." Luckily, it usually ends up being fun as well as informative. A bunch of students will probably cluster around you, dying to reveal the inside dirt.

You'll also learn what the students are like: Too studious? Too raunchy? Too radical? Too preppy? At 10:30 P.M. on a weeknight, is the atmosphere "Animal House," an academic sweatshop, or a good balance?

Are the accommodations plush or spartan? One prospective student found a dorm crawling with roaches. You won't get that information on the official tour.

### Beware of Bias

We've already mentioned the peril of an overzealous tour guide. Here are other sources of bias in a college visit:

### Timing

You visited a college on Thursday at noon. That's when many colleges are at their best. Students are buzzing around amid folks hawking hand-crafted jewelry or urging you to join their clubs or causes, all perhaps accompanied by a rock band. But if you were to arrive at 4:30, even the most dynamic college won't seem as exciting.

### Weather

No matter how great the college, rain can't help but dampen enthusiasm for it.

### The Campus

Chant this 10,000 times: "Better good teachers in wooden buildings than wooden teachers in good buildings." As mentioned earlier, it's so easy to be overwhelmed by ivy-covered buildings, lush lawns, and chiming bell towers. A beautiful campus is nice, but don't let it overwhelm other factors.

Colleges begin to melt together after a while, however, so you might want to take photos of each campus.

### After the Visit

Finish recording what you've learned on the College Report Card immediately after leaving campus. Especially if you've visited a number of colleges, it's easy to confuse key features of one with another: "Was it North Carolina-Asheville or St. John's that had great vegetarian food?"

Probably, additional questions about each college will come to mind after you leave. Write them down and send them to your college interviewer as part of a thank you note which expresses your appreciation for the time spent and the advice you received.

**The Decision**

After you get home, ask yourself four questions:

- Would I be happy living and learning with these types of students for four years?

- Would I be happy being instructed by these professors for four years?

- Would I be happy living in this environment for four years?

- Will this college help me achieve my goals?
  If it's yes to all four, you may have found your new home.
  *Congratulations!*

*Martin Nemko, Ph.D., co-author of* Cool Careers for Dummies *and author of* You're Gonna Love This College Guide *(Barron's) is an Oakland, California-based consultant to families and colleges on undergraduate education.*

# MAKING A DIFFERENCE CAREERS

**African-American Studies**  See Ethnic Studies

**Agricultural Engineers**  Design systems and strategies that preserve and protect our water and soil resources, regarding various engineering aspects of food and fiber production. Many work in developing countries helping with appropriate technology for increasing food production and quality while using human and natural resources responsibly.

**Agroecology**  (The study of sustainable agriculture — more commonly known as 'organic farming') Graduates are in demand in farming, agribusiness, teaching, research and government.

**American Studies**  Graduates find work as journalists, lawyers, government workers, teachers, business people, historical preservationists, and museum workers.

**Anthropology**  Majors find work in federal, state, and local government, law, medicine, urban planning, business, and museums. They often go on to graduate work in anthropology as well, for a career in teaching.

**Atmospheric Science**  See Meteorology

**Child Development**  Careers as adoption counselors, child development specialists, educational consultants, working with handicapped children, hospital childlife specialists and go on to graduate work for Marriage & Family Counselor degrees. They work in crisis centers, hospitals, and both private and public agencies at both the local and national level.

**Civil Engineers**  Conceive, plan, design, construct, operate and maintain dams, bridges, aqueducts, water treatment plants, sewage treatment plants, flood control works, and urban development programs. They are employed by governmental agencies at all levels and by engineering contractors, private consulting firms and in the areas of teaching, research, materials testing, city planning and administration fields.

**Community Health Educators**  Work as school health educators, community health educators, family planning educators, environmental health specialists,   occupational safety specialists, public health investigators, consumer safety investigators and OSHA inspectors.

**Conservation Law Enforcement**  Graduates find work with state and federal governments as game wardens, conservation officers, special agents for U.S. Fish & Wildlife, wildlife inspectors, border patrol agents, park rangers and state troopers.

**Economics** Prepares students for careers both nationally and internationally in business labor, government, public service, or law.

**Entomologists** (Those who study insects) Work in the area of Integrated Pest Management which is essential part of organic farming. They work to understand the role of insects in the natural world and how they interact with man. They seek safe and effective solutions to insect problems in urban environments and agriculture.

**Environmental Education** Can lead to work in park and natural preserve administration, aquarium management, environmental advocacy organizations, nature writing, photography and documentation, teaching in elementary and secondary schools, and government work for environmental agencies.

**Environmental Engineers** Work in the areas of control of air & water pollution, industrial hygiene, noise & vibration control, and solid & hazardous waste management. Graduates find work in industry, consulting firms, and public agencies concerned with air and water pollution control and water treatment.

**Environmental and Forest Biology** Careers as animal ecologists, aquatic biologists, botanists, conservation biologists, consulting biologists, environmental assessment specialists, environmental conservation officers, fisheries biologists, natural resource specialists, ornithologists, park naturalists, plant and wetlands ecologists, public health specialists, sanctuary managers, soil conservationists, toxicologists, waterfowl biologists, wildlife biologists, game biologists, entomologists.

**Environmental Health Specialists** Work for state governments enforcing and administering laws governing water, food, and air contamination, noise, land use planning, occupational health hazards, and animal vectors of disease.

**Environmental Studies** Majors find a myriad of careers from cartographers, community resource development, cultural impact analysis, to environmental lobbyist, interpretive naturalist, park managers, recycled paper promoters, to wilderness survival instructors. Graduates also find work as pollution analysts, environmental journalists, air quality aides, transportation planners, pollution measurement technicians, environmental affairs directors, recycling co-ordinators, environmental educators, energy conservation specialists and legislative researchers.

**Environmental Toxicology** Those not going on to graduate study find work with government agencies, universities, industry research and consulting firms in the areas of residue analysis, environmental monitoring, forensic toxicology, animal toxicology, environmental health and safety and pest control.

**Ethnic Studies** Graduates work in community service organizations concerned with opportunities and problems of various ethnic and racial groups. They work as affirmative action officers, Equal Opportunity representatives, human relations specialists, peace officers, ombudsmen, urban specialists, diversity directors, educational specialists and lobbyists. Preparation for graduate work in the social sciences, law and humanities, and for work in municipal, state and federal government.

**Fisheries** Work in management, law enforcement and public information-education phases of fisheries work with national and international agencies as well as with regional, state and local government. Increasing opportunities are available with private industry interested in conservation, hydropower companies, and an expanding recreation business. Careers in research, administration, or teaching.

**Forest Engineers** Work in the areas of water resources (including water supply for urban areas and ground water aquifer protection) pollution abatement, and hazardous waste management. They design and plan collection systems to store and transport water, timber and energy structures, pollution abatement systems, and energy management. Careers as energy efficiency specialists, energy planning supervisors, environmental engineers, hydrologists, pollution control engineers, road engineers, survey party chief, water rights engineers, forest engineers, cartographers, ground water investigators, and natural resource engineers.

**Forestry** Graduates find work as foresters, arborists, environmental consultants, forest ecologists, timber buyers, urban foresters, land use specialists, forest economists, interpretive naturalists, consultants, environmental scientists, outdoor recreation, environmental conservation officers, naturalists, outdoor recreation, policy makers, forest protection work, including fire, insect and disease control. Managerial work planning timber crop rotations, and evaluating the economics of alternative forest management plans. Jobs far exceed the number of graduates each year.

**Forest Ranger** Graduates find work as county park rangers, environmental conservation officers, forest firefighters, forest rangers, forestry aides, survey party chiefs, engineer's aides, and forestry technicians. Jobs in forestry and surveying fields far exceed the number of graduates each year.

**Fuel Science** Graduates find work seeking to provide reliable energy sources without adverse environmental effects. They are employed by industry, government and utilities, as well as continuing on to graduate school.

**Geology** Geologists seek new resources, while insuring the most environmentally responsible means of doing so, ensure preservation of land and water quality, formulate plans for restoration of degraded lands. Career opportunities include industry, government and education. Many students continue on to graduate school in urban planning, engineering, environmental studies etc.

**Geography** Careers with environmental and resource management, location and resource decision-making, urban and regional planning and policy questions, and transportation in government, private, non-profit and international agencies.

**Gerontologists** Work in human service positions with the elderly or preparation for graduate school.

**Human Services** Work in advocacy, program development, management, direct service and case management in child-welfare agencies, drug and alcohol programs, crisis intervention settings, group homes for adolescents, community action programs, emergency housing programs, parole and probation. May provide case management, needs assessment, advocacy, crisis intervention and stabilization, and supportive task-oriented short term counseling.

**Integrated Health Studies** See Community Health

**International Agriculture Development** Careers in helping to solve hunger problems in Third World countries. This may involve working at the local level with government, private business, church or philanthropic organizations. Equally suitable for students with or without agricultural background.

**Labor and Industrial Relations** Graduates find employment in business, government, and labor organizations as labor relations specialists, personnel and human resource specialists, researchers, organizers, consultants and professionals in mediation and arbitration. The degree is also good preparation for graduate or law school.

**Landscape Architects** Work as city planners, coastal specialists, coastal zone resource specialists, community planners, environmental planners, land designers, land use planners, landscape architects and contractors, park landscape architects, regional, site, and transportation planners.

**Landscape Horticulture** See Urban Forestry

**Land Use Planners** Work with state or federal regulatory agencies, regional planning commissions, consulting firms and municipalities.

**Marine Biologists** Find careers in marine research, education and administration in marine industries and aquaculture, as well as further graduate study and research.

**Medical Anthropologists** (The study of the relationship between culture and health - a growing discipline for persons involved with the health needs of ethnically diverse populations.) Employment areas include local, state, federal and voluntary health agencies, and preparation for graduate programs.

**Meteorologists** (Study of the atmosphere) This field is important in environmental, energy, agricultural, oceanic and hydrological sciences. Graduates find careers with industry, private consulting firms, government, or continue on to graduate school.

**Native American Studies** Graduates teach social sciences, work in tribal governments and communities, and prepare for graduate work in anthropology, history, sociology, or professional training in law or business.

**Natural Resources Planning & Interpretation** Soil conservationist, environmental journalist, natural resources librarian, park ranger, rural county planner, environmental education leader, naturalist, hydrologist, information specialist.

**Natural Resources Management** Graduates work as public affairs specialists, soil technicians, wildlife biologist/managers, plant curators, park ranger/managers, environmental planners, city planners, soil conservation planners, shellfish biologists, naturalists, and hazardous materials technicians. (See fisheries, forestry, wildlife...)

**Natural Resource Sciences** Careers in professional areas with a holistic perspective on resource management and research. Graduates are employed by all major public and private land management and wildlife organizations. They work as foresters, range conservationists, wildlife biologists, park managers, information specialists, game managers, consultants, researchers, and in developing countries.

**Oceanography** Graduates work as oceanographers, marine biologists, aquatic biologists, water pollution technicians, research assistants, earth scientists and environmental specialists.

**Outdoor Education & Interpretation** Careers in designing and administering recreation programs, guiding groups in wilderness adventures, counseling and working with diverse populations (troubled youth, handicapped people, senior citizens). Work with state, federal, private recreation departments, environmental education centers, camps, schools, groups such as Outward Bound.

**Paper & Science Engineering** Careers in recycling, paper making, waste treatment, hazardous waste management, oil spill prevention, environmental monitoring.

**Peace & Conflict** Careers in arms control and public policy, third world development and human rights, the faith community, Peace Corps, the United Nations, domestic social and economic justice, civil rights, mediation and conflict resolution. Preparation for law, journalism, education, government, and communications.

**Political Science** (The study of predicting, explaining, and evaluating political behavior, beliefs etc.) Graduates find socially relevant careers in public service, political analysis and teaching. They attend graduate school in areas such as law, teaching, social work, journalism, public administration and public policy.

**Public Administration** Graduates work in administrative positions, as well as personnel, budgeting, planning, and public relations, and in substantive policy areas ranging from health and human services and environmental protection to defense, criminal justice, transportation and taxation. Work in city and town management, regional planning commissions, the state budget office and administrative positions in education, national, and international agencies.

**Public Health** Careers as program analysts, mid-level administrators, technical staff persons, department heads in all areas of the health services delivery, and in the regulations field that require policy development, implementation, and evaluation.

**Range Management / Resource Science** Careers are available as range conservationists, range managers, natural resource specialists, environmental specialists, soil scientists, park rangers, biological technicians, and agricultural inspectors.

**Science, Technology, and Values** See Technology and Society

**Sociologists** Find work as consultants to business and government, as social change agents (such as community organizers,) politicians, educators and diplomats. They find careers as urban planners, youth counselors, employment counselors, public opinion analysts, social ecologists, industrial sociologists, correctional counselors, probation officers, health services consultants, and personnel management specialists.

**Social Workers** Work in areas of health care, services to the elderly, community practice, rehabilitation, youth work, mental health, services to children and families, substance abuse, residential treatment, the developmentally disabled and employment services. They work in nursing homes, public schools, and probation offices.

**Soil Science** Graduates work in conservation planning, wetland identification and delineation, land reclamation, sediment & erosion control, land use planning, site evaluations, waste management, soil fertility mgm't, computer modeling of nutrient and pesticide movement, and with international institutions and organizations.

**Technology and Society** Employment is found with private industry, consulting companies, environmental foundations, and government in the areas of policy analysis and formulation, planning, risk analysis and environmental impact assessment.

**Urban Forestry & Landscape Horticulture** Leads to careers in landscape design and contracting, urban forestry, park supervision, garden center management, arborists, and city foresters.

**Wildlife Studies** Wildlife biologist, wildlife manager, fish & game warden, conservation officer, range conservationist, forestry technician, park ranger, soil scientists, naturalist, environmental planner, agricultural inspector, wildlife refuge manager, preserve manager, fisheries technician, and studying rare and endangered species. Work with state and federal environmental agencies and groups such as the Audubon Society and The Nature Conservancy.

**Women's Studies** Is an asset to careers in such fields as education, social service, government, business, law, the ministry, journalism, counseling, health and child care. More specialized work is found in battered women's shelters, rape counseling services, and in displaced homemaker centers. Graduates also work as women's health care specialists, political advocates, psychologists, and teachers.

# MAKING A DIFFERENCE COLLEGES

**...**

* Please note, "Making A Difference Studies" include some minors.

# UNIVERSITY OF ALASKA, FAIRBANKS

3,900 Undergraduates    Fairbanks, Alaska

UAF students aren't afraid to be different. The University of Alaska Fairbanks isn't the right school for everyone, but if it is right for you, you can take advantage of small classes, first-rate faculty and access to hands' on research — not to mention some of the most breathtaking scenery in the world. With a low student/faculty ratio, students get lots of personal attention — more attention, in fact, than at almost any other public university in the country

The core curriculum provides students with a shared foundation of skills and knowledge. Among others, core experience achievements are expected to include:

- An intellectual comfort with the sciences — including the objectivity of the scientific method, the frameworks which have nurtured scientific thought, the traditions of human inquiry, and the impact of technology on the world's ecosystems;
- An appreciation of cultural diversity and its implications for individual and group values, aesthetics, and social and political institutions;
- An understanding of our global economic interdependence, sense of historical consciousness, and a more critical comprehension of literature and the arts;
- A better understanding of one's own values, other value systems and the relationship between value systems and life choices.

Students in the College of Natural Sciences (CNS) have one of the most exciting natural laboratories in which to learn. CNS has undergraduate programs in biology, geology, chemistry, physics, and wildlife management, all of which offer research opportunities. The college also offers two interdisciplinary programs in earth and general sciences, intended especially for those seeking teaching certificates. The research institutes associated with the college — the Geophysical Institute, the Institute of Artic Biology (IAB), the Alaska Cooperative Wildlife Research Unit — are nationally and internationally recognized. IAB manages the Large Animal Research Station just north of campus, the home of musk oxen, caribou and reindeer.

In the College of Rural Alaska, the five departments of behavioral sciences and human services — education, general studies, rural development, and vocational education — all work to prepare students to be more sensitive to cross-cultural settings and diversity. Alaskan trained teachers and social workers are in demand in Alaska.

Although primarily a graduate institution, undergraduates in The School of Fisheries and Ocean Sciences are well prepared for graduate study or to enter management, law enforcement, and/or public information-education fields related to fisheries, and often are able to find summer field work opportunities through cooperating state and federal agencies. The school operates coastal facilities at Juneau, Kodiak, Seward and Kasistna Bay, and also the 133-foot oceanographic vessel R/V Alpha Helix for seagoing research and education.

With a population of more than 70,000, the Fairbanks area offers the conveniences of a big city, yet rolling hills and spectacular panorama are only minutes away. Literally millions of acres of wilderness surround Fairbanks. Whether the sport is canoeing, climbing, running, skiing, or fishing, nowhere else compares with Alaska.

# MAKING A DIFFERENCE STUDIES

## Natural Resources Management: Forestry, Plant, Animal & Soil Sciences

Forest Protection
Introduction to Conservation Biology
Introduction to Watershed Management
Alaskan Environmental Education
Environmental Policies

Natural Resource Legislation and Policy
Environmental Ethics and Actions
Natural Resources Conservation and Policy
Outdoor Recreation Planning
Ecological Anthropology

## Fisheries / Fisheries Management

*UAF location is advantageous for the study of interior Alaska aquatic streams & lakes.*

Natural Resources Policies
Geography of Alaska
Magazine Article Writing
Wildlife Management Techniques
Alaska Native Politics

Natural Resources Legislation
Man and Nature
Congress and Public Policy
Wildlife Management – Forest & Tundra
Personnel Management

## Wildlife Biology

Survey of Wildlife Science
Wildlife Policy and Administration
Wildlife Internships
Wildlife Diseases
Biotelemetry

Wildlife Management Principles
Grazing Ecology
Waterfowl & Wetlands Ecology & Mgm't
Nutrition & Physiological Ecology of Wildlife
Wildlife Populations and their Management

## Human Services / Human Service Technology A.A.

*Interdisciplinary in approach, cross-cultural in content, and rural in orientation.*

Rural Sociology
Human Behavior in the Artic
Substance Abuse Counseling
Sociology of Later Life
Helping Role in Child Abuse & Neglect
Family in Cross Cultural Perspective

Cross Cultural Psychology
Dev. Psych in Cross Cultural Perspectives
Alcoholism: Treatment and Prevention
Community Organization & Dev. Strategies
Group Dynamics & Therapeutic Activities
Ethics in Human Service

## Rural Development: Land; Renewable Resources; Community Research & Documentation; Community Organization & Service; Local Gov't. Administration

Community Development in the North
Rural Alaska Land Issues
Resource Mgm't. Research Techniques
Tribal People and Development
Cultural Impact Analysis
Narrative Art of Alaska Native Peoples

Issues in Alaskan Maritime Development
Perspectives on Subsistence in Alaska
Community Research Techniques
Rural Social Work
Women and Development
Knowledge of Native Elders

**Women's Studies    Northern Studies    Forestry 3/2 Northern AZ. U.**
**Education    Social Work    Community Health Aide    Geology    Eskimo Studies**

Apply by 8/1

• Prior learning credit     • Weekend & evening classes     • Independent learning

Office of Admissions and Records
University of Alaska, Fairbanks
Fairbanks, AK 99775-0060

907. 474.7500
800. 478.IUAF (Alaska only)
fyadmis@aurora.alaska.edu

# ALASKA PACIFIC UNIVERSITY

325 Students    Anchorage, Alaska

"APU seeks students with a high sense of purpose and idealism about their personal future and about the future of the world. It is APU's job to help students find their individual gifts and personal paths; and to equip each with the skills, knowledge, and character they need to reach their personal goals and to improve the world."

— 1999-2000 Viewbook
Alaska Pacific University

Alaska Pacific University's educational mission is to create in its students a sense of "practical idealism." A practical idealist combines a strong commitment to bringing about societal changes with the skills and knowledge needed to be effective.

To achieve this mission, APU provides an active and experiential education. From the very first course, "Introduction to Active Learning," APU students learn how to carry out a project of personal significance with academic and professional rigor. In fact, several distinctive features of APU's curriculum are designed to enhance active, experiential learning.

Project-Based Education: Completing a project involves conceptualizing, planning, evaluating, and, finally, presenting a significant piece of work, and not just research papers. Action projects, which clearly accomplish something of value in the real world, are the essence of APU. Through directed studies, block courses, internships, and individual projects, students perfect the skills of the practical idealist. The process culminates in a required, twelve credit Senior Project that encompasses most, if not all, of a student's final semester. Senior Projects are typically done off-campus and involve significant social change work. In other words, new APU graduates are already accomplished and experienced practical idealists.

In less academic terms, while APU agrees that some of the skills required for innovation, change, and leadership are acquired in a lecture hall; they firmly believe that most of these skills are acquired through a project that has involved vision, thought, planning, and some risk of failure.

This list of recent Senior Projects and Internships speaks for itself:
- A human services student created a resource manual of social service agencies in Anchorage for the Southcentral Counseling Foundation, an Alaska Native non-profit corporation affiliated with the Cook Inlet Region, Inc.
- An environmental science student completed an internship with the Sitka Conservation Association as part of a team that analyzed the impact that the Tongass Land Management Plan (TLMP) revision had on wildlife habitat, subsistence, tourism, and fisheries.
- An education student served an internship with the Minority Leaders Fellowship in Washington, D.C., helping to set up forums and a website as well as organizing fund-raising activities.

The Block: Each of APU's three semesters begins with a four-week Block. During the Block, a student will take just one course or directed study. Having no other courses to cause conflicts, Block students have the opportunity to travel, get into the field, and out in the world.

These recent Block courses demonstrate how APU students learn experientially:

- Outdoor Studies majors take the Block course "Introduction to Wilderness Skills" where they learn the "Leave No Trace"© philosophy of camping and hiking.
- Environmental science students have traveled to Block in Borneo, Costa Rica and Baja, California to study rain forest pollution.
- Education students have traveled to remote Alaskan villages to study the role that cultural diversity plays in educating Alaska Native children and to better understand the impact that deep cultural ideals can sometimes have on educating Alaska Native children.

The Major/Minor system: APU has six areas of study: Environmental Science, Outdoor Studies, Business, Liberal Studies, Psychology and Human Services, and Education. Within these there are many majors and focus areas, such as Marine Biology, Eco-psychology, Environmental Policy, or Multicultural Education. (Students who want to "make a difference" often wonder what Business is doing on that list. But a person working with a start-up eco-tourism business or a small non-profit organization quickly discovers that social change and business often go hand-in-hand — this is to say nothing of the many ways in which business can be more responsive and responsible to the earth and its societies.)

The Major/Minor system allows students to create a personalized curriculum. The Senior Project enables them to sharpen it to a point. For instance, a student who has a gift for working with children, strong environmental and multi-cultural ethics, and an adventurous soul, would seem a natural fit as a major in education with a minor in environmental science, in addition to a student teaching assignment in a rural Alaskan village school. This could lead that student directly to becoming a state certified elementary school science teacher in a Yup'ik or Inupiat school. That is practical idealism in action. What's your gift, your purpose?

A Campus that Walks its Talk: Environmental and social consciousness and action are at the core of APU's student body, faculty and administration. Students who are socially active and motivated find that they are the majority on campus, not an alienated minority. Students run the campus recycling program and take part in volunteer social projects with United Way and Habitat for Humanity. APU's student clubs have worked together to organize programs for the homeless in Anchorage. Students with leadership positions in these clubs receive sizeable financial assistance. Approximately 18% of APU is made up of students of minority ethnicity, and that number will increase substantially in 2001 when APU opens the Morris and Thelma Thompson Living and Learning Community, a residence hall for Alaska Native students.

# MAKING A DIFFERENCE STUDIES

## Environmental Science

Environmental Assessment and Audit
Resource Economics
Environmental Chemistry
Environmental Geology
Meteorology: Weather and Climate

Principles of Forest Management
Oceanography
Environmental Ethics
Winter Ecology & Cold Weather Physiology
Natural Resources Planning and Politics

- **Conservation Biology** *An introduction to the science of preserving biological diversity, its principles, policy, and applications. Topics include extinction, ecological and genetic effects of habitat fragmentation, minimum viable population analysis, reserve design and management, the Endangered Species Act, and conflict mediation.*

## Outdoor Studies

Wilderness First Responder
Program Design for Recreational Services
Intro to Wilderness Skills
Expedition Mountaineering
Search and Rescue

Outdoor Education and Interpretive Services
Log Cabin Construction & Wilderness Living
Expedition Sea Kayaking
Outdoor Rec. Resources, Issues, &Trends
Adventure Programming & Leisure Services

- **Outdoor Leadership and Wilderness Education** *Expedition format during May. Development, application, and evaluation of outdoor leadership skills. Students will plan, organize, and lead the expedition. Decision making, teaching techniques, expedition behavior, group dynamics, risk management and environmental ethics emphasized.*
- **Faculty Bio: Roman Dial** *(M.S., U of Alaska; Ph.D., Stanford U.) Dr. Dial's research has taken him from collecting field data in Caribbean rainforests and Borneo, to studying effects of habitat destruction on Alaskan mammals. A writer and photographer, Roman has contributed to Patagonia, Smithsonian, Outside, & Mountain Bike.*

## Psychology and Human Services

Ecopsychology
Educational Psychology
Lifespan Human Development
Dynamics of Early Child Care
Intro to Counseling

Coping and Adjustment
Anthropological Psychology
Issues in Substance Abuse
Self Concept: Formation & Development
Group Process, Social Influence & Leadership

- **Applied Psychology: Intimacy, Relationships and Sexuality** *What causes one human being to become attracted to another? How are expressions of love and sexuality related? What commitments and responsibilities are implicit in an intimate relationship? Sexual orientation, abortion, reproductive technologies, gender issues.*
- **Faculty Bio: Dr. Ellen Cole's** *interests include the psychology of women, refugees and indigenous people; sex therapy; wilderness and adventure therapy; and ecopsychology. She is a licensed psychologist.*

Early decision 12/1    Regular decision 3/1
Faculty: 55% male, 45% female, 5% minority
• Field studies   • Life experience credit
• Interdisciplinary classes   • All seminar format   • Self-designed majors

Office of Admissions
Alaska Pacific University
4101 University Drive
Anchorage, AK 99508

800. 252.7528
admiss@alaskapacific.edu
www.alaskapacific.edu

# ANTIOCH COLLEGE

650 Students    Yellow Springs, Ohio

Antioch College was founded in 1852 by educational reformer Horace Mann as a pioneering experiment in education which offered the first "separate but equal" curriculum to both men and women and stressed that there should be no bars for race, sex, or creed. Today, Antioch continues to dedicate itself to the ideas of equality, "whole-person" education, and community service.

Antioch students are expected to reach beyond conventional learning. They are encouraged to become courageous practitioners, intelligent experimenters, and creative thinkers. Both the faculty and the students strive towards the common goals of refinement and testing of ideas through experience, and of extensive student participation to mold both the campus and the community.

Antioch is committed to internationalization and to peace. Antioch encourages its students to have a balanced respect for all of life — for one's self, for others, for society, and for the Earth. Empowered by their education, students are encouraged to empower others.

To accomplish its mission of enhancing classroom education with hands-on experience, Antioch has one of the most challenging cooperative education programs in the nation. Just a few examples of positions which Antiochians continue to hold include environmental science jobs in Parana State, Brazil; The National Abortion Federation in Washington, DC; and the Peace Child Foundation in Fairfax, Virginia. Each academic year is composed of three trimesters. During the Fall and Spring trimester, students enroll in three to four courses per study term. The summer trimester consists of three 4-week blocks in which students participate in a single intensive course each month. Students will begin one of two divisions which alternate use of the college campus and off-campus work experiences. One division will begin in the summer trimester. All students study full-time on campus for a total of seven 14-week trimesters. Students work full-time off campus, usually in paying jobs located throughout the country and the world, for a total of five 16-week trimesters.

The variety of experience this provides is substantial. One environmental science student, for instance, worked as an environmental education assistant on a sloop on the Hudson River, at a resource center in Minnesota, researched rare plants in Appalachia, cared for injured birds in a raptor rehabilitation project in St. Louis, and then traveled around studying issues of importance in the Northwest. The Co-op Faculty maintains a network of 300 employers who hire students on a regular basis. Advisers assist students in choosing, financing, and evaluating their co-ops, as well as dealing with unexpected problems.

During the study trimester, students take part in an academic program which relies on utilizing the strengths of each individual, a willingness to both speak and listen critically, and an international, multi-cultural focus. Professors apply their lessons to "the real world" by bringing politics, world events, and students' co-op experiences into discussions. Classes are offered in the morning, afternoon, and evening, and are evaluated not by grades, but with written evaluations. The performance of each individual in class is assessed both by the professor and the student.

Antioch recognizes that an important part of today's education involves the ability to live and work in the multinational and multicultural society of the 21st Century. In order that students learn about the geography, customs, and traditions of other peoples, the school mandates an in-depth experience of 3-12 months in a cross-cultural environment (either inside or outside of the U.S.) Students can take advantage of the Antioch Education Abroad program, which has included Buddhist Studies programs in Bodh, India, a Comparative Women's Studies Term in Europe, and a British Studies program in London.

Another integral part of Antioch campus life is Community Government. Decision-making councils consist of students, faculty, and administrators. The councils consider the many views of the community regarding administrative policy, academic programs, curriculum, budget allocations, tenure, new programs, quality of campus life and matters such as publication standards and social activities etc.

A wide variety of independent groups, such as Survivors of Sexual Offense, Third World Alliance, and Women's Center, exist on the Yellow Springs campus. Visitors often lecture or hold workshops on issues ranging from the Los Angeles Poverty Department, to ritual abuse, to Japanese theater. With the community as small as it is, everybody knows, works, and studies with everybody else. With only 650 students and 62 full-time faculty, the College nurtures close-knit relationships between students, faculty, and administration. Because of this, a common sense of responsibility for the campus prevails. This responsibility manifests itself in an extensive recycling program, a student-authored sexual offense policy, an organic garden, and more.

The College's history of experimentation, its commitment to questioning traditional values and practices, and its willingness to act on its beliefs have had a profound impact on generations of Antioch students. Their achievements represent the living legacy of the Antioch educational experience. Antioch students approach their education, as well as their lives following graduation, with a serious resolve to tackle important issues, question the status quo, and work toward constructive change. Antioch's success carrying out its basic educational mission — empowering students to make a worthwhile difference — is its proudest and most enduring tradition.

Glen Helen, the College's 1000-acre nature preserve, a registered Natural Landmark complete with medicinal springs located right across from campus, often serves as a laboratory for science-related courses. It also offers opportunities for hiking, horse-back riding, cross country skiing, canoeing, rock-climbing, rappelling and solitude.

With its Little Arts Theater, a health food store, a town library, the tiny village of Yellow Springs is a safe haven where students can find the essentials. The town offers an array of restaurants and off-beat shops, as well as seasonal street fairs. Antioch alumni, staff, and faculty account for a sizable percentage of the village's population of 4,600 people.

# MAKING A DIFFERENCE STUDIES

## Environmental Studies

Biogeochemistry

Wildlife Ecology

Earth's Surface Environments

The Marine Environment

Water and Pollution

Environmental Movements and Social Change

Environmental Botany

Environmental Journalism

Wildlife Ecology

- **Plants & People** *Plants of the world including economic, agricultural, medicinal, forest, and harmful plants, as they relate to and are used by people. How ethnic food preferences relate to available plants, economic and social basis for rain forest and other habitat destruction, and the herbal medicine tradition. Historical issues including the development of agriculture and its effects on societies.*

## International Relations and Peace Studies

*Majors learn a modern conception of the world that transcends the idea that international relations happen only between national governments and that peace is simply the absence of war. The major develops academic skills and sets up international and cross-cultural experiences that empower students as world citizens and that encourage them to think globally and act locally. Includes both negative and positive peace, which relates to direct and indirect or structural violence, and multi-disciplinary peace theories of interpersonal, inter-group, and international relations. Peace Net, a global computerized peace information network, is in the library for student use.*

Introduction to Peace Studies

The World as a Total System: Gaia and Peace

Gandhi: Truth and Nonviolence

Practicum in Peace Studies

Issues in International Politics

- **Prospects for Peace in the 21st Century** *Alternative Futures Considers probable and possible global peace developments in the 21st century. Issues include 21st century war, environmental conflict, cultural and ethnic conflict, human rights, poverty, community conflict and micro-violence as well as possibilities for zones of peace, world government, and the further development of non-violent relationships.*

- *Faculty Bio* **Patricia Mische Lloyd** *Professor of Peace studies and World Law (Ph. D., Columbia Univ.) Pat is currently visiting fellow at Kroc Inst. For Int'l Peace Studies, Univ. of Notre Dame. She is the co-founder and the current president of Global Education Institute for Teaching Justice, Peace and Human Values. She has published four books: Ecological Security and the United Nations System: Past, Present, Future; Star Wars and the State of Our Souls; Toward a Human World Order; and Perception of Social Justice as a Variable Affecting Conflict or Cooperation, War or Peace in a Social System; and over fifty articles in professional journals.*

## Women's Studies

Women in Music

The Feminist Presses 1970 -1990

Feminist Theories

Non-Traditional Literature by Women

Women in Cross-Cultural Perspective

Poetry by Women

Contemporary Latin American Thought on Women Through Literature

## Language, Literature and Culture

*Program equips students with the scholarly and critical skills they need for personal and intellectual growth and for their social contribution. The systematic placement of human belief and behavior in society and culture; ways to compare and contrast their own cultural assumptions; the historical, geopolitical and social contexts of environmental, local and global human problems. Cross-cultural studies is unique in the college curriculum; it frames inquiry and proposes strategies for problem-solving in the 21st Century.*

The World of Storytelling
Japanese Poetry
German Literature
Readings in Latin Amer. Short Story & Poetry
Readings in Native American and Chicano Literature and Culture

Human Rights: Latin America
Tribalism, Ethnicity and the Nation State
Intensive French
Intro to Japanese History, Literature & Culture

- *Faculty Bio Harold Wright Prof. of Foreign Civilizations and Language/Japanese (B.A., M.A., Univ. of Hawaii) has done further graduate research at Columbia Univ. and Keio Univ. in Tokyo. He teaches a variety of courses dealing with Japanese culture, art, history, literature, poetry translation, and language. A recipient of numerous grants and scholarships, including a 1985 National Endowment for the Arts Translators Award, he is the author of eight books, including the critically acclaimed The Selected Poems of Shumtaro Tanikawa, and Tanikawa's Map of Days. He is editing two more books of modern Japanese poetry he translated and a collection of his own original poetry. He is an active storyteller in Ohio and other parts of the U.S.*

## African and African American Studies

Literature by Black Women
Drum & Dance of W. Africa & the Caribbean
Cross-Cultural Field Program
Society Health and Disease in Africa

Race and U.S. Law
Literature by Black Women
Ideology and Form in Black Radical Thought
African-American Intellectual Thought

- **African Americans and Native Americans** *An interdisciplinary exploration of the range of interactions that characterize African American and native American lives in American history. It examines several key themes including the struggle of Native Americans and African Americans to maintain their cherished traditions and the broader phenomenon of Red/Black inter-marriage, conflict and common historical experiences.*

## Social and Behavioral Sciences

Management of Non-Profit Organizations
Fascism
Environmental Economics
Politics and Change in the Middle East
Minority Group Relations

The Economics of Developing Countries
Women in Cross-Cultural Perspective
Political Change: Non-Western Societies
Sex, Gender and Identity
Development, Sociology and Social Policy

- **Women and Minorities in Management** *Theoretical as well as practical issues concerning the expanding role of women and minorities in organizations, particularly in management positions. Diverse range of economic and organizations. Theories examined with respect to division of labor, authority-power relations, and gender/race. Career management, stereotyping, communicators, networking.*

Apply by 3/1    Faculty: 56% male, 44% female, 23% minority

- Field studies  • Co-op ed.  • Interdisciplinary classes  • Self-designed majors  • Optional SAT's
• All seminar format  • Theme Housing  • Service learning  • Vegetarian/vegan meals

Office of Admissions
Antioch College
Yellow Springs, OH 45387

800. 543.9436
admissions@antioch-college.edu
www.antioch-college.edu

# BASTYR UNIVERSITY

students   Kenmore, WA

Bastyr University's students, faculty and staff constitute a unique learning community, united by a strong commitment to the mission of improving the health and well being of the human community. The university's emphasis on the interdependence of living systems and the individual's personal responsibility for wellness provides a shared focus for all of the school's academic programs.

Founded in 1978 as a naturopathic medical school, Bastyr has grown dramatically, adopting an increasingly multidisciplinary focus. An accredited private institution, Bastyr offers a range of educational opportunities for both undergraduate and graduate students seeking study and training in natural health science and applied behavioral science fields. Integration of the knowledge of modern science with the wisdom of traditional healing methods from around the world forms the foundation for all Bastyr programs. Bastyr University's academic and research programs have received international recognition for pioneering work in science-based natural health practices.

Bastyr University's upper-division bachelor completion programs provide strongly focused junior and senior year curricula in natural health, creating a solid foundation for either continued professional study or for burgeoning job opportunities in the fitness, health and business arenas. Since Bastyr offers the last two years of the four-year undergraduate degree, the university attracts serious, goal-oriented students who have a well-defined sense of who they are and what they want to do. The result is an intensive two-year program that allows a more focused, in-depth study of the degree major than that afforded at most other institutions.

Bastyr undergraduates choose from a variety of degrees. The bachelor of science in nutrition curriculum offers a well-rounded, holistic learning base that incorporates both traditional and innovative knowledge and practices. The exercise science and wellness program provides an integrated approach to the study of physical activity and nutrition, emphasizing health and wellness. The psychology major offers a strong foundation in core psychology and research methods, plus a focus on integrating body/mind/spirit approaches with health and well-being

A new Bachelor of Science program in herbal sciences begins in 2001, and offers a thorough and scientifically-rigorous introduction to the field of herbal medicine. The bachelor's degree in applied behavioral science is an evening and weekend program, specifically designed for the needs of working adults. Additionally, Bastyr offers undergraduates entering at the junior level the rare opportunity to enter a combined bachelor/master of science degree program in acupuncture and Oriental medicine, allowing students to earn the combined academic and professional degree in under four years.

Because Bastyr is a university that trains professionals as well as educates undergraduates, students here experience a variety of perspectives in class and on campus, both from peers and from professors. The Bastyr faculty is a highly qualified community of professionals, experienced both as educators and as practitioners. More than 80% hold doctorate or terminal level degrees in their fields. Students benefit from a multidisciplinary curriculum and an integrative focus, fostered by electives available outside their major fields. Each year a number of students also work within the Bastyr University Research Institute, allowing them exposure to an active research environment.

The Bastyr main campus in Kenmore offers on-site laboratories for undergraduate and graduate use, a computer lab, a whole foods nutrition kitchen, a full-service bookstore, and the Bastyr Library. The library has over 11,000 volumes, 270 journal subscriptions, extensive audiovisual materials, Internet access, and a continuously expanding collection of materials on complementary medicine and natural health.

Bastyr students are a diverse group, ranging in age from 20s to 50s and hailing from all over the United States as well as 27 other countries. The vegetarian cafeteria (reported to be one of the best company cafeterias in the area) is a popular gathering place, not just for meals but also for socializing and study. Students are involved in the governance system of the university through Student Council and membership on the Board of Trustees and University Council. Activities include service in the medicinal and culinary herb garden and various clubs and committees (for example, the Bastyr Environmental Action Team, Herbal Ways, Nutrition Advisory Committee, the American Psychological Association, Aikido, African-American Support Group, Student Dietetics Association, Natural Products Student Reps, and various spiritual groups).

Special events like Community Day and the Talent/No Talent Show help create a sense of school identity and a feeling of community. "Brown bag lunches" and evening events feature speakers in a variety of fields. Bastyr University also participates in and co-sponsors prestigious national and international conferences each year, giving students an opportunity to consider the challenges of natural health care in a broader societal and scientific context.

A reflection of the University's commitment to healthy lifestyles, the main campus atmosphere blends quiet and activity on 50 acres, surrounded by a 300-acre state park. Students find seclusion among play fields, woods and parklands along Lake Washington. The campus is near diverse recreational opportunities among the mountains and waters of the Pacific Northwest and is also close to the rich cultural life of the greater Seattle area.

In Seattle, ten miles south of the main campus by bus or car, is the Bastyr University Natural Health Clinic, providing patient clinical services to more than 28,000 patients and providing supervisory training for all university clinical programs. The clinic is the largest natural health clinic in Washington, a state that leads the nation in complementary health care. The student health fee covers clinic visits for all enrolled students.

Bastyr offers a challenging curriculum, strong community feeling and thorough preparation for advanced studies in natural health. The bachelor's completion program at Bastyr University is provides a solid foundation for further study.

# MAKING A DIFFERENCE STUDIES

## Bachelor of Science in Natural Health Sciences: Exercise Science & Wellness

Psychology of Sports & Exercise
Sports Nutrition
Motor Learning & Development

Physiology of Exercise
Exercise Prescription & Testing
Internship for Exercise Science & Wellness

## Bachelor of Science in Natural Health Sciences: Nutrition

Whole Foods Production
Intro. to Nutrition in Natural Medicine
Nutritional Supplements & Herbs
Ecological Aspects of Nutrition

Nutrition Throughout Life
Psychology of Nourishment
Community Nutrition

## Bachelor of Science in Psychology: Health Concentration

Principles of Well-Being
Psychology of Human Relations
Healing Practices 1: Myths & Ritual
Healing Practices 2: Art as Spiritual Practice
Multicultural Issues in Psychology

Ethical Guidelines in Psychology
Health, Body Image & Human Sexuality
Psychology of the Feminine
Healing Practices 3: Mind, Body, Spirit
Psycho-Spiritual Issues in Healing

- **Holistic Interventions in Addictions** *A comprehensive study of approaches to treatment and case management, offers an integrated approach in dealing with addicted individuals. Modalities such as acupuncture for alcohol and substance abuse or herbs and aromatherapy are explored.*

## Bachelor of Science in Herbal Sciences

Philosophy, Sociopolitical & Legal Aspects of Herbalism
Plant Physiology
Plant Identification 1, 2 & 3
Herb/Drug Interactions

Pharmacy of Herbs
Nutrition for Herbalists
Herb Cultivation, Production & Quality Assurance

- **World Shamanic and Vitalistic Herbal Traditions and Practice** *Indigenous use of herbs around the world. Concepts of health and healing embraced by each of tradition studied. Principles of plant spirit medicine in a participatory fashion modeled after the shamanic tradition of learning.*

## Bachelor of Science in Applied Behavioral Science

Exploring Human Diversity
From Conflict to Collaboration
Variations of the Human Personality
Leadership to Meet Adaptive Challenges

Understanding Living Systems
Fundamentals of Helping Relationships
Community Organizing
Organizations: Structures, Theories & Change

- **Self, Service and Social Responsibility** *Students examine their beliefs about service and social responsibility; relationship between self development, sensible self-denial, and social activism.*

## Bachelor/Master of Science in Acupuncture & Oriental Medicine

Living Anatomy
Qi Practicum
Topics in Medicine: Abuse & Detox
Survey of Western Clinical Sciences
Moxibustion

Meridians & Points
Acupuncture Therapeutics
Therapeutic Nutrition
Combining Western Herbs & Chinese Medicine
Clinical Auriculomedicine

- **Topics in Medicine: HIV & AIDS** *Current diagnosis, treatment, research and issues in HIV/AIDS care, with particular emphasis on the role of acupuncture and Oriental medicine.*

Office of Admissions
Bastyr University
14500 Juanita Drive NE
Kenmore, WA 98028

425. 602.3330
www.bastyr.edu

# BELOIT COLLEGE

1,150 Students     Beloit, Wisconsin

Beloit College prepares leaders for life by emphasizing problem solving and critical thinking skills. The pace of social and technological changes taking place globally is not going to slow down. The citizens who know how to keep up with that pace, the ones who can deal with change effectively and the ones who are unafraid to ask questions will excel. A liberal arts and sciences framework provides the best learning environment for students to explore their many interests and prepare for a life of productive and active citizenship.

The concept of service is so important at Beloit that it has now made community service an integral part of the First-Year Initiatives (FYI) Program, Beloit's first-semester seminar and orientation program for new students. On "move in" day, FYI immediately links new students with an experienced professor and a group of peers. Together the class determines their community service project. The professor also serves as academic advisor and mentor until the student declares a major.

For many, FYI is just the beginning of volunteerism. Beloit students have traveled to, among other places, Guatemala, the Netherlands, Alaska and even Beloit, Alabama, doing such projects as researching acid rain, teaching, inventorying Bald Eagle populations, and building schools.

In fact, Beloit College provides grant funding for community service projects. First-year students vie for Venture Grants of up to $1,500 to fund community research projects of their choosing. Similarly, the Beloit is America Program funds innovative community internships that engage students in meaningful service projects in the city of Beloit. Beloit students' commitment to social change is evident when they graduate, too: the College is consistently ranked in the top 20 colleges/universities for producing Peace Corps volunteers.

At Beloit, students share their learning experience with peers from 49 states and 56 nations. It's just as likely that your roommate will be from New York, Oregon, or Missouri, as it is that they'll be from Finland, Zaire, or Wisconsin. What they all share, however, is this practical idealism, a deep respect for individuality, and a commitment to making diversity work.

With more than 100 clubs and organizations, you can find your cultural and social niche at Beloit — or organize a new club that suits your fancy. Students can "invent themselves" because there is no lengthy list of requirements, no rigid formula for choosing a major, no mold in which you're expected to fit. Students are encouraged to build a larger program of study by exploring social interests through an interdisciplinary minor, a second major, internships, and study abroad opportunities. There are literally hundreds of directions to go at Beloit — and Beloit is committed to providing students the resources that will allow them to make the critical and productive connections between thought and action in all aspects of their lives.

# MAKING A DIFFERENCE STUDIES

## Environmental Geology

*Department is a member of the distinguished Keck Geology Consortium, providing majors with outstanding opportunities to participate in summer research activities in US and overseas.*

Enviro Geology and Geologic Hazards
Sedimentology
Natural History
Foundations of Economic Analysis
Geologic Field Methods

Mineralogy and Crystallography
Hydrology
Challenge of Global Change
Marine Biology
Field Excursion Seminar

## Biology: Environmental, Behavioral, Medical, Molecular Biology

Botany
Behavioral Ecology
Comparative Physiology
Microbiology
Biological Issues

Environmental Biology
Population Biology
Zoology
Molecular Biology and Biotechnology
Developmental Biology

## Philosophy and Religion

Biomedical Ethics
Personal Freedom and Responsibility
Violence and Non-Violence
Hebrew Scriptures
Islam

Business Ethics
Philosophy of Science
Logic
Oriental Philosophy
20th Century Theology

## Government and International Relations

Women and Politics
Civil Liberties
Communist & Post-Communist Systems
Parties and Groups in American Politics
American Presidency

Principles of Government and Politics
The Politics of Developing Countries
Politics of Advanced Industrial Democracies
Theories of International Relations
American State Gov't. and Politics

- **International Organization & Law** *Political foundations of int'l. institutions and law. Transformation of UN, growth of specialized agencies and contemporary legal framework. Int'l. peace and security, arms control, economic development, social welfare & human rights in int'l. organizations.*

## Interdisciplinary Studies

*Individually developed majors have included Women, Environment and Change; Choreography of the Universe; Set-design for Educational TV & African Studies.*

Energy Alternatives
Liberal Education and Entrepreneurship
Sense of Place: Regionalism in America
Circumstances of Agriculture in US
Photographic Images as Recorders of History and Social Change

Town and City in the Third World
Mass Communication in a Modern Society
Women, Feminism and Science
Cultural Resource Management

### Sociology    Women's Studies    Health Care Studies

Rolling admissions    Apply by 3/1 for financial aid priority
- All seminar format    • Theme housing    • Self-designed majors    • Required community service
- Interdisciplinary classes    • Field studies    • Vegetarian & vegan meals

Admissions Office
Beloit College
700 College Street
Beloit, WI 53511-5595

608.363.2176
800.356.0751
www.beloit.edu
admiss@beloit.edu

# BEMIDJI STATE UNIVERSITY

4,300 Undergraduates    Bemidji, Minnesota

Located on the shores of Lake Bemidji at the headwaters of the Mississippi River, Bemidji State University has long been known as a college whose setting and sense of community are conducive to learning, living, and growing. As the only institution of higher education serving the baccalaureate needs of north-central Minnesota, Bemidji State recently completed its 75th anniversary by renewing its deep sense of commitment to the region, building a national reputation for quality programming, and enhancing the international perspective for its 4,300 students.

While large enough to offer more than 50 majors and 15 pre-professional programs, the university is small enough to earn its reputation as a friendly college. Understanding that all friendships require work, Bemidji State initiated a program called Responsible Men, Responsible Women, where students are exposed to concepts of civility and trust. In keeping with its philosophy of a caring campus, the university established the Service Learning Center to increase involvement in service learning as a critical component of the university curriculum.

Service is a value important to BSU students. A recent ACT study of new students planning to attend the university showed that nearly 50 percent fully expect to volunteer their time to help others on campus and throughout the community. There are ample opportunities to become involved on campus, with 84 clubs ready to satisfy any interest. These range from a very active Habitat for Humanity chapter to an Accounting Club that helps the elderly with income tax preparation. This volunteerism is officially recognized with students able to compile their work in a Student Service Transcript, which is made available to employers and others in a way similar to the normal academic record.

Situated between several major Native American reservations, the university also supports concepts of diversity and has the largest percentage of minority enrollment among the state universities in Minnesota. Bemidji State welcomes the challenge of global education. International students are actively recruited to study and live in Bemidji. At the same time, the university continues to expand its opportunities for study abroad.

Bemidji State was the first public college or university to offer single parent housing on campus. Part of the residential life complex, the one-, two- or three-bedroom apartments are dedicated to single parents with children of any age. The facility is adjacent to the campus daycare facilties and creates a ready network of single parents who trade baby-sitting services, share resources, and meet regularly to discuss common concerns.

Over the years, Bemidji State University has grown to be a comprehensive regional university offering both undergraduate and graduate degrees. Yet its mission has remained constant over time. Founded on a sound liberal education, university programs educate students so that they may live as responsible, productive, and free citizens in a global society.

# MAKING A DIFFERENCE STUDIES

## Aquatic Biology

*Prepares students for careers involving water quality and natural resource management.*

Limnology
Organic Evolution
General Ecology

Fisheries Management
Methods of Water Analysis
Scientific Communication

## Environmental Studies

*Defining and solving environmental problems caused by the actions of human beings.*

Environmental Conservation
Ecosystems Studies
Environmental Economics

Environmental Politics
Waste Management
Society and Environment

## Indian Studies and Minority Studies: Elementary Education

*Fields of emphases for educators on the Native American culture and other minority perspectives.*

American Indian Literature
Ojibwe Language
History of the Ojibwe
Social Welfare Perspectives
Curriculum Development

Ethnic and Minority Group Relations
Cultural Anthropology
Education of the American Indian
Ojibwe Crafts
Native North Americans

## Health and Community Health

*Intellectual, occupational, social, emotional, physical and spiritual factors of well being.*

Health and the Consumer
Community Health
Nutrition
Family Violence
Physiology of Exercise

A Lifestyle for Wellness
Health and Drug Education
Human Sexuality
Neuromuscular Relaxation
Women's Issues

## Psychology and Applied Psychology

*Exploring the science of behavior, cognition and affect.*

Human Sexuality
Crisis Management
Lifespan Development
Human Responses to Death
Psychosocial Adjustment to Handicapping Conditions

Family Systems
Basic Counseling
Abnormal Psychology
Interpersonal Skills

## Social Work

*Improving the quality of life for individuals, groups and communities.*

Social Work and the Law
Bureaucracy and Society
Interpersonal Relations
Human Relations
Chemical Dependency: Prevention & Intervention

Social Welfare Policy
Chemical Use, Abuse and Dependency
Family Dynamics and Intervention
Psychology of Adjustment

## Peace and Justice Studies

*Ecological balance, economic well-being, sociopolitical justice, and nonviolent conflict management.*

Global and Peace Justice Issues
Social Change
Philosophies of Nonviolence

Conflict Management
The Global Economy
Intercultural Communications

## Indian Studies

*Providing Ojibwe and other students with a viable academic area of study that is relevant to the heritage and diversity of Native Americans.*

Ojibwe Culture

American Indian Literature

Elementary Ojibwe

Contemporary Indian Issues

Tribal Government

Federal Indian Law

Contemporary Indian Issues

Survey of American Indian Art

## Women's Studies

*Creating an academic extension of the women's movement.*

Women's Issues

Feminist Theories and Critiques

Women in Literature

Ideas About Women

Women and Philosophy

The Politics of Women's Health

## International Studies

*Promoting awareness, appreciation, and knowledge of the global community we live in.*

The Global Economy

Comparative International Study

World Regional Geography

United Nations

Religion in the Modern World

Cultural Anthropology

International Conflict

Geography of Population & Settlements

## Geography: Regional and Land-Use Planning, Geographic Information Systems, Park and Recreation Planning

Human Geography

Conservation of Natural Lands

Economic Geography

Ecology

Public Administration

Land Use Analysis and Planning

Urban Geography

Environmental Conservation

Regional Planning Methods

Aerial Photography & Remote Sensing

## Applied Public Policy

*Acquiring a more sophisticated understanding of the laws, codes, social service programs and regulations that affect our daily lives.*

State and Local Politics

Introduction to American Politics

Public Economics

Markets and Resource Allocation

Benefit Cost Analysis

Public Administration

**Environmental Ed. Teaching Certificate    Minority Studies Teaching Certificate**

**Pre-Law      Pre-Fisheries & Wildlife Management     Pre-Forestry**

Rolling Admissions

Admissions Office

Bemidji State University

Bemidji, MN 5660

888. 345.1721

admissions@vax1.bemidji.msus.edu

www.bemidji.msus.edu

# BEREA COLLEGE

1500 students    Berea, Kentucky

Berea College, located in the foothills of the Cumberland Mountains, aims to fulfill its mission as a Christian school "primarily by contributing to the spiritual and material welfare of the mountain region of the South, according to young people of character and promise a thorough Christian education, with opportunities for manual labor as an assistance in self-support."

The seal of the College bears the inscription "God has made of one blood all peoples of the earth" which epitomizes Berea's belief in human-kind which should unite all people as children of God. It is hoped that men and women going out from Berea will further interracial understanding and that they will be courageous in opposing injustice and wrong.

Berea's distribution requirements for cultural area studies insures that each student will be able to demonstrate an understanding of some aspects of culture other than his or her own; a recognition of, and sensitivity to, similarities and differences in cultures; and an expanded perspective on a world of plurality of cultures. For Freshman Seminar all students select a series of courses designed to involve them in a critical study of the topic "Freedom and Justice" as it relates to the commitments of Berea College, to Appalachia, the Christian faith, the kinship of all people, or the dignity of labor. Similarly, students in the teacher education programs at Berea are asked to think deeply about the nature of teaching, learning, and schooling within the context of the college's commitments: to enable students who are economically disadvantaged; to the Christian ethic and to service; to the dignity of labor; to the promotion of the ideals of community democracy, interracial education, and gender equality; to simple living and concern for the welfare of others; and to service of the Appalachian region.

As an integral part of the educational program, each student is expected to perform some of the labor required in maintaining the institution, thus to gain an appreciation of the worth and dignity of all the labor needed in a common enterprise and to acquire some useful skill. The aim is to make available a sound education to students who are unable to meet usual college expenses, but who have the ability and character to use a liberal education for responsible, intelligent service to society.

Through the fellowship of meaningful work experiences, an atmosphere of democratic social living prevents social and economic distinctions and instills an awareness of social responsibility. Student industries include broomcraft, weaving, woodcraft and wrought iron work, the products of which are sold to the public from the student run giftshop, hotel, and catalog. Students also participate in running the college farm.

Berea's campus comprises 140 acres. Farm lands, including the experimental farms, piggery, and poultry farm cover 1400 acres. The college also owns a 7,000-acre forest.

Admission to Berea is limited to students whose families would have a difficult time financing a college education without assistance. Financial need is a requirement for admission.

# MAKING A DIFFERENCE STUDIES

## General Studies

Community Building
Freedom and Justice: The Third World
Housing: American Dream or Nightmare
Politics of Food
Immigrants and Minorities
Sacred Earth, Sacred Relationships

Health Decisions: Justice and Autonomy
Women, Society and Mental Health
Technology, Culture, Belief
Community and Spirituality
Values in Conflict
Labor, Learning and Leisure

- *One Blood, All Nations: Cultural Diversity & Environmentalism* Major issues concerning tensions between advocacy for cultural diversity and environmentalism, especially the environmental concept of a global commons. Achieve a deeper understanding of the issues contained within the concepts of kinship of all people and a way of life characterized by plain living; deeper understanding of the relatedness of these concepts; and understand how these concepts generate questions of freedom and justice.

## Black Culture

Introduction to Afro-American Studies
Slavery & Afro-American Culture
Afro-American Music: An Overview
Black Emancipation & Reform in the U.S.
Critical Issues of Black Americans in the Twentieth Century

Afro-American Literature
Contemporary Afro-American Experience
Race in America
Sub-Saharan Black African Art

## Appalachian Culture

Appalachian Literature
Appalachian Problems and Institutions
Appalachian Music

Appalachian Culture
Health in Appalachia
Appalachian Crafts

- *Community Analysis: The Appalachian Case* Study of history, demography, social structure and forces promoting social change in Appalachian rural communities. Sociological approach to understanding the concept of community, its various systems, institutions and groups. Community problem-analysis orientation. American, European, and Third-World communities examined looking at content and method.

## Child and Family Studies

Principles of Food Science
Human Environments
Family Relations
The Exceptional Child
Contemporary Family Issues

Child Development
Advanced Child Development
Guidance of the Young Child
Cross Cultural Perspectives on Family
Family Resource Management

### Nursing     Agriculture     Sociology

Rolling admissions     Student body: 80% from Southern Appalachia, 9% minority
All tuition costs are met by the college through endowment income and major fund-raising efforts.
- Field studies     • Co-op work study     • Study abroad
- Interdisciplinary programs     • Self-designed majors

Office of Admissions
Berea College
CPO 2344
Berea, KY 40404

606. 986.9341

# BETHEL COLLEGE

644 Students    North Newton, Kansas

Bethel College's 450-year-old Anabaptist heritage is the wellspring for a vibrant academic community with a tradition of combining academic excellence with a commitment to social justice, service to others, peacemaking and conflict resolution. Although Mennonite in character, there are 35 religious denominations on campus. Believing that authentic faith comes from free conviction and not from indoctrination or conformity, Bethel promotes freedom, openness, and voluntarism.

Bethel's distinctiveness, by heritage and conviction, includes a deeply-rooted commitment to peacemaking, service, and conflict-resolution. The urgency of this focus is self-evident in a nuclear world. Education has a special responsibility to seek ways to cope creatively and nonviolently with the human and environmental needs of our global community. The College seeks to study and practice ways of peacemaking and reconciliation in society both in its core curriculum and in special programs.

In a world of specialization and fragmentation the great need of our time is for coherences, to understand that we live in a world of linkages. Bethel seeks to provide an environment that integrates the worlds of faith, learning, and work. In our world of finite resources, Bethel supports a conserving desire to accent the beauty of simplicity and to live more with less. Such a goal is also a more convincing witness to the developing nations of our world and to our understanding of Christian stewardship.

All Bethel students must meet a Global Awareness requirement to prepare them to live in a shrinking world of increasing complexity. Students take a global issues seminar or spend at least thirty days in a situation exposed to a culture significantly different from their home environment. Recent international placements include rural development and environmental health in Burkina Faso; with the Migrant Farm Workers Project in Missouri; in International Development with a center for hillside sustainable agriculture; and with a Mexican environmental education organization.

Bethel's Global Studies program integrates study of our environment, development (what we do in attempting to improve our lot within that abode,) peace and justice (how we react to unequal sharing of our planet's resources). The topics are inherently interwoven and international, hence multidisciplinary and cross-cultural.

Education students are encouraged to student-teach in schools of another culture or in a multicultural setting. Interested students are encouraged to student-teach in inner-city schools, American Indian schools, or even overseas as the demand arises.

Convocation helps build community, broaden horizons, and allow exploration of basic value issues. Recent convocations included "Human Rights in the 1990's" with Bethel alumnus Curt Goering of Amnesty International, and "Housing for the Poor" with Millard Fuller, President of Habitat for Humanity International.

As a community, Bethel expects its members to guard the dignity and worth, and to promote equality and empowerment, of self and others; to value volunteerism; to work through conflicts without force, intimidation, or retreat; to promote relationships free from sexual discrimination, coercion, and exploitation; to keep the environment safe and clean; and to nurture spiritual awareness and development.

# MAKING A DIFFERENCE STUDIES

## Global Environmental Studies

Introduction to Environmental Science
Ecology
Environmental Decision-Making
Environmental Biology
Environmental Monitoring & Management
Development Economics

- **Faculty Bio Dwight R. Platt**, *Ph.D. has been Director of Sand Prairie National History Reservation. He taught at Sambalpur University in India, and was an Education Technician with the American Friends Service Committee there.*

## Global Peace Studies

Conflict Resolution Theory & Practice
Peacemaking & International Conflict
Summer Peace Institute for Teachers
Christian Social Ethics
Majority/ Minority Relations
Theories & Strategies of Social Change
Just War in American History
Public Policy for Global Issues

- **Nonviolence Theory and Practice** *Philosophical and religious foundation, theory and practice of nonviolence as a method of social change. Gandhi and M. L. King, Jr.*

## Economics & Business

Development Economics
Public Policy & Finance
Comparative Economic Systems
Public Policy for Global Issues

- **Business Ethics & Social Responsibility** *Theoretical and practical aspects of social responsibility of modern corporations as well as institutional values and goals. What role, if any, social responsibility plays in corporate activity and decision making.*

## Global International Development

*Cross-cultural understanding, appreciation for dignity of the poor and the complexity of their struggles.*

Public Policy for Global Issues
Transcultural Seminar
Principles of Sustainable Agriculture
Development Economics
Global Issues in Environment, Human Conflict and Development
Relief, Development & Social Justice
Energy Issues & Appropriate Technology
International Health
Theories & Strategies of Social Change

- **Rural Development in Central America/Mexico** *A hands-on field course about the problems and possibilities for rural development, social change, and conflict resolution. Food, population growth, urban migration and environmental degradation. Emphasis on hearing and understanding those who suffer with underdevelopment.*

## Special Education

Strategies for Behavior Management
Consultation Skills for Special Educators
Handicapped Preschool Children Practicum
Characteristics of Adolescents with Handicap
Early Intervention for Handicapped Children
Education & Psych. of Exceptional Individuals

**Off Campus Study: Biology/Anthropology Field Trip to Belize and Guatemala:** *Study of tropical marine, fresh water terrestrial biology, archaeological history and contemporary life.*

Apply by 8/15    Student body: 19% minority, 43% Mennonite

Faculty: 50% male, 50% female

- Life experience credit    • Team teaching    • Non-resident degree program
- Nursing outreach program    • Co-op work study    • Service-learning    • Vegetarian meals

Admissions Office
Bethel College
300 East 27th Street
North Newton, KS 67117-9989
800. 522.1887

# BROWN UNIVERSITY

5,500 Undergraduates    Providence, Rhode Island

Very few centers of higher education can honestly claim to offer their students the best of both worlds: the breadth and depth of a university's resources, and the intimate experience of an undergraduate liberal arts college. Brown offers this rare balance. Recently implemented "University Courses" emphasize synthesis rather than survey, and focus on the methods, concepts, and values employed in understanding a particular topic or issue. Using a single discipline or interdisciplinary approach, they introduce students to distinctive ways of thinking, constructing, communicating, and discovering knowledge. This emphasis has spawned unusual interdepartmental concentrations and programs. Biomedical researchers have worked with the departments of Philosophy and Religion to create a concentration in Biomedical Ethics. The Health and Society concentration pulls together the fields of human biology, community health, economics, and the social and behavioral sciences to examine health care systems and address policy issues at the local, national, and international levels.

Collaborations between faculty and undergraduates in research, course development and teaching have resulted in research on the impact of TV advertising on election campaigns, developing mathematical models of predator-prey interactions in marine ecosystems, and cataloguing materials for the study of race relations in Brazil.

Brown students have designed and implemented a wink-controlled wheelchair for parapalegics, converted an unused carriage house into the University's Urban Environmental Laboratory, collaborated with engineering professors to build a "clean air" automobile, and worked at a missionary hospital in Kenya.

Brown President Vartan Gregorian noted "more than ever, we need to recover a sense of the wholeness of human life and to understand the human condition.... We need to admit questions of values to the arena of discussion and debate. The moral argument of a poem, the social implications of a political system, the ethical consequences of a scientific technique, and the human significance of our responsibilities should have a place in classrooms and dormitories. To deny that place is to relinquish any claims or any attempt to link thought and action, knowing and doing."

Brown's emphasis on civic and social responsibility, and on bridging the gap between academia and the world beyond, provides opportunities to integrate community work with their academic and career goals. The Center for Public Service coordinates its activities with various academic programs, including Public Policy, Health and Society, Urban Studies, and Environmental Studies. Students volunteer with educational, social service, health, government and cultural organizations. Faculty and staff serve too: the Taubman Center for Public Policy is working with the city of Providence to develop a comprehensive antipoverty program, and the Allan Shawn Feinstein World Hunger Program tackles the issue of starvation amid plenty.

With Brown's extraordinary array of religions, ethnicities, and nationalities, students tend to find common ground through academic, extracurricular, and social interests, as well as through cultural ties. Experiencing that diversity first-hand is, for many, one of the most rewarding aspects of the Brown experience.

# MAKING A DIFFERENCE STUDIES

## Public Policy and American Institutions

Ethics and Public Policy
Woman and Public Policy
Public Policy and Higher Education
Social Welfare Policy
Political Research Methods

Environmental Regulation
Education and Public Policy
Law and Public Policy
Housing & Community Development Policy
The Price System and Resource Allocation

## Development Studies

African History and Society
Slave Community
Culture and Health
Nuclear Weapons: Technology and Policy
Women & Health Care
Burden of Disease in Developing Countries

Population Growth and the Environment
Issues in Minority Health
Gender in 20th Century American Sport
Shaping of World Views
Anthropological Issues in World Population
Possibilities for Social Reconstruction

## Biology and Medicine: Community Health

Culture and Health
Research in Health Care
Economic Development
International Environmental Issues
Red, White & Black in the Americas
The Culture of Postcolonialism

Health Care in the U.S.
Ideology of Development
Comparative Sex Roles
Social Change in Modern India
Third World Political & Economic Issues
Comparative Policy and Politics: East Asia

## Biomedical Ethics

Ethical Issues in Field of Mental Health
Ethical Issues in Pediatric Medicine
Moral Problems
Religious Ethics and Moral Issues
Ethical Issues in Research and Use of Biomedical Technology

Ethical Issues in Preventive Medicine
The Aims of Medicine
Moral Theories
Sociology of Medicine

## Sociology

Economic Development & Social Change
The Family
Social Inequality
War and the Military
Environmental Sociology

American Heritage: Racism & Democracy
Population Growth and the Environment
Race, Class and Ethnicity: Modern World
Women in Socialist & Developing Countries
Social Structures & Personal Development

- **Industrialization, Democracy and Dictatorship** *Examines the interrelations between economic development and political change. Does economic development encourage democratization in today's underdeveloped countries as it did in W. Europe? Does rapid economic change foster revolutionary movements? Does sustained economic growth require authoritarian rule? What is the impact of multinational corporations on political conditions in developing countries?*

**Women's Studies    Environmental Studies    Aquatic Biology    Urban Studies**
**Afro-American Studies    Education    International Relations    Public Policy**

Apply By 1/1

Director of Admission          401. 863.2378
Brown University
Providence, RI 02912

# BRYN MAWR COLLEGE

1100 Students    Bryn Mawr, Pennsylvania

Bryn Mawr is a liberal arts college in both the modern and traditional senses. Its curriculum is modern in offering a full range of subjects in the arts, sciences, and social sciences, but the College is also traditional in its commitment to the original sense of "liberal arts" — the studies of a free person.

Bryn Mawr believes in a broad education which prepares students to be free to question or advocate any idea without fear. This kind of education results in graduates who are determined to change society. Among Bryn Mawr graduates are the domestic policy adviser to Vice President Albert Gore; the deputy director of the U.S. Office of Management and Budget; the medical director of the only women's health clinic in Nairobi; federal judges, children's legal advocates, teachers at every level, and a much higher than usual percentage of women who are in positions to improve society — in this country and around the world.

Individual responsibility with a concern for the community are prime traits of Bryn Mawr students. The college believes that the pleasure of knowledge is insufficient if that knowledge does not lead to social action. Too many people act without knowing and too many highly educated people won't act on behalf of others. Bryn Mawr seeks students who wish to use their education, not merely for personal enrichment but to be fully contributing, responsible citizens of the world. Mary Sefranek is a good example of Bryn Mawr's philosophy in action. She was one of twenty USA Today All Academic Team winners for, among her many accomplishments, the work she has done with the Roberto Clemente Middle School in Philadelphia. Mary created a special program for this low-income, primarily Hispanic public school, including teams of Bryn Mawr student tutors and field trips. She is one of many Bryn Mawr students active in volunteer projects.

Bryn Mawr's students are from 48 states, Puerto Rico, D.C., and 51 other countries. American minorities make up 25% of the students. Several students from South Africa not only voted in the first free and open election in 300 years, they worked at the Philadelphia Absentee Ballot Center to help their compatriots vote. The unusually high percentage of foreign students means everyone learns first-hand about real world problems. Bryn Mawr is among a handful of private colleges which give financial aid to foreign students. A CBS Sunday Morning News show featured four Bryn Mawr students in a segment called "Women of the Revolution." Students from Kuwait, the People's Republic of China, Rumania, and South Africa talked about their hopes that their BM educations would be put to use for their people at home.

The Minority Coalition, an organization representing all of the minority student organizations, enables minority students to work together to increase the number of minority students and faculty, and to develop curricular and extra-curricular programs dealing with United States minority groups and non-Western peoples and cultures.

Bryn Mawr is one of the very few colleges and universities with an honor code — which characterizes a philosophy of mutual respect between students, faculty and administration.

# MAKING A DIFFERENCE MAJORS

## Geology

Mineralogy and Mineral Paragensis
Crystallography and Optical Mineralogy
Principles of Economic Geology
Tectonics

Stratigraphy/Sedimentation
Low Temperature Geochemistry
Introduction to Geophysics
Structural Geology

- **Environmental Geology** *Issues affecting land use and management of the environment including natural geologic hazards, forces shaping the earth's surface, energy sources, waste disposal, and urban planning. Labs focus on local environmental issues.*

## Peace Studies

War and Cultural Difference
Social Inequality
Schools in American Cities
Ethnic Group Politics
Germany Since 1914
Conflict and Conflict Management: A Cross-cultural Approach

Nationalism in Europe
Intransigent Conflict
The Culture of the Cold War
Great Powers and the Near East
Slavery and Emancipation: British & U.S.

## Growth and Structure of Cities

*Interdisciplinary major challenges students to understand the relationship of spatial organization and the built environment to politics, economics, culture and society. Students pursue interests in planning, art and architecture, archaeology, and in social and natural sciences including anthropology, economics, geology, sociology, and history.*

Urban Culture and Society
Ancient Greek Cities and Sanctuaries
Latin American Urban Development
Modernization
Topics in History of Modern Planning
Chinese Notions of Time and Space: Garden, House, and City

The Form of the City
Comparative Urbanism
Topics in Urban Culture and Society
Survey of Western Architecture
Ethnic Group Politics

## Anthropology

Sex, Culture and Society
African Ethology: Urban Problems
Linguistic Anthropology
Psychological Anthropology
History of Cultural Theory
Origins of Civilization and the State

Medical Anthropology
Language in Social Context
Cultural Ecology
Gender Differentiation
Traditional and Pre-Industrial Technology
Ethnography of South Asia

## Feminist and Gender Studies

Feminism and Philosophy
Patterns in Feminist Spirituality
Studies in Prejudice
Women in Science
Women in Contemporary Society: Third World Women

The Family in Social Context
Topics in European Women's/Gender History
Women in Early Christianity
Gender, Class and Culture

Apply by 1/1
• Team teaching  • Self-designed majors  • Interdisciplinary classes  • Vegetarian meals

Office of Admissions
Bryn Mawr College
Bryn Mawr, PA 19010

610. 526.5152
www.brynmawr.edu/college

# BURLINGTON COLLEGE

205 Undergraduates    Burlington, Vermont

"The chief goals of the ideal college would be the discovery of identity, and with it, the discovery of vocation."                                    — Abraham Maslow

"Burlington College is a small friendly school in a small friendly state. An alternative, liberal arts college in the Vermont tradition, this community of learners not only believes in the innate dignity of people, it believes that people should have a say in what matters most in their lives and in their education. And here they do!" says Burlington College President Daniel Casey.

Founded in 1972 as the Institute for Community Involvement, Burlington College continues its 28-year tradition of emphasizing individualized education and community action. The progressive liberal arts curriculum appeals to the broad interests of a highly diverse student body, while the small, intimate environment provides a level of support unparalleled on today's college campuses.

Above all, Burlington College treats students as individuals — individuals with important contributions to make to the intellectual spirit of the college community. These contributions become the center of college life. Working in discussion-centered classes of between eight and twelve members, students come to know each other — and themselves — well. In a classroom atmosphere that balances academic rigor and mutual support, students are challenged to discover what truly matters to them.

The respect students are given is reflected in the College's non-grading evaluation system. In each course or other learning activity, students negotiate a learning contract for the semester with their instructor, and at the end, both provide written evaluations of progress toward the learning goals they set. The evaluation period is not, then, a time to cram for exams or to please an instructor to get a grade; it is a time for reflection on what one has learned.

Because Burlington College realizes that some forms of education are best learned in alternative settings, the College provides a wide range of learning modes. Students can complete their studies by combining campus classes, action and service learning, independent study, residential and outdoor workshops, and studies abroad. Students may also cross-register, attending classes at any of the 5 surrounding colleges to meet the needs of their particular course of study.

Burlington College seeks to admit students of diverse ages and backgrounds who are mature, independent thinkers and want to be actively involved in the planning of their learning. The College looks for students who strive to make a difference in their own lives and in the larger community, who are goal-oriented, and who have a strong desire to increase awareness, knowledge, and competency.

Rich in cultural and professional resources, the city of Burlington is the college's campus. The College is housed in a renovated, turn-of-the-century building located in Burlington's Old North End. It has classrooms, a small library, an art studio, a community art gallery, computer lab, film production facilities, a student lounge, and a spectacular view of lake Champlain. Students also have borrowing privileges at nearby Trinity College and University of Vermont libraries.

# MAKING A DIFFERENCE STUDIES

## Interdisciplinary Studies

*Students can design an individualized major with their academic advisor to meet their particular academic and career needs and goals. Recent individualized majors include: Communications and Graphic Design, Counseling in Women's Health, Arts in Community, Contemporary Spiritually, Dance Movement Therapy, Community Development, Educational Media Resources, and Environmental Design.*

The City in History
In Search of American Identity
Film and Philosophy
Making a Documentary Film
Film and Psychology
The Unfinished Revolution: Racism in American History
Nature and Human Understanding: The World View of Modern Science & It's Critics

Literature and Mythology
Spiritual Traditions and Practices
Individuality, Community, and Freedom
Patterns of Wealth & Poverty: A Global Perspective
Infinity

## Transpersonal Psychology, Psychology, and Human Services

*Transpersonal Psychology is a relatively new discipline that rests upon the assumption that psychology needs both soul and spirit, and draws upon both Western Sciences and Eastern wisdom. Includes courses & workshops in tai chi, sacred art, mythology, aikido & more.*

Community Development
Lifespan Development
Organizational Theory and Behavior
Death and Dying
Mandalas: Sacred Circles of the Soul
Archetypal Psychology
Psychology of the Unconscious
Life Embodied - Experience in Wellness: Through the Mind/Body Connection

Aging Issues and Arguments
Theories of Personality
Buddhist Psychology
Social Psychology
Intro to Jungian Psychology
Intro to Oriental Medicine
Addiction

## Gender Studies

Women and Film
Intro to Gender Studies
History of Women in North America
Psychology of Women

Theory and Construction of Gender
Gender Issues in American Society
Women's Literature
Men's Lives: Gender, Intimacy and Power

## Natural Sciences

Breeding Birds of Vermont
Visioning Science
Minerals: Brick of the Earth
Winter Ecology Through Snow Travel
Issues in Reproductive Health
A River Runs Through It All: Paddling for a Greater Awareness of Vermont's Watersheds

Dynamics of the Earth's Atmosphere
Herbalism
Sustaining Agriculture in an Urban Setting
Society and Nature
Contemporary Ecological Issues

Rolling admissions     Limited housing
Student body: 84% state, 57% female, 43% male, 60% transfer
• Prior learning credit    • External degree completion

Admissions Office
Burlington College
95 North Avenue
Burlington, VT 05401

800. 862.9616
admissions@burlcol.edu
www.burlcol.edu

# UNIVERSITY OF CALIFORNIA AT DAVIS

17,500 Undergraduates    Davis, California

With 5,200 acres, UC Davis ranks first in physical size of the nine campuses of the U of California. It has 24 undergraduate programs rated among the country's top 10, including the number one botany department. The Davis campus has undergraduate colleges of Agriculture and Environmental Sciences, Engineering, and Letters and Sciences.

Major programs in the College of Agricultural and Environmental Sciences highlight multiple connections among the environment, plant and animal systems, and human health and development, all within the larger context of the quality of life in the global economy. Broad study areas are Plant Sciences; Animal Biology; Human Health and Development; and Environmental and Resource Sciences and Policies with majors in Applied Behavioral Sciences, Atmospheric Science, Environmental and Resource Science, Landscape Architecture, Soil and Water Sciences.

The Davis branch of the California Agricultural Experiment Station includes 500 faculty. In addition to lab facilities, it has approximately 3,000 acres devoted to agricultural research in experimental crops, orchards, and animal facilities. Research emphasis is placed on resource conservation and management, water and soil pollution, and regional planning. The Jepson Prairie Reserve is used to study the effects of long-term grazing, to conduct fire ecology research, and to aid in the management of native grasslands.

The Student Experimental Farm, an innovative teaching and research facility located on 25 acres of University land, is the main focus of the Sustainable Agriculture Program. Since its inception, the Farm has provided students with unique opportunities to explore alternative agriculture technologies and philosophies through classes, internships, work study jobs, and original research. Because the farm includes several acres of land that have been managed organically for over a decade, it provides researchers with a facility for conducting field research into sustainable agriculture.

The Education Abroad Program of the University of California offers a wide range of opportunities from university-based programs throughout Europe, Asia and Latin America; options for studying ethnomusicology and Balinese dance in Indonesia; study and research in a tropical cloud forest in Costa Rica; and four weeks of field work in Togo.

Outdoorsy students can take advantage of Outdoor Adventures, which rents professional quality equipment to students, and whose library contains topographic maps, trail guides, and other materials. Classes, excursions and clinics in backpacking, rock-climbing techniques, white-water rafting, kayaking, sea kayaking, mountaineering and cross-country skiing are offered throughout the year.

Ecologically aware and socially innovative, the town of Davis has a small-town friendliness and spirit of volunteerism that distinguishes it from other cities of similar size. Students comprise nearly half of the city's population, making Davis one of the state's few remaining "college towns." With 50 miles of bike paths and more bicycles per person than any other city in the nation, Davis has earned the title "City of Bicycles."

# MAKING A DIFFERENCE STUDIES

## Civil and Environmental Engineering: Transportation Planning

*Basic concepts of engineering, economics and planning in the development of policies, programs and projects.*

Construction Principles
Introduction to Transportation Planning
Transportation System Design
Energy Policy
Environmental Planning

Introduction to Air Pollution
Transportation System Operations
Energy & Enviro. Aspects of Transportation
Methods of Environmental Policy Evaluation
Public Mechanisms for Controlling Land Use

## Plant Biology (Botany)

Plants, People and the Bioshpere
Plant Ecology
Biology of Weeds
Principles of Plant Biotechnology
Conservation of Plant Genetic Resources

California Floristics
Survey of Plant Communities of California
Mineral Nutrition of Plants
Developmental Plant Anatomy
Physiology of Environmental Stresses in Plants

## Agricultural Systems & Environment: Sustainable Production Systems, Agricultural & Environmental Education, Agricultural Resource Management

Agricultural Systems and Environment
International Agriculture Development
Forage Crop Ecology
Introduction to Biological Control
Microclimate of Agricultural Systems
Environmental Law

Environmental Horticulture
Cereal Crops of the World
Greenhouse and Nursery Crop Production
Ecology and Economics
Conservation of Plant Genetic Sources
Environmental & Occupational Epidemiology

## Atmospheric Sciences

Introduction to Air Pollution
Atmospheric Dynamics
Boundary Layer Meteorology
Severe and Unusual Weather

Weather Analysis and Forecasting
Computer Methods in Meteorology
Issues in Atmospheric Science
Radiation and Satellite Meteorology

## Avian (Bird) Sciences

Intro to Poultry Science
Captive Raptor Management
Fertility and Hatchability
Nutrition of Birds

Birds, Humans, and the Environment
Raptor Migration and Population Fluctuations
Patterns in Avian Biology
Raptor Biology

- **Management of Companion Birds** *Captive propagation of birds, including trade and smuggling. Emphasis on parrots and role of captive propagation in conservation.*

## Environmental Toxicology

Toxicants in the Environment
Food Toxicology
Health Risk Assessments of Toxicants
Principles of Environmental Toxicology

Biological Effects of Toxicants
Air Pollutants and Inhalation Toxicology
Legal Aspects of Environmental Toxicology
Chromatography for Analytical Toxicology

**Chicana/o Studies    War and Peace    Women's Studies    Entomology
Environmental Studies    Environmental and Resource Sciences**

Apply by 11/30
Office of Undergraduate Admissions    530. 752.2971
University of CA at Davis
Davis, CA 95616

# UNIVERSITY OF CALIFORNIA AT SANTA CRUZ

10,100 Undergraduates    Santa Cruz, CA

Since it opened in 1965, UC Santa Cruz has won a distinctive position within the UC system as a collegiate university devoted to excellence in both undergraduate education and graduate studies and research. The residential college is an important part of the Santa Cruz experience. Every undergraduate student affiliates with one of the eight colleges while they participate in a campus wide academic program.

The theme of College Eight *Environment and Society* is an expression of concern for social, political, scientific and ethical issues within an environmental context. The fellows of College Eight are drawn from the environmental studies, community studies, biology, chemistry, psychology, and sociology. Fellowship in the college indicates the faculty's interest in the related issues of environmental quality and community development as they concern peace, justice, and human well-being. Both students and faculty develop courses, conferences and field projects. Experiential education in the form of internships and field studies offers a means bridging theory and action. These avenues provide students with the opportunity to act on their intellectual understanding under "real-world" conditions.

Kresge College is a center of innovative interdisciplinary, social, and cross-cultural programs, a place where diverse groups come together with the vision of communication across boundaries in an effort to spearhead social change. It's focus of Cultural Intersections emphasizes the create possibilities of inter-cultural exchange.

Merrill College seeks to expand its students' awareness of their own heritage and of the diversity of cultures around the world, past and present. Drawn largely from the social sciences, education, history, literature, and foreign languages, many Merrill faculty members specialize in social theory, international affairs, and social change. The college makes a special effort to be a home for students from different cultural backgrounds and for foreign students; it presents unusual opportunities to those who value multicultural perspectives.

The Agroecology Program is a research and educational group working toward the development of sustainable agricultural systems — those that maintain environmental quality and provide employment, nutritious food, and an affordable way of life while ensuring the same for future generations. The Program manages a 25-acre farm including research plots, raised-bed gardens, row crops, orchards, a solar green house, and a 4-acre garden.

Other research programs include the Adlai E. Stevenson Program on Global Security, which stimulates research, education, and policy studies on issues related to global security, conflict, and cooperation. Interdisciplinary research includes nuclear weapons, proliferation, global environmental degradation, and international cooperation on the global environment.

About 400 acres of campus wildlands are designated as a Natural Reserve. Remarkably diverse, this reserve contains redwood forest, springs, a stream, vernal pools, secondary madrone/Douglas fir forest, and chaparral. The 4,000-acre Landels-Hill Big Creek Reserve, a teaching and research facility on the Big Sur coast, includes undisturbed watershed containing numerous terrestrial and aquatic habitats.

# MAKING A DIFFERENCE STUDIES

**Environmental Studies: Sustainable Agriculture & Agroecology, Policy, Planning & Public Values, Natural History, & Wildland Conservation**

Culture and Environment
Natural History of Mammals
Capitalism and Nature
Integrated Pest Management
Environmental Assessment
Conservation Practicum
Energy Resource Assessment and Policy
Political Economy of Sustainable Agriculture in Latin America

Population, Community & Ecosystem Ecology
Natural History of Birds
Ecodevelopment
Principles of Sustainable Agriculture
Environment, Culture and Perception
National Environmental Policy
Watershed Systems Restoration

**Biology: Marine Biology; Ecology, Evolution & Behavior; Plant Sciences**

Kelp Forest Ecology
Biogeography
Biological Oceanography
Marine Botany
Field Studies of Animal Behavior

Intertidal Organisms
Biology of Marine Mammals
Systematic Botany of Flowering Plants
Infectious Diseases
Biology of Cancer

**Community Studies**

*Students actively committed to social change work on a full-time basis and designs their curriculum around a 6 month field study or internship with a community organization or agency.*

Social Documentation
California: Edge of America
Introduction to the AIDS Epidemic
Global Political Economy
U.S. - Mexico Border Region
Civil Rights Movement: Grassroots Change and American Society

Chicanos and Social Change
Mass Media and Community Alternatives
U.S. Regions & the Global Economy
Political Economy of U.S. Agriculture
Workers & Community in Industrializing Amer.

**Social Psychology**

Health Psychology
Social Psychology of Sex and Gender
Social Psychology of Bilingualism
The Social Context
Gender and Power

Chicano Psychology
Intergroup Relations
Social Influences
Psychology and Law
Organizational Psychology

**Sociology: Institutional Analysis**

Key Issues in Race and Ethnic Analysis
Development, Inequality, and Ecology
Communication and Mass Media
Drugs in Society
Sociology of Jury: Racial Disenfranchisement in the Jury and Jury Selection System

Family and Society
Sociology of Health and Medicine
Sociology of Education
Sociology of Environmental Politics

**Education**  **Earth Sciences**  **Latin American Studies**  **Economics**
**World Literature & Cultural Studies**  **Women's Studies**  **Anthropology**

Apply by 11/30    Student body: 36% minority
• Individualized majors    • Field studies    • Vegetarian meals
Office of Admissions    831. 459.4008
University of CA, Santa Cruz
Santa Cruz, CA 95064

# CALIFORNIA INSTITUTE OF INTEGRAL STUDIES

80 Undergraduates    San Francisco, California

In a world of growing complexity no one culture or tradition can provide an education broad enough and deep enough to deal with the issues it presents. The California Institute of Integral Studies is an accredited institute of higher learning where intellect, intuition, and the ageless wisdom of diverse cultures converge. Integrating the intellectual and spiritual insights of Western and Eastern traditions, education at the California Institute of Integral Studies facilitates integration of body-mind-spirit, valuing equally the emotional, spiritual, intellectual, creative, somatic, and social dimensions of being human. Students are encouraged to take an interdisciplinary approach to learning by complementing their program of study with coursework in other departments and focus on the integration of their personal growth, scholarly work, and professional skills.

The Bachelor of Arts Completion (BAC) program aims to provide graduates with the skills to respond creatively and constructively to the rapid pace of change in the contemporary world. Distinctive qualities of the program include an opportunity to explore and understand a variety of cultural, historical, ecological, and personal forces that shape individual and social experience; an environment in which to discover and develop a mature sense of vocation; and the opportunity to acquire up to 45 quarter units for demonstrated learning based in work or life experience prior to enrollment (prior learning).

To carry forward the Institute's tradition of innovative approaches to education, students are encouraged to integrate and build on their life experiences and are challenged to broaden their perspectives and deepen their knowledge. The primary way in which students in the Bachelor of Arts Completion Program progress through the year is a "cohort," or learning community. Cohort members support one another and serve as an education resource for study that is both collaborative and individualized. The core curriculum is supplemented with Special Topics courses and seminars offered in the evenings and as weekend intensives. These specialized courses have included: The Politics of Female Reproduction, The African Experience, Morality and the Human Spirit, and Speaking Writing.

Building on self-assessment of strengths and needs, students collaborate with faculty and their cohorts to design a course of study relevant to their own passionate paths. All learners participate in core seminars and design and complete a Culminating Project. Depending on their needs and interests, learners can participate in specialized study groups designed mutually by faculty and students. By challenging existing paradigms and exploring new perspectives, the student enriches the base of knowledge in the area of study; all activities are intended to support one another in creating a unified experience.

# MAKING A DIFFERENCE STUDIES

*Courses change from year to year. The course titles therefore are suggestive of types of courses offered.*

## Integrative Studies
*Explore alternative worldviews that shape human experience and challenge participants to clarify their own values and assumptions through critical and experiential research and group interaction.*

| | |
|---|---|
| The Modern Condition | Culture and Community |
| Earth Curriculum | Transformative Learning |
| Self and Society | |

## Experience, Vocation and the Development of the Self
*Focuses on individual reflective work, particularly autobiographical and journal writing. This process challenges students to examine their own underlying assumptions about themselves and the world in which they live, and to apply their new understanding in a practical way.*

| | |
|---|---|
| Culture and Community | Learning from Community |
| Research Methods | |

## Learning and Change in Human Systems
*Begins with the assumption that individuals, groups, and institutions need to "learn their way out" of the dilemmas created on the planet and in the human community. The cohort becomes a laboratory for experimenting with ways of using learning strategies to enhance personal and group capacities, and for developing flexible and creative learning processes within individuals and groups.*

| | |
|---|---|
| Systems Theory | Personal Responsibility |
| Social Ecology | Social Change |

- *Faculty Bio* **Linda Vance** *J.D., LL.M., has acted as an attorney for feminist, peace, and environmental groups in Vermont and New Mexico. Linda writes and lectures on ecofeminism and on the historical and philosophical dimensions of wilderness; she also conducts research on stream ecology.*

- *Faculty Bio* **Mutombo Mpana** *Ph.D. is originally from Zaire. Mutombo has worked with international development agencies in several African countries for over 20 years. His areas of interest include environmental studies, international development, economics, technology impact assessment, environmental ethics, transportation systems, and ecological systems.*

- *Faculty Bio* **Richard Shapiro** *MA is director of the Social and Cultural Anthropology program, and has helped shape emancipatory education in the Bay Area, particularly in developing critical, interdisciplinary, activist and multicultural education. Richard is an original member of Todos, which works with youth, social service organizations, and universities, engaging issues of social oppression and cultural identity. Richard has studied and worked with many exceptional teachers, including Michael Foucault and Herbert Marcuse. His interests include the cross-cultural study of subjectivity, sexuality and gender, social movements, and anthropology as cultural critique. Richard is also interested in movements for ecosocial justice in India, and is currently consulting on a project related to gender, equity, and sustainable development among marginalized communities in Orissa, in eastern India.*

Apply by 6/1    No housing
- Interdisciplinary classes    • Non-resident degree program    • Team teaching
• All seminar format    • Life experience credit
100% of students perform community service    Avg. 5 hours per week

| | |
|---|---|
| Office of Admissions | 415.575.6151 |
| California Institute of Integral Studies | www.ciis.edu |
| 1453 Mission St. | |
| San Francisco, CA 94103 | |

# CALIFORNIA UNIVERSITY OF PENNSYLVANIA

5,600 Undergraduates   California, Pennsylvania

California University of Pennsylvania is a state college that encourages students to take part in the life, not only of the university community, but of the wider community as well. A number of successful programs provide an opportunity for students to learn and to grow both in and out of the classroom.

In 1995, CU created a Character Education Institute to foster critical discussion of ethical issues in the academic curriculum and parental support classes, and to promote the timeless ideals of responsibility and respect. Institute activities promote the core values espoused in the US Constitution such as honesty, human worth and dignity, justice, due process, and equality of opportunity. The CEI also serves as a resource for local school districts who want to examine the idea of values education.

Vulcan ll, the university's new research vessel, provides students with access to the Monongahela River and a variety of research opportunities. Faculty and students in the environmental sciences program are working on a three-year project integrating wildlife and agriculture, and funded by the PA Game Commission, the US fish and Wildlife service, and a number of private conservation clubs. Another project involved researching acid deposition through small stream water quality analysis. For several years students in the Wildlife, Environmental and Biological Science Club (WEB) have been raising money for the purchase of acres of Colombian cloud forest to ensure preservation of that important resource.

Students in the College of Education and Human Services can choose from a variety of student teaching assignments. A special program, the Urban Teaching Center, allows participants to student-teach in Pittsburgh urban schools and live in the city. The program stresses multicultural interaction, providing students with special out-of-school cultural activities, including dinners with neighborhood groups.

Other programs encourage student teachers to become involved with education reform through hands-on activities in local school districts. Student teachers have worked with their classes to create a living biome (a Pennsylvania pond,) a butterfly garden, tropical rain forest, and a prairie grassland. Other California U students worked with an area high school to create a local cultural and historical center.

Originally part of a pilot program, the successful SHARE program matches students in need of housing with senior citizens who are interested in sharing their home. Once the program identifies a likely match, the students and the elders work out the details of the living arrangements. SHARE is only one of a number of community outreach programs coordinated through the California Area Senior Center in cooperation with CU's Gerontology Department. The University's close ties with the Senior Center enables students to use the Center for internships and/or practicums in gerontology, social work, and even journalism or public relations.

Students volunteering to work with the California Area Senior Center also participate in the Friend to Friend program, where students make a commitment to visit with an elderly friend at least once a week. Others drop by the Center on a regular basis or help with the "meals on wheels" or other outreach programs.

# MAKING A DIFFERENCE STUDIES

## Teaching Credential: Environmental Studies

Man and His Environment
Ecosystems Ecology
Wildlife Techniques
Game and Habitat Management
Physical Geography

Environmental Biology
Man and His Physical World
Outdoor Activities
Recreation and Park Administration
Human Ecology

## Environmental Resources: Environmental Pollution

Contemporary Issues in Biology
Air Quality Monitoring
Environmental Regulations
Introduction to Oceanography
Solid Waste Management
Ecosystems Ecology

Earth Resources
Economic Geography
Climatology
Coastal Geomorphology & Marine Resources
Water and Wastewater Analysis
Environmental Research Problems

## Environmental Conservation

Principles of Biology
Wildlife Techniques
Plant Ecology
Water Pollution Biology
Biometry

Biotic Communities
Soil Science
Environmental Research Problems
Conservation of Biological Resources
Ornithology

## Wildlife Biology

General Zoology
Principles of Wildlife Management
Land Use Planning
Urban Planning
Principles of Biology

General Botany
Plant Taxonomy
Mammalogy
Ichthyology
Environmental Physiology

## Urban Studies

Survey of Urban Affairs
Political Economy
Urban Transportation
Housing and Housing Policy
History of Urban America
Urban Sociology

Municipal Government
Urban Geography
Recreation for Phys./Emotionally Handicapped
Practicum in Urban Affairs
Organizational & Administrative Behavior
Community Action & Neighborhood Gov't.

**Social Work    Gerontology    Meteorology    Early Childhood Ed.**
**Special Education: Community Services/Community Living Arrangements A.A.**

Rolling admissions
• Team teaching    • Evening classes    • Field studies    • Vegetarian meals
• Over 100 service learning courses    • Interdisciplinary classes    • Life experience credit
90% of students perform over 15 hours of community service annually

Director of Admissions
California University of PA.
250 University Ave.
California, PA 15419

724. 938.4404

# CARLETON COLLEGE

1700 Students    Northfield, Minnesota

Carleton is one of the nation's most respected small liberal arts colleges, unusual for its location in the Midwest. Its vital intellectual community draws students from all fifty states and 20 other countries. Co-educational since its founding, Carleton has a long history of encouraging original thought and a sense of intellectual adventure through rigorous study of traditional academic disciplines. These disciplines are complemented by a wide offering of electives and interdisciplinary programs.

One such program appealing to some students interested in environmental studies, is the Environment and Technology concentration which explores the implementation of emerging technology public policy. Faculty in the program are drawn from several departments including economics, geology, and sociology. Other students interested in environmental studies major in the natural sciences, taking advantage of one of the strongest undergraduate programs in the country.

Carleton's setting is distinct, with a 400-acre arboretum bordering the campus. The "Arb", as it is called by students, consists of a variety of habitats including floodplain forest, wetlands, prairie, and a pine plantation. Used for both research and recreation, the arboretum is governed by the students, who decide what preservation projects are undertaken and do the actual work themselves.

Students at Carleton have a long history of activism, involving themselves in over one hundred organizations on campus. Acting in the Community Together, or ACT, is one of the most popular. Through this umbrella volunteer organization, students administer over thirty separate community-based programs. Selected as the Minnesota hub campus for the national organization COOL (Campus Outreach Opportunity League,) ACT now serves as a consultant for other campus service programs.

Carleton encourages students to engage in honest discussions on issues of difference whether based on gender, race, ethnicity, socio-economics, or political viewpoint. Through both informal discussion and coursework, the College aims to expose members of the student community to perspectives that have developed outside of, in opposition to, or in ways only dimly visible to the dominant culture in which most of us have grown up and been educated. Before first-year students arrive at Carleton, they are invited to participate in a "Common Reading" of a book such as *July's People* by Nadine Gordimer or *Donald Duk* by Frank Chin. When they arrive on campus students meet with faculty and staff in their homes to discuss the book. In order to fulfill the "Recognition and Affirmation of Difference" requirement, students must take a course centrally concerned with another culture; with a country, art, or tradition from outside Europe and the US; or with issues of gender, class, race, or ethnicity

With over 60% of its students participating in off-campus studies, Carleton operates one of the largest study abroad programs on any college campus. In an average year, Carleton students partake in 85 different programs. Whether it be in Nepal, Costa Rica, or Kenya, Carleton students gain not only an unusual academic experience, but also an invaluable personal one.

# MAKING A DIFFERENCE STUDIES

## Biology

Biology for the Humanist
Spring Flora
Marine Biology
Tropical Rainforest Ecology
Field Investigation in Tropical Rainforest Ecology (in Costa Rica)
Biology Field Studies and Research (in Australia/New Zealand)

Biology of Conservation
Introductory Botany
Ecology
Biology of Non-Vascular Plants

## Environment and Technology Studies

Information, Society and Democracy
Environmental Policy and Politics
Public Policy and the Human Fetus
Intro to Environmental Geology
Congress, Campaign Money & A National Energy Strategy

Technologies and Their Societies
Water and Western Economic Development
Environmental Chemistry
Technology Policy Project

## Sociology / Anthropology

Population and Food in Global System
Biography and Ethnography
Nationalism and Ethnicity
Islam and the Middle East
Explorations of Diaspora Populations
Conquest and Encounter: Europeans and Indigenous Peoples in the "New World"

Class, Power and Inequality in America
Economic Anthropology
Schooling and Opportunity in Amer. Society
Comparative Study of Developing Societies
Ethnology of Central America & Caribbean

## Political Science

Science, Technology and Politics
Parties, Interest Groups and Elections
Urban Politics
Political Theory of M. L. King, Jr.
International Conflict and War
Social Movements and Protest Politics

Liberal Democracy and Social Democracy
Feminist Political Theory
Urban Political Economy
Gender Discrimination & Constitutional Law
American Security and Arms Control
Urban Racial and Ethnic Politics

- **Poverty and Public Policy** *Focus on the relationship between race, class, gender and poverty in the U.S. Students will analyze various explanations for the growth of the underclass and homelessness as well as public policy strategies for reducing poverty.*

## Economics

Comparative Economic Systems
African Economic Development
Political Economy of Capitalism
Economics of the Public Sector
Environmental Health Economics
Economics of Poverty, Discrimination and the Distribution of Income

The Economics of Apartheid
Political Economy of the Third World
Economics of Human Resources
Economics of Natural Resources
Economics of Poverty

Educational Studies Concentration     Natural History Concentration
Women's Studies     African/African-American Studies
Apply by 1/15
- Team teaching    - Interdisciplinary classes    - Theme housing    - Vegetarian meals

Dean of Admissions
Carleton College
Northfield, MN 55057

507. 646.4190
800. 995.2275
admission@acs.carleton.edu
www.carleton.edu

# CLARK UNIVERSITY

2,000 Undergraduates    Worcester, MA

Typical Clark University students don't like to be called typical. They enjoy challenging convention and seeking out people who are different than themselves. These characteristics fit well in an academic community long distinguished for its pioneering research and concern for significant social issues.

Clark's culture prompts students to venture beyond the classroom and into the community, across cultures and even across the globe. In the university's own neighborhood, Main South, students are an important part of the University Park Partnership, a university-led revitalization effort that is improving the quality of life for residents and setting the standard for effective urban renewal. Students act as tutors for the neighborhood high school, help give free music lessons to local children, and include young students in academic and artistic projects. Student groups also excel in identifying the places in the city that need their help the most, whether it be at local soup kitchens, nursing homes, or elementary schools.

To encourage more students with a commitment to service to join the Clark community, the university offers Making a Difference Scholarships. These 20 scholarships, each worth $11,000 per year, are awarded to students who have demonstrated commitment to their community. In addition, these Making a Difference scholars are offered a $2,500 stipend to support projects they undertake with the University Park Partnership during the summer following their sophomore or junior years.

Clark students look beyond the local community as well. Its culture is heavily influenced by the large percentage of international students — 15 percent of undergraduate students come from more than 90 countries. That means at least one person in an average classroom, probably more, comes from another country and brings a different point of view to class discussions and projects. This sharing of cultures is also reflected in the diverse social opportunities offered on campus. One of the most popular events on campus is the international buffet, a smorgasbord of delicious food from around the world cooked by members of the International Students Association.

Faculty research involves every part of the world. In classrooms and laboratories, professors try out new ideas and recount their firsthand experience in, for example, measuring Chernobyl's radioactive fallout in Europe, or helping villagers use resources more effectively to produce food in Kenya, Somalia and Zimbabwe.

Clark was one of the first universities to offer an undergraduate major in the interdisciplinary field of Environmental Science and Policy. E.S.P. is for students who hope to find solutions to complex societal problems such as environmental protection, energy policy, technological hazards, and risk analysis. The International Development and Social Change program focuses on ways in which individuals can identify effective local action in the context of global change.

Other uniquely Clark projects, such as a cogeneration plant that recycles energy and a yearly non-profit career fair, reflect the university's commitment to encouraging students to make a difference in their world.

# MAKING A DIFFERENCE STUDIES

## Cultural Identity and Global Processes

*Dramatic growth in transnational and global phenomena has led to the existence of a global community that has significantly contributed to the demise of the nation-state. Yet, at the same time there is a resurgence of cultural identities in both regional and local contexts.*

Cultural Identities and Global Processes      Race, Migration, Gender and Ethnicity
The Creation of Nationalisms, Nationalist Cultures and Symbols

- **Culture, Consumption, & Class in Local & Global Contexts** *Focuses on consumption as it is determined culturally, ethnically, by gender and class, and impacted upon politically by both individual consumers and capitalist producers. Ways in which consumption is linked to identity values are explored. A central theme is the interplay between the forces of the world market and cultural identities, between local and global processes, and between consumption and cultural strategies.*

## Cultural / Humanistic Geography

The End of America: Los Angeles      Feminism, Nature and Culture
Culture, Place and Environment      Divided Cities, Connected Lives
Gender and Environment      Keeping of Animals: Patterns of Use and Abuse
Culture and Sport
Before and After Columbus: Ancient Middle America and Impact of the Conquest

## Regional / International Development / Political Economy

International Political Economy      GIS and Local Planning
Management of Arid Lands      Geography of the Global Economy
Political Economy of Third World Underdevelopment
African Environments and Geographical Implications

- **Gender, Work & Space** *This course examines how gender, race, class and ethnicity divide the work force and how location and space shape and sustain such divisions. Evaluates competing explanations for why women, youths and minorities hold jobs that differ distinctly from jobs held by other workers. Explores how a geographic understanding of gender, class and ethnicity can help explain the current restructuring of the global economy.*

## Environment, Society and Policy

*Interdisciplinary program that emphasizes policy questions involving the environment and the use and misuse of science and technology. The program's goal is to enable individuals to deal with technical and environmental issues in a social and political context, and to do so with an acute awareness of the short- and long-range limitations of the natural environment to respond to human interventions.*

Science, Uncertainty and Decisions      The Earth Transformed
Energy and the Campus      Cancer: Science and Society
Management of Environmental Pollutants      Environmental Toxicology
Environmental Ethics      Limits of the Earth
Tools for Quantitative Policy Analysis      Societal Analysis & Evaluation of Enviro. Hazards

## Environmental / Resource Management

Earth Systems Science      Ecological Systems
Environmental Ethics      Biosphere-Atmosphere Interactions
Environmental Policy and Management      Land Degradation
Forest and Wilderness: Values and Uses

## Peace Studies

*Peace Net, an international computer network is available for student use*

Social Psychology
Medical Ethics
Palestine, Israel and the Arab Conflict
Rescue and Resistance
Principles of Negotiation and Mediation

Psychology of Peacemaking
Race and American Society
International Division of Labor
Women and Militarism

## Philosophy

Analytic Reasoning
Social and Political Ethics
Philosophy of Religion
Social and Political Philosophy
Medical Ethics
AIDS: Ethics and Public Policy

Personal Values
Moral Problems in the Professions
The Ideal of the Educated Person
Philosophy of Language
Business Ethics

## Women's Studies

Women and Politics
Gender and the City in the U.S.
The Family
Women in Society

Gender and Environment
Feminism, Nature and Culture
Gender and Film
Feminist Critical Theory

## Physical Geography of Human Systems

Biogeography
Tropical Ecology
Earth Science and Development
Urban Ecology: Cities as Ecosystems
Environment and Disasters

Watershed Ecology
Land Degradation
Physical Environment of Arid Lands
Oceanic Islands: Geology and Ecology
Agriculture and Grazing

**Government     Sociology     Psychology     Screen Studies     Geography**
**Urban / International Development and Social Change**
**Environmental Studies     Race and Ethnic Relations**

Apply By 2/1
• Service learning     • Internships     • Interdisciplinary classes     • Field studies     • Team teaching
• Self-designed majors     • Third-world service-learning     • Vegetarian & kosher meals
• Opportunity for fifth year tuition free BA/MA programs in E.S.P. and International Development

More than 70% of classes have less than 20 students
Special interest houses include "global environment house"

Dean of Admissions
Clark University
Admissions House
950 Main St.
Worcester, MA 01610

508. 793.7431
admissions@clark.edu
www.clarku.edu

# COLLEGE OF THE ATLANTIC

260 Students     Bar Harbor, Maine

Given its name, it's probably no surprise that College of the Atlantic focuses on ecological issues. Considering that the breathtaking campus is set on the ocean in Maine, it becomes clear just how central the natural environment is to the school.

Human Ecology, the theme that defines the College's unique liberal studies program, is investigated and studied by students and faculty from many viewpoints and approaches. Each student is responsible for designing an individualized program of study. The core curriculum includes course offerings in environmental science, human studies and art, as well as writing. Students are required to fulfill a 10-week internship. International opportunities include extended study in Mexico's Yucatan Peninsula.

Students are given a great deal of academic freedom. They plan their programs according to individual interests, including independent study projects. With a student body numbering just over 260, close friendships between students are the norm. Students work closely with their peers and professors in small classes and on special projects. They receive individual evaluations of their work in addition to (optional) grades. The atmosphere is supportive and friendly while maintaining a high degree of scholarship and academic rigor.

Students are given a significant role in the school administration and campus government, which fosters a strong sense of responsibility and commitment. The very liberal student body is activist, intelligent and tolerant. College of the Atlantic students hail from all parts of the country. International students represent nearly 10% of the student population, and women outnumber men by a notable, but not overwhelming, margin.

Students are also active in the surrounding community. Service opportunities include social and educational programs such as Habitat for Humanity, AIDS education outreach, and environment-related activities in neighboring Acadia National Park. There is an active artistic community and exhibitions at COA's Blum Gallery, as well as theatrical productions in Gates Auditorium have received critical acclaim.

Although small, the oceanfront campus recently expanded with a new center for regional and international studies as well as two island lighthouse field stations. A new building for COA's Museum of Natural History is under construction.The museum features excellent environmental displays designed to raise awareness of ecological issues for museum visitors and provide educational programs for children. The College is also the home of Allied Whale, an internationally-recognized marine mammal research center. Beech Hill Farm, an 86-acre organic farm was recently donated to COA by two generous and community-minded graduates.

While the Colleges's location is decidedly quiet during the winter months, the stunning beauty of the natural surroundings offers a unique setting in which to pursue learning. College of the Atlantic seeks to nurture in its students a conservation ethic, environmental concern, and social activism enabling them to visualize and contribute to a more sustainable, just, and balanced world.

# MAKING A DIFFERENCE STUDIES

## Environmental Sciences

Animal Behavior
Biology of Fishes
Ecological Physiology
Gender and Science
Marine Ecology
Ornithology
Plant Taxonomy

Biology I and II;
Bio-Organic Chemistry
Conservation of Endangered Species
Geology
The Gulf of Maine
Plants and Humanity
Women in Science.

- **Marine Mammals**  *Biology of whales, porpoises and seals, concentrating on species that frequent New England waters, but also including other species or habitats. Study of skeletal anatomy, prey species, visits to harbor seal ledges, observation of gray seals, and whale watching.*

## Human Studies

Humans in Nature
Critical Theory to Feminist Theory
Environmental Law
International Environmental Law
International Peace In Theory and Practice
Literature and Ecology
Medicine and Culture
Philosophy of Nature
Use and Abuse of Our Public Lands

Technology and Culture
Environmental Journalism
History of American Reform Movements
Women and Men in Transition
Issues in Regional Resource Management
Literature of Third World Women
Outdoor Education and Leadership
Science and Society
Women's History and Literature

## Arts and Design

Architectural Survey
Art, Media, and Environmental Studio
Introduction to Video Production
Photography I and II
Projects in Theater Workshop

Design and Activism
Environmental Design
Presentation Skills
Primitive Art
Women in the Visual Arts.

## Teacher Certification K-12

*Approximately 20 percent of COA graduates are engaged in graduate studies or employed in the field as naturalists, environmental educators, and classroom teachers.*

Environmental Design: Learning Spaces
Perspectives on School and Society
Intro to Philosophy of Education
Qualitative Research in Schools
Mainstreaming the Exceptional Child
Schools

Art, Media, and the Practice of Learning
Mainstreaming the Exceptional Child
Learning Theory
Intellectual History of Schools
Curriculum and Instruction in Secondary

- Apply by 3/1, 4/15 for transfer    Faculty: 56% male, 44% female
Average # of students in a first year classroom: 15
- Self-designed majors  • Interdisciplinary classes    • Optional SAT's
- All seminar format   • Team teaching   • Field studies   • Life experience credit
- Required community service   • Graduate programs   • Vegetarian & vegan meals

Admissions Office
College of the Atlantic
105 Eden St.
Bar Harbor, ME 04609

207. 288.5015
800. 528.0025
inquiry@ecology.coa.edu
www.coa.edu

# COLLEGE OF ENVIRONMENTAL SCIENCE & FORESTRY

## STATE UNIVERSITY OF NEW YORK

1,200 Undergraduate Students     Syracuse, New York

When the rest of the country celebrated the first Earth Day in 1970 it finally caught up with the College of Environmental Science and Forestry. Since 1911, when the College first opened its doors, ESF began preparing scientists, resource managers, and engineers to nurture the home planet and to teach scientific principles and applications that would maintain and improve forest lands and support the wise use of natural resources. Today, ESF leads in the discovery of new knowledge and the use of new tools to deal with continuing, current, and future environmental challenges. Students in all programs at SUNY-ESF gain a coherent understanding of their natural environment and learn ways to improve its health and productivity. All students share an interest in the environment and science, design or engineering required to conserve resources and enhance the health of the Earth. SUNY-ESF has prepared people to sustain and improve the environment for almost a century.

ESF's mission is to be a world leader in instruction, research, and public service related to: understanding the structure and function of the world's ecosystems; developing, managing, and using renewable natural resources; improving outdoor environments ranging from wilderness to managed forests to urban landscapes; and maintaining and enhancing biological diversity, environmental quality, and resource options.

As the 21st century looms and society becomes increasingly concerned about the environment, members of the ESF family have timing in their favor. The future of the world may be determined by those who have broad foresight and a balance of judgment in applying scientific, technical, and sociological knowledge to guide environmental and human forces. Modern society, with its compelling demands from industry and government, needs people who think objectively and constructively, and who act creatively and responsibly. Faculty and students are committed to resolving environmental hazards, learning how to avoid future problems, and offering policy alternatives that will protect the environment and meet the needs of a global society.

Academic programs at ESF share a foundation of rigorous science and a dedication to the wise use of natural resources. The faculty's cutting-edge research becomes part of the classroom experience, and the classroom merges with the world beyond the campus. Paper science students at ESF earn real-world experience and paychecks through required summer work at leading paper companies.

Students participate in hands-on and laboratory work at the main campus and on the 25,000 acres of ESF campus outside Syracuse. The College's largest regional campus at Newcomb is located on the 15,000-acre Huntington Wildlife Forest. Faculty, undergraduates, and visiting scientists use the facility for general research and work related to forest management. The Wanakena campus is the site of the College's Forestry Technology Program. The summer session in field forestry required of environmental and resource management majors, and the dual option in environmental and forest biology and resource management, takes place at Wanakena. All locations are equipped with the latest technology.

# MAKING A DIFFERENCE STUDIES

## Environmental & Forest Biology and Resources Management - Dual Program

Plant Ecology
Diversity of Plants
Wildlife Conservation
Principles of Animal Behavior
Ecology of Freshwaters

Ecology of Adirondack Fishes
Ecological Biogeochemistry
Principles of Forest Entomology
Wildlife Habitats and Populations
Wildlife Ecology & Management Practicum

## Environmental Studies

Environmental Geology
Intro to Environmental Impact Analysis
Natural Processes in Planning & Design
American Landscape History
Environmental Studies Internship

Environmental Communication
Decision Modeling for Environmental Mgm't.
Government and the Environment
Social Processes and the Environment
Technologies: Water & Wastewater Treatment

## Landscape Architecture

Intro to Landscape Architecture & Planning
Site Research & Analysis
Plant Materials
Comprehensive Land Planning
Community Land Planning Workshop

Fundamentals of City & Regional Planning
Natural Processes in Planning & Design
Selected Readings in Environmental Studies
Professional Practice in Landscape Architecture
Negotiating Environmental Disputes

## Forest Technology and Resource Management

Forest Ecology
Timber Harvesting
Soil and Water Measurements
Forest Influences
Soils
Forest and Resource Economics

Personnel Management
Elements of Wildlife Ecology
Structure and Growth of Trees
Silviculture
Forest Protection
Natural Resource & Environmental Policy

## Forest Engineering

Water Pollution Engineering
Harvest Systems Analysis
Soil Mechanics and Foundations

Resource Policy and Management
Air Pollution Engineering
Forest Engineering Planning and Design

## Forest Technology (Ranger School) AAS Degree

# FOREST ENTOMOLOGY

Forest Roads
Fire Management
Structure & Growth of Trees
Computer Applications

# AERIAL PHOTOGRAMMETRY

Forest Pathology
Personnel Management
Forest Recreation
Elements of Wildlife Ecology

## Accelerated 5-year BS/MS Plant Biotechnology

Rolling admissions
• Field studies   • Housing at University of Syracuse   • Graduate program

Director of Admissions                     315. 470.6600
SUNY College of Environmental Science & Forestry
1 Forestry Drive                           800. 777.7ESF
Syracuse, NY 13210-2779

*College of Environmental Science and Forestry SUNY    101*

# UNIVERSITY OF COLORADO, BOULDER

19,500 Undergraduates   Boulder, Colorado

As the flagship institution of the four-campus University of Colorado system, CU-Boulder has a long tradition of teaching environmental and social responsibility to students. The campus has an international reputation for environmental education and research programs, which can be pursued through several avenues.

Environmental studies, for example — a bachelor's degree program in place for more than 40 years — features a comprehensive curricula in the basic sciences, economics, ethics, and policy that prepares students to make a difference in the real world. Its two academic tracks — one in environmental sciences, one in society and policy — allows undergraduates to specialize in areas ranging from environmental and natural resources to decision-making, planning, and public policy.

The University also offers a unique environmental studies program for undergraduates that offers course work and seminars within a residence hall setting. Courses in biology, economics, expository writing, geography, geology, mathematics and political science meet core requirements and are taught in classes of about 25 students.

All of the environmental programs on campus are buoyed by outstanding faculty members, some of whom are affiliated with internationally known campus institutes like the Cooperative Institute for Research in Environmental Science and the Institute of Artic and Alpine Research. The Mountain Research Station, located about 45 minutes from campus, features a long-term ecological study site and hosts students and faculty from around the world.

The long tradition of volunteer service on campus is underscored by the fact that CU-Boulder ranks second in the nation in the number of volunteers recruited by the Peace Corps. A total of 300 students have gone on to Peace Corps service over the past seven years, helping people in developing countries to help themselves. Since 1961, more than 1,400 CU graduates have served in the Peace Corps.

CU's International and National Volunteer Service Training (INVST) program combines academic training and fieldwork in how to start and run volunteer service organizations. During junior and senior years the 16-credit-hour INVST program features courses in global and community development, human ecology, and social change. Participating students also learn about bookkeeping, office management, program evaluation techniques and how to gain access to global computing networks.

Students can also participate in the Farrand Program, an academic program set in a residence hall, that emphasizes humanities studies. In addition to surveying western art and culture, the program offers contemporary subjects — like global ecology, film and ethics — that are taught by some of the finest University faculty. The program also provides a number of community outreach opportunities.

The new ethnic studies major promotes interdisciplinary research and teaching in Afro-American, American Indian, Asian-American, and Chicano studies, together with cross cultural and comparative race and ethnic studies. The primary focus of this major is on people of color and indigenous peoples of the US, but the study of race and ethnic issues in terms of global interactions are also important.

# MAKING A DIFFERENCE STUDIES

## Environmental Conservation

Principles of Ecology
The Environment and Public Policy
Forest Geography: Principles & Dynamics
Environments and Peoples

Conservation Practice
Remote Sensing of the Environment
Water Resource & Management of Western US
Energy in a Technical Society

## Biology: Environmental, Population and Organismic

Environmental Issues and Biology
Artic and Alpine Ecology
Ecosystem Ecology
Ecological Perspectives on Global Change

Global Ecology
Limnology (Water Ecology)
Medical Ecology & Environmental Health
Topics in Montane Ecology

## Geography

World Geographic Problems
Conservation Thought
World Agriculture
Nature and Properties of Soils

Geoecology of Alpine and Artic Regions
Migration, Urbanization and Development
Water Resources & Mgm't. of Western US
Urban Geography

## International Affairs

Political Geography
International Conflict in a Nuclear Age
Alternative World Futures
Power: Anthropology of Politics

American Foreign Policy
International Relations
Comparative Politics: Dev. Political Systems
Cross-Cultural Aspects of Socioeconomic Devlp't.

## Sociology: Population & Health; Medicine; Social Conflict; Sex & Gender

Sociology of Gender, Health and Aging
Population Control and Family Planning
Men and Masculinity
Nonviolence & Ethics of Social Action

Women, Development and Fertility
Folk Med. & Psychiatry: Chicano Communities
Social Issues in Mental Health
Sociology of Natural and Social Environments

## Anthropology

Hopi & Navajo, Cultures in Conflict
The Maya
North American Indian Acculturation
Medical Anthropology

Amazonian Tribal Peoples
Ethnography of Mexico & Central America
Analyzing Exotic Languages
Urban Anthropology

## Chicano Studies

The Mexican Revolution
The Contemporary Mexican American
Chicano Poetry
Barrio Issues

Hispanic & Native American Culture of SW
Latinos and the American Political System
Folklore, Mysticism & Myth of Hispanic SW
History of Chicanos in Amer. Labor Movement

## International and National Voluntary Service Training Certificate

*Financial aid in return for 1-2 years of humanitarian service. 6 weeks of travel to a foreign country.*

Democratic & Nonviolent Social Movements
Global Human Ecology

Facilitating Peaceful Community Change
Global Development

### Kinesiology    Peace & Conflict    Philosophy    Women's Studies
Apply by 2/15        30 service-learning courses
Office of Admissions                                303. 492.6301
University of Colorado at Boulder            www.colorado.edu
Boulder, CO 80309-0030

# COLORADO COLLEGE

1,900 students     Colorado Springs, Colorado

Students come to Colorado College knowing they will have the opportunity to explore their values and discover their place in society. Students find a community that listens and challenges, provides and delivers. Students interested in the people, cultures, and land of the American Southwest come to Colorado College for its distinguished Southwest Studies program. CC's location and programs are ideal for those whose wonder and concern for the natural world is integral to their education. The College encourages students to pursue their goals for serious independent research.

In 1970, Colorado College implemented a new schedule that allowed for in-depth study, extended field trips, and ample opportunity for independent study. the Block Plan divides the academic year into eight three-and-a-half week segments called blocks. Students take one course during each block and faculty teach only one course. Unrestricted by time and place, teachers can schedule class sessions to best suit the material. As a result, students learn through participation and "hands-on" exploration. Classes can spend entire days in the library or at a museum gathering data for research projects. Classes in geology, economics, and sociology can take prolonged field trips, studying their subject in the appropriate environment.

Because of its location and the interests of students and faculty, Colorado College has become a leader in the study of the American Southwest. Southwest Studies is interdisciplinary, asking students to understand the "big picture," to weave together various cultural and historical perspectives, the literature and language of the indigenous people, and an understanding of the area's natural environment.

With a significant representation of Native American and Hispanic students, the campus is alive with a Southwest 'flavor'. The Hulbert Center for Southwest Studies sponsors visiting scholars and events, such as the "Women of the West" or "Race, Immigration, and the Rise of Nativism in Late Twentieth Century America" lecture series. Southwest Studies classes often travel afield to visit Hispanic communities in Colorado, or to examine the Southwest terrain in the Four Corners region.

The interdisciplinary Environmental Science program is focused in the sciences while seeking the breadth — in the humanities and the social sciences — that is essential for a full understanding of environmental issues. Since 1971 nearly 100 students have bred, monitored, and studied falcons with Professor Jim Enderson, leader of the Western Peregrine Falcon Recovery Team for the U.S. Fish and Wildlife Service. Through their efforts, the Peregrine falcon is being considered for removal from the "endangered" and "threatened" lists.

At Colorado College, students' environmental interests merge into a way of life. Almost every year, students band together to form an environmental theme house. The Outdoor Recreation Committee leads trips up mountains, down rivers, and through valleys — focusing on student leadership and environmental reverence.

Students who want to get involved take advantage of the Block Plan's four-and-a-half day "mini-vacations" by traveling to places such as Denver, Chicago, or New Mexico to assist communities facing economic instability or work with Habitat for Humanity, providing decent, affordable housing for low-income families.

# MAKING A DIFFERENCE STUDIES

## War and Peace in the Nuclear Age

The Dawn of the Nuclear Age
War, Violence and the Humanities
Foundations of Nonviolence
Int'l. Human Rights: Theory and Practice

The Non-Violent Tradition in Literature
Morality in War
Freedom and Authority
War & Peace in Nuclear Age

## Philosophy

History of Environmental Ethics
Science, Technology, and Values
Asian Philosophies of Feminism
Business Ethics
Philosophy of Science

Philosophy of Feminism
Intro to Social and Political Philosophy
Philosophy of Education
Philosophy of Mind

## Southwest Studies

Geology and Ecology of the Southwest
Southwest American Indian Music
Ethnohistory of the Southwest
Arts and Cultures of the Southwest
Literature of the Southwest

Chicano Politics
History of SW Under Spain and Mexico
Southwestern Ecosystems
American SW: The Heritage and the Variety
History of the SW Since the Mexican War

## Economics and Business

Economics of Poverty
Business Ethics
Economics of Labor
Economic Development
Natural Resource Economics

Social Impact of Business
Legal Environment of Business
Political Economy of Defense in War & Peace
Economics of Discrimination
Economics of International Finance

## History

War and Society Since the Renaissance
Witchcraft & Witch Craze in Early Europe
History of 20th Century Europe
Black People in the U.S. Since Civil War

The Jews in Modern Europe
France & Italy: Fascism, War & Resistance
Women in America Before the Civil War
Women and Children in the Western Past

## Women's Studies

Gender and Science
Native American Women of the West
Feminist/Womanist Ethics
American Women in Industrial Society

Black Women, Fiction & Literary Tradition
Women, Literature and the Family
The Family Before Industrialization
Myth and Meaning

- **Ecofeminism** *Ecofeminism explores the links between systems of domination such as sexism, racism, economic exploitation, and the ecological crisis.*

### Religion    Political Economy    Sociology    Ethnomusicology

Apply by 1/15
Avg # of students in first year class: 16    80% of students engaged in community service
- Individualized majors    • Multidisciplinary classes    • Field studies
- All seminar format    • Team teaching    • Vegetarian meals    • Theme housing

Director of Admissions
Colorado College
14 E. Cache la Poudre
Colorado Springs, CO 80903

800. 542.7214
719. 389.6344
www.cc.colorado.edu

# COLORADO STATE UNIVERSITY

20,000 Undergraduates    Fort Collins, Colorado

Colorado State University has a unique mission in the State of Colorado. The land-grant concept of a balanced program of teaching, research, extension, and public service provides the foundation for the University teaching and research programs, the Agricultural Experiment Station, and the Colorado State Forest Service. In the land-grant tradition, the University emphasizes instruction and research in professional areas important to the state and nation.

The educational philosophy at CSU recognizes and respects people as individuals and as members of social groups. Because of this, the University maintains programs that contribute to interpersonal, intercultural, and international understanding. Of equal importance, education at CSU emphasizes consideration of values, for knowledge without values leaves the learner ill-equipped to make critical choices in life. CSU was honored in the Templeton Honor Role in *Colleges That Encourgage Character Development*. It was recognized for strong first year programs, faculty focus on ethics, volunteer programs, and emphasis upon civic and personal responsibility.

The College of Forestry and Natural Resources (CFNR) offers studies and professional training in the management, administration, and scientific investigation of renewable and nonrenewable natural resources. Programs include the study of fish, forests, minerals, range, watershed, wildlife, and outdoor recreation areas — their environments, products, and services. The scope of the college's programs is more broadly based than most forestry or natural resources schools. Undergraduate curricula include fishery biology, forestry, geology, landscape architecture, watershed sciences, and wildlife biology. International resources management is an increasingly important concern of the CFNR. Because it is desirable that students study abroad, the CFNR has agreements with colleges in Scotland, Australia, New Zealand, and South Africa.

College of Agricultural Sciences majors include agronomy (the science of field crops and soils), animal science, and landscape horticulture. The International Agronomy concentration is designed to meet the need of developing nations. Graduates find jobs with the Peace Corps and other agencies working in demonstration and extension positions. As new crop varieties are developed or introduced into developing countries, appropriate agronomic practices may be designed to be compatible with farming systems which can succeed in those climatic and socioeconomic constraints.

The University offers an interdisciplinary (non-degree) concentration in Youth Agency Administration. This unusual program is designed to enhance a student's academic readiness to enter a career position in the youth and human service fields. This is achieved by an emphasis in various areas of human services, organizational management, and administration in social services. Students who complete the program often find professional positions in service agencies such as Boy Scouts of America, Big Brothers/Big Sisters of America, 4-H, and the YMCA.

The Outdoor Adventure Program offers a variety of participatory programs for students and faculty. Some of the classes include wilderness survival, rock climbing, cross-country skiing, kayaking, and cycling. An outdoor resources library and rental shop are additional dimensions of this curricular-learning program.

# MAKING A DIFFERENCE STUDIES

## Range Ecology: Land Rehabilitation

Rangeland Improvements
Surface Mining Rehabilitation
Soil Fertility Management
Range Ecosystem Planning
Agriculture Experimental Design

Natural Resource Ecology
Agriculture/Natural Resource Economics
Range Animal-Habitat Interactions
Range Plant Production and Decomposition
Land Use and Water Quality

## Natural Resources Journalism

Agric/Natural Resource Economics
Environmental Conservation
Principles of Wildlife Management
Public Speaking and Discussion
Economics of Energy Resources

Attributes of Living Systems
Photojournalism
Environmental Ethics
Media and Society
Economics of Urban and Regional Land Use

## Conservation Biology

Population Ecology
Maintenance of Biotic Diversity
Disturbed Lands
Environmental Toxicology
Range Ecogeography

Environmental Conservation
Population: Natural Resource & Environment
Ecology of Landscapes
Wildlife Ecology
Politics and Natural Resources

## Entomology

Beekeeping
Aquatic Insects
Population Ecology
Insects, Science & Society

Range and Livestock Insects
International Crop Protection
Insect Pest Management
Agricultural Pesticides

## Gerontology

Perspectives in Gerontology
Social Work with Social Gerontology
Nutrition and Aging
Death, Dying and Grief
Handicapped Individual in Society

Adult Development and Aging
Biology of Aging
Housing and Design: Special Populations
Philosophy of Aging
Family Financial Resources and Public Policy

## Nonprofit Agency Administration

Intro to Nonprofit Agency Administration
Nonprofit Agency Fund Raising & Mgm't
Accounting
Human Diversity Issues
Marketing/Public Relations

Volunteer Management & Service Leaning
Management Fundamentals
Human Development & Family Studies
Social Work
Community Dynamics and Development

## Economics

Issues in Environmental Economics
Economics of Natural Resources
Labor Economics
Economics of Energy Resources

Poverty and Income Distribution
Economics of Outdoor Recreation
Economics of Urban and Regional Land Use

**Teaching Endorsement in Natural Resources    Sociology    Landscape Architecture**

Rolling Admissions

Director of Admissions
Colorado State University
Fort Collins, CO 80523

970. 491.6909
www.colostate.edu/

# CORNELL UNIVERSITY

12,750 Undergraduates    Ithaca, New York

Cornell combines both private and public education at its seven colleges. The private colleges include Engineering, the College of Arts and Sciences, and the College of Architecture, Art and Planning. The Colleges of Agriculture and Life Sciences, Human Ecology, and Industrial and Labor Relations are public institutions and, as such, their tuition is considerably lower than at the private college.

The School of Industrial and Labor Relations is a small school within a large university with about 650 undergraduates. Courses in the school are divided into six departments: Collective Bargaining, Labor Law and Labor History; Economic and Social Statistics; International and Comparative Labor Relations; Labor Economics; Organizational Behavior; and Personnel and Human Resource Studies.

The College of Agriculture and Life Sciences offers studies in Natural Resources; Entomology; Biological Sciences; Plant Sciences; Animal Sciences; Social Sciences; and Agricultural and Biological Engineering. Intercollege programs include Landscape Architecture; Science, Technology and Society; and Environmental Toxicology

The College of Human Ecology seeks to understand and improve the relations between people and their environments. Faculty and students examine relations of individuals to their family, neighborhood, workplace, and community, seeking a balance between theory and practice that will improve the quality of every day life. Majors include Human Development and Family Studies, Human Service Studies, Nutritional Sciences, and an interdepartmental major in Policy Analysis.

The university-wide program on Ethics and Public Life (EPL) is Cornell's initiative in the systematic study of the ethical dimension of public issues. In the economy we face questions of equity and justice and about the relation between prosperity, the environment, and the quality of individual lives. In constitutional law, we confront dilemmas about civil rights, freedom of speech, and abortion. In politics and government, we wrestle with questions about campaigning, character, and compromise. In international affairs, we encounter complexities of war and peace, human rights, multilateral aid, and climate change. EPL grew out of a conviction that these questions need something more than abstract philosophical discussion. Universities need to foster ways of thinking about the complex, uncertain, and urgent problems of the real world. EPL seeks to facilitate and enhance discussion of ethical issues by students whose central educational interests lie elsewhere, but whose work and lives will nevertheless be confronted with dilemmas and responsibilities for which a university eduction should prepare them.

The Center for the Environment is a campus-wide center that promotes and coordinates interdisciplinary research, teaching, and outreach activities on environmental issues. An effort to "design, develop and demonstrate ecologically sustainable communities... and transfer this knowledge to the global community to guide land and resource development" is being explored. The Center for Religion, Ethics and Social Policy is building an EcoVillage on 176 acres nearby. The goal is to build a cooperative, environmentally sensitive community. The project includes energy-efficient healthy housing, passive solar design, and biological waste treatment.

# MAKING A DIFFERENCE STUDIES

## Agricultural and Biological Engineering

Soil & Water Management
Principles of Aquaculture
Environmental Systems Analysis
Biomass Conversion Processes for Energy & Chemicals

Treatment & Disposal of Agricultural Wastes
Introduction to Energy Technology
Bioenvironmental Engineering

## City and Regional Planning

Environment & Society: A Delicate Balance
Urban Economics
Environmental Politics
Progressive City
The Global City: People, Production, & Planning in the Third World

Intro to African Development
Gender Issues in Planning & Architecture
American Indians, Planners, & Public Policy
Urban Housing: Sheltered vs. Unsheltered Society

## Rural Sociology: Development Sociology; Population, Environment & Society; Social Data & Policy Analysis

Human Fertility In Developing Nations
American Indian Tribal Governments
International Development
Technology and Society
Land Reform Old and New

Introduction to Rural Sociology
Environment and Society
Gender and Society
Population Dynamics
Gender Relations, Ideologies, & Social Change

## Biology and Society

Religion, Ethics and the Environment
Living on the Land
Writing as a Naturalist
Ecosystems and Ego Systems
Land Resources Protection Law

Ethics and Health Care
Women and Nature
Ecology and Social Change
Global Climate & Global Justice
The Politics of Technical Decisions

## Economics

Economic Development
Economic Problems of Latin America
International Trade Theory and Policy
Business Mgm't. of Worker Enterprises

Economics of Participation & Workers Mgm't.
Practice & Implementation of Self-Management
Economics of Defense Spending
Public Finance: Resource Allocation, Fiscal Policy

- ***Technological & Product Base of Worker Enterprises: Ecology & Solar Energy Applications*** *Workers self-management. & cooperation through learning about & construction of simple energy-related technologies to be produced in workers enterprises.*

## Africana Studies

Racism in American Society
Black Resistance: S Africa & N. America
Politics & Social Change in the Caribbean
Social & Psychological Effects of Colonialization & Racism

African Civilizations & Culture
African Socialism & Nation Building
Oppression & Psych. of Black Social Movement

**Women's Studies    Outdoor Education    Marine Science    Natural Resources
Int'l Agriculture    Policy Analysis    Near Eastern Studies    Human Services
Hispanic, Asian- American, American Indian Studies    Civil & Enviro. Engineering**

Apply by 1/1

Undergraduate Admissions
Cornell University
Ithaca, NY 14850-2488

607. 255.5241
www.cornell.edu

# EARLHAM COLLEGE

1,050 Students   Richmond, Indiana

Earlham is a distinctive teaching and learning community in which students build an education that is principled, humane, global, and rigorous. Founded by Friends (Quakers) in 1846, Earlham continues as a non-sectarian college firmly rooted in the values and practices of Friends. At the heart of Earlham are commitments: to upholding the value and dignity of every person; to personal integrity and academic honesty of the highest degree; to open inquiry in an interpersonally safe, but challenging, atmosphere; to increasing harmony in the world, both among humanity and between humanity and the natural environment in which we live.

President Dick Wood reflects on Earlham this way: "Earlham strives to be a special kind of learning community, one in which people are honest with others and themselves, a community in which people are encouraged to be friends, not rivals. We aspire to an academic integrity rooted in trust. Earlham's distinctive learning community rests also on another value important to Friends and, indeed, to the search for truth — respect for other persons. None of us has a monopoly on the truth....

"Earlham seeks a diversity of students and faculty. Diversity requires a heightened sensitivity in the way we listen and speak to others. We are all colleagues embarked on a shared journey to discover truth. Because we may find different paths, Earlham values individual freedom — but not at the expense of respect for those who are different or whose ideas we find disagreeable.

"Earlham values social justice and peaceful resolution of conflicts. Students and faculty have many opportunities to work for justice and to give of themselves in service. Following the example of early Friends, Earlham seeks not only to avoid violence, but to remove its causes. Students, staff, and faculty share in governing the College through a system of joint committees. As much as possible, Earlham tries to reach decisions by consensus, by arriving at what Friends call a 'sense of the meeting' that is shared by all involved...."

Earlham recognizes a responsibility for enabling students to grow in their knowledge and appreciation of American cultures, but also for challenging students through encounter with world cultures not familiar to them. Professor of English Anthony Bing says, "An Earlham education stresses the idea of global connectedness. A commitment to helping students see things from someone else's point of view. The other things compassion, understanding, humanity follow naturally."

Students often design their own majors such as Outdoor Education, Social Thought, and Museum Studies. Many students collaborate with professors on research and creative projects such as experiments in molecular biology focusing on the search for a cure for leukemia; responses of the American peace movement to Middle Eastern conflict; or seminars on women, social movements, and temperance. Students frequently participate in field study research, whether in Puerto Rico, Kenya, the Galapagos, Indiana, or in Quaker Libraries to study Quaker Women.

Student life at Earlham is enriched by a 600-acre back campus of ponds, woods, and meadows which serves as a biological field station, the site of the College's observatory and farm, and a place where students may wander, run, or ride horses.

# MAKING A DIFFERENCE STUDIES

## Conservation Biology

Ecological Biology
Ornithology
Population and Community Ecology
Field Biology Training Program at Manomet Bird Observatory, Massachusetts

Biological Diversity
Field Botany
Tropical Biology Interterm

## Environmental Chemistry

Techniques of Water Analysis
Chemical Dynamics
Instrumental Analysis
Organic Chemistry

Environmental Chemistry
Biochemistry
Quantum Chemistry
Chemistry in Societal Context

## Peace and Global Studies

Culture and Conflict
Politics of Global Problems
Conflict Resolution
Christian Ethics & Modern Moral Problems
Moral Education

Introduction to Philosophy: Food Ethics
Methods of Peacemaking
Theories of International Relations
Religious Responses to War and Violence
Technology and Arms Control

## Human Development and Social Relations

Theories of Human Development
Persons and Systems
Social Science and Human Values
Field Study
Social Relations

Human Biology
Comparative Cultures
Institutions and Inequality
Frontiers of Psychological Inquiry
Counseling & Psychotherapy

## Management

*Moral and ethical choices about how to interact with workers, and how to use the Earth's resources.*

Nonprofit Organization and Leadership
Work and Culture
Programming and Problem-Solving
Public Administration
Japanese Economic Development

Conflict Resolution
Health, Medicine and Society
Business Policy
Industrial Organization and Public Policy
Political & Econ. Development of Pacific Rim

## Japanese Studies

*Combines study of Japanese language and civilization with various disciplines, including history, political science, psychology, religion, economics, education, sociology/anthropology, and fine arts.*

Introduction to the Study of Japan
Japanese Arts
Religion of East Asia
Education and the Family in Japan

Super Japanese
Readings in Japan Culture
Politics of Japan
Senior Seminar

**African/African-American Studies    Environmental Geology    Women's Studies**
**Education    International Studies    Latin American Studies    Jewish Studies**
Apply by 2/15    Average # of students in first year class: 18-20
• Team teaching    • Individualized majors    • Service-learning    • Field studies
• Theme housing    • Interdisciplinary classes    • Vegetarian meals    • Energy conservation in effect

Director of Admissions
Earlham College
Richmond, IN 47374

800. 327.5426
admission@earlham.edu
www.earlham.edu

# EASTERN MENNONITE UNIVERSITY

1,000 Students    Harrisonburg, Virginia

Eastern Mennonite University places outstanding academics into the context of global awareness and active Christian involvement. The university's unique Global Village Curriculum builds on the belief that we are all interdependent in ways which can affect the survival or destruction of civilization. Eastern Mennonite educates students to use their talents to promote human transformation by working for peace, by creating just social structures, and by aiding access to basic human resources for life and dignity.

This educational perspective is rooted in the 450-year-old Anabaptist-Mennonite tradition. EMU's particular theological principles include Jesus as the word of God incarnate, the Bible as the authoritative guide for faith and life, the church as a community of work and worship, and discipleship as the mark of an authentic life. Discipleship implies an active faith characterized by simplicity of life, peacebuilding (which expresses itself in nonviolence, reconciliation, active pursuit of justice and non-participation in the military), evangelism, and Christian service.

The cornerstone of this approach to learning is Eastern Mennonite's Cross-Cultural Program, one of the strongest programs in international and cross-cultural education in the country. EMU students study in a wide range of international and domestic locations such as Central America, the Middle East, Europe, China, Japan, Russia, Africa, Mexico, Los Angeles, New Orleans, and American Indian reservations. On these cross-cultural study tours led by EMU's faculty, students receive an education that reaches far beyond the classroom. The larger world serves as a laboratory for testing and refining knowledge, no matter what a student's major. Eastern Mennonite students have life-changing experiences which broaden their world view and give them expanded possibilities after graduation.

On campus, Eastern Mennonite is a vibrant community bringing together students from a rich variety of cultural and religious backgrounds. A large majority of faculty have lived and served abroad. This international perspective enters the classroom, as do the perspectives of the 14% of students who are international or American multiethnic. With about 1,000 students, EMU is a good size — large enough for a full range of quality programs and activities, but small enough so students are not lost in the crowd. Personal relationships with professors are part of every student's experience.

In addition to the college's strong theater, athletic, and music programs, students participate in a wide array of extracurricular clubs and events. These include community service opportunities coordinated by student organizations. Students quickly discover that at Eastern Mennonite success is measured not only by what they achieve after graduation, but how they have developed along the way. Development of the whole person is the goal at Eastern Mennonite University.

# MAKING A DIFFERENCE STUDIES

## Biology

Environmental Science
Conservation Ecology
Food and Population

Plant Pest Management
Soil Science
Biology as Inquiry

- **Agroecology** *Explores agricultural ecosystems, especially in food deficit countries. Physical, biological, social, and economic bases of agroecology are examined using a variety of sources and case studies. An attempt is made to appreciate traditional agricultural rationality and to investigate the effects of modifications of existing agroecosystems.*

## International Business (Interdisciplinary Approach)

International Conflict and Peacemaking
Economic Development
International Business

International Marketing
Sociology of Development

- **Peace & Justice in Global Context** *Religion, theology, economic perspectives, int'l. organization, models for social change (development, revolution etc.) and missionary activity in the creation, maintenance, & change of social systems. Civil religion, Third World Theology, economic organization, and development as related to peace and justice.*

## Environmental Science

Biology as Inquiry
Environmental Science
Botany
Conservation Ecology

Applied Ecology
Agroecology
Earth Science
Soil Science

## Peace and Justice

Exploring the Peacebuilding Arts
Biblical Theology of Peace and Justice
Mediation and Conflict Transformation
Peace and Justice in the American Context

Peace and Justice in Global Context
Transformative Approaches to Justice & Peace
Justice and Compassion
History and Philosophy of Nonviolence

## Socio-Economic Development

Social Systems and Social Problems
Sociology of Development
Anthropology and Social Change
Food & Population

Transformative Approaches to Justice & Peace
Peace and Justice in Global Context
Social Policy Analysis
International Conflict and Peacemaking

## Camping, Recreation and Outdoor Ministries

Outdoor Education
Outdoor Living Skills
Camp Leadership
Introduction to Youth Ministry
Human Services Skills

Fdns. of Christian Camping & Outdoor Ministry
Technical Rock Climbing
Introduction to Youth Ministry
Recreational Programming: Design & Implementation
Sophomore Practicum

Apply by 8/1

Faculty: 60% male, 40% female    Avg. # of students in 1st yr class: 25
- Team teaching    • Field studies    • Interdisciplinary classes
- Required community service    • Self-designed majors    • Vegetarian meals
- Graduate studies in counseling, education, conflict transformation, business

Director of Admissions
Eastern Mennonite University
Harrisonburg, VA 22802

800. 368.2665
admiss@emu.edu
www.emu.edu

# EUGENE LANG COLLEGE
## NEW SCHOOL UNIVERSITY
500 Undergraduates    New York, New York

Eugene Lang College is the undergraduate division of New School University. It offers a distinctive liberal arts education with an interdisciplinary focus designed for engaged and independent-minded students. The College is a vital intellectual community which aims to foster in its students a critical self-consciousness about the process and purpose of knowing. Students at Lang College are encouraged to participate in the creation and direction of their education.

Lang students are firmly grounded in the liberal arts. They work in-depth in an area of their choosing, often doing original projects with an active faculty as a rich resource. The challenge of the experience produces graduates for whom critical thinking has become a way of life.

The liberal arts curriculum of Eugene Lang College is special. It is open and flexible; students design their own programs of study with their academic advisors. It is innovative and creative: many Lang courses explore topics that cross traditional academic boundaries and approach classic texts and traditional subjects from new perspectives. It is diverse and inclusive: Lang courses include works, voices, perspectives, and ways of knowing different peoples and different cultures. The curriculum is challenging and demanding; the small classes (15 students maximum), the emphasis on reading primary texts, the use of writing and revision as a way of learning — these hallmarks of the Lang educational program mean that students work hard and feel responsible for active participation in their classes. Most classes are conducted in seminar format. Seminars permit the most direct engagement of students with the material and the opportunity for close relationships with faculty.

Eugene Lang College offers students five broad areas of concentration, within which a student maps out an individual path. A student's particular course of study within the concentration consists of 8 to 10 courses leading to relatively advanced and specialized knowledge of an area of study. The concentrations are highly interdisciplinary, allowing students to make connections between varied modes of thought and different approaches to topics and ideas. These come under the broader headings of Cultural Studies; Mind, Nature and Values; Historical and Social Inquiry; Urban Studies; and Writing, Literature and the Arts.

Eugene Lang College believes that internships are central to undergraduate liberal education. Students earn college credit while contributing to the wider community and gaining a variety of skills available through hands-on work experience. Examples of internships include work with Madre, a women's aid organization raising money for health, prenatal, and education programs in Central America and the Middle East; the National Organization for Women; The Institute for the Development of Earth Awareness; the Interfaith Center on Corporate Responsibility; Homes for the Homeless; People Against Sexual Abuse; The Rainforest Alliance; The War Resisters League; and with The Wetlands Preserve "New York City's only environmental nightclub".

At Eugene Lang, the 'Historical Social Inquiry' study area bring together a wide range of courses from such disciplines as history, political science, economics, anthropology, and sociology. Students interested in this area of study benefit from the New School's renowned Graduate Faculty of Political and Social Science. Students may take courses in the Graduate Faculty once they are advanced enough.

"Mind, Nature and Value" is the principal study area for philosophy, religion, science and psychology — especially as the issues and questions from these disciplines exist in relation to each other and in specific social and historical contexts. Mind, Nature and Value takes as its starting point the central question: How do human beings know and live in the natural, spiritual and moral worlds they inhabit? Each field of study makes distinctive claims about how to address and answer this question.

The "Urban Studies" concentration brings a multi-disciplinary focus to bear on the history, development, politics and problems of contemporary urban life. Urban Studies is specially designed for students who seek a more direct pathway to additional training and careers in the area of public policy. The concentration makes the city an object of study and uses New York City as an educational laboratory and resource. It unites theoretical inquiry with field experience, academic internships, and urban research.

The "Writing, Literature and the Arts" concentration enables students to pursue literary studies, the writing of prose and poetry, and the discipline of theater. At the same time it seeks to establish connections among these and other art forms that are usually studied in isolation. Students examine works and traditions in a broad cultural context, framing political and aesthetic questions about issues such as the silencing and empowering of voice or changing interpretations of artistic traditions.

"Cultural Studies" permits students to develop along paths focusing directly on issues of the creation and representation of identity in social and historical contexts. In this concentration, students take an interdisciplinary approach to theories of identity and difference and to how these relate to political practice and the practical, everyday experiences of individuals.

Whatever courses a Lang student chooses, no matter what the concentration, they will involve issues and perspectives of different peoples and different cultures, including those historically underrepresented in academic study. Eugene Lang has school-wide efforts (including hiring practices) to promote sensitivity and understanding about racial, religious, and gender differences.

# MAKING A DIFFERENCE STUDIES

## First Year Studies

Ethnicity and Multicultural America
Introduction to Indo-Tibetan Buddhism
Reading Race, Writing Law
Spiritual Autobiography

Genes: The Code of Codes
Philosophy of the Sexes and Racism
Spacetime Physics from Newton to Einstein
Voyage Out: Women Write Travel

- **Is the "Good Life" Possible? Philosophy and Literature in Dialogue** *What does it mean to live the "Good Life"? How has literature attempted to answer this question? How has philosophy attempted to answer it? Is there a difference in approaches? Read selections from Plato, Augustine, Kant, and Nietzsche discussing what the Good Life is and how one might lead it. Also read four works of literature each of which portrays an individual who reflects upon and struggles with his failure to have been a good person.*

- **The Unthinkable Thought** *Imagine the moment when the apple fell on Newton's head, or Galileo saw the earth going around the Sun, or Watson and Crick stumbled over the double helix. Each of these moments produced an "Unthinkable Thought," which created a revolutionary new "paradigm" of reality, changing both science and our lives for all time. Review and discuss how science has evolved not by dispassionate logic, but by the passionate pursuit of these new "paradigms". Use this perspective to look at the origins and social implications of the paradigms of astronomy, the atom, motion, relativity, new sociology... Where are new breakthroughs likely to occur in the future.*

- Faculty Bio **Sara Ruddick Ph.D.** *(Harvard) Sara Ruddick has taught at New School University, New York University, and Haverford College. She is a consultant for Union Graduate School, on the editorial board of Peace and Justice, and a member of Network for Women in Development. Professor Ruddick received a Ford Foundation Grant for Faculty and Curricular Development in Women's Studies, and organized a conference on Simone de Beauvoir. She is a prolific writer and has been extensively published.*

## Upper Level Studies

Introduction to Anthropologies
Economics and Gender
Cultural Wars, Censorship and the Arts
All in the Family: Race in Cyberspace

Knowledge and Power, Truth and Politics
Women's Experiences of Religions
Teaching and School Reform
— (Mixed) Race Memoir

- **Masculinities in Literature** *What is it to "be a man"? What is it to be a "real man"? Following the insights of feminist criticism, explore writing by and about men assuming that, for men as for women, the scripts for behavior are shaped by society rather than biology. Readings in classic American writers such as Whitman and Melville. Explore the history of manliness in America. In modern and contemporary writers such as Kipling, E.M. Forster, Kafka, Richard Wright, Hemingway, examine how representations of manliness differ from nation to nation, from culture to culture, from subculture to subculture, and among racial, ethnic and religious groups. Follow Queer Studies in seeing male-male desire in its varied forms as crucial to the lives of men, while also setting the homoerotic within the wide range of male sexuality.*

- **Cosmopolitanism: Philosophy, Globalization and Emancipation** *Historical development of the concept of cosmopolitanism from the time of St. Paul, through it's most famous articulation in Kant, and up to recent thinkers. Invigorate intellectual historical investigation with an attempt to understand some of the most recent developments in global political life under the heading of "Globalization" e.g. the development and function of the UN, the passing of GATT, NAFTA, and other international trends.*

- *Faculty Bio* **Ann Snitow** *A cultural critic, literary scholar, and feminist theorist and activist, Ann Snitow teaches a wide variety of courses in literature, gender, and cultural studies. Well known nationally and internationally, Ann Snitow is a leading example of the "public intellectual," whose work regularly appears in such places as* The Village Voice *and* Dissent. *She has most recently established* The Network of East-West Women *which has brought scholars and activists in the women's movements in Eastern Europe and the USA together for the first time.*

## Joint BA/BFA Parsons School of Design Program — Architecture Program

Students in the architecture program have been developing mixed income housing projects for three sites in New York's depressed Lower East Side. The program was launched with a grant from Housing Opportunities for the Promotion of Equality, an organization that lends money to women and minority-owned companies. Community Access, a not-for-profit organization that develops housing, and the NY State Division of Housing and Community Renewal were involved in the project. The state initiated the project with the idea of creating useful, practical, architecturally interesting, and affordable housing.

Apply by 2/1, 5/15 for transfers
Student body: 30% state, 60% female, 40% male, 23% minority, 5% int'l.
Average # of students in a first year class: 15
Recycling and energy conservation
• Interdisciplinary classes   • Individualized majors
• All seminar format   • Kosher/ vegetarian meal option   • Internships

Director of Admissions
Eugene Lang College
65 West 11th Street
NY, NY 10011

212. 229.5665
lang@newschool.edu
www.lang.edu

# THE EVERGREEN STATE COLLEGE

3,600 Undergraduates    Olympia, Washington

Evergreen is a challenging, high energy, continually evolving community founded on the values of cooperative learning, open inquiry, and diversity. Evergreen has earned a national reputation as a pioneer in developing high quality innovative educational programs that bridge the gaps between academic disciplines. Students engage in the study of ideals, concept,s and problems that are based on real-world issues and questions. From their freshmen to senior years, students work closely with faculty who are all focused primarily on teaching and learning.

Evergreen's fundamental mission is to assist students in learning how to learn. The college prepares students to excel in a world where emerging technologies, new ideas, a changing economic climate, and cultural shifts are altering the way we organize our communities, our public service agencies, our businesses and our governments. It emphasizes the fundamental skills of communication, critical thinking, problem solving, working effectively in teams, and working across differences.

Evergreen approaches its mission through the traditional academic areas of the humanities, arts, natural sciences, and social sciences. However, the college's educational programs are transformed by a set of core beliefs that flow through everything the college does both inside and outside of the classroom. Evergreen believes:

- The main purpose of a college is to teach, and good teaching involves close interaction between faculty and students;
- Collaborative or shared learning is better than learning in isolation and in competition with others;
- Teaching across differences is critical to learning;
- Connected learning — pulling together different ideas and concepts — is better than learning fragmented bits of information;
- Active learning — applying what's learned to projects and activities — is better than passively receiving knowledge; and
- The only way to thoroughly understand abstract theories is to apply them to real-world situations.

These beliefs are reflected in the way students learn at all levels of the curriculum. Instead of taking a series of courses on separate topics, Evergreen students typically enroll in a single program that draws together different academic subjects while exploring a central theme, idea, or question. Program participants might, for example, study the theme of health-care problems by exploring real-world issues from the viewpoints of biology, history, philosophy, sociology, drama, economics, and literature.

Evergreen faculty love to teach. Their enthusiasm, their passion for teaching is infectious. The college's emphasis on students and educational innovation attracts some of the best teachers anywhere. They are hired and evaluated primarily on the quality of their teaching. Most faculty work with 23 to 25 students. Their goal is to be accessible, receptive, and open to students; teaching is never delegated to teaching assistants. At Evergreen, faculty and students are all on a first-name basis.

Freshmen typically enroll in a single, full-time, interdisciplinary program with 70 to 90 students and three to four faculty members, each representing a different academic discipline. Within this community of learners, students participate in lectures, discuss books they've read in seminars with 25 students, pursue projects with four or five students, work in labs or studios, and learn to navigate the library and other college resources. Students may stay together as a community for two quarters or an entire academic year.

More advanced students typically participate in smaller, more narrowly focused programs that strengthen skills in traditional areas of study — but always drawing on other disciplines and exploring real-world themes. Or students may choose internships, enter into group contracts to work closely with one faculty member and a small number of students, or design independent study contracts.

Rather than signing up for a prefabricated major, Evergreen students have the flexibility to design academic pathways concentrating on subject areas they are passionate about — within the range of expertise provided by faculty. These academic areas include biology, communications, computer science, energy systems, environmental studies, health and human services, humanities, language studies, management and business, marine studies, mathematics, Native American studies, performing arts, physical science, politics and economics, pre-law, pre-medicine, and visual arts.

A majority of Evergreen students complete one or more internships by the time they graduate. One student worked as a river ranger with the U.S. Forest Service in the Grand Canyon guiding researchers working on an environmental impact statement. Another worked as a marine mammal researcher documenting the travels of gray whales. Others have served as English tutors for refugees, as researchers in genetic laboratories, as support staff in shelters for abused women, and the list goes on.

Evergreen's Organic Farm has received national recognition. Thirteen acres of bustling agricultural and academic activity are located on the west edge of campus.

Student representation is encouraged in all college task forces exploring college issues or new policies, and students participate in a wide variety of organizations that provide cultural, informational, social, recreational, spiritual, and educational services and activities. Current organizations include the Asian/Pacific Isle Coalition, Bike Shop, Environmental Resource Center, American Indian Science & Engineering Society, Jewish Cultural Center, Women of Color Coalition, MEChA/Chicano Student Movement, and the Math and Science Network. Evergreen competes in the NCAA Division III conference in swimming, soccer, basketball and tennis.

Evergreen offers two undergraduate degrees, the Bachelor of Arts and Bachelor of Science, and three advanced degrees, Master of Environmental Studies, Master of Public Administration, and Master in Teaching.

Evergreen graduates tend to carry their sense of involvement and social responsibility with them in their careers as educators, social workers, counselors, microbiologists, entertainers, lawyers, journalists, health care professionals, administrators, artists, entrepreneurs, and a diversity of other occupations.

Evergreen's Tacoma Campus is located in an urban setting, and the college offers programs in five Native American communities.

# MAKING A DIFFERENCE STUDIES

**Core Studies for First Year Students** (48 credits each and team taught)

A Material World
Politics and Ideologies from the Americas
The Olympic Peninsula: Salmon, Timber and Energy

Myth & Sensibility: Eastern & Western Cultures
History: A Celebration of Place

- *Ordinary People, Extraordinary Lives: Making Meaning, Making a Difference* Many people today feel that social, economic, cultural and political problems are too big or complex to comprehend. They feel powerless to involve themselves. This program is founded on the premise that there are multiple ways individuals can address such problems, including artistic expression, religious or political activism, and community service. The program will focus on the lives and work of individuals who have responded to the issues of their times.

## Environmental Studies

Mushrooms, Culture and History
Working in Development: Learning From the Past, Creating the Future
Sustainable Forestry

Practice of Sustainable Agriculture (24-32 cr.)

Coastal Dune Ecology

- *From Public Issues to Public Policy: Environmental Activism and the Welfare State* Formation, implementation, and effects of public policy at all levels. Topics will include welfare policy and environmental policy. Tension between social goals (such as clean water or healthy children) and individual rights. The ways public issues or problems evolve into public policies.

## Culture, Text and Language

Japanese Language and Culture
Where Spirits Enter: Artistic & Literary Expressions of Religion in African Cultures in the Americas
Awakening Ireland: From the Power of the Bards to the Call of the Euro

Natural Histories: Botany, Biography, Community

- *About Time* (16 cr.) Investigates time's impact on spiritual values, world views and personal commitments, giving rise to notions of secularism and theism, tradition and progress, nature and culture, love and violence. How communication with each other is molded by our view of time. How a chosen novel, photograph, hit song, mathematical theorem, ecological niche, martyrdom... can only be deciphered through special interpretations of time.

## Scientific Inquiry

Astronomy and Cosmologies
Evolutionary Biology
Environ. Analysis: Applications of Chemistry & Geology to Issues of Surface & Ground Water

Health and Human Development
The Physicist's World

- *Whole and Holy: Alternative Herstories of Healing* To heal: deriving from the same roots as the words whole and holy. Explore healing as that which is whole and holy by examining alternative herstories — forms of healing involving body, mind, spirit, and the environment from so-called feminine perspectives. Historical roots of the healing practice, mainstream and alternative medicine. Patriarchal and reductionist effects of this on physiology, emotional literacy, and the evolution of the soul. Each student will engage in an apprenticeship, community service-learning project, an internship... go on a retreat, and develop the discipline of a healing practice (e.g., a martial art, nutritional plan, exercise routine, herbalism, goddess worship, healing touch, yoga, music, gardening or apprenticeship with an indigenous healer). From witches, midwives, and alchemists, to their takeover by corporate medicine men, we will examine the historical contexts of healing versus curing. What does the resurrection of traditional healing practices such as acupuncture, herbalism, body work, and other alternative forms of medicine have to do with the energetics of healing and the rise of personal power out of tribal authority? (16 cr)

## Expressive Arts

People of the Triangle          The Empty Stage: Theater Intensive
Horizon: Where Land Meets Sky
Envisioning Home: Finding Your Place Through Art and Music

- **Images in Context** *(48 cr.) This program examines artistic images in painting, literature, photography, and film within their social and historical contexts. It emphasizes the ways in which historical moments impact the images produced and the stories told within them.*

## Social Sciences

*Integrates anthropology, economics, history, law, political science, philosophy and sociology as ways of understanding the modern world, and as a set of tools for analyzing contemporary public problems, locally, nationally, and globally.*

Health and Human Development
Working in Development: Learning From the Past, Creating the Future
Indigenous Peoples: Identities and Social Transformation
Multicultural Counseling: New Way to Integrate & Innovate Psychological Theory & Practice

- **Growing Up in the 21st Century: Youth, Work & Families** The changing demographic, economic, cultural and social context in which American children are born, reared, educated, and prepared (or not prepared) for work and adult responsibilities. Contemporary family, parenting, and youth trends in historical and theoretical perspective. Social change and causal relationships. How race, class and gender interact with general socioeconomic or cultural trends to produce conflict, variation in the demands of parenting, the experience of growing up, work and family life, and problems such as youth violence, educational failure, and child neglect.

## Native American and World Indigenous Peoples Studies

- **Indigenous Peoples: Identities and Social Transformation** For students interested in learning about the cultural, social, and political struggles of Native Americans and other indigenous people. Focus on identity: "How are these people identified, by themselves and by others?" and "What does it mean to be identified as indigenous to insiders and outsiders?" Other social and political issues related to identity and social change experienced by people who have been invaded and colonized. Contemporary issues surrounding indigenous peoples addressed along with the economic/political ramifications of colonialism. The linguistic and cultural genocide experienced and the resulting cultural changes are highlighted. Students are given the opportunity to share what they are learning about other cultures with incarcerated youth. (16 cr)

- **Regeneration: A Celebration With the Land** Regeneration is a major concept in understanding the relationship indigenous people have to land, the politics of people and land, and policies governing land use. The program will combine focused study of Native American culture (including an analysis of the effects of natural resource policies on nature and people, and on tribal and aboriginal rights) with project work and academic research.

### Science and Human Values    MA Enviro Studies    MA Public Administration

Apply by 3/1    Faculty: 51% male, 49% female, 34% minority
• Team teaching   • Interdisciplinary majors   • Life experience credit   • Co-op education
• Study abroad   • Self-designed majors   • All seminar format
• Vegetarian & vegan Meals   • Part-time degree program

Office of Admissions        360. 866.6000 x 6170
The Evergreen State College    admissions@evergreen.edu
Olympia, WA 98505        www.evergreen.edu

# GODDARD COLLEGE

150 Students    Plainfield, Vermont

Goddard is a small college in rural Vermont dedicated to plain living and hard thinking. Founded in 1863, Goddard is recognized for innovation in education. Its mission
is to advance the theory and practice of learning by undertaking new experiments
based upon the ideals of democracy and the principles of progressive education first
asserted by John Dewey. At Goddard, students are regarded as unique individuals who
will take charge of their learning and collaborate with other students, staff, and faculty to build a strong community. The college encourages students to become creative,
passionate, lifelong learners, working and living with an earnest concern for others
and the welfare of the earth.

Progressive education is a transforming process. Traditionally, academia is about
improving skills and teaching disciplined thinking. But what about the heart, the
spirit? Of what use is a mind packed with theory and method unless it is wedded to a
knowledge of self, and to a passionate involvement with life and the welfare of the
planet? It is the whole person — intellect, passion, heart, and spirit— whose needs
are the starting point for a plan to learn, and whose purposes commit her or him to
carrying out the plan. Within and outside the college Goddard students are asked to
confront the ignorance and prejudice that engender overpopulation, nationalism and
war, alienating work, racism and sexism, homophobia, and poverty.

Never has there been a greater need for transformative education: learning that
leads individuals to see the world in a new way — as a precious jewel, unique in the
universe and facing socio-ecological issues created by the human species. Education
must lead people to search together for effective solutions, thinking globally and
acting locally, recovering the true humanity of humankind.

Goddard's smallness has contributed to the success of its graduates: students know
each other and their faculty closely; they learn to cope, to plan, to economize, to
recycle, to make do, to take initiative, to create their own recreation. They learn that
study and work, education and vocation — the work in the world that calls one to
become part of it — are inseparable.

Progressive education has its own language. The emphasis is on learning as
change. At Goddard, individuals are important, but their individuality is understood
in the context of interdependence. The words "whole" and "holistic" recur, emphasizing that persons and experiences cannot cannot be fragmented. Undergraduate campus learning is centered around Group Studies, so named to emphasize the importance of collaboration in learning.

The Goddard curriculum is different each semester, because student needs
change. Examples of possible study at Goddard typically, though not always, fall under
the following areas: The Natural and Ecological Sciences; Psychology and
Counseling; Feminist Studies; Multicultural Studies; Teacher Education; History and
Social Inquiry; Writing and Literature; Performing and Visual Arts; and the Health
Arts and Sciences.

The Work Program is a required part of the curriculum. Through it students help maintain and operate the college, at the same time reducing their tuition expenses. Two hours a week are spent on a meal team in the college dining room and kitchen; six hours a week on one of many jobs: shelving or signing out books in the library, assisting in one of many offices, operating the student bank, working in the college woods, and gardening. Work, in particular, and practical activity in general, has special importance in progressive education. Values are involved, ethical judgements may need to be made, and the social or moral worth of a product or process evaluated.

Students at Goddard also have several options for involvement in community service. They are encouraged to volunteer locally at one of the organizations in the Central Vermont area, or they can do their work program at a non-profit organization for one of their semesters. There are also new college grants for work-study students enabling them to work in the community doing a variety of service projects. These have included tutoring adults through the adult basic education program; serving as a poet in residence at a local school; volunteering in the battered women's shelter; the local library or elementary school; or doing environmental research on a nearby river. Students get credit for internships which have a service emphasis — for example, teaching at a local pre-school, or tutoring in high school. Or they can create field semester opportunities in which an internship or service activity is a key element of their time away from Goddard.

Because the faculty emphasize collaborative learning and community involvement, the college can be a bridge from self centered individualism to contributing individuality. Many students discover Goddard to be a bridge from the passive learning of lectures and exams to active, participatory learning. This parallels the exciting connection between ideas and actions, and between the creative urges to the created products. These bridges lead to the most important connection; that which a Goddard student builds between a changing self and a changing world. Goddard opens a door to one's inner self as the source of energy for learning.

Goddard College also has an off-campus study program. Students use campus facilities only during the week-long residencies that begin the off-campus semesters. They plan large-scale independent study during the residencies, carrying out their off-campus study plans and keeping in touch with their faculty mentors through correspondence.

Goddard "resource areas" are not "departments," and the studies listed for each on the following page often draw on resources from other areas. The Goddard curriculum is different each semester, because students' needs and the society change. We are, as one student said, "issue oriented". The "group studies" listed here under each area description are typical of those offered in recent years.

# MAKING A DIFFERENCE STUDIES

## Natural and Ecological Sciences

Holistic Health & Healing

Mind-Body Interaction

Global Issues & Ecology

Environmental Ed. in Elementary School

Ecology and Society

Botany for Sustainable Living

Design & Construction: Solar Greenhouse

Gaia: the Earth as an Organism

Bio-ethics

Aquatic Ecology

## Feminist Studies

*Women, a majority rather than a minority, are challenged to invent a future qualitatively different from the historic (though not, perhaps, the prehistoric) past. The feminist perspective suggests the possibility of a world characterized by resistance to violence as a way of settling interpersonal and international disputes; by the rejection of exploitation of individuals, groups, cultures, and other life forms; and by hope for a society based in life-giving wholeness, not life destroying fragmentation and competition.*

Defining Feminism: Who We Are

Goddess Religion

Lesbian Ethics

The Gender of Language

Making Feminist Sense of World Politics

History of Feminism

Women's Ways of Knowing

Women's Relationships

Women's Lives: Studies in Culture & Class

Refugee Voices: Women, Violence & Human Rights

## History and Social Inquiry

*Cultural, political, and social history are rich resources for understanding current world news. Especially relevant is "modern" history — what has happened since the late 17th century.*

The Nature of Truth & Proof

Something About the Sixties

History of Nature & Humanity's Relation To It

Technology & the Revolution of Consciousness

Global Political Economy

Who's Calling the Shots: Secret Gov't. in America

## Multicultural Studies and Cultural Anthropology

Development Problems in Third World

Intro to Navajo Culture (in Arizona)

Myths as Mirrors of Culture

T'ai Chi & Kung Fu: Philosophy & Practice

Cross-Cultural Religion & Spirituality

Cross-Cultural Health & Healing

Let Them Eat Cake: Global Economy and Its Impact on Culture

- **Mayan Studies** *Culminates in a 3 week study tour of Maya lands in Mexico including Chiapas and Yucatan. Meet farmers, community leaders, government officials, and development workers.*

## Education and Teaching

School and Society

Do it for the Children

Radical Ideas in Education

The Self and Others

- **A Sense of Place; A Study of a Bio-Region** *Students learn to find a connection to a sense of place. What it means to live here and study this region's geography, history, and ecology. How did those factors shape the people who first settled here and the people who live here today.*

## Performing Arts

African & African American Music

The Life and Times of the Guitar

Indonesian Gamelan: International Orchestra

Improvisation/Dance Theatre Performance

Rolling admissions     Faculty: 40% male, 60% female

• All seminar format   • Team teaching   • Self-designed majors

• Non-resident degree program   • Life experience credit   • Day care   • Vegetarian/vegan meals

Admissions Office

Goddard College

123 Pitkin Road

Plainfield, VT 05667

800. 468.4888

admissions@earth.goddard.edu

www.goddard.edu

# GOSHEN COLLEGE

1,000 students    Goshen, Indiana

Developing "informed, articulate, sensitive, responsible Christians" seeking to become "servant leaders for the church and the world" is the mission of Goshen College. Making a difference permeates everything about Goshen. What's more, Goshen was the first college in the nation to require international education. Operated by the Mennonite Church, one of three historic "peace churches," the college has attracted attention as a place where values are "lived as well as taught."

Central to that living out of values is Goshen's international education requirement. Since 1968, about 85 percent of GC students have fulfilled the requirement by taking part in the internationally recognized Study-Service Term (SST) program. In the program, students spend a term in a culture significantly different from that of the United States — usually at the same cost as a term on campus. Students typically spend the first seven weeks of the term living and learning in a major city, studying the language and culture of the country. The second half of the term is spent in a service-learning assignment, usually in a rural setting and often related to the student's major. Education majors teach in schools, while nursing and pre-medicine students often work in clinics and other health-related settings.

Goshen was instrumental in opening up the People's Republic of China to undergraduate students, developing the first exchange program between a U.S. college and that country. Currently, the school offers programs in Costa Rica, the Dominican Republic, the Ivory Coast, Germany, and Indonesia. Other SST sites have included Haiti, Honduras, Belize, Guadeloupe, Nicaragua, and Korea. Some students fulfill the international education requirement by taking on-campus courses focusing on intercultural studies.

But international education at Goshen isn't limited to a 13-week term in another country. Each year, around 70 students from more than 30 countries are part of the student body of 1,000. Most GC faculty leaders have lived and worked outside of the country and many bring their international experiences to the classroom. International education at Goshen also plays a significant role in the programming of the school's Multicultural Affairs Program.

Students minoring in environmental or related studies such as biology or environmental education can study at the college's nearby Merry Lea Environmental Learning Center, a 1,150-acre plot of bogs and meadow. Outdoor enthusiasts also find the center within easy riding distance by bicycle. Visitors can also spend the day hiking the trails of the facility, enjoying the hundreds of species of plant and animal life. Adjoining the campus is Witmer Woods, another source of environmental study.

The college also offers a minor in peace studies. Activities around peace include the annual peace oratorical contest, the peace play, the C. Henry Smith lectureship, Students for Shalom, public lectures and conferences. Some courses are taught in "real-world" settings, including Guatemala, Ireland, Chicago, and Washington, DC.

# MAKING A DIFFERENCE STUDIES

## Environmental Studies: Stewardship and Development

*Practicing sustainable life styles is a key part of responsible living.*

Land Management
Environmental Ethics
Economic Development
Geology
Communicating across Cultures
Field Botany

Agriculture in the Tropics
Forest Resources
Field Experience in Environmental Education
Land Resources
Liberation Theology
Entomology

## Environmental Studies: Environmental Justice

Conflict Transformation
Economic Development
Liberation Theology
Conflict Transformation
Public Policy

War, Peace, Nonresistance
Land Management
Strategies of Nonviolent Change
Community Development
Ecology

## Peace, Conflict & Justice

Prosocial Behavior
Conflict Mediation
Violence and Nonviolence
The Spiritual Path of the Peacemaker
War and Peace Systems
Healing the Wounds of Violence

Third World Theologies
War, Peace and Nonresistance
Introduction to Economic Development
Contemporary Women's Issues
Poverty and the Church

- **The Spiritual Path of the Peacemaker** *Uses biographical and autobiographical narratives alongside formal and/or theoretical writings of peacemakers. Investigates the question, "How does a peacemaker's inner spiritual journey relate to her/his peace activism work in the world?" Students will make presentations on such individuals as Mother Teresa, Thomas Merton, Thich Nhat Hanh, Dorothy Day, the Dalai Lama, Thoreau, Simone Weil, Elise Boulding etc.*

## Women's Studies

Marriage and Family
Liberation Theologies
Spiritual Writings of Women
Women's Growth and Development
Womanhood and the Cultures of the U.S.

The Bible and Sexuality
Social Problems
Contemporary Women's Issues
Women in Text and Image

## Intercultural Studies

Communication Across Cultures
Comparative Economic Systems
African Societies and Cultures
International Politics
Introduction to Linguistics
World Geography

Asian Religions
Race and Ethnic Relations
First/Third World History
International Literature
Community Development
The Far East

### Social Work

Rolling Admissions    Average # of students in a first year class: 16
- Life experience credit    • Team teaching    • Individualized majors
- Vegetarian meals    • Energy conservation

Admissions Office
Goshen College
Goshen, IN 46526

800. 348.7422
219. 535.7535

# GREEN MOUNTAIN COLLEGE

700 Students     Poultney, Vermont

"Green Mountain College seeks to prepare students for productive, caring, and fulfilling lives in a rapidly changing world. Established in a setting of natural beauty, the College takes the environment as the unifying theme underlying the academic and social experience of the campus. As a four-year, coeducational residential institution, Green Mountain aspires to build a diverse and inclusive campus community. Through a broad range of liberal arts and career-focused majors and a vigorous, service-oriented student affairs program, the College aims to foster the ideals of environmental responsibility, public service, international understanding, and lifelong intellectual, physical, and spiritual development... Drawing on its rich and varied history, the College is committed to a spirit of adventure and leadership in undergraduate higher education."

— from the Green Mountain College Mission Statement

Founded in 1834, Green Mountain College is an independent, coeducational institution named for Vermont's famed evergreen hills. In recent years GMC has refocused its mission with the aim of educating the next generation of thinkers, teachers, and leaders who will help improve and protect the world's diverse environments. GMC defines itself as an environmental liberal arts college with an international focus. GMC offers a broad spectrum of liberal arts majors and pre-professional programs. Most students choose careers or graduate school programs in traditional fields such as management, English, teaching, the behavioral sciences, and the visual and performing arts, but enter these fields with an educated awareness of environmental issues and the responsibilities of global citizenship.

In their freshman, sophomore, and senior years, all students take a three-course sequence entitled "Perspectives on the Environment": Images of Nature, Dimensions of Nature, and A Delicate Balance. This core curriculum links disparate academic disciplines to a set of common environmental concerns facing our global community.

Students select additional courses from four distribution categories — Scientific Endeavor, Social Perspectives, Humanities, and Health and Well-Being. Students in all twenty academic majors explore environmental issues together in these interdisciplinary courses. Each of the academic majors also contains courses that touch upon environmental themes, an approach GMC calls ecology across the curriculum. For example, a popular course within the English major examines the influence of nature on writers like Wordsworth and Thoreau. Students who feel that their needs are not met by traditional majors can select the option of a self-designed major.

GMC's involvement with the environment is not merely academic. To complement ecology across the curriculum, GMC offers adventure across the co-curriculum. The adventure begins with new-student orientation and extends throughout campus life. In a special outdoor orientation called the Wilderness Challenge, new students choose from a variety of activities such as mountain biking, adventure camping, hiking the Long Trail, whitewater canoeing down the Battenkill River, rappelling, or sea kayaking on Lake Champlain. To sustain the spirit and momentum begun during the Wilderness Challenge, the College's campus activities office sponsors an ambitious series of weekend outdoor activities for the entire campus community throughout the academic year.

The "Greening Green Mountain" program encourages students, faculty, and the wider GMC family to enhance recycling efforts, waste management activities, and water or energy conservation measures. Student volunteers work in the college's organic garden and with a stream bank erosion project, design greenhouses, build cold frames, and plan special Earth Day celebrations. Students have renovated one residence hall into an experiment in sustainable living. An annual Environmental Expo held on campus helps educate visiting elementary school students and their families about environmental issues.

GMC sees itself as a laboratory for developing higher levels of environmental consciousness and performance. Lessons learned — and habits transformed — in campus life have an influence far beyond the College gates, as graduates carry tested environmental values into a world in urgent need of hope and balance.

GMC also maintains a strong commitment to international education and to the promotion of cross-cultural understanding. The campus community includes students from around the globe. Numerous opportunities exist for study abroad, including exchange agreements with colleges and universities in Korea, Wales, Japan, and Mexico.

Internships and field experiences are vital components of most academic majors. This hands-on experience enables students to serve while they enhance skills, develop role models for success, and achieve a better understanding of career options.

GMC challenges students to think about other people and larger causes, and offers financial aid programs that reward not only athletic and artistic accomplishment, but also reward volunteer community or environmental service. Examples of service-learning projects undertaken by students are: community recycling, youth intramurals, centers for aging, animal shelters, environmental education, and health care agencies.

GMC's location reinforces the college's commitment to ecology across the curriculum and adventure across the co-curriculum, offering easy access to Vermont's spectacular natural resources for both outdoor study and recreation. Students enjoy mountains for climbing, hiking, biking, skiing, and snowboarding, while lakes offer skating, kayaking, canoeing, sailing, fishing, and swimming. Several major ski resorts — Okemo, Killington, Pico, and Bromley — are an easy drive from the campus.

Sports teams — soccer, basketball, volleyball, softball, tennis, golf, lacrosse, and alpine skiing — consistently bring home banners and trophies. GMC also offers an active intramural program and a wide range of action and service organizations. Among the many clubs on campus are: Environmental Club, Mountain Bike Club, Outing Club, Rugby Club, Scuba Club, Do Everything Club, and GMC Cares.

Recent GMC alumni have gone on to earn graduate degrees at such institutions as Columbia, Cal State, Drexel, the New School for Social Research, Syracuse, UNC-Chapel Hill, and the University of Vermont. They can also be found navigating the waters of Alaska's Inside Passage, teaching English to students in Korea, running marketing agencies, painting watercolor portraits, coaching cross-country skiing, and making lives — their own and others' — more productive.

# MAKING A DIFFERENCE STUDIES

## Environmental Studies

*Introduces students to increasingly sophisticated studies in biology and ecology with an emphasis on how these fields pertain to regional issues, and on the global implications of such issues as diminished biodiversity, ecosystem loss, and global warming. This interdisciplinary program is committed to developing not only scientific understanding, but also ethical, philosophical, and aesthetic approaches to the natural world.*

The Evolution Revolution

Simplicity and Sustainability

Nature in Music

Environmental Ethics

Contemporary Social Issues

Native American Perspectives

Utopias: Envisioning the Good Society

American Views of the Environment

- **The Northern Forest**  *A team-taught course with extensive field work, draws on the talents and expertise of five GMC professors to address issues from the perspectives of economics, ecology, education, and environmental philosophy. Students who enroll in The Northern Forest take only that 15-hour block course during the semester.*

- *Faculty Bio* **William M. Throop**  *Environmental ethicist, chair of the Environmental Studies Committee, recently edited the Humanities Press anthology* Renewing Nature *and published articles in* Environmental Ethics *and in Roger Gottlieb's* The Ecological Community, *among other places. When not teaching, Dr. Throop enjoys hiking (he's hiked all 46 of the 4,000-foot peaks in the Adirondacks,) canoeing, and working on his family's farm.*

## Adventure Recreation

*One of four majors, including Therapeutic Recreation, offered by the Department of Recreation and Leisure Studies. Through optional certification tracks, Adventure Recreation students can become certified whitewater canoe or kayak instructors, adventure program facilitators, open water dive instructors, mountain guides, or skiing and snowboarding instructors.*

Fundamentals of Outdoor Living

Essentials of Mountaineering (or Paddling)

Leadership and Group Dynamics

Outdoor Emergency Care

- *Faculty bio:* **J. Thayer Raines,** *widely published and the holder of numerous certifications, heads up the Adventure Recreation component of GMC's Recreation programs. In addition to his professional expertise in outdoor recreation and adventure programming, Dr. Raines is former national and current New England Ski-Archery Champion (recurve bow, classic ski).*

Rolling admissions

• Field studies  • Team teaching  • Individualized majors  • Interdisciplinary majors
• Service-learning  • Interdisciplinary classes  • Environmental housing
• SAT's may be optional  • Vegetarian/vegan meals

Dean of Admissions

Green Mountain College

One College Circle

Poultney, VT 05764-1199

802. 287.8000

admiss@greenmtn.edu

www.greenmtn.edu

# GRINNELL COLLEGE

1,300 Students    Grinnell, Iowa

Ask students, faculty, and staff what distinguishes Grinnell from other liberal arts colleges, and you will hear their agreement that Grinnell fosters a strong sense of community. At Grinnell, individuals are respected for who they are and what they believe, and differences can be expressed and appreciated. Grinnell is a place where great ideas and global issues are considered and debated. Faculty encourages debate over significant issues in the classroom. It continues throughout the campus, is carried into the community, and extends beyond Grinnell. Students leave Grinnell believing that they can and should make a difference in their careers and communities.

Grinnell is an institution informed by a pioneering spirit, a willingness to experiment, and a commitment to community. Grinnell seeks and produces good students who who take an active part in the campus community and later in the world. The college has traditionally been a community with a conscience. Grinnell's pioneering past began in 1846, when New Englanders with strong Congregational, social-reformer backgrounds established the college. Influenced by Grinnell's educational and social idealism, the College blends academic accomplishments with a sense of service to the world beyond the campus.

In 1959, Grinnell College established the Travel Service Scholarship Program, a precursor of the Peace Corps, which provided funds to send graduating Grinnell seniors to developing countries for a year to assist with language instruction, village work projects, or other special needs.

In 1989, Grinnell became the second college in the country to establish a Peace Corps Preparatory Program, a program of courses and experiential learning designed to prepare students for international volunteer service in the Peace Corps or other volunteer organizations.

"We offer an exceptional, challenging, and comprehensive educational experience," said Grinnell College president Russell K. Osgood. "We give students opportunities to transform their visions into reality. As a result, our graduates have the intellectual, professional, and social characteristics that support a lifetime of personal achievement and social responsibility."

Grinnell's pioneering present again links educational goals with society's realities. The College believes — as do leaders in business, government, and industry — that the most valued workers will analyze problems quantitatively and articulate solutions effectively within the context of the broader world. Corporations have taken note of a long-term AT&T study in which the best records for managerial progress and performance went to employees with humanities and social sciences degrees. Grinnell graduates not only join business and the professions, but they also can be found in large numbers in the Peace Corps, political campaigns, public official staffs, environmental coalitions, and public and private education. The social consciousness developed at Grinnell becomes a life-long commitment.

The interdepartmental General Science program allows students to explore other areas of the curriculum as well. It provides the broad background preferred in elementary-school teaching and in interdisciplinary science fields such as psychobiology and environmental science. A 365-acre environmental research area is also near campus.

Students who major in Chinese customarily spend the first two years on campus, the third year in the People's Republic of China, Taiwan, or Hong Kong, and return to Grinnell for the senior year. Grinnell is actively involved in Russian-American exchanges. The college annually hosts a visiting professor from Russia and offers four students from St. Petersburg the opportunity to study at Grinnell. The college sponsors its own interim study tour that allows 25 students and their instructors to visit Russia during winter break.

To introduce students to differing voices and ideas, Grinnell brings to campus many prominent thinkers. Lecturers have included: civil rights leader Eleanor Holmes Norton; the founder of United Farm Workers, Cesar Chavez; former President of Costa Rica, Oscar Arias; Ambassador George Moose '66; former U.S. Surgeon General, C. Everett Koop; and former Soviet Foreign Minister, Alexander Bessmertnykh. Symposia and conferences have focused on such topics as "Public Policy and Relative Environmental Risk," "Human Rights and Cultural Traditions," "Changing Visions of Public Service," and "Arab and Jew: The Psychology of Peace."

Grinnell students also join in campus and community life. As high school students, three-quarters did volunteer work. At Grinnell, they take part in student activities and organizations, including Environmental Action Group; Javanese Gamelan Ensemble; Students in Defense of Animals and the Environment; The Young, Gifted, and Black Gospel Choir; Amnesty International; and Model U.N. Also active on campus are the Juggling Club; Ultimate Frisbee; Stonewall Coalition; Concerned Black Students; Diversity Coalition; International Student Organization; Politically Active Feminist Alliance; Habitat for Humanity; Native American Students in Alliance; Poverty Action Now; Asian Students in Alliance; Student Organization of Latino/as; Chalutzim; Helping Hands and many more.

Many students keep one foot in the world beyond the campus by taking a part in the town of Grinnell and surrounding cities and towns — including work with Head Start, Habitat for Humanity, the Native American Tutoring Project, local school systems, and church groups. A monthly newsletter published by the Community Service Center informs the campus community of volunteer activities and opportunities. The CSC welcomes student-initiated projects and encourages students to link service activities with academic interests and career exploration.

Outdoor activities are organized by the Grinnell Outdoor Recreation Program. Students decide on the group's activities: cross country skiing, backpacking, sailing, caving, whitewater canoeing, and others. GORP provides training workshops and equipment students can use at no charge. Campus members of the Environmental Action Group promote environmental awareness and engage in nature-oriented activities.

# MAKING A DIFFERENCE STUDIES

## Environmental Studies

*Students may participate in off-campus study programs in Tropical Field Research in Costa Rica or at the ACM Wilderness Field Station.*

Ecology

Human Ecology and Adaptation

Evolution and Ecology

Resource and Environmental Economics

- ***International Politics of Land and Sea Resources***  *Analysis of the international politics of the conflict between the developed nations of the north and the developing nations of the south for control of the world's resources and over a new economic order. The impact of national decision-making processes, international organizations, cartels, and multinational corporations. Case studies on fuel, mineral, and food crises, and law-of-the-sea negotiations.*

## First Year Tutorials

Emotions

Food: Technologies and Ritual

The Rights of Minority Cultures

Mathematics and the Other Arts

Health Care

Crisis, Liberation, Justice, and Leadership

Youth in Anthropological Perspective

Latinas and their Worlds

The Technological World

Music and Nature

Nuclear Technology: Fears, Facts & Public Policy

Human Behavior in Extreme Situations

## Technology Studies

Philosophy of Technology

Bridges, Towers, and Skyscrapers

Biotechnology and its Social Impact

Sociology of Health and Illness

Evolution of of Technology

Electronic Music

Solar Energy Technologies

Technology Assessment

## Latin American Studies

Latin American Cultures

State and Society in Latin America

International Economics

Political Economy of Developing Countries

Aztecs, Incas and Mayas

Economic Development

## Global Development Studies

African Cultures

Ecology

Gender in Cross-Cultural Perspective

Resource and Environmental Politics

Nations and the Global Environment

Int'l. Politics: Conflict and Cooperation

## Sociology

Dilemmas of Third World Development

Self and Society

The Black Community

Women, Men, and Society

Human Sexuality in the United States

Social Movements in the 20th Century

Social Inequality

Race and Ethnicity in America

The Family

Contemporary Sociological Theory

**Africana Studies    Gender and Women's Studies    Anthropology**

Early decision 11/20  Regular decision 1/20

35% of students engage in community service

• Self-designed majors  • Field studies  • Interdisciplinary concentrations  • Vegetarian meals

Office of Admission

Grinnell College

P.O. Box 805

Grinnell, IA 50112-0807

800. 247.0113

641. 269.3600

askgrin@grinnell.edu

www.grinnell.edu

# GUILFORD COLLEGE

1,200 Students    Greensboro, North Carolina

"It takes a whole community to educate one person."
— African proverb

The African proverb has unique relevance for the kind of experiences you will have as a student at Guilford College. Here, learning is a cooperative effort shared by all members of the college community. Located in Greensboro, North Carolina and founded in 1837 by the Religious Society of Friends (Quakers,) Guilford College is an independent college offering a distinctive four year liberal arts and sciences education in the Quaker tradition. It is the third oldest coeducational college in the nation and the oldest in the South. Guilford's Quaker heritage stresses simplicity, integrity, compassion, tolerance, equality, hard work, enjoyment, spiritual receptivity, and concern for social justice and world peace. Growing out of this heritage, the College emphasizes educational values embodied in a strong and lasting tradition of coeducation, in a curriculum with intercultural and international dimensions, in close individual relationships between students and faculty in the pursuit of knowledge, and in governance by consensus and a commitment to lifelong learning.

While embracing many traditional educational goals and methods, the College also promotes innovative approaches to teaching and learning. Both students and faculty are encouraged to pursue high levels of scholarly research and creativity in academic disciplines. Guilford particularly explores interdisciplinary and intercultural perspectives and seeks to develop a capacity to reason effectively, to look beneath the surface of issues, to understand the presuppositions and implications of ideas, and to draw conclusions incisively, critically, and with fairness to other points of view. The College encourages the development of a "community of seekers" comprised of individuals dedicated to shared and corporate search as an important part of their lives. Such a community can come about only when there is diversity throughout the institution: a diversity of racial and cultural backgrounds, of older and younger perspectives, of beliefs and value orientations. As a community Guilford addresses questions of moral responsibility, explores issues which are deeply felt but difficult to articulate, supports modes of personal fulfillment, and cultivates respect for all individuals.

Guilford students tend to be politically aware and concerned about campus and community issues. Guilford students are involved in campus decisions in ways that contribute to their personal growth. Student opinion is respected and valued at Guilford, and students have a voice in major college decisions such as setting tuition, deciding budgets, and assisting faculty and administrators with strategic planning.

Some Guilford students choose to live in theme housing with other students who share a common interest or concern. During the year housemates discuss mutual interests and collaborate on activities and projects that increase awareness of issues in the community. In recent years, theme houses at Guilford have focused on awareness of handicapped children, gender awareness and equality, Habitat for Humanity, self esteem of young children, men against sexual assault, Greensboro Beautiful (Ecology), Guilford Geology Workshops for Children, substance abuse awareness, recycling and environmental concerns.

It is estimated that Guilford students perform more than 40,000 hours in community service each year. Students who volunteer at community agencies and area schools believe these opportunities are an important part of their educational experience. Through the program Project Community, students work with several organizations including Delancey Street, a nationally recognized two-year drug and alcohol rehabilitation program that serves as an alternative to the prison system; Turning Point, the rape crisis and child abuse agency of Greensboro; and Gateway Center, a facility that educates the physically challenged. Students collaborated with faculty and three community service agencies to develop an interdisciplinary course on homelessness, which was offered for the first time in the fall of 1996.

It has become a tradition for Guilford students to spend their semester breaks traveling to communities across the United States, helping people stricken by natural disasters or those who face the challenge of poverty. For many years, students have helped residents of Johns Island, South Carolina, with construction and renovation work on housing and area facilities. Other semester break work trips have brought Guilford students to the Cherokee Indian Reservation in North Carolina, to southern Florida to assist residents recover from the damage from Hurricane Andrew, and to Houston, Texas, to rebuild a community center.

One of the most important advantages of a Guilford education is that students have the opportunity to work directly with faculty. Faculty who are involved with research projects will often include their students in the project. To his courses in criminal justice, for example, Barton Parks brings his own extensive experience of the judicial system. He helped start a successful dispute settlement center which mediates everything from neighborhood disagreements to criminal charges. Student interns are active participants in the operation of the center.

Psychology professor Richard Zweigenhaft, coauthor of *Jews in the Protestant Establishment* and *Blacks in the White Establishment?*, is also an avid basketball player and has developed a course on the psychology of sports. Zweigenhaft encourages students to undertake independent research projects. A recent collaboration between Zweigenhaft and student Michael Cody on The Self-Monitoring of Black Students on a Predominantly White Campus was published in the *Journal of Social Psychology*.

A collaborative program entitled Teaching in the Multicultural Classroom was developed by Guilford student Darlene Whitley and sociology/anthropology professor Vernie Davis. The program, presented to public school teachers and principals in Guilford County, North Carolina, presented anthropological concepts and examined cultural situations faced by teachers and administrators. The program encouraged teachers to use the multicultural makeup of a student body as a constructive resource.

# MAKING A DIFFERENCE STUDIES

## Geology

| | |
|---|---|
| Physical Geography | Historical Geology |
| Environmental Geology | Marine Geology |
| Energy and Natural Resources | Hydrology |
| Crust of the Earth | Exploration Geophysics |

- **Seminar West**   *Summer course, including four weeks of camping and hiking, to study the American West. Geologic process of mountain building and erosion and their impact on man - history, prehistory, environment, literature and art.*

## Justice and Policy Studies

*Offers students study and participation in community service, focusing on the criminal justice system and related public service institutions, including community based organizations.*

| | |
|---|---|
| Intro to Criminal Justice | Youth in Trouble |
| Trust and Violence | Building Community |
| Conflict Resolution Strategies | Ethics in Justice and Policy Studies |
| Criminal Justice Policy and Practice | Media and Community Relations |
| Public Administration | Punishment and Corrections |

- **Family Violence**  *Wife abuse, child sexual abuse and rape/sexual assault. Causal factors, psychology of victim and offender, societal impact, treatment & intervention strategies.*

## Religious Studies

| | |
|---|---|
| Myth, Dream, Metaphor | History of Religion in America |
| Religion and Social Issues | Quakerism |
| Islam | Hebrew Bible |
| Feminist Theology | East Asian Religions |
| Primitive Myth | History of Christianity |

## Peace and Conflict Studies

| | |
|---|---|
| Peace, War and Justice | Nonviolence: Theories and Practice |
| Community and Commitment | Personal and Social Change |
| Conflict and Cooperation | Women/Body/Voice |
| Revolutionary Central America | Personal and Social Change |

## Education Studies

| | |
|---|---|
| Education Inquiry | Contemporary/Historical Issues in Education |
| Learning and Teaching | Field Study in Cross-Cultural Education |
| Processes of Elementary Teaching | Processes of Secondary & K-12 Teaching |

**Sports Medicine     Women's Studies   3/2 Physician Ass't. Training/ Wake Forest U.**

**Environmental Studies   3/2 Pre-Forestry/ Duke    Economics    International Studies**

Early decision 12/1     Regular decision 2/1     Average # of students in first year class: 14
- Self-designed majors  • Team teaching  • Vegetarian meals  • Eight int'l. programs
- Theme housing  • Life experience credit  • Third-world service learning
- 50% of students engaged in community service

Director of Admission
Guilford College
5800 W. Friendly Ave.
Greensboro, NC 27410

800. 992.7759
336. 316.2100
admission@rascal.guilford.edu
www.guilford.edu

**Friends World Program** senior student on project site in Kenya with a traditional folk healer. He studied spirituality and healing in the U.S., India, China, Costa Rica, and Kenya.

Natural Resources Management students at **Sterling College** work with draft horses even in Vermont's snowy winters.

**Green Mountain College** attracts active learners interested in environmental issues. GMC takes an educational approach college officials call "Ecology Across the Curriculum" and "Adventure Across the Co-curriculum".

**Pitzer** student, Brian Schoeck, with internship mentor, Don Woo, Director of the Inland Empire West Resource Conservation District, discussing community garden projects in Ontario, California.

# HAMPSHIRE COLLEGE

1200 Students    Amherst, Massachusetts

In 1970, 200 students came to Amherst, Massachusetts to take part in an extraordinary new experiment in liberal arts education. Hampshire College has since grown to 1,200 students, and its position in higher education is secure. But true to Hampshire's original philosophy, an atmosphere of challenging accepted ideas and of intellectual and social ferment, still permeates the college.

Hampshire's innovations include: breaking down barriers between academic disciplines and fostering an integrated, dynamic view of knowledge; actively involving students in their own education; and connecting academic work to "real-world" issues and problems. All faculty and courses are organized into four Schools:  Humanities and Arts, Social Science, Natural Science, and Communications and Cognitive Science. An anthropology professor daily rubs elbows with historians, psychologists, and political scientists. Faculty trained in different disciplines often "team up" and offer courses together. For instance "Women's Bodies, Women's Lives," was taught by a physiologist, a writer, and a sociologist.

Hampshire's founders were convinced that students would be better prepared for a rapidly changing society if they were also expected to carry out research and independent projects, and to pursue internships and field studies. The student headed to law school works for a Congressional representative in Washington; a student concerned about the problems of refugees goes to SE Asia to work for the Red Cross.

Virtually all Hampshire students incorporate internships or other off-campus experiences into their academic programs. The Program in Public Service and Social Change assists students in finding placements in human service agencies or social action organizations. The College maintains close ties with all study and service programs in Third World Countries. Students are also required to perform community service, and to incorporate a non-Western or multicultural perspective into their work.

Students collaborate with faculty mentors to design an individualized program of study. Concentrations typically embrace several subjects — a student concentrating in environmental studies might take courses in biology, politics, Third World studies, even literature. She might work at a local conservation area, or conduct research on the effect of habitat destruction on local wildlife populations. In the absence of course requirements, students design programs that reflect their most passionate interests and concerns. The typical question, "What's your major?" might elicit "Well, I'm interested in health care in Third World countries, so I'm taking pre-med courses and studying African history and reading about the philosophy of medicine. Next term I'll be working in a rural clinic in Nigeria."

Some 85% of Hampshire students go on to graduate or professional school. Almost 20% run their own businesses, everything from restaurants to yogurt companies, to design-and-construction firms. Still others are working as physicians, writers, lawyers, college professors, scientists, school teachers, and social workers. Having learned at Hampshire to take charge of their own lives, and to change the society around them, the college's alumni are engaged in doing just that.

# MAKING A DIFFERENCE STUDIES

**School of Natural Science:**
**Agricultural Studies, Coastal & Marine Studies, Women and Science**
*Agricultural program centers around facilities which include the Farm Center, bioshelter, a hydroponics lab, solar aquaculture, nitrogen fixation, and passive solar energy. Women and Science studies scientific theories about women and the impact of these theories on women's lives, health and nutrition, and on how women's participation in science might impact science.*

Marine Ecology
Environmental Science and Politics
Agroecology
Biology of Poverty
Women's Bodies, Women's Lives
Agricultural Research & Technology in Developing Countries

Pollution and Our Environment
Sustainable Agriculture
The Science of Disarmament
Health in America Before Columbus
Land Degradation and Society

**School of Social Science**
*Focuses on problem areas in faculty's interests in social institutions and social change.*

Culture, Gender, and Self
Poverty and Wealth
Third World Development
Land Degradation and Society
Inter-American Environmental Economics

Poverty, Patriarchy, and Population
Politics of the Abortion Rights Movement
Psychology of Oppression
World Food Crisis
Making Social Change

**School of Humanities and Arts**

Art and Revolution
Technoculture
Caribbean Crossing
Chicano Narratives
Latin America History Through Fiction

Women's Lives, Women's Stories
The Harlem Renaissance
Feminist Challenges to Art History
Ethnic Expression in America
Gender, Race, and Class: U.S. History

**School of Communications & Cognitive Science**

Culture Industries
Producing Cable and Community TV
Political Culture
Moral Issues and the World of Work

Moral Theory
Culture and Human Development
Developmental Language & Learning Disorders
Eurocentrism in Philosophy

**Population and Development**
*How fertility, mortality, and migration issues are shaped by colonialism, gender inequality, the organization of economic production, and international division of labor.*

- *Faculty Bio* **Benjamin Wisner** *has worked for 21 years in Africa, Asia, and Brazil with popular struggles to satisfy needs for food, water and sanitation, health care, shelter, and education. Recent research has concerned socially appropriate technology for co-production of food and biomass energy, land reform, and refugee settlements.*

**Education Studies     Food, Resources, & Int'l. Policy     Third World Studies
Feminist Studies     Peace & World Security     Civil Liberties & Public Policy**
Apply by 2/1     Faculty: 50% female, 50% male, 14% minority
Hampshire College has 5000 sq. ft. of solar collectors for energy conservation.
- Required community Service  • Team teaching  • Self-designed Majors  • Vegetarian meals

Director of Admissions
Hampshire College
Amherst, MA 01002

413. 549.4600
www.hampshire.edu

# UNIVERSITY OF HAWAII AT MANOA

13,000 Undergraduates    Honolulu, Hawaii

The University of Hawaii at Manoa is located in Honolulu's lush green Manoa Valley. Much like Hawaiian cities, the mix of people from all over the world bring with them the cultures and lifestyles of many lands, insuring a stimulating experience that goes beyond simple education. The cultural diversity of the student body insures an appetite for international culture, and the university community serves as the venue for year-round plays, concerts, dance and films.

Throughout its history, the University has emphasized studies related to the distinctive geographical and cultural attributes of Hawaii. Geographical location generates interest in oceanography, marine sciences, Asian and Pacific studies, and interdisciplinary studies of tropical environments, problems, and resources. The physical characteristics of Hawaii focus academic attention in such areas as tsunami research, volcanology, astronomy, and astrophysics. The state's multi-ethnic culture and close ties to Asia create a favorable environment for the study of diverse cultural systems, including linguistics, genetics, philosophy, and interracial relations.

Hawaii's incredible environment provides a focal point for much of the pioneering research done by the University's natural scientists. In the human realm, the University's social scientists are uniquely able to inquire deeply concerning the impact on people's knowledge of Hawaii's unique blending of cultures, heritage, and the social life of these islands.

The Hawaii Institute of Marine Biology, (HIMB) a research institute within the School of Ocean and Earth Science and Technology, provides facilities and services supporting research and education in marine biology. Research into the life processes of marine plants, animals, and microbes covers a broad range of topics, including coral reef biology and ecology, tropical aquaculture, behavior of reef animals, management of marine ecosystems, and coastal biogeochemical processes. HIMB is unique in its close proximity to a well-equipped laboratory, to a major university campus, and to sub-tropical environments.

The School of Hawaiian, Asian, and Pacific Studies (SHAPS) brings together nine research centers related to geographic regions in Asia and the Pacific, and is establishing new projects related to cross-cultural research topics. The centers for Chinese, Japanese, and Southeast Asian studies are the largest in the nation; the Center for the Soviet Union in the Pacific and Asian Region and the centers for Hawaiian, Pacific Islands, and Philippine studies are the only ones of their kind. SHAPS and its centers sponsor lectures, colloquia, conferences, film festivals, and special events such as the Grand Kabuki, Chinese martial arts performances, and the SE Asian Studies Summer Institute.

The University of Hawaii at Manoa has made a commitment to the study of Asia far greater than any other university in terms of numbers of languages taught, areas studied, and faculty specialists employed. This provides a unique opportunity to students interested in Asia. Interdisciplinary programs draw upon the disciplines of anthropology, art, economics, geography, history, religion, sociology, and theater.

# MAKING A DIFFERENCE STUDIES

## Botany

Plants and Pollution
Plants in the Hawaiian Environment
Ethnobotany
Natural History of Hawaiian Islands
Hawaiian Ethnobotany

Resource Mgm't & Conservation in Hawaii
Ecology of Hawaiian Coastal Algae
Inside Tropical Rainforests
Vegetation Ecology
Plant Evolutionary Diversity

## General & Enviro. Science; Island Environments; History & Nature of Science

Intro to Science: Hawaiian Environments
Technology and Ecology Forum
Endangered Species
Man and Energy in the Island Ecosystem
Natural Science as a Human Activity

Women and Genetics in Society
Environmental Issues
The Atoll
Human Role in Environmental Change
Island Ecosystems

## Geography/Environmental Studies & Policies: Resource Systems; Urbanization, Population & Regional Development; Remote Sensing & Computer Applications

Resource Management in Asia-Pacific
Ecological Concepts and Planning
Tropical Agrarian Systems
Plants, People and Ecosystems
Conservation and Resource Management

Planning in Developing Countries of Asia
Atmospheric Pollution
Environment and Culture
Hazard and Human Decision
Energy Resources

## American Studies

Diversity in American Life
Filipino Americans
American Environments: Survey
Nonethnic Minorities
Race and Racism in America

Japanese-American Experience
Contemporary Hawaiian Issues
Television in American Life
American Ideas of Nature
Native America: Hawaiians & White Conflict

## Anthropology

Technology and Culture
Pacific Island Cultures
Ecological Anthropology
Polynesian Cultures
Pre-European Hawaii

Aggression, War and Peace
Ethnographic Field Techniques
Medical Anthropology
Micronesian Cultures
Melanesian Cultures

## Agronomy and Soil Sciences

*This department is one of only a few in the nation with a special commitment to linkages with the developing world, and the only one fully dedicated to crops and soils of the tropics.*

Agroforestry Systems
Soil, erosion and Conservation
Soil Physics
Lab Techniques in Microbial Ecology

Pasture Management (tropical emphasis)
Soil Fertility
Farming Systems Research & Development
Techniques of Plant/Soil Analysis

**Civil Engineering    Hawaiian Studies    Entomology    Pacific Island Studies**
**Social Work    Peace Studies    Women's Studies    Zoology**

Student body: 58% Asian-American, 7% Native American
Apply by 6/15

Director of Admissions                    808. 956.8975
University of Hawaii at Manoa
Honolulu, HI 96822

# HENDRIX COLLEGE

1,150 students    Conway, Arkansas

Hendrix College is a selective liberal arts college located in central Arkansas at the foothills of the Ozark Mountains. In The Statement of Purpose, Hendrix declares its "dedication to the cultivation of whole persons" and its intention to "prepare its graduates for lives of service and fulfillment in their communities and the world." Hendrix encourages its students to develop "powers of ethical deliberation and empathy for others; discernment of the social, spiritual, and ecological needs of our time; and a sense of responsibility for leadership and service in response to those needs".

For Hendrix, "cultivation of whole persons" includes preparation for meaningful work, satisfying personal relationships, and opportunities for leisure. It also involves global awareness, respect for life and environment, sensitivity to suffering of others, and a desire to help build communities that are compassionate, participatory, peaceful, and free.

Hendrix offers numerous opportunities for volunteer work and service-learning. Eighty percent of Hendrix students volunteer each year, working at homes for abused women, planting organic gardens, tutoring underprivileged children, finding homes for abused animals, and assisting at a local sanctuary for abandoned elephants. One course, State of the World, includes five hours of volunteer work a week as its "laboratory." The course involves various readings in world affairs, environmental ethics, and spirituality, assisting students to "think globally" even as they "act locally."

Beginning in 2002, Hendrix will offer a single course required of all students, "Foundations of World Cultures." Students will be introduced to art, literature, history, and philosophy from various world cultures. Students will also be required to complete at least one course in "Challenges for the Twenty-first Century." These courses will involve attention to environmental despoliation, population, underconsumption among the world's poor, and overconsumption among the world's affluent.

Numerous student organizations offer opportunities for advocacy for human rights, the environment, and animal welfare. They include Amnesty International, Habitat for Humanity, Regional AIDS Interfaith Network, Student Activities that Value the Earth, and the Volunteer Action Center. A student-initiated recycling program has had a significant impact on campus waste disposal.

Hendrix graduates regularly gain admission to the finest graduate and professional programs in the country. Others pursue opportunities for service through the Peace Corps, Teach for America, Heifer Project International and other related organizations. Hendrix recently received an award from the Peace Corps for the high number of graduates who have completed service in the Peace Corps.

Hendrix encourages students to study and travel abroad — whether through formal study abroad programs or a two-week experience in the rain forests of Costa Rica at the conclusion of the Field Ecology course. The College enrolls students from 35 states and 8 foreign countries. Eighyt-five percent of Hendrix students live on campus, fostering an intimate community in which students and faculty members interact in all aspects of campus life.

# MAKING A DIFFERENCE STUDIES

## Interdisciplinary Studies

*Through the Interdisciplinary Studies program students may petition to design their own major, combining courses from several departments or areas to explore an area of particular interest. Students pursuing an Interdisciplinary Studies Major work with a faculty committee specially appointed by the Registrar. Examples of some Interdisciplinary Majors currently underway include: African Studies & Anthropology; Ecology & Society; Ecology, Society, & Politics; Environmental Education; Environmental Studies; Gender Studies; Holistic Health; International Relations & Global Studies; Non-Profit Leadership; and Sustainability & Global Awareness.*

## Anthropology & Sociology

| | |
|---|---|
| General Anthropology | Cultural Anthropology |
| Cultures of India | Cultures through Film |
| Ethnographic Methods | Psychological Anthropology |
| Global Studies Seminar | Medical Sociology |
| Gender and Family | Racial and Ethnic Minorities |
| The Urban Community | Environmental Sociology |
| Social Inequality | Social Change |

## Gender Studies

| | |
|---|---|
| Gender and Environment | Women and African Literature |
| Gender in Medieval Literature | Gender in African History |
| Introduction to Gender Studies | Social Inequality |
| Gender, Sexuality, and American Politics | Gender and Family |

## Philosophy & Religion

| | |
|---|---|
| Ethical Issues | Ethics |
| Feminist Thought | The Philosophy of Whitehead |
| Religion in a Global Context | African-American Religion |
| Mysticism, Meditation and Prayer | Buddhism |
| Religion, Animals, and the Earth | Native American Religions |

## Politics

| | |
|---|---|
| Current Affairs in Global Politics | Global Politics I: History and Theory |
| Current Issues, Problems, and Events | Latin American Politics |
| Asian Politics | Public Policy Process |
| Politics of the Middle East | African Politics |

## Psychology

| | |
|---|---|
| Social Psychology | Advanced Social Psychology |
| Psychological Services in the Community | Psychology of Women |
| Learning and Cognition | Personality Assessment |

Apply by 1/15    Avg. # of students in 1st year classroom: 15
• Field studies    • Student environmental audits    • Service-learning
• Interdisciplinary Classes    • Team teaching    • Self-designed majors    • Vegetarian Meals

Director of Admissions
Hendrix College
1600 Washington Avenue
Conway, AR 72032

501. 450.1362
www.hendrix.edu

# HUMBOLDT STATE UNIVERSITY

6,675 Undergraduates     Arcata, California

Set between redwood groves and the Pacific Ocean, 275 miles north of San Francisco, Humboldt State University is a campus of choice, not convenience. The northernmost institution in the California State University system, the campus tends to attract from afar students who are more adventurous and self-reliant. The intimate, natural setting and small class sizes foster friendliness and close faculty/student relationships. Undergraduates enjoy uncommon privileges: broad access to computers, equipment, and laboratories including the University forest, greenhouse, marine laboratory, and electron microscope. HSU is traditionally known for its sciences and natural resources programs such as forestry and wildlife

The intimacy of the campus mirrors the sense of community along California's North Coast. In the small-town atmosphere, students learn they can make a direct, positive difference in the lives of others. And they do, through programs for senior citizens, recycling, science outreach, legal counseling, health education, and others. Many students acquire a long-lasting sense of social commitment, as evidenced by Humboldt's historically high proportion of graduates entering the Peace Corps.

The University welcomes the challenges and opportunities of a diverse and rapidly changing society. To this end, it is a community striving to value diversity, to be inclusive, and to respect alternative paradigms of behavior and value systems. The mission of Humboldt State includes the development of a fundamental understanding of the interdependent web of life; and cultivating capacity for self-initiative, self-fulfillment, and autonomous and responsible action.

Humboldt State has a remarkable array of resources. Students from fisheries, oceanography, geology, biology, and other majors get a chance to test experiments and work on research projects at the University's Marine Laboratory in the coastal town of Trinidad, not far from the main campus. The nearby bay and Pacific Ocean provide rocky and sandy intertidal and subtidal habitats for further study. HSU also has a seagoing vessel available for the primary purpose of providing instructional experiences on the ocean. Students also find instructional and research opportunities at a 300-acre Dunes Preserve managed by HSU on behalf of the Nature Conservancy. The dunes, bounded by the Pacific and the River Slough, contain rare natural coastal habitats where research can be conducted in a protected ecosystem. A recently acquired 4,500-acre ranch is being used by students in a wide variety of disciplines.

At the edge of Humboldt Bay is a 150-acre sanctuary which benefits students in botany, fisheries, environmental resources, engineering, biology, wildlife, and natural resources interpretation. Among the projects are: a national model natural wastewater treatment process designed by a HSU professor; a co-generation system using methane digesters; and an aquaculture program devoted to rearing salmon, trout, and oysters in treated wastewater. Students interested in appropriate technology have a unique opportunity at the Campus Center for Appropriate Technology. Students combine theory and practice at the center — a live-in, working demonstration home — including photovoltaic and wind electric systems, a solar hot water system, a greenhouse passive heating system, a composting privy, a graywater system, and organic gardens.

144

# MAKING A DIFFERENCE STUDIES

## Environmental Resources Engineering

Principles of Ecology
Environmental Health Engineering
Environmental Impact Assessment
Solid Waste Management

Introduction to Design
Renewable Energy Power Systems
Solar Thermal Engineering
Air Quality Management

## Forestry: Forest Resource Conservation

Wilderness Area Management
Forest Resources Protection
Natural Resource Management in Parks
Forest Ecosystems and People

Remote Sensing & Geographic Info. Systems
Advanced Forest Ecology
Forest Administration
The Forest Environment

## Oceanography

General Oceanography
Sampling Techniques and Field Studies
Estuarine Ecology
Beach & Nearshore Processes
Solid Earth Geophysics

Biological Oceanography
Physical Oceanography
Marine Primary Production
Zooplankton Ecology
Field Cruise

## Environmental Science: Environmental Ethics

Environmental Ethics
Environmental Politics
Dispute Resolution
Case Studies in Environmental Ethics

Water Pollution Biology
Technology and the Environment
Sociology of Wilderness
The Conservation Ethic

## Appropriate Technology Minor

*Especially useful for Peace Corps or overseas development work.*

Whole Earth Engineering
Technology and the Environment
Politics of Appropriate Technology in the Third World

Appropriate Technology
Politics of Sustainable Society

## Natural Resources: Interpretation and Planning

Natural Resource Economics
Oral Interpretation
Natural Resources Public Relations
Intro. to Natural Resources Interpretation
Resource Planning in Rural Communities

Nature Writing
Intertidal Ecology
Interpretive Graphics
Natural Resources and Recreation
Environmental Impact Assessment

## Water Resource Policy

Forest and Range Soils Management
Systemic Geography
River Morphology
Watershed Management

Western Water Politics
Water Resource Development
Intro to Water Quality
Water Law

**Rangeland Resources   Peace & Conflict   Fisheries   Social Work   Wildlife   Enviro. Toxicology**
**Indian Natural Resource, Science & Engineering    Indian Teacher & Ed. Personnel**

Apply by 11/30    Avg. 1st. year class size: 24
• Prior Learning Credit    • Individualized Majors    • Service-Learning    • Theme Housing

Admissions and School Relations          707. 826.4402
Humboldt State University                www.humboldt.edu
Arcata, CA 95521

# IONA COLLEGE

2,555 Undergraduates     New Rochelle, NY

Iona College takes its name from the isle of Iona located in the Inner Hebrides, just off the west coast of Scotland. It was to this tiny island that the Irish monk Columba came in A.D. 563 to establish an abbey from which missionaries went forth to teach and evangelize. The island of Iona became a center of faith and culture that contributed significantly to the civilization of Western Europe. The name Iona signifies the college's fundamental purpose: a synthesis of culture and faith and faith of life. Enriched by the cultural multiplicity within our society, the college further expresses this tradition in terms of action on behalf of justice and of participation in the transformation of the world.

There is a vision for Iona that its constituents be engaged in the task of building a concerned community. Iona believes that through this experience its members will be better prepared to work toward such a community within their families, places of employment, and neighborhoods, as well as in the nation and the world.

Iona seeks to educate students through intellectual discipline and a developing awareness of self, based upon increasing understanding of their cultural, religious, and social heritage. Iona endeavors to develop informed, critical, and responsive individuals who are equipped to participate actively in culture and society.

Iona's Center for Campus Ministries offers vast opportunities for students in the areas of Peace and Justice Education and volunteer service activities. Student groups at Iona include: Amnesty International, Project Earth, and Pax Christi that put a focus on helping to change the world today. On-campus activities such as environmental awareness, multicultural education, and a Holocaust remembrance reflect Iona's unique commitment to creating positive change. The College's commitment to leadership as an institution dedicated to Peace and Justice is evident every November when the college celebrates the "Week of the Peacemaker" recognizing the great works of peacemakers throughout history. The week-long celebration includes lectures, seminars, and performing arts events. Past visitors on this week include Mother Theresa, Coretta Scott King, the Dalai Lama, and 'geologian' Thomas Berry.

Another natural way for students to express their faith is through service activities. Iona students serve communities locally at soup kitchens; Project S.W.A.P. (Stop Wasting Abandoned Property), an inner-city rebuilding project; the Midnight Run, in which students bring food, clothing, and companionship to NYC's homeless; and the Lord's Pantry in which students deliver meals to homebound patients with AIDS. Students serve regionally as well, travelling during winter and spring breaks to Appalachia to assist in building homes in poor communities while learning about the history and culture of the Appalachian region. There is also a semester-long program in Bonita Springs, Florida, where students work with migrant workers. Iona students even serve internationally and have travelled to El Salvador to live in local communities while helping to build cinder block homes. There are service learning credit options for many of these programs.

# MAKING A DIFFERENCE STUDIES

## Biology: Ecology

*The Department has a collaborative internship for students to do research with the Osborn Laboratories of Marine Sciences of the NY Zoological Society at the NY Aquarium.*

| | |
|---|---|
| Ecology | Microbiology |
| Oceanography | Microbial Ecology |
| Invertebrate Zoology | Science, Technology and Society |
| The Life of Green Plants | Parasitology |
| Genetics | Assessing the Environmental Future |

## Peace and Justice

*All faculty have made a commitment to directly address issues of peace and justice in a global and/or ecological perspective. Three week summer intensive courses in Ireland and with Native Americans of the Lakota tribe in South Dakota.*

| | |
|---|---|
| War and Peace in American Society | Conflict Solving for Children |
| Sacred Cosmology | Race to Save the Planet |
| Ethics and Business | Health Care Ethics |
| Contemporary Peacemakers | Latin American Politics |
| The Homeless of New York | Environmental Health |
| Service Learning: Appalachia | Service Learning: Urban Immersion |

- **Iona Peace Institute in Ireland** *The opportunity to experience Ireland's social and political realities, its spirituality, and its cultural achievements in an integrated and lively way. Analysis of the roots of injustice, notably Ireland's "Great Famine" and "troubles," and exploration of possible routes to resolution of injustice and reconciliation.*

## Economics

| | |
|---|---|
| Health Economics | Economics of the Arts: Performing & Visual |
| Economics of Labor | Economics of Poverty and Discrimination |
| Urban Economics | Women in the Labor Market |
| Public Finance | Assessing the Energy Future |
| Economics of Global Resources | Enviro. Economics & Sustainable Development |
| Changing Role of Women in the Economic Development of the U.S. | |

## Political Science

| | |
|---|---|
| American Political Thought | International Relations |
| Politics and Criminal Justice | Peace and Justice in the Contemporary World |
| Politics and the Mass Media | Campaign Politics |
| Third World: Politics of Development | Latin American Politics |
| Soviet and E. European Systems | Public Administration |

**Social Work    Gerontology    Urban Studies**

**Women's Studies    International Studies    Philosophy**

Rolling admissions    Average # of students in first year class: 22

• Service-learning   • Life experience credit

• Team teaching   • Vegetarian meals   • Weekend & evening classes

Office of Undergraduate Admissions    800. 231.IONA

Iona College    www.iona.edu

715 North Ave.

New Rochelle, NY 10801

# LONG ISLAND UNIVERSITY
## FRIENDS WORLD PROGRAM
250 in FWP    Southampton, New York

"While all life is being threatened by increasing military might and ecological ruin, a rising tide of quiet voices from all parts of the world reminds us that only knowledge inspired by justice and compassion has the power to save us and save the life sustaining power of the earth. We must listen to and learn from such farsighted scholars, professionals and others and search for those emerging concepts — globally applicable and globally acceptable — which can provide a basis for a saner future"
                    — Morris Mitchell, First President, Friends World College

Very few colleges offer a program like Friends World — experiential education by total immersion into other cultures. The Program stands alone in two important ways. The first is its faith in students. Friends World (FW) believes that intelligent young men and women have the ability and the right to be deeply involved in determining their own educational plans. FW trusts them to be capable of gathering, absorbing, and synthesizing knowledge through their own experiences. The second is the FW belief that all nations of the world need citizens who are educated to see beyond their own borders and who recognize that as individuals they share the responsibility for the future of the planet.

With campuses throughout the world and a faculty drawn from twenty countries, FW is uniquely international. The Program is designed to ensure that students spend a significant portion of their college years outside their homeland so that they might collect different perspectives on issues of global concern. Students are required to study in two or more foreign cultures while earning a U.S.-accredited B.A. degree. With the help of faculty advisors, students design individual programs of learning according to their personal interests and goals. Classroom study must be complemented with field experience and internships. The Program's goal is to provide a balanced liberal arts education including fluency in at least one foreign language and an appreciation of the culture and values of several world regions.

In addition to the North American Center, located in Southampton, NY, Friends World operates Centers in England, China, Japan, Costa Rica, Israel, and India. Study through the East African Center is currently suspended but expected to be available again in the near future. Students may also enroll in FW's traveling Comparative Religion and Culture program, a year-long option that concentrates on a more focused curriculum and visits sites in Asia and the Middle East.

Friends World admits freshmen and transfer students. In addition, students who attend other institutions may enroll for a semester or a year as visitors. Friends World also offers associate status to individuals who wish to take advantage of the Program's resources for a semester or a year but who do not seek college credit. Students develop study plans in an individualized area of concentration. Examples of concentrations designed by former students include: Cross-Cultural Studies, Comparative Education, Arts and Literature, Agroecology, Music and Media, Education and National

Change, Environmental Studies, International Development, Holistic Health, Creative Writing, Globalization and Society, Indigenous Peoples, and Women's Studies.

Friends World students do not receive letter grades. Each semester, they submit a portfolio of learning to their faculty advisor who responds with a narrative evaluation. A student's permanent record consists of the list of courses taken, the credits earned each semester for each course, and the accumulated evaluations. Students contract for and earn an average of 15 credits per semester.

Typically, study begins at the North American Center with an examination of the theory and practice of experiential education, as well as coursework on foundation topics such as composition, ecology, economics, cultural studies, philosophy, community health, and history. After a semester in residence on the Southampton campus, students embark on a ten-week self-designed internship or research project. The second semester concludes with the group's return to Southampton for reflection, presentations, and further coursework. In years two and three, students repeat the pattern in overseas Centers: the first semester provides structured area studies and language training, and the second semester allows students to pursue independent projects in their areas of concentration. Senior students synthesize their FW experiences by designing and carrying out a senior thesis or project.

Friends World students have their education enriched by working with many leading professionals and specialists and with highly-respected organizations.

Graduates of Friends World hold a variety of jobs and positions. Many students eventually enroll in graduate programs in a field first explored as a FW student. Alumni have reported employment as a substance abuse counselor, physical therapist, hospice administrator, animal trainer, computer programmer, elementary school teacher, musician, local government official, embassy official, college professor, carpenter, park naturalist, and legislative aide, as well as in a wide variety of other professional and socially-responsible positions.

Founded in 1965 by the New York Yearly Meeting of Friends (Quakers), Friends World became a program of Long Island University in 1991. Approximately 250 students are currently enrolled in the program. The first-year class typically enrolls 60-75 students, representing diverse ethnic and economic backgrounds. Although non-sectarian, FW is still respectful of its Quaker roots and expects students to become involved in service both to the institutional community and the local neighborhood. First-year students are required to involve themselves in an action project such as tutoring, land preservation, sustainable development, or community health.

Campus facilities are literally as varied as the world. Southampton College of Long Island University offers full access to Friends World students who wish to integrate a more traditional campus experience into their studies.

# MAKING A DIFFERENCE STUDIES

*Experiential projects, field studies, seminars, workshops, individualized majors, service learning.*

**North American Center**  *Student projects have included study of family histories in ethnic neighborhoods, "green" business outreach, herbal medicine, animal behavior research. Group seminars:*

Agroecology
Zen and Psychology
Holistic Health
History of Activism

Environmental Activism
World Religions
Cultural Perspectives of the USA

**South Asian Center**  *Student projects have included: art of henna and rangoli, historic sites, rural health projects, dance forms of various traditions, conservation & wildlife. Group seminars:*

By Women - About Women
Basic Sanskrit

Philosophy and Practice of Yoga
Indian Cuisine

**Latin American Center**  *Student projects have included study of: women and violence, rural development projects, the plight of children, ethnic music and theater, eco-tourism. Group seminars:*

Central America Today
Environmental Issues

Women's Issues in Latin America

**Middle East Center**  *Student projects have included: modern challenges to religion, conflict resolution and the young, sacred space and its expression in different religions. Group seminars:*

Politics and Identity
Comparative Mysticism
Comparative Perspectives on Israeli & Palestinian Society

Field Work Methodology
Women in Transition

**China Center**  *Student projects have included study of: major Chinese philosophers, traditional Chinese medicine, activism, environment and the state, economic reform and women. Group seminars:*

Calligraphy and Ideographs
Introduction to Chinese Customs

Martial Arts and Qi Gong,

**European Center**  *Student projects have included: global marketing, progressive education systems, European Union policies, immigrants and their integration into London. Group seminars:*

Multicultural London
Ireland in Perspective
Literature of Social Change

British Class System
Changing Face of Eastern Europe

**East Asian Center**  *Student projects include study of: disaster relief practices, food & society, history of Japanese cinema, shiatsu massage, traditional arts & Buddhism, workers in Japan. Seminars:*

Writing Workshop
Intercultural Communication

Photography and the Darkroom
Introduction to Eastern Philosophy

**Program in Comparative Religion & Culture**  *Student projects: ecology & Buddhism, religion & the peace movement in Mid East, religion & feminism in Islam, approaches to life & death. Seminars:*

Methodology of Comparative Studies
Religion and Society in Taiwan, India, and the Middle East

Religion and Social Change

Rolling admissions    Faculty: 60% female, 40% male, 68% int'l.
• Individualized majors  • Interdisciplinary classes  • Service learning  • Team teaching
•All seminar format  • Vegetarian meals  • Life experience credit

Office of Admissions
Friends World Program,  LIU
239 Montauk Highway
Southampton, NY 11968

631. 287.8465
fw@southampton.liunet.edu
www.southampton.liu.edu/fw/

# SOUTHAMPTON COLLEGE
## LONG ISLAND UNIVERSITY
1,200 Students     Southampton, New York

Southampton College's commitment to the environment began when it opened in 1963. The seacoast location was chosen for access to a wide variety of marine environments for study. Located on the eastern tip of Long Island, the college is in one of the most ecologically beautiful and fragile areas of the country. Bordering on the Atlantic Ocean with miles of barrier beach, dunes, salt marshes, bays, pine barrens, endangered wildlife, and a fragile groundwater aquifer, the area is a kind of living environmental laboratory. With four environmental studies majors offered, Southampton is a very strong destination for students interested in the environment.

The Environmental Science Program offers a unique multidisciplinary curriculum developed by faculty in consultation with employers in the environmental field. Southampton prepares young scientists to deal with some of the world's most critical environmental issues. In Environmental Biology, problems may include the effects of harmful substances on ecosystems, tropical deforestation, the loss of biodiversity, and the protection of wildlife resources. In Environmental Chemistry, chemicals in water, soil and air; hazardous waste management; acid rain; ozone depletion and global cycling of toxic substances are studied. Environmental Geology explores such topics as pollution of surface and ground water, coastal processes, sedimentation, and erosion.

Southampton is one of the few institutions that offers an undergraduate degree in Marine Science. In the past 25 years, the Marine Science program has graduated 28 Fulbright Scholars, an extraordinary record for a small school. A fully equipped Marine Station houses aquaculture and water quality labs, teaching labs and classrooms, and research equipment. Southampton has the largest concentration of undergraduate marine and environmental science faculty on the East Coast. They bring a diversity of backgrounds and interests to the Environmental Programs — from environmental planning and management to marine natural products; from energy conservation to beach processes; from environmental law to marine mammals.

The Environmental Studies major prepares students for careers in environmental planing and policy. The course work and field experiences are aimed at helping students develop essential tools and skills in economic analysis and decision making, natural resource management and computing.

The Environmental Education program's main emphasis is interpretive naturalism — how we explain the natural world to others and how we use the natural environment to teach scientific principles and aspects of environmental concern.

"SEAmester," allows students not only to study the ocean environment, but to live it. For nine weeks students travel on board a 125-foot schooner modeled after a turn of the century fishing schooner. Students earn up to 16 academic credits while sailing almost 3,000 miles, stopping at selected ports of call to examine unique ecosystems, or "heaving to" for oceanographic stations at sea — while studying coastal ecology, navigation, and marine science. Field work ranges from a study of the finest Caribbean reefs to the mudflats of North Carolina.

# MAKING A DIFFERENCE STUDIES

## Marine Science: Marine Biology, Chemistry, Geology

Introduction to Cell Biology
Quantitative Chemical Analysis
Geochemistry
Marine Operations and Research
Physical Oceanography
Coastal Processes and Marine Geology

Plant Biology
Marine Ecology
Biology of Plankton
Evolution
Mineralogy

## Environmental Science: Biology, Chemistry, Geology

Ecology
Environmental Inventory
Physical Geology
Environmental Law
Technical/Scientific Writing

Microcomputer Analysis and Report Writing
Biochemistry
Hydrology
Environmental Impact Assessment
Chemical Oceanography

- **Environmental Chemistry**   *A multidisciplinary study of the sources, reactions, transport, effects, and fates of chemical species in water, soil, and the atmosphere, and the influence of human activity on these chemicals. Biogeochemical cycles, water pollution and treatment processes, microbial transformations of pesticides in soils, trace metals, sources and reactions of atmospheric pollutants and their effects.*

## Environmental Studies

Society and the Environment
Environmental Sociology
Regional Planning & Enviro. Protection
Alternate Agriculture and Society
Field Biology

Public Policy
World Population Problems
Environmental Psychology
Ethics
Coastal Zone Resources

- **Global Environment**   *Study of international relations from an environmental perspective and an analysis of efforts by the UN in improving the human environment.*

## Sociology

Society Through film
Social Problems
Community Field Service
Social Minorities

The Community
Contemporary Issues in Drug Abuse
The Sociology of Aging
Cross-Cultural Child Development

- **Science, Technology and Society**   *Historical, ethical, ecological, and social perspectives are used to define the broader context in which the practice of science and the adaptation of technology occur. Value free science is discussed with reference to Nazi doctors and development of the atomic bomb. Technological displacement of workers, social responses to "killer" diseases, high risk and nuclear technologies.*

### Environmental Education      Biology      Psychobiology

Rolling admissions      Avg # of students in first year classroom: 20

- Field studies   • Co-op work study   • Student environmental audits   • Interdisciplinary classes
- Required community service   • Life experience credit   • Vegetarian meals

Office of Admissions
LIU, Southampton
Southampton, NY 11968

800. 548.7526
scinfo@sand.liu.edu
www.southampton.liu.edu

# UNIVERSITY OF MAINE

10,000 Undergraduates    Orono, Maine

In the spirit of its land-grant heritage, the University of Maine is committed to the creation and dissemination of knowledge to improve the lives of its students and Maine citizens in their full social, economic, and cultural diversity. In 1980 the University was accorded Sea Grant College status by the Federal government.

The College of Forest Resources at the University of Maine is one of the oldest and strongest forest resources programs in the United States. Its strength comes from a commitment to quality education, research and public service. CFR is divided into three departments: Forest Biology, Forest Management, and Wildlife. Faculty in these departments teach both graduate and undergraduate courses and serve as academic advisors. Bachelor of Science degrees are offered in Forest Engineering, Forestry, Recreation and Park Management, Wildlife Management, and Wood Technology.

Maine offers diverse opportunities to study wildlife in a variety of natural environments ranging from the coast — with its sea birds, marine mammals, and eagles — to the more mountainous northern boreal forest occupied by moose, loons and marten. Students in the University's Wildlife Management program are exposed to wildlife issues in national parks, wildlife refuges, state management areas, and small and large tracts of privately-owned land. Internships and cooperative education opportunities are available with state, federal, and private organizations.

The Darling Marine Center is the marine laboratory of the University of Maine system and functions as a research and teaching facility. Located on the Gulf of Maine, its coastal habitats include rocky shores, march, beaches, and mudflats. The new 12,000 sq. ft. Flowing Seawater Laboratory serves as a multifunctional facility for culturing and experimenting with a wide variety of living marine organisms.

The Canadian Studies Program at UM offers the greatest number and range of courses of any university in the country. Canadian Studies is a study valuable for students entering fields of education, business, international relations, and government, where knowledge of Canada is increasingly important. For twenty years, students in the Canada Year Program have attended Canadian Universities such as Memorial University in Newfoundland, University of Prince Edward Island, Dalhousie University in Nova Scotia, McGill University in Quebec, and University of British Columbia.

The University recognizes the increasingly global context of economic, social, scientific, technological, and political issues, as well as the evolving multicultural dimensions of contemporary society. UM's Women in the Curriculum Program improves the quality of education for all students by helping to ensure that the experiences and perspectives of women are part of the University curriculum. It continues a long-standing effort toward revising existing courses so that they represent equally the experiences, values, contributions, and perspectives of both women and men and so that classroom climate in all courses is equally hospitable to both female and male students.

# MAKING A DIFFERENCE STUDIES

## Forest Biology -Five year program

Forest Ecology
Conservation Biology
Tropical Deforestation
Forest Wildlife Management

Forest Protection
Artificial Regeneration
Wildlife Conservation
International Conservation

- *Sustainable Tropical Forestry* *Strategies to produce and extract products from tropical forests in sustainable ways and to provide employment for indigenous people.*

## Bio-Resource Engineering

Intro to Bio-Resource Engineering
Energy and Society
Energy Efficient Housing
Irrigation and Water Supply Design

Water Supply and Waste Management
Engineering for Sustainable Agriculture
Soil and Water Resources Engineering
Aquatic Food Webs

## Natural Resources: Resource/Environmental Economics, Soil & Water, Marine Sciences

Natural Resource Economics and Policy
Public Finance and Fiscal Policy
Introduction to Public Policy
Shellfisheries Biology
Aquatic Food Webs

Resource Economics
Forest Economics
Marine Fisheries Management
Fundamentals of Environmental Engineering
Algae Growth and Seaweed Mariculture

## Sustainable Agriculture

Insect Pest Management
Engineering for a Sustainable Agriculture
Agricultural Ecology
Agricultural Pest Ecology

Soil Organic Matter and Fertility
Sustainable Animal Production
Pesticides and the Environment
Principles and Practices of Sustainable Agric.

## Public Administration

Foundations of Public Administration
Health Care and Human Services
Ethical Issues in Health Care
Medical Anthropology

Critical Analysis in Public Administration.
Urban Politics
Topics in City and Town Management
Industrial Workers in America

## Recreation & Park Management: Interpretation

Conservation Biology
Environmental Interpretation
Wilderness and Wild River Management
Field Ornithology

Aspects of the Natural Environment
Visitor Behavior and Management
Field Natural History of Maine
Geology of Maine

## Peace Studies

Humanistic Economics
Hunger as an Issues in Social Welfare
Violence in the Family
Hunger in U.S. and the World
Race and Culture Conflict

Latin America: Reform and Revolution
Religion and Politics
International Conservation
Economic Development
Education for Intercultural Understanding

**Land Use Planning**   **Wildlife Mgm't.**   **Natural History & Ecology**   **Women's Studies**

Apply By 2/1

Admissions Office
University of Maine
Orono, ME 04469-5713

207. 581.1561

# MANCHESTER COLLEGE

1,075 Students    Manchester, Indiana

Manchester College has a long tradition of combining learning and values. Its goal, as presented in the mission statement, is "to graduate people who possess ability and conviction." Manchester recognizes that change cannot come from conviction alone, that those who ardently desire to build a better world need real world skills to accomplish those goals. At Manchester College, skills and abilities are developed through rigorous preparation in a student's academic major(s) and broad coursework in the liberal arts. Graduates leave well trained for graduate school or their first job.

Manchester's mission statement also speaks best to its core values: "Within a long tradition of concern for peace and justice, Manchester College intends to develop an international consciousness, a respect for ethnic and cultural pluralism, and an appreciation for the infinite worth of every person. A central goal of the College community is to create an environment which nurtures a sense of self-identity, a strong personal faith, a dedication to the service of others, and an acceptance of the demands of responsible citizenship." Manchester College is an independent, co-educational college in the liberal arts tradition, and is committed to continue in the tradition of social concern which is a mark of the Church of the Brethren, its supporting denomination.

The learning environment at Manchester College emphasizes an open exchange of thoughts and ideas. Students are taught to ask tough questions and search for satisfying answers. The curriculum allows varied combinations of majors and minors, both in allied fields (e.g. history and political science) and across disciplines (e.g. physics and peace studies, music and gender studies). Students can take advantage of travel opportunities through international studies programs (a semester or year at campuses in Brazil, China, France, Ecuador, England, Germany, Greece, Indonesia, Japan, Spain, and Mexico), and during the three and a half week January Session. Recent January Session classes have gone to Spain, Morocco, Costa Rica, Mexico, Vietnam, Egypt, England, Florida, India, and Nicaragua. January Sessions have included NASA research; health, fitness and wellness internships; field experiences in peace studies, social work and psychology, and many other off campus opportunities.

Manchester's emphasis on developing abilities and convictions shapes the academic and extra-curricular experiences of students in every major. Action-oriented student groups are open to all students. They include Amnesty International, the Environmental Group, Habitat for Humanity, prison visitation teams, Death Penalty Awareness, Women's Advocacy Group, and many others. Students also participate in the Peace Choir, retreats, coffee houses, concerts, lectures and discussion forums, and in local and national conferences.

The Peace Studies Institute offers college-wide conferences featuring speakers, debates on issues of public policy, and workshops. Manchester also offers an unusually large number of scholarships to students majoring in Peace Studies.

Other special resources include the 100 acre Koinonia Environmental Center, including a 5-acre natural lake and woods, just 11 miles from campus. Koinonia has become a retreat and learning center for church and college groups

# MAKING A DIFFERENCE STUDIES

## Environmental Studies: Interpretation, Education and Technical Studies

*Over 20 years old, this program was founded before "environmentalism" became popular.*

Environmental Philosophy
Plant Taxonomy
Science and the Environment
Field Biology
Environmental Economics

Environmental Studies Practicum
Ecology
State and Local Politics
Environmental Science
Historical Geology

## Peace Studies:
## Interpersonal & Intergroup Conflict, Int'l. & Global, Religious & Philosophical

*The Peace Studies program, founded in 1951, was the first in the nation. Nearly all majors participate in a Peace Studies practicum, an internship, or a year of study abroad.*

Current Issues in Peace and Justice
Religions and War
Philosophy of Civilization
International Politics
Confucian and Buddhist Worlds
Microeconomics

Literature of Nonviolence
Analysis of War and Peace
Environmental Philosophy
Conflict Resolution
The Brethren Heritage
Peace and Justice

## Social Work

*The Social Work program has an excellent reputation among professionals in the region, resulting in a strong placement rate for interns and graduates.*

Introduction to Human Services
Social Service Policy
Social Welfare as an Institution
Juvenile Delinquency

Human Behavior and the Social Environment
Race and Minority Group Relations
Gerontology
Social Work Practice

## Psychology

*Students interested in psychology and conflict resolution find an exceptional opportunity in Manchester's mediation program — the Reconciliation Service — one of only a few in the country where students are active participants in mediating disputes for students and outside groups.*

Cross-Cultural Psychology
Psychology of Mediation and Conciliation
Psychology of Learning

Psychology of the Young Adult
Counseling Theory and Practice
Psychology of Childhood

## Gender Studies

*Based on the theory that gender is a cultural construct, not a naturally given aspect of personality, Gender Studies calls on us to reflect on the role gender plays in our lives and in society.*

Introduction to Gender Studies
Feminist and Womanist Theology
Self and Society
Women in European History

Women in Literature
Women in the Arts
Women in American History
Feminist Theory

Rolling admissions

Faculty: 57% male, 43% female • Average # of students in a first year classroom: 20
• Service-learning • Self-designed majors •Interdisciplinary classes & majors
• Team teaching • Field studies • Theme housing • Vegetarian & vegan meals

Admissions Office
Manchester College
604 E. College Ave
N. Manchester, IN 46962

800. 852.3648
219. 982.5055
admitinfo@manchester.edu
www.manchester.edu

# MARLBORO COLLEGE

290 Students    Marlboro, Vermont

"If we are to survive, it will take a combination of an objective mind and a humane spirit. Marlboro strives to develop both qualities and hence we leave prepared to confront these issues in a meaningful way."
— Tadd Lazarus, M.D. '78, Spellman Center for HIV Related Disease

Founded in 1946 in the hills of southern Vermont, Marlboro College's goal is to teach students to think clearly, learn independently, develop a command of written language and aspire to academic excellence, all while participating in a self-governing community. Marlboro's insistence on independent thought, clearly expressed vision, and responsibility toward others has produced compassionate and involved world citizens dedicated to making a difference in their own lives and in the world around them. Many Marlboro students begin college with boundless idealism. Marlboro encourages this idealism by helping each student build on his or her skills and experience to become a more effective member of both the campus and global community.

Essential to a Marlboro education is the Plan of Concentration, within which students design a course of study tailored to their interests. The Plan is a two-year process in which juniors and seniors research and write an academic project; each Plan is as unique as the student who develops it.

Students study under the close guidance of one or two faculty members who suggest a coherent sequence of coursework in small classes (ranging in size from two or three students to 10 or 12) and one-to-one tutorials. However diverse, Plans share a common outcome. Every Marlboro graduate knows that he or she has gained the ability to define a problem, set clear limits on an area of inquiry, analyze the object of study within those parameters, evaluate the results of research or artistic production, and report articulately on the outcome of a worthy project. These are very important and powerful skills in the arena of progressive change.

The world is becoming a more volatile place, threatened by exploding populations, dying ecosystems, and a resurgence of ethnic hatred. Marlboro's World Studies Program, run in association with the School for International Training in Brattleboro, VT, works from the premise that we must develop an understanding of — accept and celebrate — the world's diversity through intercultural work and education.

The World Studies Program is designed to help motivated students acquire the cultural framework, practical skills, and intellectual tools necessary to analyze global developments in the light of differing cultural values and traditions. Students study broadly within the liberal arts, focusing increasingly on a particular area of inquiry. They acquire foreign language proficiency and cross-cultural skills and, in their junior year, experience living, working, and conducting research in a different culture.

Interns have traveled to over 30 different countries worldwide, from Russia to Bali, and return holding not only a broader global perspective but also increased insight and maturity. They complete their studies by producing a finished Plan of Concentration — a work that fuses their academic and intercultural experience in a world view, one which is often continued in their later work.

Outside the World Studies Program students arrange study-abroad semesters or internships, both in other countries and at other colleges and universities in the United States. Marlboro College's new academic partnership with Huron University in London will extend numerous exchange and internship opportunities to students and faculty in all curricular areas.

The College also sponsors several field trips each year including: scientific expeditions to tropical, desert, or mountain environments; outdoor adventures in mountain climbing or white-water rafting; and a theater trip to England each winter. Those remaining on campus enjoy an annual intercultural lecture series, presentations from fellow students returning from internships, and international nights that feature the food, music and films of different countries.

To the faculty at Marlboro, the term "Environmental Science" is synonymous with the term "Human Ecology", that is, a study of the way that humans interact with their environment. Such a broad definition suggests that an interdisciplinary approach is warranted, and indeed, students should study the environmental sciences from the special perspective and knowledge of the arts, humanities, social sciences and natural sciences.

The integration of various disciplines into a coordinated approach to environmental questions is the challenge of this field. Each student majoring in environmental science must develop an in-depth familiarity with one or more approaches to problem solving. One cannot, for example, reasonably address the problems associated with acid rain without knowing something about biology and ecology, resource economics, public policy and political institutions, international relations, environmental chemistry, and meteorology.

Marlboro's interdisciplinary nature also allows great flexibility for students who wish to study gender issues. Students focus on women's studies throughout the curriculum. Like studies in environmental sciences, a broad perspective in all areas of the liberal arts, coupled with a specific focus within a discipline or cross-discipline, provide each student with multi-faceted and thus, more informed work.

Along with the academic challenge, Marlboro has a tradition of community service. To some degree this can be attributed to a highly distinctive aspect of Marlboro: the Town Meeting structure within which many college decisions are made. Town Meeting serves as a training ground for the College community to participate in the democratic process and to assume a considerable measure of personal responsibility for the health of the community at Marlboro and beyond.

Marlboro also offers a very active Outdoor Program, including such activities as rock climbing, backpacking, spelunking, canoeing, cross-country skiing, and winter camping in places ranging from Vermont's Green Mountains to the Southwest deserts.

# MAKING A DIFFERENCE STUDIES

## Environmental Studies: Coursework & Tutorials

*Broad study develops an aesthetic sense in the arts, an appreciation of the foundations of civilization in the humanities, a view of the inner workings of past and present human societies in the social sciences, and a firm grounding in physical and biological principles in the natural sciences. Advanced students focus their studies to a specialized goal.*

| | |
|---|---|
| Environmental Economics and Policy | Genetics & Evolution |
| Atmosphere, Weather & Climate | General Ecology |
| Global Environmental Issues | Culture & Ecology of the Western U.S. |
| Conservation Biology & Policy | Global Atmospheric Change |

## Plans of Concentration in Environmental Studies

| | |
|---|---|
| Coastal Zone Management Act | Wetland Policy and Protection in Vermont |
| Energy Policy Issues | Role of Wildlife in Community Development |
| Tropical Deforestation | Forest Practices and Management in the U.S. |

Resource Management with focus on Solid Waste and Resource Recovery Strategies
Relation Between Range Management and Public Policy on Grazing of Public Land

- **Ethnobiology**   *This course includes three distinct but interrelated segments: 1) an examination of how people in different cultures classify plants and animals; 2) a study of contemporary and historical events in the Americas in which resource consumption, environmental destruction, and native land rights are linked; and 3) a brief survey of medical anthropology, the study of medical belief systems within particular cultural contexts.*

## World Studies Program: Coursework & Tutorials

*World Studies Program students are expected to gain a general education through the liberal arts and to develop skills as international citizens. These general goals include: an introductory knowledge of world history and cultures; an understanding of contemporary global issues; competence in cross-cultural communication; recognition of difference in cultural values; experience working and learning in another culture; proficiency in a second language; and a basic knowledge of one world region (geography; economic and environmental systems; culture and history).*

| | |
|---|---|
| World Studies Colloquium | African Politics |
| Topics in Human Understanding | Designing Fieldwork |
| Professional Development | Introduction to World Politics |
| Latin American Area Studies | Language in Culture |
| 20th Century World | Finding an Internship |
| Theories of Development | |

## Plans of Concentration in World Studies

| | |
|---|---|
| Gender and Healing in Tunisia | Cultural Responses to Development in Uganda |
| Tibetan Subcultures in Exile | History, Language, & Ethnic Identity in Ireland |
| Tourism and Tradition in Balinese Dance | Changing Roles of Women in East Africa |

- **Twentieth Century World**   *An introductory seminar for World Studies students. The course is designed to help students situate themselves in time and place, and begin to think historically, culturally, and geographically. Classes discuss concepts and issues relevant to the contemporary world, and to historical experience, in global comparative contexts.*

## Gender Studies

*Gender Studies are conducted throughout the curriculum under the auspices of various disciplines, such as American studies, philosophy, world studies, art history, literature, sociology, psychology, and the sciences. In almost all cases, gender studies are interdisciplinary.*

Women's History

Women on Women

Toni Morrison

Misogyny, Melodrama & Myth: The Art of 18th Century Europe

Gender in World Cinema

Feminism: Theory & Practice

Gender Issues in International Development

### Plans of Concentration in Gender Studies

Working Women in the Progressive Era

Feminism and Drama

A Feminist Critique of Philosophy of Science

Women, Science and Objectivity

Artistic Development of Modersohn-Becker, O'Keefe, and Virginia Woolf

Contemporary African-American Women & The Search for Identity

The Relationship between Women and Nature in Victorian Post-colonial Fiction

## Economics

Economic Systems

Environmental Policy

Philanthropy, Advocacy & Public Policy

Economics of Globalization

U.S. Capitalism

Organizations, Environments & Public Policy

Topics in U.S. Environmental History

Intermediate Microeconomics

Decision Making: Individual, Interactive and Collective

### Plans of Concentration in Economics

Role of Wildlife in Community Development   Water Quality Management in the U.S.

Fdn. & Structure of European Community Law  Evolution of Monetary & Financial Institutions

Environmental Economics, Policy and Activism in Developing Nations

## Biology

General Biology

Plants of Vermont

Animal Behavior

Comparative Animal Physiology

Conservation Biology & Policy

Ethnobiology

Genetics & Evolution

General Ecology

Human Physiology

Ornithology

### Plans of Concentration in Biology

Ethnobotany

Physiological Plant Ecology

Population & Community Ecology

Cell Biology

Biochemistry

Genetics

Apply by 3/1

Faulty: 62% male, 38% female, 6% minority   Avg. # of students in a first year class: 8

- Team teaching   • Self-designed majors   • Interdisciplinary classes & majors
- Field studies   • All seminar format   • Smoke-free, substance free dorms
- Vegetarian & vegan meals   • Graduate programs   • Many buildings on campus are passive solar.

Director of Admissions

Marlboro College

South Road

Marlboro, VT 05344-0300

802. 257.4333

800. 343.0049

admissions@marlboro.edu

www.marlboro.edu

# MENNO SIMONS COLLEGE

Winnipeg, Canada

Menno Simons College is located in the inner city of Winnipeg on the University of Winnipeg's campus. The U of W is a liberal arts & science university that places its primary emphasis on undergraduate education. Menno Simons College, an affiliated college of The University of Winnipeg, offers solely two degrees: Bachelor of Arts Degees in International Development Studies (IDS) and Conflict Resolution Studies (CRS)

The College prepares students from diverse backgrounds for participation in local and global communities through an education that addresses conflict, inequality, and poverty. The College combines the values of peace, justice, and service with high standards of academic excellence in the fields of Conflict Resolution and International Development. Rooted in the tradition of the Mennonite Anabaptist faith, the College's interdisciplinary programmes are provided in affiliation with other disciplines at the University of Winnipeg and with other institutions in the community. Menno Simons College values interactive learning and facilitates this by limiting class size. MSC students register in, and receive degrees from, the U of Winnipeg.

International Development Studies (IDS) is an interdisciplinary liberal arts major that challenges students to explore the causes and consequences of processes that promote some individuals, communities, and nations while excluding others. IDS students are prepared for citizenship in an increasingly interdependent global community, and are encouraged to envision paths towards a transformed, just world.

The IDS Program offers students the opportunity to gain practical experience in the development field through local and international practicum experiences. Partnerships have been developed with local community development agencies, and international opportunities are available through a variety of Canadian international development agencies. Past practicum opportunities have included: community development in Winnipeg's inner-city; research on development issues in Bangladesh, Brazil, and Haiti; and teaching English as a Second Language in Lebanon and Jamaica.

Conflict Resolution Studies seeks to understand the nature and dynamics of human conflict, and to look at appropriate alternatives for dealing with conflict in ways which develop healthy relationships and prevent violence. Conflicts are analyzed from an interdisciplinary perspective together with topics such as violence, power, justice, peace, communication, culture, war, conflict transformation, and dispute resolution. CRS prepares students to understand and interact constructively in response to personal, local, and global conflict situations.

Many international agencies, like the International Institute for Sustainable Development, Mennonite Central Committee, and the Canadian Foodgrains Bank which are headquartered in Winnipeg, facilitate study of the international aspects of these topics.

Winnipeg, situated on the historic banks of the Red and Assiniboine rivers, has a vibrant multicultural flavor. Its urban, multicultural, and agricultural character ideally situate it for the study of development and conflict at the community level.

# MAKING A DIFFERENCE STUDIES

## International Development Studies

Rural Development

An Analysis of Development Aid Policies

Voluntary Simplicity

Mennonite Community And Development

Global Processes And Local Consequences

Human Impact on the Environment

Gender and Global Politics

Urbanization In The Developing World

Introduction to International Development

Crisis, Vulnerability And Development

Environmental Sustainability: A Global Dilemma

Do No Harm: Conflict & Humanitarian Aid

Population Geography

Ethnography of South America

Indigenous Peoples And The Industrial State

Energy, Resources and Economic Development

- **Poverty-Focused Development**  *The failure of modern development efforts to eradicate poverty in the South (Asia, Africa, and Latin America) has led to a widespread belief that alternative participatory, grassroots development projects are the solution. Course examines historic efforts at participatory development, including community development and cooperative formation, then considers the growing attention given nongovernmental organizations and grassroots movements today. Reviews contemporary strategies to enhance productivity through economic interventions such as credit programs and agricultural extension, or human interventions such as education and health provision. Sustainability issues are considered with reference to the enhancement of social capital.*

## Conflict Resolution Studies

*MSC encourages students to consider a double major, i.e. an MSC interdisciplinary major plus a major from one of the traditional disciplines or a double major in CRS and Int'l. Development Studies.*

Introduction To Conflict Resolution Studies

Conflict As Creative Catalyst

Models For Conflict Transformation

Human Rights and Civil Liberties in Canada

Models For Conflict Transformation

Conflict Within Faith Communities

Restorative Justice

Aboriginal Spirituality

Social Change

Mediation Skills: Dealing With Anger

Cross-Cultural Issues In Conflict Resolution

Conflict And Communication

Environmental Perception and Human Behaviour

Conflict And Culture

Conflict and the Construction of the Other

Race and Ethnic Relations

Environmental Economics

Peace Theory And Practice

Faith and Justice

Programme Planning, Monitoring And Evaluation

Conciliation Skills

Issues in Sustainable Cities

- **Conflict & Development Issues In Indigenous Communities**  *Explores dynamics of indigenous peoples globally, with special reference to the Canadian context, within the broad frameworks of development and conflict resolution. Key elements of indigenous culture and worldview. From the perspective of conflict resolution studies, inter- and intra-group conflict and conflict resolution processes involving indigenous communities will be explored. From the perspective of int'l. development studies, processes of marginalization and underdevelopment will be presented to understand the indigenous communities' social, economic and political situation. Strategies for community development and conflict resolution highlighted as means to achieve transformation.*

The University of Winnipeg

Admissions Office

515 Portage Avenue

Winnipeg, Manitoba

Canada R3B 2E9

204. 786.9159

adm@uwinnepeg.ca

www.uwinnipeg.ca/~msc/

# UNIVERSITY OF MICHIGAN
## SCHOOL OF NATURAL RESOURCES AND ENVIRONMENT
400 Undergraduates    Ann Arbor, Michigan

Established in 1927, the University of Michigan School of Natural Resources and Environment (SNRE) is the first of its kind in the world. For seventy years, its mission has been to educate future leaders to be effective and innovative stewards of the environment. The School's academic program is interdisciplinary in scope, providing undergraduates with a background in liberal arts and sciences with an emphasis upon building analytical, problem-solving, and communication skills. With approximately 400 undergraduate students and 200 graduate students, SNRE provides a close-knit community environment. At the same time it offers students the advantages of attending a large research institution. Teaching and building community are valued aspects of the school's program.

Most students pursue one of three academic concentrations: Resource Ecology and Management, Environmental Policy and Behavior, or Landscape Design and Planning. Individualized concentrations are also possible. The Resource Ecology and Management concentration is designed for students interested in pursuing field- and science-oriented studies of natural resource systems, such as aquatic or terrestrial ecosystems, wildlife, remote sensing, and soils. Students in the Environmental Policy and Behavior concentration focus their study upon the human and societal aspects of natural resource and environmental problems. Landscape Design and Planning is intended for junior or senior students interested in becoming landscape architects, environmental planners, or urban planners.

There are over 600 extracurricular organizations for students attending the University of Michigan, several of which are populated with SNRE students. Among the most popular are: Students Organized to Recycle and Reuse Organic Waste, Environmental Justice Group, Minorities in Agriculture and Natural Resources, Environmental Action, Rainforest Action Movement, and the Wildlife and Conservation Society. SNRE students are also involved in campus service organizations such as Project SERVE, Alternative Spring Break, and Amnesty International.

Many SNRE courses are taught with field or lab components. The Ann Arbor area features extensive wetland, inland lake, river, and forest ecosystems provide unique opportunities for research. SNRE uses several properties near the campus including the Matthaei Botanical Gardens, Nichols Arboretum, Stinchfield Woods, and the Saginaw Forest. Additionally, students may attend programs and classes held at the University of Michigan Biological Station in northern Michigan, or they can participate in the University's "Geology in the Rockies" program in Wyoming. There are many study-abroad opportunities available through SNRE and the School for Field Studies, which enable students to pursue their studies in an international setting.

SNRE students may participate in the University's Living Learning Community Programs which typically feature theme housing and exciting research opportunities in an environment more like that of many smaller schools. These provide an opportunity to develop leadership skills in a stimulating environment.

# MAKING A DIFFERENCE STUDIES

## Environmental Policy and Behavior Concentration

Environmental Law
Environmental Justice: Domestic & Int'l.
Environmental Politics & Policy
International Environmental Policy
Native American Perspectives
Intro. to Environmental Policies: Race, Class & Gender
Ecotourism for Ecodevelopment in National Parks & Protected Areas: Third World

Applications of Environmental Justice
Environmental Education & Natural Resources
Women and Environment
Natural Resource Internship Program
Small Group Organization & Advocacy Planning

- **Environmental Thought and Activism** *Race, class, and gender approach to examining history of American environmental activism (1850-present). Identifies the major period of environmental mobilization and significant forms of environmental activism among the white middle class, white working class and people of color. Influence of social class, race, gender, and of environmental, and labor market experiences upon environmental perception and the kinds of environmental ideologies they develop. Rise of major environmental paradigms and the factors that make them influential.*

- **Environmental Ethics and Policy** *Critically examines selected issues in applied environmental ethics including: duties to future generations, animal rights, biocentrism, ecocentric "land ethics", and global environmental justice. Deep ecology, social ecology, feminist ecology, economic rationality, and ecological sustainability. Multicultural inspirations that might enrich western environmental ethics arising from Judeo-Christian, Hindu, Buddhist, Native American, and Australian aborigine traditions.*

## Resource Ecology and Management

Advanced Forest Ecology
Aquaculture
Biology & Management of Insects
Ecological Restoration
Imaging Radar as a Remote Sensor
Remote Sensing of Environment
Wildlife Behavior and Ecology

Agroforestry
Aquatic Entomology
Conservation of Biological Diversity
Ecology of Fishes
Multiple Use Forest Management
Wetland Ecology
Woody Plants: Biology & Identification

- **Tropical Conservation & Resource Management** *Multidisciplinary course examines underlying problems of tropical conservation and natural resource mgm't. Ecological, socio/political, and economic aspects. Complexity of social, political, and economic factors that interact with environmental ones to limit, enhance, or affect the conservation and management of resources. Interactions between conservation, development, and Third World peoples.*

## Landscape Design and Planning

Construction Materials and Detailing
Landscape Architecture Design
Landscape Architecture History
Site Engineering

Elements and Principles
Landscape Architecture Design Theory
Plant Materials for Landscape
Visual Communications

Apply by 2/1     Avg. # of students in a first year class: 85
- Team teaching   • Self-designed majors   • Field Studies   • Service-Learning
Interdisciplinary classes   • All seminar format   • Theme Housing   • Vegetarian Meals

Office of Undergraduate Admission
University of Michigan
1220 SAB/515 E. Jefferson
Ann Arbor, MI 48109-1316

734. 764.1316
snre.help@umich.edu
www.snre.umich.edu

# MIDDLEBURY COLLEGE

2,000 Students    Middlebury, Vermont

Middlebury is well-known as one of New England's outstanding small, residential, liberal arts colleges of long tradition. It was founded in 1800 and in 1883 became one of the earliest co-educational institutions. Middlebury is distinguished for its long international and multicultural tradition. Middlebury seeks those who wish not only to learn about themselves and their own traditions, but to expand their vision — to see beyond the bounds of class, culture, region or nation. Indeed, it could be said that the central purpose of a Middlebury education is precisely this transcendence of oneself and one's own concerns.

Since World War 1, the College has operated internationally-known language programs. Middlebury views languages both as a means of communication and as ways to learn more about a culture or a discipline. Four out of ten Middlebury students spend at least one semester abroad, experiencing another culture first-hand and bringing their new perspectives back to campus.

At Middlebury, the New England tradition of the town meeting takes on an international dimension at many of our symposia. His Holiness the Dalai Lama – the exiled spiritual and political leader of Tibet – spent a week on campus as part of a conference called "The Spirit and Nature Symposium." A symposium on South Africa had international speakers and a large audience: 140 American public radio stations.

First Year Students at Middlebury are required to elect one of a number of seminars designed to make connections among a number of traditional academic disciplines. Recent topics have included: Environmental Issues for the Nineties; Crises and Resolution; Thinking About War; and Cries of Injustice, Black Protest and the Civil Rights Movement.

Efforts are under way at Middlebury to "green" the campus. The College has decided it is important to incorporate what it teaches in its daily workings. Everything from course work, to meals and energy conservation is being scrutinized.

Middlebury College has a very active volunteer service program. Over 600 students volunteer each year. One of the oldest programs is Community Friends, in which students work with individuals in need from the following groups: children between the ages of 6-12, the elderly, and people with mental retardation and mental illness. Students also read to the blind and renovate affordable housing. Students take ungraded internships for credit in various areas, from a clinic for parasitology in Thailand to the office of a local attorney.

The College has a partnership with De Witt Clinton High School (Bronx, N.Y.) whose student population is 99% minority. De Witt Clinton teachers have participated in workshops with Middlebury faculty, and students have conducted teaching internships at the high school during winter term. Middlebury also has three regional "diversity task forces" designed to help recruit and retain students of color. In addition a rural outreach program focuses on first-generation, college-bound students of modest financial means.

# MAKING A DIFFERENCE STUDIES

## First Year Seminars

Theory and Practice of Nonviolence  
Stories About Women  
Voices Across Social Groups: How Do We Talk To Each Other?  
Women and World Politics: Questions About Gender  
Social Class & Ethnic Relations in America  
Moral and Ethical Decisions in Public Life

## Environmental Studies: Conservation Biology; Environmental Geology; Enviro Economics; Geography; Environmental Policy; Environmental Perspectives in Literature & Writing; Philosophical & Comparative Perspectives; Human Ecology

*Environmental Studies is one of the most popular majors at Middlebury.*

Visions of Nature  
Ethics and the Environment  
Social Movement and Collective Action  
Environmental Economics  
Freedom, Faith and Ecology  
Environmental Economics  
Methods in Ecology  
Environmental and Natural Resource Policy  
Native Peoples of North America  
Environmental Geology  
Religion, Ethics and the Environment  
Perspectives on the Environmental Movement  
Natural Science and the Environment  
Philosophy of Nature

## Geography

The Geography of Development  
Population Geography  
Surface Water Resource and Development  
Energy Fuels and Mineral Development  
Economic Geography  
Geographic Perspectives on Middle East  
Social Aspects of Environmental Issues  
Women in the City

## Northern Studies

Polar Biota: Flora*  
Artic and Alpine Environments  
Northern Archaeology*  
Public Policy in Circumpolar North  
Northern Resource Conflicts  
Political Economy Of Resource Mgm't.*  
Northern Legal Issues  
Arctic Policy Studies*  
Indigenous Cultures of Circumpolar North*  
Community Development in Circumpolar North*

* These classes are offered at the Center for Northern Studies in Wolcott, VT

## Sociology/Anthropology: Social Inequality, Social Policy Issues, Health and Society

Women, Culture and Society  
Indian Society  
Sociology of Women  
Social Movements and Collective Action  
Medical Anthropology  
Medical Sociology  
Native Peoples of North America  
American Community Studies  
Women in Social Thought  
Chinese Society and Culture  
Sociology of Education  
Race and Ethnicity

### Women's Studies     Third World Studies

Apply by 1/ 15

• Internships   • Self-designed majors   • Field studies  
• Third-world study abroad   • Mystic Seaport Program

Admissions Office  
Middlebury College  
Middlebury, VT 05753-6002  

802. 443.3000

# UNIVERSITY OF MINNESOTA

28,000 Undergraduates    Minneapolis, Minnesota

At the University of Minnesota, students in the College of Liberal Arts integrate fields of knowledge through interdisciplinary and thematic courses. They have the opportunity to examine values, ethics, and social responsibility and to learn about the cultural diversity of the world and U.S. society. Students also have opportunities for active learning, such as internships and study abroad. Carlson School of Management is known for its particular emphasis on socially responsible business practices.

The College provides a variety of programs to enhance or personalize chosen degree programs. Programs such as the Honors Program, the Martin Luther King Program — and those offered through the Office of Special Learning Opportunities, the Foreign Studies Office, and the Career Development Office — help students get the most from their undergraduate experience. Students earning a Bachelor of Individualized Studies (BIS) design their own program with three areas of concentration. The program must have a coherence based on stated academic objectives. Also available is an individually designed interdepartmental major — a program with an interdisciplinary theme that meets the students' individual academic interests. Established interdepartmental majors include African, American, East Asian, Jewish, Latin American, Middle Eastern, urban and women's studies, and international relations.

In order for students to transcend the boundaries set by major European and North American educational traditions, B.A. and B.I.S. degree students are asked to examine cultures substantially different from their own. At least two courses are required dealing with the cultures of Asia, Africa, Latin America or with traditional Native American cultures. Students are also required to take a course in U.S. Cultural Pluralism, with a primary focus on social and cultural diversity and with special attention to race and ethnicity.

Field-experience learning at UM is a form of study in which community resources are used to explore the questions and issues raised in the classroom. Students work in a paid or volunteer positions, usually in locations such as a museum, social service agency, government office, or community program. The fieldwork (sometimes called an internship or practicum) takes place off campus, but is carried out under the direction of a faculty member.

The College of Natural Resources seeks to increase the economic, social and environmental benefits of our most important renewable resources. The CNR offers six majors: Fisheries and Wildlife; Forest products; Forest Resources; Natural Resources and Environmental Studies; Recreation Resource Management; and Urban Forestry. Most majors require completion of a 31/2 week summer term at Lake Itasca Forestry and Biological Station, at the source of the Mississippi River. The College's Cloquet Forestry Center includes more than 3,700 acres of virgin and second-growth timber in a major forest products manufacturing area. Forest Resources seniors spend their fall quarter at the center taking 18 credits of field-oriented instruction.

# MAKING A DIFFERENCE STUDIES

## South Asian & Middle Eastern Languages & Cultures

The Religion of Islam
Women in India: Role and repression
Beginning/Colloquial Arabic
Folklore of India
Buddhism

The Qur'an as Literature
Islam and Communism
Persian Poetry in Translation
Tribal Peoples and Cultures of S. Asia
Gandhi and Non-violent Revolution

## Journalism and Mass Communication

Media in American History and Law
Public Affairs Reporting
Supervision of School Publications
Mass Media and Popular Culture
Communication & Public Opinion

Visual Communication
Community Newspaper
Racial Minorities & the Mass Media
Mass Media and Politics
Mass Communication & Public Health

## Urban Forestry

Urban Forest Management
Insect Pest Management
Nursery Management & Production
Plant Propagation
Forest Genetics

Forest Economics and Planning
Farm and Small Woodlands Forestry
Herbaceous Plant Materials
Landscape Management
Strategy and Tactics in Project Planning

## Paper Science & Engineering

Bio & Enviro Science of Pulp & Paper
Pulp and Paper Operations
Analysis of Production Systems

Analysis and Design of Wastewater Systems
Analysis and Design of Water Supply Systems
Renewable Nat. Resources/Developing Countries

## Resources and Environmental Protection

Land Economics
Pollution Impacts on Aquatic Systems
Organic and Pesticidal Residues
Environmental Policy
Technology and Western Civilization

Resource and Environmental Economics
Assessing the Ecological Effects of Pollution
Ethics and Values in Resource Management
Ecology & Mgm't of Fish & Wildlife Habitats
Resource Dev. & Environmental Economics

## Environmental Issues and Planning

Economic Dev. of American Agriculture
Energy Research Use
Recreation Land Policy
Politics, Planning and Decision Making
Politics of the Regulatory Process

Resource Dev. & Environmental Economics
Assessing the Ecological Effects of Pollution
Environmental Policy
Management of Recreational Lands
Impact Assessment and Enviro Mediation

**Forest Biology/Harvesting/Resources  Fisheries & Wildlife  Waste Mgm't.**

**Water/Soil Resources  Int'l. Relations  Women's Studies  African-Amer. Studies**

**History of Science & Tech.  Sociology  Landscape Architecture  Philosophy**

Rolling admissions

Office of Admissions
University of Minnesota
Minneapolis, MN 55455

612. 625.2006
admissions@tc.umn.edu

# CSU, MONTEREY BAY

2300 Students    Seaside, California

California State University, Monterey Bay is the California State University system's 21st campus for the 21st Century. Founded in 1994, CSUMB is located on the beautiful and historic Monterey Peninsula area on California's central coast. With its truly innovative curriculum, CSUMB is preparing students to become socially and professionally capable and well-rounded. CSUMB's academic programs are designed for people of diverse backgrounds who want to work hard at learning, have fun while learning, and consciously add value to their lives through the learning they do.

The vision for CSUMB includes a model pluralistic-academic community where all learn and teach one another in an atmosphere of mutual respect and pursuit of excellence. Graduates will have an understanding of interdependence and global competence, distinctive technical and educational skills, the experience and abilities to contribute to a high-quality workforce, the critical thinking abilities to be productive citizens, and the social responsibility and skills to be community builders. The curricula is student- and society-centered and is of sufficient breadth and depth to meet statewide and regional needs, specifically those involving both inner-city and isolated rural populations (Monterey, Santa Cruz, and San Benito counties).

CSUMB's innovative curriculum is outcome based rather than "seat time" based; that is, students will be assessed in terms of what they actually know and what they can do rather than how many classes they have completed or how many tests they have passed. Graduates will have mastered seven learning outcomes which are:
- Effective and ethical communication in at least two diverse languages;
- Cross-culturally competent citizenship in a pluralistic and global society;
- Technological, aural, and visual literacy;
- Creative expression in the service of transforming culture;
- Ethics, social justice, and care for one another;
- Scientific sophistication and value for the earth and earth systems; and
- Holistic and creative sense of self.

The seven goals are achieved by demonstrating competencies including technology, language, cross-cultural competence, and service to the community. Service learning is an important and integral component of CSUMB's vision, philosophy, and educational programs. All students must complete two service learning courses. Service learning involves active learning — drawing lessons from the experience of performing service work that meets community needs, as defined and determined by the communities. Typical courses include: Monterey Bay — A Case Study in Environmental Policy; Marine and Coastal Management — Integration of Science and Policy; and Fieldwork in Multicultural Child Care.

At CSUMB, the class size is kept small and students work side by side with faculty to develop their unique learning paths. CSUMB has state-of-the-art technology, and works with several high-tech industries right on campus.

It takes a special kind of pioneering student to succeed at CSUMB. Students must be adaptable, be able to appreciate rigorous academic programs, and want to play an active part in a dynamic and diverse educational evolution.

# MAKING A DIFFERENCE STUDIES

## Human Communication

*Emphasizes community building, peaceful co-existence, the development of individual and group potential, effective and ethical decision making. Covers traditional fields such as American Studies, Chicano/Latino Studies, Communication, Ethics, Ethnic Studies, History, Humanities, Journalism and Media Studies, Liberal Arts, Oral History, Pre-Law and Women's Studies.*

Communication, Culture and Conflict
Latina Life Stories
Communication and Gender
Critical Political Analysis in Everyday Life
Oral History and Community Memory

Communication Ethics
Free Speech and Responsibility
Linguistic Diversity and Language Barriers
History of Politics in the Americas
Linguistic Diversity and Language Barriers

## Global Studies

*Encompasses issues of human well-being and survival, environmental degradation, persistent global poverty, racial and gender violence, and how various peoples interface with technology.*

World Economy
Third World Issues & Cultures
Introduction to Global Studies

Changing Politics of Global Life
The Chicano Community
Global Organizations & the United Nations

## Earth Systems Science and Policy: Ecological Systems, Environmental Economics & Policy, Marine Science

*Teaches students to view the earth as a complex system of interacting components including the anthrosphere, atmosphere, biosphere, geosphere, and hydrosphere. A key factor in solving many of the serious challenges confronting our world (developing sustainable food and energy resources, reducing pollution, minimizing impact of natural disasters) is the ability to analyze and understand complex interactions between physical, biological, and socio-political processes.*

Ecosystem Modeling
Environmental Chemistry
Ecosystem Hindcasting
Environmental Dispute Resolution
Advanced Watershed Systems

Water issues in California
Conservation Biology
Habitat Biodiversity
Environmental Politics
Ecological Economics

## Collaborative Human Service

*As the program matures, it will offer courses with an emphasis of collaboration in the context of health services, criminal justice, mental health, and parks and recreation.*

Civic Community
Women's Leadership Development
Public Policy Analysis
Empowering Communities

Personal Renewal & Organizational Development
Services and Support for Children & Youth
Systems Mgm't. in Human Services Delivery
How to Develop a Full-Service Charter School

Reinventing Leadership: Facilitative Leveraging to Dissolve Barriers to Collaboration

Apply by: 11/30
Student body: 55% minority, 60% transfer     Faculty: 68% male, 32% female, 53% minority
• Service learning   • Interdisciplinary classes   • All seminar format   • Self-designed majors
• Team teaching   • Field studies   • Life experience credit   • Vegetarian meals

Student Information Center
CSU Monterey Bay
100 Campus Center
Seaside, CA 93955-8001

831. 582.3518
Student_Info_Center@monterey.edu
www.monterey.edu

# NAROPA COLLEGE

400 Undergraduates    Boulder, Colorado

Nestled in the foothills of the majestic Rocky Mountains on 3.7 acres in the center of Boulder, Colorado, Naropa College provides a unique educational environment that balances personal meaning and creative expression with academic excellence. The degree programs cultivate a spirit of openness, critical intellect, and the development of effective action, while transmitting the principles of awareness and wisdom.

Naropa College was founded in 1974 by Tibetan meditation master and scholar Chögyam Trungpa and is patterned after Nalanda University — an 11th century Indian university renowned for joining intellect and intuition, and for its appreciation of various contemplative traditions. Naropa offers a full four-year undergraduate program in a wide range of majors, as well as M.A. and M.F.A. degrees at the graduate level. An active Study Abroad program, in both Bali and Nepal, mixes academic study and experiential learning with the philosophy, music, painting, dance, and traditional awareness practices of each country.

The Naropa College faculty is remarkable in its diversity and achievements. They are distinguished by a wealth of experience in the professional, artistic, and scholastic applications of their disciplines. They are committed to a heart-felt philosophy that brings out the individual insight and intelligence of each student. In addition to its outstanding core faculty, an international community of scholars and artists is consistently drawn to Naropa because of its strong vision and leadership in higher education. The faculty and student body at Naropa form a close-knit community, and this relationship between the students and faculty is a unique part of the educational experience. Naropa offers small class size, a low teacher/student ratio, and a vibrant atmosphere of creative risk-taking; an integration of intellect and intuition is modeled and encouraged. Drawn from over 39 states and 10 countries, Naropa students represent a wide range of life experiences, ages, cultures, and backgrounds. Activism, altruism, and community involvement are among the many notable characteristics of Naropa's unique student environment.

Naropa seeks students who have a strong appetite for learning, enjoy experiential education in an academic setting, and have demonstrated an ability to live independently. Non-traditional students and all those with a high school degree or GED are welcome to apply. The Office of Admissions reviews learning done outside the traditional college classroom (and CLEP scores) in addition to academic transcripts. Naropa gladly accepts international students, although certain language and financial requirements apply.

The campus and surrounding grounds include The Naropa Performing Arts Center, a meditation hall, the Allen Ginsberg Library, Naropa Gallery, and Naropa Cafe. Naropa also has a new campus in North Boulder. The city of Boulder (population 100,000), 25 miles northwest of Denver, was rated by *Outside Magazine* as one of the top ten places to live for health and outdoor recreation.

# MAKING A DIFFERENCE STUDIES

"When human beings lose their connection to nature, to heaven and earth, then they do not know how to nurture their environment. Healing our society goes hand in hand with healing our personal, elemental connection with the phenomenal world."

— Chogyam Trungpa Rinpoche

### Environmental Studies

*Integrates science, spirit, and personal engagement in a broad multidisciplinary environmental curriculum with specialization in Anthropology, Ecology, Ecospirituality, Horticulture, & Native American Studies.*

Small Farm Management

Deep Ecology

Edible Plants and Survival Skills

Field Ecology

Vegetable Garden

Sustainable Communities

Ecology Practicum

Eco-Literature

Restoration Ecology and Changing Landscapes

Field Botany

Permaculture

Ethnomedicine Seminar

- **Nature, The Sacred, and Contemplation** *The pure mindful experience of Nature often leads to a personal emotional relationship, sometimes referred to as spiritual, sacred, or mystical. Individual, cultural, and contemplative dimensions of such a relationship. Integrates experiences and contemplation outdoors with teachings from contemplative traditions, ecological knowledge, and observations as a naturalist.*

### Contemplative Psychology: Buddhist & Western Psychology; Jungian Psychology; Psychology of Health & Healing; Transpersonal & Humanistic Psychology

*Prepares a student for any occupation requiring subtlety in interpersonal relationships, particularly in the helping professions.*

Psychology of Healing

Healing and Music

Body Cosmology and Natural Healing

The Geshtalt Approach

Archetypes and Collective Unconscious

Tibetan Medicine

Psychology of Meditation

Psychology of Shamanism

Dynamics of the Intimate Relationship

Healing in Cross-Cultural Perspective

Teaching Children in Contemplative Tradition

Buddhist Psychology: Maitri & Compassion

### Early Childhood Education

*Emphasizes personalized teacher education with teaching skills drawn from the holistic and spiritual traditions of Montessori, Waldorf, and Shambala. Graduates are preapproved by the state for certification as group-leader qualified preschool teachers, directors of child care centers, and private kindergarten teachers.*

Buddhist Educational Psychology

Cultural Anthropology & Social Change

Teaching & Learning Styles

Contemplative Parenting

Body Mind Centering

Nourishing the Teacher

Child Development and Creativity

Educational Admin. of a Child Care Center

- **Foundations of Contemplative Education** *Lays the ground for discovering the full-blown richness and dignity of ourselves and children. Study and practice the essentials of contemplative education psychology in order to apply its wisdom to teaching young children. Through an exploration of the traditional Shambala and Buddhist approaches to working with states of minds, you prepare for teaching with vigor, freshness, and openess. Encounter concepts and emotions directly, gently, and creatively. Develop disciplines of mindfulness/awareness and contemplative educational observation, a natural extension of awareness practice. These practices enable you to perceive and bring forth children's true natures without prejudice and aggression.*

## Inter-Arts Studies

*Encourages students to practice their primary discipline while exploring other art forms and contemplative practices. The focus is on collaboration and the creative process. Four areas of concentration include: Dance/Movement, Dance Therapy, Music, and Theater Studies.*

Body Mind Centering
The Dance of Haiti
Dance Therapy

The Dance of West Africa
Contact Improvisation
Contemplative Arts Practice

- **Dance Therapy 11** *Focus on developing movement relationships through empathic movement and verbal exchange. This discipline supports increasing intimacy — the ground of the healing relationship and, eventually, of participation in and support of another's process. Increased authenticity of presence and movement.*

## Religious Studies

*Major world religions as living traditions in both historical and contemporary perspectives.*

Contemplative Christianity
Meditation Practicum
Contemplative Islam/Sufism
Buddhist Civilization
Women, Sufism, & Islam: Womanist Perspectives

Contemplative Religions of China and Japan
Tibetan
Contemplative Judaism: The Knowing Heart
Contemplative Hinduism

## Traditional Eastern Arts

*The only degree program in the country offering training in the Traditional Eastern Arts of Aikido, T'ai-chi Ch'uan, and Yoga. Focus is integration of body, mind, and spirit through practices grounded in meditative awareness and physical acumen.*

T'ai Chi Chu'an
T'ai Chi Ch'uan: Sword Form
Shambala Meditation Practicum
Ikebana: Japanese Flower Arranging
Bugaku: Japanese Court Dance

Aikido
Yoga
Kyudo: The Way of the Bow
Japanese Tea Ceremony

## Study Abroad: Nepal and Bali

*Program provides a thorough introduction to the living traditions of meditation, philosophy, music, painting, and dance presently flowering in both Nepal and Bali. Both programs infuse the cross-cultural educational experience with awareness of the personal journey.*

Meditation Practicum
Balinese Gamelan Orchestra
Arts and Culture
Kathmandu Valley:Traditional Culture, Developing Nation

Buddhist Traditions
Balinese Dance
Independent Study and Travel

## Visual Arts

*Eastern and Western art disciplines. Hands-on studio approach with studies in art history and portfolio/gallery presentations. Drawing, color theory, figure studies, watercolor, painting, calligraphy, brush stroke, thangka painting, and ceramics/sculpture.*

Rolling admissions     Student body: 90% transfers    75% over 25 years of age
- All seminar format  • Service-learning  • Self-designed majors  • Life experience credit
- Interdisciplinary classes & majors  • Graduate programs  • Vegetarian & vegan meals

Director of Admissions
The Naropa College
2130 Arapahoe Ave.
Boulder, CO 80302

303. 546.3572
800. 772.6951
admissions@naropa.edu
www.naropa.edu

The McLean Environmental Living and Learning Center at **Northland College** is one of the most ecological dorms in the world. Resource saving features include a wind tower, photovoltaics, solar panels, and greenhouses.

A mother and her child in Cedar Apartments, a unique single parent housing complex on the **Bemidji State University** campus. Bemidji State was the first public college or university to offer single parent housing on campus.

Work and community service are integral parts of student life at **Warren Wilson College**. Environmental studies majors often choose the organic garden work crew.

Environmental Science students at **Alaska Pacific University** doing field research at Ship Creek which runs through Anchorage and is the destination of millions of returning salmon each year.

# NEW COLLEGE OF CALIFORNIA

200 Undergraduates    San Francisco, California

New College is a place where students are intellectually challenged to make a difference — in an atmosphere that is, above all, personal and encourages people to see themselves not as isolated individuals, but as human beings who are part of a community.

To be sure, the New College community is diverse, and not only in the usual aspects of ethnicity, class, and orientation. Diversity also means recognizing that we are all complex beings who can nevertheless come together for a common purpose in this case, embarking on a journey of academic exploration that mines the wisdom of the past in order to raise the hope of a future that is more humane for everyone.

This unusual combination of concern both for the particularities of each individual and for the welfare of the society as a whole — mediated through real concern for the situation of each person at the school — makes New College the unique place it is. If you choose to join this unusual community, one thing is certain: your life in its many aspects — intellectual, spiritual, social, emotional — will never be the same. And you will make a difference.

New College's School of Humanities — Weekday BA Program is committed to an undergraduate education that fosters:

• Critical Thinking — This doesn't mean just questioning the facts or logic of an argument. It also means understanding the social and cultural situations in which knowledge is produced, and grounding knowledge in ethical principles and application to daily life.

• Interdisciplinary Learning — Knowledge may need to be organized into distinct areas or disciplines, but students should be able to move freely between them and use the concepts of each to reveal what others leave out.

• Diversity — Individual experience is shaped — and society is divided — by income and social class, by race and ethnicity, by gender and sexual orientation. New College is committed to bringing this diversity into education, and to building trust and solidarity across social divisions by rediscovering shared needs and values.

• Activism — New College wants students to connect learning to their life experience and current lives outside the classroom. The College helps them create positive change in society, both while in school and after graduation. All New College students, for example, do community internships or field studies.

• Community-Building — For New College, building community is both a means and an end. Community is built in everyday interaction: in classroom dialogue and in common projects. This community in turn enhances learning while helping envision and work for the common good.

The curriculum is organized into three clusters: Community and Global Studies; Cultural Studies; and Arts, Music, and Literature. Within each cluster are several emphasis areas, but students can construct their own from courses offered by any cluster. The emphasis area is focused in a Senior Project. Learning options include tutorials, independent study, field study, and a practicum.

The New College World Studies Project is an academic field-program designed to facilitate communication and develop relationships between the New College community and friends and colleagues in other parts of the world. The World Studies Project enables students to take an active role in their education by connecting classroom learning with the outside world through field experience, while promoting an understanding of world cultures. The international community that grows out of these experiences fosters understanding through communication among peoples of varying social, economic, and cultural backgrounds. New College hopes to carry this vision of a truly global community into the twenty-first century.

A component of the project, the Semester Abroad Program, enables students to immerse themselves fully in other cultures in conjunction with a three to four week academic study tour. Undergraduate and graduate academic credit is available, but non-credit participants are also welcome. Within this educational framework, participants search for community solutions to social and cultural conflicts by looking at the complex relationships between politics, economics, culture, geography, and spirituality.

The Weekend College Completion Program is an accelerated, upper-division program study culminating in a BA in Humanities. The program was designed for self-motivated, disciplined working adults who have completed approximately 45 units of transferable college credit, or who can combine transferable units with credit awarded for earlier life experience and/or general subject matter testing through CLEP.

Twelve months of study, divided into three 4-month trimesters, combines interdisciplinary seminars one full weekend each month with supervised independent study and journal work. The cohort method creates learning groups that pass through the entire program together, providing a common context for concentration either in interdisciplinary humanities or individually-designed emphasis areas.

Culture, Environment, and Sustainable Community is also a Weekend BA Completion Program. Located just north of San Francisco in Santa Rosa, this one-year degree program is designed for people interested in the interdependence of culture, meaning, politics, ecology, and community — and who want to use their knowledge to create sustainable alternative communities. Its focus is on developing a critical perspective on the history and present condition of modern society, and on learning new ways to conceptualize solutions to contemporary problems while acquiring the skills to concretely solve them.

This three-part program features a structured 12-month curriculum of core seminars; individualized research and study leading to an undergraduate thesis; and optional co-curricular activities including workshops, activist projects, community building rituals, and social gatherings. Cohorts of up to 20 students will meet in the core seminars once a month, remaining in contact with each other throughout the program.

# MAKING A DIFFERENCE STUDIES

## Community & Global Studies

*This cluster immerses students in the lives of communities anywhere — from just around the block to halfway around the world. This program makes sense of the new global economy and its impact on culture, ecological problems and solutions, and social movements. Fieldwork and internship opportunities allow students to work for change while they prepare themselves for graduate school and/or socially relevant careers.*

## Anthropology & Sociology

*In this interdisciplinary approach, as a basis for responding creatively to our reality, other cultures are studied in detail, while inquiring into our own: global interdependence in a context of unequal power relations and political, economic, and cultural struggle.*

## Ecological Studies

*Analyzes various areas of human interaction with the environment, while seeking ecologically-conscious alternatives. Students work in both the classroom and the community, learning through dialogue, creative problem-solving, and internships with local environmental groups.*

Nature as a Concept
Eco-Literacy: Introduction to Ecology

Eco-Logics / Eco-Nomics
Issues in Environmental Activism

## Integrated Health Studies

*The history and politics of health care - its ethical dilemmas, cultural, social, economic, and psychological dimensions, and its role in the community — as well as cross-cultural and alternative perspectives on health together with practical, health-related work.*

Medical Anthropology
Health Promotion and Awareness
Living Anatomy Through Movement
Social and Psychological dimensions of Health and Medicine

Political Economy of Health Care
Feminist Theory and Women's Health
Health Studies: Strategies for Change

## Media and Society

*Blends a core curriculum examining the three "contexts" of the "global media society" — theoretical, political-economic, and cultural- historical — with one-on-one mentorships covering media fields like film, TV, journalism and hands-on internships in local radio, newspapers, PR, advertising, etc. (www.newcollege.edu/media studies/)*

## Cultural Studies

*Culture represents the social production of meaning; it shapes both the self and the self's relation to society. This cluster provides critical tools for making sense of our relationship to the world we live in drawing on history, aesthetics, psychology, economics, literature, religion, science, and theories of gender, sexuality, race, and ethnicity.*

## Cultural Histories: Latin America

*Some see culture as a form of social control, others as a field of resistance and play. Cultures are environments we inhabit: subcultures, microcultures, mass culture, popular culture, middlebrow and high cultures. How these work, where they came from, and where they're going.*

Cultures of Resistance in Latin America
Contemporary Cuba
Contemporary Issues of the Americas
Popular Health in the Americas
Women and Political Terror; The Literature of South American Women Writers

Latin American History Through Literature
Literature of Latin American Women Writers
Murals: Images of Latin America
History, Narrative, & Ideology in Latin America

## Psychology

*To understand the mind, we must understand the social worlds in which minds are born and live. Foundation in development, therapy, and investigation of the unconscious aspects of social life. How does an ideology that justifies domination become anchored in the dominated? What lets people rape, torture, and kill other people designated as "the enemy"?*

## Gender Studies

*What is gender? How many genders are there? How many sexual orientations? Is gender different from sex? What roles do race and class play in all this? Feminist and queer theory as well as history, psychology, law, literature, sociology, anthropology, and media studies help us understand.*

Creativity, Sexuality, and the Sacred
Cultural Notions of Self and Sexuality
Perspectives on Lesbian/Gay Experience

Queer Cultures, Queer Spaces
AIDS and Society
Fundamentalism & the Religious Right

## Politics & Society

*Contemporary critical thinking challenges established versions of history and politics. Emerging movements demand accountability to women, queers, ethnic "minorities," to working-class and poor people, and to the biosphere. This emphasis area analyzes power relations, explores critiques of the status quo, and seeks viable alternatives.*

Political Economy
Political History of San Francisco
Global Political Economy

Social Problems/Social Visions
Critical Moments in 20th Century US History
Schooling, Inequality, & Social Change

## Arts, Music, & Literature

*Examines the history of art forms and media, their connection with society, and the ways they've been used to change people's attitudes and ways of knowing. In this context, "art"is not only for self-expression, but also for social critique and communal celebration, for political challenge and spiritual focus, and for training the senses and enlarging the imagination.*

## Arts and Social Change

*Acquire the skills to bring imagination to life through Performance, Movement/Dance, Video, and Visual Arts. Students learn to apply these skills in education, community organizing, therapy, and activism as well as personal art making. Simultaneously, they explore how other cultures have defined similar kinds of creative activity.*

Arts and Learning
Performance/Urban Ritual
Joy of Movement
Drama Therapy

Arts and Social Change
Community Theater Making
Video Arts
Screenwriting and Propaganda

## Writing, Literature, & Publishing

*Literature and its composition from an historical, social, and international perspective, exploring the role of the writer as witness, agitator, and activist. Letterpress printing and desk-top publishing.*

Rolling admissions  No housing
Faculty 53% male, 47% female, 40% minority

- Service learning   • Weekend & evening classes   • Required practicum   • Field studies
- Team teaching   • Self-designed majors   • All seminar format   • Life experience credit
- Interdisciplinary classes & majors   • Optional SAT's   • Graduate program   • Distance learning

Office of Admissions
New College of California
777 Valencia St.
San Francisco, CA 94110

415. 437.3460
888. 437.3460
www.newcollege.edu

# NEW COLLEGE OF CALIFORNIA
## CULTURE, ECOLOGY, & SUSTAINABLE COMMUNITY
North Bay Campus, Santa Rosa, CA

In 1998, the New College of California established its North Bay Campus Center for the Study of Culture, Ecology, and Sustainable Community in Santa Rosa north of San Francisco. The campus offers a BA Completion Program with an emphasis in Culture, Ecology, and Sustainable Community.

The mission of this program is to help create a just, sacred, and sustainable world. We seek to do this by educating students who can heal both people and the earth; who can engage in resistance to the further destruction to humans, other living things, and the planet; who can build sustainable alternative institutions and finally create a consciousness shift to a more wholistic, ecological paradigm. Through the curriculum, students learn the "languages" of critical thinking, imagination, empathy and compassion, and of activism necessary to accomplish these tasks.

The programs focus on developing a critical perspective of the history and present condition of modern society, while learning new ways to conceptualize solutions to modern problems and acquiring skills to build a sustainable future.

Students, with their advisors, design a program of study that suits their own particular interests and needs. Some students will develop intellectual and theoretical theses; others will seek approaches to changing the existing system, while still others will acquire the knowledge and skills for guiding alternative communities and institutions. Through individualized study and research, students may emphasize their study in areas such as politics, health, ecology, cultural critique, alternative systems, global studies, or an interdisciplinary area of their own design.

The program comprises twelve months of study, divided into three semesters, leading to a Bachelor of Arts degree with an emphasis is Culture, Ecology, and Sustainable Community. Working with an academic advisor, students entering with at least 42 semester units combine the various program elements into a degree completion plan that meets their needs. The basic semester structure consists of: core seminars; an academic journal; a senior thesis; and a group or independent study, or internship. Students may develop a Prior Learning Portfolio for up to 30 academic credits to complete their degree.

One weekend a month, students attend on-campus Core Seminars that are organized into three semesters over the program's one-year period. Each weekend contains three seminars organized as part of a year long course of 1 2 seminars each.

Students may pursue their interest in a particular area through guided group or independent study arranged through their advisors. These may include workshops and courses at New College or other institutions not part of the Culture, Ecology, and Sustainable Community Program. Guided group/independent study is also available for students to meet breadth requirements for the B.A. degree e.g. Quantitative Reasoning, Scientific Reasoning, Art and Literature.

Students develop their own areas of concentration through their Senior Project, through individualized study, and research under the guidance of an Academic Advisor. Students may concentrate their degree in areas such as ecology, education, alternative health, activism, global studies, or an interdisciplinary area of their own design. Up to 30 units are directly focused in the student's area of interest. Beginning in the year 2000, there will be two new developed areas of concentration: Environmental Entrepreneurship and Biodynamic Agriculture.

Internships in appropriate community agencies, environmental/political organizations, and intentional communities are available for students to pursue for additional credit or for thesis topics, etc.

Many students have prior life experience that is equivalent to college level learning. Students may apply for as much as 30 units of credit (one full academic year).

The Academic journal allows students to reflect on and to integrate the program into personal and professional development. It challenges students to consciously examine their relationship to culture, society, and self. The Senior Thesis offers the opportunity for a year-long research project in an area of academic, professional, or activist interest. The project may involve internship work and/or research in the field.

## MAKING A DIFFERENCE STUDIES

### Environment, Civilization and Development
*The Saturday morning seminar is a year-long in-depth analysis and critique of industrial civilization and its self- generated crises. Sample seminar topics are:*

| | |
|---|---|
| From Hunter-Gatherer to Industrial Society | Technology and Civilization |
| Development: Exporting Civilization | Globalization and its Discontents |

### Sustainable Community and Cultural Renewal
*The Saturday afternoon seminar is an exploration of existing and potential alternatives to the dominant culture that hold the promise for creating a parallel universe/future society that is just, sacred, and sustainable. Seminar topics include:*

| | |
|---|---|
| Intentional Community | Deep Ecology |
| Eco-Psychology | Appropriate Technology |
| Eco-Cities and Eco-Villages | Alternative Economics & Community Currencies |
| Environmental Justice | Natural Building and Alternative Architecture |

### Politics, Culture and Society
*The Sunday morning session is a series of radical philosophical seminars on politics, science, the environment, culture and spirituality, integrating community and democracy, overcoming scientific reductionism, the philosophy of ecology, indigenous knowledge, and on spirituality, justice & ethics, and corporations & social responsibility.*

### Integrative Seminar
*Sunday afternoon features an Integrative Seminar, a time for reflection, questions, further exploration and integration of the topics of the Core Seminars.*

| | |
|---|---|
| Michael J. McAvoy | 707. 568.0112 |
| Academic Director | 707. 568.0114 Fax |
| North Bay Campus  New College of California | |
| 99 Sixth Street | |
| Santa Rosa, CA 95401 | |

# NORTHLAND COLLEGE

880 Students    Ashland, Wisconsin

The abundant natural beauty of the northern lakes and forests of Lake Superior country provide the perfect setting for a school like Northland. Over twenty five years ago the faculty of this one hundred and six year-old college committed themselves to a new vision: a liberal arts/environmental college. Since then the idea that our natural and social worlds — and the knowledge they support — are inextricably connected, has flourished and matured at Northland.

A premise of Northland's educational mission is that we must strive to free ourselves from the alienating and self-destructive assumption that humans live in isolation from the natural environment. The essence of human existence is that we live in two worlds: the world we have created and the world that created us. We dwell simultaneously in the human realm of institutions, cultures, and ideas as well as in the life-giving realm of nature. As long as we separate these two realms we can never feel completely at home — at peace with ourselves and our environment. In our quest for wholeness, we affirm our deepest humanistic values.

Northland is unique in that it does not restrict its study of the relationship between humanity and nature to a few courses in ecology or environmental studies. Almost a third of Northland's courses may be said to have some clear relevance to environmental issues. If the human and the natural world are as intimately interwoven as we believe, that relationship can and should be, analyzed and appreciated from all perspectives: scientific, political, anthropological, philosophical, literary, artistic, and recreational. A concern for the natural world around us runs throughout Northland's curriculum and co-curricular activities. Northland gained national recognition by receiving the Certificate of Environmental Achievement from Renew America in association with the National Environmental Awards Council. Northland has also received national recognition for outstanding science and math programs.

As a liberal arts college Northland strives to bring about the maximum intellectual, social, personal, and physical development of its students. In the long run a liberal arts education is the most practical form of training. The world is quickly changing and tomorrow's problems cannot be anticipated. Success in the future will depend on the ability to cope with the unknown, to acquire new skills as the need arises, and to gather knowledge about factual situations that could hardly have been imagined a decade earlier. A technical, overly specialized training prepares for today; a liberal arts education prepares for tomorrow.

A small college, Northland fosters an atmosphere in which there is a distinctive concern for both the individual human being and the natural world. Northland offers a value-sensitive education focusing on the liberal arts as a vehicle for understanding the disciplines, techniques, and knowledge needed to function effectively in the modern world. Northland focuses on the study of our interactions with the environment, ranging from aesthetic and spiritual values derived from the great Northwoods and Lake Superior, to complex social and scientific issues. There is also emphasis on the study of human behaviors and interaction through traditional majors and interdisciplinary programs in such areas as environmental studies, outdoor education, cross-cultural and global understanding, education, and business.

Emphasis is placed on individual relationships with faculty, on field experience, internships and independent study, on exposure to other cultures and travel abroad, as well as on cooperative and experiential learning. The faculty is committed to including environmental subject matter or methodologies in their classes whenever appropriate. Several classes are team taught in a multidisciplinary approach. Northland's 4-4-1 calendar year offers many opportunities for travel to other countries.

Several environmental and social issue-conscious groups are active on campus. The Sigurd Olson Environmental Institute is the environmental education outreach arm of the college. The Timber Wolf Alliance, Loon Watch, and the Bi-National Forum are among its sponsored programs. The Institute also provides educational programs to increase public understanding of the Lake Superior bio-region and environmental issue,s as well as in-service training in environmental education for teachers.

In keeping with Northland's commitment to apply in practice what it teaches about environmental issues and ways to develop a sustainable future, the new Environmental Living & Learning Center residence was designed with hundreds of environmental considerations in mind. Among the special features are a 20 kilowatt wind tower, three photovoltaic arrays, fourteen solar hot water panels, and composting waterless toilets. The apartments have passive solar design and share two greenhouses to be operated by the residents. Students joined architects and others on the campus committee to select the most environmentally friendly materials. The College has adopted a goal of achieving zero-discharge for eliminating waste materials. A campus-wide recycling program and a pesticide policy was initiated at Northland ten years ago, and an environmental energy audit is done once a year. The Environmental Council, a college-wide task force, is designed to serve as the vanguard of environmental consciousness on campus.

Lake Superior, the Apostle Islands, Chequamegon National Forest, and dozens of freshwater lakes offer a natural setting for field studies. Outdoor Education majors may spend a full semester at the Audubon Center of the North Woods. Academic adventures abroad provide in-depth exposure to international culture and environments. Examples include the study of rainforest ecology in Costa Rica, tropical lowland ecology of Mexico, the mammals of Kenya, and natural history of the Galapagos.

Northland students have interned with the Fish and Wildlife Service, the Department of Natural Resources, nature centers, the U. S. Forest Service, Great Lakes Indian Fish and Wildlife Service, Olson Environmental Institute, businesses, and other organizations. Students started a volunteer service organization on campus to work with groups in Ashland as well as a service-learning program.

Northland also trains regional school teachers for expanded emphasis on the environment in Wisconsin classrooms, and the Apostle Island School, a cooperative educational venture with elementary and middle schools.

At Northland, students participate in many outdoor activities and excursions, from sea kayaking and biking, to backpacking and cross country skiing. The outdoor orientation program for freshmen gives new students an opportunity to canoe or kayak, to study native woodland skills, or to participate in other small group outdoor experiences. The College also offers Wild Careers, a special week-long summer program for high school students wanting to explore environmental careers.

# MAKING A DIFFERENCE STUDIES

**Teacher Certification: Environmental Studies & Education (Grs. 1-9, 6-12), Native American Studies.**

Concepts of Biology
Environmental Public Policy
Sociology of the Environment
Ecology

Environmental Education Curriculum Review
Concepts of Earth Science
Environmental Law
Teaching Practicum

- **Environmental Citizenship** *Holistic investigation of what it might mean to live at peace with the earth, including philosophies, alternative lifestyles, and management skills necessary for participating in a democracy.*

## Environmental Studies: Social Sciences

Sustainable Development
Environmental Ethics
Public Administration
Applied Problem Solving
Native Peoples and Rainforests

Environmental History
Expository Writing
Internship
Economics of Citizenship
Global Resource Issues

## Environmental Studies: Natural Sciences

Environmental Modeling
Land and Water Use Planning
Land Forms
Dendrology

Concepts of Biology
Populations
Remote Sensing
Pollution Biology

## Environmental Studies: Humanities

Humanity and the Environment
Environmental Policy Analysis
Arctic Environments

Cultural Ecology
The Nature of Sound
Art in the Environment

## Native American Studies

*Program includes credit and non-credit courses, workshops, and technical assistance to residents of reservation communities.*

Introduction to Ojibway Language
Native American History to 1890
North American Indian Cultures
Native American Song and Dance
Native American World Views

Native American Cultures of Wisconsin
Native American History 1890 to Present
American Indian Literature
Native American Arts and Crafts
American Indian Law

- **Ethnobiology** *A study of native American beliefs and values regarding the natural environment. Use of plants and animals to meet basic needs, i.e. food, shelter, clothing, medicines, etc. The course is oriented toward field work and projects incorporating the traditional lifestyle of Native American people.*

## Government: Environmental Policy

Environmental Public Policy
Land and Water Use Planning
Sociology of the Environment
Environmental Ethics

Seminar in Environmental Law
Environmental Citizenship
Microeconomics
Policy Analysis Techniques

- **Global Resource Issues** *Analysis of growing human pressures on scarce resources and fragile ecosystems as a result of population increase, national public policy, and corporate policies — with special view to the potential for human conflict generated: e.g. by the oil crisis, desertification, and competition for minerals.*

## Natural Resources: Resource Management; Land & Water; Wildlife & Fish Ecology

Natural Resource Field Study
Woodland Plants
Environmental Impact Analysis
Land / Water Regulations

Wildlife Management
Intro to GIS
Aquatic Invertebrates

## Outdoor Education: Natural History; Special Populations; Native American; Recreation & Leisure Services; Adventure Education

*Teaching Assistantships, Field Activities, Outdoor Education Practicums*

Whitewater Canoeing
Orienteering
Group Process and Communication
Camp Counseling and Administration
Therapeutic Recreation Design
Basic Wilderness Skills
Urban Ecology

Rock Climbing
Introduction to Outdoor Education
Winter Exploration and Interpretation
Search and Rescue
Environmental Education Curriculum
Philosophy & Theory of Experiential Education
Ecological Ecosystem Interpretation - Nat. Science

## Conflict and Peacemaking

*Major has four components: Peace Strategies, Values & Ethics, Skills, and World Systems*

War, Peace and Global Issues
Environmental Citizenship
Theory and Practice of Nonviolence
Human Relations Workshop
Global Resource Issues
Social Change and Social Movements

Nuclear Age
Exploring Alternative Futures
Conflict Resolution
Sociology of the Third World
Group Process and Communication
Conflict and Peacemaking

## Government: Social Welfare Policy

Economics of Labor
Social Problems
Nature of Inequality
Social Change & Movements
Microeconomics
Global Resource Issues

Conflict Resolution
Crime, Deviance and Criminal Justice
Sociology of the Community
Population
Issues in Political Thought
Introduction to Public Administration

## Sociology/Anthropology

Cultural Ecology
Sociology of Community
Sociology of the Third World
Group Process & Communication
The Nature of Social Inequality

Human Conflict
Sociology of the Environment
Exploring Alternative Futures
Modern Japanese Social Thought
Social Change and Social Movements

### Forestry Dual Degree/Michigan Tech U    Government    Education

Apply by: 5/1    Avg. # of students in a first year classroom: 25-30
• Student environmental audits • Field studies • Individualized majors
• Service-learning • Team teaching • Theme housing • Interdisciplinary classes
• Optional SAT's • Non-resident degree program • Vegetarian & vegan meals

Director of Admissions
Northland College
1411 Ellis Ave.
Ashland, WI 54806

715. 682.1224
admit@wakefield.northland.edu
www.northland.edu

# OBERLIN COLLEGE

2,950 Students    Oberlin, Ohio

As long as there has been an Oberlin, Oberlinians have been changing the world. As an institution and as a community, Oberlin is characterized by a heady spirit of idealism. Do Oberlinians arrive with the conviction that a single person's efforts can have far-reaching effects, or does Oberlin instill this idealism in them? Most likely it is a combination of the two, one reinforcing the other. Whatever its source, the results of this idealism are dramatic. It impels Oberlinians to be open to new perspectives, to rethink their positions when necessary, to speak their minds, and to strive to make the world a better place. This spirit of idealism, this sense of conviction, unites the many different individuals in the Oberlin community. Students, faculty members, and alumni believe they can change the world.

What unifies this diverse and often opinionated group of students into a community of scholars? First, they are all extraordinarily committed to academic achievement. Second, their vision and progressive thinking — that Oberlin spirit of idealism — allows them to seize every opportunity as a learning experience. They educate one another on important issues and they work to solve problems on campus, in the community, and in the world. Their ongoing debate is evidence of their willingness to confront issues that society often chooses to ignore. Oberlin students put their idealism to work on a variety of issues. Reflecting Oberlin's traditional concern for the betterment of humanity, about 30% of Oberlin graduates work in the field of education. Alumni also stay close to important social causes.

Oberlin was the first coeducational college in the country. Three women graduated in 1841, becoming the first women in America to receive bachelor's degrees. The admission of women caused Oberlin to be the center of controversy over coeducation for years. Similarly, Oberlin decided to admit blacks in 1835 in exchange for financial backing by two wealthy abolitionists. As a result of this decision, by 1900 nearly half of all the black college graduates in the country - 128 to be exact - had graduated from Oberlin. To put it in even greater historical perspective, in 1835 the state of Ohio was still debating whether to allow blacks to attend elementary and secondary schools, while Southern states were drafting even stricter slave codes.

Once set on this progressive course, Oberlin became a center for abolitionism. The progressive impulse that inspired Oberlin's commitment to minorities and social justice in the 19th and 20th centuries spurred innovations in academic and campus life. Programs focusing on cultural diversity have been part of Oberlin's new-student orientations since the early 1980's. While Oberlin has never been a utopia, neither has it been willing to give up its quest for perfection. In 1991 Oberlin began requiring students to take at least nine credit hours in courses that deal with cultural diversity in order to graduate. Faculty members are also incorporating material on the environment, the experience of minorities and women, and other new areas into current courses, as well as developing new courses in these areas.

Freshman and sophomore colloquia are interdisciplinary, seminar style courses in which enrollment is limited to 10 first-year and five second-year students. This small size allows students to become familiar with the give-and-take nature of class discussions at the college level. Recent colloquia included "The Religious Thought of Mahatama Gandhi," "The Personal is Political: Representations of Activist Women in American History," "The Palestinian-Israeli Conflict," and "Explaining Social Power."

Students frequently work as research assistants for their professors. Biology students have assisted in research on the use of rock dust to remineralize soil and increase its fertility. Six students worked on a sociology survey investigating problems encountered by local low-income people. More than 350 Oberlin students particpated in a year-long planning process with architects and the wider Oberlin community to ensure that Oberlin's new Adam Josph Lewis Center for Environmental Studies would not only house environmental studies courses, but would itself embody the principles of environmentally sustainable architecture. The building is powered by sunlight and causes no discharge or disposal of toxic materials.

In keeping with Oberlin's tradition of community service and social activism, Oberlin formed a chapter of the Bonner Scholars Program on campus in 1992. The program provides scholarship funds to first generation and low-income students by providing the equivalent of a full work-study award to students who complete ten hours of community service per week during the school year.

Off-campus study is quite popular and, by graduation, about half of each class has spent at least one semester studying away from Oberlin. Nearly two dozen programs are available in countries such as Ireland, England, France, China, Kenya, Liberia, Nigeria, Sierra Leone, Japan, Costa Rica, Spain, India, and Scotland. The Mystic Seaport program, a wilderness program, and an urban planning and historic preservation program with Columbia university are among other options.

For members of the Oberlin Student Cooperative Association (OSCA), cooperative houses and dining rooms are as much a statement of political conviction as they are place to live and eat. OSCA, a student run business with a $1.6 million operating budget operates four room-and-board co-ops and four board-only co-ops on campus. Members emphasize the democratic nature of decision making in each co-op and in the organization as a whole. Working together also saves students money: the board fee charged by co-ops is about 30% less than that charged in College dining halls, and the fee for a double room was 15% less. Co-ops purchase food from local family farms and send work crews every week to help in harvesting on the farms.

Oberlin has more than 100 extra-curricular organizations. Some of the most popular are the various community service, environmental, human rights, multi-cultural and Lesbian/Gay/Bi-sexual groups.

Oberlin's Experimental College is a student-run organization which sponsors courses (for limited academic credit) taught by members of the community — faculty, students, administrators, and townspeople. Each year a very heterogeneous list of subjects is offered including crafts, special interests, community service, and academic subjects not found in the regular curriculum.

# MAKING A DIFFERENCE STUDIES

## Environmental Studies

Environment and Society
American Environmental History
Environmental Education Practicum
Environmental Economics
Organic Agriculture

American Environmental Policy
Ecology and the Environment
Energy Technology
Colloquium on Sustainable Agriculture
Conservation Biology

Environment, Current Destitution, Future Generations and Moral Responsibility

* **Oberlin and the Biosphere**  *Examines food, energy, water and materials flows, and waste management on the Oberlin campus; what enters and what leaves the campus community. Attention will be given to mines, wells, forest, farms, feedlots, dumps, smokestacks, outfall pipes, and alternative technologies and practices. Students participate in a joint research project.*

## Black Studies

Practicum in Black Journalism
Education in the Black Community
African-American Drama
Pan-African Political Perspective
African-American Women's History

West African Dance Forms in Diaspora
Modern African Literature
Traditional African Cosmology
Cinema and Society: Racial Stereotyping
Langston Hughes and the Black Aesthetic

## Women's Studies

The Challenge of Gender and Race
Experiences of Religious Women
Issues in Language and Sexuality
Gender, Race and Rhetoric of Science
The Emergence of Feminist Thought

Turning Points in Women's History
Nature and Statue of Women
Paid & Unpaid Work: Sexual Division of Labor
Power and Marginality: Women & Develop't
Women in the Transition from Socialism

Feminist Theory and Challenge of Third World Feminism

## Sociology

Community and Inequality
Urban Sociology
Gender Stratification
Race and Ethnic Relations
The City and Social Policy

Youth Subcultures, Movements & Politics
Revolution and Reform in Latin America
Sociology of the Black Community
State, Society & Social Change: Latin America
Social Change in Contemporary Societies

## Religion

Issues in Medical Ethics
Themes in Christian Ethics
Christian Social and Political Thought
Zen Buddhism
Mysticism in the West

Islamic Spirituality and Mysticism
History of African-American Relig. Experience
Religion and the Experience of Women
Taoism
Selected Topics in Early Judaism

Christian Utopias and Communitarian Movements

## History

Latinos in the U.S.
Roots of Feminist Analysis

Race, Class and Gender in the Southwest
History of Vietnam

Nourish or Punish? Ideologies of Poverty in 18th and 19th Century England
Caribbean History: Slaves and Slavery in the New World
Peasant Movements and the Agrarian Condition in Latin America

## Economics

Poverty and Affluence
Labor Economics
Economic Development in Latin America
Economics of Discrimination

Public Sector Economics: Health Care Policy
Environmental Economics
Environmental & Resource Economics
Econ. of Land, Location & the Environment

- **Introduction to Political Economy** *Economic problems of unemployment, inflation, the distribution of income & wealth, and the allocation of resources. The basic tools of analysis for studying these problems are developed and the role of public policy in securing economic objectives is explored.*

## Politics

Political Change in America
Government and Politics of Africa
Public Policy in America
Emergence of Feminist Thought
Political Economy of Women in Late Industrializing States

Federal Courts and the Environment
Urban Politics
Third World Political Economics
Nuclear Weapons and Arms Control

## Law & Society

Philosophy and Values
Christian Social & Political Thought
Economics, Ethics and Values
Equal Protection of the Law
Moral Problems in Relig. Perspective

Social & Political Philosophy
Deviance, Discord and Dismay
Reproductive Biology in the 80's
Individual Responsibility
Turning Points: American Women's History

## Latin American Studies

Folklore and Culture of Latin America
Dirty Wars and Democracy
Hispanics in American Politics
Revolution and Reform in Latin Amer.
Latin American History: Conquest and Colonialization

Economic Development in Latin America
State, Society and Social Change
Int'l. Political Economy / North-South Relations
Female and Male in Latin American History

## Anthropology

Native American Literature
Immigration and Ethnicity in US
Immigration and Ethnicity in Israel
Ancient Civilizations of New World

Engendering the Past
Ideology, Power and Prehistory
Jewish Society and Culture in Middle East
Anthropology of Sub-Saharan Africa

### Third World Studies     East Asian Studies

Apply by 1/15
50%+ of students engaged in community service    Avg. # of students in a first year classroom: 20
- Internships    • Interdisciplinary classes    • Theme housing
- Self-designed majors    • Student environmental audits    • Vegetarian & vegan meals

Admissions Office
Carnegie Building
Oberlin College
101 Professor Street
Oberlin, OH 44074

800. 622.OBIE
216. 775.8411
college.admissions@oberlin.edu
www.oberlin.edu

# OHIO WESLEYAN UNIVERSITY

1,850 Students    Delaware, Ohio

Ohio Wesleyan is a dynamic liberal arts university that seeks to prepare students for informed, ethical, productive, and satisfying lives in the world community. The University strives to maintain an environment that both challenges and supports: that encourages individuals while it respects diverse opinion, that promotes personal growth and demands social responsibility, and that links today's learning with tomorrow's possibilities. The goal of Ohio Wesleyan is to prepare young men and women to know what they believe and why they believe it.

Since its founding in 1842, Ohio Wesleyan has been a leader in values-centered education, a place where public service and community leadership are the natural outcomes of an outstanding academic experience. The core of the academic program is its professors: distinguished scholars, accomplished teachers, and dedicated mentors.

Ohio Wesleyan links liberal arts learning with the civic arts of citizenship. The academic program and co-curricular life work together, fostering students' awareness of their role as responsible citizens of society. "National Colloquium" involves the entire University community in a semester-long examination of a complex public issue. Past topics have included racism, population and the environment, ethics and health care.

Ohio Wesleyan's unusually broad curriculum blends traditional classroom learning with hands-on experience through research, independent study, internships, and off-campus experience. Involvement is the theme of co-curricular life: from student political groups and media operations to athletics and intramurals; from the Environment and Wildlife Club to Amnesty International; from "improv" theater and modern dance to religious groups and a respected Greek system.

Public service is an Ohio Wesleyan tradition. Each year an extraordinary percentage of the student body participates in some form of community service. "Leadership for Tomorrow," a seven-week series of workshops, helps students develop and refine leadership skills in organizational and personal areas of their lives. Students try to "leave the woodpile a little higher than we found it." Most years, some students spend spring-break working in health clinics in the Dominican Republic, learning about Third World poverty, neocolonial economics, and health delivery systems. Recently Ohio Wesleyan was one of only 16 organizations in the country selected to host a Summer of Service project in the Clinton administration's National Service Program.

Fully 18 percent of Ohio Wesleyan students are either U.S. minorities or foreign students. This multicultural presence is a source of enrichment for all members of the community. OWU also participates in an exchange program with predominantly black Spelman College and Morehouse College in Georgia. Cross cultural understanding is further enhanced in the residential area. Among the "small living units" are the House of Black Culture, Women's House, and the Peace and Justice House.

Students graduate from Ohio Wesleyan with heightened awareness of world issues and a commitment to put their skills, insights, and concern for others to work in the world.

# MAKING A DIFFERENCE STUDIES

## Environmental Studies

Ecology and the Future of Man
Ornithology
Environmental Plant Biology
Economic Geography
Human Ecology

Plant Communities and Ecosystems
Environmental Chemistry
Biology and Tropical Nations
Technology & Environmental Ethics
Marine Biology

- **Island Biology** *Characteristics of islands and analysis of why island organisms provide superior examples for the study of evolutionary, ecological, and behavioral phenomena. This course includes a required trip to the Galapagos Islands.*

## Politics and Government

Civil Rights and Liberties
Judicial Process and Policy-Making
Democracy & Its Critics
American Political Thought
Global Issues: Human Rights, Terrorism, Arms & Arms Control

American Politics & The Mass Media
Equality and American Politics
Public Administration
Public Opinion and Political Behavior

## Sociology/Anthropology

Crime and Deviance
Race and Ethnicity
Science and Society
Gender in Cross-Cultural Perspective
Population Problems

Peoples and Cultures of Africa
Peoples and Cultures of the Pacific
Health and Illness
Magic, Witchcraft and Religion
Social Inequality  Self and Society

## Economics

National Income and Business Cycles
Comparative Urban Economics
Economic Development
Introduction to Game Theory
Public Finance

Economic History
International Economics
Labor Economics and Problems
Monetary and Fiscal Economics
The Economic Growth of Modern Japan

## Women's Studies

Literary Perspectives on Women
Women in Antiquity
Women in American History
Psychology of Women

Gender and Identity
Gender in American Society
Philosophy and Feminism
Gender in Cross-Cultural Perspective

- **Sociology of Feminism**    *Liberal, Radical, Socialist Feminism, Third World & Lesbian Feminism. Under/un-paid labor, rape & violence against women, women's self-help movement.*

## Urban Studies

Population Problems
Economic Geography
Contemporary Amer. Landscape Problems
Urban Society

Comparative Urban Economics
The World's Cities
Technology and Environmental Ethics
Judicial Process and Policy Making

Apply by 3/1
• Internships  • Study abroad  • Individualized majors  • Combined degree program

Director of Admissions
Ohio Wesleyan University
Delaware, OH 43015

800. 862.0612 (in Ohio)
800. 922.8953 (outside Ohio)

**Audubon Expedition Institute's** unique field studies program takes students on extended bus tours to different regions of the country. (See travel section.)

**Goddard College** equally values internal knowing (through such practices as yoga) and external action in the world. Goddard is a place for hard thinking and plain living.

**Grinnell's** commitment to social responsibility has been a large part of its history. Students are encouraged to link community service to their academic interests. Here students raise money to help the needy.

**Prescott College** students design their own majors - from natural history to outdoor experiential education and environmental conservation - and many take advantage of the college's Southwest location.

# UNIVERSITY OF OREGON

17,250 Undergraduates    Eugene, Oregon

In the September/October 1996 issue of Mother Jones magazine, the University of Oregon ranked first in a list of activist campuses in the United States. Why? The UO produces more Peace Corps volunteers than any American university its size and ranks 15th overall nationwide. The UO was also the top school in the nation in voter registration for the 1996 presidential election. UO students are making a difference.

Recognized nationally and internationally as a research university committed to liberal arts and sciences education as well as professional preparation, the University of Oregon offers students more than 100 comprehensive programs, including professional schools of architecture, business, education, journalism, and music. Open discussion, exploration, questioning, and sharing information are what the UO values. If you're curious, open-minded, and willing to challenge yourself, you'll love it here.

The UO has developed innovative programs to ensure that its undergraduates have access to seminars, discussion groups, and other small-class settings encouraging direct interaction with the institution's finest teachers and researchers. Freshman Interest Groups (FIGs), for example, create social support groups based on academic interests, by placing participating freshmen in small-class settings with students who have similar interests or majors. Freshman Seminars are small, discussion-oriented classes that allow freshmen to sample what's available academically at the University of Oregon—putting our most respected professors in touch with our newest students.

More than 250 student-run organizations and activities enhance students' educational experiences outside the classroom. The Solar Information Center (SIC), for example, promotes a higher awareness of the importance of conservation and renewable energy. SIC sponsors a quarterly lecture series on local, regional, and global energy issues and publishes a quarterly newsletter. The Institute for a Sustainable Environment fosters research and education on environmental issues at the University of Oregon. The Institute's programs encompass environmental themes in the natural sciences, the social sciences, policy studies, humanities, and the professional fields. Because environmental problems are seldom adequately addressed by a single discipline, the Institute is particularly concerned with encouraging cross-disciplinary environmental research, education, and public service. Other student-run groups — such as OSPIRG (Oregon Student Public Interest Research Group), Students for Government Integrity, and the award-winning Student Recycling Program — allow students to work together towards creating a better world.

Education continues beyond the borders of the Eugene campus. Students can participate in internships or community service experiences within the Eugene/Springfield community or travel abroad through one of the University's nearly 70 overseas study/international exchange programs. The University also has two off-campus facilities: the Pine Mountain Observatory and the Oregon Institute of Marine Biology (OIMB). OIMB, situated on 107 acres of coastal property along Coos Bay, offers an interdisciplinary course encompassing marine ecology, marine mammals and birds, and biological oceanography, as well as opportunities for individualized study.

University of Oregon's more than 170,000 graduates include leaders in business (Charles Lillis of Media One), journalism (Ann Curry, of NBC's "The Today Show," and Randy Shilts, author of *And the Band Played On* and *Conduct Unbecoming*), education, science, and the arts (Ken Kesey, author of *One Flew Over the Cuckoo's Nest*). Three Pulitzer Prize winners, two Nobel Prize winners, six U.S. senators, and six Oregon governors are also among UO's distinguished alumni.

The University of Oregon is located in Eugene (pop. 126,500), a city known for its commitment to individuality, in the heart of the Willamette Valley. Both the Willamette and McKenzie rivers run right through town, and are bordered by 250 miles of bike paths and running trails. The Pacific Ocean is one hour west; snow-covered peaks are one hour east. The student-run Outdoor Program organizes trips to these and many other beautiful destinations between and beyond. Program activities include biking, hiking, kayaking, mountaineering, and windsurfing.

## MAKING A DIFFERENCE STUDIES

### Architecture: Landscape and Interior Architecture
*All are five-year programs subscribing to the concepts of green architecture and sustainability.*

Architectural Form and Urban Quality
Hydrology and Water Resources
Natural Resource Policy
Solar Heating
Passive Cooling

Housing in Society
Landscape Preservation
Preservation and Restoration Technology
Urban Farm
Settlement Patterns: Japanese Vernacular

### Planning, Public Policy & Management: Planning & Community Development; Social Policy Development; Resource Development & Environmental Mgm't.

Communities and Regional Development
Environmental Health
Managing Fiscal Austerity
Energy Policy and Planning
Planning & the Changing Family

Contemporary Housing Issues
Planning in Developing Countries
Managing Nonprofit Organizations
Neighborhood and Community Revitalization
Planning and Social Change

### Environmental Studies

American Environmental History
Conservation Biology
Environmental Politics
Population Ecology
Urban Geography

Solar Heating
Architectural Form and Urban Quality
Community, Environment, and Society
Gender and International Development

### Ethnic Studies

Asian Americans and the Law
Intro to the Asian American Experience
Intro to the Native American Experience

Chicanos and the Law
Intro to the Chicano and Latino Experience
Minority Women: Issues and Concerns

### Peace Studies

American Radicalism
Political Ideologies

Political Geography
Systems of War and Peace

## International Studies

Aid to Developing Countries
International Protection of Human Rights
Population and Global Resources
Global Ecology
International Community Development
Anthropological Perspectives on Health & Illness

Environmental Planning
Introduction to World Value Systems
Rich & Poor Nations: Conflict & Cooperation
Ethnology of Tribal Societies

## Education

Cultural Diversity in Human Services
Family Policy
Innovative Education
Mental Health
Self as Resource

Change in Educational and Social Systems
Community Organization and Social Planning
Interventions with Individuals and Families
Learning Environments for Diverse Students
Professional Communication & Collaboration

## Women's Studies

Global Feminisms
Lesbian and Gay Studies
Postcolonial Women Writers

Feminist Perspectives: Identity, Race, Culture
History and Development of Feminist Theory
Sexuality

## Human Services

Issues and Policies in Human Services
Mind and Society
Family Policy
Child Welfare Services
Cultural Diversity in Human Services

Innovative Education
Organizational Intervention
Mental Health
Prevention Strategies
Community Organization & Social Planning

## Journalism

The Mass Media and Society
Women, Minorities, and Media
Communications Law
Media Management and Economics
Cultural Approaches to Communication

Advertising as a Social Institution
Journalism and Public Opinion
Third World Development Communications
Mass Media Ethics
International Journalism

**Outdoor Pursuits Leadership    Burmese, Thai, Indonesian Languages**

Apply by 2/1    Faculty: 58% male, 42% female
Avg. # of students in a first year class: 26
• Interdisciplinary classes & majors    • Co-op work study    • Team teaching    • Theme housing
• Self-designed majors    • Student environmental audits    • Vegetarian & vegan  meals

Office of Admissions
240 Oregon Hall
University of Oregon
Eugene, OR 97403

541. 346.3201
800. BE-A-DUCK
uoadmit@darkwing.uoregon.edu
www.uoadmit.uoregon.edu

# PENN STATE UNIVERSITY

59,700 undergraduates at 17 campuses    Rural Central PA.

Penn State, founded in 1855 and designated Pennsylvania's land-grant university in 1863, is irrevocably dedicated to a threefold mission of teaching, research, and public service. Even though the idea of the land-grant university — higher education in service to the public good — dates to Abraham Lincoln's time, Penn State and its sister institutions across the nation are constantly finding new ways to make land-grant ideals relevant in a constantly changing world. At Penn State, this idealism, rooted in practicality and the wisdom of experience, remains a great attraction to today's students.

Penn State's enrollment makes it one of America's 10 largest universities, but it was one of seventeen public institutions cited as attractive alternates to Ivy League schools for academic quality and ambience in Richard Moll's *Public Ivys*. One reason for this popularity is that teaching has remained central to the University's mission.

Penn State's University Scholars Program offers unusually flexible and rigorous courses of study for students at all Penn State locations and in all majors. Students have all the benefits of a small, selective, private college, and the resources of a major research university. The program believes that those with special talents have special obligations to others. The program offers seminars and workshops on topics of service, leadership, and travel grants, and provides support for exemplary student-initiated projects that enhance communities and/or the moral ecology. Scholars may also take advantage of summer and service/learning programs that carry academic credit. These activities offer experiences in cultures around the world to students who are, at the same time, making a real contribution to local communities. Experiences include international work camps, helping a Mexican village build a basketball court at a community center, and projects organized in consultation with Native American organizations.

The College of Agricultural Sciences is involved in teaching and programs in such far-flung locations as Egypt, Kenya, Poland, Swaziland, and Ukraine. Students in an interdisciplinary minor in international agriculture (INTAG), gain an awareness of and an appreciation for the interrelationships and interdependence of the nations of the world, find out what resources are available to solve international problems, study the impact of technology transfer across cultures, and acquire skills in development work.

Shaver's Creek Environmental Center offers environmental studies and an interpretation laboratory. The Center promotes positive attitudes about the Earth, provides opportunities for experiential learning and research, and encourages individual and group development. It is the only center that holds both federal and state licenses to use birds of prey in its public education program.

Engineering education, one of Penn State's traditional strengths, is also more diverse than one might assume. The Minority Engineering Program recruits, and works to retain, underrepresented minority students. The Women in Engineering Program aids in recruiting and retaining women in engineering programs at Penn State, and assists in creating a more positive environment for women students.

# MAKING A DIFFERENCE STUDIES

## Human Development & Family Studies

Communities and Families
Family Development
Infant and Child Development
Biocultural Studies of Family Organization
Personal and Interpersonal Skills

The Helping Relationship
Observation with Pre-School Children
Adolescent Development
Policy and Planning for Human Development
Adult-Child Relationships

## Health Policy & Administration

Health Services Organization
Health Services Policy Issues
Health Systems Management
Principles of Public Health Administration
Field Experience in Health Planning

Intro to Environmental Health
Health Care & Medical Needs
Health Planning Methods
Population and Policy Issues
Comparative Health Systems

## Community Studies

Community Systems
Social and Behavioral Change
Environment, Energy & Society
Comparative Community Development
Issues in Community Physical Design

Youth and Societies
Housing Problems & Policies
Evaluation of Community Service Programs
Power, Conflict & Community Decision Making
Planning of Community Social Services

## Educational Theory and Policy

Education in American Society
Global Education
Education and Status of Women
Ethnic Minorities and Schools in U.S.
Intro to Philosophy of Education

Introduction to Comparative Education
Education in Socialist Societies
Education in Latin America and Caribbean
Anthropology of Education
Education in Africa

## Labor and Industrial Relations

Industrial Relations
Practice of Collective Bargaining
History of the American Worker
Collective Bargaining Trends
History of American Organized Labor

Employment Relationship: Law and Policy
Women, Minorities and Employment
Labor-Management Relations
Occupational Health: Policy and Practice
Industrial Psychology

## Public Service

Public Finance
Regional Economics
Urban Geography
Community Organization

Economics of Public Expenditures
Housing Problems and Policies
Planning and Public Policy
Urban Sociology

## Architectural Engineering

Solar Energy Building System Design
Environmental Systems in Building

Solar Passive Design & Energy Conservation.
Soils Engineering

**Enviro Ed. Teacher Certificate   Medical Anthro.   Forestry   Health Education
Rehabilitation Services   Agronomy   Wildlife & Fisheries   Science, Tech. & Society**
Rolling admissions

Undergraduate Admissions Office        814. 865.5471
201 Shields Building                   admissions@psu.edu
Penn State University                  www.psu.edu
University Park, PA 16802-1294

# PITZER COLLEGE

850 Students    Claremont, California

Founded in 1963, Pitzer is a coeducational liberal arts college with a progressive educational philosophy. Enrolling approximately 850 men and women, Pitzer College is part of a uniquely stimulating higher education environment consisting of five schools known collectively as the Claremont Colleges. Together, these Colleges bring a vast range of courses and facilities to Pitzer students. Indeed, students on this campus have the best of two worlds — enjoying a level of resources usually associated with mid-sized universities together with the close student-faculty relationships found within small, human-scale colleges.

Pitzer College offers no short cuts to intellectual discovery, no guarantees as to the kind of person you'll be when you graduate. It does, however, offer a setting rich in possibilities, and if Pitzer graduates are more creative, more independent of spirit, and more willing to seek new answers, then it could be that the opportunities unique to Pitzer helped to make them this way. Because of Pitzer's curricular strengths, it tends to attract students that concern themselves with the critical social and political issues facing our world. Most students arrive at Pitzer already committed to various social or political issues. Once at the College, they're encouraged to develop these interests to a greater degree; to take them further and test them harder. But mostly, the ideals that bring people to Pitzer continue to guide them after graduation. A Pitzer graduate who becomes a lawyer is as likely to use those skills in the public defender's office as in a corporate law firm. The graduate who goes on to earn an M.B.A. may opt not to work on Wall Street, choosing instead to help run a foundation raising money to fight a deadly disease.

Pitzer presents a unique opportunity for exploration of the self, the world around us, and our involvement in that world. The College believes that students should take an active part in formulating their individualized plans of study, bringing a spirit of inquiry and adventure to the process of academic planning. Rather than enforcing traditional requirements, Pitzer provides the following guidelines to students and faculty advisors in order that students will fulfill the College's educational goals:

• Breadth of Knowledge: By exploring broadly the programs in humanities and fine arts, natural sciences and mathematics, and the social and behavioral sciences, students develop understanding of the nature of the human experience — its complexity, its diversity of expression, its continuities and discontinuities over space and time, and of those conditions which limit and liberate it.

• Understanding in Depth: Through the study of a particular subject in depth, students experience the kind of mastery which makes informed and independent judgment possible.

• Critical Thinking, Formal Analysis, and Effective Expression: Through juxtaposing and evaluating the ideas of others, and through participation in various styles of research, Pitzer students develop their capacities for critical judgment. Through exploration of mathematical and other formal systems, students acquire the ability to think in abstract, symbolic ways. Through written and oral communication, students acquire the ability to express their ideas effectively.

- Interdisciplinary Perspective: By bringing together the perspectives of several disciplines, students gain an understanding of the powers and limits of each discipline and of the kind of contribution each can make to an exploration of the significant issues. Pitzer wants its students to learn the differences and the connections between different disciplines, as well as developing the ability to look at a situation from different perspectives.

- Intercultural Understanding: By learning about their own culture and placing it in comparative perspective, students come both to appreciate other cultures and to recognize the ways that their own thinking and actions are influenced by the culture in which they live.

- Concern with the Social Consequences and Ethical Implications of Knowledge and Action: By examining the social consequences and ethical implications of the issues they explore, students learn to evaluate the effects of individual actions and social policies and to take responsibility for making the world in which we live a better place.

Since its founding in 1963, Pitzer College has committed itself to educating students to be effective and responsible citizens of communities organized at a local or global level. Such citizenship is fostered through the effective engagement of our students in local communities, in conjunction with a strong theoretical and applied curriculum. The Center for California Cultural and Social issues is the institutional structure through which we support community-based research efforts, build new research out of our internship and field-based courses, and allow for assessment of these programs. The Center provides research and project awards to both faculty and students to facilitate innovative work.

Because of the emphasis on classroom teaching and a student-faculty ratio of 12 to1, students and teachers are colleagues in the educational process; faculty do not draw a hierarchical distinction between themselves and the students. The average class size is 18 students and, to facilitate discussion, is often taught in seminars rather than lectures.

Internships are a popular way to apply theories to practical experience, and many Pitzer students have begun fulfilling careers through the internship program. Internships affirm Pitzer's commitment to connecting knowledge and action, and provide opportunities to link students to social issues in Los Angeles communities — thus developing feelings of social responsibility. Independent study allows students to create a curriculum that meets their individual needs and goals. Through this program, students work individually with faculty to create a course and to work through the materials.

External programs in over 100 locations throughout the U.S.A. and abroad have become a part of the curriculum for the majority of Pitzer students. With programs offered in China, Ecuador, Italy, Nepal, Turkey Venezuela, Wales, and Zimbabwe, as well as an urban studies program in Ontario, California, Pitzer's External Studies program goes far beyond the traditional. The program provides students with opportunities for intensive language study, internships, independent research, homestays, and significant interaction with peoples of other cultures.

# MAKING A DIFFERENCE STUDIES

## Environmental Studies

*Environmental Studies can provide an integrated, unifying perspective on life, as well as a program for radical change.*

Chemistry and the Environment
Environmental Arts and Action
Environments Workshop
Environmental Policy
Plants and People
Ethnoecology
Reading and Painting the Landscapes

Ecology, Human Rights and Development
The Desert as a Place
Enviro. Awareness & Responsible Action
Theory & Practice of Environmental Education
Off the Mother Road
Population and Society

- **Consciousness, Environment & Self: Multicultural Perspectives** *How perception of the natural environment, self, and society result in different ways of knowing the world. Notion of "consciousness" as reflected in diverse spiritual, social, and political forms and practices. How "western" & "eastern" perspectives differ, but also coalesce.*

## Freshman Seminars

At Your Service
Crossing Borders
Living Emma Goldman's Life
The Family East and West
Us vs. Them: The Role of Ethnicity in Modern Politics

Contemporary Economic Issues
Deconstructing Disney
Oppression and Marginalization
Science & the Rationalization of Racism & Sexism

## American Studies

Native Americans & Their Environments
Sociology of Popular Culture
Mall, Movies and Museums: The Public Sphere of Modern America

Women of the Historic American West
Sociology of the Family

## Asian Studies

Applied Asian American Psychology
Asian American Women's Experience
(Mis)Representations of Asian and Asian Americans

Asian American Experiences
Intro to Asian American Experience

## Black Studies

African and Caribbean Literature
Blacks in American Politics
Race, Class, and Power
Survey in African American Fiction
Industrialization & Social Change in Southern Africa

Black Women, Feminism and Social Change
History of African American Women in U.S.
Pan-Africanism and Black Radical Traditions
The Politics of Race

## Chicano Studies

Introduction to Chicano Studies
Latino Politics
Contemporary Issues of Chicanas & Latinas

Latinas in the Garment Industry
Applied Community Psych. in Latino Populations

## Science, Technology and Society

Mathematics in Many Cultures
Media and Society
Science & Technology in the Modern World
Scientific Explanation

Mathematics, Philosophy & the Real World
Philosophy of Science
Science, Technology and Politics
Sociology of Health and Medicine

## Media Studies

Anarchy and the Internet
Documentary Media
Imagined Communities
Language of Film

China & Japan Through Film and Ethnography
Feminist Documentary and Production
Intro to Latin American Literature and Film
Mexican Film History

- **Women and Film**   *An investigation of both the oppressive and oppositional potential of the fiction film as it either captures or constructs cultural understandings of women's sexuality, agency and identity. This introduction to feminist film theory and scholarship will consider the representation of women in a variety of classic Hollywood film genres as well as how women represent themselves in both Hollywood and avant garde film and video.*

## Gender and Feminist Studies

Feminist Political Thought
Religion in Medieval East Asia
Whitman and Dickinson
Women of Color in the US

Politics of Gender
Violence in Intimate Relationships
Women in the Third World
Women of the Historic American West

## Organizational Studies

China and Japan: Economy and Society
Labor Internships
Political Psychology
Sociology of Work and Occupations

Economic Development
Manufacturing Tales
Social Responsibility and the Corporation

- **Human Resource Management & Organizational Analysis**   *Explores contemporary issues related to the human side of organizations. Examine practices and beliefs present in the field today. In addition, the local and global  ramifications resulting from changes seen in the working environment will be highlighted*

## Political Economy

International Political Economy
Public Choice
Third World and the Global Economy
State and Development in the Third World

Agricultural Development in the Third World
Politics of Water
Issues of Int'l. Trade Development Policy

## International and Intercultural Studies

The World Since 1492
Culture and Power
The Third World & the Global Economy
Progress & Oppression: Ecology, Human Rights, & Development
Chinese Philosophy, Culture & Traditional Medicine
Theory and Practice of Resistance to Monoculture: Gender, Spirituality, and Power

Nature, Movement & Meditation in Qigong
African Politics and Society: Zimbabwe
Ecology and Culture Change

Apply By 2/1

Student body: 30% minority     Faculty: 64% male, 56% female, 28% minority
Average # of students in first year classroom: 18
Full recycling and energy conservation programs in effect since founding of college in 1963
- All seminar format   - Self-designed majors   - Field studies   - Study abroad
- Team teaching   - Multidisciplinary classes   - Vegetarian meals

Office of Admission
Pitzer College
1050 North Mills Ave.
Claremont, CA 91711

909. 621.8129
800. 748-9371
admission@pitzer.edu
www.pitzer.edu/

# PORTLAND STATE UNIVERSITY

10, 215 Undergraduates    Portland, Oregon

Portland State University (PSU) is Oregon's only urban public university and is defined by its relationship with the community. PSU is committed to the delivery of quality academic programs for undergraduates and graduates. These programs are integrated with a campus-wide commitment to community service, and to collaborative strategies linking faculty and students in learning and research experiences that bear directly on the problems and opportunities of the community and state.

Portland State has won praise from scholars nationwide by replacing its traditional general education requirements with an inquiry-based interdisciplinary undergraduate program that meets the needs of today's students. The undergraduate experience at PSU offers many of the advantages found at small selective private schools, but at the price of a public university. The general education program, called University Studies, is designed to facilitate the acquisition of the knowledge, abilities, and attitudes which will form a foundation for lifelong learning among its students. This foundation includes the capacity and the propensity to engage in critical thinking, to use various forms of communication for learning and expression, to gain an awareness of the broader human experience and its environment, and to appreciate the responsibilities of persons to themselves, each other, and to their communities.

Freshmen and Sophomores enroll as small groups in interdisciplinary inquiry courses each taught by teams of five faculty, facilitated by peer mentors, and supported by dedicated high tech classrooms and labs. Upper division students enroll in clusters of theme-related courses that offer in-depth learning as well as advanced skill development in communication, information technologies, group work, and research. Many of the inquiry and cluster courses contain elements of service learning. The general education program culminates in a two-term six-credit Senior Capstone course. These students are organized in small interdisciplinary teams to apply and interpret their undergraduate learning experience in a community-setting focused on a real-life issue. The capstone also offers an opportunity to connect with potential employers and gain work experience, while addressing a priority need of the community.

Service learning is also integrated into many courses in the majors; more than 200 courses at PSU involve some aspect of community-based learning. One example is the Center for Columbia River History, which engages undergrads in history and related research disciplines and educational programs to enhance understanding of River Basin history. Using folklore, geology, literature, history, economics etc, the project asks small Oregon communities to focus on changes since the big dams were built.

PSU offers thirty-two bachelor's degrees in Arts and Sciences, Business Administration, Education, Engineering and Applied Science, Fine and Performing Arts, Social work, Urban and Public Affairs, and Extended Studies.

Located around a tree-lined city park in downtown Portland, PSU offers access to jobs, shopping, sporting and cultural events, and relatively low-cost housing. The campus has strong connections with its immediate neighborhood and the University district is becoming a model urban community with a blend of retail, business, housing, education, recreation, and transportation services.

# MAKING A DIFFERENCE STUDIES

## Community Development:

## Community Organization & Change/Housing & Economic Development

*One of only a few undergrad programs nationwide in the growing field of community development. Trains citizen activists and professionals empowered to take leadership roles in public affairs. Interdisciplinary approach includes anthropology, communications, cultural studies, ecology, environmental studies, history, political economy, social psychology, and urban design.*

Methods of Community Development
Probability and Statistics
Urban Economics
Housing Development
Communication in Groups

Theory & Philosophy of Community Devlp't
Sophomore Inquiry in Community Studies
Downtown Revitalization
Neighborhood Conservation & Change
Afro-American Community Development

## Environmental Studies: Environmental Science & Environmental Policy

Science and Policy Considerations
Institutions and Public Change
Environmental Ethics
Culture and Ecology
Soils and Land Use

Environmental Risk Assessment
Environmental Economics
Urbanism and Urbanization
Groundwater Geology
Epidemiology of Cancer

## Child and Family Studies

*Collaboratively designed by faculty and professionals in cooperation with community agencies*

Child in Society
Anthropology of the Family
Preparation for Early Intervention Settings
Child Psychology
Interdisciplinary Perspectives on Children & Families

Family in Society
Admin. of Programs for Children & Families
Health Promotion Programs: Children & Youth
Survey of Exceptional Learners

## Geography

The Developing World
Urban Geography
Resource Management
Hydrology
Water Resource Management

Geography of Portland
Problem of World Population & Food Supply
Biogeography
Metropolitan Economic Geography
Cultural Geography

## Health Education: Community Health/Health & Fitness Promotion

Drug Education
Emotional Health
Stress Management
Principles of Environmental Health
Communicable Diseases and Chronic Health Problems

Foundations of Health Education
Epidemiology
Determinants of Health Behavior
Planning & Evaluation: Health Educ. Programs

### Environmental Engineering (Minor)    Women's Studies    International Studies
### Anthropology    Psychology    Sociology

Student body: 55% transfer, 17% minority      Apply By: 6/1
• Interdisciplinary classes    • Team teaching    • Over 200 classes with service learning (all majors)

Office of Admissions
POB 751
Portland State University
Portland, OR 97207-0751

503. 725.3511
askadm@osa.pdx.edu
www.pdx.edu

# PRESCOTT COLLEGE

500 Students    Prescott, Arizona

It is the mission of Prescott College to educate students of diverse ages and backgrounds to understand, thrive in, and enhance our world community and environment. Reality and intelligence are culturally relative. Prescott College regards learning as a continuing process and strives to provide an education enabling students to live productive lives while achieving a balance between self-fulfillment and service to others. Students are encouraged to think critically, with a sensitivity to the human community and the ethics of the biosphere.

A liberal arts college with a very strong environmental component, the College's broad academic program utilizes classroom work, independent studies, library research, and field studies. Students are expected to demonstrate competence in individually-designed study programs and to possess two breadths of knowledge beyond their major area of study. Prescott's educational philosophy stresses experiential learning and self-direction within an interdisciplinary curriculum. Programs integrate philosophy, theory, and practice so that students can synthesize the knowledge and skills to confront important value issues and make personal commitments.

In addition, the College expects its graduates to demonstrate: integration of the practical and theoretical aspects of human existence; integration of the spiritual, emotional, and intellectual aspects of the human personality; sensitivity to and understanding of one's own and other cultures; and commitment to responsible participation in the natural environment and human community.

Prescott College's programs and process are individualized in ways that reward the student personally and intellectually. Since learning takes place in different ways for different people, education at the College is self-directed. Prescott College wants its students to be problem-solvers by the time they graduate; therefore students are introduced to real, often original, problems with all their accompanying complexity and frustration. The College also wants its students to know how to adapt in a changing world.

Beginning students usually participate in introductory classes or structured field projects, working closely with faculty members and other students. Small classes promote participation and allow for flexibility to meet individual interests and needs. As students demonstrate their ability to assume increased responsibility they pursue a broader range of learning experiences, and emphasis is placed on internships and independent studies. Students may serve in apprentice relationships with faculty, often serving as assistant teachers, co-researchers, and expedition leaders.

Many of the courses at Prescott College have strong field components, and some are conducted entirely in the field. Students may live and study in a cultural context outside their normal experience. One-month blocks allow for intense immersion in one course — often entirely in the field — whether it be a fishing village in Mexico, the alpine meadows of Wyoming, or a local social service clinic.

Prescott College helps students become impassioned learners, sensitive listeners, practical idealists, and entrepreneurial leaders. The College believes that the following facets of education are crucial:

- A close relationship with faculty members in which learning is achieved through personal exchange, sharing, and commitment;
- Small classes designed with student participation, in which teachers continually challenge students to articulate their beliefs in speech and writing;
- Independent studies and projects — working with a supportive advisor to plan, accomplish, and evaluate a significant endeavor;
- An interdisciplinary approach to learning where students are challenged to construct complex understandings of real-life situations rather than simplistic, monolithic, rote understandings;
- Experiential, adventurous learning in the real world where students also learn responsibility, appropriate risk-taking, group leadership, and collaborative skills.

Examples of independent studies completed by Prescott College students include: Ethnographic Field Study in Mexico, Deep Ecology Through Literature, Native Alaskan Cultural Studies, Multicultural Education, and Developing Sustainable Communities. Internships have included work with Woodswomen in Minnesota; working with the Arizona Nature Conservancy performing restoration ecology and conservation; working with the Caribbean Conservation Corps in Costa Rica; and doing mountain search and rescue in Denali National Park, Alaska.

Three off-campus field sites complement the Prescott facilities: the Rim Institute, Wolfberry Farm, and the Kino Bay Center. The Rim Institute is located on 24 forested acres in the Mogollon Rim area of the Tonto National Forest at an elevation of 6,300 feet. The College utilizes the Rim Institute to provide a viable curriculum dedicated to the themes of personal growth, spiritual renewal, and planetary healing, and incorporating the arts, human development, and environmental education.

About 15 miles north of Prescott, the College has acquired 30 acres of land to develop a farm dedicated to education, demonstration, and research in Agroecology. Wolfberry Farm serves as the outdoor classroom for the summer program in Agroecology as well as a place where students can carry out independent studies and senior projects.

The Kino Bay Center is located in Kino Bay, Mexico, on the Sea of Cortez. This field station is used for a variety of courses such as Coastal and Cultural Ecology of Kino Bay, A Sense of Place, Field Methods for Intertidal Ecology, and Marine Conservation. The Center also serves as a launching point for sea kayaking courses and as a meeting place for many Mexican and American researchers.

# MAKING A DIFFERENCE STUDIES

## Environmental Studies

*Students have designed majors in Environmental Education, Natural History, Human Ecology, Environmental Conservation, Ecological Design, and Agroecology.*

| | |
|---|---|
| Agroecosystems of the Southwest | Enviro. Restoration Thru Riparian Ecology |
| Coastal Ecology of the Gulf of California | Colorado Plateau: Nature, Culture, Conservation |
| Ecological Design | Issues of Global Food Production |
| Environmental Geology | Ecology and Natural History of the Southwest |
| Marine Invertebrate Ecology | Wetland Ecology and Management |

## Adventure Education

*Students have designed majors in Adventure Education, Outdoor Experiential Ed., Wilderness Leadership, Therapeutic Use of Wilderness, and Outdoor Program Administration.*

| | |
|---|---|
| Aboriginal Living Skills | Alpine Mountaineering |
| Avalanche Forecasting | Methods in Experiential Education |
| Explorers and Geographers | Expeditionary Kayaking |
| Outdoor Education and Recreation | Outdoor Program Administration |
| Wilderness Leadership | Gender Responsible Adventure Education |

- **Sea Kayaking and Marine Landscapes** *Sea kayaking in Baja, California, learning basic techniques of sea kayaking, sea living, and sea safety. Basic concepts of marine, coastal & desert ecology, geology, oceanography, and conservation issues. Interacting with native people who work in and inhabit these areas. Snorkeling, observing, and recording marine invertebrates.*

## Integrative Studies

*Students have designed majors in Human Development, Education, Religion & Philosophy, Peace Studies & Conflict Resolution, Cultural & Regional Studies, Sustainable Community, Psych & Ecopsychology.*

| | |
|---|---|
| Addiction and Recovery | Christian Tradition: An Interpretation of Love |
| Counseling Theories | Dreamwork Intensive |
| Expressive Arts Therapies | Family Systems Theory |
| Human Rights Seminar | Interpersonal Communication |
| Latin American History | Nature and Psyche |

## Arts and Letters

*Students have designed majors in Fine Arts, Photography, Performing Arts, Spanish, Writing and Literature.*

| | |
|---|---|
| Alternative Processes of Photography | African Inspired Arts & Drumming |
| Bookmaking As Art | Dance and Improvisation |
| Intercultural Communication | Introduction to Fiction Writing |
| Literary Journal Practicum | Movement Theater |
| Reading & Writing About Natural History | Interpreting Nature Thru Art & Photography |

- **Intercultural Communication** *Applications and ramifications of interactions between cultures with different value orientations; examines specific cultures, including US non-dominant cultures; implications of global industrialization, and ethics of overseas development.*

Apply by 2/1, 9/1　　No housing

• Mentored studies • Self-designed majors • Field studies • Interdisciplinary classes • Optional SAT's
• Life experience credit • Adult degree program • M.A. Program • Vegetarian & vegan meals

| | |
|---|---|
| Admissions Office | 800. 628.-6364 |
| Prescott College | 520. 776.5180 |
| 220 Grove Ave. | rdpadmissions@prescott.edu |
| Prescott, AZ 86301 | www.prescott.edu |

# UNIVERSITY OF REDLANDS

1,500 Students    Redlands CA

The University of Redlands is one of the oldest and most respected liberal arts universities in the west, but it is not a college that dwells on its past. Comfortable with tradition but emboldened by experimentation, Redlands believes that a classical education in the arts, letters, and sciences is most powerfully applied to the world we inhabit when students are thoroughly invested in its creation. The University seeks to build a community of questioning, compassionate, and internationally aware students who can effect change in the world.

The University is an eclectic place with a broad range of backgrounds and lifestyles — a place where diversity is defined in the broadest possible terms. This has created a rarity in higher education: a place where artists, business majors, feminists, evangelical Christians, activists, scientists, athletes, and others can find common ground amidst significantly differing belief systems. Redlands is not a utopian society — our diversity does not deny fundamental differences — but the University rejects the limitations imposed by both intolerance and political correctness.

The academic programs at Redlands reflect an interest in providing a wide-ranging and multi-disciplinary intellectual experience: the creative writing program, led by five full-time, working writers is one of the finest programs of its kind in the west; environmental studies utilizes state-of-the-art computer mapping technology and a thorough grounding in science, economics, and ethics to search for workable solutions to ecosystem degradation; communicative disorders provides theoretical and clinical experience within a liberal arts curriculum; and our strong government and international relations programs prepare leaders who will effectively shape public policy for years to come. These examples, in addition to 28 other academic majors, offer an uncommonly varied palette of courses and programs to choose from.

The University encourages each of its 1500 students to construct an educational course of study that engages their academic work with the local community and the world at large. This is done largely through ambitious foreign study and Community Service Learning programs. Students utilize one January term for a community service project that can take place in locations across the country and overseas. The University's Community Service Learning office coordinates hundreds of projects that have included work at a home for battered women, language translation in Bosnia, community relations work for the L.A. Police Department, construction of Habitat for Humanity homes, and AIDS education programs. From this experience, students discover a commitment to community-building that extends well beyond their time in college.

To deepen students' cultural literacy and awareness, Redlands has assembled over 60 foreign study programs that help bring alive one's sense of what it means to be a world citizen in the modern age. By spending a semester as a "guest" of another culture, students learn first-hand the complexities and discomfort of cultural assimilation, the richness of newly appreciated intellectual traditions, and the simple joys of new friends, new food, and new music. Redlands students have studied at the world's greatest universities in the U.K., Europe, and Asia where they have learned in educational environments quite different from the U.S. They have also settled into cities and villages throughout Africa, Asia, and Latin America, discovering cultural, political, and artistic traditions largely unfamiliar to American students.

The most unusual aspect of the University of Redlands' innovative approach to education is The Johnston Center for Integrative Studies, home to 10 percent of the University's student population. Founded in 1969 at the peak of the experimental college movement in the U.S., Johnston is the most unorthodox expression of Redlands' approach to higher education. Johnston students have almost total freedom to hand-craft their educational program by designing individually created classes and majors, and they receive narrative evaluations for their courses rather than letter grades. Most Johnston students choose to live together in the Johnston Complex, where group decisions within the community are made using a weekly Quaker-style community meeting. Johnston students attempt to create an atmosphere of academic and social idealism, where ideas are vigorously debated and humanistic values are cherished.

Recent Johnston Center student-created majors include Religion and Transformation; Biochemistry and Neurobiology; Comparative Folklife Studies; Computer Science/Mystical Traditions & Ethics; World Development; Ecological Anthropology; Feminism and Politics; Education: Theory, Practice & Alternatives; Environmental Community Planning; and Psycholinguistics, Psychology and Healing.

Redlands is not an overtly political campus, but public activism is encouraged and supported. While a broad range of political perspectives exist within the student body, activism on campus frequently originates from the left, with issues of animal rights and vegetarianism, environmentalism, and sexual politics currently on the forefront. Organizations like the Brotherhood of Rangi Ya Giza and Women of Many Shades are multi-racial groups dedicated to cultural awareness and solidarity, and have been active on campus regarding issues of culture and race. More traditional venues for involvement and leadership are available such as student government, the student newspaper, and a nationally competitive Division III NCAA athletic program.

The University is located in Redlands, California, a small suburban city of 70,000 people, that was recently listed as one of southern California's "most livable cities". Just north of the campus is the San Bernardino mountain range; to the east sits the highest peak in southern California, Mt. San Gorgonio (11,500') and three ski resorts. Joshua Tree National Park is just over the mountains and is home to some of the most beautiful scenery in the desert southwest.

The Redlands campus is considered one of the most beautiful in the west. Greek-revival and Spanish-influenced architecture predominates, and most residence halls border a 7-acre, tree-lined quadrangle. A modern student center is the hub of campus activity, and the University recently built the Stauffer Center for Science and Mathematics, an $18 million Biology/Chemistry laboratory building and accompanying classroom.

# MAKING A DIFFERENCE STUDIES

## Government and International Relations

Slavery and the Constitution
Constitutional Law
Liberty and Authority: Women and Politics in Latin America
Political Philosophy: Power and Morality: Asian Politics and Development

American Parties and Interest Groups
Modernization and the Politics of Ethnicity

## Environmental Studies

Environmental Design Studio
Issues in Ecology
Biosystems Modeling
Spatial Information System

Ethics and the Environment
Energy and the Environment
Urban and Environmental Economics
Global Environment

## Latin American Studies

Mexican-American Literature
Comparative Politics and Development
Brazil
Hispanic Poetry
Mediating Cultures

Women and Politics in Latin America
Latin American Civilization
Ways of Seeing: Art & Social Reality in Mexico
Power & Social Change in Global Economy
Latina Literature

## Women's Studies

Women's Issues Across the Curriculum
Feminist Ethics
Women, Sexuality and Western Religion
Women in Collective Action

Contemporary Feminist Theory
Economics of Race and Gender
Feminist and Womanist Theologies

## Race and Ethnic Studies

Eliminating Racism
Class and Inequality
African American Literature
Debating Change in the Modern West

Teaching Diverse Students in U.S. Schools
Urban Sociology
Economic Dynamism & Challenge for America
Columbus & Cowboys: Revisiting Frontier History

## Economics

Economic History
Industrial Organization and Public Policy
International Trade
Money, Banking and Financial Markets

Economics of Race and Gender
Urban and Environmental Economics
Business Cycles and Economic Forecasting

## Sociology and Anthropology

African Society
Fieldwork and Ethnographic Methods
Sociology of Work and Family
Political Economy
Women and Collective Action

Classical Social Theory
Deviance; Crime and Delinquency
Social Movements
Community Social Change
Peoples of the American Southwest.

Apply by 12/1     Student body: 32% minority, 12% int'l.
Faculty: 55% male, 45% female, 5% minority
• Interdisciplinary classes   • Team teaching   • All seminar format   • Theme housing
• Field studies   • Required community service   • Individualized majors   • Vegetarian & vegan Meals

Office of Admissions
University of Redlands
1200 E. Colton Ave.
Redlands, CA 92374

800. 455.5064
admissions@uor.edu
www.redlands.edu

# RUDOLF STEINER COLLEGE

250 Students    Fair Oaks, California

Rudolf Steiner College strives to provide a creative educational environment for men and women of diverse ages and backgrounds who seek a deeper understanding of the challenges of modern life and wish to develop new capacities as a basis for their life's work, for social service, and cultural renewal.

Founded on the spiritual scientific work of Rudolf Steiner, the College has as its mission to provide programs that:

- Awaken independent thinking and healthy judgment about the deepest issues of human life;
- School powers of perception;
- Cultivate and enrich artistic faculties;
- Strengthen capacities for practical life.

The view of the human being as an individuality encompassing body, soul, and spirit is central to the programs of the College, along with an emphasis on the cultivation of the inner life as a source of strength, creativity, and initiative. Programs strive to address the students' quest for the knowledge, insight, and moral imagination needed to bring balance and healing to human beings, communities, and the earth itself.

Rudolf Steiner College offers upper division and graduate level courses. Most students are between the ages of 22 and 45 with a few younger and a few older. Most have already earned at least one academic degree. The cosmopolitan community is comprised of students and faculty from many different countries. They have explored some of the world through travel, study, work; many are also raising families. They come seeking to make a difference.

Self-Development Through the Arts: Students seek to make a difference for the world by cultivating the imagination, insight, and initiative required to address modern problems. The arts are studied as a basis for sensitivity, and to deepen perception, social awareness, and balance of soul.

Waldorf Education: Making a difference for the next generations. Waldorf education (K-12 curriculum) seeks to cultivate balanced human beings by educating head, heart, and hand in harmonious interplay. People preparing to teach in Waldorf schools study: human development, based on the assumption that a human being is a spiritual being; curriculum appropriate to different age levels; and several arts. Waldorf education is the fastest growing independent education movement world wide. Upon graduation, teacher placement is 100%; with most graduates getting multiple job offers.

Bio-Dynamic Gardening and Goethean Studies: Students seek to make a difference for the earth itself. Bio-dynamic gardening seeks to work with, rather than against, life forces in the growing of plants. Goethean Studies, initiated by scientist/artist Johan von Goethe, cultivates the powers of observation by bringing together outer and inner experiences.

Those who have successfully completed at least two years of general education courses, may enroll in Rudolf Steiner College programs leading to a B.A. in Anthroposophical Studies or Waldorf Education.

# MAKING A DIFFERENCE STUDIES

### Foundation Program

*One-year full-time and two-year weekend options. This speaks directly to the quest for deeper understanding of the human being, to a yearning for self-knowledge and higher wisdom of the world. It is designed to introduce and explore the insights and endeavors of Rudolf Steiner, as well as focusing on artistic development and personal growth. Evolution of consciousness in history, art, and music. Personal biography and life cycles.*

| | |
|---|---|
| Introduction to Waldorf Education | Eurythmy (Movement) |
| Spiritual Streams in American Literature | Choral Singing |
| Painting, Drawing, Sculpture | Parsifal: The Quest for the Holy Grail |
| Movement and Spatial Dynamics | World Evolution and Spiritual Development |
| Karma and Reincarnation | Philosophy of Freedom |

### Waldorf Teacher Education Programs

*Full-time, part-time, certificate; B.A. & M.A. options. San Francisco weekend/summer option. Preparation for early childhood, elementary, or high school teaching in a Waldorf school (over 700 schools worldwide). Practice in presenting subjects from fairy tales to mathematics in an artistic way.*

| | |
|---|---|
| Storytelling, Gardening | Puppetry and Festivals for the Young Child |
| Learning and Development | Speech, Eurythmy, Music |
| Inner Work of the Waldorf Teacher | High School Curriculum Subjects |
| Painting, Drawing, Crafts | Teaching Science in the Elementary Grades |
| Psychology of Adolescence | Working With Colleagues |

Teaching Math, Science, Languages, History, and Geography
Teaching Science in the Elementary Grades

### Arts Program

*Watercolor painting: veil and wet-method. Use of these techniques in the Waldorf curriculum and art therapy. Supplemental studies of singing, eurythmy (movement), and clay sculpture.*

### Biodynamic Gardening Course

*Soil preparation, composting, Bio-dynamic preparations and sprays, crop rotation, Earthly and cosmic forces in plant growth. Pest management, seed saving.*

### Goethean Studies Program

*Goethe's theory of knowledge as a path to deepened perception and higher cognition. Botany, color study, meteorology, comparative morphology, and study of sacred geometry, Gaia/Sophia and the alchemy of the soul. Exploration of science through artistic media.*

Rolling applications
Student Body: 20% international    Faculty: 80% female, 20% male
• Part-time, weekend, and summer study    • Vegetarian lunch

| | |
|---|---|
| Admissions Counselor | 916. 961.8727 |
| Rudolf Steiner College | 916. 961-8731 (fax) |
| 9200 Fair Oaks Blvd. | rsc@steinercollege.org |
| Fair Oaks, CA 95628 | www.steinercollege.org |

# RUTGERS STATE UNIVERSITY OF NEW JERSEY
## COOK COLLEGE

3,285 Undergraduate Students    New Brunswick, N.J.

Cook College is one of four residential undergraduate colleges on the New Brunswick campus of Rutgers University. Although the college is a professional school offering B.S. degrees solely in programs in environmental sciences, food, nutrition, marine sciences, and natural resources, the university's vast array of courses, student life programs, academic activities, and offerings in the arts are also available and convenient.

Cook College was formerly known as Rutgers' College of Agriculture and Environmental Sciences, and it shares its campus with the New Jersey Agricultural Experiment Station. The College combines a rural setting on the outskirts of New Brunswick with state-of-the-art laboratory and research facilities in biotechnology, food science, bioremediation, geographic information systems, marine and coastal sciences, and sustainable agriculture.

Cook College has long been recognized as the national leader in land-grant college curriculum innovation. The Department of Environmental Sciences was the first of its kind in the nation. The College thus broadens the established land-grant agricultural mission to include its environmental effects and, ultimately, the environmental problems of urban and suburban development. The transition to Cook College in 1973 reflected the faculty's commitment to a multidisciplinary, problem-oriented undergraduate program. This program now includes the social, cultural, aesthetic, and ethical dimensions of problems in food, agriculture, natural resources, and the environment — in addition to the scientific and technical aspects that had been the focus of the land-grant colleges.

The current curriculum, which became effective for the Class of 1997, emphasizes the mastery of skills and competencies for lifelong learning, as well as the ability to apply them in the professions for which the College prepares its graduates. A required "Perspectives on Agriculture and the Environment" course introduces entering students to the mission of the College and the complexity of environmental problems. A capstone "Junior-Senior Colloquium" requires students to work as a team drawn from a variety of majors, to propose solutions to a well-defined "real world" problem. A stated goal of the new curriculum asserts that to sustain the integrity of our ecosystem, students should develop the ethical sensitivity and the analytical skills to address questions of social responsibility, environmental ethics, moral choices, and social equity.

Because of the complexity of environmental problems all students, regardless of major, are required to master the basic concepts of biology, ecology, the physical sciences, economics, and domestic policy process. Students must also develop oral and written communication skills, an appreciation for the arts and modes of critical response, and an awareness of cultures other than their own. Requirements in quantitative methods, computer applications, professional ethics, and foreign languages are specified for the particular fields of study. Finally, all students are required to undertake a project in experience-based education — preferably but not necessarily related to the major — such as a Cooperative Education placement, independent research on-campus or off, or a community-service activity.

President Clinton launched AmeriCorps at Rutgers because the university had in place the most ambitious community service program of any large, research-oriented state university. Although AmeriCorps was originally intended for students in the liberal arts colleges, a number of Cook College majors are developing their own local community service activities under the auspices of this program.

The Cooperative Extension Service is an integral part of the land-grant college missions. In New Jersey this program is as involved in air and water resources, Youth-at-Risk programs, Urban Gardening projects, and nutrition programs for urban families as it has been traditionally devoted to the agricultural extension service and 4-H. The College's experiential-education requirement is intended to provide even more of our students with opportunities to work on projects throughout the state with extension faculty members.

Cook College offers traditional land-grant college programs in agricultural, animal, atmospheric, food, nutritional, and plant sciences. Discipline-based programs in the natural sciences, journalism, communication, and public health are offered in cooperation with other faculties of the university, but Cook students focus on the application of these disciplines to problems in the environment or human health.

Nine multidisciplinary majors are open only to Cook students. All minor programs of study offered in New Brunswick are open to all undergraduates. A Cook student, for example, could major in animal science and minor in women's studies, and a liberal arts student could major in history and minor in animal science at Cook. The nineteen minor and certificate programs offered by Cook College allow a journalism student, for example, to specialize in environmental risk communication, or a pre-med biochemistry major to focus on human nutrition.

Rutgers University offers eight Study Abroad programs in thirteen countries. Cook College has also established programs focusing on agriculture and the environment with Technion Institute in Israel, the University of Reading in England, and the University of Natal in South Africa. In addition, regularly offered courses involve field work in Newfoundland, Alaska and Puerto Rico. The college also participates in a consortium of mid-Atlantic agriculture colleges.

An organic farm was established on campus in 1993, operated by students who remain in New Brunswick for the summer. The farm is a CSA (community-supported agriculture), selling start-up shares to university faculty and staff. The shareholders and student farmers consume approximately 25% of the produce; the balance is donated to local soup kitchens and food banks who are pleased to receive fresh, wholesome organic produce. Students, for their part, learn the fundamentals of organic gardening and the complexities of distributing fresh produce — skills which can be applied to backyards and possibly to sustainable commercial enterprises in the future.

# MAKING A DIFFERENCE STUDIES

## Environmental Planning & Design

Environmental Design Analysis
Legal Aspects of Conservation
Land Planning and Utilization
Conservation Vegetation

History of Landscape Architecture
Land Economics
Horticulture in the Residential Environment
Weather, Climate & Enviro. Design

## Bioenvironmental Engineering (5 year dual degree program)

Environmental Systems Analysis
Solid Waste Treatment Systems
Conservation Ecology
Applied Principles of Hydrology
Organic Crop Production

Air Pollution Engineering
Solar Energy
Energy Conversion for Biological Systems
Environmental Statement & Impact
Land & Water Resources Engineering

## U.S. or International Environmental Studies

Research Methods in Human Ecology
Population, Resources and Environment
Rural Communities
Environmental Teacher Education
International Environmental Policy

Environment & Development
Economics of World Food Problems
Social & Ecol. Aspects of Health & Disease
Rural Development
Economics of Peasant Agriculture

## Environmental Sciences

Solid Waste Management and Treatment
Soils and Their Management
Air Pollution Control
Environmental Health
Soil Ecology

Pollution in Int'l. Perspective
Problems of Aquatic Environments
Hazardous Wastes
Water Resources-Water Quality
Pollution Microbiology

## Environmental Policy, Institutions & Behavior

Politics of Environmental Issues
Population, Resources and Environment
Human Ecology
Environment and Development
Social & Ecological Aspects of Health & Disease

Behavior and Environment
Energy and Society
Rural Communities
Global Environmental Processes & Institutions

## Natural Resources

Forest & Wildlife Conservation
Principles of Applied Ecology
Wetland Ecology
Natural Resource Administration

Field Ecology
Conservation Ecology
Environmental Law
Fishery Management

**Marine and Coastal Sciences    Integrated Pest Mgm't.    Agroecology**

**Forest Resource Mgm't.    Public Health    Fishery Science    Water Resources**

**Wildlife Science    Enviro. Health Science    Enviro. Journalism & Mass Media**

Apply by 1/15, transfer 3/15
• Field studies  • Team teaching  • Self-designed majors  • Multidisciplinary classes
• Service-learning  • Vegetarian meals

Undergraduate Admissions
Rutgers University, Cook College
New Brunswick, NJ 08901

732. 445.3770

# SAINT OLAF COLLEGE

3,000 Students    Northfield, Minnesota

St. Olaf provides an education committed to the liberal arts, rooted in the Christian Gospel, and incorporating a global perspective. In the conviction that life is more than a livelihood, a St. Olaf education focuses on what is ultimately worthwhile and fosters the development of the whole person in mind, body, and spirit.

St. Olaf strives to be an inclusive community, respecting those of differing backgrounds and beliefs. Through its curriculum, campus life, and off-campus programs it stimulates students' critical thinking and heightens their moral sensitivity; it encourages them to be seekers of truth, leading lives of unselfish service to others; and it challenges them to be responsible and knowledgeable citizens of the world.

This liberal education cherishes a sense of continuity with the past, finding in the past not rigid, dead paradigms, but the vital wisdom of experience and the recognition of errors we should aspire not to repeat. Alive to change, this education celebrates the venturesome spirit of risk-taking ancestors who sought freedom, and it welcomes all who seek a similar adventure. It finds in this daring spirit of earlier generations the roots of compassion for others of diverse origins.

At St. Olaf, liberal education accepts the intriguing challenge of communication under the conditions symbolized by the destruction of the Tower of Babel and the confusion of tongues. It accepts the responsibility to listen, study, and speak with all our brothers and sisters of every tongue and race. A cross-cultural component in the core curriculum insures that every St. Olaf student gains some insight into significant aspects of non-western culture or minority cultures of North America.

About 500 students participate in the St. Olaf International Studies Program each year. Typically, they study in Africa, Asia, Europe, Latin America, the Middle East, and the former USSR. More than half of every graduating class has studied abroad at least once. Options include one month interim courses, semester, and year-long programs. All the programs add a cross-cultural dimension to a liberal arts education and aid in developing a global perspective.

Study/Service programs provide students with a challenging and independent study-abroad experience. It offers an international experience combining academic study and active participation with nationals in rural and urban settings through local organizations. Programs provide enriched learning experiences through immersion in a local situation — in most cases in the Third World, and opportunities to make a contribution to the local community through a service project.

St. Olaf students participate in numerous volunteer services, regularly visiting with juvenile offenders, with the physically and mentally impaired, with senior citizens in local hospitals and retirement centers, and serving as big brothers or sisters.

St. Olaf's Paracollege offers an alternative means of earning the B.A. degree. Paracollege students develop individualized plans for their education. Students implement their goals through a variety of educational options — especially tutorials, where they explore topics of their choice with the guidance of a faculty member — and seminars, which are small discussion courses frequently team-taught by professors from different disciplines.

# MAKING A DIFFERENCE STUDIES

## Environmental Studies

Introduction to Environmental Studies
Canyonlands Geology
Coastal Biology in California
Environmental Ethics
Ecological Principles

American Ecological History
Desert Ecology
Winter Ecology
Water Resources Management
The Land, American History and Culture

## Women's Studies

Women's Health
Women in the Visual Arts
Family and Economy
American Feminist Thought
Family & Gender in Cross-Cultural Perspective

Philosophy and Feminism
Dance, Gender and the Church
Women and Judeo-Christian Tradition
Women in America

## American Racial and Multicultural Studies

Introduction to ARM Studies
Native-American-White Relations
Race and Class in American Culture
Contemporary Native American Issues

From Wounded Knee to Red Power
Ethnic Music
Black American History
Dance in America

## Economics

Energy Economics
Entrepreneurship
Ethical Management
Labor Economics

Environmental Economics
Economics of Health Care
Economics of the Public Sector
Environmental Policies and Regulations

*Development Economics* *The study of economic, political, and institutional requirements necessary to bring about relatively rapid and large-scale improvement in the standards of living for Third World populations in Latin America, Asia,and Africa. Major theories of economic development are employed to analyze specific problems such as population growth, poverty and hunger, agricultural stagnation, industrialization, export-led growth and debt.*

## Sociology

Men and Women in American Society
Social Problems and Social Change
Sociology of Global Interdependence
Encountering the "Primitive" Tribal and Peasant Societies
Forging a Latin American Culture: Indians, Conquerors and Revolutionaries

Contemporary Native American Issues
Race and Class in American Culture
Culture, Conflict and Nonviolence

## Latin American/Latino Studies

The U.S. and Peoples of Latin America
Politics of Developing Nations
Problems in Political Development
Modern Mexico

Development Economics
Latin American Literature
Culture and Civilization of Latin America
Progress & Poverty: Modern Latin America

## Family Resources

*"The family" as a focus for a discipline in higher education has increased in significance as the well-being of individuals and families has become an area of major national concern.*

Family Relationships
Child Development in the Family
Nutrition in the Community
Maternal and Child Nutrition

Lesbian and Gay Issues
Human Sexuality
Family Resource Management
Marriage

## Interim (January) Studies

Biomedical Ethics
Economic Justice: Government vs. Market
Women and Work in Africa
Wilderness in American Life
Human Relations in Cross-Cultural Perspective (abroad)

Public Policy and the Family
Liberation Theology
Freudian & Buddhist Psychology
Ethics, Animals & the Environment

## Paracollege Seminars

Planning for the 21st Century
The Legacy of Columbus
Family, Gender and Economy
Feminism and Philosophy
Gender in the 1990's: New Women? New Men?
Saving Wild Places: The American Conservation Movement

Red, Black and White in American Religion
Religion, Theology and Ecology
Economics of Resource Depletion
Global Climate Change

## Interdisciplinary Courses

Values
Science, Technology and Values

Peace and Violence
Spain and Latin America from 1491 to 1992

## Around the World — The Global Semester

*In cooperation with a St. Olaf coordinator at the American University in Cairo, Egypt, and with staff members from Bangalore, India; Taipei, Taiwan; and Kyoto, Japan, St. Olaf students may spend the fall semester and the Interim studying sociocultural developments in the non-western world.*

- **India Studies** *After an intensive ten-week orientation term including language study, partici-pants spend six months in Pune living with Indian families, and enroll at Tilak Maharashtra Vidyapeeth where they continue language instruction and engage in other studies.*

- **Biology in South India** *Following a five week study and orientation session in Madras, stu-dents do independent study/internships in rural and/or urban health care, agriculture, fishing village, and mountain ecology.*

- **Indonesia** *Students work as teaching assistants in the English Dep't at Nommensen University in Sumatra, and at Satya Wacana Christian University in Java.*

- **New Guinea** *Students work with English conversation programs or participate in local church activities such as religious education classes or alcohol abuse prevention. Ten weeks of course work are followed by ample time to visit villages.*

**Africa and the African Diaspora    Hispanic Studies**
**Social Work    Philosophy**

Apply By 3/1
Faculty: 60% male, 40% female, 13% minority    Avg. # of students in first year classroom: 21
• Interdisciplinary classes • Field studies • Internships • Third-world service-learning
• Team Teaching   • Self-designed majors   • Evening classes   • Vegetarian & vegan meals
• Energy conservation and campus wide recycling policies in effect

Director of Admissions
St. Olaf College
1520 St. Olaf Ave.
Northfield, MN 55057-1098

800. 800.3025
admissions@stolaf.edu
www.stolaf.edu

# SAN FRANCISCO STATE UNIVERSITY

20,725 Undergraduates    San Francisco, California

The society of the future is studying on San Francisco State University's campus today — the broadest mix of race, ethnicity, culture, age, and life experience likely to be found anywhere. Surrounded by one of the world's most ethnically rich cities, and with students enrolled from across the nation and more than 90 countries, SFSU helps prepare students with the skills and insight necessary to succeed in a pluralistic society and global economy.

A dynamic, cosmopolitan city, San Francisco is a global center of business, technology, and culture. As a laboratory for meaningful work-study and community involvement, for personal growth and recreation, San Francisco and the greater Bay Area help make SFSU an ideal place to live and to learn.

SFSU students consistently stand out as independent and creative thinkers and doers who contribute to their community and to the world. Because the University believes a multicultural, multiethnic community is the most productive environment for learning, students of all backgrounds will find San Francisco State a welcoming place. The campus reflects California with its various colors, lifestyles, and experiences.

SFSU professors are winning awards, doing cutting-edge research — even discovering planets — often while working side-by-side with their students. The faculty include winners of the Pulitzer Prize, the MacArthur "Genius" award, and Guggenheim Fellowships among others. Excellent teaching is the faculty's highest priority.

The Community Involvement Center provides academic credit, training, supervision, and support for students performing community service. This interdisciplinary program based on reciprocal learning, sharing, and teaching offers the opportunity for personal growth and career skills development. Regardless of major, students may choose to learn through community service and work in such settings as Rain Forest Action Network, Greenpeace, and a variety of agencies devoted to AIDS -related, health care, homelessness , family service, legal issues and human rights .

The NEXA program is an established part of the curriculum using team teaching by faculty drawn from the Creative Arts, Humanities, Science and Engineering, Ethnic Studies, Health and Human Services, and Behavioral and Social Sciences. NEXA courses bring convergent perspectives to the "two cultures" of science and humanities, and investigate means for reconciling these domains of knowledge.

The Romberg Tiburon Center for Environmental Studies, SFSU's marine and estuarine research and teaching facility on San Francisco Bay, is the site of continuing studies to maintain the Bay's health and ecology. Situated on a stunning and historically rich stretch of coastline, on one of the largest and most urbanized estuaries in the U.S., RTC serves as an ideal laboratory for a broad range of environmental studies.

The International Relations Department and other related departments offer forums for the expression of the widest range of ideas about matters of international significance, and places an emphasis on closing the gap between expert knowledge of world affairs and popular understanding. Students interact with faculty, visiting experts, and interested laymen to analyze and understand the complicated patterns, processes, and institutions of international relations.

# MAKING A DIFFERENCE STUDIES

## NEXA Program — Science and Humanities: A Program For Convergence

Science and Culture
Business and Culture
The Nuclear Revolution
Science as a Social Process
Animal Rights: Multidisciplinary Exploration

Mythic and Scientific Thought
The Feminist Revolution
Explorations of the Future
Computers in the Arts and Humanities
The City in Civilization

## Labor Studies

Know Your Work Rights
Union Structure and Administration
Organizing in the Workplace
Collective Bargaining

Women and Work
Affirmative Action
Labor and Government
Labor in an International Perspective

## Urban Studies

Policy Analysis
Urban Growth Management
Urban Health Policy
Homelessness and Public Policy
Race, Poverty, and the Urban Environment

Urban Politics and Community Power
Politics, Law and the Urban Environment
Urban Housing
Urban Environmental Design
Alternative Urban Futures

## Holistic Health Minor

Holistic Health: Western Perspectives
Holistic Health and Human Nature
Chinese Body-Mind Energetics
Environmental Health
Ethics of Medicine

Holistic Health: Eastern Perspectives
Psychosomatics and Stress Management
Fd'ns. of Biofeedback & Self-Regulation
Healing Practices of the World
Traditional Sciences of Indian America

## Intercultural Skills

Cultural Awareness
Intercultural Communication
Culture and Personality
Language and Culture

International Negotiation
Sociolinguistics
Intracultural Communication
Ethnic Relations: International Comparisons

## Health Education

Health in Society
Women's Health — Problems and Issues
AIDS: Contemporary Health Crisis
Health Promotion in Ethnic Communities

Drugs and Society
Health Aspects of Aging
Environmental Health

## La Raza Studies

Oral History and Traditions
La Raza Community Organizing
La Raza Journalism
Acculturation Problems of La Raza
Central Americans in the U.S.

Socioeconomics of La Raza
La Raza Women
Latino Health Care Perspectives
Indigenismo
Community Mental Health

### Non-Western/Cross-Cultural Musical Arts    Counseling    Marine Biology

Student body: 93% state, 62% minority, 57% transfer    Apply during November

Director of Admissions
San Francisco State University
1600 Holloway Ave.
San Francisco, CA 94132

415. 338.1113
www.sfsu.edu

# SARAH LAWRENCE COLLEGE

1,050 Students     Bronxville, New York

Sarah Lawrence, a coeducational liberal arts college, offers a unique education to students who want to shape their own curriculum with the guidance of a talented faculty. Sarah Lawrence was the first college in the United States to propose that education should be shaped to fit individuals and have a sustained commitment to their needs and talents, and the first to realize that genuine learning engages the imagination as well as the intellect. Other innovations include:

- A seminar/conference system where students learn in small interactive classes (limited to 15 students) and private tutorials. The student/faculty ratio of 6:1 is one of the lowest in the country.
- Faculty advisers, called dons, with whom students work to design individual programs of study. The don also teaches the student's First Year Studies Seminar, meets weekly with first-year students, and provides ongoing guidance throughout the undergraduate years.
- Written evaluations for coursework, with grades kept on file for graduate school applications only.
- No graduate assistants, instructors, or adjunct lecturers. Each professor is fully a teacher, available to first-year through fourth-year students.

Sarah Lawrence endows students with the efficacy and will to make a difference in their own lives and in others. They are given the resources and support needed to study their areas of interest with intensity and to explore the moral, social, and political implications of the subjects studied.

The College was a pioneer in incorporating field work into its curriculum. Students can arrange to receive academic credit for interning at numerous social and political organizations if they work with a faculty member to explore and write about an academic aspect of their experience. Past field-work sites include the NAACP Legal Defense Fund, the American Civil Liberties Union, the Landmark Preservation Commission, and the Mount Sinai Center for Occupational and Environmental Medicine. Theater and dance students participate in outreach groups that work with area public schools.

In an expansion of its field-work option, Sarah Lawrence recently initiated an effort to develop service/learning courses in which all class participants do field-work in a social service or public policy organization; their combined experiences are formally integrated into the course content.

Sarah Lawrence prepares students for global citizenship — to meet the challenges of living and learning in a multicultural world. In recognition of this, the College has been named a member of the International 50, a select group of schools that graduate a disproportionately high number of people entering careers in international affairs, or areas of government or academia with an international focus.

# MAKING A DIFFERENCE STUDIES

## Public Policy

Economics of the Environment
The Meaning of Work
Global Economic Development
Women, Families & Work
Changing Places: Social/Spatial Dimensions of Urbanization

Survival & Scarcity: Resources for the Future
Econ. Policy & the Environment of the Future
Science, Technology & Human Values
Ecological Principles: Science of Environment

## Political Science

African Politics
Politics of American Elections
Drugs, Trade, Immigration: U.S.-Mexico Relations in the Late 20th Century
Nuclear Weapons: Selected Explorations of their Impact on Modern Life
Is America a Democracy? Class, Race, Gender, & Political Participation
Politics & History: Conservative, Radical & Liberal

Politics & Government of Latin America
Perspectives on Politics & Society in 20th Cent.

## Area Studies

Images of India
Islam, Flower in the Desert
Literature of Exile
Asian Religion
Middle East History & Politics
African Identities: Lives in Contemporary Sub-Saharan Africa

Culture & Society: Anthro Perspectives
Chinese & Japanese Literature & History
Tradition & Change in Modern China
Russian History, Literature & Politics
Latin American Literature & Politics

## Sociology

Crime & Deviance Theory
Contemporary Urban Lives
Social Movements & Social Change
Colonialism, Imperialism, Liberation: Third World Perspectives

Inequality: Social & Economic Perspectives
Social Theory: Class, Race, Gender & the State
African-Americans & Social Science Research

## Psychology

Education: Theory & Practice
Moral Development
Ethnicity, Race & Class: Psychosocial Perspectives
Ways of Knowing: Gender and Cultural Contexts
Deception & Self-Deception: The Place of Facts in a World of Propaganda

Social Development Research Seminar
Social Psychology

## Women's Studies

Equality & Gender
Mothers & Daughters in Literature
Women in Asian Religions
The Female Vision: Women & Social Change in American History
Theories & Methodology of Women's History & Feminism

Psychology of Women
Gender, Sexuality & Kinship
Women & Resistance in the Muslim World

Student Body: 30% state, 70% female, 30% male, 20% minority     Apply by February 1
• Service learning   • Individualized programs   • Interdisciplinary courses   • Field studies
• Seminar/conference format   • Continuing education   • Vegetarian cafe

Office of Admissions
Sarah Lawrence College
Bronxville, New York 10708

914. 395.2510
800. 888.2858
www.slc.edu

# SEATTLE UNIVERSITY

3295 Undergraduates  Seattle, Washington

Seattle University, founded in 1891, is the largest independent university in the Northwest. A teaching institution, it is one of the 28 Jesuit universities in the United States. The University's mission has four central themes: Teaching and Learning, Education for Values, Preparation for Service, and the Growth of Persons. These provide an intellectual environment promoting the growth of creative, ethically-aware individuals with the skills, values, and motivation to lead and serve their communities and professions.

Seattle University has been consistently ranked by *U.S. News and World Report* as one of the best comprehensive universities in the West. This is due in part to its developmental and unified Core Curriculum which embraces the unique tradition of Jesuit liberal education. The three phases of this Core Curriculum are: Foundation of Wisdom, Person in Society, and Responsibility and Service. Together they provide a developmental approach to educating students for a life of service, a foundation for questioning and learning, and a common intellectual experience for all students.

Seattle University has a solid environmental institutional philosophy and culture. The University recycles or composts more than 50% of its waste. Close monitoring of campus lighting, heating/cooling, and transportation makes Seattle U. a community leader in energy conservation. The campus is also certified as a Backyard Wildlife Sanctuary. In 1981 Seattle U. was the first university to initiate Integrated Pest Management, relying on alternative strategies to develop a balance of nature by allowing beneficial insects to control non beneficial insects.

Seattle U. was recently selected as one of five "lead institutions" in a national program — "Theological Education to Meet the Environmental Challenge" — initiated by the Program on Ecology, Justice, and Faith, and The Center for Respect of Life and the Environment. In response, Seattle University has been preparing its students, through three undergraduate environmental programs, for careers which maintain a clean natural environment while attaining a sustainable economic environment .

Seattle University's Bachelor of Arts in Ecological Studies is unique. Grounded in the concept of ecology, the study of one's home, it explores the complex web of human-nature relationships constituting earth's many ecological systems. The fully integrated program focuses on earth (geological science,) life (biological science,) human (social science,) and spirit (humanities).

The Ecological Studies program aims to develop sufficient ecological and scientific literacy to understand the function of natural ecological systems and the nature and complexity of human interactions with these systems. Students not only understand the historical context of ecological issues, but will develop a multi-perspective strategy for addressing them. The program considers local, national and global issues; students learn about local and regional ecosystems and the attitudes of human cultures towards these ecosystems. Coursework leads students to consider ecological dimensions of natural science, politics, history, philosophy, and religion. As part of Seattle University's Jesuit identity, students consider the importance of the spirituality of nature and the critical role of spirituality and ethics to ecological issues.

# MAKING A DIFFERENCE STUDIES

## Ecological Studies

*Collaboration with community and environmental leaders through four service-learning courses.*

Introduction to Geosystems
Human Ecology and Geography
Environmental Politics *
Religion and Ecology *
Statistical Methods

Introduction to Ecological Systems *
Environmental History
Environmental Philosophy *
Internship and Colloquium
*indicates service-learning*

## Psychology: Addiction Studies

Addiction: Law and Public Policy
Group Process in Treatment
Addiction and the Family
Intro to Alcohol and Drug Addiction
Field Experience

Counseling — Alcohol and Drugs
Case Management and Record Keeping
Ethics for Addiction Professionals
Pharmacology of Alcohol and Drugs
Intervention Techniques

## Environmental Engineering

Engineering Geology
Soil Mechanics
Water Supply & Waste Water Engineering
Environmental Law and Impact Studies

Environmental Engineering Chemistry
Surface and Ground Water Hydrology
Solid and Hazardous Waste Engineering
Engineering Design Course Series

## Theology and Religious Studies

Spiritual Traditions: East and West
The Gospel of Jesus Christ
Church as Community
Biomedical Ethics

Women and the Hebrew Bible
Women and Theology
Jesus and LIberation
Religion and Ecology

- **Creation Spirituality**   *The Christian search for a God whose presence continues in ongoing Creation and of human connectedness with the natural world. Reflection on Taoism and Zen Buddhism, contributing to environmental courtesy and personal harmony with the universe.*

## Psychology: Addiction Studies

Addiction: Law and Public Policy
Group Process in Treatment
Addiction and the Family
Intro to Alcohol and Drug Addiction
Field Experience

Counseling — Alcohol and Drugs
Case Management and Record Keeping
Ethics for Addiction Professionals
Pharmacology of Alcohol and Drugs
Intervention Techniques

## Political Science: Public Administration

Principles of Public Administration
Local and State Politics
Citizenship
Diversity and Change
Native American Politics and Protest

The Policy Process
Public Sector Analysis
Planning, Budgeting & Information Systems
Leadership in the Public Sector
Urban Politics and Public Policy

Apply By: 3/1

- Field studies   - Service-learning   - Third world service-learning   - Interdisciplinary classes

Office of Undergraduate Admissions
Seattle University
900 Broadway
Seattle, WA 98122-4460

206. 296.5800
admissions@seattleu.edu
www.seattleu.edu/

# SHELDON JACKSON COLLEGE

200 Students    Sitka, Alaska

Sheldon Jackson College is for the student choosing a decidedly different and bolder path through life. The campus is located on the western shore of Baranof Island in Southeast Alaska. Encircled by mountains and settled between ancient forests and the Pacific Ocean, it provides a vast wilderness classroom for education and discovery. Within walking distance of campus students can investigate tidelands and old-growth spruce and hemlock forests, observe freshwater estuaries, muskeg, and high alpine meadows — or kayak through Sitka Sound, paddling past sea lions and humpback whales. The campus borders on the 16.8 million acre Tongass National Forest, the largest temperate rain forest in North America.

While many colleges make commitments to ethnic diversity and cultural sensitivity in attempting to create a multicultural learning environment, Sheldon Jackson College provides the reality of such a community. Alaska Natives currently comprise twenty-eight percent of our student body. Some of these students come from villages in Alaska where subsistence hunting, fishing, and gathering are essential to survival. Others celebrate their native heritage within a westernized society. The Annual Gathering of the People celebrates the heritage, culture and current experiences of Alaska's Native Peoples — complete with dancing and a potluck dinner in which traditional Native foods (seal, whale, herring eggs, moose, and Eskimo ice cream) can be sampled. This is a College of rich cultural and geographical diversity. Overall, students come from 40 states and several foreign countries. At Sheldon Jackson diversity is something you encounter in the residence hall as well as in the classroom.

Sheldon Jackson believes that it is important for students to explore and develop the spiritual component of their lives, and to commit themselves in very practical ways to the application of that understanding in the profession of service. SJ is affiliated with the Presbyterian Church, and while providing an education in which the exploration of Christian faith and values is nurtured, it challenges students to develop a sensitivity to other faith traditions. The Community Service Program provides opportunities for students to volunteer while receiving tuition assistance for service.

The Environmental Awareness Team and Outdoor Recreation Program sponsor a very successful city-wide Spring Expo to celebrate Earth Day, complete with Intertribal Native drumming, an Eskimo blanket toss, sea kayaking, a river traverse, climbing wall session, snorkeling, tree planting, and bald eagle release from the Alaska Raptor Rehabilitation Center.

The Wilderness Orientation Program allows new students to participate in a wilderness adventure which could include sea kayaking, a hike to the crater of Mt. Edgecumbe on nearby Kruzof Island, and a sampling of wild edibles. Opportunities abound for students to become involved as explorers and caretakers of the ancient forests and Pacific Ocean which surround Sheldon Jackson College. Sea kayaking, hiking, camping, scuba diving, hunting, and fishing are all popular pastimes.

# MAKING A DIFFERENCE STUDIES

## Aquatic Resources: Aquaculture, Fisheries, Marine Biology

*Sheldon Jackson has the only college-owned private salmon hatchery in the U.S. Hands-on work experience includes culturing shellfish and algae, taking eggs, and collecting samples.*

Salmonid Culture
Fish Health Management
Mariculture
Ecosystem Analysis
Marine Invertebrate Zoology

Marine Biology
Water/Genetics/Nutrition
Oceanography
Fish Ecology
Micro Economics

- **Fish Husbandry** *Hydraulics and hatchery plumbing, fish rearing containers, carrying capacity calculations, programming of fish growth, fish nutrition, fish disease, marking and tagging of fish, and computer applications of fish husbandry.*

## Natural Resource Management & Development

Surveying and Mapping
Field Studies in Resource Management
Native Perspectives on Resource Mgm't.
Natural Resource Policies and Law
Economic Considerations in Natural Resources

Forest Ecology
Forest/Range Soil
Photogrammetry
Wildlife Ecology and Management

## Outdoor Recreation

Outdoor Survival
Hiking
Sea Kayaking
Outdoor Leadership
Outdoor Recreation Planning

Small Business Management
Public Speaking
Environmental Interpretation
Rock Climbing and Mountaineering

## Business Administration

*Prepares graduates for making intelligent business decisions based on analytical, moral, ethical and environmental decisions; making decisions from an international/global perspective; and conducting business in a manner that accommodates different cultural expectations.*

Environmental Issues and Business
Personnel and Labor Relations
International Business

Ethics
Techniques Developing Creativity
Principles of Management

- **Native Issues in Business** *Issues and problems important to Native Alaskans as they relate to business, society, and the physical environment. Topics include Alaska Native Corporations, cultural and environmental issues; accommodating-integrating Native perspectives and cultural sensitivity into business; multiculturalism; and the future of Native Alaskans in business.*

### Education    Forestry Technology Certificate    Fish Husbandry Certificate

Student body: 30% minority (21% Alaska Natives) 40% transfer
Rolling applications    Average # of students in first year class: 10
- Service-learning programs    • Individualized majors    • Required community service
- Interdisciplinary classes and majors    • Optional SAT's

Director of Admissions
Sheldon Jackson College
801 Lincoln St.
Sitka, AK 99835

800. 478.4556
907. 747.5221

# SIMON'S ROCK COLLEGE

322 Students     Great Barrington, Massachusetts

Simon's Rock College of Bard is devoted solely to the academic acceleration and enrichment of the "younger scholar"; that is, the student who, after the tenth or eleventh grade, is ready to leave secondary school for serious undergraduate education. Elizabeth Blodgett Hall, the founder of Simon's Rock, understood the yearning of many younger American students to be taken seriously as thinkers and citizens. Her mission in founding Simon's Rock was to create a community where the habits and enthusiasms of scholarship and friendship could develop unfettered by preconceived notions of age and grade level biases.

In 1979 Simon's Rock became part of Bard College. Through that affiliation the College's resources were expanded and its mission was renewed and enhanced, while the unique identity of Simon's Rock has been preserved. Both Simon's Rock and Bard share a strong commitment to quality undergraduate education, and to innovation, and to the reform of American secondary education.

Because students enter Simon's Rock after the tenth or eleventh grade, they differ in their preparation for college work. The first year curriculum embraces common intellectual enterprises while accommodating and strengthening the background and interests of each entering student. All students admitted to Simon's Rock enroll in the Associate in Arts degree program. During their first two years, they complete a coherent core curriculum that makes up approximately half of their total academic load.

Simon's Rock offers two options for completing a Bachelor of Arts (B.A.) degree. Students eager to pursue their interests in several areas, and those who wish to continue their ongoing work with Simon's Rock faculty, may choose to pursue the interdisciplinary program at Simon's Rock. In this program, advanced course work is completed in concentrations including Arts and Aesthetics; Environmental Studies; Intercultural Studies; Literary Studies; Natural Sciences; Social Sciences; and Women's Studies or studies in one or more complementary areas. Students may create individualized programs by combining advanced seminars, tutorials, and independent research projects under the guidance of the faculty. These on-campus opportunities may be supplemented with study-abroad programs, off-campus field projects, and internships.

Students may also select a major from a wider range of topics offered through a new joint B.A. program with Bard. The thesis, a requirement of both B.A. programs, is a year-long research or creative project that explores a substantive issue in depth.

Upperclass students in Environmental Studies are encouraged to enroll in at least one internship program. Recent internships have included the Massachusetts Audubon Society, the Center for Ecological Technology, and The School for Field Studies. Interns have been involved in assessment of wetlands, stream and lake alterations, and a study of the human perceptions of aesthetics in natural and built environment. Scholarships are also available for environmental studies majors.

The core faculty at Simon's Rock is active in feminist scholarship. Women's studies features speakers from around the country on topics such as feminist interpretation of education and sexual difference, and feminist challenges to objectivity.

# MAKING A DIFFERENCE STUDIES

## Environmental Studies

Environmental Studies
Environmental Management
Aquatic Biology
Nature and Literature
Animal Behavior

Principles of Ecology
Ecological Methods
Limnology
General Botany
Issues in Cultural Ecology

- **Ethics and Environmental Issues** Examines ethical concepts and their implications for environmental problems. Students analyze environmental issues using ethical guidelines. By considering long and short term goals and courses of action and consequences, students gain expertise in decision making and communicating.

- Faculty Bio **Donald Roeder** Dr. Roeder was a consultant to the Canadian gov't. for an environmental-impact study of oil and gas pipelines in the Northwest Territories. He was Ass't. Director of the Environmental Studies Internship Program on Cyprus for the Cypriot government. He has done lake management studies in Massachusetts and New York, and pollution studies of rivers in Boston and the Hudson Valley. He is an Associate Professor in the Graduate School of Environmental Studies at Bard College.

## Intercultural Studies

Recent senior theses include: The Element of the Sacred in the Folk Tales of the Peul: Revolutionary Change within the Indian Community of Guatemala; Alchemy East and West: A Path to the Self, the Other, the One; The Literature of Decolonialization.

Latin America
The Arab World
Music of East Asia
Cultural Encounters
Revolutionary Russia

The European Community
Music of India
Women Writers of Spanish America
Issues in South African Development
Political Economy of the Middle East

## Women's Studies

Women's Studies is committed to the integration of theory and practice and grounded on the principle that the personal is political. Consequently, all students in the major undertake a practicum in a non-academic situation where issues they have considered theoretically may be addressed practically.

- Faculty Bio **Barbara Resnik**, Art History, Social Science, Women's Studies (B.A. Sarah Lawrence; J.D., Cardozo School of Law, Yeshiva University) Ms Resnik is an attorney, graphic designer, and printmaker. She has taught constitutional law, art history, and studio arts at Fairfield U. and Queens College. Her interests include issues of race, class, gender, and the law; art and media in contemporary culture; and population policy and reproductive rights. She has served as exhibition designer for numerous galleries and institutions. Her work is included in many private collections.

Apply by 7/1    Avg. age: 16
20 full scholarships available to outstanding entering students.
• Field studies    • Team teaching    • Interdisciplinary classes    • Vegetarian meals

Admission Office
Simon's Rock College
84 Alford Rd
Great Barrington, MA 01230

800. 235.7186
admit@simons-rock.edu
www.simons-rock.edu

# STANFORD UNIVERSITY

6,575 Undergraduates     Palo Alto, California

At Stanford, students are engaging in community service in growing numbers. Service has become part of student life in classrooms, in the residences, and in extracurricular programs. According to recent senior surveys, over 70% of undergraduates are involved in public service during their Stanford careers. Numerous student service organizations have taken root in the ethnic community centers, student residences, and religious organizations on campus. In addition, the Haas Center for Public Service serves as a focal point for public and community service locally, across the U.S., and overseas. By engaging students in the widest variety of service activities — through hands-on action, policy research, or community problem solving — the Center enriches their education and inspires them to commit their lives to improving society.

The act of service is only the beginning for the Stanford-educated citizen who seeks to make an impact in society. Volunteer work does not end with the completion of a "service action;" rather, it provides an experiential foundation for intellectual work, including academic scholarship, that attempts to answer questions raised by the service experiences. The Haas Center serves as a hub for building study-service connections on campus and for linking Stanford with the outside community: by encouraging students to seek faculty sponsorship of service projects, by supporting the creation of service-learning components in existing courses; and by developing intensive study-service programs such as Stanford in Washington and the Public Service Scholars' Program.

Interest in study-service connections is growing among Stanford students and faculty. More than 50 courses integrate public service activity with study. Courses with service-learning components have been created in American Studies, Anthropology, Chicano Fellows, Children and Society, Communication, Earth Systems, Education, English, Feminist Studies, History, Human Biology, Linguistics, Native American Studies, Psychology, Public Policy, Sociology, and Urban Studies.

A few of the courses at Stanford with a service component include: The Process and Practice of Community Service; Aging: From Biology to Social Policy; Children and Society Program Internship; The State of Public Education in Urban Communities; Women in the African-American Freedom Struggle; The Impact of AIDS; The Meaning of Being Handicapped; HIV/AIDS Training Education; Policy Making at the Local and Regional Level; and an Urban Studies Community Organization Option.

Among the most intensive courses is History Professor Al Camarillo's colloquium, "Poverty and Homelessness,", in which students gain an understanding of the nature of poverty and homelessness from readings and from class discussions, and from a two quarter experience working with homeless families or individuals at shelters. The most extensive venture is the Community Service Writing Project. Now in its seventh year, this joint project of the Haas Center and the Freshman English Program has involved over 1,000 freshmen, matching students with more than 100 community agencies that need newsletter articles, grant proposals, public education materials, and other kinds of writing. The project aims to give students a chance to write outside the academic setting, where their work will reach an audience beyond the teacher and will serve a purpose for its readers. More than 400 freshmen sign up for the program annually.

# MAKING A DIFFERENCE STUDIES

## Civil Engineering

Water Resources
Environmental Planning Methods
Ethical Issues in Civil Engineering
Building Energy Laboratory
Environmental Science & Technology

Building Systems
Small Scale Energy Systems
Environmental & Natural Resource Economics
Air Quality Management
Environmental Planning Methods

## Children and Society

*Emphasis is on public policy and includes research and field experiences.*

American Education and Public Policy
Federal & State Policy: Education & Children
Current Trends in Policy Making
Adolescence
Communication and Children

Children, Civil Rights, & Public Policy in US
Understanding Research: Children & Schools
Children and Society
Urban Youth and Their Institutions
Language & Culture of Urban Youth

## Ethics in Society

*Honors program open to majors in every field and may be taken in addition to a dep't major.*

Introduction to Moral Theory
Medical Ethics
Distribution of Income and Wealth
Character and the Good Life
Contemporary Theories of Justice

The Ethics of Social Decisions
Economics and Public Policy
Computers, Ethics, and Social Responsibility
Ethics and the Built Environment
Ethics of Devlp'.t in the Global Environment

## Urban Studies: Community Organization, Urban Planning, Architecture & Urban Design

Urban Politics
The Multicultural City in Europe
Education of Immigrants in Cities
Gay and Lesbian Urban Youth
The Politics of Development

The Urban Underclass
Group Communication
Process & Practice of Community Service
Organizational Decision Making
Utopia & Reality in Modern Urban Planning

## Feminist Studies

Virgin Mary and Images of Power
Gender and Society
Gender, Power and Justice
Women and Technology
Harassment and Discrimination

Women, Sexuality, and Health
Women in the Health Care Debate
Women — Transition to Democracy: Latin America
Women in Higher Education
Status, Expectations, and Rewards

## Anthropology

Ethnographic Film
Ecological Anthropology
Medical Anthropology
Sociocultural Studies of Biotechnology

Peasant Society, Economy & Environment
Conservation & Community Devp't: Latin Amer.
Cultural Approaches to Education & Devp't
Ethnography of Communication

- *Archaeology and Education at Zuni Pueblo, NM* Learn archaeology and current conditions of pueblo life, while living at pueblo and teaching and tutoring Zuni HS students.

Apply by: 12/15

Office of Undergraduate Admission
Old Union - 232
Stanford University
Stanford, CA 94305-3005

650. 723.2091
www.stanford.edu

# STERLING COLLEGE

90 Students    Craftsbury Common, Vermont

The rural beauty of Vermont's Northeast Kingdom surrounds Sterling College, and the location enhances the twin focus of the curriculum: humans' relation to nature, and human relations within community. Sterling's mission statement clearly expresses that the College is a learning community cultivating the wisdom, skills, and values needed for sustainable living. Sterling has received national attention for blending environmental studies, hands-on skills, and outdoor group challenges into integrated learning experiences. Sterling College grants Associate's and Bachelor of Arts degrees.

Sterling's program of studies includes experiential components, field studies, living and working in a community, challenge experiences, as well as traditional academic coursework. During the Associate degree program, students enroll in a core curriculum, and select electives in the areas of wildlife management, forestry, agriculture, and outdoor leadership. Students study the scientific principles of ecology, the history and philosophy of human relationship with nature, and current problems or conflicts over resource use and management.

Practical hands-on skills-development courses include Woodlot Practices, Farm Workshop, and Organic Vegetable Production. In the Practicum in Experiential Education students experience the importance of community, of trust, and of effective communication through participation in group initiatives and personal challenge. Second-year students participate in a ten-week off-campus internship. Interns typically work with federal land management agencies, sustainable farms, wildlife rehabilitation centers, or outdoor leadership programs.

Students in their final two years of study select a concentration in the areas of Wildlands Ecology and Management, Sustainable Agriculture, or Outdoor Education and Leadership. Bachelor's degree candidates design a program of studies and a Senior Project. During the third year of studies, students have the opportunity to enroll in field programs such as the Colorado Field Semester, or in overseas study programs sponsored by Sterling College or other colleges. Students may also enroll as non-matriculated students, arrange an exchange semester at other colleges offering relevant courses, or develop an in-depth independent study.

Fourth-year students spend their fall semester on campus in core courses largely determined by their concentrations, while finalizing plans for their Senior Projects. The Project is an integrated learning experience in which students develop the theoretical knowledge necessary to tackle a real problem in their fields of study, and then work on the planning and implementation of solutions. The fourth year concludes with the students presenting the  results of their Senior Projects to the Sterling community and the public. This is a final exercise in synthesis and public speaking. Graduation concludes their Sterling College careers.

The nature of Sterling's curriculum makes it best suited to students who are willing to commit to full-time participation. Students living on campus are required to participate in the non-credit community-work program. Participation in the work program results in a reduction in tuition. Students above the age of 21 have the option of living in off-campus housing after their first year of study.

# MAKING A DIFFERENCE STUDIES

## Associate of Arts in Resource Management (first two years)

*Study of the manipulation of resources to meet specific objectives. Investigates the relationship among resources and the short - and long-term effects of manipulation. Focuses include water, soil, fisheries, forage, forestry and wildlife resources.*

Writing And Speaking To The Issues
Humans Ecology
Tools and Their Applications
A Reverence for Wood
Woodlot Practices
Exploring Alternative Agriculture
Fish and Wildlife Management
Economics and The Environment
Advanced Wilderness First Aid

Environmental Science
Practicum in Experiential Education
Ecology
Farm Workshop
Resource Management: Watersheds
Animal Science and Lab
Vertebrate Natural History
Triumphs of the Human Spirit
Wilderness First Responder

- **Practicum in Experiential Education (Bounder)** *Challenge activities to promote group problem-solving and individual initiative. Activities include a ropes and initiative course, preparation for winter camping and a four-day expedition, and flat and whitewater canoeing and backcountry navigation. These activities promote a forum for understanding group interaction and reactions to challenge.*

- *Faculty Bio* **Perry Thomas** *(B.A Biology, Dartmouth College; M.A Teaching Biology, Northern Arizona U; Ph.D. Biology, NAU) Perry teaches Statistics & Research Methods, Conservation Biology, and Systems Thinking. Perry also advises students in the Wildlands Ecology and Management concentrations, and assists in Practicum in Experiential Education.*

## Bachelor of Arts: Wildlands Ecology & Management, Outdoor Education & Leadership, Sustainable Agriculture

International Forestry and Wildlife Issues
Forgotten Arts
Exchange Semester
Statistics and Research Methods
Psychology of Groups
Outdoor Photography
Human Nutrition
Conservation Biology
Draft Horse Management

Field Ecology
Snow Physics and Avalanches
Community Service Project
Systems Thinking
Practicum in Experiential Education
Nature Writing
Natural Science and Lab
Recreation Policy and Management
Outdoor Leadership

- *Faculty Bio* **Edward (Ned) Houston** *(A.B. summa cum laude, Architectural Sciences, Harvard, Phi Beta Kappa; M.A., Social Ecology, Goddard College), Ned Houston, Dean of Sterling, teaches People and Animals, Literature Of The Rural Experience, and Triumphs Of The Human Spirit. A teacher for twenty-eight years, Ned enjoys a particular interest in interdisciplinary learning and systems diagnosis.*

**Short Term Programs for Adults**: Immersion Practicum in Sustainable Agriculture, Wildbranch Writers' Workshop, Rural Matters, Outdoor Leadership (grades 8-12)

Rolling admissions    Faculty: 50% male, 50% female
• Team teaching   • Self-designed majors   • Service-learning   • Interdisciplinary classes
• Field studies   • Required community service   • Optional SAT's   • Vegetarian & vegan meals

Admissions Office
Sterling College
Craftsbury Common, VT 05287

802. 586.7711
800. 648.3591
admissions@sterlingcollege.edu
www.sterlingcollege.org

# SUNBRIDGE COLLEGE

200 Undergraduates    Chestnut Ridge, NY

Without question, a student's experience at Sunbridge is different than the form of learning one finds at almost any other institution of higher learning. Seminar work is combined with artistic and practical activities to provide a new way for students to approach learning. Intense study expands out to movement, music, art, sculpture, etc. By virtue of the unique curriculum, students have a rare opportunity to meet themselves and their value systems in a fresh light.

An anthroposophical college chartered by the N.Y. State Education Department, Sunbridge is founded on the research and insights of Rudolf Steiner, the Austrian philosopher and scientist. Rudolf Steiner presented an image of the human being based on the physical, psychological, and spiritual dimensions of human life. This threefold picture inspired the Waldorf educational movement, as well as extensive work in areas such as curative education, social and economic development, agriculture, medicine, science, and the arts. Anthroposophy, or spiritual science, holds at its core the needs and nature of human life as a whole.

Waldorf education, initiated by Steiner in 1919, is one of the largest and fastest growing independent educational movements in the world. It represents a long-practiced method which has deeply researched the meaning of a holistic approach to education. In Waldorf teacher-training, a study of the nature of the whole human being, from birth to maturity, is part of the learning process. Related to this is the question of the teacher-trainee's self-development, which is taken up in depth. A renewed understanding of human society, in terms of the totality of the arts, sciences, and humanities is also undertaken, so that the child's faculties can be developed out of a complete experience of human life.

There are more than 600 Waldorf schools worldwide, and graduates of the Waldorf Teacher Training and Early Childhood Education program find ready employment with the growing number of Waldorf schools (over 160) in North America. Others come to seek a new life-direction, for example, in the realms of business, science, and the arts. Sunbridge's student population spans several generations and hails from a wide variety of countries; students have the experience of meeting many different people who are also looking at the world and their places in it.

Sunbridge College is located 30 miles north of New York City — allowing students to avail themselves of the City's many offerings while enjoying the natural surroundings of the College. Visitors to the College community find an established Waldorf school, a school of movement (eurythmy,) a center for the care of the elderly, a food co-op, and a homeopathic pharmacy — all within walking distance. Social life revolves around Holder House, an attractive modern student residence. Many meals and other activities take place in the College's "Main House" dining facility. The College campus is also the venue for numerous lectures, workshops, stage performances, and conferences of general and specialized interest during the course of the year.

# MAKING A DIFFERENCE STUDIES

## Orientation Year

*A full-time program which gives a foundation in Rudolf Steiner's organic view of the world through intensive courses in spirituality, arts and sciences, and the humanities.*

Evolution of Consciousness

The Philosophy of Freedom

Social Development

Projective Geometry

Gardening

Sculpture

Astronomy

Eurythmy (art of movement)

The Legend of Parzival

Human Development

Music

Painting

## Teacher Training

*A one-year, full-time program (Orientation Year, or equivalent, a prerequisite) which prepares students for teaching in Waldorf Elementary or High Schools. Option for master's degree.*

Child Development and Learning

Painting

Inner Development of the Teacher

Practice Teaching

School Organization and Administration

Language Arts

Remedial Education

Science

Curriculum Development

Sculpture

## Early Childhood Education  (with option for Master's Degree)

*A one-year, full-time program which is a preparation for teaching in Waldorf kindergartens. Students have also found it a valuable training and preparation for work with young children in nursing, social work, and daycare. Option for master's degree.*

Early Childhood Development

Language, Imagery and the Small Child

First Grade Readiness

Music and the Young Child

Festivals

Practice Teaching

Puppetry

Rhythmic Games

Handwork

Speech

## Teacher Education

*Over the course of 6 weeks during each year, students experience a program that integrates studies in Steiner's spiritual science and Waldorf education for Elementary school. The program comprises three summer courses plus short, on-campus intensives, and continuing course work in the student's geographical area. Three year program.*

### Handwork, Woodwork, & Clay Modeling Program  (3 yr. part time)

### Art of The Actor (1 yr. in N.Y.C.)    Master's Degree In Waldorf Education

### Non-Profit Administration & Community Development (2 yr. part time)

### Biodynamic Gardening and the Environment

Rolling applications     Student body: 40% state, 35% int'l.    Avg. age: 30
• Evening programs in general studies & Waldorf education
• Summer Programs - educational & general topics  • Talks, workshops & conferences
• Center for Life Studies (family, parenting, adult development)  • Vegetarian meals available

Sunbridge College                                914. 425.0055
285 Hungry Hollow Rd
Chestnut Ridge, NY 10977

# SWARTHMORE COLLEGE

1,325 Students    Swarthmore, PA

If you want to make a difference in the world, Swarthmore College will encourage and support you all the way. Swarthmore is widely known for academic excellence; what insiders also know is that the academics serve a larger mission to train students to ask hard questions, to explore how things are, and then to act to improve their world. At Swarthmore, you'll get a philosophical and academic background that will prepare you for a life of service to your community.

On a practical level, at Swarthmore you'll find scholarships for activists, funding for student-run social action projects, and a fully-staffed volunteer clearinghouse that matches students with organizations that need help. You can even choose a concentration such as Peace and Conflict Studies or Environmental Studies which will prepare you to make a profession of changing the world. Courses in social action combine academic study with classes spent actually tutoring poor children or working with residents of a housing project to improve access to medical care. There's nothing as powerful as the combination of theory and personal knowledge: students come away knowing their own power and how to use it effectively.

Swarthmore's campus is populated by people who believe not only that they can make a difference, but that they must. You'll meet professors who are involved in international struggles for peace and justice, and students who spend their breaks not in Aspen, but in Guatemala or Northern Ireland.

Swarthmore's academic atmosphere is as exhilarating as it is demanding, because every course is informed by the belief that things can change if one is willing to take risks and do the work. At Swarthmore, you'll find cynicism blessedly rare.

At Swarthmore there are many opportunities and support systems for idealism. Each year six entering students are awarded Lang Scholarships which give them up to $10,000 to support a social action project which they design and carry out themselves. For instance: a housing rehabilitation project started by a Lang Scholar over ten years ago is now carried forward by the people who were able to buy the houses at low cost through the project. (Students must apply for the Lang Scholarships when applying to the College.) Any student may apply to the Swarthmore Foundation for a grant up to $2,000 for a social service project of their own design.

CIVIC (Cooperative Involvement as Volunteers in Communities) has a full time staffer that supports students in volunteer work. CIVIC itself runs seven volunteer programs and puts students in touch with 200 other organizations that need volunteers — from soup kitchens to AIDS care. CIVIC also teaches the skills and sensitivities volunteers need to be effective and provides copiers, computers, paper, and experience to students who are working to make a difference.

There are many other opportunities at Swarthmore, and students can make of them what they will. Follow the lead of the student who has built her entire senior year around a project to make health care accessible in hard-hit housing projects. She is researching residents' needs and preferences, organizing care with a local hospital, identifying and training people who are willing to help their neighbors tap into the system, and writing reports and papers on her experience—all for credit.

# MAKING A DIFFERENCE STUDIES

## Environmental Studies
*Students take related courses as diverse as religion and engineering, and conclude with a practical senior project. One recent project: building a prototype house of straw bales — strong, well-insulated, cheap, biodegradable, and not prone to fire, rats, or mildew.*

Chemistry in the Human Environment
Water Quality and Pollution Control
Religion and Ecology
Swarthmore and the Biosphere
Food and Famine

Intro to Environmental Protection
Marine Biology
Solar Energy Systems
Economics of Environment & Nat. Resources
Problems in Energy Technology

## Peace and Conflict Studies
*As a college founded by Quaker pacifists, Swarthmore has a strong tradition of pacifism buttressed by a large and comprehensive peace library.*

War and Cultural Difference
Power, Authority and Conflict
Race and Foreign Affairs
War and Peace
Nonviolence: Theory and Practice

Defense Policy
Nonviolence and Violence in Latin America
Comparative Politics: Comp. Democratization
Peace Movement in the US: Women & Peace
Managing Conflict: Interpersonal to Int'l.

## History
*The investigation, from various points of view, of those ideas and institutions — political, religious, social, and economic — by which people have endeavored to order their world.*

European Revolutionary Tradition
Sex and Gender in Western Traditions
Nationalism and National Identity
Black Culture and Black Consciousness

Labor in Society and Culture
Revolution to Capitalism: Contemporary Russia
European Jewry's Encounter with Modernity
History of Manhood in America, 1750-1920

- **Murder in a Mill Town** Examines primary source documents concerning the trial of a Methodist minister for the 1833 murder of a female factory worker in Mass. Topics include gender, sexuality, industrialization, religious revivalism, and mental illness

## Sociology and Anthropology

Latin American Society and Culture
Explorations of Diaspora Populations
Social Inequality
Cultural Representations
Wisdom and the Healing Arts: A Multi-cultural Study of Healing

Indigenous Resistance & Revolt in Latin Amer.
Language and Culture
Ecology, Peace, & Development in El Salvador
Psychological Anthropology

## Education

Educational Psychology
Environmental Education
Political Socialization and Schools
Political Economy of Education
Women and Education

Child Development and Social Policy
Ethnographic Perspectives in Education
Counseling: Principles and Practices
Urban Education
Arts as Community Service — Social Change

Apply by 1/1
• Service learning • Self-designed majors • All seminar format • Team teaching
Interdisciplinary classes • Field studies • Vegetarian meals

Office of Admissions
Swarthmore College
Swarthmore, PA 19081

610. 328.8300
www.swarthmore.edu/Home

# TUFTS UNIVERSITY

4,550 Undergraduate Students    Medford, Mass.

"...[A] college works out abroad from itself, beyond the circle of its graduates, sending its energies forth through all other institutions, and down through all classes, even the most unlettered."

— Hosea Ballou 2nd, First President of Tufts

Since its founding in 1852, Tufts University's commitment to using knowledge, skills, and scholarship for active public leadership has broadened traditional definitions of service, citizenship and education. At Tufts, the responsibility of each individual to their local, national, and international communities is a basic tenet of the University's mission and philosophy. Public service is promoted across the curriculum from the College of Engineering and the Sackler School of Biomedical Sciences, to the College of Liberal Arts, the Fletcher School of Law and Diplomacy, and the Urban and Environmental Policy Program.

Tufts is a community of scholars dedicated to change through service. Many courses and departments employ community service as a method of enhancing classroom learning and performance of service. Service-learning courses can be found in Education and Child Study, as well as in Mechanical Engineering and Chemistry. Many other courses have a public service content — that explore, for example, different facets of public decision-making or the nature of community problems.

John DiBiaggio, President of Tufts and ardent supporter of service learning is committed to making public service a hallmark of a Tufts education: "We are using all the best educational innovations of this century to produce a corps of thinking, caring men and women dedicated to bettering their society." Tufts works to enhance the public service education, research, and community outreach activities of students and faculty through the Lincoln Filene Center, the Public Service Task Force, the Center for Environmental Management, and many other organizations and disciplines dedicated to education for active citizenship. By sponsoring conferences and forums, courses, and fellowship/internship opportunities, Tufts acts as a catalyst connecting people and resources in new ways and developing new approaches to public problems.

Building on a tradition of service, Tufts' students engage in developing new initiatives for public service. Many organizations not only participate in, but create venues for, community service. Tufts' largest and oldest community service organization is the Leonard Carmichael Society with a core membership of 700 students participating in 23 ongoing programs annually. Many cultural groups, such as the Pan-African Alliance and the Asian Community at Tufts, have long-standing service commitments to nearby ethnic communities. Groups such as Environmental Consciousness Outreach and Oxfam Cafe also inform the student body on local, national, and international challenges to community and the environment.

Tufts' commitment to citizen education does not simply start with matriculation and end with graduation; through the Community Service Option, students may dedicate their time, and energy to serving social needs before, during, and after their years at Tufts. Newly accepted students may defer admission for one year if they commit to a minimum of twenty-five hours of community service during that time. Current undergraduates may postpone two academic semesters to do service.

# MAKING A DIFFERENCE STUDIES

## Environmental Health

Environmental Biology & Conservation
Introduction to Community Health
Environmental Law
Public Health
Exposure Assessment

Environmental Systems Engineering
Wastewater Plant Design
Hazardous Materials Safety
Fate &Transport of Enviro Contaminants
Public Administration

## Community Health

*Multidisciplinary approach to health sciences and care. How anthropology, medicine, history, sociology, psychology, economics, ethics, political science, public health, and biology, affect communities' strategies to promote health and cope with disease. Factors in health and illness; formation of health care policy with a look at other countries; and institutions that plan, regulate, and deliver health care.*

Domestic Violence
Occupational and Environmental Health
Health and the Law
Challenge of World Hunger
Disease and Difference

Intro to Hazardous Materials Management
Human Health and Risk Assessment
Addiction
Contemporary Issues in Health Policy

## Architecture: Social Focus

Introduction to the City
Urban and State Politics
Urban Sociology
Land Use and Planning Policy
Environmental Facilities for Children

Public Administration
Cognitive Psychology
Housing Theory
Urban & Environmental Planning & Design
Designing Educational & Therapeutic Enviro's

## Child Study

The Child and the Education Process
Personal-Social Development
Language and the New Immigrant
American Sign Language and the Deaf
Social Policy for Children and Families

Developmental Crises
Community Field Placement
Fostering Literacy Development
Child Advocacy Educational Rights
Rights of Children to Social Services

## International Relations

Topics in International Development
Economics of Food & Nutrition Policy
International Global Human Rights
Cross Cultural Political Analysis
Cold War America

Natural Resources & Environmental Economics
Sociology of War and Peace
Political Economy of World Hunger
Non-Governmental Actors in Int'l Relations
African Politics

**Peace & Justice    Environmental Studies    Women's Studies    American Studies
Science, Technology, & Society    Economics    Civil & Environmental Engineering**
Early decision 11/15 or Regular decision 1/11
• Handicapped programs and accessibility    • Theme housing    • Service learning
• Individualized majors    • Interdisciplinary classes
• Early admissions programs to Fletcher School and School of Medicine

Office of Undergraduate Admissions    617. 627.3170
Tufts University    uadmiss/inquiry@infonet.tufts.edu
Bendetson Hall    www.tufts.edu/as/uadmiss
Medford, MA 02155-7057

# UNITY COLLEGE

525 Students    Unity, Maine

Unity College recognizes that we are custodians of a fragile planet. The College intends to graduate individuals with firm values, a sense of purpose, and an appreciation of the web of life. Unity graduates are professionally effective and environmentally responsive, recognizing their responsibilities as passengers on this fragile planet. They understand that, as global citizens, they must assume a leadership role in the stewardship of the earth.

Unity College exists for the student whose love of the outdoors is reflected in career choices. Unity students typically place a premium on jobs that do not require sitting behind a desk, thus Unity combines academic rigor with equally demanding field experience. Education at Unity can be the first step to a position with a state park, wildlife refuge, nature education center, or wilderness recreation organization.

Unity students come from diverse backgrounds, but they share a spirit of independence and a love of nature. They are individuals who welcome the opportunity to participate actively in their own education and in the life of a small college community.

To succeed at Unity College, students must bring a willingness to have their ideas questioned — and possibly changed. Students must be prepared to accept new challenges that expand their limits. Climbing an ice-covered mountain demands courage and commitment; waking up at 4 a.m. to go out in the field and conduct a small mammal survey requires determination.

Unity College has a special location: the mountains, lakes, and rocky coast of Maine offer innumerable opportunities to camp, hunt, hike, canoe, and fish. At Unity, students experience the personal growth that comes from awareness of the connections linking human beings with the natural environment. Nearby habitats as diverse as ocean, mountains, freshwater wetlands, and lakes provide the opportunity for hands-on study of a variety of ecological systems.

Most Unity students gain work experience in their major field as part of their education. Students may choose credit-bearing internships, cooperative education work experiences, or summer employment to supplement classroom learning. Positions with state and federal agencies, businesses, or nonprofit organizations enable students to apply academic knowledge to real working situations. Typical internships have included work with the Environmental Defense Fund, the American Rivers Conservation Council, and the U.S. Environmental Protection Agency. Other internships have included Hurricane Island Outward Bound, Connecticut Audubon Society, Volunteers for Peace, and numerous nature centers and summer camps.

Unity's campus has a sense of open space that reflects the value the College places on the outdoors. The 200-acre campus has an agrarian feel; in the warm months cows graze adjacent to the residence halls. Over 100 acres of campus land have been designated a tree farm used for educational and recreational purposes. In addition to its campus property Unity owns more than 320 acres of land including frontage on Lake Winnecook, a Wetlands Research Area, and a 230-acre tree farm with a working sawmill.

# MAKING A DIFFERENCE STUDIES

### Environmental Policy

Environmental Pollution
Environmental Law
Natural Resource Policy
Technical Writing
Soil Science

Land and Water Law
Geology of Environmental Problems
Freshwater Ecology/Limnology
Social Problems
State & Local Government

### Urban and Community Forestry

Supervisory Management
Landscape Fundamentals
Forest Tree Diseases & Insects
Biology
General Chemistry

General Ecology
Urban Forest Management
Arboriculture
Conservation History
Soil Science

### Outdoor Recreation Leadership

Wilderness First Responder
Leadership
Group Process
Cross Country Skiing
Adventure Ropes Course

Wilderness Skills & Techniques
Program Planning
Enviro Education: Methods & Materials
Canoeing
Mountaineering

### Conservation Law Enforcement

Introduction to Criminal Justice
Courtroom Procedures
Forest Fire Prevention & Control
Geology of Environmental Problems
Environmental Law
Wildlife Law Enforcement

Conservation Law Enforcement
Firearms Training
North American Wildlife
Interpersonal Relations
Freshwater & Marine Fishes
Conservation Biology

### Environmental Education (note - not a teaching credential)

Introduction to Outdoor Recreation
Conservation History
Environmental Ed: Methods & Materials
Group Process
Educational Psychology

Art Media Techniques
Education of Exceptional Youth
Instruction Practices & Curriculum Develp't.
Orienteering & Backpacking
Current Environmental Education Problems

### Park Management

Park Planning, Design & Maintenance
Conservation Biology: Aquatic
Wildland Recreation Policy
Interpersonal Relations
Weather and Climate

Preprofessional Development in Park Mgm't.
Park Administration and Operations
Natural Resource Policy
Landscape Fundamentals
Geology for the Naturalist

### Ecology    Forestry    Aquaculture    Fisheries    Wildlife

Rolling admissions    Avg. # of students in first year classroom: 20
• Team teaching    • 35 Service learning classes — available in all majors
• Field studies    • Interdisciplinary classes    • Individualized majors    • Vegetarian meals

Dean of Admissions                    207. 948.3131
Unity College
Unity, ME 04988-0532

# UNIVERSITY OF VERMONT

8,000 Undergraduates    Burlington, Vermont

The University of Vermont and State Agricultural College blends the academic heritage of a private university with service missions in the land-grant tradition.

Environmental Studies is a University-wide undergraduate curricular option offering students several challenging academic programs. This option is one of UVM's most distinctive and popular academic programs — unique nationally in its breadth and interdisciplinary nature. The program includes undergraduate education, research, and community service programs dedicated to the study and improvement of the cultural and natural environments essential to the quality of life.

The School of Natural Resources is actively committed to diversity; biodiversity in natural communities and cultural diversity in human communities. A major goal of the School is to develop men and women as leaders in the stewardship of renewable natural resources — our forests, wildlife, fish, water, and land. An Honors Project, open to qualified juniors and seniors encourages original thought and creativity. The School includes academic programs in: Environmental Studies, Forestry, Natural Resources, Natural Resources Planning, Recreation Management, Resource Economics, Water Resources, and Wildlife and Fisheries Biology, and provides a holistic framework that complements traditional natural resources curricula.

UVM reaffirmed its commitment to environmental values by hiring a full time coordinator for its Environmental Council. The council, a group of students, faculty, alumni, and others recommend ways the University can reduce environmental impacts and expand environmentally-related research, education, and service. Current student projects include reducing junk mail, designing ecologically sound buildings, and socially responsible investing. The council is working on indicators of sustainability for the University, a campus arboretum, and use of hazardous materials in laboratories.

UVM's Center for Service-Learning provides structured experiential programs and volunteer placements within the context of public service. Through the Vermont Internship Program in service-learning, students get involved in the community by filling real needs and link their experience with a structured academic program. Typical placements involve health and human services, law and justice, or governmental, environmental, and educational organizations.

The Community Service Program provides ways for students to get involved as volunteers. They participate in one-time events such as Hunger Clean Up or Into the Streets, work several hours per week at a local agency, or make a year-long commitment. The Alternative Spring Break allows students to increase their social awareness through service in an economically disadvantaged environment away from Vermont. Reflection on and examination of the cultures and circumstances are built into the program. The Center also offers a Community Service Trek, a week-long experience for incoming first-year students prior to the first week of classes.

The Living/Learning Community Service Leadership Suite offers students the opportunity to live together while becoming involved in community service projects, and to study the philosophical and practical aspects of service-learning.

# MAKING A DIFFERENCE STUDIES

## Agroecology (Sustainable Agriculture)

Agriculture & Resource Economics
Alternatives for Vermont Agriculture
Integrated Forest Protection
Soil Erosion & Conservation
Insect Pest Management
Agroecology

Agriculture in the Third World
Energy Alternatives
Biosphere (Gaia) Ecology
Ecological Vegetable Production
Environmental Economics
Composting

## Agricultural & Resource Economics: Int'l. Development & Rural Economy

Comparative Economic Systems
Rural Planning
World Natural Environments
Intro to Urban & Regional Planning
Land Economics Issues

World Food, Population & Development
Agriculture, Planning & Project Development
Anthropology of Third World Development
Community Organization & Development
Rural Communities in Modern Society

## Natural Resources

Forest Ecology
Water as a Natural Resource
Int'l Problems in Natural Resource Mgm't.
Wilderness & Wilderness Management
Race & Culture in Natural Resources

Effect of Human Activities on Lake Champlain
Environmental Policy
Assessing Environmental Impact
Ecological Aspects of Nat. Resource Conservation
Environmental Aesthetics & Planning

## Wildlife and Fisheries Biology

Wildlife Conservation
Fisheries Biology
Florida Ecology Field Trip
Uplands Wildlife Ecology

Ornithology
Wildlife Habitat & Population Measurements
Wetlands Ecology & Marsh Management
Marine Ecology

## Early Childhood and Human Development

Intro to Early Childhood & Human Dev.
Public Policy and Programs for Elders
Infancy
The Emerging Family

Contemporary Issues in Parenting
Family Ecosystems
Personal & Family Development in Later Life
Human Relationships and Sexuality

## Communication Science and Disorders

Voice and Articulation
Disorders of Language
Current Research in Language Acquisition
Audiological Assessment

Fundamentals of Hearing
Disorders of Speech
Physiological Phonetics
Habilitation of Hearing Impaired Children

## Women's Studies

Images of the Goddess
Women & Public Policy in Vermont
Feminist Theory
Women, Society & Culture
History of Women in US

Women & Society
Studies in Gender & Religion
Women in Development: Third World Countries
Psychology of Women
Women in the U.S. Economy

### Social Work    Environmental Studies    Teaching Credential: Enviro Studies (7-12)

Apply by 2/1

Director of Admissions
University of Vermont
Burlington, VT 05405

802. 656.3370

# WARREN WILSON COLLEGE

750 Students    Asheville, North Carolina

Warren Wilson College is located on a beautiful 1,100-acre campus in a mountain valley that American Indians called "Swannanoa", meaning "land of beauty". Over the years the setting has inspired community, creativity, learning, and a sense of harmony with the environment. The mission of Warren Wilson College is to provide a liberal arts education combining academic study, participation in a campus-wide work program, and required community service. Each component of this triad plays an important role in the education of the whole person — within a learning environment that promotes wisdom, understanding, spiritual growth, and contribution to the common good.

Warren Wilson College affirms a commitment to spiritual growth and social responsibility; it invites to its educational community individuals who are dedicated to personal and social transformation, and to stewardship of our natural environment.

Students have constituted the core work-force for the College since its founding more than a century ago. Today each residential student works 15 hours each week on one of more than 100 work-crews that help run the college, and the work helps offset the cost of room and board. The work-crews give students experiential learning opportunities in their fields of study. For example, pre-veterinary students care for the hogs and cattle on the 300-acre College farm; education majors assist in the Head Start Program at the Early Learning Center; and other students provide support to the English department or work in one of the computer centers.

The work crew is not the only commitment Warren Wilson students make outside the classroom. Each student is responsible for giving 100 hours of community service in the Asheville community, their own home town, or in another country before graduation. The College believes that service to society enables students to make a difference in the world and to better understand the needs of the others. Service projects include working at homeless shelters, building homes with Habitat for Humanity, serving as Big Brothers and Big Sisters, establishing tree plantations in Nicaragua, and developing water collection systems in Kenya.

Warren Wilson's student body of 750 comes from 42 states and 21 countries. The College also provides many opportunities for students, faculty, and staff to learn about different cultures well beyond the campus, whether they be in a different part of the United States or a different part of the world.

The Warren Wilson WorldWide Program was recently instituted to give each student a chance to work, learn, and serve abroad. From summer- to semester-long trips in countries ranging from Ireland to India, the WorldWide program offers cross-cultural experiences that help students discover how their academic studies and the College mission triad come alive in the field, in our global community, and in connection with our fragile planet.

Ninety-three percent of students and 40 percent of faculty and staff live on campus. Because students, faculty and staff live, work and serve together, there is a strong sense of community. The size of the college enables students and staff to be involved and challenged with community leadership roles. The staff meets biweekly for a staff forum at which issues, goals, and ideas are communicated and acted upon. The student caucus also plays an important role in the college's short- and long-term plans. It meets each week to discuss student issues, to communicate ideas and concerns to the administration, and to make policy recommendations.

The four-term calendar (students typically take two or three classes per term) allows concentration in a few subjects at a time. Not only are classes small, but there are ample opportunities for independent tutorials.

Community members meet often to address issues concerning sexism, diversity, peace issues and other global and local topics. Students and staff are particularly sensitive to environmental issues. Warren Wilson has been recycling on campus for more than a decade. Student work-crews are completely responsible for the program, which includes curbside pickup for campus buildings and residences. Soon to be constructed is the Eco-Dorm, a dormitory planned by both students and the administration that will be constructed with sustainable principles in mind.

Students and staff have participated for more than 20 years in the archaeological excavation of an American Indian village on the campus. Further reflecting the special heritage of its Southern Appalachian location, Warren Wilson offers a program in Appalachian music including instruction in the more common instruments used in the genre. Students and staff join together to create an Appalachian String Band which performs for campus activities.

Capitalizing on its mountain location Warren Wilson is in partnership with North Carolina Outward Bound, and the outdoor leadership major has become one of the College's most popular fields of study.

On weekends students may stay on campus to enjoy a play, a performance or music, see an art exhibit, go to dances, or create their own entertainment. Or they may go to downtown Asheville for a poetry reading, a movie at the Fine Arts Theatre, or a meal at one of the many restaurants in and around Asheville. The College's location just outside Asheville, in the Blue Ridge Mountains, provides many fascinating opportunities for students including kayaking, mountain biking, caving, and rock climbing.

One applicant to the college wrote: "I'm lured to Warren Wilson College because of many things: the triad, the location, the classes, the cows, the kindness of the staff and students. I have found in my visit to the College a respect for life that coincides with my own. Very simply, I felt at home there, I felt that I had found an environment that would allow me to grow, that would unbiasedly witness a portion of the continuous evolving of my life." All of these things combine to make Warren Wilson College the community and learning environment that it is, a place where students come to grow.

# MAKING A DIFFERENCE STUDIES

**Environmental Studies: Environmental Analysis; Environmental Education; Plant Biology & Horticulture; Forest Resource Conservation; Environmental Policy; Wildlife Biology**

Horticulture
Forest Biology
Community and Regional Studies
Wilderness: Past and Prospects
Environmental Impact Assessment
Thinking Globally, Acting Locally
Methods and Materials in Environmental Education

Conservation of Natural Resources
Aquatic Ecology and Water Pollution
Environmental Issues for the 90's
Introduction to Environmental Education
Environmental Policy
Wildlife Management

- ***Discovery Through Wilderness*** *Interdisciplinary learning experience that involves extensive study of a geographical area which is largely wilderness. The course challenges participants to explore their personal limits and to integrate knowledge from several academic disciplines. In the classroom, students study the history, geology, politics, culture, ecology, and resources of the region. The class then travels to the region for a month of camping and backpacking. Past trips have visited New England, Atlantic Canada, the Pacific Northwest, and Caribbean islands.*

- *Faculty Bio:* ***Dr. Mark V. Brenner*** *(B.S., U of Wisconsin — Stevens Point, M.S. and Ph.D., U of Washington) is the chair of the Environmental Studies Department. Mark's specialty is aquatic ecology and the ecological effects of pollution. He has assisted a number of students with research projects related to aquatic ecology and pollution. Currently Mark is working with waste recycling research, composting techniques, and waste from aqua-culture. For fun Mark plays on Warren Wilson's volleyball team and leads the Discovery Through Wilderness - Pacific NW trip.*

## Biology

Field Natural History
Field Ornithology
Evolution
Plant Morphology

Ecology
Animal Behavior
Immunology and Infectious Disease
Special Topics in Biology

## Peace Studies

Introduction to Peace & Conflict Studies
Lifestyles of Nonviolence
Resolving Conflict: Global and Local

Special Topics in Peace Studies
Politics of Peace
Current Issues of Peace and Justice: America

## Social Work

The Aged: Issues and Interventions
Social Welfare as a Social Institution
Micro-Practice: Individuals
Field Instruction
Macro-Practice: Communities, Organizations, and Policy Development

Substance Abuse: Issues and Interventions
Human Behavior in the Social Environment
Micro-Practice: Groups and Families
Social Work in the International Community

## Religion

Social Ethics in Story Theology
Religious America: Four Distinct Paths
Heaven on Earth: Religious Lifestyles in 19th Century America

Eastern Religions
Christ and Contemporary Culture

- ***The Sacred/Secular Search*** *This course explores fundamental questions concerning the nature of religion. Eastern and Western religions, innovative and traditional examples of religious practice are examined. Particular attention is paid to the relationship between "religious" and "secular" claims upon one's time and energy; diverse rivals for our "ultimate concern" are studied, whether or not they bear overt religious labels.*

## Intercultural Studies

*This interdisciplinary field provides a foundation for further study and work in private or govern-ment international agencies, conflict resolution, and global development.*

Economic Development
Mahatma Gandhi
Human Behavior in Social Environment
Global Issues
Intercultural Communication
Poverty and the American City

The Holocaust
Worlds of Change
Latin American Civilization
Social Work in the International Community
Development Agencies at Home & Abroad
Cross Cultural Field Study

- **International Development Practicum** *This course involves participation in a work-study overseas service field project of the international development program. Emphasizes providing a useful service to a local community program through use of appropriate skills.*

## Appalachian Studies

Introduction to Appalachian Studies
Appalachian Folk Arts
Archaeological Field School
Southern Appalachian Term

Folk Tales and Storytelling
Appalachian Folk Medicine
Native Americans of the Southeast
Introductory Anthropology

## Outdoor Leadership

*Prepares you for a leadership role in the professional field of outdoor adventure education. Focus on education, facilitation, and experiential learning methodologies. Interpersonal skills and leadership skills such as group process, conflict resolution, program planning, and administrative issues.*

Leadership for Adventure Education
Wilderness Skills and Techniques
Rock Climbing
Group Process
Program Planning and Design
Winter Camping

Outdoor Recreation Activities
Wilderness First Responder
Initiatives for Adventure Education
Outdoor Leadership Internship
Survey of Exceptional Child Education
Org. & Admin. of Adventure Education Program

> *Faculty Bio* **Ed Raiola** *(B.A., California State U; M.A., U of Northern Colorado; Ph.D., Union Graduate School) I consider myself a catalyst: an educator who facilitates opportunities for people to challenge their expectations and preconceived limitations about what they can and cannot do. All of us need to keep growing and learning in order to make a positive difference in society. I see education in general and outdoor education in particular as encouraging people to become responsible choice-makers. Without knowledge or emotion relating to the earth, we lose a sense of commitment and loyalty to it. Hobbies: biking, cooking, travel, hiking, and mountaineering.*

## History and Political Science

The Holocaust
Civil War and Reconstruction
Poverty and the American City
Politics of Developing States

Latin American Civilization
History of Black Experience in America.
Mahatma Gandhi: Experiments With the Truth
Amer. Immigrant Experience Thru Ethnic Lit.

**Human Studies     Philosophy     Psychology   3/2 Pre-Forestry with Duke**

Apply by 3/15     Avg.# of students in a first year classroom: 15
- Work program   • Service-learning   • Core/multidisciplinary classes   • Self-designed majors
- Third world service-learning   • Required community service   • Vegetarian & vegan meals

Office of Admission
Warren Wilson College
P.O. Box 9000
Asheville, NC 28815

828. 298.3325
800. 934.3536
admissions@warren-wilson.edu
www.warren-wilson.edu

# UNIVERSITY OF WASHINGTON

20,500 Undergraduates    Seattle, Washington

The University of Washington has made pubic service one of its top priorities and has initiated intensified collaboration with city leaders, especially Seattle's public schools. The University is one of only three institutions invited to contribute to a Campus Compact publication on exemplary college service programs.

Students are actively involved in the community in a variety of meaningful ways, both within and alongside the curriculum. "This means that students are challenged to take an active role in constructing meaning and to recognize the ethical dimensions of making meaning" says Kim Johnson Bogart of the Carlson Leadership and Public Service Office. Many faculty include community service in their courses, and more recently, others have joined them in providing service learning options in their courses. Service learning is incorporated in courses in philosophy, mathematics, Asian American studies, and sociology, among others. A recently inaugurated interdisciplinary major in Community and Environmental Planning has community service as a principle strand of its two-year degree program.

The UW College of Forest Resources holds a position of national and international leadership in both instruction and research. Its location in one of the world's largest forest regions provides unique opportunities for field classes and research, actual management of forested lands, exposure to wood-based industries, and awareness of resource-use issues. About one hundred fifty undergraduate and two hundred graduate students are taught by more than fifty faculty members. Thus, students enjoy small classes and close association with faculty.

The Charles Lathrop Pack Demonstration Forest, of approximately forty-two hundred acres, located south of the University is the focal point for on-the-ground academic work in forest management, resource science, and forest engineering. Research centers in the Cedar River watershed are utilized by the College for studies in forest hydrology and mineral cycling in the forest ecosystem.

The marine environment is a dominant factor in the Pacific Northwest. It is not surprising, therefore, that the University has a long tradition of commitment to teaching, research, and public service in the marine and freshwater area. The College of Ocean and Fishery Sciences is comprised of the School of Fisheries, Marine Affairs, Oceanography, Applied Physics, and the Washington Sea Grant Program.

The School of Fisheries maintains joint programs with the College of Forest Resources, the School of Marine Affairs, the Institute of Environmental Studies, and the School of Oceanography. It searches for ways to use stocks of fish and shell fish more effectively, and cultures aquatic plants and animals. It is also concerned with the impacts of pollution, industry, and human population pressures on the environment.

The College of Architecture and Urban Planning and the Department of Mechanical Engineering have jointly created facilities for studying energy usage in buildings. One facility contains direct-gain and Trombe wall passive-solar test bays, and tests alternative envelope insulation types. A second facility compares energy-efficiencies for houses built to various standards.

# MAKING A DIFFERENCE STUDIES
# COLLEGE OF FOREST RESOURCES

## Urban Forestry
*Role of plants and ecosystems in urban environments; role of people in mgm't of urban forests.*

Landscape Plant Recognition
Landscape Plant Selection
Computers in Enviro Design & Planning
Public Outreach in Urban Horticulture
Site Planning

Curatorial Practices in Public Gardens
Landscape Plant Management
Urban Plant Protection
Wetland Ecology & Management
Ecological Concepts & Urban Ecosystems

## Forest Resources Management

Forest Transportation
Forest Stand Dynamics
Wildlife Biology & Conservation
Forest Management & Economics
Forest Planning & Project Management

Forest Ecosystems
Intro to Forest Resources Management
Forest Protection
Wilderness Preservation and Management
Management of Wildland Recreation

## Conservation of Wildland Resources

Introduction to Wildland Conservation
Forest Resources
Dendrology and Autecology
Forest Policy and Law
Economics of Forest Use

Wildlife Biology and Conservation
Social Functions of Forest Ecosystems
Physical Aspects of the Forest Environment
Wilderness Preservation and Management
Natural Resources Utilization & Public Policy

- **Global Change & Forest Biology** *Ecological & Biological effects of atmospheric pollutants, acid precipitation, and climate change on forest trees and ecosystems. Potential climate changes are compared to current and historical climates.*

## Wildlife Sciences

Wildlife Field Techniques
Wildlife Biology and Conservation
Wildlife Seminar
Social Functions of Forest Ecosystems
Plant Identification

Biology and Conservation of Birds
Range and Wildlife Habitat
Human Culture and Wildlife Conservation
Quant've Assessment of Wildlife Populations
Application of Computers to Nat. Res. Problems

## Forest Products & Engineering

*Evaluate engineering, economic, biological, environmental, and social aspects of forest multiple-use management, as affected by access, harvest, transportation, and timber use.*

Forest Surveying and Transportation
Creativity and Innovation
Snow Hydrology
Forest Harvesting
Hillslope Stability and Land Use

Timber Harvesting Management
Introduction to Soil Mechanics
Wildland Hydrology
Microclimatology
Hillslope Hydrology

Apply by 2/1

Director of Admissions
University of Washington
Seattle, WA 98195

206. 543.5150

# WASHINGTON STATE UNIVERSITY

16,000 Students at four campuses    Pullman, Washington

Founded by the Legislature in 1890 as the State's land-grant university, Washington Sate University is today a four-campus university with a growing national reputation. WSU offers a liberal arts education balanced with practical instruction in professional and technical fields. Quality teaching and a special student experience in and out of the classroom are hallmarks of a WSU education.

The University includes the historic home campus in Pullman, a pleasant college town of 24,000 in the agriculturally rich Palouse region of southeast Washington, and three new campuses in Spokane, the Tri-Cities, and Vancouver.

WSU has a number of unique programs that prepare students to make a difference in society. For example, the University offers:

- The nation's most comprehensive educational program in pollution prevention. Students learn to assess business and industrial practices to identify ways to keep pollution from occurring;
- A speech and hearing program aimed at training Native American students to work with their own people who have communication disorders 5 to 15 times more often than the general population;
- Sustainable agriculture and integrated pest management; and
- The Extended Degree Program, using various teaching technologies, that allows Washington residents in the rural areas of 16 counties to take junior and senior year courses to complete a bachelor's degree in social sciences.

One of the state's two public research universities, WSU is known for teaching and research that makes a difference in people's lives, and in the state's industries and professions. Current studies range from cancer prevention to analog-digital computer chips, from disease-resistant crops to qualities of successful marriages, from education reform to animal health. WSU faculty work in an array of developing countries on agricultural, animal health, and educational projects to improve the quality of life.

International elements can be seen in many of WSU's academic programs. They are part of a comprehensive effort to increase student understanding of diverse cultures, economies, political systems, and environments. A pair of world civilization courses, required for undergraduates students, is at the heart of WSU's nationally recognized core curriculum. WSU is one of the top universities receiving funding from the Agency for International Development.

Highly regarded academic programs include the famous Edward R. Murrow School of Communications with one of the country's top broadcasting programs; the biological sciences, especially biochemistry; the College of Veterinary Medicine, known for a commitment to animal well being; and sociology.

# MAKING A DIFFERENCE STUDIES

**Environmental Science & Regional Planning: Agriculture; Enviro. Education; Human or Cultural Ecology; Enviro. Quality Control; Transportation; Nat. Resource Mgm't.**

Topics in Radiation Safety
Environmental Impact Statement Analysis
Environmental Ethics
Environmental Policy
Environment and Human Life

Natural Resource Policy & Administration
Hazardous Waste Management
Human Issues in International Development
Econ. Development & Underdevelopment
Advanced Resource Economics

## Bio-Agricultural Engineering — Five year program

Conservation Engineering
Irrigation Engineering
Agricultural Processing and Environment
Drainage System Design

Global Agricultural Engineering
Soil and Water Engineering
Hydrology
Irrigation Water Requirement

## Soil Resources & Land Use: Soil Conservation & Sustainable Agriculture

Soil Conservation
Botany
Remote Sensing:Terrain Evaluation
General Ecology
Soil Microbial Ecology

World Agricultural Systems
Soil & Water Conservation and Management
Soil Analysis
Forestry Application /Airphoto Interpretation
Soil-Plant Relationships in Mineral Nutrition

## Entomology: Integrated Pest Management

Pest Management Internship
Insects and People
Toxicology of Pesticides
Urban Entomology
Pesticides and the Environment

Urban Entomology
Beekeeping
Systems of Integrated Pest Management
Insect Ecology
Biological Control: Arthropod Pests & Weeds

## History

History of Medicine
Native Peoples of Canada
History of Cuba & the Caribbean
History of Women in American West

North American Indian History
History of the Pacific Northwest
Politics of Developing Nations
Gandhi & 20th Century India

## Child/Consumer/Family Studies

Patterns of Chicano Families
Family Housing Decisions
Families in Crises
Perspectives on Aging
Management Experiences With Families

Guidance of Young Children
The Child and Family in Poverty
Women in Management
Curriculum for Young Children's Programs
Adolescent and Early Adult Development

**Enviro. Engineering   Peace Studies   Women's Studies   Geology**

**Natural Resources Mgm't: Wildlife; Range; Forestry; Wildland Recreation**

Apply by 8/1

• Co-op education   • Service-learning   • Team teaching   • Individual majors   • Veg. meals

Director of Admissions
Washington State University
Pullman, WA 99164

509. 335.5586

# WESLEYAN UNIVERSITY

2,775 Students   Middletown, Connecticut

Wesleyan has long been known as an institution committed to preparing students with such a diverse education that they are poised to make a difference upon graduation. Nationally known for its long-standing commitment to a multicultural student body, Wesleyan's students boast a diversity of ideas, interests, and viewpoints, together with their diverse socio-economic, geographic, and international backgrounds. The interaction of these factors on a small campus, coupled with top-notch academic departments, enables Wesleyan students to understand "the big picture". Wesleyan graduates are involved at all levels of public and private service, education, community organization, and academia.

The Center for Afro-American Studies sponsors a wide range of academic, social, and cultural events open to the entire university community. Established in 1974, the Center's annual roster of events includes a lecture series, jazz concerts, dance performances, art exhibits, a spring film series, and a Fellows Program designed to encourage students and faculty members to meet informally.

The Mansfield Freeman Center for East Asian Studies presents a continuing program of interesting exhibitions, concerts, courses, lectures, and special events. The Center is a place to meet distinguished visitors and faculty, and to learn from first-hand observers about current political and cultural events — from the repercussions of Tiananmen Square to contemporary theater and philosophical trends. Majors in East Asian Studies are able to have a concentration on either China or Japan, but the societies and cultures of both countries are treated as an interrelated field of study. Most majors study abroad during their junior year, making it especially important to begin required language and history courses as early as possible.

Wesleyan's Science in Society curriculum has been designed to help students explore systematically the interrelations between scientific knowledge, society, and the quality of human life. The Earth and Environmental Science department emphasizes field work on the coast and inlands of Connecticut, and is known for the cohesiveness that its field experiments help create. Faculty have taken students to Central America, Newfoundland, Montana, Greece, Italy, and elsewhere.

Students have been involved in a broad range of internships in hospitals, museums, television stations, architectural firms, publishing companies, and educational institutions. The College Venture Program places students for 3-6 months in positions such as advocate for the homeless, research assistant, and teaching.

All students are encouraged to become involved with the local community and to use the Office of Community Service as a resource for volunteer opportunities. The OCS supports for student-run tutoring programs, and offers mini-grants to students who create programs for local children, and sponsors service projects. In 1997, for the first time, community service was a voluntary option for entering students, and 40% of the class of 2001 elected to participate in over 15 community service projects in Middletown.

# MAKING A DIFFERENCE STUDIES

## Earth and Environmental Science

Physical Geology: Our Dynamic Earth
Geology of Connecticut
Coastal and Estuarine Environments
Invertebrate Paleontology
Water Resources

Introductory Oceanography
Environmental Geology Seminar
Principles of Geobiology
Coral Reef Ecology & Geology (in Belize)
Global Change

## Science in Society

Philosophy of Science
Sociology of Health and Illness
Policy Implementation
Sociology of Science and Technology
Discourse, Text and Gender: A Feminist Methodology?

History of Scientific Thought to 1700
Myths and Paradigms
Cultural Studies of Scientific Knowledge
Public Policy Analysis

## Women's Studies

*Areas of study include Women and History, Gender in Cross-Cultural Context, Gender and Society, Gender and Representation, and Science and Gender.*

Feminist Ethics
Women in History and Memoir
Domesticity & Gender — Mid 19th Century
Modernity, Gender and War
Psychology of Gender: Cultural and Historical Perspective

The Newest Minority
Feminism in Global Perspective
Women, Health and Technology
Women and Political Power

## Government

The Moral Basis of Politics
Unheavenly Cities
Educational Policy
Caring, Rights, and Welfare
Conflict in the Middle East

Urban Politics
Strategies of Political Mobilization
Expert Knowledge & Political Accountability
Comp. Welfare States in Europe & America
Arms Control and Global Security

## Afro-American Studies

Education and the Urban Poor
Making the Underclass
Black Politics in Urban America
Toni Morrison
Power and Poverty in Postindustrial Cities

Religions of Afro-American Peoples
Women of Color and Identity
Race, Gender and Ethnicity in America
Other than Black and White
Education and the Urban Poor

## East Asian Studies

Introduction to East Asian Music
Traditional China
Taoism: Visionaries and Interpreters
Salvation and Doubt
Japanese Film & Japanese Society

Japanese Literature 1700-1945
Tibetan Buddhism
Twentieth Century Japan
Women in Buddhist Literature
Politics & Political Development in China

Apply by 1/1
• Individualized majors   • Interdisciplinary majors & classes   • Co-op studies
• Theme housing   • Vegetarian & vegan Meals   • Graduate programs

Dean of Admissions
Wesleyan University
Middletown, CT 06457

203. 685.3000
admissions@wesleyan.edu
www.admiss.wesleyan.edu

# WESTERN WASHINGTON UNIVERSITY
## FAIRHAVEN COLLEGE
400 Students    Bellingham, Washington

Fairhaven College is an undergraduate learning community, within Western Washington University, defined by five attributes: 1) interdisciplinary study; 2) student-designed studies and evaluation of learning; 3) examination of issues arising from a diverse society; 4) development of leadership and a sense of social responsibility; and 5) curricular, instructional, and evaluative innovation.

Fairhaven's interdisciplinary curriculum is centered on the process of inquiry as well as on the development of knowledge. Classes are small, and most are held in a seminar format where the use of primary sources and student participation is essential. Classes are interdisciplinary, often problem-focused, and students use the methods and the research tools of the varied disciplines to examine these problems. Students learn to engage respectfully in discussion, to value and respect different world views, and to appreciate multiple voices reflecting the diversity of experience in our society. Narrative self-assessments and written faculty evaluations of student learning replace letter grades.

Fairhaven students can choose to develop a self-designed interdisciplinary concentration (major) integrating several areas of study, or they can choose an established major in another college within WWU. The Fairhaven Concentration allows flexibility in designing a program to meet academic and personal goals. Interdisciplinary in nature, it places responsibility for its design and development in student hands and allows them to incorporate independent study projects, internships or study abroad experiences within their frame of study. Recent Fairhaven Concentrations have included: Latin American Studies; Inequality and Social Change; Viewing and Marketing the Outdoors through Media; Sustainable Living through Art, Ecology and Communication; Creative Writing and Psychology in Human Service; Women, Law and Policy; and Contemporary Political and Economic Issues in Native America.

Independent Study projects enable students to take responsibility for the direction and content of their education. These projects have included: Multicultural Women's Literature; Wilderness First Aid; Alternative Healing; Wetlands Restoration; History of Native American Education; and Grant Writing.

Fairhaven's curriculum provides a wide range of liberal arts coursework quarterly. Students draw from Fairhaven's courses and in coursework from other departments at WWU. The interdisciplinary courses in Fairhaven's Core Curriculum replace WWU's general university requirements and elective seminars allow opportunities to study many different ideas and issues, and to reflect on current changes in the world. Recent seminars include: Pacific Rim Studies; Mediation Across Cultures; Awareness Through the Body; Regional Ecologies; Art and the Environment; Death and Dying; Scriptwriting; and Organic Gardening.

# MAKING A DIFFERENCE STUDIES

*Note: Fairhaven resource areas are not "departments," and the studies listed for each often draw on resources from the other areas.*

## Law and Diversity
*A rigorous two year program aimed at developing skills and knowledge necessary for law school. Open to any student interested in law, social justice and legal assistance for diverse populations — particularly those with potential for becoming leaders and role models in ethnic and other communities under-represented in the legal profession.*

American Legal System
Gender & Law
Politics of Inequality
Law and Morality

Political Economy and the Law
Government Power Under the Constitution
Civil Rights: Power, Privilege and Law

## History, Culture and Society
Comparative Cultural Studies
Street Youth: Drugs, Gangs, Sex and Soul
Society and the Individual

Judaism as a Civilization
Amer. Constructions of Race, Sex and Gender
Issues in Contemporary Mexican Society

Cross-Cultural Education: Understanding Race, Ethnicity, and Power in the Classroom
Suzie Wong to Miss Saigon: Asian Presence in Hollywood

## Nature, Science and the Environment
Organic Gardening
Ethnobotany
Alternative Futures

Patterns in Nature
Regional Ecologies
Evolution of Technology

- **Alternative Energy Sources** *Class will provide the tools necessary to intelligently make choices about our individual and social energy futures. In addition to exploring the political history of power trust development (and its current manifestation), we will learn from presentations and hands-on field experience about energy from solar, hydro, wind, and atmospheric elements; energy storage technology; charge control equipment; and power conditioning devices.*

## Human Development, Personal Identity and Socialization
Awareness Through the Body
Spiritual Psychology: Becoming Conscious
Human Aggression

Native American Women
Women of Color in the US

- **Social Activism and Making Change** *Opportunity for students to develop or improve their ability to be more effective and knowledgeable social activists. How people make change in their communities at a grassroots level. How and why are action groups formed? Who joins and why? Does the organization operate through a cooperative or command structure? Are they directed at helping immediate victims or addressing causes? Is community interest affected by race, class, sexual orientation, gender, mental state, appearance, or age of victims?*

### Arts, Self-Expression & Creativity

Apply quarterly    Faculty: 54% female, 46% male, 27% minority
Avg # of students in a first year class: 15    Avg. age: 25
- Service learning   • All seminar format   • Self-designed majors
- Field studies   • Team teaching   • Vegetarian meals

Admissions Coordinator
Fairhaven College
Western Washington University
Bellingham, WA 98225-9118

206. 650.3682
Jackie.McClure@wwu.edu
www.ac.wwu.edu/~fhc/

# WESTERN WASHINGTON UNIVERSITY
## HUXLEY COLLEGE OF ENVIRONMENTAL STUDIES

500 Undergraduates    Bellingham, Washington

Are you concerned about the environment and like the challenge of problem solving with others; do you want a career where you can make a difference? The faculty, staff, and students at Huxley College of Environmental Studies share your genuine concern for the environmental well-being of the earth.

A diverse student body of more than 500 undergraduate and 50 graduate students from around the world come to Huxley College with a commitment to hands-on environmental problem solving. As a graduate of Huxley College you will take your place among the more than 2,000 alumni who have active, rewarding careers throughout the world. Alumni are employed as leaders in education, directors of environmental agencies, administrators in conservation groups, and as key managers in national and international organizations. Huxley graduates are making a positive impact internationally by their participation in environmental decision making.

Huxley is one of six colleges that, together with the Graduate School, comprise Western Washington University — consistently recognized as one of the outstanding public institutions of higher education in the West. Established in 1968, Huxley is one of the oldest environmental colleges in the nation. The College's academic programs reflect a broad view of our physical, biological, social, and cultural world. This innovative and interdisciplinary approach makes Huxley unique, and it has won national and international recognition thanks to its comprehensive upper-division and graduate programs.

Students pursue specialization in their chosen fields, gaining breadth through interdisiplinary coursework. Courses at Huxley are primarily upper-division (junior and senior level). Students enter the College with a foundation in science and social studies. They may design independent programs within Huxley and cooperative programs with other departments of the University. Faculty and staff are readily available to collaborate with students' initiatives in learning. In addition to their classroom work, students participate in internships and may serve with faculty and staff on college committees.

Huxley College contends that the more people know about their environment in its interdependent detail, the better they will be able to make decisions relative to a quality of life that depends on the environment. To this end the College teaches and researches, in an interdisciplinary and systematic way, the complex issues and problems of the natural environment and its social overlay. Huxley is a gathering place and focus for those genuinely concerned about the environmental well-being of the earth.

The Institute for Environmental Toxicology and Chemistry provides opportunities for research and education in the effects of toxic substances on aquatic and terrestrial species. The Institute for Watershed Studies provides opportunities and specialized equipment for freshwater and watershed studies. A marine laboratory on Fidalgo Island provides facilities for marine students.

# MAKING A DIFFERENCE STUDIES

## Environmental Studies

Environmental Disturbances
Environment and Resource Policy
Fundamentals of Ecology or Biol. Ecology
Social Impact Assessment
Environmental Risk Management
Landscape Ecology

Human Ecology
Environmental History and Ethics
Elementary Organic Chemistry
Environmental Impact Assessment
Oceanography

## Environmental Science: Aquatic Ecology; Marine Ecology; Terrestrial Ecology; Environmental Chemistry; Environmental Toxicology

Ecology
Environmental Physiology & Biochemistry
Air Pollution
Water Quality Lab
Intro. to Marine Pollution and Toxicology

Introduction to Environmental Toxicology
Energy & Energy Resources
Environmental Impact Assessment
Conservation of Biological Diversity
Aquatic Ecology/Lab

## Planning & Environmental Policy: Planning; Human & Intternational Studies; Geography; Environmental & Resource Management

Introduction to Planning
Environmental Systems
United States Environmental Policy
Map Reading and Analysis
Planning Studio

Urbanization: Processes and Patterns
Environmental Impact Assessment
Analysis of Areal Data
The Planning Process
Urban Economics

## Environmental Studies: Economics concentration

Economics, Environment & Natural Resources
Geography of the World Economy
Intermediate Macro-Economics
Energy Economics
Environment and Resource Policy

Developing World
Population and Resources
Environmental Economics
Resource Economics
Environmental History and Ethics

## Mass Communication & Environmental Education

*Skill development courses in four relevant areas: Newswriting; Editing; Reporting; Introduction to Broadcasting; Broadcast Communication; Television News Production (Feature Writing)*

Environmental Education
The History of Conservation in America
Environmental Interpretation Methods
Introduction to Mass Media
Mass Communications Theory and Research

The Environmental Education Curriculum
The American Literature of Nature and Place
Advanced Environmental Writing
The Press and Society
Introduction to Social Psychology

Outdoor Education & Interpretation    Education/Environmental Studies (Elementary)

Apply by: 3/1    Student body: 94% state, 61% female, 39% male, 16% minority

Director of Admissions
Huxley College
Western Washington University
Bellingham, WA 98225-9009

206. 650.3520
www.wwu.edu
www.ac.wwu.edu/~huxley/

# UNIVERSITY OF WISCONSIN, STEVENS POINT
## COLLEGE OF NATURAL RESOURCES
1,600 CNR Students    Stevens Point, Wisconsin

The College of Natural Resources (CNR) is widely regarded as the leading under-graduate program in natural resources in the United States. It began in 1946 with the nation's first conservation education major. The conservation education program pro-vided a broad background in natural resources management, ethics, and philosophy for high school teachers. In 1970 the College was formally established and is now the largest undergraduate program in North America, with over 60 faculty and staff, 1600 undergraduates, and 70 graduate students. The strength of the program is the inter-disciplinary education of its students. All students take coursework in forestry, wildlife, water resources, and soils before focusing on their major.

All of CNR's faculty are committed to undergraduate education; over one fourth have received the coveted excellence in teaching recognition at UW Stevens Point.

UWSP is located on the north edge of Sevens Point in Portage County, the geo-graphic center of Wisconsin. Portage County is located within an ecological "tension zone" that separates northern plant and animal communities from those in the south. As a result, the county has a rich diversity of flora and fauna. A general inventory of the county includes: 160,000 aces of forest land, 32,000 acres of wetlands, 31,000 acres of public lands within a 20 mile radius of campus, 64 streams and 135 lakes.

Students at CNR are are involved. The College has 16 student-professional organizations with over 650 active members. Student organization members gain skills and experience in leadership development, communications, public relations , and practical application of their knowledge. Over 150 students hold paying intern-ship positions — earning in excess of $300,000 annually — with 56 state, federal, and private agencies throughout the United States.

The College emphasizes field experience in all curricula and operates three field stations. Treehaven, a 1,200-acre field station near Tomahawk, Wisconsin, serves as a year round conference center as well as a base for our summer camp and short cours-es. All CNR students participate in a six week summer camp field experience at Treehaven, or attend a similar program in Europe. The Central Wisconsin Environmental Station (CWES) is a 500-acre facility on Sunset Lake, 17 miles east of Stevens Point. CWES is a year-round conference and education center. The Schmeeckle Reserve is a 200-acre nature preserve, adjacent to the UWSP campus, that provides a field laboratory for many UWSP classes as well as an extension of the city park program.

CNR international programs allow students to gain a global perspective on resource management. The three international programs coordinated by the CNR are: the European Environmental Studies program in Poland and Germany for 6 weeks; a semester abroad in Australia, New Zealand, & the Fiji Islands; and an inter-im trip to study rain forest ecology in Costa Rica for 3 weeks.

Graduates of the CNR are in great demand. Students have many job offers and overall, 80 -100% either go to graduate school or find jobs in their fields.

# MAKING A DIFFERENCE STUDIES

## Wildlife

Wildlife Ecology
Wildlife and Society: Contemporary Issues
Wildlife Diseases
Wildlife Population Dynamics
Human Dimensions of Wildlife and Fisheries Management

Wildlife Forum
Principles of Captive Wildlife Management
Management of Wildlife Habitat
Nonconsumptive Uses of Wildlife

## International Resource Management

International Resources Management
Processes of Sociocultural Change
Peoples of Central & South America
World Populations & Resources
United Nations at Work

Internship
International Economics
Latin American Development
Introduction to Environmental Study
Environmental Psychology

## Resource Management (Conservation): Secondary Teaching Certification

Foundations of Environmetal Education
Environmental Policy
American Environmental History

Resource Economics
Population Problems
Environmental Degradation: World Survey

## Environmental Education: Elementary & Middle School

Intro to Enviro Study & Enviro Education
Environmental Field Studies
General Ecology

Environmental Field Studies
Environmental Ethics
Physical Environment Under Stress

## Captive Wildlife Management

Animal Physiology
Wildlife Diseases
Animal Behavior
Museum Methods

Principles of Captive Wildlife Management
Techniques of Captive Wildlife Management
Wildlife Economics
Animal Parasitology

## Environmental Communication

Natural Resources and Public Relations
Interpretive Publications
Planning for Interpretation
Interpersonal Communication
Film Laboratory

Interpretive Signs, Trails and Waysides
Interpretation for Visitor Centers
Oral Interpretation Methods
Basic Broadcasting Laboratory
Local Production of Media

## Natural Resources: Environmental Education & Interpretation; Land Use Planning; Youth Programming & Camp Management

Environmental Interpretation Practicum
International Resource Management
Integrated Resources Management
Environmental Law Enforcement
Park Interpretation

Citizen Action in Environmental Education
Resource Economics
Environmental Issues Investigation
Natural Resource and Public Relations
Soil Conservation & Watershed Inventory

**Urban Forestry Mgm't.    Soil Science    Aquatic Toxicology    Groundwater Mgm't.**

Rolling admissions

College Of Natural Resources          715. 346.2441
University Of Wisconsin — Stevens Point
Stevens Point, WI 54481

# YALE UNIVERSITY

5,200 Undergraduates    New Haven, Connecticut

At Yale, education is achieved by dialogue — between roommates and classmates; between students, teachers and texts; and between the university and the city in which it is located. The richness of this dialogue reflects the richness of the Yale community, which attracts talented students from all over North America and the world. Everyone at Yale encounters difference and is challenged in his or her assumptions and beliefs. At the same time, the student body of 5,200 undergraduates is large and heterogenous enough that all students can find the support they need to develop and articulate their concerns.

One such support is the residential college system. Every student belongs to one of 12 residential Colleges throughout his or her years at Yale. Students live and eat in the residential College community, which draws from a cross-section of Yale's diverse undergraduate population and is small enough to be familiar and close-knit.

Students at Yale also learn about being part of a larger community that extends beyond the campus to include New Haven, a city whose roots stretch back to the 1600's. More than 50 percent of the student body is involved in volunteer work in this community, whether addressing critical social issues, tutoring at a local school, or volunteering at a soup kitchen. Dwight Hall, the umbrella organization for undergraduate community-service groups, is the largest such organization on any college campus in the US.

In more than 200 undergraduate social, political, and cultural groups — and in more than 30 publications — students are able to voice opinions about campus, national, and international issues. Among these organizations are cultural houses for Yale's minority communities, single-issue groups like the Student Environmental Coalition, the Yale Hunger and Homelessness Action Project, and the Yale Journal for Human Rights.

Among major universities, Yale is distinctive for the number of courses with comparatively small enrollments. Of its 2,000 courses, 85 percent have fewer than twenty-five students. Equally important, professors at Yale are dedicated to undergraduate teaching. Widely respected senior professors and young aspiring scholars share their passion and knowledge in classes, and in one-on-one conversations during office hours. Quality student-faculty relationships are often cited as one of Yale's most important strengths.

Every student's course of study is self-selected and unique. Without requiring specific courses, each student takes a broad sampling in humanities, arts, sciences, and social sciences. Yale's extensive array of academic resources offers undergraduates unparalleled opportunities to explore and learn. With its combination of breadth and depth, Yale starts students on a path of learning that lasts throughout their lives.

Yale stays abreast of new philosophies of education and recognizes that, in a complex world, people need to develop a broad cultural and ethical awareness. Interdisciplinary majors respond to these and other issues: International Studies focus on global socioeconomic, environmental, and political change; Ethics, Politics, and Economics examines the institutions, practices, and politics that shape our world. Within many majors there are "tracks" for students interested in special subtopics, such as the new track in Geology — Earth, Environment, and Resources.

# MAKING A DIFFERENCE STUDIES

## Ethics, Politics and Economics

*Constructive responses to natural and social hazards, allocation of limited social resources (medical care) or morally sensitive political issues (affirmative action) require close knowledge of their political, economic, and social dimensions, and a capacity to think rigorously about the basic questions they raise.*

Classics of Ethics, Politics & Economics
Culture and Social Criticism
Enviro. & Development in Third World
Comparative Political-Economic Systems
Welfare Economics, Social Choice and Political Theory

Liberalism and Its Critics
Ethics in International Relations
Gender, Race, and the State in America
The Politics of Parental Authority

## Economics

Labor Economics
Economics of Developing Countries
The Economics of Population
Int'l Trade, Development & Environment
Economic Problems of Latin America

Health & Social Consequences of Economic Devlp't
Economics of Natural Resources
Topics in Labor Economics
Corporation & State in 20th Century Capitalism
From Plan to Market in Russia & Eastern Europe

## History

War and Society in the U.S.
American Labor in the 20th Century
The Balkan Lands and Peoples
Colonial Latin America
Suburbanization of America: Social History

China in Western Minds
The Holocaust in Historical Perspective
Amer. Missionaries & W. African Christianity
New Deal Liberalism and Its Critics
Excellence & Equity: Competing Goals in Amer. Ed.

## Literature

Identity & the Landscape in Literature
Science and Literature
Self-Representation and Technology
Art and Ideology
Postcolonial Literatures

Modern French Feminisms
Cultural Perspectives in Chinese Literature
The Problem of Evil
The Writing of History After the Holocaust
Problems in Cultural Criticism

- **Totalitarian Humanity: Literature & History** *Ideological-totalitarian regimes of the twentieth century in which intellectuals and artists played a visible role both of support and of defiance. Focus on Soviet terror and the Jewish Holocaust as well as on Yugoslavia. Nationalism, linguistic culture, utopian ideologies, terror and resistance.*

## Political Science

Multinationals and the State
Ethics in International Relations
Public Opinion
Politics of National Security and Law
Political Economy of East Asian Newly Industrialized Countries

Intelligence and Covert Operations
Environment & Development in Third World
The U. N. & Maintenance of International Security
Religion & Politics in Comparative Perspective

### Women's Studies    Anthropology    Psychology    Geology & Geophysics
Apply by 12/31
- Individualized majors  • Multidisciplinary classes  • Team teaching  •Vegetarian/vegan meals

Office of Undergraduate Admissions
Yale University
P.O. Box 208234
New Haven, CT 06520-8234

203. 432.9300
www.yale.edu

# MAKING
## A
# DIFFERENCE

• • •

## FIELD STUDIES

• • •

## SUMMER INSTITUTES

• • •

## TRAVEL PROGRAMS

• • •

## ACTIVIST TRAININGS

• • •

# ARAVA INSTITUTE FOR ENVIRONMENTAL STUDIES

Kibbutz Ketura, Israel

The Arava Institute for Environmental Studies offers a year or semester of intensive hands-on learning in the scenic Arava Valley of southern Israel. Situated near the Jordanian and Egyptian borders, AIES serves as a regional center for conservation and environmental protection activities, and for developing ties between Middle Eastern and international university students. Arava Institute offers the foremost environmental studies program in Israel and the Middle East. The Institute is based at Kibbutz Ketura, an agricultural settlement situated in the Arava desert, 50 kilometers from Eilat, Israel's Red Sea resort, and Aqaba, the adjacent Jordanian port city.

The Institute's curriculum is divided into three main tracks: environmental policy, environmental sciences, and environmental ethics. Students are required to take basic courses in each of these areas. They also select from a series of related electives. While the Institute prefers students to complete a two-semester program, it is possible to attend for one semester only. Taught in English, AIES courses are designed to provide university students with the technical literacy, the familiarity with public policy, and the comprehension of philosophical concepts necessary to participate actively and effectively in environmental matters. Academic credits are given through the internationally-recognized Tel Aviv University Overseas School.

Specific projects and training, including areas such as wildlife captive breeding and repatriation, coral preservation, sustainable agriculture, and environmental activism and advocacy, contribute to a holistic educational experience. The Institute's location allows it to focus on issues concerning desertification, water conservation, sustainable architecture, wastewater treatment and reuse in agriculture, and marine environment preservation.

Students examine regional environmental issues from an interdisciplinary perspective with a diverse group of students from Israel, the Palestinian National Authority, Jordan, Egypt, and nations outside the Middle East including the US, Canada, Sweden, and China. They participate in multi-day trips exploring natural and cultural sites in Israel and the Middle East, with a focus on environment and development issues. A recent trip focusing on regional water issues included a visit with Shimon Peres, former Israeli Prime Minister. Opportunities abound to learn about the challenging and growing environmental movement in the Middle East through classes, trips, and a bi-weekly Speakers Forum.

The AIES faculty is comprised of academics and practicing professionals who offer students a solid theoretical grounding in environmental studies, as well as the practical skills required for conservation activities. In addition, leading experts from the Arab world are integrated into the teaching program, offering supplementary seminars and lectures during the semester.

| American Friends of Tel Aviv Univ. | (800) 665-9828 |
| or | TAUOAA@aol.com |
| Arava Inst. for Environmental Studies | 927.7.635.6618 |
| Kibbutz Ketura, Israel | ketura-aies@ketura.ardom.co.il |
| | www.ardom.co.il/heilot/ketura/aies |

# AUDUBON EXPEDITION INSTITUTE
## NATIONAL AUDUBON SOCIETY
100 Students    Based in Belfast, Maine

The Audubon Expedition Institute offers an extraordinary educational journey. AEI's philosophy comes directly from years of creating and living in our unique educational environment — North America. The journey, which began as an educational experiment twenty five years ago, has become a sought after educational model.

Nature has always been and continues to be our best teacher. The places we have visited, and the people who inhabit them, have guided our curriculum. AEI has changed and grown as environmental and student needs have changed. The lessons have been transforming, and through our experiences we have created an academic program that speaks to the environmental and educational needs of today.

AEI offers an opportunity to actively experience nature and people as parts of a whole. The Institute's program fosters a thorough understanding of the world of plant, animal, air, earth, and spirit — the world where community, relationships, and life are of primary importance.

Through small-community living, AEI challenges students to experience and examine life. By using the school community as a microcosm of larger systems, students learn to apply fresh insights and skills from their lives both to the political and social structure of society, and to the workings of natural systems.

AEI believes in open and honest communication as a route to personal growth. We foster the development of clear and honest written and verbal communication, and a healing and open relationship with ourselves and others, in order to promote interpersonal understanding.

Audubon's program promotes educational excellence through structured self-directed field studies, hands-on experience, and traditional academics. AEI integrates challenging outlooks with progressive ways of learning in nature to encourage the evolution of independent thinking, self-discovery, and scholastic competency.

Each student is encouraged to cultivate individual spiritual growth. Developing a spiritual relationship with the environment is of primary importance in understanding the inherent connections between people, nature, and culture. AEI encourages a lifestyle that leads to the integration of humanity and nature. By providing ethical, philosophical, and practical skills development in ecological studies, we prepare the individual for a life of service as a global citizen. AEI invites students to consider that their physical, emotional, intellectual, and spiritual well-being can lead to global health. The Institute encourages students to approach their relationship to the Earth with the care and reciprocity that allows all persons to seek their fullest potential.

Participation in AEI's Bachelor's degree program is an exciting opportunity for a student to broaden his or her experience while preparing for careers in education, public policy, conservation, small and non-profit business, industry, science, or environmental work. The environment becomes your educator as you immerse yourself in the study of culture and nature. Students develop skills in such diverse subjects as ecology, geology, English, psychology, history, and anthropology, and meld the sciences with the humanities to bring a holistic overview to each student's journey in education. The faculty members guide students in expanding their communication skills and broadening their environmental outlook. Each student's vision is cultivated through direct contact with diverse cultural groups, studies in nature, idea exchanges among students and faculty, and analysis of expedition experiences.

Undergraduate students may participate in the field program for one semester, a full year (two semesters), three semesters, or two years (four semesters). AEI's Quest Program described below is an individually-designed Independent Study/Internship that takes place during a student's third year. Students may wish to participate in Audubon Expedition Institute programs immediately following high school, as a post-graduate year instead of taking a year off before college. Credits taken with AEI can generally be applied towards a student's undergraduate degree. Many students come as sophomores or juniors in order to enhance their classroom experiences. Most colleges accept credit either directly from AEI or from Lesley College in Cambridge, Massachusetts with which our program is affiliated.

Students can receive a Bachelor of Science degree in Environmental Studies from AEI and Lesley College. The undergraduate program sequence of 64 AEI credits (equivalent of four traveling semesters), plus 64 additional liberal arts credits can be arranged in several ways. Up to 3 semesters taken with AEI may be applied to the following degrees granted by Lesley College: B.S. in Education, B.S. in Human Services, B.A. in Liberal Studies, B.S. in Self-Designed majors, or an A.A. in Liberal Arts.

Quest is a student-designed, junior or senior year personal "expedition" to seek educational and career settings that complement the Audubon/Lesley B.S. degree. Quest may take the form of an internship, an apprenticeship, an independent study project, or a combination of these during the third year.

A limited number of Advanced Placement high school students may also enroll in the AEI program. Students are given the opportunity to challenge themselves academically in a supportive experiential setting, while earning both their final high school credits and Lesley College credits. Students take the combination of high school and college courses while traveling and participating fully as Expedition members. They are involved in every aspect of the educational process, from selecting and planning activities to carrying them out and evaluating them. The Advanced Placement program is only offered during a student's final semester of high school.

Audubon Expedition Institute also has a 2-year, fully accredited graduate program offering a Master of Science in Environmental Education.

# MAKING A DIFFERENCE STUDIES

*Following is a sample of AEI programs and regions visited. While no one bus visits all of these places in the course of a year, nor has all the experiences listed, this list gives a brief glimpse of the scope of the program.*

**Pacific Northwest Semester: SW British Columbia, Washington, Oregon, N. California**

Explore strikingly different ecosystems including the Sierra Mountains, the Hoh Rain Forest, and Mount Saint Helens. Listen to a Makah Indian story-teller recite legends in her traditional tongue, investigate highly controversial logging practices, study sea lions on the Oregon coast, and hike on trails through old-growth redwoods.

**Southwest Semester: Arizona, New Mexico, Southern Utah, Southern Colorado**

Backpack, explore, and ski cross-country among the canyons, buttes, mesas, and desert ecosystems of the Four Corners area. Discover and explore ancient Anasazi cliff dwellings and then experience the ceremonies of their descendants, the Hopi Indians. Water scarcity, grazing, and mining are major environmental struggles in the Southwest.

**Southeast Semester: Florida, Georgia, Louisiana, S. & N. Carolina, Tennessee**

From wading through the Everglades in search of unusual birds, to West Virginia hiking in the Smoky Mountains during the spring wildflower extravaganza, the Southeast provides a rich tapestry of folklore and natural history. Talk with old-time musicians, wrestle with development issues, visit a citrus plantation, and work to protect endangered wildlife.

**Mountain/Plains Semester: Wyoming, Colorado, Montana, South Dakota**

Rocky Mountain geology, grassland ecology, national park mgm't, water issues, and endangered species are the academic backdrop for this semester. Discover the difference between Lakota-Sioux Indian and European/American influences upon this bioregion, and explore some of North America's best known parks.

**Canadian Maritime/New England Semester: Newfoundland, New Brunswick, Nova Scotia, Maine, New Hampshire, Vermont, Massachusetts**

Glacial geology, coastal and tundra ecology, and forest biology accent this semester. Spend a day with an old-time fisherman, canoe in the northern Maine woods, and be immersed in a tide-pool during a day of estuarine ecology. Issues involving forest management, acid rain, and hydro-electric projects are highlighted.

*These experiences translate into course work in the following manner:*

**First Year Courses**

| | |
|---|---|
| Ecology of Place | English as a Means of Self-Expression |
| People, Land and Traditions | Physical Education: Camp & Outdoor Ed. |
| Learning Communities | Physical Education: Health and Wellness |

• **Ecology of Place** *Survey the biomes, ecosystems, microsystems, and geological features which comprise the bioregion. The ability to visualize and conceptualize geologic processes and principles which have shaped the earth and its life are emphasized. Understanding of the interrelationships of all life as well as humanity's position in the natural world is stressed. Examine natural systems with a deep ecological perspective in addition to a more traditional scientific approach.*

## Second Year Courses

Applied Ecology

Practicum in Environmental Education

Human Diversity

Methods of Independent Learning & Self-Directed Study

Eco-Philosophy

Special Topic in Ecology

- **Eco-Philosophy** *Our post-industrial society is in the midst of a transition, with the outcome still unknown. This course offers students an opportunity to personally explore a newly-emerging ecological world view which pursues wisdom and is spiritually alive, life-oriented, socially-concerned, and environmentally-sensible. At the core of this philosophical journey is the art of asking questions that open hearts and minds to a healthy dialogue. In this time of deep personal and social change, such questions encourage us to expand our ecological consciousness and increase our reverence for natural wisdom.*

## Third Year "Quest" Courses

Voice of Nature

Survey of Personal Growth

Environment As Educator

Internship

- **Life Systems Communication** *Examines the functioning of earth's ecosystems on a global scale. Based on the Gaian hypothesis that the planet Earth is alive and that all life has a common interest in self-preservation, this course identifies the basic communication processes between critical ecological and geological systems. Earth communication is compared to the various means by which people communicate.*

- Faculty Bio **Susan Klimczak** *(M.S. Environmental Ed., Lesley College). Susan worked for nine years as an engineer specializing in communications. Her work includes community organizing around feminist issues, renovating shelters for the inner city homeless, volunteering in a prison, and living on a permaculture demonstration farm. A published writer, she is enthusiastic about Environmental Justice, sustainable agriculture, multi-cultural education, as well as Quaker and Eastern philosophy.*

- Faculty Bio **Hank Colletto** *(M.S. Environmental Ed., Lesley College). Hank has been part of a consensus-run community land trust where he built a solar, earth-bermed home, and was active in grassroots environmental organizations. As an energy conservation consultant, Hank presented workshops on photovoltaics, superinsulation, solar construction techniques, and solar heating. His work as an environmental education trip leader adds to the foundation of his teaching career. Hank's humor and storytelling are an integral part of the bus experience and he finds particular joy in guiding students on a transformative journey in search of their dormant inner wildness.*

Apply by: Fall semester & full year — early decision1/1, preferred admissions 3/1

Spring semester —- early decision 9/1, preferred admissions 11/1

Additional per semester credit fee if arranged through Lesley College.

Average age: 19    Faculty: 50% male, 50% female

- Team teaching  • Individualized majors  • Exclusive seminar format
- Service-learning  • Student environmental audits  • Vegetarian meals

100% of students do community service.

Audubon Society Expedition Institute

P.O. Box 365

Belfast, ME 04915

207. 338.5859

AEI@audubon.org

www.audubon.org/audubon/aei.

# BIOSPHERE 2 CENTER
## COLUMBIA UNIVERSITY SUMMER PROGRAMS
60 - 75 students — Arizona        14 students — Baja California, Mexico

Columbia University Biosphere 2 Center programs offer students a variety of ways to learn about the environment and planetary stewardship. Students design and run experiments inside Biosphere 2 itself. They work side-by-side with internationally noted researchers studying one of the most critical issues of the future. Students explore the desert Southwest from the Grand Canyon to the Gulf of California.

In the mid-1980's, in the foothills of the Santa Catalina Mountains, Space Biosphere Ventures constructed an award-winning set of research facilities  focused on exploring the dynamics of life in closed systems. These facilities included the world-renowned Biosphere 2, a 3.15-acre research facility with seven biomes focusing on those environmental regions found at 30 degrees north and south of the equator. It houses a tropical rainforest, a million-gallon ocean with living coral reef, a desert, savannah, marshland, human habitat, and intensive agricultural area. Cutting edge research and education programs on the effects of global warming and greenhouse gasses have been the focus of the facility since Columbia took over its management in 1996.

The programs at Biosphere 2 are interdisciplinary in their approach. This means that while you study biology, geology, botany, political science, history, and economics you don't take different courses for each of these topics. Instead, you will study an environmental issue from the perspective of each of these disciplines at the same time. This teaches you about the intersections between subjects, and it also teaches you how to respect and understand the complexities of opposing viewpoints.

The programs focus on team-based projects, giving students the opportunity to learn how to create successful working groups — an invaluable skill for college and beyond. Students utilize the latest in computer technology and complex systems management theory to problem-solve. The goal is not to make each person an environmental scientist, rather to provide each student with the tools to approach decision-making with a critical eye and to understand the impact of their actions on all members of planet Earth.

Student-life programs help students discover the unique and interesting cultures and natural wonders of the desert Southwest. Programs include social, cultural, and athletic activities. Each class is unique in its personality and helps to shape the list and mix of activities.  Weekend shuttle service is provided for the students. Special events have included Native American heritage celebrations, astronomy, Latin dance lessons, canyon and mountain hiking trips, and lots more.

Biosphere 2 programs welcome — and are designed to work best with — a diversity of students. Students from around the United States and the world have participated in each of our programs. Students come from schools representing all areas of the U.S. and from such countries as Nepal, Sri Lanka, Austria, Bulgaria, Mexico, and Canada.

# MAKING A DIFFERENCE STUDIES

*Students may choose to participate in either the semester-long (fifteen weeks) program or summer programs ranging in length from two to six weeks.*

### The Earth Semester

A comprehensive, interdisciplinary study abroad experience. Explore the Southwest desert on field trips, interpret data from your own original research, participate in team-based projects on the future of planetary stewardship, and study the history of planet Earth. This program is open to students who have completed at least the first semester of college. (16 credits from Columbia University)

### Island Conservation and Biogeography in the Sea of Cortez (2 weeks)

Program takes place aboard a ship and on the islands of the Southern Baja peninsula in Mexico. Study islands as models of the impact humans have on environments. This program is open to students who have completed at least their junior year in high school. Mid-June

### Earth Systems Field School (6 weeks)

Session 1 (Earth Camp) is a field geology and ecology course which studies how the Earth and environment has evolved to its current state, especially looking at the impact of humans. Students explore the Southwest desert from the Grand Canyon to the Gulf of California, and the Biosphere 2 research facility. Open to students who have completed at least their sophomore year in college. (6 credits) Beginning of June to mid-July.

### Earth Systems Field School, Session 2 - Planetary Stewardship (4 weeks)

This is a management course which teaches students the basics of environmental science from a whole-Earth perspective, while teaching them to be good managers of the planet and their lives. This course focuses on the tools necessary to be good managers, giving skills which will be useful to students regardless of their career aspirations. Open to students who have completed at least their junior year in high school. Mid-July to mid-August

Hiking is required in each of the programs, sometimes up to 15 miles each day in high heat and altitude conditions. Each student is strongly encouraged to discuss the program with his/her family physician prior to program participation.

Rolling admissions, apply early
Costs vary by program, depending upon length and number of college credits awarded.
Financial assistance is available. Scholarships from $500 to full-tuition.

Office of Student Affairs   800. 992.4603
Columbia U's Biosphere 2 Center admissions@bio2.edu
32540 S. Biosphere Road  www.bio2.edu
Oracle, AZ 85623

# CENTER FOR AGROECOLOGY &
# SUSTAINABLE FOOD SYSTEMS
## UNIVERSITY OF CALIFORNIA, SANTA CRUZ

Each year the Center's Apprenticeship in Ecological Horticulture provides 35 students with an intensive, six-month training course in basic organic gardening and farming techniques. The Apprenticeship has developed into an internationally recognized program that blends the virtues of hands-on experiential learning with traditional classroom studies. Apprentices work with staff at the campus's 25-acre Farm and at the 4-acre Alan Chadwick Garden to gain experience in the entire cropping cycle, from soil preparation and plant propagation to harvest and marketing.

The goal is to provide a diverse mix of students with an intensive education in organic growing methods and concepts, and the promotion of food and agricultural systems which are environmentally sound, socially responsible, economically viable, and beneficial to communities around the world.

Apprentices receive more than 200 hours of formal instruction in the classroom, in small group classes in the field, and on field trips designed to broaden their exposure to different aspects of sustainable agriculture. The core curriculum covers topics such as soil science, soil fertility management, botany, biological management, crop planning, and marketing. Apprentices are exposed to the different aspects of growing plants organically both on the scale of a hand-dug garden and of a tractor-cultivated field.

While classes provide the conceptual framework for the course, much of the learning happens as apprentices work side-by-side with staff in the gardens and fields. Over 800 hours of hands-on training give apprentices a concrete context for the concepts and methods learned in classes and demonstrations. Visiting speakers, brought in to increase the range of topics covered, are drawn from the rich pool of agricultural scientists, extensionists, farmers, and gardeners in our area. Apprentices take field trips to different farm and garden operations, and to interesting horticultural and agricultural sites in and around Santa Cruz.

The apprentices selected to attend the course each year are interested in practical training that will prepare them to run their own operations and/or to teach others. Graduates have made a positive impact in the world as:
- Instructors in international development programs;
- Community garden leaders, school garden teachers, & horticultural therapists;
- Successful organic farmers and gardeners;
- Advocates for economic models such as community supported agriculture;
- Developers of teaching gardens for the homeless; and
- Environmental educators and writers who teach the importance of sustainable agriculture to groups, organizations, and the general public.

A Certificate in Ecological Horticulture is awarded by UC Extension and gives 20 extension credits which might be transferable. Second-year apprentices act as assistant managers and field instructors. Traditionally, seven are hired on at the end of the Apprenticeship to work through October of the following year.

# MAKING A DIFFERENCE STUDIES

The Chadwick Garden was established by the late Alan Chadwick, a master horticulturist who pioneered both an organic gardening method and an apprenticeship model. This Garden is where the French intensive method of horticulture first gained recognition in the US. Under Chadwick's direction, a cadre of dedicated student and community volunteers transformed a steep, brushy hillside into an incredibly diverse garden that stands as a graphic example of how marginal land can be transformed into a productive garden.

The Farm supports several acres of vegetable and fruit crops, together with perennial and annual flowers and herbs. Apples, pears, plums, kiwis, and persimmons grow in the Farm's two orchards. The 10-acre Farm includes crops for the Community Supported Agriculture project. The hand-dug garden area features vegetables, flowers, and herbs for the direct-market stand, and a demonstration nutrition garden.

Although the Farm and Garden are less than a mile apart, they differ in soils, topography, microclimate, and history, requiring different management strategies at the two sites.

### Growing Methods

*Plant propagation, organic greenhouse techniques, crop planning, French-intensive bed preparation, transplanting and sowing, crop care, cultivation, seed-saving, and irrigation.*

### Botany

*Botanical characteristics and requirements of specific vegetable crops, herbs, flowers, fruits, and trees, and how they may be combined in a farm or garden.*

### Soils

*Soil science, soil/plant interactions, soil fertility management, composting, and cover cropping.*

### Pests and Diseases

*Weeds and organic weed control, vertebrate and invertebrate pests, insect pests, plant diseases, and organic pest and disease control.*

### Marketing

*Post-harvest handling, marketing strategies and outlets, small farm/garden management, and Community Supported Agriculture (CSA) management.*

The Apprenticeship runs continuously from mid-April to mid-October. This program involves strenuous physical work five days a week. Examples of daily activities include bed preparation, transplanting, seed sowing, watering, weeding, composting, harvesting, produce handling, storage, and marketing. Rotational positions of responsibility, such as cooking, cleaning, greenhouse managing, watering, and market coordinating.

Apprentices will get the maximum out of this experience by coming prepared financially, physically, and emotionally, to make the program their singular focus for the six-months.

Apply by 11/1 for U.S. residents & Canadians  9/1 for international applicants
Scholarships available for students of color

Apprenticeship Applications          831. 459.2321
Center for Agroecology & Sustainable Food Systems
University of California, Santa Cruz       alindsey@cats.ucsc.edu
1156 High Street                           http://zzyx.ucsc.edu/casfs/appr.html
Santa Cruz, CA 95064

# CENTER FOR GLOBAL EDUCATION

100 Students     A Program of Augsburg College, Minnesota

The Center for Global Education at Augsburg College offers six undergraduate academic programs abroad for students from colleges and universities throughout the U.S. and Canada. These unique study programs: bring you face-to-face with people struggling for justice; give you hands-on opportunities to meet and discuss current issues with people at the grassroots level; expand your worldview and challenge your perceptions about global justice and human liberation; and provide you with a life-changing experience and the foundation for a job that can make a difference in the world.

These six programs are currently available for sophomores, juniors and seniors at any college or university in the U.S. or Canada. The Center has consortial arrangements with many colleges and universities, allowing you to participate in our programs without changing schools.

What makes the Center's study abroad programs unique?

- Experiential Education: Integrate solid academic work with real-life experiences.
- Diverse Guest Lecturers: Learn directly from local people involved in some of the most important issues of our time.
- Living/Learning Community: Reflect on your learning experience in a community of students interested in similar issues.
- Family Stay: Spend several days to several weeks living with local families and participate in their daily life and activities.
- Regional Travel: Broaden your perspective on the cultural history and current social and political struggles in the region through group travel experiences.

Programs in Mexico and Central America require one previous college-level course in Spanish or its equivalent. Students from over 200 colleges and universities in the U.S. and Canada have participated in the Center's academic programs abroad. The Center also coordinates numerous one- to three-week programs in Mexico, Central America, and Southern Africa.

What have previous students said about the programs?

"A person who is sincere about ... questioning himself/herself has everything to gain from this experience. It has deepened my understanding and widened my perspective on the world immeasurably. A wonderful, deeply gratifying experience."

"This was an adventure in empowerment — being confronted with so many other realities made me look so much more critically into my own. Thanks!"

"My experience in Mexico with this program will always be remembered in a positive light and it has influenced the directions I have pursued professionally. Thanks for running the program and giving such a great experience to so many."

"Keep up the tremendous work! I owe the Center my focus and my career path."

"I think this experience was the most important part of my college career. I highly recommend it to anyone interested."

# MAKING A DIFFERENCE STUDIES

**Mexico/Central America**

## Crossing Borders: Gender And Social Change In Mesoamerica (Fall Semester)

Engage in gender analysis of key social, economic, political, and cultural issues; explore the interconnectedness of race, class, and gender; and learn first-hand from both women and men who are involved in struggles for sustainable development and social change. Based in Cuernavaca, Mexico with travel to Chiapas and Guatemala. Orientation at US/Mexico border.

## Gender and the Environment: Latin American Perspectives (Spring Semester)

Explore socio-economic and political issues with a focus on the impact of environmental policies on the lives of women and men from varying economic classes and ethnic groups in Mexico and Central America. Based in Cuernavaca, Mexico with travel to El Salvador and Guatemala.

**Guatemala, El Salvador, & Nicaragua**

## Sustainable Development & Social Change in Central America (Fall & Spring)

Explore the life and culture of the people of Guatemala, El Salvador, and Nicaragua. Improve Spanish language skills while living with families in Guatemalan highlands. Study the role of the Church and social injustice in El Salvador. Examine economic development and the impact of social change movements in Nicaragua.

**Namibia/South Africa**

## Multicultural Societies in Transition: Southern African Perspectives (Fall Semester)

Examine the reconciliation process ending the era of apartheid. Explore the rich mosaic of cultures in Namibia. Challenge yourself to confront your own attitudes toward race and class. Based in Windhoek, Namibia with travel to South Africa.

## Nation Building, Globalization & Decolonizing The Mind: Southern African Perspectives (Spring Semester)

Learn from Namibia and South Africa as they struggle to build nationhood and deal with the legacies of apartheid and colonialism; the challenges posed by rapid globalization; under-and unequal development; and the long-term process of decolonizing the mind. Based in Windhoek, Namibia with travel to South Africa.

| | |
|---|---|
| The Development Process | Social Stratification: Gender, Class and Ethnicity |
| Sustainable Economic Development | Contemporary Social Movements in Central Amer. |
| Internship | Environmental Theology and Ethics |
| The Church and Social Change | Women in Comparative Politics |
| Political and Social Change in Namibia: A Comparative Perspective | |
| Namibia and South Africa: A Historical Perspective | |

Rolling admissions thru 4/1
Average group size: 20 students    Faculty: 50% male, 50% female, 70% minority
• Team teaching  • Service-learning  • Interdisciplinary classes  • Vegetarian meals
• Financial aid from your institution usually applies  • Scholarships available

Center for Global Education
Augsburg College
2211 Riverside Avenue
Minneapolis, MN 55454

800. 299.8889
globaled@augsburg.edu
www.augsburg.edu/global/

# COOL LEADERS

The COOL Leaders Program is a year-long intensive leadership training and development program for college students who are actively involved in campus-based community service and service-learning programs. The primary purpose of COOL Leaders is to help strengthen and expand service programs by providing increased training and support for emerging student leaders.

The COOL Leaders Program provides training for college students to develop and utilize their service and leadership skills. The goals of the program are to provide students with:

- Practical skills training that will make the student a more effective leader on campus and in the community;
- Exposure to a variety of other campus, regional and national organizations in the field of community service, heightening the opportunity for networking and learning; and
- Resources and support to promote the improvement of service programming on their campuses.

COOL Leaders receive skills workshops, resource materials, on-going support, training from COOL staff and other service leaders three times per year, alumni mentoring, monthly mailings, and a dedicated e-mail discussion group (list-serv) just for them.

Students interested in applying to the COOL Leaders Program must be active participants in an established campus-based service organization or service-learning program. The applicant should have at least one year of demonstrated student leadership involvement on campus.

Each school will be asked to sponsor the travel and registration cost for all training activities. COOL though will be responsible for all food and lodging costs during the summer and fall training components. A limited number of scholarships are available.

Campus Opportunity Outreach League
1531 P Street, NW, #LLa
Washington, DC 20005
www.COOL2SERVE.org/COOLleaders.html

# ECO-DESIGN EXPERIENCE

A Program of the San Francisco Institute of Architecture    Oracle, Arizona

The Eco-Design Experience (EDE) is an opportunity to study with Phil Hawes, Ph.D., who studied with both Frank Lloyd Wright and Bruce Goff. Mr. Hawes was the architect of Biosphere 2, in Oracle, Arizona. EDE emphasizes: the classic mentor-apprentice relationship; focuses on sustainable design and building with local materials; renewable energy; food production with Permaculture; natural wastewater treatment systems; water harvesting; and more.

Courses are conducted by hands-on construction and by classroom work that includes selected readings in ecological subjects, discussions, and the writing of short papers. The overall goal is to practice resolving design problems ecologically, and to operate from the point of view of sustainability.

For over thirty years Director Hawes has worked exclusively on ecological projects as an architect, planner, building contractor, and teacher. Phil was the chief architect of the Biosphere 2 Project near Oracle, AZ for seven years. Biosphere 2, a unique experiment using a holistic approach to research the ecology of closed systems, contained 3800 species of life, including eight humans. It was closed-off from the outside world and was internally sustainable and self-sufficient designed to be like Planet Earth.

The essential intention of the Eco-Design Experience is: to become skilled in the theory and practice of creating ecologically sustainable buildings and communities by investigating and integrating a broad spectrum of subjects and to accomplish this through learning-by-doing which is reinforced, by talks, slide and video presentations, and design sketch-projects. There are at least 6 hours of instruction and/or discussion each day plus reading assignments. Classes vary in length from 3 days to 6 weeks. Credit is granted from the San Francisco Institute of Architecture.

Theory learning includes concepts of bioregions, deep ecology, site planning, restoration ecology, rainwater harvesting, passive and active solar, and ecovillage design. Alternative construction methods studied include: adobe, strawbale, cob, stone, rammed earth, and ferrocement.

Hands-on participation is the primary method used at the Eco-Design Experience. In this way conditions promoting elements of mystery, uncertainty, and of the unexpected — in transforming theory into practice — are encountered. Students get practical experience in: designing and building a greenhouse; ferrocement work building rainwater collection tanks, light- weight vaulted roofing panels, a bioremediation pond; designing and building with strawbales; installation of photovoltaic panels and wind generators; and permaculture work with native and heirloom plants, tree planting and more.

Students also help in the kitchen and perform minor maintenance.

Eco-Design Experience
PO Box 5209
Oracle, AZ  85623

520. 896.3303
1-877. 208 6673 (toll free)
philhawes@theriver.com
http://personal.riverusers.com./~philhawes

# THE UNH-ECOQUEST PROGRAM

The University of New Hampshire's Department of Natural Resources and the Environmental Conservation Program serve as a catalyst, engaging its students in the process of preparing themselves professionally and personally to serve as 21st Century leaders in achieving a more sustainable human society. The UNH EcoQuest program, established in 1998, is designed for students who have already embarked on their quest for an understanding of how our planet functions, and for the acquisition of practical research and management tools that will lead to greater sustainability.

EcoQuest offers students from a diversity of disciplines an opportunity to immerse themselves in a rigorous field-based program in applied ecology, resource management, and environmental policy. The program is based on New Zealand's North Island along the shores of the vast, intensively utilized, Hauraki Gulf and associated watershed. Students from the UNH and other accredited institutions participate in the EcoQuest program at its field center — a four-acre coastal and subtropical organic orchard and vegetable garden. This includes a rammed-earth house constructed with ecologically appropriate technology and materials, and a library and field laboratory. Students live in seaside dormitory facilities while they are at home base.

The unique geologic history and island biogeography of isolated New Zealand, combined with its relatively low human population, make it a superb natural laboratory for ecological studies. The EcoQuest focus is conservation biology and ecosystem management. Participants carry out field research on species, habitats, and community interactions in the context of NZ's progressive environmental policies.

The EcoQuest philosophy is based on the concept that sustainable societies can exist only if their citizens exhibit, through action, a commitment to improve their relationships with each other and with the earth. Thus, service learning is a key component of the student's experience. EcoQuest is working to empower a new generation of multi-skilled, hands-on, proactive ecosystem decision-makers. Maori culture and its importance in matters of environmental custodianship and protection plays a key role in the EcoQuest approach. The EcoQuest mission is to:

- Provide participants an intensive inter-disciplinary education in biology, applied ecology, environmental policy, and sustainable management of land, water and air;
- Focus on practical field-based research and problem solving, while bringing together facets needed to resolve issues at the interface of people and the environment;
- Develop awareness of cultural, political, social, economic, and environmental influences in working to achieve sustainable outcomes;
- Encourage development of the heart and spirit as well as the mind and the body.

Students learn to integrate the knowledge and skills they acquire to address questions such as: How are New Zealand's habitat management strategies addressing threats of irreversible extinctions and alterations? What are the biological, economic, and political opportunities and constraints for expanded aquaculture, eco-tourism, and recreational activity in the Hauraki Gulf? How do the different resource-use regimes affect sustainability? What is the role played by the Maori people and the Treaty of Waitangi in resource management policies and practices?

To address these questions students learn to analyze and understand the complex environmental and economic issues of:

- sustainable development
- marine biosecurity
- rehabilitation of habitats
- riparian management
- forestry and agricultural practices
- ecotourism
- biodiversity
- wildlife recovery
- environmental indicators and monitoring
- shellfish farming and enhancement
- watershed management

EcoQuest is situated at the epicentre of a diverse range of ecological, cultural, commercial, and recreational landscapes and activities. Within three hours travel, students have the opportunity to experience varied coastal and marine environments, protected off-shore island sanctuaries, agricultural lands, substantial wetland and riparian ecosystems, lowland and montane forests, and snow covered alpine ranges.

EcoQuest offers two annual 15-week semester programs for 16 credits, and one 5-week program for 8 credits. Credits are provided through the University of New Hampshire and are transferable to other institutions. Most of the learning occurs in the field, with a high instructor to student ratio. Student numbers range from 10 to 24, with a professional staff of 6 to 10 and numerous specialist lecturers including some of New Zealand's foremost scientific experts and resource managers. Semester students travel to many locations around the country to do comparative studies of different ecosystems and effects. Summer students concentrate on studies of the ocean, islands, estuaries, and coasts of the gulf. Each semester-participant will also do a directed research project, usually in concert with two or three teammates.

Students investigate key elements of diverse ecosystems and the often devastating effects of introduced pests, weeds, and other human impacts on the environment. Most short studies are components of on-going research and monitoring initiatives. Students engage with New Zealanders, both Maori and those of mainly European origin, and thus have opportunities for rich cultural exchanges.

**Fall or Spring semester UNH courses** (16 credits)

Evolution, Biodiversity, and Community Ecology in Geographically Isolated New Zealand
Ecosystem Management and Restoration Ecology in New Zealand
Environmental Policy, Planning, and Economics in New Zealand's Political Context
Applied Directed Research on Sustainable Resource Use in the Hauraki Basin, New Zealand

**Summer session UNH courses** (8 credits)

Environmental Policy, Planning, and Economics in New Zealand's Political Context
Evolution, Biodiversity, and Community Ecology in Geographically Isolated New Zealand

Director of Admissions
UNH-EcoQuest New Zealand
Department of Natural Resources
215 James Hall
Durham, NH 03824

603. 862.2036
ecoquest@unh.edu
www.ecoquest.unh.edu

# INSTITUTE FOR SOCIAL ECOLOGY

Plainfield, Vermont

The Institute for Social Ecology (ISE) was established in 1974 and incorporated in 1981 as an independent institution for the purposes of education, research, and outreach in the field of social ecology. For over a quarter of a century, the ISE has inspired individuals involved in numerous social-change movements to work toward a directly democratic, liberatory, and ecological society.

Social ecology advances an interdisciplinary framework drawing on studies in the natural sciences, philosophy, feminism, anthropology, social and political theory, and history. It provides a coherent, radical critique of current forms of hierarchy and other anti-ecological trends, recognizing that the ecological crisis is rooted in a social crisis. At the same time, social ecology suggests that creative human enterprise can remake society, reharmonizing people's relationship to the natural world by harmonizing our relationship with each other. By integrating theory and practice social ecology offers a reconstructive, communitarian, ecological, and ethical approach to society.

The educational programs of the Institute for Social Ecology have served more than 2,000 students from around the world. A growing international network of social ecologists has been attracted to study at the ISE from such countries as Ethiopia, New Zealand, Chile, Iran, Greece, Bhutan, Australia, Sweden, Sri Lanka, Uruguay, the Sudan, Puerto Rico, Germany, Guatemala, Nepal, Japan, Norway, Ireland, Korea, Indonesia, and Canada.

ISE's mission is to enhance people's understanding of their relationship to the natural world and to each other. That understanding, by necessity, involves the deepening of our awareness of self and society which helps us to think critically and to expand our perception of creative potentialities for human action. The purpose of the Institute for Social Ecology is the preparation of well-rounded human beings who can work effectively as participants in the process of social and ecological reconstruction.

The programs of the Institute offer a college-level curriculum. ISE also offers lectures, workshops and other learning activities throughout the year, and hosts a variety of conferences, activist meetings, and community events. The ISE's renowned summer program features the three-week Planning, Design, and Construction for Sustainable Communities, and the month-long Ecology and Community.

The ISE location allows it to offer both hands-on experience and a contemplative setting for study. Nestled in the rural Vermont countryside, the ISE's facility n offers indoor and outdoor class-rooms, a library, reading room, bookstore, organic gardens, a swimming pond, camp sites, and spectacular views of the Green Mountains.

# MAKING A DIFFERENCE STUDIES

**Summer Programs**

**Planning, Design, and Construction for Sustainable Communities**

*Using the ISE's 50-acre site on Maple Hill as a laboratory, students devote their time to the study of design principles which can be assigned to any design task: a building, a garden, an orchard, or a campus. There are demonstrations, hands-on projects, and discussions on:*

Layout and Design Principles
Permaculture and Ecological Restoration
Principles of Sustainability
Appropriate Technologies

Drawing, Drafting, and Mapping
Construction Techniques
Organic Agriculture

**Ecology and Community**

*This month-long residential learning experience at the ISE offers an intensive series of workshops and practica in the field of social ecology. Ecology and Community offers participants an opportunity to study and live together in a community setting that reflects the ISE's belief in self-reliance, democracy, and participation. There are a variety of educational activities, from studies on activist history and strategies, to philosophical explorations of society and nature, to work in the gardens. Areas of study include:*

Key Concepts in Ecofeminism
Ecological Movements and Social Activism
Toward Directly Democratic Communities

Culture & Resistance in the Global Economy
Radical Agriculture & Ecological Technology
Public Education and Community Action

The facilitators bring an unusual combination of theoretical depth and activist experience to bear on the study of social ecology. They offer a wide range of professional and practical expertise, and a deep commitment to exploring and expanding the ideas of social change as expressed through social ecology.

Institute for Social Ecology
1118 Maple Hill Road
Plainfield, Vermont 05667

802. 454.8493
ise@sover.net
//ise.rootmedia.org/

# INSTITUTE ON PHILANTHROPY & VOLUNTARY SERVICE
## INDIANA UNIVERSITY

Do you think it is important to give something back to your community? Are you active in organizations on your campus that promote volunteering and civic involvement? Do you know that millions of college students volunteer to help other people every day? Would you like to learn more about why philanthropy is so important for American society? Have you wanted to learn more about the historical roots of philanthropic activity and the ethical values that support them? If so, accept the challenge to live, learn, and intern at the Institute on Philanthropy and Voluntary Service.

The Institute offers a six-week residential program for college undergraduates from across the nation who are engaged in tutoring, mentoring, and other kinds of service programs on and off their campuses, and who are interested in careers in the nonprofit sector. As an Institute participant, you will:

- Deepen your understanding of the history and ethics of philanthropy and volunteering.
- Explore the role of the nonprofit sector as an alternative to government in solving social, economic, and other social problems.
- Gain practical experience through an internship with a nonprofit organization.
- Learn about the importance of a free-market economy to the creation of wealth.
- Meet nationally prominent leaders in philanthropy and voluntary service.
- Identify opportunities for fulfilling careers in nonprofits, particularly in foundation and corporate contribution programs.

Classes taught by faculty of the Center on Philanthropy are held four days a week. You earn six credit hours from Indiana University upon successful completion. Applicants to the Indiana University Summer Institute on Philanthropy and Voluntary Service must be college undergraduates entering their junior or senior year. Applicants should have a strong academic record and some involvement with volunteer activities. Apply early to increase your chances of acceptance into the program.

The experience, knowledge, and contacts you will gain will be valuable assets, and can increase your prospects in getting a job or applying to graduate school.

- **The Role of Philanthropy in American Life** *What is philanthropy, and what roles does it play in American life? Why is it so widespread in our country? What does it accomplish? By looking at some major works in the philanthropic tradition, as well as the work of contemporary observers and experts, the course explores the history, economics, and politics of philanthropy.*

- **The Ethics and Values of Philanthropy** *Are philanthropic impulses of value? If so, why, to whom, and under what conditions? Is there really something called altruism, or is it just self-interest by another name? Are there special ethical standards that people engaged in philanthropic enterprises should be held to? What are the ethical and moral traditions of philanthropy.*

Apply by 4/15    Scholarships available

The Fund for American Studies
IU Summer Institute on Philanthropy & Voluntary Service
1706 New Hampshire Ave., NW                philanthropy@tfas.org
Washington, DC 20009                        www.tfas.org

# INTERNATIONAL HONORS PROGRAM

60 Students

"I will never forget the many people who unselfishly shared their lives with me this year, and I hope that parts of me will also live on with my new friends and host families in different countries. They have given me the most beautiful gifts of all: the strength to face the challenges that lie ahead, the courage to find my own limits and to push them further, the hope that I can help to make the world a better place, and the determination to really make a difference."

— Laura Sessions, IHP '95, Oberlin College '96

Founded in 1958 the International Honors Program, in cooperation with Bard College, offers a small group of 30 students per program the opportunity to: study and travel around the world; work with an international faculty; meet with a variety of leaders, activists, and academics in each country; and live with families in most locations. IHP has two study/travel programs: the two-semester *Global Ecology: Culture, Ecology and Justice* and the one-semester *Cities in the 21st Century: People, Planning and Politics.*

The itinerary for the 2000-2001 Global Ecology program is: Washington DC, England, Tanzania, India, New Zealand, Mexico, and Boston. This year's program will combine academic study — in the areas of ecology, biology, cultural anthropology, and sociology — with on-site examination of governmental policies and independent projects concerned with ecological balance, the environment, social movements and indigenous cultures. The Cities in the 21st Century program will travel to New York, Mumbai (Bombay) India; Johannesburg and Capetown, South Africa; Rio de Janeiro and Curitiba, Brazil; and Washington, D.C. In this semester-long program students will study political science, urban planning, anthropology, and environmental issues in these Mega-cities.

The two-semester 2000-01 Global Ecology program will be the eleventh year with guidance from Edward Goldsmith — publisher of *The Ecologist* magazine, author, and winner of the Right Livelihood Award (alternative Nobel Prize). Other faculty include ecologist Jim Kettler from Bard College Graduate School of Environmental Studies; Jerry Hembd, economist trained at Stanford University, and Patricia Mangan, visiting professor at Mount Holyoke College. IHP leadership is provided by at least two professors in each country with contributions from local academics, environmental experts, and activists including Peter Bunyard in England, Fatma Alloo in Tanzania, Smitu Kothari in India, Peter Horsley in New Zealand, and Gustavo Esteva in Mexico.

The one-semester 2001 Cities in the 21st Century program, in its third year, was developed in conjunction with Janice Perlman, founder and president of the Mega-Cities Project, Inc. — a non-profit organization dedicated to finding innovative solutions to the problems of the world's largest cities. Also on the IHP faculty planning and teaching team are Lisa Peattie, Senior Lecturer in Anthropology at MIT; Hans Spiegel, former Chair of Department of Urban Affairs and Planning at Hunter College; and Melvin H. King, retired faculty political leader at MIT's Department of Urban Studies and Planning. On-site international leadership is provided by Yoland

Trevino in Mumbai, India; George Mathabane and Sally Frankental in South Africa; Claudia Macedo and Henri Acselrad in Rio de Janeiro, Brazil; and Cleon dos Santos in Curitiba, Brazil.

Each program is composed of approximately 80 percent undergraduates and 20 percent recent graduates, mid-career professionals and, occasionally, teachers on sabbatical. Although course work is at the undergraduate level, some students have obtained partial graduate credit for their work with IHP. Students come from a mix of academic backgrounds; while many are majoring in ecology, urban issues, or related fields, recent IHP students have also brought to the program an interest and expertise in art, philosophy, architecture, engineering, politics, music, and history.

IHP encourages and supports an active network of alumni and, in 1994, established a formal mentoring program to connect recent graduates with students from the past 40 years of IHP. Alumni and incoming students have access to a private on-line conference on the Internet where information is shared and many practical questions are answered.

# MAKING A DIFFERENCE STUDIES

## Global Ecology (two semesters: September - May)
## Ecology and Ecosystems

Through visits to key habitats in each country, study first-hand ecology, threats to survival and conservation, and land-use management issues. Fieldwork-based projects in habitats to be visited — including salt marshes, mangroves, tropical forest, and aquatic systems — are an important component. Readings by Odum, Aber and Melilo, Pomeroy, Schlesinger, Weins, and related journal articles.

## Cultural Anthropology

Using comparative cultural and historical readings, and examining societies and cultures first-hand, explore the differences in definitions and uses of "nature" and "environment" and critically appraise how these have an impact on practical matters — even on the survival of peoples and habitats. Readings by Malinowski, Geertz, Boserup, Nash and Descola are complemented by ethnographic literature from each country visited.

## Nature, Culture, and Justice

Interrelationships between ecology, society, and economy are discussed as an integral part of the sustainability debate. Consider the two "moral pillars": environmental responsibility and social justice. Topics include: energy use in particular energy systems; resource depletion, efficiency and renewability; global climate change and the basics of atmospheric chemistry; agricultural and industrial activities; consumerism and markets; health issues and diseases of the environment; ecological world views; environmental ethics and deep ecology; and solutions for achieving sustainability. Readings by Lovelock, Bunyard, Margulis, Sagan, Ho, and Tudge. Guest lecturers provide additional material.

## Social Movements

This course will look at how social movements — which are demanding greater local autonomy, environmental and gender justice, and more democratization and accountability from state and other national and global economic actors — are articulating alternative visions of society. There will be meetings with leaders and others directly involved with social movements. Readings will include an overview of theoretical and empirical literature on environmental justice and social movements.

## Economic Development

Development as related to ideas of scientific, technological, and industrial progress, and whether present development strategies are truly sustainable. Review of such key events as Bretton Woods, establishment of the World Bank, and GATT. Analysis of the "politics of aid" and the effect of development on agriculture, water development projects, and forestry. Readings by Daly, Sachs, Shiva, Esteva, Costanza, Lappe, Brown, Berry and others.

## Independent Study

This course is designed to allow students to pursue individual interests. The emphases are on creativity, relevance to the student's academic program and goals, and taking advantage of the unique sites and resources offered by the IHP Global Ecology curriculum.

## Cities in the 21st Century  (One Semester: January - May)

## Urban Politics: How Decisions are Made

The course focuses on the political process and, in particular, group interests. Who exercises power in cities? What are the sources of their power? Specific topics of study will include: government structures; relationship between city and regional institutions; role of NGOs and the private sector; approaches to government funding and project financing.

## Culture and Society in World Cities

How do people identify and bound various social groupings? What places in the city are of symbolic importance to people? What are the celebrations and festivities? Who participates in them? The course will examine how these elements combine to form the rich layers of multicultural urban society.

## Urban Ecology: Sustainable Urban Environment

Examines service delivery and public policy. What is the potential for making these processes of transformation more efficient and less polluting? What are the relative contributions to waste and pollution of industries, public transport, private automobiles, and private individuals and families? You will look a which groups are working to solve these problems.

## Urban Planning: Guiding the Development of Cities

This course introduces students to the basic elements of urban studies. Focus on the history of cities, worldwide urbanization, urban design and planning basics, the role and impact of urban architecture, elements of a livable city, patterns of urban industrialization, metropolitan growth and the relationship between urbanization and poverty.

## Global Ecology Itinerary (September 2000 - May 2001)

- **Washington, D.C.** (2 weeks)  Get started, meet students, first assignments! Challenge and learn from policy makers in Congress, the World Bank, USAID and the Environmental Protection Agency. Opportunity to meet government officials as well as representatives of environmental advocacy organizations such as Friends of the Earth, Worldwatch Institute, and Development Gap, and many more.
- **England** (6 weeks)  Experience first homestay and farm stays, study in Cornwall at the Worthyvale Manor Ecological Center, and in Cambridge. Meet with biologists, activists, historians, and political leaders.
- **Tanzania** (5 weeks)  Explore the fragile island ecosystem of Zanzibar, home to mangrove swamps and endangered species. On the mainland in Dar es Salaam, examine development issues of a major port city. Assess game preserve ecology and land management issues. Meet with leaders of Tanzania's environmental movement.

- **India** (7 weeks)  Start in Mumbai (Bombay), follow up with time in small villages. Confronting first-hand the problems of population, health issues, energy, and development. View eco-restoration initiatives, sustainable agriculture projects, and biodiversity conservation programs. Meet with a wide variety of representatives from government and non-government organizations.
- **New Zealand** (6 weeks)  Meet environmental and Maori leaders, senior government officials, and business leaders in the capital city of Wellington. Debate a range of ecological and ethical issues with leading-edge academics at Massey University in Palmerston North. Then, examine communities from South Island base in Christchurch.
- **Mexico** (6 weeks)  Start with homestays and meetings in Mexico City, then live and study in Oaxaca. Explore the ecology of the surrounding valley and learn about the culture of local Mixtec and Zapotec communities. Meet local environmental and political leaders.
- **Boston** (1 week)  Wrap up! Boston-area leaders share their experience in community development issues. Meet with lectures and guests from Boston University, MIT, Harvard, and with country coordinators and faculty who help to synthesize the year.

## Cities in the 21st Century Itinerary (January 2001 - May 2001)

- **New York (1 week)**: Get started in one of the earliest mega-cities and a global hub of information, art, capital, labor, and transportation. Explore diverse neighborhoods, markets, and housing; learn how to 'read' a city. Meet classmates and faculty, undertake first assignments and orientation.
- **Bombay, (Mumbai) India (4 weeks)** By 2015 Bombay may be the second largest city in the world. Meet with ecological and social activists, including spokespersons for the Hindu Nationalists Movement and organizers of pavement dwellers.
- **Johannesburg, South Africa (5 weeks)** While living at the University of Witswatersand in Johannesburg, meet with students and academic leaders — as well as with urban policy leaders who, a few years ago, were in prison or were political refugees. Field trips will be to Soweto and Alexandria. In Cape Town contrast the awe-inspiring natural beauty with the apartheid legacy townships. Meet with government representatives, business and religious leaders, local activists, and entrepreneurs.
- **Rio de Janeiro and Curitiba, Brazil (5 weeks)** In Rio you will explore the workings of successful social and environmental public policies, as well as the historic city-center renovation in progress. Meet with community leaders from different NGOs. In Curitiba you will study an exemplary model of urban planning. Spend time at the Open University of the Environment, and meet the creative individuals who designed such innovations as Theater in the Quarry and the Light House Schools.
- **Washington, D.C. (1 week)** Wrap up by meeting policy-makers in Congress, the World Bank, USAID, and other agencies, as well as Washington-based advocates working on urban sustainability issues at home and abroad.

Apply by: Global Ecology - 1/1 (early decision)  3/15( regular deadline)
Cities in the 21st Century: 6/15 (early decision)  10/1 (regular deadline)
Global Ecology: $22,950    Cities in the 21st Century: $13,650      Airfare $3,900
Faculty: 50% male, 50% female
• Field studies    • Team teaching    •Full academic credit    • Homestays

International Honors Program        617. 267.0026
19 Braddock Park                         info@ihp.edu
Boston, MA 02116                        www.ihp.edu

# LIVING ROUTES

Ecovillage Education Consortium — University of New Hampshire

Bring your education to life and learn skills needed to help heal our planet and build sustainable communities. Why study in a classroom when you can be:

- Identifying rare medicinal plants in a rainforest in southern India;
- Building a straw bale house on a green kibbutz in Israel;
- Gardening in the Australian subtropics watched by a group of Wallabies;
- Designing ecological communities in western Massachusetts and upstate NY;
- Monitoring a "Living Machine" waste treatment facility in Scotland or
- Meditating at Thich Nhat Hanh's Buddhist monastery in southern France.

These are just a few of the many real-life learning opportunities available through Living Routes - Ecovillage Education Consortium. All programs are based in unique communities around the world that are striving to create cooperative lifestyles in harmony with their local environments. These "ecovillages" are refining social and ecological tools — such as consensus decision making, ecological design, community-scale renewable energy systems, and organic farming — that offer positive visions and alternatives for humanity and the planet.

Living Routes programs are based on our belief that:

- Humans *must* learn how to live sustainably, in harmony with each other and the natural world;
- The best way to learn about sustainability is not to read about it in books, but to actually live it;
- Ecovillages are some of the best places to gain first hand experiences in sustainable living.

On each program twelve to sixteen students from diverse backgrounds, ages, and academic pursuits join with faculty to create their own "learning community" within a variety of "living communities". Dialogues with experienced community members, together with service work, internships, and participation in daily rhythms and activities, all facilitate a deep understanding of community life.

In addition, students develop individual and group goals, discuss readings, lead seminars, practice yoga and meditation, pursue independent studies, write essays and papers, visit areas of natural beauty, and create learning portfolios of their work in order to ground and deepen their understanding. In the process, students immerse themselves in the fields of ecological design, sustainable community development, globalization, and international relations.

Living Routes is working closely with the Global Ecovillage Network (www.gaia.org), the Fellowship for Intentional Community (www.ic.org), and a growing consortium of ecovillages, colleges, and universities to create these globally-connected yet regionally-developed programs.

All programs are accredited and some partial scholarships are available.

# MAKING A DIFFERENCE STUDIES

## Geo Communities Semester: France, India, USA (Fall/Spring)

Twelve-day orientation in NH; ten days at Plum Village, Thich Nhat Hanh's Buddhist monastery in southwest France; ten weeks in southern India at Auroville, an international community of 1500 people; two weeks at Mitraniketan, a Gandhian community promoting village renewal; and one week re-entry at the Sirius Community in western MA. Host school: U of New Hampshire (12 credits)

Studies in Sustainable Community Design   Internship in Sustainable Development
Ecological Worldview Education            Problems in Human Relations to their Enviro.

## Findhorn Community Semester: Scotland (Fall/Spring)

Two-day orientation in Edinburgh, Scotland; thirteen weeks in Northern Scotland at the Findhorn Foundation Community, a thriving ecovillage and spiritual community of 350 people from over 20 countries; and one week on the Isle of Erraid in a rural community associated with Findhorn. Host school: Pacific Lutheran U. (16 credits)

Human Ecology                    Art in Community:
Learning to See/Learning to Draw  Psychology of Community
Writings on Community

## Crystal Waters Permaculture Practicum: Australia (January)

Three weeks at Crystal Waters, a Permaculture community on 640 acres of land in subtropical Queensland, Australia. Semester program will include an expanded itinerary of ecovillages in Australia. Host school: Pacific Lutheran U. (4 credits in Environmental Studies)

## Summer Institute in Sustainable Living: USA (Summer)

Four weeks at Sirius Community — a spiritual community, education center, and ecovillage in western MA; two weeks at EcoVillage at Ithaca, an ecological cohousing community in upstate NY. Semester program will include an expanded itinerary of ecovillages on the east coast. Host school: Greenfield Community College, UNH (8 credits)

Introduction to Ecological Living          Eco-Action Seminar and Field Placement
Intro to Sustainable Energy — Solar Living  Sustainable Agriculture — Organic Gardening

## Green Kibbutzim Semester: Israel (Semesters to begin in 2002)

Two weeks at Kibbutz Gezer, home of the Green Kibbutz Group; ten weeks at Kibbutz Lotan, a Permaculture community in the Arava; two weeks visiting communities in Galilee, with a four day wilderness trip and four days of silent retreat. Host school TBA (16 credits)

Studies in Sustainable Community Design   Spirituality in Ecology
Permaculture Design                        Internship in Sustainable Development

Living Routes                    888. 515.7333
Ecovillage Education Consortium  413. 259.0025
72 Baker Rd.                     info@LivingRoutes.org
Shutesbury, MA 01072             www.LivingRoutes.org

# RAINFOREST CONSERVATION

The non-profit Rainforest Conservation Fund offers high quality/low cost Rainforest and Marine Biology workshops in Belize, Costa Rica, and Ecuador. Each is approximately two weeks in length and hosted by highly respected non-profit organizations in each country. During these workshops you will spend most of your time in the field with local guides and biologists studying rainforest ecology, wildlife, biodiversity, medicinal uses of native plants, natural history, rainforest conservation, land management, local cultures, archaeology, geology, and much more.

Rainforest Conservation Fund Workshops have been designed to create a better understanding of the many complex issues surrounding the conservation of precious tropical resources. You will return home enlightened and, hopefully, even more committed to conservation — not only in the tropics, but in your part of the world as well.

The 1999 the rainforest workshops included participants from across the U.S., Canada, Europe, and the Far East. Forty-six universities were represented by faculty and students, along with community college and high school groups, science professionals, and lay people with an interest in natural history and other topics covered in our programs. Your participation in these valuable experiences helps support a variety of rainforest conservation projects in Latin America. College credit is available.

## MAKING A DIFFERENCE STUDIES

**Belize: Rainforest Ecology - Marine Biology — Mayan Archaeology (2 weeks)**

Hosted by the Belize Tropical Education Center and their staff of biologists and naturalist guides, the TEC promotes environmental education and scientific research. Evening presentations on the local flora and fauna, conservation, and Belizean history. Become familiar with conservation projects involving the green iguana, yellowhead parrot, and manatee. Travel to a Creole community and a baboon sanctuary, where conservation groups and local subsistence farmers protect Black Howler Monkeys. This is followed by three days in the heart of a Mayan archaeological site, surrounded by more than 229,000 acres of pristine tropical forest — home to a vast abundance of wildlife including monkeys, cats, coatimundi, and more than 300 species of birds.

The group then travels to a 4.5 million-acre conservation area, the largest protected area in Central America, where over 70 species of mammals and 390 species of birds have been recorded. Visit the Natural History Center, Blue Morpho Butterfly Farm, the Medicinal Plant Trail, and the spectacular 1400 year-old Mayan site of Xunantunich. Visit the world's only Jaguar Reserve and the community of Dangriga, where you will observe colorful Garifuna drumming and dancing.

During the second week the focus changes to Marine Biology, as your group travels to South Water Caye situated on Belize's Great Barrier Reef — largest in the Western Hemisphere, second largest in the world. The pristine waters around South Water Caye support a variety of marine ecosystems. Participants will be taught to snorkel and explore ecosystems filled with coral, anemones, starfish, spectacular fish, and dolphins. Evening presentations on Marine Biology topics.

**Costa Rica: Rainforest Ecology, Geology, & Conservation (12 days - June, July, Aug.)**

Study rainforest ecology, conservation, land management, and geology, and participate in a reforestation project. Visit the Quaker community of Monteverde and the surrounding Cloudforest Reserve. Characterized by a cool climate and lush vegetation, Monteverde is home to three species of monkeys, sloths, coatimundis, kinkajous, the spectacular quetzal, red-eyed tree frogs, and blue morpho butterflies. Visit Santa Elena to discuss conservation and reforestation projects with villagers. Travel to Arenal Volcano — the most active in the Western Hemisphere — for an evening hike. On clear nights, red-hot molten lava can be seen shooting hundreds of feet into the sky. Travel to Palo Verde National Park which, with both wetland habitats and tropical dry forest, has one of the largest concentrations of waterfowl and shorebirds in Central America. Then, take a boat trip down the Tempisque River to observe crocodiles, large iguanas, howler monkeys, and a wide variety of birds.

Travel to a national park which protects both the largest remaining stand of tropical dry forest in Central America and the nesting sites of endangered sea turtles. Visit the Ecological Museum and Butterfly Garden near Abangares. You'll help in a reforestation project, mist net vampire bats, and go on a night hike in the rainforest. Evening presentations on topics including local cultures, the medicinal uses of rainforest plants, sustainable uses of rainforests, and Costa Rican/Central American history.

**Ecuador: Rainforest Ecology — Quichua Indian Village (2 weeks- June, July, August)**

Workshop takes place at the Jatun Sacha Biological Station in the upper Amazon basin of eastern Ecuador. Take a spectacular bus ride to the village of Tena and travel over the Andes to an elevation of 13,000 feet, then down into the upper Amazon basin. Experience and discuss alpine and cloudforest ecosystems and study flora and fauna of Amazonian Ecuador.

The region around Jatun Sacha is one of the most biologically diverse in the world with 520 bird species, 750 different kinds of butterflies, and over 100 species of orchids. You'll participate in the mist-netting of birds; study rainforest ecology; take part in a reforestation project; visit the local Plant Conservation Center; have a "solo experience" in the rainforest. You'll visit an animal rehabilitation center and view monkeys, tapirs, ocelots, and other animals native to the region, and learn about the medicinal uses of rainforest plants from a local Shaman. Then visit the Shaman's home and the nursery, where many herbal remedies are grown; also see a Quechua Indian village, observing how they live in harmony with the surrounding rainforest. Quechua Indian guides, using interpreters, will explain how they hunt, fish, and garden. Activities include evening story-telling, Indian music, sampling local food, making pottery, and observing the use of blow-guns.

**Honduras    Peru    Panama    Alaska    Hawaii**

Apply by April 15
Costs for all trips are around $1,000 plus international airfare.

Rainforest Conservation Fund          616. 776.5928
29 Prospect NE, Suite #8              877. 967.7467 (toll free)
Grand Rapids, MI 49503               rainforest@mail.org

# RUCKUS SOCIETY

"We wanted to create a program where people could learn skills and take action rather than sit around and argue about issues."

— J. R. Roof, Ruckus Board of Directors

The Ruckus society provides training in the skills of non-violent civil disobedience to help environmental and human rights organizations achieve their goals.

Direct action has long been a catalyst for social change. The conscious disobedience of unjust laws can capture the depth of injustice in a single powerful moment — creating an inspiring, deeply resonating energy. From the struggle for civil rights to the development of the modern environmental movement, creative nonviolent protest has played a critical role in galvanizing activists, educating the public, and shaping debate over many important issues. Effective protest, however, does not always happen spontaneously. It often requires careful planning, preparation, and the participation of experienced activists.

Since its formation in October of 1995, Ruckus — a California non-profit — has trained and assisted hundreds of activists in the use of non-violent civil disobedience. We either bring activists to us or we go to them. We have assisted dozens of organizations, large and small. Our showcase venue is Action Camp. Through Camp trainings, we help people learn the skills they need to practice civil disobedience safely and effectively. Trainings contain cerebral elements as well as physical, like classroom-style instruction for action planning, communicating with the media, and non-violent philosophy and practice. Safety and non-violence are integral themes of each subject taught. Wherever the location and regardless of the subject, Ruckus condemns and does not train activists in any technique that will destroy property or harm any being.

Ruckus has shared skills with recognized frontline organizers from all over the world — activists combating authoritarian regimes, multinational corporations' ecological obliteration, and human rights abuses. U.S. News and World report call it "basic training for tree huggers". The New York Times asked, "can green rads be tamed?" and a spokesperson for B.C. Lumber interests stated, "it's just insanity." Flattering praise indeed.

In addition to providing training and support, Ruckus also aids and abets a growing number of organizations in action planning, logistics and tactics, preparing staff and volunteers for high-profile direct actions. Ruckus helps to create actions and images that penetrate the fog of media blackouts, draw public attention, and get a positive reaction. Ruckus actions for organized labor, human rights, and environmental battles are covered by media world wide.

The Ruckus Society depends on talented, committed people to help train others to be effective with non-violent civil disobedience. Trainers come to Ruckus Action camps and actions from all over the country.

*Editors note: If you were thrilled and inspired by the World Trade Organization protests in Seattle, here's a group that provided training for some of the more creative protests.*

# MAKING A DIFFERENCE STUDIES

## Nonviolence

All participants go through a nonviolence training session — even if you've done them before. History, philosophy and technique will be covered. Lots of role playing.

## Scouting

One session in camp, a trainer-led scout, and a practice scout. Workshop uses off-camp sites as examples. Reading maps and photos, dealing with authorities, intro to security, access dealing with barriers, brainstorming for action possibilities. Night scouts and evasion.

## Action Planning and Coordination

Two sessions, the first being the nuts and bolts of coordinating. Discussion of non-arrest actions, protests, and demos. Secrecy, site management, dealing with authorities, etc.

## Climbing

For direct actions: basic ropework, belaying, rappelling, knots, harness, and hardware. Anchors, hammocks, and platforms, equipment care and repair. Protest situations such as tree sits, bridge blockades, building climbs, stack climbs, etc. will be illustrated, discussed, and practiced.

## Electronics

Electronics and direct actions radio communications and discipline; determining your communications needs. Discuss exotic but available technology: scanners, frequency analyzers, use of computers and databases. A level of technology that is within reasonable reach — in terms of money and sophistication — of activists will be taught.

## Blockades

The brown-bread basics of direct action. Among the subjects we will demonstrate, discuss and practice are: tree sits, tripods, lockboxes, railboxes, barrel blockades, vehicle blockades, water blockades, bridge actions, cattle guard blockades, putting up blockades, etc. Learn how to lock your head to something.

## Media Training

Overview of how the news media operates. Discussion and strategic thinking about the newsworthiness of direct actions; a checklist of nuts-and-bolts tasks necessary for a successful action; and practical experience in crafting leads and soundbites, pitching the story, "spin control", and message delivery.

## Banner workshop

Banner types, design, and fabrication in respect to site conditions (low-high wind, etc), anchoring durability, length of use, graphics mediums, and applications. Banner types will include: handheld, pole supported, flag, and suspended/hanging.

## Political theater training

Development and use of effective guerrilla theater. Students discuss various opportunities within campaigns to make use of humor, drama, and pageantry to move their agenda forward. Puppet making and costume design will be discussed in depth.

The Ruckus Society
2054 University Ave. #204
Berkeley, CA 94704

510. 848.9565
ruckus@ruckus.org
www.ruckus.org

# THE SCHOOL FOR FIELD STUDIES

The School for Field Studies (SFS) provides motivated young people with an experience-based education in environmental problem solving. Since its inception in 1980, SFS has given more than 9,500 students the unique opportunity to conduct hands-on field studies and research which address some of the most critical environmental issues facing the world.

Rainforests don't fit under a microscope. In SFS programs, students come face-to-face with complex environmental problems. Lectures and field research occur in the actual ecosystems where the problems exist. This provides dramatic real-life examples, which help students integrate theory with practice. Students are able to make immediate and real contributions toward sustainable management of natural resources. SFS seeks to make tomorrow's leaders more environmentally literate, and to give them a diverse set of skills that can help prepare them for the future.

SFS programs are taught using the case study method. Each case study, focusing on a particular environmental issue, is examined from a number of disciplinary perspectives including ecology, economics, political science, and more. Faculty members present information from various perspectives, and then integrate the lectures to give students exposure to the interdisciplinary nature of environmental problem solving.

Program participants come to SFS from a variety of colleges, universities, and secondary schools nationwide, and they have diverse academic backgrounds. SFS teams typically consist of approximately 30 students and 3 or 4 faculty members. In both summer and semester programs, SFS students are actively involved in all aspects of research and day-to-day living. This team approach to learning and problem solving is the basis for the SFS educational model.

SFS has six centers worldwide, and each offers both semester and 30-day summer programs. Participants receive college credit for 4 courses during the semester, and one course in the summer.

SFS semester-length programs require successful completion of one college level biology or ecology course. Applicants to semester programs must be at least 18 years of age and should have completed one semester at a college or university.

SFS summer programs require applicants to be at least 16 years old, and to have successfully completed at least their junior year of high school. Most summer participants have completed at least one college biology or ecology course. Talented and motivated students with no ecology background have, however, had comparable academic success.

Financial aid is available for qualified SFS students and is need-based. Historically, one third of all participants have received aid in the form of scholarships and/or interest-free loans.

# MAKING A DIFFERENCE STUDIES

## The Center for Coastal Rainforest & Fisheries Studies — Vancouver Is., British Columbia

**Semester Program: Coastal Rainforests & Marine Resources**

*Summer Program: Conserving Marine Resources & Coastal Rainforests*

Coastal Ecology

Principles of Resource Management

Directed Research

Economic & Ethical Issues in Sust. Development

## The Center for Rainforest Studies — Australia

**Semester Program: Tropical Rainforest Management**

*Summer Program: Tropical Reforestation (8 weeks/8 semester credits)*

Rainforest Ecology

Environmental Policy & Socioeconomic Values

Principles of Forest Management

Directed Research

## The Center for Marine Resource Studies —British West Indies

**Semester Program: Marine Resource Management**

*Summer Program: Marine Parks Management*

Tropical Marine Ecology

Principles of Resource Management

Enviro. Policy and Socioeconomic Values

Directed Research

## The Center for Wildlife Management Studies — Kenya

**Semester Program: Wildlife Ecology and Management**

*Summer Program: Community Wildlife Management*

Techniques of Wildlife Management

Wildlife Ecology

Environmental Policy & Socioeconomic Values

Directed Research

## The Center for Sustainable Development — Costa Rica

**Semester Program: Studies in Sustainable Development**

*Summer Program: Strategies for Sustaining Tropical Ecosystems )*

Tropical Ecology & Sustainable Devel.

Principles of Resource Management

Economic & Ethical Issues in Sustainable Devel.

Directed Research

## The Center for Coastal Studies — Baja, Mexico

**Semester Program: Conserving a Critical Coastal Ecosystem**

*Summer Program: Conserving Coastal Diversity*

Coastal Ecology

Economic & Ethical Issues in Sustainable Devel.

Principles of Resource Management

Directed Research

*All Fall and Spring semester programs are 16 credits.

*All 30 day summer programs are 4 credits.

Tuition for semester programs: $12,125 - $13,150 (plus transportation)
Average tuition for summer courses: $2975 - $3795 (plus transportation)

School for Field Studies
16 Broadway
Beverly, MA 01915-4499

(508) 927-7777
(800) 989-4418
www.fieldstudies.org

# SIERRA INSTITUTE
## UNIVERSITY OF CALIFORNIA EXTENSION, SANTA CRUZ

At the end of his sophomore year the young John Muir left the University of Wisconsin for what he called the "university of the wilderness". He traveled to the Sierra Nevada mountains in California and began a lifelong adventure in learning directly from nature. It is that first-hand contact with the natural world that Sierra Institute programs seek to provide.

Sierra Institute offers academic field courses taught entirely in wildlands — students never enter a campus classroom. For up to a full academic quarter, students form small traveling field schools, backpacking through the western U.S., Central and South America.

Program coursework is diverse, interdisciplinary, and always focused on specific places. You can study field ecology and natural history in Utah's canyon lands, California's Sierra Nevada, or the rainforests of Belize. If you study environmental ethics and philosophy in the Sierra, you will read John Muir and Gary Snyder while following in their footsteps. In the Pacific Northwest you experience old growth forests, northern spotted owls, clearcuts, and conservation biology while studying public lands management.

Whether studying natural science or nature philosophy, Sierra Institute students all share a common experience — their classroom is alive. There is an immediacy to coursework that enhances and supplements the educational process. Academic and experiential learning combine to create a richness rarely found on campus. The direct knowledge of the rhythms of the natural world that students get by learning outside also fosters a deep sense of place.

All instructors have advanced degrees and are skilled wilderness leaders with appropriate first aid training. Programs are approved by the Environmental Studies Board at the University of California, Santa Cruz. Courses are at the lower or upper-division undergraduate level.

Group size is limited to 12–13 students. All instruction takes place outdoors, usually on a series of backpack hikes ranging from 4–14 days long. Yet the physical pace is slow, allowing participants to sink into the place and come to know it well — no prior backpacking experience is necessary. Because of the small group size, daily lectures and discussions are usually lively and always intimate.

A Sierra Institute experience can serve as a powerful springboard back into the university life that surrounds — and increasingly threatens — the backcountry. Many students, upon returning to campus, are inspired to work on the environmental problems facing society. One recent student remarked that, "until Sierra Institute I had thought environmental issues were not worth discussing because they were hopelessly unsolvable. Now I know there exist positive solutions and that change is possible".

Sierra Institute seeks to combine critical perspectives with profound personal experience, and to stimulate an overall ecological literacy. It asks students both to understand the ecology of their place and to work toward sustainable living in school and beyond. In an urban culture that continues to separate itself from its wild roots, we need educational opportunities that reconnect culture with nature. It is just these bonds that Sierra Institute programs foster.

# MAKING A DIFFERENCE STUDIES

*Sierra Institute field programs can vary from year to year. These are a recent example.*

## SUMMER (application deadline April)

### Mountain Ecology: The High Sierra (June-July)

This 8-week program explores the ecology and natural history of John Muir's high Sierra. Most of the hiking routes and "classrooms" are in forests and meadows above 9000 feet in Yosemite and the north-central Sierra.

### Spirit in the Mountains: Idaho Wild (June-August)

There are rich bonds between human creativity, and nature — this program explores these key interrelationships while hiking in Idaho's spectacular Sawtooth Mountains. Methods include the cross cultural analysis of myth and poetry, environmental ethics, and the art of journal writing. Focus on the contemporary ecofeminism and deep ecology movements.

- **Wilderness At Risk**  *This is a hands-on field course in conservation biology and ecosystem management in the North Cascades of Washington. Hiking on both sides of the Cascades, you encounter owls and ancient forests, public lands managers, grassroots activists, and more. Courses are: Ecosystem Management and Wilderness Education.*

Other Sierra Institute summer offerings include environmental ethics in the Olympic Mountains, public lands politics in Montana, and natural history / ecology in Northern CA.

## FALL (application deadline mid-July)

### Mountains, Canyons, Mesas: Southern Rockies Field Studies (Sept.-Oct.)

From the peaks of the Colorado Rockies to Mesa Verde and the canyons of the Four Corners country, this program explores southwestern field ecology and environmental issues. Broad introduction to the natural history and resource conflicts of this fascinating region.

Introduction to Natural Ecosystems, Contemporary Environmental Issues
Wilderness Education

### California Wilderness: Nature Philosophy and Religion (Sept.-Oct)

California's landscapes are diverse — the desert of Death Valley, the High Sierra, the Big Sur coast, and secret ranges in the north. These are places that help spark our exploration of nature's influence on American philosophy, religion, ethics, and literature. This program affords provocative reflection at the boundary of nature and culture.

Perspectives On Nature                 American Nature Philosophers
Wilderness Education

## WINTER (application deadline early November)

*Sierra Institute international winter programs in Central and South America are unique and very popular. Unlike other field programs abroad, you are not based out of a field station. Instead, you immerse yourself in the natural and cultural landscapes of our neighbors to the south. You travel with the locals on public transportation, live and work with villagers, and backpack in the bush far from any tourist routes.*

### Rainforest Field Studies: Guatemala and Belize (Jan.-March)

The natural history and ecology of Guatemala and Belize are the focuses of this field program. Together with your instructors you live and work with Maya villagers in the Guatemala highlands, explore the temples and forests of Tikal National Park, visit an agoforestry research station, backpack in Belize's wildest mountains, and camp on a Caribbean coral-reef caye. The protection of tropical ecosystems and human cultural adaptations, past and present, are emphasized.

Wilderness Education            Evolution & Conservation of Neotropical Diversity
Natural and Cultural History of Central American Rainforests

### Endangered Wildlife: Chile (Jan.-March)

Enter into the fascinating world of ecosystem planning and international conservation politics through study of the huemul and it's habitat. The secretive huemul deer is one of the country's most endangered species. You will backpack into several mid-elevation study- sites in the Andes, search for remnant huemul populations, meet with Chilean campesinos, foresters, and conservationists, and contribute to ongoing research to protect Chile's wild places from development.

Wildlife Conservation in Chile        Ecosystem Management
Wilderness Education.

### SPRING (application deadline early January)

### Desert Field Studies: The Canyons of Time (April-May)

Natural history and nature writing are combined in this program that explores the slickrock country of pinyon pine and juniper, of Ed Abbey and Terry Tempest Williams. The combination of ecological observation, and exploration of landscape and self through writing is powerful.

Natural History of the Colorado Plateau       Introduction to Nature Writing
Wilderness Education

### Nature and Culture (April-May)

Program explores the interconnections between human cultures and landscapes, from Death Valley to Mount Shasta and the Siskyou Mountains of wild southern Oregon. Using interdisciplinary studies from ecology, environmental history, literature, and anthropology, the role of wild nature in shaping people and their world views comes alive.

Cultural Ecology                Contemporary Environmental Issues
Wilderness Education

Other spring offerings include Sierra Field Studies: California Wilderness: Nature Philosophy and Religion. (See Fall descriptions.)

- Field Studies   • Team Teaching
- Multidisciplinary Classes   • Vegetarian & Vegan Meals

Sierra Institute                  831. 427.6618
UC Extension                  sierrai@cats.ucsc.edu
740 Front St. Box C          www.ucsc-extension.edu/sierra
Santa Cruz, CA 95060

# WILDLANDS STUDIES PROGRAM
## SAN FRANCISCO STATE UNIVERSITY

Wildlands Studies is a unit of San Francisco State University's College of Extended Learning. The program invites you to join field teams in a search for answers to important environmental problems affecting endangered wildlife and threatened wildland ecosystems. Now entering its 18th year, Wildlands Studies offers onsite field research projects throughout the US and around the world. You can choose among 34 wildlife, wildland, and wildwater projects in the US Mountain West, Alaska, Hawaii, New Zealand, Canada, Belize, Thailand, or Nepal.

Wildlands Studies projects are exciting and challenging opportunities for which previous fieldwork experience is not required. In backcountry settings, you will acquire and directly apply field-study skills while examining firsthand the issues of wildlife preservation, resource management, conservation ecology, and cultural sustainability.

Your fellow team members will come from diverse US and Canadian locations, a mix that provides ample substance for trailside conversations and new friendships. In most cases there will be no more than 9-14 team members working with project faculty. Small teams are best suited for sharing energies, responsibilities, and discoveries.

Wildlands Studies projects occur entirely in the field, and while there is time for solitude and relaxation, they are not vacations. Fieldwork sometimes means long days and uphill trails in weather that is not always ideal, but that is a rare and fascinating opportunity to explore wildland firsthand while striving toward shared goals with experienced researchers and new friends. Students earn 3-12 upper division semester units per project. Units earned are transferable to both semester and quarter system colleges throughout North America.

As concerned students you can join a Wildlands team and help in the effort to solve critical problems facing wildlands and wildlife populations. Wildlands Studies programs afford a rare chance to gain an intimate introduction to the ecology of fascinating and remote ecosystems, while taking part in field studies of significance to the region's future. All necessary skills of data acquisition and analysis are taught onsite.

Wildlands programs will expose you to a stunning flux of new information. In the field you will discover how boundaries separating subjects — like wildlife behavior, biogeography, conservation biology, and cultural ecology — tend to dissolve, and information appears as a richly integrated text. A primary goal is to teach you to read this text in critical and meaningful ways.

A cooperative, experiential approach is at the heart of WS's educational philosophy. Education is most effective when students are involved in the learning with all their faculties. Expect to become an active member of a small community, learning from all aspects of your daily life. The way in which learning occurs is as important as the content of any particular discipline. Questions, and the thoughts and processes behind the answers, may be as valuable as the answers themselves. Wildlands approaches field studies the same way you might approach a glacier, a fern, or a friend: first with direct experience and observation, then with questions about how the conclusions drawn tie into personal and global conditions.

Using an interdisciplinary approach of rigorous ecosystem/wildlife observation and experimental field investigation, students consider the complex network of inter-related biological, ecological, and social processes which shape wildernesses and the wildlife populations they support. Throughout, students develop and sharpen their skills in creative and critical thinking. While considering wildlands and wildlife from a variety of perspectives, students integrate what they are learning about a particular landscape into a wider framework of social, ecological, and educational concerns.

Developing self-confidence in new and challenging environments is an important part of Wildland's programs. Expect to arrive excited and prepared for a rewarding academic, social, and physical experience.

## MAKING A DIFFERENCE STUDIES

*Wildlands Studies field programs take place year round, and run from approximately 3 weeks during the summer to a full academic or summer term.*

### Canadian Corridor Project

Two field-teams will participate in an extensive search for elusive and endangered gray wolf populations, one of the west's rarest predators now recolonizing western US mountain ecosystems. Students gain onsite instruction and direct participation in key field research activities — including howling surveys, wolf habitat examination, prey-base investigation, and wolf sign identification — as they strive to document wolf presence and assess wildland habitats for their ability to support wolves.

### Yellowstone Endangered Species

Combine firsthand field observation and evaluation — of the ecological relationships and habitat needs for recovery in the wildlands of the Greater Yellowstone Ecosystem — of the Gray Wolf, the Grizzly Bear, the Bald Eagle, and the Peregrine Falcon.

Working in the largest essentially intact ecosystem in the temperate zones of the earth, team members will gain a firsthand understanding of the ecological parameters and wildlife management-complexities surrounding efforts to recover Yellowstone's endangered wildlife.

### Thailand Ecosystems and Cultures

Students take part in a rare onsite examination of Thailand's wild ecosystems and the environmental challenges they face. Working onsite, the Wildlands Studies team will use several of Thailand's National Parks as models to investigate the biological ecology of Southeast Asia, and how the Thai people's interaction with wild nature shapes emerging conservation strategies. The goal during the ten weeks in Thailand is to explore how the people of Southeast Asia might hope to balance economic development, biological conservation, and cultural survival.

**Himalayan Ecosystems   Big Sur Wildlands   North Cascades Wilderness   New Zealand
Birds of Prey & Bighorn Sheep   NY Adirondacks   American Wildwaters   Belize**

Wildlands Studies
3 Mosswood Circle
Cazadero, CA 95421

707. 632.5665
wildlnds@sonic.net
www.wildlandsstudies.com/ws

# MAKING
## A
# DIFFERENCE

• • •

## GRADUATE
## PROGRAMS

# A FEW WORDS ON THE GRADUATE PROGRAMS

THE GRADUATE PROGRAMS listed on the following pages are an eclectic smorgasbord. There are health studies (from acupuncture and community-based medicine, to hospice); Peace Corps degree programs — for people planning service therein and folks who have already returned; "consciousness" programs; and human rights and education studies. You'll find non-profit management and sustainable development programs profiled, as well as "green" and social change or social improvement studies. Quite a few are singular and/or interdisciplinary (i.e. Earth Literacy) and hence, hard to categorize. I have, nonetheless, made a brave (or foolhardy) effort to categorize the programs in the page footers to make the section more user-friendly, but a program listed under "environment" might fit as well under "anthropology", and another program categorized as "education" would fit equally well under "social action". A few programs listed at the start are not categorized at all. Consequently, you are invited to journey through these pages with an adventurous spirit.

The data type of information you typically find in graduate guides (date program founded, number of students, GRE info, # of volumes in library, apply by etc.) is absent here — I'd rather tell you about program content, values, and goals. If you find the program interesting, contact it for more information.

As you may have already learned, investigating graduate programs can be arduous. Had even half the programs contacted for infomation responded, this section would be a separate book. The spotty response also accounts for the apparent over-representation of some institutions, and the conspicuous absence of others. Nonetheless, you will find herein a thoughtful and inspiring mix. It should be noted that some programs, rather than sending a profile, gave permission to edit materials from their websites. If in your search you find some programs which would make a good addition to the Guide, please email me information about them for the next edition.

A few profiles of some unique graduate schools are also offered in the front of this section.

Thank you for joining the true, meaningful, luminous world-wide web of caring and committed people working together to make a difference.

Miriam Weinstein
sageworks@igc.org
www.making-a-difference.com

# UNIVERSITY OF CREATION SPIRITUALITY

"UCS has sprung from the hope of our time: to awaken awareness of the sacred in our work and everyday lives. At its core are cosmology, deep ecumenism, Earth awareness, and the emerging consciousness of women and indigenous peoples. It is from this broad source that faculty, students, and staff will find the heart of their work and efforts to build community... People often ask: 'What does one do with a degree in spirituality?' I answer: Everything. You can do everything better when the Source of your life comes together with your living of it. You can become a better parent, a better spouse, a better citizen, a better human being, a better business person, secretary, artist, athlete, theologian, therapist, educator, politician — a better warrior on behalf of social and environmental justice, on behalf of the young, the old, and the future."

— Matthew Fox, President

Creation Spirituality integrates the wisdom of western spirituality and global indigenous cultures with the emerging scientific understanding of the universe, and the passionate creativity of art. It is the earliest tradition of the Hebrew Bible and was celebrated by the mystics of medieval Europe. Creation Spirituality provides a solid foundation and a holistic perspective from which to address the critical issues of our times — the revitalization of religion and culture, the honoring of women's wisdom, the celebration of hope in today's youth, the wisdom to be learned from deep ecumenism, the spiritual traditions of the world's religions, and the promotion of social and ecological justice. Creation Spirituality is concerned with developing theologies and practices within religion and culture which promote personal wholeness, planetary survival, and universal interdependence.

This liberal arts Master's degree requires 32 credits of study — either in the full-time 9-month program, or a 2-year Weekend of the Spirit which allows students to complete the degree in 2 or more years of weekend courses. These programs are now affiliated with Naropa University (see next page).

The Doctor of Ministry program is open to people of all professions who are eager to reinvent the workplace and contribute to deep societal transformation. Social workers, doctors, lawyers, artists, therapists, clergy, and social activists alike have enrolled in this program. Students are predominantly working adults who come from all parts of the nation and the world. Students integrate the week-long intensives offered six times a year into their full lives with minimal disruption.

| | |
|---|---|
| Intensive in Creation Spirituality | The New Cosmology |
| Reinventing Work | Dancing Sacred Texts |
| Men's Rites of Passage | Tai Chi and Art |
| Sustainable Communities | Perspectives: Ecofeminism & Ecopsychology |

Admissions Coordinator
University of Creation Spirituality
2141 Broadway
Oakland, CA 94612

510. 835.4827
www.creationspirituality.com/

# NAROPA UNIVERSITY

Accredited since 1986, Naropa University in Boulder, Colorado is a non-sectarian liberal arts school founded in 1974 by Tibetan meditation master and scholar, Chogyam Trungpa. The aim of education at Naropa is to uncover wisdom, cultivate compassion, and develop the intellectual knowledge and skills necessary for effective action in the world.

Naropa's approach to learning embodies the spirit of many contemplative traditions around the world, and is based in the practice of cultivating one's awareness of the present moment. Naropa seeks resourceful students who have a strong appetite for learning and enjoy experiential education in a rigorous academic setting. The faculty and students form a close-knit community, and this relationship is an integral part of the educational experience.

Naropa University offers six M.A. degrees, one M.F.A. and one M.L.A. degree, in addition to a four-year undergraduate program. Graduate areas of study are as follows:

Contemplative Psychotherapy (M.A.) combines the wisdom traditions of Buddhism and Shambhala with Western, humanistic psychotherapy. Somatic Psychology (M.A.) trains students in body-centered psychotherapy, offering concentrations in both Psychotherapy and Dance/Movement Therapy. Transpersonal Counseling Psychology (M.A.) integrates psychology and spirituality with concentrations in Art Therapy, Music Therapy, and Counseling Psychology. Graduates of all M.A. psychology programs meet academic requirements for the Licensed Professional Counselor credential examination in the state of Colorado. Naropa's Art Therapy program is approved by the American Art Therapy Association, and the Music Therapy program is approved by the American Association for Music Therapy.

The Buddhist Studies program provides an in-depth study of Buddhism as a literary, religious, and cultural tradition with concentrations in Contemplative Religion, Engaged Buddhism, and Tibetan or Sanskrit Language.

Environmental Leadership (M.A.) explores a contemplative study of ecosystems, sustainable communities, horticulture, and ecology, and emphasizes compassionate engagement with environmental issues.

Gerontology and Long-Term Care Management (M.A.) teaches a creative and compassionate approach to elder care, and leads to licensure as a nursing home administrator.

Writing and Poetics (M.F.A.) provides a supportive and vital writing community, concentrations in poetry and prose, with additional coursework in translation, letterpress, and outreach.

Creation Spirituality (M.L.A.) through Naropa's Oakland, CA branch campus, integrates the wisdom of western spirituality and of global indigenous cultures, with the emerging scientific understanding of the universe.

Director of Admissions
Naropa University
2130 Arapahoe St.
Boulder, CO 80302-6697

303. 546.3572
800.772-6951 (outside CO)
admissions@naropa.edu
www.naropa.edu

# SAN FRANCISCO INSTITUTE OF ARCHITECTURE

"The real architects are the young ones, regardless of age, with continuing enthusiasm, imagination, industry, inventiveness, curiosity and dedication to architecture for all people as their reason for being... By such examples we continue to renew faith in the creative spirit and its potentials."

— Bruce Goff, *As An Architect*

SFIA is a new kind of school of architecture and ecological design. It was created to offer new alternatives in design education while retaining the best features of exceptional traditional schools. SFIA is creating one of the first and most comprehensive programs in Ecological Design in the U.S. and developing curricula and textbooks in cooperation with other schools in an emerging Ecological Design Consortium.

A unique 75 unit Master of Ecological Design is offered. SFIA also offers low-cost optional courses in affiliation with the Ecological Design Program at Merritt College in Oakland. This allows some students to earn academic credit with SFIA, while paying very low community college fees.

SFIA offers a three-year Master of Architecture degree program for committed students from other disciplines. This follows the pioneering program at the University of California in Berkeley that has been adopted by many other universities across the U.S. SFIA is privileged to have the support of faculty and speakers of extraordinary achievement, who work outside of the academic tradition. This policy is patterned after the internationally esteemed Architectural Association in London.

While following many well-proven traditions in education, SFIA is also testing new approaches to solve long-standing problems. Research studies challenge the value of competitive design studios, the jury system, arbitrary criticism, and subjective grading. SFIA has introduced dozens of innovative practices to deal with these issues.

SFIA offers open enrollment for re-entry students, students from other professions and trades, and other promising students — regardless of academic background. And it offers academic credit for work in architectural offices. These policies are in the tradition of the long-established Boston Architectural Center.

SFIA is pursuing state licensing and accreditation.

Ecological Studio/Workshop
Bamboo: An In-Depth, Hands-On Intro
Ecological Design & Organic Agriculture

Site & Sun: Bioclimatic Design
Urban Ecology: Planning The Eco Ark
Laboratory Principles Of Ecological Design

San Francisco Inst. of Architecture
Information Office
Box 749
Orinda, CA 94563

925. 299.1325
sfia@aol.com
www.sfia.net

# WESTERN INSTITUTE FOR SOCIAL RESEARCH

Since 1975, the Western Institute for Social Research (WISR) has offered mature adults opportunities to design their own individualized B.A., M.A., and Ph.D. programs. Dedicated to social change, students and faculty are people committed to changing today's oppressive patterns — of race and gender relations, of wealth and poverty, of extreme power and powerlessness — in peaceful and constructive ways.

WISR combines theory and practice, demonstrating that high quality, academic study and full-time work on community problems can go together — that each, in fact, enhances the other. All students do active reading, writing, thinking, and discussing while they continue wrestling with specific practical problems in their work and/or other community involvements. Each student builds a personal learning plan and works with the guidance of faculty, other students, and community resource people on problems he/she deeply cares about.

WISR is a small, multicultural learning community. Students, faculty and Board members are engaged in a living experiment in cooperation among people of different racial, cultural, and personal backgrounds. People know each other personally, and procedures are human-scaled. Active collaboration with others, not competition and distance, lend richness and interest to each person's learning process.

Not many universities or colleges combine these kinds of commitments and ways of learning and teaching. The founders of WISR were people who had worked in other "innovative" colleges, and who got together to fill some gaps they saw being left open. The result after 25 years is a vital, changing, and deeply involved group of people who are helping each other to operate a living laboratory for multicultural education and social change.

Students meet regularly with faculty to design, or receive feedback about, their academic projects — their readings, written papers, jobs, internships, and community involvement. The majority of WISR students are working full-time. While most live in the San Francisco Bay Area, a few students live in other parts of California — and even occasionally outside of California and in foreign countries.

In 2000, 40 graduate and undergraduate students were enrolled at WISR, ranging in age from their 20's to their 60's. Students at WISR are all strongly motivated, mature people who are actively engaged in the work of the communities where they live, as well as in their own personal growth. WISR graduates are very successful in going forward in such careers as directors of non-profit agencies, college professors, licensed counselors, and self-employed writers and activists.

Program areas include Bachelor's and Master's Degrees in Psychology, Human Services and Community Development and Social Sciences, a Master's Degree in Education and an interdisciplinary Ph.D. in Higher Education and Social Change.

Western Institute for Social Research    510. 655.2830
3220 Sacramento St.                       www.wisr.edu
Berkeley, CA 94702

# BOTANY
## UNIVERSITY OF HAWAII AT MANOA

Hawaii's location provides the best opportunity in the United States for hands-on botanical exploration of both marine and terrestrial tropical ecosystems. Moreover, the isolation and geology of the islands has produced a unique flora, and a context to probe questions of systematic, evolutionary, and ecological diversity that are unmatched by any other location on earth. The interaction of Hawaiian and introduced species provides a rich assemblage of conservation problems, and offers many opportunities to study resource management, restoration, and preservation.

The Botanical Sciences Graduate Program in the College of Arts and Sciences offers M.S. and Ph.D. degrees in Botanical Sciences. The Botany Graduate Program offers training in a wide range of botanical specialties, although emphasis is placed on terrestrial and marine plant ecology, evolution, and systematics. The Hawaiian Islands are home to many rare endemic plant species, and the Hawaiian Islands provide a unique environment for studies of island evolution, conservation biology, ethno-botany, tropical plant ecology, and alien plant invasions.

A wide range of taxa are studied by faculty and students in the Botany Graduate Program including marine and terrestrial angiosperms, algae, fungi, and ferns. The Hawaiian Islands provide excellent opportunities to study physiological ecology, adaptation, and genetic differentiation. Many students learn and apply techniques for DNA analysis to address questions relating to plant ecology, population genetics, evolution, or species hybridization.

The program is affiliated with the National Parks Service, the Harold L. Lyon Arboretum, the Kewalo Marine Laboratory, and the Hawaii Institute of Marine Biology. Further arrangements can be made with the National Tropical Botanical Gardens and the Volcanoes and Haleakala National Parks, among others.

The Botany Department offers a variety of facilities for general use in graduate research including greenhouse space, growth chambers, an electron microscopy suite, dark rooms, an herbarium, and on-site computers for data processing, graphics, word processing, and email.

Separate graduate programs in Plant Molecular Physiology and Plant Pathology are offered through the College of Tropical Agriculture. Programs in ecology, evolution, and conservation biology are offered through the Ecology, Evolution and Conservation Biology Graduate Specialization Program.

Dr. George Wong
Graduate Program Chair
Department of Botany, St. John 101
University of Hawaii
3190 Maile Way
Honolulu, HI 96822

808. 956.8369
gwong@hawaii.edu
www2.hawaii.edu/graduate/

# ETHNOBOTANY
## WASHINGTON UNIVERSITY

Doctors' Walter and Memory Elvin-Lewis in the Biology Department at Washington University specialize in Ethnobotany. Studies in collaboration with the laboratory of Dr. Walter Lewis among the Amazonian Jivaro and other adjacent mestizo and Indian groups that still successfully practice ethnomedicine, have been underway since 1982. Whenever in vitro and in vivo studies were applied to validate their pharmacopeia it became evident that their preferences continued to identify pharmacologically active plants e.g., in the use of potentially stimulating beverages, to prevent tooth decay, remove teeth, promote parturition, treat skin infections, malaria, hepatitis B, delta hepatitis, and to significantly enhance wound healing. Of interest to this laboratory is the use of biodirected anti-infective assays to isolate potentially therapeutic anti-viral, anti-bacterial, and other anti-infective agents.

Studies begin in the field by developing an inventory of candidate plant species. Appropriate surveys are conducted to identify those most valued and, whenever possible, to correlate these with therapeutic observations made by collaborating clinicians. Selected species are then studied in order to isolate the active principles in collaboration with experts in natural products, organic and synthetic chemistry, diagnosis, or molecular virology, and microbiology.

Empirical selection continues to be an important factor in identifying plants with potential therapeutic value. Prioritizing preferred plants by epidemiological methods has invariably shown that the most popular are also the most efficacious. The concept of ethnomedical/dental focusing, evolved in this laboratory, has been applied to understanding the therapeutic value of plants used in folk dentistry and medicine worldwide.

The Program in Plant Biology at Washington University has made outstanding contributions to the plant sciences. The research areas of the member laboratories span the breadth of plant biology. A major emphasis is placed on using plants as an experimental system for the molecular genetic dissection of key processes, including photosynthesis, plant growth regulator action, environmental response, transcriptional control, and DNA modification.

Professors Lewis
Program in Plant Biology
110A Busch Laboratory, Box 1137
Washington University
St. Louis, MO 63130

elvin@wustlb.wustl.edu

# BUILDING DESIGN
## ARIZONA STATE UNIVERSITY

The Master of Science with a major in Building Design is dedicated to the development of new knowledge useful to the arts and sciences of building design, and to the integration of that knowledge into the building design process. The program emphasizes: 1) the ecological importance of energy-conscious design and construction; and 2) the development of research, information systems, and management processes suited to the planning and design of complex buildings.

The Master of Science degree is intended to be an advanced post-professional degree for architects, or a graduate specialization of students possessing baccalaureate degrees in related fields such as engineering, business, computer sciences, or the physical or environmental sciences. It is not intended to serve as a first professional degree in architecture. It is instead structured to educate a new generation of scholars and practitioners who will bring appropriate technology and management techniques to the building and rebuilding of humane and supportable environments.

Concentrations are offered in Computer Aided Design, Energy and Climate, and Facilities Development and Management. The Energy and Climate concentration educates students to become experts in energy efficient design and technology. The program is concerned with the relationships among climate and site, thermal and visual comfort, energy demand and consumption. Courses establish a basic core of knowledge of the principles of the natural energies available at the building boundary due to climate and site; thermal and optic behavior of building materials and components; passive and low-energy architectural systems for heating, cooling, and lighting; and appropriate integration with mechanical systems.

Building Environmental Science
Experimental Evaluation
Environmental Control Systems
Bioclimatic Design Studio

Energy Environmental Theory
Energy & Climate
Passive Cooling and Heating
Building Systems Simulation Studio

The Graduate Programs Coordinator
School of Architecture
Box 871605
Arizona State University
Tempe, Arizona, 85287-1605

480. 965 2507
arch.grad@asu.edu
www.asu.edu/caed/architecture/programs

# CONFLICT ANALYSIS & RESOLUTION
## GEORGE MASON UNIVERSITY

The Institute for Conflict and Analysis and Resolution (ICAR) offers an M.S. and Ph.D. in the new field of Conflict Resolution. ICAR provides training and technical assistance to governmental and nongovernmental organizations and to academic institutions worldwide. The Institute for Conflict Analysis and Resolution offers the Ph.D. and the Master of Science degrees in Conflict Analysis and Resolution. Both degree programs are among the first in this field and are part of the mission of the Institute: to advance the understanding and resolution of significant and persistent human conflicts among individuals, small groups, communities, ethnic groups, and nations.

Major research interests include the analysis of conflict between and within nations; ethnic, religious, and identity groups; organizations and social classes; the exploration of conditions attracting parties to the negotiation table; the role of third parties in dispute resolution; and the testing of a variety of conflict intervention methods in community, national, and international settings. ICAR offers academic program in: International Negotiations, Mediation, Peacekeeping, and Organizational and Inter-Agency Conflict.

The Master of Science in Conflict Analysis and Resolution is a two-year professional program that prepares students for practice through the integration of theory and conflict resolution processes such as negotiation, mediation, third-party consultation, and analytical problem solving. Students study the theory, methods, and ethical perspectives of the field and apply this knowledge in laboratory-simulation and workshop courses, and in field internships. The latter are contracted with agencies in the Washington area and elsewhere, including abroad.

In addition, students can take a two-semester, six-credit course in the Applied Practice and Theory (APT) program. APT students become part of a continuing team applying analytical methods and intervention processes to a variety of local and regional conflict situations under the guidance of clinical faculty members. Graduates of the MS program work in a variety of settings where conflict resolution is useful: business, government, religious organizations, court systems, educational institutions, community centers, and conflict resolution consulting firms.

Enhancing the Institute's degree programs are three additional components: research and publication, a clinical and consultancy program, and public education.

Major research interests include: the analysis of deep-rooted conflicts and their resolution; the exploration of conditions attracting parties to the negotiation table; the role of third parties in dispute resolution; and the testing of a variety of conflict intervention methods in community, national, and international settings.

Institute for Conflict Analysis & Resolution   703. 993.1300
George Mason University   jdrake@gmu.edu jdrake@gmu.edu
Fairfax, VA  22030-4444   www.gmu.edu/departments/ICAR/

# CONFLICT TRANSFORMATION
## EASTERN MENNONITE UNIVERSITY

The Institute for Peacebuilding at Eastern Mennonite University supports the personal and professional development of individuals as peacebuilders and strengthens the peacebuilding capacities of the institutions they serve. The Institute offers The Conflict Transformation Program (CTP), leading to an M.A.degree in conflict transformation.

Open to people from all parts of the world and all religious traditions, the program is an outgrowth of the long-standing Mennonite peace-church tradition. As such, it is rooted in the Anabaptist values of peace and nonviolence, social justice, service, reconciliation, personal wholeness, and appreciation for diversity. The program also builds upon extensive Mennonite experience in domestic and international service in disaster response, humanitarian relief, socio-economic development, conciliation, and restorative justice.

CTP believes that today's conflicts call for long-term strategies that address root causes of conflict, develop strategic approaches to conflict transformation, and promote healing of relationships and restoration of the fabric of the human community. The program is committed to encouraging conflict transformation and peacebuilding efforts at all levels of society in situations that are complex, protracted, violent, or potentially violent. Students best suited for the program are those who have had experience working across cultures — in the U.S. or internationally — in conflict transformation or related areas such as humanitarian assistance, criminal justice, or development.

The M.A. equips students to understand the multiple forces operating in a given conflict and to engage in action to transform it constructively. Depending on the nature of the conflict, transformation may involve a range of peacebuilding activities: from advocacy to mediation, from humanitarian relief efforts to programs in social, political, or economic reconstruction. Graduates work in a broad range of areas:

- refugee resettlement organization in the Shenandoah Valley;
- refugee work in Tanzania under the auspices of the Maryknoll Fathers;
- trauma healing with the Christian Health Association of Liberia;
- peer mediation in schools and counseling at-risk children;
- program development and human rights work in Guatemala and El Salvador;
- environmental conflict consultancy in Virginia; and
- peacebuilding organization evaluations in Cambodia, Vietnam, and Thailand.

The Institute for Peacebuilding provides the applied practice and research component of the CTP. It supplies direct services in the form of trainings, consultancies, peace-process design, conciliation, mediation, and action-oriented research.

The M.A. program is intentionally designed to accommodate busy practitioners by offering full and limited-residency formats, thus minimizing the need for students to be away from their work for long periods of time.

Conflict Transformation Program
Eastern Mennonite University
Harrisonburg, VA 22802-2462

540. 432.4490
800. 710.7871
CTProgram@emu.edu
www.emu.edu/ctp/ctp.htm

# CONSERVATION BIOLOGY & APPLIED ECOLOGY
## FROSTBURG STATE UNIVERSITY

The graduate program in Applied Ecology and Conservation Biology at Frostburg State University, established in 1976, enables students to gain scientific training in addressing conservation issues — especially those pertaining to ecosystem fragmentation, conservation or development conflicts, and integrated resource management. The program addresses both domestic and international issues, since the need of professionals is broad-based and global. Frostburg has inter-institutional agreements — with universities and national agencies in the African countries of Malawi and Zimbabwe, the Central American country of Nicaragua, and in Trinidad, West Indies — that facilitate the international dimensions of this program.

The Conservation Biology Program addresses both local and global problems associated with conflicts between human development, and conservation of biodiversity. It prepares graduates for professions that require specialized training in maintaining biodiversity, and for work with environmental consulting firms, national and international conservation organizations, and state and federal agencies.

To provide expanded research opportunities, the program is presented in cooperation with the Appalachian Environmental Laboratory, one of the three research institutes of the Center for Environmental and Estuarine Studies.

An additional significant feature is the local environment. Frostburg State University is located high within the Allegheny Mountains, surrounded by mountain slopes, meadows, swamps, bogs, shale barrens, lakes, and streams. This variety of habitat provides students with a fine opportunity for ecological and environmental study in both natural and altered environments.

Conservation and Population Genetics
Conservation of Natural Resources
Resource & Environmental Economics
Plant Ecology
Environmental Planning
Wildlife Habitat Ecology and Analysis

Island Biogeography and Reserve Design
Ethics, Economics, and Politics in Conservation
Methods of Research in Biological Sciences
Conservation of Natural Resources
Ecosystem Ecology and Analysis
Ornithology

Coordinator
Dr. Gwen Brewer
Dept. of Biology
Frostburg State University
101 Braddock Road
Frostburg, MD 21532-1099

310. 687.4306
www.fsu.umd.edu

# CONSERVATION BIOLOGY
## UNIVERSITY OF SOUTHWESTERN LOUISIANA

Conservation Biology students can pursue studies in biodiversity, systematics, environmental toxicology, wetland restoration, coastal ecology, organismal evolution, behavioral ecology, and conservation genetics through the Department of Biology at University of Southwestern Louisiana. The department offers a M.S. in Biology and a Ph.D. in Environmental and Evolutionary Biology. The department consists of 30 faculty members, including a very active Research Faculty; 60 graduate students; and 7 support-staff members.

Research scope and possibilities are expanded by diverse Adjunct Faculty, who serve both as major professors and as committee members. The adjuncts are largely associated with the USGS National Wetlands Research Center (NWRC) located on campus, and with the Louisiana Universities Marine Consortium Marine Laboratory (LUMCON) located in Cocodrie, Louisiana.

Facilities on campus are augmented by the new 50-acre Environmental Research Annex, located about 6 miles from the main campus. Several vehicles and small boats are available for field research. Large marine-research vessels are available at the LUMCON Marine Laboratory.

USL is located in Lafayette in the heart of Acadiana, the area of southern Louisiana settled by "Cajun" French exiles from Nova Scotia. Within a short drive of campus, students can work in the Atchafalaya Basin and Delta (the largest bottomland hardwood forest in the Mississippi Drainage), coastal marshes and prairies, beaches and barrier islands, and upland pine forests.

*James B. Grace  Plant ecology and conservation, exotic species, wetland and prairie ecology, plant life histories, statistical models of natural communities.*

*Clinton W. Jeske  Waterfowl and shorebird biology, avian and reptile physiological ecology, migration ecology, international avian conservation.*

*Paul Klerks  Environmental toxicology, long-term effects of environmental pollutants, adaptation to environmental changes, detoxification mechanisms, ecology of zebra mussels and other invading species, biology of fishes and oligochaetes.*

*Mark Konikoff  Aquaculture of fishes and crustaceans, life history and ecology of fish, water quality analysis.*

*Paul L. Leberg  Ecology and evolution of vertebrates, population viability and extinction, genetic diversity, habitat disturbance and management, conservation genetics of bats and poeciliid fish, statistics, simulation modeling, introductions and translocations, migration and breeding ecology of seabirds and songbirds.*

Dr. Karl Hasenstein
Graduate Coordinator
Department of Biology
P.O. Box 42451
Lafayette, Louisiana 70504

318. 482.6750
hasenstein@usl.edu
www.usl.edu/~khh6430/

# COMMUNITY & ECONOMIC DEVELOPMENT
## NEW HAMPSHIRE COLLEGE

The CED program enables students from across the United States and around the globe to work together in applying economic principles for building sustainable, socially concerned programs. The program provides education, training, and technical assistance, and develops new models for community economic development through the affiliated Institute for Cooperative Community Development.

Community Economic Development is a strategy enabling people to develop the economy of their community by benefiting the greatest number of its residents; it is a systematic and planned intervention promoting economic self-reliance and focusing on issues of local ownership and the capacity of local people; it is a program that helps consumers become producers, users become providers, and employees become owners of economic enterprises; it is a method of building efficient, self sustaining and locally controlled initiatives that support both profitable ventures and effective social programs; and it is a commitment to working within the context of a community's social, cultural, and political values.

New Hampshire's CED program is an alternative to orthodox models of development. It embodies the belief that social and economic institutions must operate in a way that guarantees an equitable allocation of opportunities and resources for all people in a society; that equitable institutions can only be achieved and maintained through community participation and awareness; and that social and economic development programs are most effective when they address the needs of the community as articulated by representatives of that community. Concern and care for the environment is a key element of the development process.

Examples of CED programs include worker-owned businesses; producer and consumer cooperatives; revolving loan funds and other financial strategies; micro-enterprise development programs; community-managed health delivery; parent-owned child care centers; and neighborhood redevelopment land trusts.

The CED Program emphasizes a learner-centered model in its approach to education. Participants visit a variety of Community Economic Development projects. and attend conferences and workshops covering related topics. This one-year residential program leads to a Masters of Science in CED with a specialization in International Development. A one weekend a month program is also offered for non-local students.

Training of Trainers
Housing and Land Use
Economics and Development
Micro Enterprise Development
Resolution

Appropriate Technology and Development
History and Philosophy of Development
Health Planning and Policy for Development
Development as a Tool for Conflict

Michael Swack
CED Program
New Hampshire College
2500 North River Road
Manchester, NH 03106

603. 668.3130

# INTERNATIONAL DEVELOPMENT
## UNIVERSITY OF DENVER

The faculty of the Graduate School of International Studies (GSIS) accepts the notion that "development" is a broad and somewhat ambiguous concept and thus presents a program that is both interdisciplinary and cross paradigmatic. As a result, the program allows a high degree of flexibility both in terms of the pursuit of individual interests and the variety of courses offered. Congruent with the realities of international life, courses depict the very nature of a complex, interdependent world and incorporate sociological, anthropological, historical, political, economic, and ethical perspectives on problems of development.

The International Development program focuses on political, economic, and social problems that face developing countries, and provides students with a basic understanding of their interrelated features. Each student pursuing a concentration in development must begin their course work by completing Introduction to Development. This course evaluates the meaning of development, and presents alternative interpretations that incorporate problems of power and the environment. Modernization theory, dependency theories, and theories of imperialism are presented, and issues of growth and reform are examined. Thus, this course imparts the basics of development and is the foundation from which students can build their own concentration.

Other fields and concentrations complement work conducted in development studies. A student is free to choose to work extensively in international economics, comparative politics, international technology management, human rights, international security, or in some specific geographic region of the world. While seminars are constructed so as to provide the needed methodological skills and research techniques to analyze more general issue-oriented problems, the student is encouraged to apply these skills to their own particular intellectual concerns.

Additionally, the visiting speaker's series, the international student body, and the faculty and student exchanges arranged with several universities around the world, significantly enlivens the atmosphere at GSIS.

Flexibility is the cornerstone of the development concentration at GSIS. The development program at GSIS is unique because of its flexibility and interdisciplinary nature. The greatest advantage of the development concentration at GSIS is its flexibility, and GSIS encourages students interested in development to explore interrelated fields and concentrations.

Admissions Counselor                         303. 871.2989
Graduate School of International Studies
University of Denver
Denver, CO 80208

# SOCIAL CHANGE & DEVELOPMENT
## JOHNS HOPKINS UNIVERSITY

In stressing the primacy of local initiative, the Johns Hopkins Program on Social Change and Development (SC&D) affirms the importance of community. The community provides the framework within which individuals develop their abilities and modern interest groups compete. Relationships depend upon the moral responsibility of community members and the internal sanctions of accountability, complemented by a public life that rejects paternalism. Locally-initiated development stresses the knowledge, leadership, and creativity of the poor themselves, many of whom are often suspicious of development directed by centralized government or by outsiders.

The SC&D Program hopes to contribute to the process by which development practitioners learn from those whom they would serve. SC&D seeks to provide a holistic comprehension of society, culture, and the challenges of low-income families. Many in the field of development welcome new emphases on the market economy as these accentuate initiative, spontaneity, diversity, and even consumerism.

Many individuals working in development and academia share these "participatory" values, but few academic programs have risked placing them up front as their credo. One factor encouraging the SC&D Program to do so is the exciting community of alternative-paradigm doers and thinkers in Washington.

The SC&D community interacts with people coming from the local level in developing countries and with leaders of innovative neighborhood initiatives in inner-city Washington. Out of this interaction comes a rich flow of "best practice" cases, evaluations, and self-reflections about "participation" and "empowerment". There are few other places in the world in which so many innovations in development are being discussed by people who are also trying them out.

To encourage focused career preparation, the program helps each student develop a theoretical or functional concentration in his or her studies at the School of Advanced International Studies, frequently deepening an interest acquired in grassroots work before entering the program. Many students define their functional fields broadly, choosing such areas as primary and secondary education, the rural-urban interface, the informal economy, or maternal and child health; some have focused on concerns that affect only certain countries, concentrating on refugee work, for instance, or the particular challenges of small nations.

| | |
|---|---|
| Entrepreneurship & Development | Cross-Cultural Perspectives on Social Org. |
| Theories of Social Change & Continuity | Management Principles of NGO's |
| Assisting Refugees — Values, Issues & Practical Matters | |
| Health Problems and Practices in Developing Countries | |

Margaret Frondorf                     202. 663.5691
SC&D Assistant Director
Nitze School of Advanced International Studies
1740 Massachusetts Ave. N.W.
Washington DC 20036

# EARTH LITERACY
## SAINT MARY-OF-THE-WOODS COLLEGE

Earth Literacy is interdisciplinary learning that fosters the capacity to understand the natural world in order to ensure sustainability of the planet as a habitat for life. The 36-hour Master's degree program grounds participants in the theory and practice needed to work effectively toward a just Earth Community. The curriculum includes 24 hours of team-taught courses exploring Earth Literacy, and using the perspectives of the natural and social sciences, the humanities, the arts and spirituality. Twelve hours are devoted to internships and practica which provide the experience and skills needed within each person's area of interest.

The Program format uses distance learning. Each of 6 required courses has a 5-day campus residency to build community among participants and to utilize the campus as a learning resource; preliminary and follow-up work are completed at home.

The program's goals are: to understand the world as a web of elegant, complex, and integrated systems; to develop skills in identifying and solving problems; to formulate effective strategies for change; to foster development of a personal world view which integrates the individual into the web of life; to experience and celebrate the beauty, mystery, and wonder inherent in the Universe; and to recognize community as a sustaining force for transformation.

The learning outcomes are an understanding of the foundations and principles of natural and socio-cultural communities and the systems by which they function; an understanding of the connection between long-term sustainability of the planet and just systems and practices; an understanding of the natural world as primary referent in which humans are derivative. Students will learn to apply analytical, evaluative, and integrative/synthetic skills; to gather, analyze, interpret, and use relevant data; to demonstrate problem-solving and negotiating skills; to deepen a biospiritual integration giving expression to the relationships of self to, with, and in the world and leading to unity of being and doing; to effectively communicate values and concepts which are transformative through the arts, humanities, and sciences; to initiate, implement, and evaluate just and holistic strategies for change; and to develop personal strategies for sustaining the change agent role.

The 1200-acre campus includes trails, varied natural habitats, the White Violet Eco-Justice Center, and ecologically managed farmlands, orchards, and gardens.

Faculty include Dr. Sharon Ammen, Theater and Literature; Dr. Constance Bauer, Anthropology; Dr. Rebecca Goff, Biology; and Dr. Paul Salstrom, History.

Concepts of Earth Literacy
Nature and Cultures
Healing Earth

Principles of Evolution and Change
Justice and the Earth

Mary Lou Dolan CSJ
Earth Literacy Program
Saint Mary-of-the-Woods College
Saint Mary-of-the-Woods, IN 47876

812. 535.5160
mldolan@woods.smwc.edu

# EXPERIENTIAL EDUCATION
## MANKATO STATE UNIVERSITY

The basic tenet of experiential education is that when learning is integrated with the activities of everyday life, learning becomes more effective and engaging. Persons interested in the service-learning movement will find this program of particular value.

The Master of Science degree program in Experiential Education at Mankato State University is the oldest graduate degree program of its kind in the United States. Originally started in 1971 as a joint venture between Mankato State University and Voyageur Outward Bound School, the Master's program is now housed in the University's Department of Educational Leadership and has expanded its vision and developed an ever-increasing number of options for graduate students. Although there is still a strong and viable tradition of involvement in outdoor-oriented activities, the department is committed to the idea that experiential education is much broader than wilderness programming.

The first fundamental assumption of the Master's program is that there is more to the knowing process than much of traditional education assumes. Graduate students in the program are encouraged, even required, to leave the classroom and develop meaningful learning experiences for themselves. Whether their interest is in outdoor programming, classroom teaching, administration, or psychological interventions for example, the program gives students academic credit for testing ideas. The program is designed for strongly self-directed individuals who want to experiment with new educational ideas.

The other fundamental assumption of the Master's degree program in Experiential Education is that raw, direct experience must be complemented with careful thought and reason. In this light, the core seminars are oriented toward analysis of and questions about the fundamental theory of experiential education. In addition to the core seminars, students can develop their reasoning abilities by taking graduate-level elective courses of their own choosing. The goal of the program is to unite practical skills with scholarly abilities in the interest areas of the individual student.

The program enables students to use experience as a means of instruction. The program promotes direct participation and involvement in a number of activities, followed by periods of reflection and analysis — a process based on the assumption that experience needs to be interpreted and internalized in order to have value.

The department has a limited number of graduate assistantships available, including some as instructors of the on-campus ropes course.

Educational Leadership Department
MSU 52
POB 8400
Mankato State University
Mankato, MN 56002

507. 389.1005
www.mankato.msus.edu/dept/edlead

# HIGHER EDUCATION & SOCIAL CHANGE
## WESTERN INSTITUTE FOR SOCIAL RESEARCH

This interdisciplinary Ph.D. program provides individualized learning and professional training for educators, community service professionals, community activists, and other adults concerned with the relations between social change, education, and community service or development in everyday practice. Examples of specific objectives are: the preparation of teachers for innovative college and university programs; assisting the personal and intellectual growth of leaders in community service organizations; helping to advance knowledge of ways to meet the needs of low-income and ethnic-minority communities; and contributing to the education and knowledge of professionals in such fields as education, community services, and counseling.

Students in the Ph.D. program critically examine existing programs and institutions; innovative models and practices; the social/cultural/political forces that influence institutions and programs, local communities, and professional practices; and the creative potential of new kinds of learning and teaching processes.

Examples of areas of concern to Ph.D. students are multicultural education, community-based adult literacy programs, health education, the educational effectiveness and social impact of self-help groups, the professional education of counselors concerned with creative practices that consider the larger social context, and the educational practices in formal school and college settings.

This Ph.D. program enrolls very mature and capable adults who are able to do creative, specialized work in one or more areas pertaining to the education of adults for social change. Ph.D. students at Western Institute learn how to create useful knowledge for educators, community-based professionals and leaders, and lay people who are interested in using educational processes to address social problems.

Some examples of individually designed student coursework include: Action-Research Theories and Methods; Theories of Social Analysis and Change; Multicultural Education; Social Change through Cross-Cultural Contact; Educational Theories and Metaphors; Adult and Continuing Education; Gender Roles and Culture; African Philosophy; American Indian Cultural Perspectives; Trauma Education; and Men, Women and War.

For a more in-depth look at Western Institute for Social Research, see their profile under that name at the beginning of this section.

Western Institute for Social Research        510. 655.2830
3220 Sacramento St.
Berkeley, CA 94702

# INTERNATIONAL EDUCATION

## BILINGUAL/BICULTURAL EDUCATION
## PEACE EDUCATION / FAMILY & COMMUNITY
## TEACHERS COLLEGE — COLUMBIA UNIVERSITY

Teachers College offers interdisciplinary degree programs in Comparative and International Education and International Educational Development, with emphases in Bilingual/Bicultural Education, Economics and Education, Family and Community, Language and Literacy, Peace Education, Comparative and International Education, and International Educational Development.

The programs in International Educational Development and Comparative and International Education offer advanced preparation for professional careers in a wide range of teaching, policy and evaluation, administrative, and research roles. In the Bilingual/Bicultural Emphasis special attention is directed to the role of bilingualism as a major resource in education for democratic pluralism and intercultural understanding.

The Family and Community Education program examines issues in the basic processes of education with families, such as the social construction of family memories, the mediation of television and other forms of technology by families, and the changing configurations of education in community settings. When extensive immigration and transnational migration are taking place, as they are in many areas of the world today, the connections between global culture and the cultural resources of families and communities come to be of critical importance for educators and policymakers.

Outdoor Educational Programs
Comparative Education
Postcolonial Studies of Education
Education for Global Security
Issues and Institutions in Int'l. Educational Development
Preparation of Instructional Materials for Developing Countries
Educational Planning in Int'l. Education Dev.: Ethnicity, Gender, Human Rights
International Education and the United Nations

The Family and Television
Education in Community Settings
Education & Development of Nations
Education for Global security

International Education
Teachers College
New York, NY 10027

212. 678.3710
tc.info@columbia.edu

# TEACHER EDUCATION
## SCHOOL FOR INTERNATIONAL TRAINING

With a focus on applied classroom practice, the academic program that leads to the Master of Teaching (M.A.T.) degree is designed to prepare graduates for a successful career in language education. Concentrations offered are English to speakers of other languages (ESOL), French, and Spanish. The program can be completed as a one-academic-year program or in a two-summer format specifically designed for working teachers. In the one-year program, students may choose either single or double language concentrations.

The teaching internship, supervised by program faculty members during the winter quarter, is a period of rapid professional growth as the student is called upon to put theory into practice in the classroom and to make individual choices regarding teaching styles and approaches. Internship sites in the U.S. are located primarily in New England. Overseas sites used in recent years include Mexico, Singapore, El Salvador, Morocco, and South Africa. The practical focus of the program serves to equip graduates to achieve a high professional standing in their field.

During course work, interactive seminars, and small group projects, students listen, share, debate, and challenge their learning. In the field, during the teaching internship or professional practicum, they test and refine their classroom learning and develop the practical experience to contribute successfully as professionals. All programs combine on-campus study with a professional practicum.

Students in the academic-year format are eligible for public school certification after a second teaching internship during the fall following the course work. There is also an optional endorsement in bilingual-multicultural education (BME) available. The Summer M.A.T. Program consists of two 8-week sessions in consecutive summers, with the teaching practicum supervised by program faculty members during the interim year. The format brings together experienced ESOL, French, and Spanish teachers from all over the world who can earn the M.A.T degree with out having to take time off from their jobs.

Admissions                                          802. 258.3282
School for International Training
PO Box 676
Kipling Road
Brattleboro, VT 05302

# WALDORF TEACHER TRAINING
## RUDOLF STEINER COLLEGE

Rudolf Steiner College offers a 30-semester-hour Master of Arts in Waldorf Education. An applicant must qualify for the Waldorf Teacher Education diploma program at Rudolf Steiner College and have already earned a B.A. degree. Upon successful completion of the diploma, an additional 3-week summer session plus a thesis or artistic project completes the M.A. requirements. Summer courses deepen the student's understanding of Waldorf Education and of mainstream education; further develop powers of perception; give advanced experience in an artistic discipline; and prepare the student for education-related research, including the use of computers.

A qualified student who has completed a Waldorf Teacher Education diploma at another institution may satisfy the Rudolf Steiner College M.A. program requirements by completing three 3-week summer sessions and the thesis or project.

The best way to take advantage of this advanced program in Waldorf Education is to enroll after having several years of Waldorf teaching experience.

The conversation among teachers and experienced teacher-students allows profound insights to arise for all the participants. In this field of education, sharing with others engaged in similar striving gives support to each for truly making a difference. (Experienced Waldorf teachers may enroll in individual summer courses without applying for M.A. candidacy.)

For a more general idea about Waldorf education, read the undergraduate profile for Steiner College. Interested persons might also look into the work of Professor Douglas Sloan at Teachers College — Columbia University.

Admissions Counselor              916. 961.8727
Rudolf Steiner College
9200 Fair Oaks Blvd.
Fair Oaks, CA 95628

# AGRICULTURAL & BIOLOGICAL ENGINEERING
## CORNELL UNIVERSITY

A diversity of interests, and an integration of engineering with physical and biological sciences, characterize graduate study and research in agricultural and biological engineering at Cornell. Courses are taken in several colleges and numerous departments. Graduate theses typically blend analytical and experimental work, and draw on Cornell's strong programs in physical, biological, and engineering sciences. Theses reflect the variety of faculty strengths and interests, and the talent of the graduate student group we are fortunate to attract.

One of the professors has International Agriculture and Food Processing interests, so many of his students look at helping those in lesser developed countries to find ways of storing their post-harvest crops before taking them to market for sale (i.e which type of small structure set up near the fields will keep freshly picked fruits/vegetables fresher or cooler in the hot weather).

Cornell University has also just recently signed a degree program certification with Dr. Mark Gearan (US Peace Corps Director). The program now offers a Masters of Professional Studies (Peace Corps), in which students do a year of course work followed by 2 years of service.

Graduate study at Cornell is organized into 94 major fields, independent of traditional colleges and department units; Agricultural and Biological Engineering is one of these fields. Members of the Department of Agricultural and Biological Engineering, and of other departments, may be elected to membership in the Graduate Field of Agricultural and Biological Engineering as appropriate to their interests.

Within the Field of Agricultural and Biological Engineering there are nine research specialization areas: Biological Engineering, Energy, Environmental Engineering, Environmental Management (MPS only), Food Processing Engineering, International Agriculture, Local Roads, Machine Systems, Soil and Water Engineering, Structures and Environment

Within the Field of Agricultural and Biological Engineering there are four degree options. These are the Master of Science, the Doctor of Philosophy, the Master of Engineering (Agricultural and Biological), and the Master of Professional Studies (Agriculture) programs. All programs require full-time enrollment for timely completion of the degree.

Graduate Student Coordinator
Agricultural and Biological Engineering
207 Riley-Robb Hall
Cornell University
Ithaca, NY 14853

607. 255.2173
abengradfield@cornell.edu
www.cals.cornell.edu/dept/aben

# ENVIRONMENTAL SCIENCES AND ENGINEERING
## UNIVERSITY OF NORTH CAROLINA AT CHAPEL HILL

### SCHOOL OF PUBLIC HEALTH

The Department of Environmental Sciences and Engineering (ESE) was founded in 1921 as a program of instruction and research in sanitary and civil engineering. Since that time, it has become one of the largest graduate environmental education and research programs in the United States. Faculty and students represent a broad range of disciplinary backgrounds, including specialties within biology, chemistry, economics, engineering, mathematics, microbiology, physics, policy, and toxicology.

ESE is one of the few degree-granting units at a research university that integrates environmental science, engineering, and policy analysis. ESE also collaborates with units in UNC's School of Public Health; School of Medicine; School of Business; departments of Biology, Chemistry, City and Regional Planning, Economics, Geology; and curricula in Ecology, Marine Sciences, Public Policy Analysis, and Toxicology.

The Master of Science in Public Health is designed to develop the science base of the field of public health with specialization in one or more of the areas in environmental sciences and engineering. The Master of Public Health is designed to provide professionals in the health care and health-related areas with a broad base of knowledge of the field of environmental science and engineering, and an understanding of its relationship to public health. Emphasis is placed on understanding the scientific principles underlying environmental health.

The Master of Science in Environmental Engineering develops the engineering skills and technical knowledge base for entry into professional engineering. The Ph.D. in Environmental Sciences and Engineering is granted by the Graduate School, and the curriculum of study is individualized according to each candidate's interest area.

Research and teaching in ESE has steadily expanded to encompass the chemical, biological, toxicological, and physical aspects of environmental and engineered processes, as well as the social, political, and legal considerations of managing the quality of water, soil, and air resources. Faculty hold advanced degrees in fields ranging from chemistry, microbiology, and engineering to economics, planning, and public administration. Research is conducted individually, jointly, and interdisciplinarily.

The department is organized into six administrative program areas which define and administer the curricula: Air, Radiation and Industrial Hygiene; Aquatic and Atmospheric Sciences; Environmental Health Sciences; Environmental Management and Policy; Water Resources Engineering; Environmental Modeling.

Student Services
Dep't. of Enviro. Sciences & Engineering
School of Public Health, CB #7400
University of North Carolina at Chapel Hill
Chapel Hill, NC 27599-7400

919. 966.3844
www.sph.unc.edu/env

# ENVIRONMENTAL ANTHROPOLOGY
## UNIVERSITY OF WASHINGTON

Environmental Anthropology is an interdisciplinary graduate program based in the Department of Anthropology. Its purpose is to provide a coherent framework for graduate students wishing to study environmental issues from an anthropological perspective, while building and maintaining strong interdisciplinary connections. Like other graduate programs in the department, study in Environmental Anthropology will lead to M.A. and Ph.D. degrees in Anthropology.

The program in Environmental Anthropology (EA) considers human-environment interactions across the full range of sociocultural variation, and from the earliest human societies to the contemporary global system. It endeavors to understand environmental problems and knowledge not only from a western scientific standpoint, but also from the multiple and often conflicting perspectives of members of various local or indigenous cultural systems. These goals require familiarity with concepts and methods in various sciences: social, biological, and physical; hence EA is inherently interdisciplinary.

While environmental problems are widely recognized as matters of great public and scholarly concern, far more attention has been focused on physical and biological dimensions of these problems than on social, cultural, and historical dimensions. A primary aim of EA is to redress this imbalance. Since sociocultural and environmental phenomena shape each other through a process of mutual influence, EA fosters an integrated analysis of their interaction. The primary areas of interest within the EA Program include:

- indigenous environmental knowledge (e.g., ethnobiology);
- social and cultural causes & consequences of environmental modification;
- environmental conservation and sustainability;
- culturally-appropriate environmental economics; and
- political ecology of economic and environmental change.

Depending on their particular interests or backgrounds, students in the program may focus on ethnographic or archaeological contexts for the study of human environment interaction; and they may work in any region of the world. The present EA core faculty focus their research on (Native) North America, Mesoamerica, the South Pacific, and (paleolithic) Europe. The University of Washington has long been a premier center of environmental studies, and offers a particularly rich array of faculty and courses in this area.

Eric Smith
Grad. Program in Environmental Anthro.
Box 353100
University of Washington
Seattle, WA 98195

206. 543.5240
easmith@u.washington.edu
www.anthro.washington.edu

# ECOSYSTEM RESTORATION
## NIAGARA COLLEGE, CANADA

This unique postgraduate program combines expertise from the Centre for Environmental Training and the Horticultural Centre and prepares students to assist in the maintenance and rehabilitation of natural ecosystems through both government and private sector initiatives. The program provides a combination of theory, demonstration, practice, and optional working experience, developing a broad range of competencies for application in the field of ecosystem restoration.

With the increasing attention being paid to disturbed ecosystems, focus has been shifted towards the rehabilitation of these sites in an ecologically responsible manner. This provides students with a comparative advantage in the ecological and environmental labor market. Students are involved in practical projects with community groups and with industry in the development of solutions to ecological challenges. Ecosystem Restoration students are capable of performing: vegetation quadrant surveys; water quality and quantity evaluation; soil property characterization; collection and storage of seeds; various propagation techniques; long-term restoration management strategies; map design and interpretation; stream channel naturalization design and implementation; slope stabilization utilizing bioengineering methods; invasive species control; wildlife habitat creation; flora and fauna site inventories.

Niagara College's Glendale Campus is nestled alongside the Niagara Escarpment, a world-recognized biosphere. The campus is a 68-acre living lab that showcases the College's environmental programs, ecological conservation, horticultural applications and agriculture. These themes combine and showcase the conversion of two major sewage lagoons, each of seven acres, into ecological reserves for community enjoyment and education. The site is being developed to link with a trail and conservation areas immediately adjacent to the campus while ongoing projects are focused on the lagoons.

On campus, students are establishing a benchmark inventory of flora and fauna; others are conducting cattail reproduction experiments at the lagoons — one of the few producing cattail marshes for migratory stop-offs in the Niagara Region. The campus can also be used for the development of native species, natural meadows, and other experimental areas for study and ecological development. The program accesses new state-of-the-art environmental laboratories, greenhouses, propagation areas, arboretum, and an experimental natural storm drainage system.

Plant Material Management
Wild Species Management
Data Collection and BioMap
Project Management
Ecological Engineering

Hydrology Restoration
Floral Identification
Natural Channel Design
Soil Sciences
Ecological Restoration Issues

Centre for Enviro. Training
Niagara College
135 Taylor Rd., R.R. #4
Niagara-on-the-Lake, Ontario
L0S 1J0 Canada

905. 641.2252, ext. 4470
enviro@niagarac.on.ca

# ENVIRONMENTAL RESTORATION
## NORTHERN ARIZONA UNIVERSITY

Academic study, research, and practical ecological restoration projects are brought together in an innovative program newly created by Northern Arizona University. Students can incorporate a restoration emphasis into their undergraduate and graduate programs. A unique undergraduate research or fieldwork opportunity complements the coursework, allowing students to gain solid work experience in conjunction with an independent project to investigate and apply restoration principles on the ground.

"Northern Arizona is an ideal natural setting for ecological restoration," said Dr. Wally Covington, program director. "We are surrounded by ecosystems of outstanding beauty and tremendous natural and cultural value, like the Grand Canyon and the forests and grasslands of the Colorado Plateau. But many of these landscapes have been severely degraded over the past century as a consequence of livestock grazing, old-growth tree harvesting, and exclusion of the natural frequent fire regime. Our goal is to bring together managers, scientists, and all people concerned with the management of these ecosystems to build a consensus on appropriate methods for restoring and sustaining ecosystem health."

Among the projects currently underway are collaborations with the Bureau of Land Management, National Park Service, Forest Service, and the Arizona National Guard. A central theme is the integration of science and management. Ecological restoration treatments are designed as landscape-scale experiments. As treatments are put in place, the effects on grasses, trees, wildflowers, animals, and soils are carefully monitored. Results from initial treatments are applied to refine the next set of restoration prescriptions. This adaptive approach to wildland management holds promise for dealing with urgent environmental problems in a rational and open way.

This new University program will support student researchers in investigating a broader range of questions. For example, "herbaceous plants and shrubs make up the greatest species diversity and wildlife habitat resources in southwestern forests. As they decline, we see ecosystems become less complex and more fragile, but far too little is known about how to restore these diverse and productive communities," said Dr. Margaret Moore, ecology professor. A great variety of issues, ranging from conservation genetics to the sociology of public policy-making, are open for motivated students to explore. Funding comes from the state of Arizona and outside research grants, with strong backing from the School of Forestry and the College of Ecosystem Science and Management.

Program in Environmental Restoration    520. 523.9011
Northern Arizona University              www.nau.edu
Box 15016
Flagstaff, AZ 86011

# ENVIRONMENTAL SCIENCE & ENGINEERING ECOSYSTEM MANAGEMENT & RESTORATION
## THE OREGON GRADUATE INSTITUTE

The Oregon Graduate Institute is a private, graduate-only technical university dedicated to contemporary scientific research and education. The Department of Environmental Science and Engineering offers interdisciplinary graduate study leading to the degrees of Master of Science (nonthesis and thesis) and Doctor of Philosophy. The nonthesis and thesis M.S. programs can be completed in 1 year and 2 years, respectively. The Ph.D. program takes 4 to 5 years to complete.

The coursework is highly relevant to modern environmental science and engineering. The 18-month Environmental Systems Management program combines training in environmental science with innovative instruction in the management of technology. The Ecosystem Management and Restoration program integrates rigorous environmental science principles, laboratory and field applications, risk assessment, project management, and policy regulation into a cohesive curriculum.

The faculty members are active in grant-supported research and have expertise in groundwater hydrology and geochemistry, aquatic chemistry of organic and inorganic pollutants, estuarine and coastal hydrodynamics, trace organic analysis of air and water, and nutrient cycling in watersheds. The department's low student-faculty ratio allows for close interactions with faculty.

Graduates are prepared for work in industry, government, or for the pursuit of further work in academia. M.S. graduates work at the various major environmental firms throughout the country and at government agencies. The Ph.D. graduates are now faculty; scientists at laboratories of the Environmental Protection Agency, U.S. Geological Survey, and Department of Energy; or environmental program managers at private, state, federal, and international agencies.

Dr. Patty Tuccalina  
Dep't. of Environmental Science & Engineering  
Oregon Grad. Institute of Science & Technology  
P.O. Box 9100  
Portland, OR 97291-1000  

800. 685.2423  
503. 690.1086  
admissions@admin.ogi.edu  
www.ese.ogi.edu

# ENVIRONMENTAL STUDIES
## UNIVERSITY OF CA, SANTA CRUZ

Human societies rest on an ecological foundation and are sustained by ecosystem processes, biological diversity, and genetic resources. Threats to this foundation imperil societies and peoples' well-being, challenging us to maintain the integrity, diversity, and resilience of existing ecological and agricultural systems and of the human societies that depend on them. Environmental problems are among the most serious of current issues. The challenge of harmonizing societies' environmental practices and choices with ecological sustainability, economic necessity, social justice, democratic participation and human well-being, requires people prepared to respond to both ecological and social problems. This poses a historic challenge to graduate training to address complex social and ecological problems from an interdisciplinary viewpoint.

The Ph.D. program in the Department of Environmental Studies at UCSC provides training for students committed to addressing these issues. Disciplinary and interdisciplinary capabilities are essential for effective analysis of environmental issues and to work effectively with others in universities and the commercial, public, and nonprofit sectors. Viable solutions must address social and economic factors as well as scientific and technological questions.

The program draws from two areas of knowledge: ecology and social science. Primary interests in ecology range from conservation biology to agroecology. Interests in social science bridge environmental policy analysis and political economy of the environment (which examines the deeper social processes through which institutions that structure our social and ecological agendas have been constructed).

The social science component includes politics, economics, human geography, social theory, and planning. Emphasis is placed on social factors that drive ecological change in natural and managed systems, thus affecting sustainability; design and evaluation of policies and institutions aimed at resolving environmental dilemmas; and integration of conservation and social justice in planning and development.

The Environmental Policy area stresses the question of social choice, drawing on concepts from political science, welfare economics, and moral philosophy. It analyzes how public decisions are made in democratic societies and responses of economic actors to policy choices. Political economy emphasizes the importance of culture, history, and power relations in constructing beliefs, values, and social structures. Emphasis is placed on transformation of values and institutions to reconcile social and ecological priorities. The Conservation and Resource Ecology area emphasizes the protection, restoration, and management of populations and communities of native species.

Research and teaching in Agroecology and Sustainable Agriculture examines systems of food and fiber production that can be sustained over long periods of time and are compatible with protection of both cultural and biological diversity.

UC Santa Cruz
Environmental Studies, Ph.D. Program
339 Natural Sciences 2
Santa Cruz, CA 95064

831. 459.2634
gradadm@cats.ucsc.edu
//graddiv-19.ucsc.edu/gradstudies/index

# ENVIRONMENTAL STUDIES
## UNIVERSITY OF WISCONSIN — MADISON

The University of Wisconsin-Madison's excellent academic reputation and progressive political climate have attracted many social and scientific innovators, including some of America's leading environmentalists.

Here, John Muir studied more than a century ago before departing for the mountains of California, where he founded the Sierra Club and lobbied successfully for creation of the national park system. Here, Aldo Leopold established the first wildlife management department at any university and penned his conservation classic *A Sand County Almanac*. Here, Gaylord Nelson earned a law degree en route to becoming one of the U.S. Senate's leading environmental advocates and the "father" of Earth Day.

The university today is home to hundreds of professors with environmental expertise of one kind or another. About 150 of them, representing 50-plus academic disciplines, converge in the Institute for Environmental Studies (IES), which promotes interdisciplinary environmental instruction, research, and outreach programs.

The institute offers more than 80 graduate-level courses with the university's academic departments. It also offers: Master's degrees in Conservation Biology and Sustainable Development, and Water Resources Management; Master's and Doctoral degrees in Environmental Monitoring, and Land Resources; a "dual degree" (with the UW Law School) combining any of these degrees with a law degree; and graduate-level certificates in air resources management, and energy analysis and policy.

IES's 200-plus graduate students hail from throughout the United States and around the world. Many come not only with outstanding academic backgrounds but with years of professional experience. More than 1,100 people have earned graduate degrees or certificates through IES since its creation in 1970. The majority of the institute's alumni work in government (30 percent), business and industry (21 percent), or academia (15 percent); others work for citizen organizations and international agencies.

The University offers a growing number of opportunities for students to lead and/or participate in innovative on-campus demonstrations of ecological restoration, resource reuse and recycling, and other "environmentally friendly" projects.

University of Wisconsin-Madison's foreign-student population is second or third largest in the U.S., and the University is strongly oriented toward international and global concerns.

Senior Student Services Coordinator 608. 262.0651
Institute for Environmental Studies
University of Wisconsin-Madison
70 Science Hall, 550 N. Park St.
Madison, WI 53706-1491

# GEOGRAPHY AND URBAN STUDIES
## TEMPLE UNIVERSITY

Temple University's Department of Geography and Urban Studies offers an M.A., and an interdisciplinary Ph.D. linked with Anthropology, History, Political Science, or Sociology. GUS graduates find careers in community service, planning and public administration, environmental management, geographic information systems management, and social change efforts.

Key features of the program include diverse students and faculty, close personal attention, an issue-oriented curriculum that provides exposure to practice-based learning, and opportunities for funded research, internships, and international study. GUS has linkages with African-American Studies, Asian Studies, Environmental Studies, Latin American Studies, and Womens Studies.

Students are afforded opportunities to work with individuals and resources of the Geographic Information Systems (GIS) and Cartography Laboratories, Institute for Public Policy Studies, Paley Library Urban Archives, and Social Science Data Library.

The program has had 40 graduates in the last five years, with a current enrollment of 34 students in the master's program, and 3 in the Ph.D. program. Recent graduates have had a 95% employment rate within six months of graduation.

*Sanjoy Chakravorty: Development theory, third world urban and regional development, inequality, GIS and spatial analysis*

*Robert J. Mason: Environmental management, land use planning, non-governmental organizations, Japan*

*Michele Masucci: Water resources management, GIS and society, information technologies, planning theory*

Chair
Graduate Admissions Committee
Dep't. of Geography & Urban Studies
309 Gladfelter Hall
Temple University
Philadelphia, PA 19122-6089

215. 204.7692
www.temple.edu/gus

# RURAL GEOGRAPHY
## NORTHERN ARIZONA UNIVERSITY

The Department of Geography and Public Planning at Northern Arizona University offers a graduate program in Rural Geography. The Master of Arts in Rural Geography provides an advanced degree for geographers who will work in the area of rural, environmental, and small town analysis. The strength of the program and the faculty lies in the areas of:

- Rural, small town, and Native American planning and development;
- Natural Resource development in rural areas;
- Tools of spatial analysis specifically appropriate for conducting research and solving problems in rural areas (including geographic information systems, computer cartography, and remote sensing);
- Climate and geomorphology of arid lands and mountain regions;
- Recreation and tourism geography; and
- Areas studies: West and Southwest US, Colorado Plateau, Pacific Rim (Latin America, East and Southeast Asia).

There is a growing need for professionals with skills that are particularly applicable to the needs of small towns, rural and natural areas, and Native American reservations. The Department has close working relationships with local, city, and county planning agencies, and with Native American reservations in Arizona. Paid internship positions with these agencies are often possible. Opportunities also exist for cooperative projects with the USGS facilities located in Flagstaff and the numerous National Park Service facilities located throughout northern Arizona.

Northern Arizona University is situated within one of the largest ponderosa pine forests in the world. Located at 7,000 feet, atop the scenic and historic Colorado Plateau, the campus is 80 miles from the Grand Canyon. The Navajo and Hopi reservations are but two of the many Native American communities within easy driving distance. This setting offers students a rich variety of opportunities to study environmental, rural, and small town problems and practices. Flagstaff, the Verde Valley communities to the south, and the Native American reservations are all dynamic and growing places. Combined with the diverse recreational and resource opportunities in the surrounding national forests and parks, these areas provide many issues for rural geography students and classes to explore.

Leland Dexter
Program in Rural Geography
Northern Arizona University
Flagstaff, AZ 86011
Box 15016
Flagstaff, AZ 86011

520. 523.6535
lrd@alpine.for.nau.edu
www.nau.edu

# COMMITMENT TO UNDERSERVED PEOPLE
## COLLEGE OF MEDICINE, UNIVERSITY OF ARIZONA

Since 1993, The U of Arizona College of Medicine has provided a unique opportunity in the Commitment to Underserved People (CUP) program for Arizona residents or WAMI students. CUP is a student run - student- directed program. Students decide if there is a need to change or update a program, and the responsibility for the development and success or failure of the program lies with them. The College of Medicine provides technical, educational, and programmatic support. Training session provide program specifics, technical skills, and background knowledge.

Programs are developed by students based on their desire to work with a particular population. Students learn to establish connections with community organizations, set meetings and timelines, and the 'how to' of program development.

Under the supervision of an attending physician, students administer and staff a clinic for refugees, primarily from Central America. Patients are case-managed through a church which provides the only medical care for this population. Patients have many problems caused by years of absent or poor medical care. In addition, many have been victims of torture and have had harrowing trips from their country of origin. The resulting psychological problems take a toll on the refugees' mental and physical health. Students draw blood for labs, give immunizations, provide patient intake, maintain medical records, and perform translation services.

Medical students in the CUP program travel with residents and an attending nurse practitioner to a local shelter for homeless men, providing care and triage to men in the shelter system. The nurse practitioners see the men for follow-up care. CUP students also provide care to the women and children staying at a domestic violence shelter. The psycho-social aspects of caring for an abused population helps sensitize students to working with abused and displaced women who would otherwise not receive health care, since many are without insurance or the means to pay.

In Medical Students Educating Teens, students provide health education at a teen shelter; to young women in a halfway house emerging from substance abuse treatment; and to other at-risk populations. Subjects include contraception, sexually transmitted diseases, HIV, nutrition, and decision-making; and smoking prevention in several elementary schools located in a poor part of the community.

In the Guadalupe Clinic students work with Dr. John Molina, providing healthcare to the Yaqui Indians. When Dr. Molina was a CUP student, he expressed a desire a to serve his home community. While working for the Indian Health Service, Dr. Molina began seeing patients in the economically depressed community in which he spent his childhood. Now Dr. Molina's program has received nonprofit status and sees patients several days a week.

Carol Galper                    520. 626.2351
University of Arizona College of Medicine
Program in Community Responsive Medicine
1247 N. Warren
Tucson, AZ 85724

# HEALTH AND HOUSING

## BOSTON UNIVERSITY SCHOOL OF PUBLIC HEALTH
## JOHNS HOPKINS UNIVERSITY SCHOOL OF NURSING

The AmeriCorps Health and Housing Fellows Program's mission is to provide an opportunity for Returned Peace Corps Volunteers (RPCV) to continue their commitment to service while training for the health professions. The program's distinct objectives are to:

- Develop and refine a service-learning model for students of public health and community nursing, directly serving populations at risk;
- Provide public health and nursing students with first-hand experience of the everyday lives of the people they serve;
- Establish permanent and working linkages between community agencies and health professions schools.

A long-term objective of the program is to attract RPCVs to careers in community health. This program represents a collaboration among a number of institutions including Boston University School of Public Health (BUSPH), Johns Hopkins University School of Nursing (JHUSoN), the Peace Corps, and AmeriCorps. The schools recruit RPCVs and others with extensive community service experience, and provide them with training and education for a career in public health and community nursing. Fellows work on community-identified projects during graduate study.

At BUSPH, RPCVs are assigned to public housing authorities where they live in family or elderly developments and organize residents around health strategies for improving nutrition, the prevention of drug and alcohol abuse, teen pregnancy, violence, and HIV/STD infection. Fellows at JHUSoN work at transitional housing projects in inner-city Baltimore where they provide a variety of health and social support services to previously homeless families.

BU has nine public housing authorities which provide the Fellows with a rent-free living unit and a stipend. JHUSoN Fellows work in groups at three transitional housing sites with nursing faculty supervision. All Fellows receive educational awards from AmeriCorps and each institution provides partial tuition assistance.

Both sites have seen a considerable amount of success in the two-plus years they have been operating. Some of these successes include: 1785 hepatitis B vaccinations given in Baltimore city schools; 894 people screened for blood pressure and 744 for blood sugar at the Hollander Ridge Transitional Housing site as part of ongoing health sessions; and 7 tenant resource centers established at public housing authorities.

Sarah Dowley                                          617. 638.5036
Boston University School of Public Health    scd@bu.edu
80 East Concord St.
Boston, MA 02118

# HOMELESS AND INDIGENT POPULATION HEALTH OUTREACH PROJECT
## UMDNJ-ROBERT WOOD JOHNSON MEDICAL SCHOOL

HIPHOP (the Homeless and Indigent Population Health Outreach Project) is a student run organization at UMDNJ-Robert Wood Johnson Medical School involving over 120 medical and physician-assistant students, faculty/staff, and community representatives. HIPHOP provides a variety of health outreach services to an underserved population and fosters responsible citizenship while encouraging a lifelong commitment to community service.

The major components of HIPHOP (Clinic/Home Visit, Health Workshops Project, MOMS Project) link student-learning objectives with the health related needs of the community. The Clinic/Home Visit Project increases access to health care during evening hours, while enabling students to gain clinical experience and exposure to primary care and community health. The Health Workshops Project consists of two educational programs: SHARRP (the Student Health Awareness and Risk Reduction Project) and STATS (Students Teaching AIDS To Students). Through these programs, HIPHOP tries to reach the youth of the New Brunswick community and promote healthy living and responsible behavior. The MOMS project pairs medical students with expectant mothers. The student is encouraged to attend all of the mother's clinic visits while serving as a source of support and friendship for her.

Currently, HIPHOP offers two credit electives (SHARRP and Clinic/Home Visit) and three non-credit electives (STATS, MOMS, HCOA-Health Care Organization and Administration). HIPHOP works to provide ongoing service with local soup kitchens and family shelters. Monthly Grand Rounds seminars are given in which distinguished faculty and speakers are invited to address issues important to the practice of community-oriented primary and preventive medicine in an underserved population. In addition, HIPHOP helps to coordinate World AIDS Day activities and local community health fairs, and is teaming up with the Cancer Institute of New Jersey. Everyone is encouraged to provide service to the members of New Brunswick and neighboring communities.

HIPHOP, the Homeless and Indigent Population Health Outreach Project, is entering its six year in existence at Robert Wood Johnson Medical School-UMDNJ Piscataway Campus. HIPHOP is a student driven organization administered by a Steering Committee.

HIPHOP                           732. 235.4198
RWJMS - Dep't. ECM               hiphop@umdnj.edu
675 Hoes Lane                    www2.umdnj.edu/hhopweb
Piscataway, NJ 08854

# INTERNATIONAL & DEVELOPMENT HEALTH
## LOMA LINDA UNIVERSITY

This program prepares graduates to fill leadership roles in government and non-government agencies that are active in the field of public health and development. Applicants must have a master's degree in public health or a related field, at least two years of experience in professional public health practice, and appropriate career goals and prospects.

Professionals in the field of international health are employed by a variety of agencies and organizations working in the field of development and health care. These include government agencies — both host country and donor government agencies, non-government organizations, and intergovernmental and church related entities. Roles include planning and management of health and development programs, education of health care professionals, communication support to health care services and research.

Students prove their ability to apply their learning in a "real world" setting. During a ten-week field practicum, they demonstrate their ability to function as a public health professional in a cross cultural setting.

Programs are designed to meet the needs of professionals working in developing countries or for international agencies. Curricula are based on a recognition of the need for technology and organization appropriate to cultural and economic realities. Interdisciplinary programs combine public health knowledge with competence in techniques applicable to the developing country context, and/or to medically underserved communities and social groups within developed countries.

Cross-Cultural Health Education
Agriculture in Development
Population Dynamics
Delivering Primary Health Care Services
Integrated Community Development
Health and Behavior Change
Refugee Health
Women in Development
Systems
Grant and Contract Proposal Writing
Program Planning and Evaluation
Children
Evaluation of Int'l. Health & Development Programs

Advanced Seminar in International Health
Issues and Programs in Family Planning
Epidemiology of Infectious Disease
Dynamics of Sociocultural Change
Principles of Environmental Health
Violence: Global Public Health Perspective
Methods of Cross-Cultural Communication
Comparative Health & Development

HIV/AIDS: Implications for Public Health
Interventions for High-risk Infants &

Program in International Health
School of Public Health
Loma Linda University
Nichol Hall, Rm 1511
Loma Linda, CA 92350

909. 824.4575
www.llu.edu

# HOLISTIC HEALTH
## JOHN F. KENNEDY UNIVERSITY

J.F. Kennedy University is a community of educators, practitioners, and students who share a vision of personal and societal transformation. The programs and courses are designed to provide a balance between academic learning and experiential understanding. The intention is to honor all aspects of consciousness and to promote a fuller integration of body, mind, and spirit. Collectively, students use the structure of an academic setting to learn the skills that will prepare them to seek new career paths, while profoundly deepening their self-knowledge.

The 68-unit M.A. in Holistic Health Education is designed for individuals pursuing careers as consultants, educators, or practitioners in the field of holistic health. It is the only degree program in the United States that combines training in education and communication with the study of holism, the body, and movement as they apply to individual, group, and family well-being.

Students have the opportunity to develop their personal and professional vision by combining required courses with electives from throughout the school. By choosing the appropriate electives, students may prepare themselves for professional work with clinical health teams or in health agencies, teaching, and consulting services. They may also prepare to bring holistic health approaches into pastoral counseling, the allied health professions, or the social and life sciences.

Students complete a 12-unit professional skills sequence that provides training in classroom techniques or workshop development, as well as field training in a professional setting in the student's area of interest. A 15-unit individualized component allows students a variety of options. You may choose a concentration in either Wellness or Somatics, or take a wide variety of electives within the department or from other programs within the school (e.g., consciousness studies, transpersonal psychology, or arts and consciousness).

Paradigms of Consciousness
Cross-Cultural Issues
Concepts of the Body
Social Transformation
Movement Seminar
Personal Assessment and Life Planning
Mind/Body Approach to Self-Care

Principles of Holistic Health
Effective Communication
Body Nutrition and Health
Group Process
Physiology and Psychology of Stress
Support Group Facilitation
Body-Oriented Psychotherapies

The Graduate School for Holistic Studies
John F. Kennedy University
12 Altarinda Road
Orinda CA 94563

925. 254.0200
holistic@jfku.edu
www.jfku.edu

# HOSPICE

## MADONNA UNIVERSITY

Madonna University offers a Master of Science in Hospice degree. Hospice provides support and care for persons in the last phase of incurable disease so that they may live as fully and as comfortable as possible. Hospice recognizes dying as part of the normal process of living and focuses on maintaining the quality of remaining life. Hospice affirms life and neither hastens nor postpones death. Hospice exists in the hope and belief that through appropriate care, and the promotion of a caring community sensitive to their needs, patients and their families may be free to attain a degree of mental and spiritual preparation for death that is satisfactory to them. Hospice offers palliative care to terminally ill people and their families without regard for age, gender, nationality, race, creed, sexual orientation, disability, diagnosis, availability of a primary care giver, or ability to pay (National Hospice Organization).

The Hospice faculty of the College of Nursing and Health at Madonna University believes in the hospice philosophy as defined by the National Hospice Organization. In accordance with this belief our purpose is to comprehensively prepare individuals to serve diverse client populations during the terminal phase of life; to perform effectively as members of an interdisciplinary team whose goal is to enhance the quality of life by focusing on the physical, psychological, social, emotional, and spiritual needs of the hospice patient and family; and to become leaders in the hospice movement by their expertise in their cognate area and research skills.

Students who complete the graduate program in hospice education will be able to understand the past and current hospice movement; analyze hospice models of care that support palliative, interdisciplinary interventions in an advanced hospice practice; and analyze advanced bereavement models and relevant interdisciplinary theories that support bereavement counseling and spiritual interventions in advanced hospice practice. Additionally they will be able to evaluate current transcultural, ethical / moral, and legal issues pertaining to hospice patients and families to develop a professional code of conduct in advanced hospice practice.

History & Philosophy of Hospice
Advanced Holistic Palliative Care
Hospice Seminar/ Practicum
Power, Politics, & Health Policy
Conversation and Reconciliation
Pastoral Counseling
Pastoral Care of the Sick
Pastoral Counseling Within a Family Setting

Dimension of Bereavement
Transcultural, Legal and Ethical Issues
Theoretical Basis for Nursing Practice
Disciplined Inquiry in Nursing
Moral Theology
Ministry to the Elderly
History & Philosophy of Hospice

Hospice Program
Madonna University
36600 Schoolcraft Road
Livonia, MI 48150-1173

734. 432.5667
kellums@smtp.munet.edu
//ww3.munet.edu/gradstdy/mshospice.htm

# NATUROPATHY, ACUPUNCTURE, ORIENTAL MEDICINE, NUTRITION

## BASTYR UNIVERSITY

A leader in the study of natural healing practices, Bastyr University is an accredited private institution, internationally recognized as a pioneer in the study of natural healing. Its multi-disciplinary curriculum integrates the knowledge of modern science with the wisdom of ancient healing methods and traditional cultures from around the world. Bastyr University's mission is to serve as a leader and a vital force in the improvement of the health and well-being of the human community through education, research, and community health care.

Bastyr University is a true community bound together by an abiding concern for human health and wellness and a passionate dedication to the natural modalities of healing. The recurring themes of natural healing, rigorous scientific inquiry, individual empowerment, and personal responsibility for health bring focus to Bastyr University's programs and people. The university's role as a change agent is integral to that focus.

Bastyr University offers an exceptional naturopathic medical education. With an international reputation for leadership in science-based natural medicine, the Bastyr doctoral program integrates scientific and holistic viewpoints by demanding achievement, dedication, and an open heart and mind in an atmosphere of scholarly inquiry.

Naturopathic physicians are primary health care practitioners who, while they conventionally diagnose and treat disease, are focused on treating the whole person and promoting optimal health. The philosophical principles which underlie the practice of naturopathic medicine form the foundation of the Bastyr medical program:

- Utilization of therapies that first do no harm;
- Prevention of disease through healthy lifestyle and control of risk factors;
- Recognition and encouragement of the body's inherent healing abilities;
- Treatment of the whole person — physical, emotional, mental, and spiritual;
- Identification and treatment of the causes of disease rather than the elimination of symptoms;
- Patient education and cultivation of an attitude of personal responsibility for one's health;
- An acknowledgment of the possibility of everyone's achieving a state of wellness.

Naturopathic practice blends centuries-old knowledge of natural, nontoxic therapies with current advances in the understanding of health and human systems. The scope of practice includes all aspects of family care — from pediatrics to geriatrics — and relies on a broad spectrum of modalities, including botanical medicine, nutrition, homeopathy, hydrotherapy, naturopathic manipulation, and counseling. A Naturopathic Midwifery option is also available.

The Naturopathic Medicine program is a 4–5 year advanced degree program of 315 graduate credits. Candidates for admission into the Naturopathic Medicine Program are expected to present strong academic credential and demonstrate maturity and humanitarian qualities.

Oriental medicine, a discipline that bridges the medicines of East and West, is one of the fastest growing health care professions in America today. Bastyr University, with its broad curriculum and deep respect for both traditional methods and rigorous Western science, is an ideal setting for comprehensive acupuncture and Oriental medicine training.

The program at Bastyr University integrates the rich history of Chinese acupuncture methods with the study of modern medical sciences and the contemporary practice of acupuncture and Oriental medicine. Clinical training is guided by experienced Asian - and Western-trained acupuncturists at the Bastyr Natural Health Clinic and at various off-site clinic placements. An exciting adjunct to the clinical internship is the option of a clinical intensive at the Chengdu University of Traditional Chinese Medicine in China.

Bastyr University's MSAOM graduates are qualified for licensure as acupuncture practitioners and trained in safe and effective care of their patients whether working independently or in collaboration with other health care professionals in an integrative medical setting.

The first year of the MSAOM program provides students with a basic foundation in both traditional Chinese medicine (TCM) and in basic Western sciences.

Curriculum in the second year offers continued studies in traditional Chinese medicine and clinical application, including the Acupuncture Therapeutics series and advanced TCM Techniques. Students have the opportunity to begin providing direct care to patients as student interns. The clinical program is the main focus of the third year of study. Clinical training focuses on both acupuncture and Chinese herbal medicine at the Natural Health Clinic.

A small program with an exceptional faculty, the Bastyr University Master of Science in Nutrition program integrates the physical, psychological, behavioral, and educational aspects of human nutrition, balancing a "whole foods" approach with a rigorous understanding of human biochemistry and nutrient metabolism. Students have two options of study: the Research Track, which culminates in a thesis, and the Clinical/Counseling Track, which emphasizes nutrition counseling skills.

Nutrition graduates may work as community and outpatient clinic nutritionists, as nutrition consultants to the food and fitness industries, as nutrition counselors on a holistic health care team or as Certified Nutritionists in the state of Washington. A Bastyr graduate has the knowledge and skills necessary to help others achieve and maintain optimal health through informed food choices.

Bastyr University
14500 Juanita Drive NE
Kenmore, WA 98028-4966

425. 823.1300
425. 602.3100 Admissions
www.bastyr.edu

# ACUPUNCTURE

## NORTHWEST INSTITUTE OF ACUPUNCTURE AND ORIENTAL MEDICINE

Established in 1981, the Northwest Institute of Acupuncture & Oriental Medicine (NIAOM), offers three- and four-year Master's degree programs in acupuncture and Traditional Chinese Medicine. NIAOM is a non-profit educational institution dedicated to providing the highest quality academic and clinical programs, as well as affordable healthcare to the community.

Community service has always been an important part of NIAOM's mission. Many students choose the program because of this commitment, and for the breadth of opportunities it offers them to carry it out. In addition to the main clinic located on campus, NIAOM has fourteen community clinics in settings like a county jail, a nursing home, several AIDS/HIV clinics, an in-patient drug and alcohol treatment facility, a clinic serving homeless youth, and the county hospital. These clinics provide patients with accessible, affordable, holistic healthcare close to where they live, and NIAOM's students with a better education through opportunities to work with a broad cross-section of the community presenting a great variety of conditions, needs, and concerns. Students complete a minimum of 150 observation hours in NIAOM's clinics, and 700 intern hours treating patients under faculty supervision.

Students complete a total of 132 academic credits in the M.Ac. program and 168 academic credits for the M.T.C.M. degree. They learn the theory and practice of Traditional Chinese Medicine, including diagnosis, needling techniques, herbal medicine, nutrition, bodywork, Tai Ji and Qi Gong. Coursework also includes a grounding in Western science and medicine. The faculty includes experienced practitioners of Chinese medicine and other healthcare specialties, trained in China and in the West.

NIAOM's programs are authorized by the Washington State Higher Education Coordinating Council; are accredited by the Accreditation Commission for Acupuncture and Oriental Medicine; and are acceptable for Federal student financial aid. NIAOM's graduates are eligible to sit for the National Commission for the Certification of Acupuncture and Oriental Medicine exams, which is required for licensing in most states. Licensing laws vary by state, but NIAOM's programs meet the current requirements of most US states that license acupuncturists. NIAOM is located in the Fremont district of Seattle. Using the principles of feng shui as a guide, the school has created a nurturing, supportive environment conducive to natural healing and enhanced learning opportunities. Spectacular views of Lake Union and the Cascades add to the beauty of the campus. The nearby Burke-Gilman bike trail provides students a popular way to get to campus.

NIAOM admits students once a year in the fall. Admission requirements include three years of college credits, including introductory courses in biology and psychology.

Roberta Castorani, Admissions Advisor  
NIAOM  
701 N. 34th Street, Suite 300  
Seattle, WA 98103  

(206) 633-2419  
(206) 633-5578 Fax  
admissions@niaom.edu  
www.niaom.edu

# HUMAN RIGHTS & HUMANITARIAN AFFAIRS
## COLUMBIA UNIVERSITY

Responding to the need to prepare personnel and institutions to deal with all forms of violence and social conflict, the Human Rights and Humanitarian Affairs (HRHA) concentration focuses on both research and advocacy skills. The curriculum prepares students for different advocacy professions — particularly law; monitoring and reporting; policy analysis; NGO development; and the protection of refugees and displaced persons, especially women and children. Degrees offered are a Master's in International Affairs and a Master of Public Affairs.

The HRHA concentration offers a broad range of approaches to human rights, including advocacy in its various forms, as well as reporting and empirical research. Courses also offer training in the new range of skills needed to address recent problems of refugees and displaced persons, conflict resolution, peace-making, and democracy-building. HRHA offers the most extensive array of human rights courses of any university in the world.

Students are encouraged to accept internships with the many human rights-related organizations based in New York, and to seek additional field experience overseas during summers. Funding for summer internships is available through both the Human Rights Center and the School of International Affairs. Recent local placements have included Human Rights Watch, the Lawyers Committee for Human Rights, and the Open Society Institute. Overseas, many of the placements are with human rights organizations in countries such as Argentina, Brazil, Colombia, Mali, Nepal, Peru, South Africa, Thailand, and Zimbabwe.

Students are encouraged to specialize in their chosen interest and to develop necessary skills such as monitoring; research and documentation; fundraising; lobbying; public relations; human rights education and training; communication technology; policy-making and policy analysis.

Courses are taught by internationally recognized scholars in the field, and by experienced advocates for human rights organizations such as Human Rights Watch, The Lawyers Committee for Human Rights, and the United Nations.

Graduates find work in human rights monitoring, refugee advocacy, disaster relief, peacekeeping, women's issues, child welfare, and development work.

Refugees and Displaced Persons
UN Peacekeeping: Case Studies
Human Rights & International Affairs
Report Writing for Human Rights

International Affairs
International Law
Women and Human Rights
Human Rights and Social Justice

Patrick Bohan, Admissions Director
International Affairs Building 408
420 W. 118th St.
Columbia University
New York, NY 10027

212. 854.2479
pb3@columbia.edu

# HUMAN RIGHTS
## UNIVERSITY OF DENVER

The study of Human Rights at the Graduate School of International Studies (GSIS) is designed to provide opportunities for in-depth consideration of the rights of individuals and collectives, in the context of international relations. Students analyze specific policies of countries and investigate international regimes with a view to the protection of human rights.

GSIS offers a unique program devoted to understanding conflicting perspectives in human rights as a field of study. Though many would agree that human rights abuses challenge the "New World Order" championed at the end of the Cold War, there is still no consensus regarding what constitutes human rights and how they should be implemented. A clear understanding of human rights is thus vital to the development of a comprehensive human rights agenda for the twenty-first century. To meet this need, GSIS has developed an interdisciplinary program examining human rights from economic, sociological, anthropological, historical, political, and cultural perspectives.

The courses are designed to provide the student with a foundation for a rigorous and critical examination of several topics: legal and organizational aspects of human rights; human rights issues of particular countries and regions; themes of contemporary relevance considered from a human rights perspective for example, immigration, refugees, genocide, nationalism; and more theoretical issues such as the affinity, if any, between human rights and democracy, social justice and the marketplace, or realism and democracy.

Specialization in Human Rights may be acquired at two different levels: first, by completing a trilogy of required courses for the concentration; or, second, by completing four additional courses enabling the student to receive a Certificate in Human Rights.

Additionally, the Center on Rights Development enlivens the atmosphere at GSIS by housing a Documentation Center; running a speakers' series; by publishing the journal *Global Justice*, as well as monographs and books; and by offering fellowships and internships to graduate students pursuing human rights activities and research.

The program offers many advantages: a highly flexible program with none of the rigidity of a specialized degree — a flexibility congruent with the ever-changing needs of a dynamic international environment.

The Human Rights program has grown into a versatile, lively, and serious course of study for those interested in pursuing a career in monitoring and promoting human rights. The Consortium on Rights Development links GSIS, the College of Law, and the Iliff School of Theology in an effort to promote the study of Human Rights.

Admissions Counselor
Graduate School of Int'l. Studies
University of Denver
Denver, CO 80208

303. 871.2989
www.du.edu/gsis/ma_inthumri.html

# HISTORY OF CONSCIOUSNESS
## UNIVERSITY OF CA, SANTA CRUZ

History of Consciousness is an interdisciplinary graduate program centered in the humanities, with links to the social sciences and arts. It is concerned with forms of human expression and social action as they are manifested in specific historical, cultural, and political contexts. The program stresses flexibility and originality, and is focused on problems rather than disciplines. Although the program prepares students to teach in particular fields, it emphasizes questions that traverse a number of different approaches.

Although History of Consciousness does not have formal tracks, it does emphasize certain topics and approaches in its seminars and research groups. These include: comparative cultural studies; ethnographic methods; feminist theory; theory of contemporary visual culture; the historical analysis of social movements; political and economic analyses of late capitalism; historical and cultural studies of race and ethnicity; psychoanalysis; lesbian and gay theory; semiotics; theory and history of religions; and social studies of science and technology.

Over its 30 years of existence, the History of Consciousness program has won increasing recognition as a leader of interdisciplinary scholarship. Graduates currently find employment in a wide range of disciplines, including literature, women's studies, science studies, anthropology, sociology, American studies, cultural studies, ethnic studies, communications, and philosophy.

History of Consciousness has strong cooperative relations with associated faculty from other campus programs — scholars who offer seminars and participate in advising, qualifying exams, and thesis committees. Cross-disciplinary work in graduate courses offered in other departments is encouraged. Research organizations such as the UCSC Center for Cultural Studies and the Chicano/Latino Research Center also provide venues for collaborative work.

Applications are invited from students with backgrounds and interests in the humanities and social sciences, and are especially encouraged from individuals with a clear idea of the project they wish to undertake.

*Angela Y. Davis    Feminism, African American studies, critical theory, popular music culture and social consciousness, philosophy of punishment (women's jails and prisons)*

History of Consciousness
218 Oakes College
University of California Santa Cruz
Santa Cruz, CA 95064

(831) 459-2757
(831) 459-4616
//humwww.ucsc.edu/histcon/HisCon.html

# INTERNATIONAL & INTERCULTURAL MGM'T
## SCHOOL FOR INTERNATIONAL TRAINING

The School for International Training (SIT) uses language and cross-cultural training to prepare volunteers for service abroad. Students at SIT are true partners in determining the course and success of their learning. By the time they come to SIT, many students have lived and worked with cultures and in countries other than their own, and many speak a second language. SIT graduates are entrepreneurial by nature, are culturally-sensitive and well-prepared to make a difference in their fields, communities, and the world.

The experiential educational approach often utilized in the SIT classroom offers students the opportunity to act and react, and to make connections between theory and practice. Because the program requires students to take responsibility for their own learning, SIT appeals to mature, experienced learners, regardless of age. Students learn how to construct and progressively build upon their own experience. In addition to the body of knowledge typically acquired in a classroom or laboratory setting, graduates master a set of applicable competencies appropriate to their career goals in a supportive and goal-oriented environment with a low faculty to student ratio.

The academic program — leading to the Master of International and Intercultural Management degree — develops the intercultural, managerial, and training skills necessary for careers in international and intercultural professions. The program is based on the College's philosophy of learning through experience, and combines on-campus academic study with a minimum six-month professional-level practicum appropriate to the student's area of interest. Students write a professional paper and present their work to their colleagues and program faculty.

Course work focuses on project management, development administration, training and organizational development, intercultural communication, and leadership and managerial skills. There are three areas of concentration: international education, training and human resource development, and sustainable development. Alumni work in such fields as sustainable development, community development, exchange management, global education, international student advising, cross-cultural training, and refugee relief. They work with organizations such as CARE, NAFSA, Oxfam, the United Nations, and the American Field Service International.

Admissions                                          802. 258.3282
School for International Training
PO Box 676
Kipling Road
Brattleboro, VT 05302

# INTERNATIONAL SECURITY POLICY
## COLUMBIA UNIVERSITY

An interdisciplinary program of courses and professional internships that prepares students to analyze a broad range of political, military, and economic problems in security. The Master of International Affairs in International Security provides a solid conceptual foundation for dealing with military strategy and technology, defense economics, regional conflicts, multilateral peacekeeping arms control, and diplomatic alternatives to the use of force. The program is designed to prepare students for the rapidly expanding agenda of problems that have evolved since the end of the Cold War.

Most ISP courses are taught by members of Columbia University's Political Science department, many of whom are associated with the Institute of War and Peace Studies. Others are associated with School of Interntional and Public Affairs regional institutes.

Additional courses are offered by University research scholars, faculty from other universities, and practitioners from Washington and New York who have served in the State Department, Pentagon, National Security Council, Congressional staffs, United Nations, and elsewhere.

There is one field trip each year, alternating between a U.S. military installation in one year, and government offices in Washington D.C. in the other. Students have a chance to see something of both operational and policy-making aspects of U.S. national security policy. Past trips have included Fort Bragg, NATO headquarters in Brussels, the House Armed Services Committee, the Bosnia Task Force, International Security Affairs, and the Arms Control and Disarmament Agency.

Graduates have been hired by the U.S. Departments of State and Defense, Arms Control and Disarmament Agency, intelligence agencies, the United Nations, public interest organizations, and other areas.

Conflict & Cooperation
General Problems in Int'l. Security
Weapons, Strategy War
American Strategies in World Politics
Causes of War
Third World Security Issues
Political Economy of National Security
War, Peace, & Strategy in the 20th Century
Nuclear Weapons, Strategy, & Arms Control

Security Issues in South Asia
Military Force
Countries and Regions
Politics UN Peacekeeping
Diplomacy & International Bargaining
War & Alliance in the Third World
Nationalism & Contemporary World
Limited War & Low Intensity Conflict

International Security Policy
School of International and Public Affairs
Columbia University
420 W. 118th St.
New York, NY 10027

212. 854.7325

# INTERNATIONAL SECURITY
## UNIVERSITY OF DENVER

Just a few years ago, many believed that the end of the Cold War and the heralding of a "New World Order" would result in a sharp reduction in global conflict, and a decline in the importance of and interest in security studies. Instead, a variety of troubling cases has presented major new challenges to scholars and policy-makers in the field of security.

Desert Storm demonstrated the continuing danger of major interstate conflict. The diminishing U.S. presence in Asia and Europe, coupled with the instability of the former Soviet Union, raised new concerns over security in those regions. Savage ethnic conflicts posed dilemmas regarding the viability and costs of humanitarian intervention. The long-standing problem of proliferating weapons — both conventional and of mass destruction — received belated recognition as an ominous and growing global threat. Finally, increasing disparities between rich and poor states and regions, the ongoing population explosion, environmental degradation, and the surge in communicable diseases has inspired calls to expand security studies to encompass the spectrum of global threats.

The International Security concentration at the Graduate School of International Studies (GSIS) has been designed to meet these challenges and further explore the central issues of instability and revolution, repression and other forms of violence, international conflict and war, the danger of nuclear holocaust, great-power intervention, and the promotion of domestic and international peace and justice. The program is highly flexible. Within the international security studies program, diverse courses are offered which cater to the interests of all students. These courses cover the spectrum of international security studies, from traditional courses such as U.S. National Security policy to non-traditional courses such as Human Rights and International Security, Future Issues in Security, and Nationalism and Ethnic Conflict.

The program offers many advantages. In particular, it offers a highly flexible program with none of the rigidity of a specialized degree — flexibility congruent with the ever-changing threats emerging in a dynamic international environment. The flexibility of the program encourages students to explore theoretical and topical issues which influence the emerging international system. The relaxed educational atmosphere at GSIS encourages active student participation and lively debate.

There is no greater challenge at the end of this century than to understand and resolve conflicts. The Security Concentration has been designed to provide in-depth understanding of the nature of current security problems and evolving approaches to addressing and (hopefully) resolving them. Interdisciplinary inquiry is designed to stimulate research into alternative approaches to the field.

Admissions Counselor                          303. 871.2989
Graduate School of International Studies
University of Denver
Denver, CO 80208

# INTERNATIONAL SERVICE
## INTERNATIONAL PARTNERSHIP FOR SERVICE-LEARNING

Combine rigorous academic study with substantive community service in two nations for one year and receive a British Master's degree. The International Partnership for Service-Learning, in cooperation with its affiliated universities in Britain, Mexico, and Jamaica, sponsors a one-year program leading to a British Master's degree in International Service.

Students elect to study and serve for the fall semester either in Kingston, Jamaica or in Guadalajara, Mexico. During the semester they serve in a community agency and earn 16 hours of credit through academic courses. For the spring semester all students go to England where they continue their studies, earning 16 hours of credit. Here, students serve in a London-based agency and begin work on the Master's thesis. All service is with a community agency and matches students' skills and interests. Examples of agencies include orphanages, homeless shelters, and health clinics.

During June and July in England students prepare their Master's thesis using experiences, observations, and research from their semesters of service and learning. The thesis takes the form of a proposal — to a development, relief, education, or policymaking body — in which a social/cultural/economic problem, a budget, and evaluation procedures are described. The thesis, along with course work and service experience, is evaluated by an international panel of Partnership practitioners and academics.

These studies and resulting degree prepare participants for work and careers with international, non-profit, private and voluntary organizations, as well as with governmental and inter-governmental agencies, in areas such as development, relief, education, and social services. Combining academic studies and community service, the program gives future professionals both the practical knowledge which comes from working in service agencies at the grass roots level and the theoretical framework and analytical skills developed from formal academic study. Degree recipients are able to develop informed programs and policies, and to provide leadership in international and local service and educational organizations.

The affiliated universities are distinguished and fully recognized institutions of higher education, validated to award graduate degrees by their respective governments and ministries of education. The universities are the University of Technology in Jamaica, the Universidad Autónoma de Guadalajara in Mexico, and the University of Surrey, Roehampton in England. All have a long history with and commitment to community service and the study of social administration. The degree is awarded by the University of Surrey, Roehampton.

Int'l. Partnership for Service-Learning
815 Second Avenue, Suite 315
New York, NY 10017

212. 986.0989 )
212. 986.5039 Fax
pslny@aol.com
www.ipsl.org

# LANDSCAPE ARCHITECTURE

## UNIVERSITY OF MICHIGAN

### SCHOOL OF NATURAL RESOURCES & ENVIRONMENT

Landscape Architecture (LA) at the University of Michigan is offered as a graduate specialty within the School of Natural Resources and Environment (SNRE). The Master's constitutes a first professional degree for students with or without prior design training, and an advanced degree to students with previous training from undergraduate programs in Landscape Architecture. The Master's of Landscape Architecture is unique for its strong emphasis on an ecological approach to design and planning at all scales, and its attention to a broad range of professional skills and knowledge. It is also distinctive because it is offered within the context of a professional school of natural resources and environment. The emphasis of the program is on design and planning based on a clear understanding of environmental and cultural factors, and a direct integration of ecological and socio-behavioral sciences.

All Master's students are required to complete a Master's opus as their capstone experience. Some students elect to write a thesis which explores their particular research in the Resource Ecology and Management concentration. Others work with Resource Policy and Behavior students, in teams of 6-8, on projects addressing resource problems for real-world clients. This is a terrific opportunity for SNRE students to apply their knowledge and skills to particular environmental problems or situations. The third option, a practicum, is available primarily for two-year students for whom LA is a 2nd professional degree (e.g., they have received a bachelor's degree).

Students can also develop dual degree programs in combination with many university departments including Urban Planning, Architecture, and Resource Planning at the School of Natural Resources and Environment.

Graduates of the School find work at local, state, national, and international levels, with non-profit organizations; colleges and universities; and the private sector. Examples of positions held by recent graduates include Landscape Architect, Urban Planner, Vice President, Associate Professor, and Environmental Planner.

Plant Materials for Landscapes
Woody Plants: Biology and Identification
Site Planning and Engineering

History of Western Landscape Architecture
Land Use Planning and Design
Master Planning & Design for Parks &
Recreation Landscape Design Theory

Graduate Admissions Team
1024 Dana, SNRE-OAP
University of Michigan
Ann Arbor, MI 48109-1115

734. 764.5453
snre.gradteam.@umich.edu
www.wnre.umich.edu/

# LANDSCAPE DESIGN
## CONWAY SCHOOL OF LANDSCAPE DESIGN

The Conway School of Landscape Design is a small, ten-month graduate program in environmentally sound site design and land use planning. The program is intensive and inventive, the work professional and creative, and the setting unique. Students come from throughout the country and occasionally from other nations to the village of Conway, Massachusetts, to study and work with a close-knit learning community in a converted house and barn.

The Master of Arts program is structured around professional-level work for residential clients, municipal agencies, and non-profit organizations. Through these projects, students produce the drawings and reports characteristic of the designer/planner while learning technical skills and developing intellectual abilities. Integrated throughout is a strong emphasis on communication skills and ecological processes.

The mission of the Conway School is to explore, develop, practice, and teach design of the land that is environmentally and ecologically sound. It seeks to:

- Provide graduates with the basic knowledge and skills necessary to practice design of the land which respects nature as well as humanity;
- Develop ecological awareness, understanding, respect, and accommodation in its students and project clients; and
- Produce project designs which fit human use to natural conditions.

The School's mission guides decision-making at every level: who is hired, what projects are undertaken, how courses are structured, and what offices and sites are visited on field trips. While the program is thoroughly based in ecological beliefs and practices, the focus of the education remains design of, and on, the land rather than environmental science.

The Master of Arts in Landscape Design is an academic degree rather than a professional one. The Conway School's program does not offer as much instruction time as longer Master of Landscape Architecture programs, especially in design history, engineering aspects of design, or graphics techniques, and it offers no specialized instruction in computer aided design (CAD). Rather, the M.A. in Landscape Design offered at the Conway School represents an integrated curriculum where classes complement design practice. Instruction occurs in a small, intimate, and supportive environment. There is an unambiguous emphasis on environmental responsibility, oral and written communication skills, and project management. The emphasis given human and community issues in planning and design, and oral and written communication, make this a Master of Arts program.

Conway School of Landscape Design
P.O. Box 179
Conway, MA 01341-0179

413. 369.4044
conway@csld.edu
http://www.csld.edu/

# ENVIRONMENTAL LAW
## VERMONT LAW SCHOOL

Vermont Law School's environmental law specialization has consistently been ranked one of the best in the country by surveys of law school environmental faculty. VLS offers the traditional core legal curriculum and a series of experiential programs, in addition to emphasizing environmental and public interest law. This combination prepares students for practice in any locale and legal environment. The School's location in a small Vermont town encourages an unusual balance between academic rigor, and the sense of community and strong ethical values for which Vermont is noted.

The mission of the Environmental Law Center is to educate for stewardship: to teach an awareness of underlying environmental issues and values;, to provide a solid knowledge of environmental law; and to develop skills to administer and improve environmental policy. Environmental law and policy are often about change and, since change can be threatening to those who benefit from the status quo, it is no surprise that consensus on environmental issues is difficult to achieve. For that reason, environmental professionals understand that sound environmental policy must be formed at the intersection of politics, law, science, economics, and ethics.

"The Environmental Law Center combines the core strengths of the School with the talent and expertise of leading environmental practitioners and scholars to provide an unmatched interdisciplinary training for lawyers and other professionals who seek to serve in the field of environmental law and policy." — Dean L. Kinvin Wroth.

The goal of the Master of Studies in Environmental Law is to educate leaders who will fashion and carry out environmental policy grounded on the stewardship ethic. Specifically the M.S.E.L. aims to:

- Develop knowledge of the environmental goals and standards embodied in U.S. law, and of the legal mechanisms used to achieve those goals;
- Develop an understanding of the political, economic, cultural, institutional, and scientific mechanisms by which environmental policy is shaped;
- Explore the ethical bases for environmental policy;
- Provide a basic understanding of ecological concepts that govern the relationship of living organisms within the biosphere;
- Introduce students to international environmental issues such as ozone depletion, global warming and conservation of biodiversity; and
- Examine the concepts of hazard, risk, and uncertainty and their role in and effect upon environmental policy.

In addition to its regular curriculum, the M.S.E.L. Programs offers a special fellowship and courses which are of specific interest to First Nations Members.

| | |
|---|---|
| Vermont Law School | 800. 227.1395 |
| Chelsea Street | admiss@vermontlaw.edu |
| South Royalton, VT 05068 | www.vermontlaw.edu |

# PUBLIC INTEREST LAW
## NEW COLLEGE OF CALIFORNIA SCHOOL OF LAW

New College of California School of Law is the oldest public interest law school in the country. From its inception 25 years ago, New College has been a leader in the effort to link law and social justice using critical legal analysis, apprenticeships, clinical electives, and a supportive environment to help students of different races, income levels, and social backgrounds succeed. The desire at New College has been to provide an outstanding legal education to people who plan to use their legal knowledge to redress injustice, and to change the status quo.

In addition to providing excellent and rigorous preparation for the bar exam, our aim is to make sure that every student receives the practical skills training needed to become an effective public-interest attorney. New College places great emphasis on teaching the intricacies of existing legal rules and doctrines; it also supplements these standard elements of legal education with readings and discussions offering a critical perspective — on the moral and ethical assumptions of existing law — and on the role of law in achieving social change.

The overall goal is to provide students with a thorough grasp of both the analytical and practical skills required of any good lawyer, while enabling them to challenge assumptions embedded in the law where they should be challenged. The School also assists students in developing their own moral vision of how the law should serve others.

The Law School is ideally located for the study of law. It is within easy walking distance of San Francisco City Hall, and of various California and federal courts. Major libraries, government offices, the State Bar of California, and various law firms where our students apprentice, are also nearby.

San Francisco's progressive legal community provides ample opportunity for law students to become involved in a variety of public interest pursuits: from providing legal services to the poor; criminal defense work; environmental protection advocacy; and advising socially conscious small businesses. In addition, the diverse neighborhoods of San Francisco provide students with unique and exciting opportunities beyond the walls of the classroom.

New College offers an innovative and refreshing educational program. It has an inspiring legacy and a motivated community of students, professors, administrators, alumni, and friends. New College strives to keep the flame burning for justice, equality, and human understanding while training sensitive, talented, and principled legal professionals. The College knows that public interest lawyers need to be creative and resourceful in finding ways to accomplish their clients' goals.

Director of Admissions                415. 241.1300 x314
New College School of Law
50 Fell St.
San Francisco, CA 94102

# INTERNATIONAL & PUBLIC SERVICE MGM'T.
## DEPAUL UNIVERSITY

As of 1997, a master's degree in International Public Service Management, "a practical alternative for people whose business isn't just business" has been offered at DePaul University. The program combines a liberal arts education in international studies with hands-on training in the technical skills necessary for public service management. Students who devote their careers to public service are discovering that need has no borders in a DePaul University program that trains future leaders of nonprofit programs with international missions.

Graduates of the program could work as program officers and administrators for large nonprofit public service organizations that operate across borders. Such organizations include the International Red Cross and smaller, transnational agencies focusing on local issues.

In the tradition of St. Vincent de Paul, our first responsibility is to our students and graduates and all who benefit from or are served by them — their clients, coworkers, and citizens of our urban and international society. We respect the dignity and recognize the merit of each person, as we work in partnership to build a multiracial, multicultural, and international community among us.

The Public Services Graduate Program prepares graduates for effective management of nonprofit organizations and government agencies, and fosters the development of sound public policies affecting the delivery of social services. Programs of instruction, research, and community involvement prepare adult learners to pursue administrative careers in a broad range of public service organizations. Following the tradition of St. Vincent de Paul, the Public Services Graduate Program devotes special attention to policies and practices that promote social equity through the delivery of affordable, quality services to those in greatest need.

Degree and certificate programs are interdisciplinary, drawing primarily upon sociology, economics, political science, law, and the human-service professions. The curriculum balances theoretical and applied approaches to the contemporary challenges of administration and policy analysis.

Public Services Graduate Program      312. 362.8441
DePaul University      pubserv@wppost.depaul.edu
243 S. Wabash, Room 600
Chicago, IL 60604-2304

# NON-PROFIT MANAGEMENT
## UNIVERSITY OF JUDAISM

Combining leadership and learning, the University of Judaism's mission is to educate men and women who are destined to take part in shaping the future of society. The University of Judaism (UJ) offers fully accredited undergraduate and professional graduate degree programs. UJ's liberal arts College has been selected by U.S. News and World Report as one of the leading institutions of its type. The University offers four graduate degrees: the Masters in Education, the Masters in Behavioral Psychology, the Masters in Hebrew Letters (Conservative Rabbinical Ordination), and the Masters of Business Administration (MBA) in Non-Profit Management. Gifted students and distinguished scholars from around the world are attracted to programming that is designed to stimulate and nourish a passion for intellectual excellence, scholarly inquiry, meaningful spiritual growth, and vital engagement with the arts.

The Lieber School of Graduate Studies of the University of Judaism offers an MBA geared specifically to students planning careers in the non-profit world. This service sector is the economy's fastest growing segment and, with more than 1.2 million not-for-profit organizations in the United States, there is a tremendous demand for well-trained managers. The MBA is designed to meet this growing need by training professionals for middle and upper management positions in cultural, educational, religious, social service, and health care organizations. Courses — in finance, ethics, accounting, fund-raising, marketing, human resource management, organizational and individual behavior, and public relations — blend traditional business management with training in areas unique to the not-for-profit sector. The program focuses on the ethical, managerial, and humanistic issues of non-profit organizations.

MBA students may also complete a Certificate in Jewish Communal Studies. The program emphasizes the historical, social, and moral principles vital to the contemporary Jewish community. Most courses are offered in the late afternoon and evening to provide time during the day for students to gain hands-on experience and to accommodate working students. In addition, students complete a 600-hour internship, and a thesis. Recent internship placements have included: The World Recreation Center for the Deaf, Big Brothers, The Jewish Federation, and Tree People.

For managers already holding a master's level or higher degree, who want to enter the non-profit sector, the University of Judaism also offers a 10-course program focusing on management skills and theory. Generous financial subsidies and fellowships are available for all UJ academic programs. The University of Judaism is open to students regardless of race, religion, nationality, or ethnic background.

Dean of Admissions and Financial Aid
University of Judaism
15600 Mulholland Drive
Bel Air, CA 90077

310. 476.9777
888. UJ-FOR-ME
admissions@uj.edu
www.uj.edu

# NONPROFIT MANAGEMENT
## NEW SCHOOL UNIVERSITY
### (NEW SCHOOL FOR SOCIAL RESEARCH)

The Master of Science (M.S.) Degree Program in Nonprofit Management at the Milano Graduate School of management and Urban Policy at New School prepares students to assume increasingly important positions of leadership in the nonprofit sector. The program combines theory with practice and provides students with knowledge and skills in areas such as nonprofit governance; general management; fund raising and development strategic planning; program development; financial and human resources management; policy analysis and problem solving; ethics; and marketing.

There are more than 30 nonprofit management courses to choose from, as well as courses in the Milano School's other masters programs in Human Resources Management, Health Services Management and Policy, and Urban Policy Analysis and Management. Courses may be also taken on a non-degree basis.

This program/school is outstanding because the courses are specialized and applied. The program is distinctive because very few nonprofit management programs in the country offer a full M.S. in Nonprofit Management. The nonprofit management program is not a concentration of courses in an MBA or MPA program, but rather a "stand alone" degree in nonprofit management. This program is the only one of its kind in the New York metropolitan area. Students have opportunities, within the context of the courses, to work with nonprofit organizations.

Religious Nonprofit Organizations and their Role in Community Building

| | |
|---|---|
| Social Movements and Advocacy | The Role of Nonprofit Organizations |
| International Nonprofit Sector | Community Health Programs |
| Women and Health: Past and Present | Race and Public Policy |
| Community Development | Children, Youth, and Family Policy |
| Techniques of Counselling | Group Processes: Facilitation & Intervention |

*Dr. Pier Camille Rogers has conducted studies of the representation of people of color in nonprofit leadership and management in the U.S., and on diversity and nonprofit boards.*

*Dr. Dennis Derryck has thirty years experience both in research and executive management positions. His expertise includes economic and community development, institutional strategic planning; and program development.*

Nonprofit Management Program             212. 229.5950
Milano Graduate School of Mgm't. & Urban Policy     www.newschool.edu/academic/gs
New School University
80 Fifth Avenue, Suite 405
New York NY 10011

# NATURAL RESOURCES

## THE UNIVERSITY OF MONTANA

### THE SCHOOL OF FORESTRY

The School of Forestry at The University of Montana offers a broad set of programs in renewable natural resources. Graduate degrees offered are Master of Science, Master of Ecosystem Management, and Doctor of Philosophy. Primary areas of study are Forestry (nearly all natural resource management emphases), Recreation Management, Resource Conservation, and Fish and Wildlife Biology. Approximately 115 graduate students are enrolled in the School; one-third are doctoral students. Fellowships and teaching or research assistantships are available, and most graduate students are funded through some or all of their graduate study. A joint degree program is offered with the Fish and Wildlife Biology program at Montana State University.

Field studies characterize much of the coursework and thesis research. Research is carried out through the Montana Forest and Conservation Experiment Station. The Station operates a 28,000-acre experimental forest and a 3,400-acre experimental ranch within about 30 and 50 miles, respectively, from the Missoula campus. The Station also has access to an additional 6,000-acre ranch along the east face of the Rocky Mountains, just south of Glacier National Park.

The University of Montana, located in Missoula, is known for outstanding programs in natural resources and environment, creative writing, avian biology, legal practice, and Native American Law. Missoula is surrounded by mountains and wilderness areas, and has a river running through it. It is a major natural resources center with a regional office of the USDA Forest Service, numerous offices of other federal and state agencies, and national and regional offices of many non-profit natural resource and environment organizations.

Dr. Donald Potts, Associate Dean
School of Forestry
University of Montana
Missoula, MT 59812

406. 243.5521
request@forestry.umt.edu
www.forestry.umt.edu

# RESOURCE ECOLOGY AND MANAGEMENT
## UNIVERSITY OF MICHIGAN
### SCHOOL OF NATURAL RESOURCES & ENVIRONMENT

Human populations have dramatically altered most ecosystems on earth, yet continue to rely on these ecosystems for food, water, fiber, and recreation. Managing our ecosystems for multiple use creates an ever-increasing demand for scientists trained in the sustainable management of natural resources. Such scientists may focus on particular resources such as forests, fisheries, wildlife, but also must understand interactions between these organisms and the environment — including natural and human influences. The Resource Ecology and Management (REM) graduate concentration in the School of Natural Resources and Environment is a national leader in research and teaching on such complex issues of sustainable resource and ecosystem management.

The REM program at the University of Michigan is unique in that it pays attention to issues of large scale, integrating physical, biological, and social concepts into the understanding of natural resource problems. The Resource Ecology and Management concentration is an outstanding choice for making a difference in the conservation of biological resources for future generations. The program uses the latest ecological theory, field observations, and management practices to provide an education that allows scientists to integrate biological and social components of resource management into actions that are significant, large scale, and sustainable for future generations.

All master's students are required to complete a master's opus as their capstone experience. Some students elect to write a thesis which explores their particular research — REM, Landscape Architecture, and Resource Policy and Behavior students work together on projects in teams of 6-8 to address resource problems for real-world clients.

Students concentrating in REM further specialize in aquatic or terrestrial ecosystems. REM students might further focus on conservation biology and ecosystem management. An aquatic ecosystems course of study might include fluvial ecology, ichthyology, the ecology of fishes, aquatic invertebrates, water resource policy, and fishery management. Students in the terrestrial ecosystem plan might expect to study forest ecology, soil properties and processes, forest hydrology and watershed management, conservation biology, wildlife behavior and ecology, tropical conservation, or the biology and management of insects.

Graduates of the School are employed at the local, state, national, and international levels; in non-profit organizations, colleges, and universities; and in the private sector. Positions held by recent graduates include: Aquatic Ecologist; Environmental Scientist; Fisheries Research Biologist; Project Scientist, and Assistant Professor.

Graduate Admissions Team
1024 Dana, SNRE-OAP
University of Michigan
Ann Arbor, MI 48109-1115

734. 764.5453
snre.gradteam.@umich.edu
www.wnre.umich.edu/

# PHILANTHROPY
## INDIANA UNIVERSITY

The Indiana University Center on Philanthropy offers a Master of Arts in Philanthropic Studies — a program that focuses on the history, culture, and values of philanthropy. While other programs focus on the "how" of nonprofit management, this program focuses on the "why": the social, cultural, political, and economic roles played by philanthropy and nonprofit organizations in both contemporary and historical settings. Students in this program investigate the broader theoretical issues of philanthropy from a variety of perspectives. The 64 faculty members come from history, public administration, economics, American studies, religious studies, and many other departments, for a truly interdisciplinary program.

The M.A. in Philanthropic Studies is a 36-credit-hour graduate program, which includes core courses, electives, an internship, and a thesis. Dual degrees exist with nonprofit management, economics, history, and nursing. Several scholarships and assistantships are awarded each year to incoming students. Also, there are two minority fellowships for persons underrepresented in the field of philanthropy.

The Executive M.A. program allows individuals — who cannot come to Indiana University for the traditional program — the opportunity to earn the full master's degree. Students in this program correspond electronically with their instructors and classmates, and come to the campus one week per summer for each course they take. Scholarships are also available to incoming students in the executive program.

Approximately 70 students are currently pursuing the Master of Arts in Philanthropic Studies. Individuals from at least 25 different states and several foreign countries have ventured to Indianapolis to study philanthropy. Some are early-career students who come directly from college, but many are mid-career students who come with several years of relevant work experience. There is also great diversity in the undergraduate backgrounds and future goals of the students because of the interdisciplinary nature of philanthropy.

Center on Philanthropy
Indiana University
550 W. North St.
Indianapolis, IN 46202-3162

800. 854.1612
maphil@iupui.edu
www.philanthropy.iupui.edu

# PUBLIC POLICY

## TUFTS UNIVERSITY

The graduate Department of Urban and Environmental Science at Tufts University offers a two-year master's degree to prepare public-spirited individuals for challenging careers in government, nonprofit organizations, citizen advocacy groups, and the private sector. The mission of the department is to educate a new generation of leaders, "practical visionaries", to face complex problems in public policy. Distinctive features of the program include an interdisciplinary approach; an emphasis on values, democratic principles, and citizen initiatives in setting public agenda; an appreciation of the centrality of nonprofit organizations in implementing programs; and a concern for the local and distributive aspects of public policy.

Students receive a Master's Degree in Public Policy with concentrations either in Environmental Policy (natural resource management; pollution prevention; chemicals, health and the environment; or international environmental policy) or in Urban and Social Policy (community development and housing; social welfare policy; or child and family policy). Students also have the option of developing individually tailored specializations in consultation with their advisers. The program normally takes the equivalent of two years full-time study, although it is possible to be enrolled in the program on a part-time basis.

The curriculum emphasizes practice as well as theory, linking academic instruction with policy issues defined by communities and public agencies. Practical planning and research experience is provided to students through their participation in field projects. Students work in teams for clients from a variety of organizations — including government, community, or non-government agencies — to evaluate existing initiatives and to formulate alternative policy approaches to actual problems. A required internship gives students additional experience working in a professional setting.

Students may be enrolled exclusively in UEP; in a joint-degree program with the Departments of Civil and Environmental Engineering, Biology, Economics, or Child Development; or in a three-year dual-degree program with the Fletcher School of Law and Diplomacy. The department also has a collaborative master's degree in agriculture, food, and environment with the School of Nutrition, Science and Policy.

Tufts is located in the Boston area.

Ann Urosevich
Urban and Environmental Policy
Tufts University
97 Talbot Ave.
Medford, MA

617. 627.3394
www.tufts.edu

# PUBLIC POLICY AND MANAGEMENT
## CARNEGIE MELLON UNIVERSITY
### H. JOHN HEINZ III SCHOOL

The H. John Heinz III School of Public Policy and Management at Carnegie Mellon University provides a Ph.D. program in Public Policy and Management, and Masters programs in Arts Management, Public Policy and Management, Health Care Policy and Management, Information Systems. A mid career Masters program in Public Management is also offered.

The programs offered at the Heinz School provide students with an opportunity to gain strong analytical and quantitative skills while specializing in particular policy areas including: Economic Development, Financial Analysis, Sustainable Economic Development, Environmental Policy, and Information Systems. The programs combine the interdisciplinary structure of Carnegie Mellon University and provide students with an opportunity to gain practical skills through required internships for the majority of the masters programs.

*Alfred Blumstein: Professor of Operations Research, Criminal Justice Systems and Policy, and Director of the National Consortium of Violence Research.*

*Richard Florida: Professor of Regional Economic Development  Research interest in economic transformation of advanced industrial societies, and Director of the Center of Economic Development.*

*Linda Babcock: Associate Professor of Economics  Research interests in collective bargaining and dispute resolution, labor economics, behavioral economics.*

*Dan Martin: Associate Professor of Arts Management and Director of the Arts Management Program. Areas of research include not-for-profit organizational structure, and the practical application of information and computer technology in the arts management process.*

*Ramayya Krishnan: Professor of Management Science and Information Systems. Research interests in information networking and decision support systems, electronic commerce, and data privacy.*

Ms. Sandra Day  
Heinz School of Public Policy & Mgm't.  
Carnegie Mellon University  
5000 Forbes Ave.  
Pittsburgh, PA 15213  

412. 268.2164  
www.heinz.cmu.edu

# RESOURCE POLICY AND BEHAVIOR

## UNIVERSITY OF MICHIGAN SCHOOL OF NATURAL RESOURCES & ENVIRONMENT

The Resource Policy and Behavior (RPB) concentration draws from economic, political, psychological, anthropological, and other social models of human behavior to enable students to understand the social dimensions of resource controversies, and to devise and analyze strategies to intervene in these issues. In other words, its focus is two-fold: understand human behavior at all levels of social organization and then mobilize to change that behavior.

Intelligent decision-making and informed applied research must be grounded solidly in the social and natural sciences. Since RPB is housed in the School of Natural Resources at the U Michigan, the program is distinctive in that it allows students the ability to study policy and behavior within a scientific framework. The multidisciplinary setting provided by SNRE, and the depth of social science and professional schools at U Michigan, provide fertile ground for learning about real-world problems. These factors provide students with the professional skills to make a difference.

All master's students are required to complete a master's opus as their capstone experience. Ecology and Management concentration, Landscape Architecture and RPB students work together on projects in teams of 6-8 students to address resource problems for real-world clients.

Students concentrating in RPB can choose an emphasis on either policy or behavior. Those pursuing environmental policy further specialize in resource policy or resource planning. Those concentrating in behavior emphasize advocacy, behavior, or environmental education. RPB concentrators might further specialize in conservation biology and ecosystem management or environmental justice issues.

RPB has formal joint-degree programs with the Center for Russian and East European Studies, Corporate Environmental Management Program with the U Michigan Business School, and Environmental Law with the U Michigan Law School. Many other possibilities for dual programs also exist.

A resource policy/planning course of study might include courses in resource policy administration, aquatic ecosystems, conservation biology, negotiation skills, environmental law, water resource economics, and water resource policy. Students focusing on human behavior in an environmental context might study research methods in environment and behavior, conflict management, conservation behavior, social impact assessment, environmental education, and small groups and advocacy planning.

Examples of positions held by recent graduates include: Legislative Aide; Project Manager; Attorney; Endangered Species Lobbyist; Policy Analyst and Associate Professor.

Graduate Admissions Team
1024 Dana, SNRE-OAP
University of Michigan
Ann Arbor, MI 48109-1115

734. 764.5453
snre.gradteam.@umich.edu
www.wnre.umich.edu/

# SOCIAL POLICY
## HELLER GRADUATE SCHOOL, BRANDEIS UNIVERSITY

Since its founding in 1959, the Heller Graduate School has been committed to developing new knowledge and insights in the fields of social policy, and health and human services management. Faculty members and students actively engage in examining policies and programs that respond to the changing needs of individuals and social groups in society. Heller and its nationally renowned research centers have pioneered in a variety of policy areas including: health, children, youth and families, aging, disabilities, mental health, substance abuse and work, inequality, and social change. The faculty represents many social science disciplines and includes both scholars and practitioners. Heller offers graduate programs designed explicitly to bridge the gap between theory and practice: a Ph.D. in social policy, a Master of Management (M.M.), a Master of Business Administration (M.B.A.) in human services, and a M.S. in Sustainable International Development.

The Heller School's M.M. and M.B.A. programs train leaders to manage a wide range of health and human services organizations. The curriculum uniquely combines social policy with cutting-edge management education — cross-training students not only to identify the issues and needs of disadvantaged groups, but to address those needs through effective and efficient program design and management within the complex and changing environment of health and human services. The M.M. and M.B.A. programs offer the option of three specialized tracks — health care and child, youth and family services, and elder and disabled services. Students can also choose to self-design a concentration from our other policy specializations. This allows students interested in careers in a specific area of human services to pursue a course of study that emphasizes both management and policy in that field. A final Team Consulting Project enables students to apply management and analytical skills in a real-life context. The full-time accelerated program takes fifteen months, beginning in June each year and finishing in August of the following year. Part-time and evening study are available.

Students in Heller's Ph.D. Program in Social Policy pursue a course of study that provides intensive scholarly preparation in general and specialized social policy areas, honed research skills, and a strong working knowledge of various social science disciplines. The course of study is interdisciplinary, based on economics, sociology, and political science. Courses in social welfare, policy analysis, and research methods combine with those in substantive areas of interest for an integrative approach to social policy. Students must complete fifteen courses and a comprehensive paper in the social sciences as well as successfully defend, both orally and in writing, a policy research dissertation. The doctoral program educates students for careers in teaching, research, social planning, administration, and policy analysis. Students benefit from association with an expert research staff in six policy centers conducting nationally significant projects in a wide range of areas.

Students in the M.A. program in Sustainable International Development (SID) consider the state of world development, and probe issues that will affect future generations. They also broaden the skills necessary to plan, negotiate, implement, monitor, and evaluate development programs. SID has gained international recognition as an innovative degree program, examining models of development for their achievements in reducing poverty and inequality, in raising quality of life, and in conserving the environment. SID seeks fresh thinking about complex relationships, bridging areas of concern reserved traditionally to scientists or social scientists, policy makers, human rights advocates, or development practitioners.

SID aims to impart the knowledge and skills necessary to design and manage local, regional, national, or international development. The program suits early to mid-career professionals from governmental or non-governmental entities who are assuming responsibility for: enterprise creation; poverty reduction; bio-diversity and natural resource management; refugee settlement and disaster mitigation; food security; and civil society institutions. SID has an innovative professional curriculum that includes a year in residence studying with senior researchers and field level development practitioners, and a second year field project, internship, or advanced study applying and evaluating methods and models of development.

*Former Secretary of Labor Robert B. Reich; University Professor Maurice B. Hexter Professor of Social and Economic Policy, J.D., Yale. Work and inequality.*

*Stuart Altman; Sol C. Chaiken Professor of National Health Policy, Ph.D., UCLA. Healthcare policy.*

*Andrew B. Hahn, Research Professor and Associate Dean for University Relations, Ph.D., Brandeis. Labor Market Studies*

*David G. Gil, Professor of Social Policy, D.S.W., Pennsylvania. Social welfare, inequality.*

*Constance W. Williams, Associate Professor and Director of the Ph.D. in Social Policy Program, Ph.D., Brandeis. Family and children, race, class, culture.*

*Jack P. Shonkoff, Professor of Social Policy and Dean, M.D., NYU. Pediatrics, child and family policy.*

Full-time students complete the Master's Program in fifteen months, a considerable advantage in cost and time over equivalent two-year programs. Part-time students finish in two to three years. Evening students typically take two courses per semester and finish in three to four years.

Office of Admissions
The Heller Graduate School
Brandeis University
MS 035
Waltham, MA 02254-9110

781. 736.3820
HellerGS@.brandeis.edu
//heller.brandeis.edu

# POPULATION AND RESOURCE STUDIES
## STANFORD UNIVERSITY
### MORRISON INSTITUTE

The world's population is increasing by eighty million people each year. This growth profoundly affects our environment, the pressure on natural resources, and the capacity of many nations to achieve sustainable socioeconomic development. The problem that we face is how to stimulate economic development to meet rapidly expanding human needs, while ensuring that we do not destroy the natural resources and environment on which all life ultimately depends.

A new kind of scholar is required to address the many components that contribute to this enormous endeavor, one familiar with global issues through the perspectives of population biology, economics, and the social and medical sciences. The search for new approaches to these complex problems demands interdisciplinary cooperation and new modes of collaboration and communication.

Stanford University's response to concerns about population-related global issues, and to the research and educational needs pertaining to them, is the creation of the Morrison Institute for Population and Resource Studies. The Institute is led by Director Marcus W. Feldman, Wohlford Professor of Biological Sciences. This interdisciplinary program brings together faculty members and courses in numerous departments and programs: Chemistry, Human Biology, Biological Sciences, Genetics, Mathematics, Civil Engineering, the Hoover Institution, the Public Policy Program, Statistics, Anthropological Sciences, Cultural and Social Anthropology, Economics, Sociology, the Medical School, and the Center for Conservation Biology.

The Institute's objective is to lead this interdisciplinary study of population growth and its effects on social structures, national economies, resource availability, and the environment throughout the world. The three major facets to this endeavor — research, education, and contribution to the formation of policy — overlap in the major programs of the institute.

Through the training program, the institute helps sponsor research projects by Stanford students, usually in fieldwork that contributes to their dissertations and to the study of population problems (e.g., on-site study of population growth as a factor in the destruction of the tropical forests of Latin America). About eighty students have been supported in this way, with the numbers growing each year. In addition, a couple dozen interdisciplinary courses are available, and students majoring in Human Biology and Public Policy can specialize in population studies.

The annual Winter Colloquium, which is available for course credit, presents a range of lectures designed to highlight the significance of an interdisciplinary perspective by drawing on the physical, natural, medical, and social sciences.

Morrison Institute for Population and Resource Studies
Stanford University
Stanford, CA                          www.stanford.edu/group/morrinst/programs.html

# PSYCHOLOGY
## ANTIOCH UNIVERSITY, LOS ANGELES

Antioch University's model of clinical education brings the real world into the classroom. The MA in Clinical Psychology (MAP) prepares students for a variety of professional roles in today's emerging systems of mental health service delivery. Students receive training in short-term therapy, and in groups, individual, and family therapy. Antioch's socially aware and ethically sensitive education focuses on the development of each student as an individual. Eclectic in orientation and pragmatic in spirit, the program prepares students for licensure as a Marriage, Family and Child Counselors (MFCC).

If a student wishes to pursue an M.A. in Psychology, but is not interested in MFCC licensure in California, Antioch offers the flexible individualized M.A. in Psychology. Students design an individualized plan of learning activities in concert with a faculty advisor. Some take courses in Graduate Management, combining psychological practice and organizational management.

Recent concentrations in the program include: domestic violence, parenting education, substance abuse counseling, conflict resolution for children, death and dying, children's creativity, existential psychology, counseling African-American elders, career counseling, and transpersonal psychology.

Antioch helps students develop as professionals through continuing education workshops, professional development seminars, and mentoring with experienced clinicians. Clinical training placements are considered an integral part of educational and professional development. Antioch's Clinical Training Office finds, evaluates, authorizes, and lists potential clinical training placements for students. Clinical skills are developed through hands-on experience with expert supervision in Antioch's more than 200 clinical placement settings. Clinical Training and Career Resource Day provides students and alumni with the opportunity to network with job sites, and to receive the latest information on job opportunities in a rapidly changing marketplace.

The Antioch University Counseling Center, a nonprofit mental health center since 1974, is a training site for selected students in the MA in Clinical Psychology Program. Group workshops, career counseling and testing are available.

Antioch's 72-unit MAP is designed for working adults, and provides education meaningful for your personal development. It can be completed in 18 months, or more slowly by part-time enrollment, and offers flexible scheduling with choices of day and evening classes. Written narrative evaluations are used instead of grades.

In the one-day-a-week program, students complete all required courses in six consecutive quarters of full-time study with classes typically scheduled from 8:30 a.m. to 6:30 p.m. The remaining requirements are scheduled individually by students.

Office of Admissions
Antioch University, Los Angeles
13274 Fiji Way
Marina del Rey, CA 90292

310. 578.1080
admissions@antiochla.edu
www.antiochla.edu

# COMMUNITY PSYCHOLOGY
## UNIVERSITY OF LA VERNE

The Department of Behavioral Sciences at the University of La Verne meets the challenges of the changing dynamics in professional psychology with a Doctor of Psychology (Psy.D.) degree in Clinical-Community Psychology. ULV's Psy.D. program provides a distinctly integrative degree following a practitioner-scientist model. The ULV program will prepare graduates to provide a broad range of clinical services and assume an expanded psychosocial role in the community. The clinical-community model offers an ecological perspective which emphasizes that individual behavior can best be understood within the context of interactive systems that are multi-level, multi-dimensional, and multi-directional. The capstone experience of the program — the dissertation — will integrate the candidate's skills and knowledge to address relevant professional issues in clinical and community settings.

The University of La Verne's Psy.D. program is secular in orientation and is designed to meet the criteria for pursuing eventual accreditation by the American Psychological Association. ULV Psy.D. graduates will be trained to provide direct clinical services, consultation, program evaluation, and research services in a broad array of settings. Graduates are expected to pursue psychologist licensure upon completion of all pre-doctoral and post-doctoral requirements.

For several decades, ULV's Department of Behavioral Sciences has enjoyed a position of leadership in undergraduate and graduate education in psychology, counseling, sociology, anthropology, and human services. The multi-disciplinary faculty consists of 14 full-time professors and numerous part-time instructors who are committed to teaching excellence and collaborative, interdisciplinary student-faculty research. Our faculty serve as mentors through their own careers in the Behavioral Sciences, strengthening the link between the University and the community through their professional affiliations.

The capacity for self-awareness and an appreciation of the psychotherapeutic process are important aspects of an individual's development as a clinician. The program encourages this process by requiring students to complete at least 40 hours of personal psychotherapy during the program and prior to the pre-doctoral internship.

The Psy.D. program is designed to meet all of the academic and pre-doctoral clinical requirements for California licensure in psychology. Because licensure requirements vary among states, students interested in practicing psychology outside of California should consult with the licensing board in the state where they intend to practice for information on eligibility in that state.

Graduate Student Services
University of La Verne
1950 3rd Street
La Verne, California 91750

909. 593.3511 ext. 4244
www.ulv.edu/~psych/HOME.html

# ECOPSYCHOLOGY AND INTEGRATED ECOLOGY
## INSTITUTE OF GLOBAL EDUCATION

The Institute for Global Education (IGE) offers Applied Ecopsychology and Integrated Ecology Ph.D. and M.S. Degree programs, and transferable graduate and undergraduate courses through online distant learning. IGE researches and provide education that supports the United Nations manifesto for environmentally-sound personal growth and social justice.

The nature-connected psychology cooperative program reduces college course-work and Ph.D. and M.S. degree costs by 70%. This is done by incorporating students' prior learning experiences, and through online support — group education with experts. It is open to environmentally caring individuals with interests in psychology, wellness, or personal and global peace. When appropriate, participants obtain M.S. degree waivers for their past training, professional, and life experiences

IGE specializes in nature-connected psychology: the Natural Systems Thinking Process (NSTP). This science enables people interested in education, counseling, nature interpretation, wellness, peace, mental health, or social work to discover how our excessively nature-separated lives stressfully separate our psyche from its nurturing origins in nature. This disconnection produces the insatiable wants that disturb our sentient inner nature and fuel our most challenging problems. Students learn to reverse this destructive process. They master thoughtful nature-reconnecting activities that help them make conscious sensory contact with natural areas. This dissolves stress by satisfying our deepest natural loves, wants, and spirit.

NSTP employs an intelligent, healing searchlight of sunshine from nature itself, and enables your intellect to think in supportive ways that include your hands, heart, and nature.

Greenwich University, which bestows the degrees for these programs is accredited in Australia, with branch operations in Hawaii.

*Program Director: Applied Ecopsychologist Michael J. Cohen, Ed.D., faculty at Greenwich U, Portland State U, and the Institute of Global Education. For 45 years he has founded and directed environmental outdoor education programs including the National Audubon Society Expedition Institute at Lesley College. His books include the award winning "Connecting With Nature: Creating Moments That Let Earth Teach". Dr. Cohen conceived the 1985 National Audubon International Symposium and Conference "Is the Earth a Living Organism?", and is the recipient of the Distinguished World Citizen Award.*

Institute of Global Education
Dep't. of Integrated Ecology
P.O. Box 1605
Friday Harbor, WA 98250
or
Greenwich University

360. 378.6313
nature@pacificrim.net
www.ecopsych.com

www.greenwich.edu

# PSYCHOLOGY
## SONOMA STATE UNIVERSITY

The Psychology Department at Sonoma State, working in conjunction with Extended Education, offers Master of Arts degrees in several areas of psychology. Students who have been accepted in the past have been those particularly concerned with personal meaning and growth, mature in their sense of self-direction, and capable of developing and communicating their personal goals. The program's goal is, essentially, to impart learning that has relevance to human experience.

With Creative Arts Therapy, a range of subjects in the creative arts therapies are taught primarily through small-group learning experiences and supervised field work. This completes the first part of the credential process with the American Art Therapy Association.

Depth Psychology is a new structured two-year curriculum which explores Jungian and archetypal psychology through work with cross-cultural symbolism, mythology, art, religion, ritual, and dreams. It combines core classes with independent supervised Master's thesis work.

The Organization Development program is a two-year evening program that combines theory with practical field experience. This special focus M.A. emphasizes development of competence in emerging models of leadership, consultation, and change. Designed for a small group of mid-career individuals who move through the two-year curriculum together, students develop the personal awareness, interpersonal competence, and conceptual understanding required for effective practice in organization development.

In the Mentor/Portfolio Model for Humanistic/Transpersonal Psychology concentration, students work closely with a mentor to design individual programs that combine core courses, individual and small-group learning experiences, opportunities for teaching, internships, and workshops that focus on a selected interest area. It serves students interested in a psychology career in a number of areas, including public and private education, writing and publication, community activism, and consultation. It can also enhance a particular career in psychology in which a student may already be engaged. All of the interest areas in humanistic/existential/transpersonal psychology involve independent learning experiences rather than classroom experiences. Faculty are qualified to guide students in many areas, and successful application depends upon the availability of a qualified mentor.

This M.A. does not prepare students for the M.F.C.C. license in California.

Sally Tomlinson
Graduate Admissions Coordinator
Special Sessions M.A. in Psychology
Sonoma State University
Rohnert Park, CA 94928-3609

707. 664.2682
sally.tomlinson@sonoma.edu
www.sonoma.edu/psychology/

# HOLISTIC SCIENCE

## SCHUMACHER COLLEGE, ENGLAND

Schumacher College, in partnership with the University of Plymouth, has launched the first postgraduate program in the world to offer an M.Sc. in Holistic Science. The program provides an integrated framework of study and research that recognizes the changes occurring in science as it goes beyond interdisciplinarity to the understanding of complex wholes and their emergent properties at the levels of organisms, communities, ecosystems and the biosphere. These changes are also responses to the limitations of conventional science in dealing with crises in the state of the environment, in food production, health, community structure, and quality of life.

It has become evident that basic assumptions need to be re-examined so that values and ethics become integral to scientific practice, instead of add-ons. Holistic science includes qualities as well as quantities in our understanding of nature, our relationship to it and to each other. We are moving from a science of manipulation to one of participation in natural processes which are too complex to be controlled but which we can influence, for better or for worse. Core courses cover methodology, philosophy, the sciences of complexity as they have developed in physics, chemistry and biology, and applications to a diversity of complex systems — from individual organisms through communities to the global level of the geobiosphere — Gaia.

Schumacher College is focusing its attention on ecological economics and development issues; the links between philosophy, psychology and ecology; and the new understandings arising out of recent scientific discoveries. The College was founded in 1991 upon the twin convictions that the world view which has dominated Western civilization has serious limitations, and that a new vision is needed for human society, its values and its relationship to the earth. The College explores innovative forms of learning for sustainable living with distinguished thinkers and scientists such as Fritjof Capra, James Lovelock, Vandana Shiva, James Hillman, and Theodore Rozsak.

The College offers rigorous enquiry to uncover the roots of the prevailing world view; it explores ecological approaches which value holistic rather than reductionist perspectives and spiritual rather than consumerist values. It also offers a learning experience that is consistent with a holistic philosophy.

A significant component of study and research at Schumacher College will be participation in the communal life of the College. This provides an opportunity for teamwork and experiential learning through interaction with the diversity of highly motivated, informed and talented people who attend the short courses. This will complement and extend the emphasis on participation and cooperative enquiry that is an integral aspect of holistic science.

The Administrator  
Schumacher College  
The Old Postern, Dartington  
Devon TQ9 6EA, UK.

44 (0)1803 865934  
schumcoll@gn.apc.org  
www.gn.apc.org/schumachercollege/

# ACTION FOR A VIABLE FUTURE
## SONOMA STATE UNIVERSITY

The Hutchins School of Liberal Studies at Sonoma State University, in partnership with the department of Interdisciplinary Studies and Extended Education, offers a Master's program with the theme "Action for a Viable Future". The program is designed to move from the theoretical study of contemporary problems to actual implementation of a plan for social action. Students begin their program in an intensive, 9-unit seminar entitled Critical Inquiry: A Preparation for Action and Change. In this introductory course, the group explores the roots of environmental and social justice issues and the mechanisms of change, with an emphasis on learning research techniques. After students branch out to explore individual interests, they come back together to combine experiences and insights in the project design and implementation phase. Throughout the process, there is an emphasis on forming a vibrant learning community; the final project may be undertaken individually, in teams, or in small groups.

Each student's Plan of Action will address an issue they find of concern. Several students may choose to work on the same issue from different angles. For example, if the issue is education for the disadvantaged, some may work with a prison population; some may work at the policy level; some may develop appropriate curricula; some may instigate remedial programs. If the issue is environmental deterioration, some students could work on organizing work crews; some could work on media exposure; and again, some could work on curricula for schools.

The faculty include Dr. Francisco Vazquez, with extensive bi-cultural experience in Mexico and the United States; Dr. Mutombo M'Panya from Zaire, who also teaches at California Institute of Integral Studies; and Paula Hammett, Associate Librarian at SSU's library. The designer of the program is Dr. Ardath Lee who holds an M.A. and a Ph.D. in English, as well as M.A. degrees in Humanities and Art History. Dr. Lee has been involved in interdisciplinary and re-entry education since the early 1970s.

As this is a "hybrid" program that requires students to take both Extension and regular SSU classes, the cost for the program varies from semester to semester. The initial nine-unit seminar is at the Extension per-unit fee. The next fifteen units are at the normal CSU graduate studies rate; the final six units of seminars again cost the Extension "going rate" per unit. Financial aid and scholarships are available.

The program is in the experimental stage: the first cohort started their first seminar class in Spring 2000. Pending evaluation of the curriculum, the earliest a new group would be started is Fall 2001. If you are interested in the program, contact the administrative coordinator and ask to be put on a contact list.

Beth Warner
Administrative Coordinator
Action for a Viable Future
Hutchins School of Liberal Studies
Sonoma State University
Rohnert Park, CA

707. 664.3977
beth.warner@sonoma.edu

# SOCIAL WORK
## BOSTON UNIVERSITY

The Boston University School of Social Work is committed to education that furthers social and economic justice in the urban environment. The School strives to incorporate this commitment into its curriculum, programs, and activities, and is particularly concerned with the empowerment of all oppressed groups.

The primary aim of the School of Social Work is to educate professional social workers who will become leaders in a complex multicultural society. They will possess the knowledge and skills to address the needs and potential of individuals, families, groups, organizations, and communities. The School offers an integrated program of study, including clinical and macro social work methods. Full-time and part-time programs leading to the Master of Social Work, Joint degrees with the School of Public Health (M. S.W./M.P.H.), the School of Theology (M.S.W./M.T.S. or M.S.W./M.Div.), and the School of Education (M. S.W./M.Ed or M. S.W.Ed.D.) are offered. In addition, the School of Social Work has an advanced standing program for graduates of an undergraduate social work program accredited by the Council of Social Work Education. Students transferring from other graduate social work programs are also accepted.

In both classroom and field, professional education is divided into four broad categories of instruction: human behavior in the social environment, social welfare policy, social work research, and methods used in social work practice. The School of Social Work's multimethod social work practice program offers the opportunity to concentrate in clinical social work practice (with individuals, families, and groups) and macro social work practice (community organization, management, and planning).

*Maryann Amodeo, Clinical Associate Professor, M.S.W., Syracuse; Ph.D., Brandeis. Substance abuse identification and intervention skills.*

*Melvin Delgado, Professor, M.S., Columbia; Ph.D., Brandeis. Social welfare, issues of populations of color, cross-cultural practice.*

*Lena Lundgren-Gaveras, Assistant Professor, M.S.W., Ph.D., Chicago. Public welfare dependency, urban poverty, unemployment policy.*

*Susan Stern, Associate Professor, M.S.W., Michigan; Ph.D., Chicago. Family and marital conflict, childhood aggression, child abuse, adolescent mental health and delinquency.*

Boston Univ. School of Social Work        617. 353.3765
264 Bay State Road                        busswad@bu.edu web.bu.edu/ssw/
Boston, MA 02215

# HUMANITIES AND LEADERSHIP IN CULTURE, ECOLOGY, AND SUSTAINABLE COMMUNITY

## NEW COLLEGE OF CALIFORNIA

New College of California's North Bay Center for the Study of Culture, Ecology, and Sustainable Community in Santa Rosa (north of San Francisco), offers a Master's degree in Humanities and Leadership with an emphasis in Culture, Ecology, and Sustainable Community. The program seeks to help create a just, sacred, and sustainable world by educating students who can: heal both people and the earth; engage in resistance to further destruction to humans, other living things, and the planet; build sustainable alternative institutions; and create a consciousness shift to a more wholistic, ecological paradigm. Students learn the "languages" of critical thinking, imagination, empathy, compassion, and the activism necessary to accomplish these tasks.

The M.A. Program consists of a 36-unit, 12-month program combining classroom learning with in-depth research projects enabling students to become leaders in the field of culture, ecology, and sustainable community. The program offers seminars in culture, ecology, and sustainable community; social theory; and leadership skills development for creating social change. Students develop their own areas of concentration through the Field Research and Master's Thesis/Project. Concentrations have included Eco-Dwelling and Design, Alternative Medicine, Appropriate Technology, Eco-psychology, Bio-remediation, etc. Two concentration areas — Environmental Entrepreneurship and Biodynamic Agriculture — have set curricula.

Each month, students interview a leaders seeking to discover how they became a leader — what skills they needed to develop, what barriers they overcame, and the strategies they are using to create a better world. Interviewees have included Joanna Macy, David Brower, Helena Norberg-Hodge, Jerry Mander, Susan Griffen, Alice Walker, Kevin Dannaher, Helen Caldicott, and Carl Anthony.

Using the global media society as an arena of inquiry, students explore the larger context in which issues of cultural renewal and sustainability are situated. The critical lenses of economics, psychology, anthropology, sociology, and politics are explored. The Ecology, Social Change and Leadership component focuses on critical thinking, problem solving, and strategic skills development. A core seminar helps students build leadership skills in specific areas of cultural transformation and ecological activism including critical thinking and problem solving, planning and strategy, social marketing, and impact assessment.

Distance learning is possible by combining attendance at seminars one weekend a month while conducting the thesis or project in your own community. Students are attending from as far as San Luis Obispo, Humboldt County, and the Sierras.

Michael McAvoy, Academic Director
New College of California
North Bay Campus Center for the Study of
Culture, Ecology and Sustainable Community
99 Sixth Street
Santa Rosa, CA 95401

707..568.0112
www.newcollege.edu/northbay

*Sustainability*

# SUSTAINABLE DESIGN
## UNIVERSITY OF VIRGINIA

The Institute for Sustainable Design (ISD) was created at the University of Virginia's School of Architecture by former Dean William McDonough to "render visible" viable alternatives to conventional design and practice in human production. The ISD has since fostered development of new creative tools for sustainable design by facilitating creative interdisciplinary collaborations among faculty and students. The Institute has advocated innovative design approaches and restorative action based on principles that recognize the interdependence of ecology, equity, and economy.

Much of the work and public outreach conducted by the Institute has focused on the complex land-use issues confronting communities across Virginia and the nation. The goal has been to promote revolutionary and creative thinking toward more environmentally intelligent and sustaining strategies in land use planning and development practices as alternatives to the natural and social environmental degradation and the economic inefficiencies inherent in conventional approaches.

More recently the work at ISD has been informed by recognition of the crucial role played by the global marketplace in the pursuit of a more sustaining future, and by the need to integrate and organize large-scaled enterprises around principles of intelligent economic, environmental, and equitable principles. ISD's work interests have evolved towards the development of more environmentally sustaining business practices.

The Institute's objectives are: to render visible human practices damaging to the built and natural environments and to human and ecological health; to articulate strategies of change that celebrate the concepts and promise of a sustaining and delightful world; to be a living laboratory for the incubation and testing of innovative and sustainable practices and technologies; to engage industry to enable ethical and prosperous commerce; to be an effective agent of change; and to create tools to make possible the successful transfer and implementation of sustainable practices and technologies.

ISD's guiding principles are: sustainable solutions integrate concerns for ecology, economy, and equity; sustainable solutions require interdisciplinary collaboration and action; all sustainability is local; in the cycles of the natural world nothing is wasted, and everything old becomes food for something new; and designers must take the lead in pressing for and inventing sustainable alternatives to conventional design and production practices.

To strengthen its role in the development and implementation of sustainable commerce, the Institute is relocating to the UVA's Darden School of Business campus and being renamed the Institute for Sustainable Design and Commerce. The ISD pursues applied research opportunities for faculty and student members of UVA's university community and does not offer formal academic programs.

Diane M. Dale, Director
Institute for Sustainable Design
Campbell Hall
UVA  P.O. Box 400122
Charlottesville, Virginia 22904-4122

804. 924.6454
uva-isd@virginia.edu
arch-admissions@virginia.edu.
http://minerva.acc.virginia.edu/~sustain/

# SUSTAINABLE SOCIETIES
## NORTHERN ARIZONA UNIVERSITY

The Master of Liberal Studies in Visions of Good and Sustainable Societies is an interdisciplinary program for people seeking to create models of community for the twenty-first century. The program is offered to adult learners who seek a broad and integrated perspective on the complex issues of contemporary society. The degree program is organized around the curricular theme — Visions of Good and Sustainable Societies — that cuts across many academic areas including anthropology, the arts, business, economics, environmental science, gerontology, psychology, sociology, religion, technology, and women's studies.

Students work with a faculty advisor to develop an emphasis appropriate to their interests. For example, some students have emphasized ethics and leadership, spirituality and health, women's studies, or aging — all in relationship to strengthening community life. A 6-hour final integrative project can be a traditional research thesis, a creative work, or an applied research project in your community.

As part of a community of learners that respects the experiences and insights of mature students, you can study models of communities as well as environmental and social issues of immediate importance to regional, national, and international communities. The program is appropriate for students who are committed to the connection between thought and action. Secondary school teachers, working in the humanities or the social and natural sciences, also find this program particularly appealing.

The program is tailored to students who wish to pursue graduate study on a part-time basis. Courses are offered on a flexible schedule — including summers, evenings, and weekends.

Northern Arizona University is one of a small group of colleges in the Historically Black Colleges and Universities/Minority Institutions Environmental Technology Consortium that are making a concerted effort to green their education, and to particularly reach out to native and minority populations in the process.

Dr. Sandra Lubarsky
Master of Liberal Studies Office
Northern Arizona University
Flagstaff, AZ 86011-6031

520. 523.9359
Sandra.Lubarsky@nau.edu

# SUSTAINABLE SYSTEMS
## SLIPPERY ROCK UNIVERSITY

The Master of Science in Sustainable Systems (MS3) program at Slippery Rock University is charged with preparing students to face the pressing environmental challenges of the future by considering sustainability as the underlying framework for action. Students study and practice sustainability through the integration of agriculture, natural resource management, and the built environment. Particular emphasis is given to the design and management of productive systems that reflect the diversity and resilience of natural systems. The program embraces the human element in the landscape, searching for sustainable ways to satisfy food, energy, shelter, and other material and non-material human needs.

To achieve these goals, students take interdisciplinary coursework as the core of the program and select one of three focal tracks - Agroecology, Built Environment, Sustainable Resources Management - or an interdisciplinary track in which to concentrate. These academic courses include exercises in creative design and problem solving, as well as laboratory and field experiences. A host of non-curricular opportunities for learning and practicing sustainability are available through the Macoskey Center, the surrounding community, internships, and other campus-related projects.

The MS3 Program is a 37 credit-hour program, and both thesis and non-thesis options are available. The Agroecology track core courses include: Sustainable Agriculture Techniques; Sustainable Agricultural Practices in Plant and Animal Husbandry; and Fertility Considerations. Built Environment track courses consist of Design and Resource Development for Energy Conservation; Healthy Building Systems and Materials; Alternative Energy and Engineering for Sustainable Systems; and Site Building Feasibility Studies. The Resource Management track courses include: Sustainable Forest Management, Restoration Ecology, and Open Space Planning.

An on-campus facility serves as a host to a variety of educational, research and social activities associated with the MS3 Program. Conceived by the late Dr. Robert A. Macoskey, this Center promotes the transition to sustainable systems through education, research, and demonstration. The Center includes organic community and market gardens, a small woodlot, a composting research and demonstration project, and a restoration ecology project. Harmony House, a renovated farmhouse located at the Macoskey Center, serves as a gathering area for program activities and serves as the residence for two graduate assistants. It has been redesigned for energy efficiency, indoor air quality, and utilization of environmentally friendly materials.

Foundations of Sustainability
Design for Sustainable Landscapes
Soils as a Resource

Applied Ecology or Ecosystem Management
Design Graphics & Problem Solving
Sustainable Systems Seminar

Dr. Karen Kainer
101 Eisenberg Classroom Building
Slippery Rock University
Slippery Rock, PA 16057-1326

724. 738.2622
karen.kainer@sru.edu

# WOMEN'S SPIRITUALITY
## CA. INSTITUTE OF INTEGRAL STUDIES

The California Institute of Integral Studies offers a M.A. in Philosophy & Religion and a Ph.D. in Humanities in Women's Spirituality dedicated to the liberation of women's spirits, minds, and bodies. It is one of the first accredited graduate programs in women's spirituality in the world.

The Women's Spirituality Program offers in-depth studies of the cultural, historical, and spiritual experiences of women across the millennia and around the world. Integrating academic scholarship with a celebration of the feminine energies of the divine through ritual, song, dance, and dreams, students and faculty explore the creative gifts of women from many spiritual traditions.

The program encourages an embodied scholarship that encompasses cultural history, the arts, ritual, bodywork, movement, and activism. Students often enter the Women's Spirituality program to pursue careers in teaching, research, or writing — or to enhance existing careers in such fields as the media, psychotherapy, the ministry (lay or clerical), social action, public policy, hospice work, or in women's health and health advocacy.

The core curriculum is enhanced by public programs that bring leading voices in women's spirituality to the Institute, as well as by for-credit journeys abroad to women's sacred sites in Malta, Greece, Turkey, and the British Isles.

Visiting faculty and workshop presenters include: Carol P. Christ, Susan Griffin, Deena Metzger, Vicki Noble, Marion Rosen, and Starhawk.

Archaeomythology of Culture & Psyche
Ecofeminist Philosophy
Women's Mysteries & Sacred Arts
Philosophy & Religion
Mary, Goddess of the West
Women & Religion: Reclaiming the Sacred Feminine

Body Wisdom: Women & Healing
Partnership Studies
Feminist Research and Integral Scholarship
Community Service: Spirituality in Action
Midwifing Ecstasy: Sacred Movement & Song

*Mara Lynn Keller, Ph.D., Philosophy, Yale University; Program Director   Ancient Goddess cultures of Crete and Greece, holistic philosophy, ecofeminism, peace issues.*

*Riane Eisler, J.D., Macro-historian, co-director of The Center for Partnership Studies.*

*Elinor Gadon, Ph.D., History and Culture; Program Founder. Art and culture of India, world religions, mythology and women's cultures.*

*Joanna Macy, Ph.D., State University of New York, Syracuse, Buddhist scholar, systems scientist, ecological and social activist.*

*Arisika Razak, MPH, Health Care Administration, UC Berkeley, nurse midwife, performance artist, dancer. Reproductive health, ritual, embodiment of the sacred, perinatal care of African American women.*

*Charlene Spretnak, M.A., English, University of California/Berkeley  Pioneer in the framing of women's spirituality, ecofeminism, and Green politics movements.*

CA Institute of Integral Studies          415.575.6155
1453 Mission St.                          www.ciis.edu
San Francisco, CA 94103

# WOMEN'S SPIRITUALITY
## NEW COLLEGE OF CALIFORNIA

**Women's Spirituality M.A. Program**

Drawing on the grass-roots Women's Spirituality and Ecofeminist movements, the Women's Spirituality M.A. Program reclaims women's history and pre-history, spiritual experience and creative expression. The visual and symbolic languages of art and mythology are integrated with oral traditions and written language, honoring a multiplicity of expressions. This feminist learning community, located in the heart of the Mission District of San Francisco, offers strong mutual support and mentoring, encouraging the development of new theory through an integration of scholarly research, spirituality, activism and the arts.

The philosophy of feminist education enables each woman to contribute her scholarly achievements in a non-hierarchical structure. It allows for a re-examination of the nature of knowledge and information and the restoration of women and all other sentient beings to their rightful position in history, the correction of omissions, exploration of new forms, creation of new visions and re-visions. In keeping with New Colleges's mission of social activism, feminist education attempts to balance theory and practice. New College emphasizes the advising relationship between each student and a member of the faculty, and encourage students to be active participants in their course of study.

Affiliated Faculty (The Wise Women's Council) - a circle of scholars and practitioners - includes: Lucia Chiavola Birnbaum, Jalaja Bonheim, Sandy Boucher, Zsuzsanna Budapest, Elinor Gadon, Genny Lim, Joan Marler, Vicki Noble, Donna Read, Papusa Molina, Namonyah Soipan, Starhawk, and Luisah Teish.

| | |
|---|---|
| Women Healers: Hands and Hearts on Fire | Women's Spirituality Group |
| Rites of Passage: Shamanism and Healing | Ecofeminism |
| Archaeomythology: the Goddess of Prehistory | Justice and the Divine: Healing the Split |
| Art as Sacred Process | The Language Myth, Symbol, and the Body |
| Holy Well, Sacred Flame: Relationship and Practice with Community and the Living Earth | |
| Women and Buddhism | Women, Spirituality & Cultural Transformation |
| Creativity, Sexuality and the Sacred | Fem. Research Methodology & Crit. Analysis |

*Anica Vesel Mander, Ph.D. Women's Studies, The Union Institute Co-director of the Women's Spirituality Program. Fluent in French, Italian, Serbo-Croatian, German, Spanish and Latin, her research focus includes international debate on multiculturalism, gender, language, and identity.*

New College of California
741 Valencia Street
San Francisco, CA 94110

888. 437.3460
415. 437.3460
www.newcollege.edu

# PEACE CORPS

# MASTER'S INTERNATIONALIST

◆ ◆ ◆

# RETURNED

# PEACE CORPS FELLOWS

# GRADUATE PROGRAMS

## (CHECK THEM OUT!)

◆ ◆ ◆

# PEACE CORPS
# MASTER'S INTERNATIONALIST
# PROGRAMS

FOR MORE THAN TEN YEARS, the Peace Corps has joined forces with colleges and universities across the United States to provide a unique academic experience through the Master's International Program (MI Program). First established at Rutgers University in 1987, the MI Program has provided hundreds of students the opportunity to incorporate Peace Corps Volunteer service into a Master's degree program. These "Student-Volunteers" forward their own professional and personal goals, and develop technical expertise that is valued by people in developing nations throughout the world.

The Peace Corps collaborates with colleges and universities to offer the MI Program in numerous different degree programs. Students may pursue studies in public health, forestry, agriculture, English teaching, business, non-profit management, or urban planning. They are placed in Peace Corps assignments overseas where they are able to apply theoretical knowledge learned in the classroom to practical, real-life settings.

Participating in the MI Program is demanding, but the rewards — both to you and to the people you serve — are great. We encourage you to consider the MI Program as you look to build your professional career.

Mark D. Gearan
Director

## Deciding between Peace Corps and Graduate School?

Since 1987, the Master's International Program has made this decision easier for hundreds of prospective students and Peace Corps Volunteers. A cooperative partnership between the Peace Corps and colleges and universities, the Master's International Program, provides a unique opportunity to incorporate Peace Corps service into a graduate degree program. The program combines a minimum of one year on-campus study with the training and field experience for which the Peace Corps is renowned. Upon completion of the program, Master's International (MI) graduates possess both an excellent academic credential and international field experience — an attractive combination for prospective employers.

The MI Program is offered in disciplines where the Peace Corps can provide relevant field assignments. The specific degree(s) offered by each school will vary.

## Master's International students as Peace Corps Volunteers

Since the Peace Corps' inception in 1961, its mission has remained unchanged:
- To provide Volunteers who contribute to the social and economic development of interested countries;

- To strengthen Americans' understanding about the world and its peoples — to bring the world back home.

More than 145,000 Americans have joined the Peace Corps since the agency was established. They work for two years, sharing their technical expertise, creativity, flexibility, and dedication with people all over the world. Peace Corps Volunteers live and work in local communities, encouraging small enterprise, protecting the local environment, improving agricultural production, promoting sound health and sanitation practices, and teaching English to students who recognize the language as a means to economic and educational opportunity. Master's International students bring a strong knowledge base to their overseas assignment, making them highly valued by the people with whom they work. MI students also enjoy the benefit of having a faculty advisor in the United States who can provide technical support and advice. Over the last 35 years, the needs of Peace Corps' host countries have evolved, and requests for Peace Corps Volunteers with strong technical skills have increased. Host countries are increasingly requesting Volunteers skilled in forestry, agriculture, business and non-profit management, English teaching, public health, and urban planning.

## What will I do as a Peace Corps Volunteer?

MI students are placed in projects relevant to their course of study. Some of the many projects in which MI students have worked are:

A public health project in Madagascar to introduce improved nutrition and hygiene practices to school children and their mothers;

An agricultural project in Nepal introducing more efficient crop production, pest management, seed production and storage techniques in order to increase both food production and income;

A forestry project in Albania to promote the integration of forestry with current agricultural practices, working with farmers to help increase farm income and conserve local natural resources;

A business project in Kenya to assist entrepreneurs in gaining practical business skills, including inventory management, accounting, marketing, and accessing credit;

A project in Kyrgyzstan to teach English to secondary school students and to introduce new teaching methodologies to local English teachers.

## What are the benefits of being a Master's International Student?

In addition to receiving excellent training and practical experience, Master's International students receive a number of benefits from the Peace Corps, including:
- Transportation to and from the country of service;
- Living and housing expenses;
- Full medical and dental care;
- Vacation time and allowance;
- Cancellation or deferment of certain government-backed educational loans;
- $5,400 readjustment allowance upon completion of 27 months of service ;
- Career counseling and support; and
- Non-competitive eligibility for Federal government jobs upon completion of full term of service.

Most participating Master's International schools offer academic credit for Peace Corps service. In addition, several schools provide scholarships or tuition waivers for these credits. Depending on their availability at specific universities, Master's International students may also compete for research or teaching assistantships.

### How do I apply to the Master's International Program?

Master's International students must apply and be accepted to both the Peace Corps and at least one of the participating Master's International schools. The Peace Corps application will be evaluated based on the agency's selection criteria for Volunteers, including medical and legal clearances. The application to the school will be evaluated based on the school's own admission requirements.

To be eligible for Peace Corps service, you must be a U.S. citizen, in good general health, and at least 18 years of age. Married couples without dependent children may be accepted, but both spouses must qualify for a Volunteer assignment.

We recommend that your Peace Corps application and the application for admission to the MI school be submitted simultaneously, using the admission deadline of the school as a guide. This allows enough time for the necessary medical, legal, and other clearances from Peace Corps to be completed.

### When will I receive my Peace Corps assignment?

While you are completing your course work, your Peace Corps application will be kept active with the Peace Corps Office of Placement which is responsible for assessing and placing applicants. Peace Corps' host countries submit requests for Volunteers approximately six months prior to the scheduled start date of training.

### How is this different than entering graduate school and Peace Corps separately?

As a MI student, you earn academic credit for your Peace Corps service. In many cases, the school will waive the cost of these credits. You will have the benefit of your faculty advisor's technical expertise and support as you identify and address areas of need overseas. In addition, you will return to the United States with two years of professional international experience incorporated into your graduate degree.

### Does the Peace Corps provide financial support to MI students?

The Peace Corps does not provide scholarships to MI students. However, some student loans can be deferred or cancelled, and all costs associated with your Peace Corps experience are covered by the Peace Corps including transport, medical care, and living expenses. In addition, the Peace Corps provides a $5,400 readjustment allowance which is paid to you at the end of your assignment. Most schools provide students with an opportunity for research or teaching assistantships, scholarships, or a tuition waiver for the cost of credits earned while in the Peace Corps.

Peace Corps Recruitment    800. 424.8580, option "2,", ext. 1812
Washington, DC 20526      masters@peacecorps.gov

# AGRIBUSINESS

You might work in Ecuador advising and training small-scale farmers on improved farming techniques, post-harvest handling, quality control, marketing, and management.

## ARIZONA STATE UNIVERSITY EAST

The School of Agribusiness and Resource Management and the Center for Agribusiness Policy offer a MS degree in Agribusiness. Prepares students for assignments in agribusiness management and for volunteer and development activities. Courses cover issues such as: advanced agribusiness marketing, management and finance, food management, int'l. agricultural techniques, and world agricultural development.

*Benefits:* Students may earn up to six credits for their Peace Corps service.

Dr. Julie Stanton      480. 727.1126
Morrison School of Agribusiness & Resource Mgm't.
ASU East, 7001 E. Williams Field Rd. #0180
Mesa, AZ 85212      jstanton@asu.edu

## SANTA CLARA UNIVERSITY

The Leavey School of Business and Administration at Santa Clara University offers a M.B.A. with a specialization in Agribusiness. Prepares students for careers in the food and agribusiness industry, and to contribute to more effective Volunteer service in agriculture economics/farm management, and advanced business development. On-campus course work is complemented by a mentor program, internships, and international study tours.

*Benefits:* Scholarships, assistantships and loans. 6 quarter units for PC service.

S. Andrew Starbird, Ph.D.      408. 554.4086
Director, Institute of Agribusiness      sstarbird@scu.edu
Leavey School of Business Administration      fai@scu.edu
Santa Clara University
Santa Clara, CA 95053

# AGRICULTURE

You might work in Gabon to introduce more efficient crop production, pest management, and storage techniques.

## COLORADO STATE UNIVERSITY

CSU offers Master's degrees through five departments in the College of Agricultural Sciences: Agricultural and Resource Economics; Animal Sciences; Bio-agricultural Science and Pest Management; Horticulture and Landscape Architecture; and Soil and Crop Sciences. A Master's of Agriculture is also offered.

The thirty semester credit program of study is individually designed to meet students' professional/career objectives, and needs of the Peace Corps and host country.

*Benefits:* Eight to ten credits for Peace Corps service; competitively-based scholarships; and research and teaching assistantships may be available.

Barbara Jares                                    970. 491.6793
The Peace Corps Master's Int'l. Program          bjares@global.colostate.edu
CSU Office of Int'l. Programs
315 Aylesworth Hall NE
Fort Collins, CO 80523-1024

*or* Dr. Jack Fenwick                            970. 491.6907
Department of Soil and Crop Sciences             fenwick@ceres.agsci.colostate.edu
College of Agricultural Sciences
Ft. Collins, CO 80523-1170

## CORNELL UNIVERSITY

The MPS/Agriculture program has an emphasis on conservation of natural resources, sustainable farming systems, and on various aspects of international development such as population, nutrition, planning, policy, or agriculture. The program prepares students to assume a leadership position in development programs, in government and non-government organizations, or in the private sector. Twenty four of the 30 credit hours will be earned at Cornell prior to entering the Peace Corps.

After two semesters of academic work, students undertake their Peace Corps assignment. Students are encouraged to enroll for one more semester of study following Peace Corps service for further extension and refinement of their learning.

*Benefits:* Up to six credit hours may be earned for Peace Corps service.

James Haldeman                                   607. 255.3037
Box 14, Kennedy Hall                             jeh5@cornell.edu
Ithaca NY, 14853

## UNIVERSITY OF GEORGIA

UG offers a Master's Degree from the College of Agricultural and Environmental Sciences. The program is designed for students from a wide variety of backgrounds who desire further studies in international research and development. The MIP is offered in several departments including Agricultural and Applied Economics, Horticulture, and Crop and Soil Sciences. Candidates acquire a solid working knowledge of crop and animal production practices, sustainable agricultural production, water quality and availability, biodiversity, and an introduction to the economic aspects of international agricultural development. Thesis and non-thesis options.

*Benefits:* One MI assistantship per year is available. First year assistantship recipients eligible for a waiver of out-of-state fee on tuition. PC service may count for credit.

Julianne V. Stewart                              706. 542.7803
Program Coordinator                              jstewart@uga.edu.
International Agriculture
118 Four Towers Building
The University of Georgia

# PURDUE UNIVERSITY

Purdue University School of Agriculture offers a M.S. in Entomology with special emphasis in crop extension, crop protection, and integrated pest management. The program provides students with working knowledge of crop production, integrated pest management principles and practices, and economic aspects of international agricultural development. The program is tailored to student's interests, background, and career goals. Students will pursue a non-thesis master's option in the Department of Entomology. However, the Purdue MI curriculum involves nearly all of the academic disciplines in the School of Agriculture, thus providing the student with a broad educational base in agriculture, natural resources, and the food system.

*Benefits:* Part of the requirement for the M.S. in Entomology is a "creative project" which will be based on work done overseas; a 1/4 to 1/2 time assistantship is available.

Dr. Chris Oseto
Department of Entomology
Purdue University
West Lafayette, IN 47907

317. 494.4554
chris_oseto@entm.purdue.edu

# WASHINGTON STATE UNIVERSITY

WSU offers the MI degree option in the College of Agriculture, Human and Natural Resources. Students may enroll in the Departments of Natural Resources. Forestry, Range Management, Wildlife Management, Crops and Soils, Agriculture Economics, Entomology, or Horticulture depending on their past experiences, education, and interests. Program prepares students to serve in PC assignments in agroforestry, crop extension, and environmental management. They complete a year of graduate course work at the University prior to their Peace Corps assignment. Thesis and non-thesis options.

*Benefits:* Three to six credits are granted for Peace Corps service; no guaranteed financial aid, but some fellowships and assistantships may be available.

Sally Burkhart, Ass't. to the Director
International Programs
PO Box 645110
Washington State University
Pullman, WA 99164-5110

509. 335.1348
sburkhar@wsu.edu

# BUSINESS

## MONTEREY INSTITUTE OF INTERNATIONAL STUDIES

The Fisher Graduate School of International Business  at the Monterey Institute of International Studies offers an International MBA degree that prepares Peace Corps Volunteers for international business development. Students in the two-year MBA program take the first year of core courses from September to May. They complete the International Business Plan during the summer and take the following fall semester of courses. They enter Peace Corps service early the next year and, afterwards, return to Monterey for their final semester of study. The courses at MIIS prepare students for a Peace Corps assignment working with businesses in an advisory capacity.

*Benefits:* Students satisfy the language component of their degree program while in the Peace Corps, but do not earn actual credits; half tuition scholarships are available for the final semester of study following Peace Corps service.

Christy Herlick Gibson
Academic Programs Associate
Fisher Graduate School of Int'l. Mgm't.
Monterey Institute of International Studies
425 Van Buren Street
Monterey, CA 93940

831. 647.6586
Christy.Gibson@miis.edu

## UNIVERSITY OF THE PACIFIC

The Eberhardt School of Business offers a MBA degree in conjunction with the Peace Corps. The program prepares students for their service as Business Development Volunteers. Peace Corps service fulfills the internship requirement for the degree program. The University offers both a standard and an accelerated MBA curriculum. Students spend either one or two semesters on campus before Peace Corps service, and return for a final semester to complete their course work.

*Benefits:* MI students can apply their PC service towards completion of the internship requirement; for each semester following their Peace Corps service, students are forgiven 1/3 of their tuition costs through a graduate assistantship.

Dr. N. Peery, MBA Program Director
Eberhardt School of Business
University of the Pacific
3601 Pacific Avenue
Stockton, CA 95211

(209) 946-2642
npeery@uop.edu

# CIVIL & ENVIRONMENTAL ENGINEERING

You could work at the local level in Thailand to survey, plan, and supervise construction of water resource improvement projects, such as water systems, wells, and latrines, to ensure access to clean drinking water.

## MICHIGAN TECHNOLOGICAL UNIVERSITY

Michigan Technological University offers a Master's of Science in Civil Engineering and Environmental Engineering. The degree requires 3 quarters of course work, totaling 45 quarter units of academic study, prior to Peace Corps service. Students are required to take courses derived from the areas of civil/environmental engineering, project management/leadership/consensus building/environmental policy, and environmental microbiology/public health biology. Accredited bachelor's degree in engineering required.

*Benefits:* To 9 credits of independent study for PC service; tuition for credits earned through PC service waived; graduate TA's and positions as hourly graders available.

> Dr. James Mihelcic
> Dep't. of Civil & Enviro. Engineering
> Michigan Technological University
> 1400 Townsend Drive
> Houghton, MI 49931-1295
>
> 906. 487-2324
> jm41@mtu.edu

# ENVIRONMENTAL EDUCATION

You might work in Nicaragua to promote sound conservation techniques among local farmers and assist teachers in integrating environmental awareness in their curriculum. Also see Florida International University listing in Forestry/Natural Resources Mgm't.

## UNIVERSITY OF NEW MEXICO

The UNM College of Education offers a Master of Arts in Parks and Recreation with an emphasis in either Environmental Education or Parks and Recreation Administration. Students receive one year (3 semesters) of academic preparation in their field of study before entering service as PC Volunteers. The program consists of a minimum of 45 semester units covering issues such as: multicultural environmental education, organization and administration of parks and recreation agencies, community relations, leadership development, urban and rural natural resources planning. Minority participation is encouraged. Bachelor's degree with major in parks, recreation, leisure studies, environmental education, or a related field is required.

*Benefits:* 12 credits for Peace Corps service. Out-of-state tuition is very affordable, MIP students are eligible for various in-state financial aid opportunities after the first semester.

> Paul S. Miko, Ph.D
> College of Education
> The University of New Mexico
> Johnson Center, 112C
> Albuquerque, NM 87131-1251
>
> 505. 277.8172
> http://coe.unm.edu/MIP_main.htm.

# FORESTRY/NATURAL RESOURCES MGM'T.
## COLORADO STATE UNIVERSITY

Colorado State University offers Master of Science programs through five departments in the College of Natural Resources: Earth Resources (Watershed Science); Fishery and Wildlife Biology; Forest Sciences; Natural Resources Recreation and Tourism; and Rangeland Ecosystem Science. Master's programs in international watershed management, natural resources management, and the graduate program in ecology are also available. Thirty semester credits are required to complete the program. The program of study is individually designed to meet the students professional/career objectives, taking into consideration the needs of the Peace Corps and the host country. Students apply to individual department and indicate desired specialization.

*Benefits:* Eight semester credits for Peace Corps service; competitively based scholarships; research and teaching assistantships may be available.

Dr. Freeman M. Smith  970. 491.5678
Peace Corps/MI Liaison  freeman@cnr.colostate.edu
International School of Natural Resources
Colorado State University
Ft. Collins CO 80523-1401
*or*
Barbara Jares  970. 491.6793
Peace Corps Master's Int'l. Program  bjares@global.colostate.edu.
CSU Office of International Programs
315 Aylesworth Hall NE
Fort Collins, CO 80523-1024

## FLORIDA INTERNATIONAL UNIVERSITY

The Department of Environmental Studies, College of Arts and Sciences offers a MS in Environmental Studies with a concentration in biological management. The program prepares students in areas of forestry, agroforestry, and environmental education, and for volunteer and development activities generally. The MIP consists of a minimum of 36 semester units of academic study, in which 20 of the units are expected to be completed before students begin their Peace Corps assignments. Courses cover issues such as: restoration ecology, sustainable development, environmental resource policy, environment and development, tropical forest conservation, and protected area mgm't.

*Benefits:* Students may earn up to six credits for their Peace Corps service.

Mahadev Bhat  305. 348.1210
Graduate Studies Program  bhatm@fiu.edu
Florida International University
University Park, ECS 333
Miami, FL 33199

## UNIVERSITY OF IDAHO

The University of Idaho offers a Masters of Natural Resources Management through its College of Forestry, Wildlife and Range Sciences. The program aspires to help prepare students for careers in natural resources management and administration rather than research. Students must complete 28 semester credits in four emphasis areas (management, human dimensions, ecology, and tools and technology). Coursework may be completed in two or three semesters. All MI students will participate in a 1 credit colloquia focusing on Natural Resources Management in the context of the Peace Corps. Degrees are granted as a terminal degree, with no thesis.

*Benefits:* No credits can be earned for Peace Corps service, however financial assistance and scholarships are available.

Dr. Michael R. Whiteman  208. 885-8984
Director, International Programs Office  208. 885-2539
Morrill Hall 216,  whiteman@uidaho.edu
University of Idaho
Moscow, Idaho 83844-3013

# MICHIGAN TECHNOLOGICAL UNIVERSITY

MTU School of Forestry and Wood Products offers a MI Program for students with an interest in forestry and Peace Corps service. Students with or without a forestry, environmental studies, or natural resources background are encouraged to apply. The program is designed for students who have liberal arts degrees. However, adjustments are made for students with natural resources, forestry, and environmental studies backgrounds. Students spend one academic quarter at the 4000+ acre Ford Forestry Center, learning fundamental forestry skills. Two more quarters are spent at the main campus completing course work involving traditional forestry, general ecology, and international forestry. Thesis, project, and course work degree options.

*Benefits:* To nine graduate quarter credits for PC service; $500 work study allowance for first year MI students.

| | |
|---|---|
| Dr. Blair Orr | 906. 487.2291 |
| School of Forestry and Wood Products | bdorr@mtu.edu |
| Michigan Technological University | //forestry.mtu.edu/peacecorps |
| 1400 Townsend Drive | |
| Houghton, MI 49931-1295 | |

# UNIVERSITY OF MINNESOTA

The University of Minnesota College of Natural Resources offers a Master of Science Degree in Forestry. The program requires a minimum of 44 graduate credits. Students entering the program without natural resource backgrounds may need additional courses to achieve the necessary background. Participants spend three quarters on campus prior to Peace Corps service, and take a full course load of 10-15 credits per quarter. After completion of the Peace Corps assignment, students will return to the University for one or two quarters to complete the degree requirements.

*Benefits:* Between four and eight credits are awarded for Peace Corps service; tuition fellowships and partial grants are available on a competitive basis.

| | |
|---|---|
| Dr. Kenneth Brooks | 612. 624.2774 |
| Prof. & Director of Grad. Studies in Forestry | kbrooks@forestry.umn.edu |
| College of Natural Resources | |
| University of Minnesota | |
| 235 Natural Resources Administration Bldg. | |
| 2003 Upper Buford Circle | |
| St. Paul, MN 55108-6146 | |

# UNIVERSITY OF MONTANA

The School of Forestry offers students interested in international conservation and resource management the opportunity to combine academic course work with a Peace Corps experience. Students may earn a Master's Degree (thesis or non-thesis option) in Forestry (Forestry, Resource Conservation, Recreation Management) or Wildlife Biology. A total of 30-36 credits are required to complete a master's degree.

Candidates usually attend school for at least one year prior to two years of service in the PC. The course of study specifically designed for MI students includes courses in ecology, tropical forest management, development sociology, and int'l. resource mgm't.

*Benefits:* 4-6 credits can be earned for PC service; teaching assistantships available.

Dr. Steven Siebert
School of Forestry
University of Montana
Missoula, MT 59812

406. 243.4661
siebert@forestry.umt.edu

## N. CAROLINA STATE UNIVERSITY

Graduate students enrolled in the College of Forest Resources, Department of Forestry can pursue a Master of Forestry, Master of Natural Resources, or a Master of Science degree in Forestry or Natural Resources. The MIP consists of a minimum of 36 semester hours of academic study for the Master of Natural Resources and the Master of Forestry degrees, or 30 semester hours of academic study for the MS. The program prepares students for Peace Corps assignments in forestry (primarily agroforestry) and/or natural resources management (emphasis on environmental education), and for volunteer and development activities generally.

*Benefits:* 6 units for Peace Corps service. Research assistantships available on competitive basis to students pursuing research-based MS degree.

Erin Sills
Department of Forestry
Box 8008
North Carolina State University
Raleigh, NC 27695

919. 515.7784
sills@cfr.cfr.ncsu.edu

## WASHINGTON STATE UNIVERSITY

WSU offers the MI degree option in the Department of Natural Resources (forestry, range management, wildlife management) in the College of Agriculture, Human and Natural Resources, and in the multidisciplinary program in Environmental Sciences and Regional Planning. Both programs prepare students to serve in forestry or natural resource management. Former MI students in these programs have developed educational programs preparing them to serve in Peace Corps assignments in agroforestry, crop extension, and environmental management. They must complete a year of graduate course work at the University prior to their Peace Corps service. In most cases, students return to WSU for a semester after service to write their thesis or project report. Thesis or non-thesis options.

*Benefits:* Three to six credits are granted for PC service; no guaranteed financial aid, but some fellowships and assistantships may be available on a competitive basis.

Sally M. Burkhart
Ass't. to the Director, Int'l. Programs
French Administration 328
Washington State University
Pullman, WA 99164-1034

509. 335.2541
sburkhar@wsu.edu

## U OF WISCONSIN AT STEVENS POINT

The College of Natural Resources offers a MI Program in Forestry/Natural Resources. The program combines a minimum of one year of advanced training in forestry/natural resource management, with two subsequent years of Peace Corps service followed by a final semester on campus. Both thesis and non-thesis options are offered — the former preparing more for careers in research, the latter for careers in management.

*Benefits:* Six credits hours are earned for PCs service; occasional scholarships.

Dr. Hans G. Schabel
Professor of Forestry
College of Natural Resources
University of Wisconsin
Stevens Point, WI 54481

715. 346.4230
hschabel@uwsp.edu

# INTERNATIONAL ADMINISTRATION
## UNIVERSITY OF DENVER

The University of Denver offers a Master of Arts in International Administration through the Graduate School of International Studies (GSIS). Students will earn a minimum of 90 quarter-hour credits, which include sixty-two (62) credit hours of coursework. Participants choose from among three concentrations: Development, Global Political Economy, and Policy Analysis. Participants will spend four quarters on campus prior to Peace Corps service, and will carry full course loads of 14-18 credits per quarter.

*Benefits:* 15 credit hours for foreign language are waived for MIP participants. 15 credit hours towards an internship requirement and the standard research paper requirement for the degree; waive tuition for the 15 credits earned during PC experience.

Andrew J. Burns
Director of Admissions & Student Affairs
Office of Admissions
Graduate School of International Studies
University of Denver
2201 Gaylord St.
Denver, CO 80208

303. 871.2544
877. 474.7236
anburns@du.edu

# NON-GOVERNMENT ORGANIZATIONAL (NGO) DEVELOPMENT/NON-PROFIT MANAGEMENT

You could work in Jordan with a social service organization to improve the effectiveness of women's income-generating activities. You would provide assistance to institutional strengthening by providing hands-on instruction in identifying community aspirations, developing a mission statement, and strategic long-range planning.

# RUTGERS UNIVERSITY— CAMDEN

The Rutgers University-Camden MI Program offers a Master's degree in Public Administration (MPA), with a concentration in international development administration. Qualified participants are placed in assignments that best match their skills and experience. Students in international development policy and administration will spend two semesters and one winter term studying at the University. Students then complete nine study credits for Rutgers University while serving abroad with the Peace Corps. MPA graduate students receive training in the formation, implementation, and evaluation of public policy and administration. Special course work will focus on international development. Students may choose to emphasize particular areas, including non-profit/NGO management and development, international community development, and international municipal management.

*Benefits:* Students receive nine credits for Peace Corps service; assistantships and financial aid are available on a limited and competitive basis.

Sandra Cheesman-Cattefesta          609. 225.6353
Grad. Dep't. of Public Policy & Administration
Rutgers University
401 Cooper Street
Camden, NJ 08102

# SCHOOL FOR INTERNATIONAL TRAINING

The School for International Training offers a Master of International and Intercultural Management degree. Program aims to train students in managing NGOs in diverse settings. The curriculum develops intercultural competencies to insure that students succeed in their experience. The Program has three phases: A 9-month on-campus study, Peace Corps service, and a two-week Capstone Seminar and paper. Students must also meet a language requirement. Many of SIT's staff and faculty are former Peace Corps Volunteers or former Peace Corps staff and trainers.  For more information see listing in graduate section.

*Benefits:* PC service fulfills professional practicum requirement. SIT grant, work-study, scholarships are available; Financial Aid application priority deadline April 1.

Marshall Brewer          802. 258.3265
SIT Admissions
P.O. Box RSOPS
Brattleboro, VT 05302-0676.

# ILLINOIS STATE UNIVERSITY

Illinois State University offers a non-profit management/community development concentration through the Master's programs in Political Science or Economics. Students are trained to meet Peace Corps' need for Volunteers with skills in community service administration and non-profit/NGO management. Master's International students complete 12-18 months of study, including the applied-focus core courses shared by the existing ISU Peace Corps Fellows Program in applied community and economic development.

*Benefits*: MI students may apply Peace Corps service toward completion of the degree's internship requirement. Tuition and fees are waived during Peace Corps service.

Director  
Unit for Community & Econ. Development  
Master's International Program  
Illinois State University  
Campus Box 4200  
Normal, Illinois 61790-4200

309. 438.8685  
UCEDinfo@ilstu.edu

# PUBLIC HEALTH/NUTRITION

You might work in Guatemala to assist the local school system in upgrading its health education curriculum by teaching young school children about nutrition and hygiene, and training local teachers in health education.

## UNIVERSITY OF ALABAMA AT BIRMINGHAM

MI students pursue a Master's of Public Health degree in International Health (60 credit hours), which focuses on health issues in developing countries. A joint program in epidemiology and IH is also available. IH coursework includes tropical and infectious diseases, nutrition, environmental hygiene, reproductive health, disaster relief, and program planning. Students complete 53 credit hours/five quarters before leaving for Peace Corps service. PC service satisfies the program's field experience requirement. Students in the School of Public Health must be enrolled during the term in which they graduate, but are not required to return to campus.

*Benefits*: Nine credit hours are earned for PC service.

Maria L. Smith, MPH Coordinator  
Int'l. Health Unit, 217 Ryals Bldg.  
UAB School of Public Health  
1665 University Blvd.  
Birmingham, AL 35294-0022

205. 975.9749  
msmith@lab.soph.uab.edu

## BOSTON UNIVERSITY

The MI Program at Boston University aims to provide practical public health research, management, and training skills to students for immediate application in Peace Corps service. The joint program is an ideal way to earn a Master of Public Health degree while gaining the international experience necessary to develop a career in the competitive field of international health. With careful planning, the MPH degree can be completed in three full-time semesters. There are seven concentrations to choose from within the School of Public Health: international health, maternal and child health, epidemiology and biostatistics, environmental health, health services, social and behavioral sciences, and health law. Courses are designed to provide skills that are both practical and relevant to the developing country environment. Relevant experience in some field of health is helpful, but not required.

*Benefits*: Up to 8 credits for PC service; financial aid and favorable loan terms are available. Certificate courses are offered at a reduced tuition rate.

Joseph Anzalone, MPH Director
Program Management Unit
International Health
715 Albany Street, T4W
Boston, MA 02118-2526

617. 638.5234
josanz@bu.edu

## U. OF CALIFORNIA AT BERKELEY

University of California-Berkeley offers a Master's in Public Health with emphasis in community health education, public health nutrition, maternal and child health, and epidemiology. In a typical four-semester academic program, the first three semesters will be spent on the Berkeley campus. In the winter of the second year, the student will begin their two-year Peace Corps service. After their assignment, students return to the School of Public Health for a fourth semester, integrating the international experience with final course work.

*Benefits:* No credits earned for Peace Corps service; financial aid is available.

Rick Love
School of Public Health
University of California - Berkeley
Berkeley, CA 94720

510. 643.8452
ricklove@uclink2.berkeley.edu

## EMORY UNIVERSITY

The Rollins School of Public Health (RSPGH) offers a Master of Public Health degree in conjunction with the Peace Corps' MIP. Graduate students enrolled at Emory will be required to complete 42 semester units of academic study towards their MPH. The MIPPH will award three credits toward the thesis/special study requirement for the MPH degree at RSPH contingent upon successful completion of overseas services as a Peace Corps Volunteer. While students are overseas, they will be expected to submit quarterly activity/research reports. The program is designed to improve the MIPPH Peace Corps Volunteers' ability to make positive, sustainable contributions to improving the health and well-being of the communities in which they serve.

*Benefits:* Tuition and fees will be waived for the three credit-hour thesis/special study requirement. Financial aid is available on a competitive basis.

James C. Setzer
Senior Associate/Program Coordinator
Department of International Health
The Rollins School of Public Health
Emory University
1518 Clifton Rd., NE
Atlanta, GA 30322

404. 727.3338
setzer@sph.emory.edu

## GEORGE WASHINGTON UNIVERSITY

The Department of Health Care Sciences hosts a Master's of Public Health which offers several tracks of special interest to Volunteers, including health promotion/disease prevention, and international health. Program completion will require 33-36 credit hours and will take 10 to 12 months. A degree in one of the health professions, substantial experience in the health field, and proficiency in a foreign language are desirable.

*Benefits:* PC service satisfies 2-3 required credits toward the MPH degree; partial scholarships, federal traineeship support, federal loans, and work-study are available.

> Karen Helsing; Administrative Officer      202. 994.4473
> The GW Center for Int'l. Health            iphklh@gwumc.edu
> Ross Hall 125
> 2300 I Street, NW
> Washington, DC 20037

## UNIVERSITY OF HAWAII

The School of Public Health offers a Master's in Public Health as well as the opportunity to obtain significant overseas work experience in health. Persons accepted into both the School of Public Health and the Peace Corps will typically complete a year of full-time academics at the SPH, and then complete their Peace Corps health assignment. Following Peace Corps service, an additional semester at the SPH may be needed to complete requirements for the master's degree. About 30-36 credits are needed to complete the program. Previous employment, and/or significant voluntary work experience in a health agency or health-related service setting is desirable.

*Benefits:* Three to nine credits can be awarded for Peace Corps service; MI students are eligible for, but are not guaranteed a tuition waiver; SPH Alumni Association scholarships are available.

> Nancy Kilonsky, Assistant Dean      808. 956.4543
> Student Services Office - D204
> University of Hawaii
> 1960 East-West Road
> Honolulu, HI 96822

## LOMA LINDA UNIVERSITY

Loma Linda University School of Public Health offers a Master's in Public Health through the Department of International Health. The curriculum is based upon the recognition of the need for technology and organization appropriate to cultural and economic realities. The program combines public health knowledge with competence in techniques applicable to the developing country context. Students complete five quarters of academic work for a total of 55 quarter credits. The first four quarters are completed at LLU; the last quarter is a field practicum that participants will satisfy by completing two years of Peace Corps service. Students can also work as teaching assistants during their time on the LLU campus.

*Benefits:* Twelve quarter credits can be earned for the field practicum component of Peace Corps service; tuition waiver by the University for the field practicum.

> Dr. Barbara Anderson
> Associate Professor
> Department of International Health
> Loma Linda University
> Loma Linda, CA 92350

> 909. 824.4902
> 800. 422.4558
> banderson@sph.llu.edu

## U. OF NORTH CAROLINA AT CHAPEL HILL

The goal of the UNC School of Public Health MI Program is to provide practical public health research, program planning, policy and management skills for students entering Peace Corps service. Master's Degrees are offered in Maternal and Child Health, Nutrition, and Health Policy and Administration. The Maternal and Child Health Department accepts applicants with two years of community health experience from a variety of health and human service fields, including social work. The MI Program consists of one year of study and two years of Peace Corps Volunteer service. The student's Peace Corps service may provide a focus for a master's paper.

*Benefits:* Six credits for Peace Corps service, traineeships and graduate assistantships available; tuition remission for out-of-state students; full academic year tuition and fees scholarships available on a limited basis for North Carolina residents.

> Dr. Deborah Bender
> Research Assoc. Prof. & MIP Coordinator
> Dep't. of Health Policy and Administration
> School of Public Health
> University of North Carolina
> Chapel Hill, NC 27599-7400

> 919. 966.7383
> deborah_bender@unc.edu

## OKLAHOMA STATE UNIVERSITY

The Department of Nutritional Sciences offers a Master of Science degree, requiring the completion of 34 credit hours. A basic nutrition course is a prerequisite of the program. Academic course work begins during the summer; students are eligible for Peace Corps service following twelve months of study. Four credit hours are earned for Peace Corps service, but enrollment in the research credit hours occurs after the student returns to OSU. During the final semester at OSU, students complete the thesis requirements and the final two credit hours.

*Benefits:* Up to four credit hours can be earned for PC service.

> Dr. Barbara Stoecker
> Dep't. of Nutritional Sciences, Rm. 425
> Oklahoma State University
> Stillwater, OK 74078-0337

> 405. 744.8289
> chrom@okway.okstate.edu

# TULANE UNIVERSITY

As a MI student at Tulane you will earn a Masters of Public Health. The MI begins his or her program at Tulane and finishes with two years of service in the Peace Corps. The School waives five credit hours for MI students. Thus, you will be required to complete 40 of the 45 credits. If you are in the Tropical Medicine department you will complete 36. Successful completion of the academic course and project requirements will result in the awarding of the master's degree.

*Benefits:* Five credit hours waived for PC service; Dean's Grant of $3500 during the second semester of their course work, contingent upon Peace Corps service.

Dr. E. Elaine Boston, Assoc. Dean
School of Pub. Health & Tropical Medicine
Tulane University
1501 Canal Street, Suite 700
New Orleans LA 70112

800. 676.5389
mastersintl-1@mailhost.tcs.tulane.edu

# TEACHING ENGLISH TO SPEAKERS OF OTHER LANGUAGES (TESOL)

## AMERICAN UNIVERSITY

The MI Program enables participants to qualify for Peace Corps TESOL assignments through graduate work leading to an MA in TESOL. MIP/MA TESOL participants can qualify for Peace Corps assignments in secondary school TEFL instruction, university English teaching, and university level English teacher training. At the completion of the program, participants are ready to enter the job market with excellent academic credentials and significant overseas teaching experience. Students are waived from the three-credit TESOL Practicum course based on their Peace Corps teaching experience. It is recommended that native English speakers have at least one other language than English.

*Benefits:* Six credits are earned for the Cooperative Education Field Experience; tuition is waived for these six credits during Peace Corps service. Students are required to complete a portfolio and pass an oral comprehensive exam.

TESOL Program
Dep't. of Language and Foreign Studies
American University
4400 Massachusetts Ave., NW,
Washington, DC 20016-8045

202. 885.2582
tesol@american.edu

## CAL STATE U AT SACRAMENTO

The Department of English at CSUS offers a Master of Arts in teaching English to speakers of other languages (TESOL) for MI students. The program consists of 27 units of course requirements, six units of elective courses, and a thesis option. MI students complete 18 units before their Peace Corps service. When overseas, participants will complete several projects, to be designed in consultation with the program's advisor prior to leaving campus. Peace Corps Volunteer service will serve as an elective for the degree. Upon returning to the CSUS campus, students' final semester will consist of nine units of coursework.

*Benefits:* Six credit hours for PC service; assistantships, grants, loans, and work-study positions; job placement during graduate program and following graduation.

Dr. Linda Callis-Buckley
TESOL Coordinator
English Department, CSUS
6000 'J" Street
Sacramento, CA 95819-6075

916. 278.5394
buckleyl@saclink.csus.edu

## FLORIDA INTERNATIONAL UNIVERSITY

The College of Education, Department of Educational Foundations and Professional Studies offers a MS degree in TESOL. The program is designed to prepare student participants in teaching secondary-level English, teaching university-level English, or English teacher training, and for Volunteer and development activities generally. The MIP consists of a minimum of 36 semester credit hours of study based on courses such as: Developing ESOL Language and Literacy, Educational Psychology, Applied Phonetics, Curriculum Development, and Language Acquisition.

*Benefits:* Students may earn up to six credits for their Peace Corps service.

Dr. Patricia Killian
Educational Foundations & Prof. Studies
College of Education
FIU, University Park Campus
Miami, FL 33199
*or*
Farley Ferrante
Peace Corps Coordinator

305. 348.3418
killianp@fiu.edu


305. 348.3641
fferra01@fiu.edu

## MONTEREY INSTITUTE OF INT'L. STUDIES

The Graduate School of Language and Educational Linguistics at the Monterey Institute of International Studies offers a MA in Teaching English to Speakers of Other Languages (MATESOL). Upon completion of one year at MSIS, the Peace Corps places them as high school or university English teachers overseas. Students must complete 37 units: 26 units are completed during the first two semesters at MIIS, and 11 units during the third semester at MIIS following PC service. MI TESOL students are not charged for 8 of the 12 units during the final semester.

*Benefits:* Four credits for an independent study based on PC experience; tuition waived for eight of the final 11 units of course study remaining after PCs service.

Dr. Ruth Larimer, Associate Dean
GSLEL
Monterey Institute of International Studies
425 Van Buren Street
Monterey, CA 939831

831. 647.4185
rlarimer@miis.edu

## SCHOOL FOR INTERNATIONAL TRAINING

The School for International Training has been an innovative leader in the field of language teacher education for over 30 years. The MA in Teaching program emphasizes the development of effective teaching skills through course work that is experiential, practical, and participatory. MI students earn a minimum of 32 credits during the one-academic-year program including a supervised two-month-long teaching internship at a choice of sites in the US or overseas between semesters.

Students may also choose to further develop ideas of particular interest in an independent professional project (six credits). They may also obtain certification for teaching ESL in US public schools (with or without the Bilingual-Multicultural Endorsement), either before or after Peace Corps service.

*Benefits:* Up to 12 credits for PC service, six for the second teaching internship and six for completion of a thesis; $1000 SIT grant, work study, scholarships.

| | |
|---|---|
| Admissions Counselor | 800. 336.1616 |
| SIT | 802.258.3267 |
| P.O. Box 676 | admissions@sit.edu |
| Kipling Road | |
| Brattleboro, VT 05302 | |

# URBAN PLANNING

You might work in El Salvador assisting communities manage their services, water systems, and administrative and financial planning through the promotion and support of local development.

## FLORIDA STATE UNIVERSITY

The Department of Urban and Regional Planning offers a professional Master's Degree in Planning with opportunities to specialize in one of six areas including: planning for developing areas, housing and community development, transportation, comprehensive land use, environment, and health. MI participants specialize in planning for developing areas, but may take electives from the other specialization areas. The typical MI program will take 48 semester hours over two years, including an internship and 21 hours in the core curriculum common to all specializations.

*Benefits:* To three credit hours for Peace Corps service; scholarships, and grants are available for MI students who demonstrate need.

| | |
|---|---|
| Dr. Rebecca Miles-Doan | 850. 644.4510 |
| Dep't. of Urban & Regional Planning, R-117 | pdoan@coss.fsu.edu |
| Florida State University | |
| Tallahassee, FL 32306 | |

# RETURNED PEACE CORPS FELLOWS
## USA PROGRAM

Editor's note: On the following pages you will find a sample of the Peace Corps Fellow/USA graduate programs. Although they are offered especially to returned Peace Corps volunteers, some of the programs offer a comparable educational experience for non-Peace Corps students. If you find one of interest to you, contact the program and enquire further. These are very rich, experiential programs. There are many more teacher training programs not listed here. Visit their websites for a complete listing.

ARE YOU INTERESTED IN A GRADUATE DEGREE or certificate program that will provide hands-on practical experience? Is the cost of graduate school a concern? Would you like to apply your Peace Corps skills to assist underserved U.S. communities?

If the answer to any of these questions is "yes", then consider the Peace Corps Fellows /USA Program. As a Returned Peace Corps Volunteer (RPCV), you have the opportunity to continue your professional development and fulfill the "third goal" of the Peace Corps through the Fellows/ USA Program. For two years, you lived and worked in places unknown to many Americans. The "third goal" of the Peace Corps is to bring the world back home" and put your Peace Corps experience to work in the United States. The legacy of your Peace Corps service is not confined to your country of service. It is enhanced through your interaction with neighbors, students, and colleagues in the United States. Additionally, as a Peace Corps Fellow, you will receive financial assistance or reduced tuition for coursework while applying the lessons learned as a Peace Corps Volunteer

The Fellows Program can help you take what you have learned overseas and use it to build a better future, rather than storing it away as a memory of a once-in-a-lifetime experience. Whether you are still overseas, recently returned home, or thinking about a career change, examine the benefits of the Peace Corps Fellows Program.

In exchange for a two-year commitment to work in a community that needs your help, you can earn a master's degree and establish your career. A local university, with financial support from foundations, government agencies, corporations, and individual donors, will assist you in this process. You may receive any number of benefits such as tuition assistance, yearly stipends, housing, paid employment, and health benefits. The exact nature of the award varies with each university. In addition, through the Fellows Program you can form personal and professional relationships and expand your understanding of the United States and the world. There is no better way to bring home your Peace Corps experience and to make a difference — for your community and yourself — than through the Peace Corps Fellows/USA Program.

Peace Corps Fellows/USA Program
1990 K St. N.W., Room 9500
Washington, DC 20526

800. 424.8580, press "2", then ext. 2259
fellows@peace corps.gov
www.peacecorps.gov/fellows/index.html

# COMMUNITY & ECONOMIC DEVELOPMENT
## CARNEGIE MELLON U

The H. John Heinz III School of Public Policy and Management offers a Master of Public Management degree. Fellows work in public housing communities assisting residents in designing and implementing economic development plans, crime and violence reduction, and building a computer-based Neighborhood Information Network. Fellows are assisted by city officials and Heinz School faculty. Evening classes allow Fellows to work at their projects during normal working hours.

*Benefits:* Scholarships and stipends available.

Dr. Harry Faulk, Associate Dean      412. 268.2195
The Heinz School                     hf0c@andrew.cmu.edu
Carnegie Mellon University
5000 Forbes Ave.
Pittsburgh, PA 15213-3890

## DUQUESNE UNIVERSITY

The A. J. Palumbo School of Business Administration awards a MBA to RPCV's. Fellows work in community and economic development organizations associated with Duquesne's-Community Collaborative Project. The Graduate Center for Social and Public Policy awards a Master of Arts in Social and Public Policy, with concentrations in Policy Analysis and Administration or Conflict Resolution and Peace Studies. Fellows work in organizations such as Conservation Consultants, the Green Building Project, and a citizens council on program development, proposal writing, housing management, business development, and environmental programs.

*Benefits:* Stipends, partial or full tuition scholarships.

Dr. G. Evan Stoddard,Director        412. 396.5179
Center for Social & Public Policy    stoddard@duq2.cc.duq.edu
215 College Hall
Duquesne University
Pittsburgh, PA 15282
*or* Dr. William D. Presutti, Assoc. Dean   412. 396.6269
Palumbo School of Business Admin.    presutti@duq2.cc.duq.edu
704 Rockwell Hall
Duquesne University
Pittsburgh, PA 15282

## FLORIDA INSTITUTE OF TECHNOLOGY

The College of Science & Liberal Arts and Engineering awards a Master of Science in any of nine environmentally related degree programs or a Doctor of Philosophy in seven environmentally related degree areas. Other doctorate degrees awarded include Education Specialist and Doctor of Education. The Graduate Environmental Program is a two-year program designed for RPCVs with bachelor's coursework and Peace Corps experience in an environmentally-related area. Program offers degrees in four environmental areas: science, engineering, management, and education. The Program combines coursework in a selected M.S. degree program with a related internship. Regional partners include federal, regional, and county environmental agencies; school districts; and conservation organizations.

*Benefits:* Tuition and stipend support contingent upon fund-raising efforts intended to provide a 90% tuition waiver and a stipend commensurate with University Teaching (GSA) and Research (GRA) assistants.

Tom Marcinkowski                    407. 674.8946
PC Fellows Program                  marcinko@fit.edu
Science Education Department
150 W. University Boulevard
Melbourne, FL 32901-6975

## ILLINOIS STATE UNIVERSITY

The two-year program provides training in Community and Economic Development, including field experience in rural communities. Fellows earn a Master's Degree in Economics, Political Science, or Sociology by completing two to three semesters of coursework and applied workshops, as well as 11 months of hands-on work in development projects in mainly high poverty rural and urban areas.

*Benefits:* Full tuition waiver and graduate assistantships during the first year; full tuition waiver and monthly stipend during the second year (of community work).

The Director                              309. 438.8685
Community & Economic Development          UCEDinfo@ilstu.edu
PC/ACED Fellows Program                   http://lilt.ilstu.edu/uced
Illinois State University, Campus Box 4200
Normal, Illinois 61790-4200

## JOHNS HOPKINS UNIVERSITY

Fellows work at the Johns Hopkins Hospital and community health clinics in a variety of roles. A concentration in family and community health nursing is offered to Fellows committed to working with underserved populations. Fellows are placed in sites such as a transitional housing program working with residents to improve health and social status through case management, health education, and parenting education. Curriculum prepares Fellows for practice in underserved communities.

Degrees are awarded in BS in Nursing; MS in Nursing (community health nursing, nurse practitioner); dual degrees in Nursing and Public Health, and Nursing and Business.

*Benefits:* Special consideration for admission; scholarships, grants, and loans; Peace Corps Fellows Scholarship covers a portion of tuition costs.

Mary O'Rorke, Director of Admissions      410. 955.7548
Johns Hopkins U School of Nursing         ororke@son.jhmi.edu
525 N. Wolfe St.
Baltimore, MD 21205

# LOYOLA MARYMOUNT UNIVERSITY

Fellows work for the Housing Authority of the City of Los Angeles to establish and maintain an effective community and economic development effort on the part of the Authority. Degree awarded is a Master of Business Administration.

*Benefits:* Partial or full tuition scholarships; stipends are usually available.

Dr. Rachelle Katz, Assoc. Dean
Loyola Marymount University
7900 Loyola Blvd.
Los Angeles, CA 90045-8387

310. 338.2848
rkatz@lmumail.lmu.edu

# MARQUETTE UNIVERSITY

The Graduate Schools of Business, Communication, Political Science, Philosophy, and Public Service awards Master's degrees in Business, Public Service Communications, Political Science, or Philosophy with core courses in urban studies.

Fellows expected to complete the master's program in two years and work in the 21-month community service leadership program.

*Benefits:* Substantial tuition and fee allowances, and a monthly salary.

Dr. Thomas J. Jablonsky
Director, Institute for Urban Life
Marquette Universit
P.O. Box 1881
Milwaukee, WI 53201-1881

414. 288.5300
Thomas.Jablonsky@marquette.edu

# U OF MARYLAND, BALTIMORE COUNTY
## THE SHRIVER PEACEWORKER PROGRAM

Various degrees are awarded with focus on four areas of social concern: education, economic and community development, juvenile justice, and health. The Peaceworker Program is a two-year program integrating graduate study, community service, and ethical reflection enabling Fellows to adapt their experience as Peace Corps volunteers to solving problems confronting America's cities. Participants develop an intellectual framework to identify and respond to the ethical and spiritual dimensions of urban problems, and the leadership and facilitation skills necessary for effective work in the community. Graduate study in the humanities, sciences, and professional schools is available. Fellows are placed in part-time community service positions correlated with the Peaceworkers' graduate study.

*Benefits:* Funded at graduate assistant level: full tuition, $13,000 stipend, health care.

Peter Antoci, Coordinator
Shriver Peaceworker Program
The Shriver Center at UMBC
1000 Hilltop Circle
Baltimore, MD 21250

410. 455.2493
antoci@gl.umbc.edu

# MICHIGAN STATE UNIVERSITY
## CENTER FOR URBAN AFFAIRS

Joint MA, MS and PhD degrees awarded in Urban Studies with over 15 programs including: Urban Planning, Resource Development, Social Work, Sociology, and Criminal Justice. Fellows work with residents and resident-based organizations in public housing to identify community concerns and develop effective responses to problems.

*Benefits:* Graduate assistantship for one or more semesters; in-state-tuition; tuition waiver for six credit hours per semester, monthly stipend.

Dr. Rex LaMore, State Director,
Center for Urban Affairs
Michigan State University
1801 West Main St.
Lansing, MI 48915-1097

517. 353.9555
lamore@pilot.msu.edu

# NEW HAMPSHIRE COLLEGE
## GRADUATE SCHOOL OF BUSINESS

Fellows can choose the weekend program or the international program designed for international students and RPCVs who want to practice in the developing world. Fellows in the weekend program commute to New Hampshire one weekend per month during the 17-month program, while working in their home community. In the 12-month international (ICED) residential program, Fellows participate in graduate studies along with professionals from developing countries. MS in Community Economic Development or International Community Economic Development awarded, dual degrees in CED and Business Administration.

Two years experience working in community development or related field; or commitment to community economic development/community service through a minimum of five years experience in CED or related field is required.

*Benefits:* Special consideration for admission, scholarships, grants and loans; PC Fellows Project Award $1,000 for project development and/or implementation.

Woullard Lett, CED Administrator
New Hampshire College
2500 N. River Road
Manchester, NH 03106-1045

603. 644.3103
wolett@minerva.nhc.edu

# UNIVERSITY OF NEW ORLEANS
## COLLEGE OF URBAN & PUBLIC AFFAIRS

The U. of New Orleans College of Urban and Public Affairs has a long and distinguished record of service to the diverse communities of the New Orleans area. Fellows are placed with nonprofit agencies or local units of government actively involved in community development projects. Placements include Neighborhood

Housing Services, Community Resource Partnership, and a neighborhood development collaborative. Masters degrees awarded in Urban and Regional Planning, Urban Studies, and Public Administration; and a Ph.D. in Urban Studies.

*Benefits:* Fellows appointed as Grad Assistants and receive waiver of out-of-state tuition costs. $850-$1,000/ month stipend for Masters level, $1,000-$1,250/ month for Doctoral level.

Jane S. Brooks, A.I.C.P. 504. 280.6514
College of Urban and Public Affairs cupa@uno.edu
University of New Orleans
3100 Cleburne Avenue
New Orleans, LA 70148

## NEW SCHOOL UNIVERSITY
### MILANO GRADUATE SCHOOL OF MGM'T & URBAN POLICY

The Milano Graduate School offers MS degrees in four concentrations: Urban Policy Analysis and Management, Nonprofit Management, Health Services Management and Policy, and Human Resources Management, and a joint BA/MS degree. The Schools' partnership with the New York City Housing Authority enables students to work on high priority projects integrated throughout the curriculum, and will also involve a paid summer internship. Potential topics include welfare reform, economic development, youth services, crime prevention, and transportation.

*Benefits:* Special consideration for admission, grants, loans, and college work study.

Joseph K. Encarnacion 212. 229. 5462
Assistant Director of Admissions encarnaj@newschool.edu
Milano Graduate School of Mgm't. & Urban Policy
New School University
66 Fifth Avenue, 7th floor
New York, NY 10011

## UNIVERSITY OF NORTH TEXAS
### SCHOOL OF COMMUNITY SERVICE

The Center for Public Service at the University of North Texas operates several sustainable healthy neighborhood programs in the Dallas/Fort Worth Metroplex. Field placements are available with the Environmental Alliance for Senior Involvement, and the Educational Consortium for Volunteerism.

The Department of Sociology offers a Ph.D. in Community Development. MS in Applied Economics, Sociology, Criminal Justice, Applied Gerontology, Behavioral Analysis and Rehabilitation, Social Work and Addictions; Master of Public Administration; M.S. in Interdisciplinary Studies in Sustainable Communities, or Volunteer & Resource Management degrees awarded.

*Benefits:* Special consideration for admission; scholarships, grants, loans, and college work-study. Peace Corps Fellowships are also available.

Dr. Martin Jaeckel, Director
Sustainable Communities Studies
or Cathy Davidson, Coordinator
Peace Corps Fellows Program
Center for Public Service, UNT
P.O. Box 13438
Denton, TX 76203-6438.

940. 565.4630
mjaeck@scs.unt.edu
940. 565-3474
davidson@scs.unt.edu

# UNIVERSITY OF OREGON
## RESOURCE ASSISTANCE FOR RURAL COMMUNITIES

RPCVs are invited to participate in the Resource Assistance for Rural Communities (RARE) Program leading to a Master of Community and Regional Planning. Qualified applicants live and work in a rural community for one year helping to improve environmental and economic conditions. This is a Learn & Serve Higher Education demonstration program. RPCVs may apply for RARE placement prior to enrollment, part-way through, or upon completion of a master's program.

Demonstrated skill and training in community development, working with representatives, and/or environmental education is required.

*Benefits* : $1,000 per month stipend and an educational award of $4,275 for completing 1,700 hours of service, 9 credit hours, and qualify for in-state tuition.

Prof. David Povev, Director RARE
or Scott Craig, Ass't Director RARE
RARE Opportunities, PPPM Hendricks
University of Oregon
Eugene, OR 97403

541. 346.3812
541. 346.3889
darkwing.uoregon.edu—cpw//rare/rare.html
dpovey@oregon.uoregon.edu

# SANTA CLARA UNIVERSITY
## FOOD & AGRIBUSINESS INSTITUTE

This two-year degree program in the Leavey School of Business and Administration leads to an MBA with a specialization in Food and Agribusiness Management. The agribusiness program prepares students for a management career in the food industry. Fellows are expected to complete an internship at a non-profit agency involved with delivering food and/or nutrition assistance such as a food bank or the Sacred Heart Community Service. Programs supplementing on-campus course work include international study tours, mentors, and conferences.

*Benefits:* Full and partial scholarships are available through the Institute. Assistantships and loans are available.

Dr. S. Andrew Starbird, Director
Institute of Agribusiness
Leavey School of Business and Administration
Santa Clara University
Santa Clara, CA 95053

408. 554.4086
sstarbird@scu.edu

# UNIVERSITY OF SOUTH CAROLINA

## CENTER FOR CHILD & FAMILY STUDIES

Master of Social Work and Master of Public Health dual degree with a concentration in public health social work awarded. Fellows are part of a specialized education and training program to provide South Carolina with qualified public health social workers. Students attend the dual degree program full-time for three years and must commit to four and one-half years of post-graduate employment. The emphasis is on community practice and leadership in disease prevention and health promotion in a public health setting.

*Benefits:* All tuition, books, and academic fees, annual stipend of $10,000.

Gail Reid, MSW, LISW      803. 777.9407
*or* Sarah Cleary, MSW      gailr@cosw.cosw.sc.edu
The Center for Child and Family Studies
College of Social Work
University of South Carolina
Columbia, SC 29208

# TEXAS SOUTHERN UNIVERSITY

## SCHOOL OF TECHNOLOGY

Master's degrees in Business Administration, Public Administration, Science of Industrial Technology, City Planning, Transportation Planning and Management, and Ph.D. in Technology, and a concentration in community development are offered. The Community Development Leadership Program provides a comprehensive approach to leadership training. Fellows share expertise in areas such as: home maintenance, business creation, health maintenance, cross-generational programs, construction, and community education. Activities include researching needs in housing, day care, community organizing; program development, and proposal writing.

*Benefits:* Special consideration for admission; tuition support, scholarships, tuition forgiveness, waivers of out-of-state residency requirements and others.

Prof. Joshua Hill, Interim Dean      713. 313.1853
School of Technology      tchajxhill@tsu.edu
Texas Southern University
3100 Cleburne Avenue
Houston, TX 77004

# WESTERN ILLINOIS UNIVERSITY

## ILLINOIS INSTITUTE OF RURAL AFFAIRS

Master's Degrees in Economics, Geography (Regional and Rural Planning), Business Administration, Public Administration, or Health Education and Promotion are awarded. In two years, Fellows complete a Master's degree and obtain specialized training and experience in community development. For their graduate assistantship,

Fellows work in development projects. Fellows serve a paid 11-month internship in a rural community, providing hands-on assistance and leadership for local development projects.

*Benefits:* Full tuition waiver and graduate assistantships, and internship salary. Educational award upon completion of community service.

Dr. John Gruidl
Illinois Institute for Rural Affairs
Western Illinois University
518 Stipes Hall
Macomb, IL 61455

800. 526.9943
309. 298.2237
John-Gruidl@ccmail.wiu.edu

# EDUCATION

## DEPAUL UNIVERSITY

### URBAN TEACHERS CORPS

DePaul's Urban Teacher Corps program, in cooperation with inner-city Chicago public schools, is recruiting RPCVs to teach full-time and pursue a Master's degree and an Illinois teaching certificate at the elementary level. Program begins with a three week intensive orientation and provides certification by the end of the following summer. RPCVs teach during the week at schools with mentor teachers assistance. University course work is completed through all-day Saturday sessions.

*Benefits:* $2,000 scholarship, reduced tuition rates. Approximately $15,000 for ten-month internship. Scholarships and relocation stipends may be available.

Kathy Vandlik
Center for Urban Education
DePaul University
2320 N. Kenmore
Chicago, IL 60614

773. 325.7170
ajakymiw@teacher.depaul.edu

## NORTHERN ARIZONA UNIVERSITY

### PEACE CORPS FELLOWS PROGRAM

At Northern Arizona University, Fellows enroll in three consecutive summer school terms for 12 hours each term. During the school year, Fellows teach in schools on rural reservations, with Arizona temporary certification. At the end of the third summer, Fellows receive a standard teaching certificate. Doctoral Fellows spend their first year in the program as graduate assistants, and then serve for two years as site instructors in the teacher preparation program. They may conduct research in association with the work of teacher training on reservation sites.

Successful teaching experience in the Peace Corps, successful second language acquisition, and demonstrated sensitivity to cultural differences required. In addition to this, doctoral Fellows must have experience working with diverse populations.

*Benefits:* One-time relocation stipend of $1,000; 50% support for tuition for three summer sessions. Doctoral Fellows receive a $16,840 stipend and tuition credit.

Dr. Daniel Kain  
Peace Corps Fellows Program  
Center for Excellence in Education  
NAU, Box 5774  
Flagstaff, AZ 86011-5774  

520. 523.7023  
520. 523.7122  
dlk@nauvax.ucc.nau.edu

## PACIFIC OAKS COLLEGE

A Quaker-founded institution, the college philosophy states in part that each person has a unique identity and human potential which they contribute to the lives of all those with whom they come in contact. Experiential learning is emphasized. Portfolios and personalized evaluations replace tests. The Internship Program is a 14-month, summer-to-summer program which provides field supervision and teacher support. Fellows may continue at Pacific Oaks to obtain a MA in Human Development.

RPVC's must have successfully completed a full two-year service in which their primary assignment was elementary education.

*Benefits:* ±$8,000 tuition costs; placement assistance for salaried teaching positions.

Ramona Young  
Teacher Education & Credentials Program  
Pacific Oaks College  
5&6 Westmoreland Place  
Pasadena, CA 91103  

626. 397 1334

## SAN FRANCISCO STATE UNIVERSITY

The Peace Corps Fellows Program at SFSU combines full-time teaching in urban inner-city schools with evening coursework leading to a California Teaching Credential and/or a Master's Degree in Education. Participants may enroll in any graduate program offered by the School of Education. A master's degree designed for PC Fellows who have satisfied California teaching certification requirements, based upon overseas teaching experience, is available. PC teaching experience required.

*Benefits:* In-state residency for fee determination; $1,500 scholarship; $400 relocation stipend; free housing during first month; employment opportunities.

Dr. Andrew Dubin  
College of Education  
San Francisco State University  
San Francisco, CA 94132  

415. 338.1300  
fellows@sfsu.edu

## TEACHERS COLLEGE AT COLUMBIA UNIVERSITY

Fellows are placed in full-time, salaried positions in public schools throughout New York City, and attend Teachers College classes part-time in the evenings and on weekends. In addition to a MA, New York State Teacher Certification and New York City Licensing can also be obtained. The positive and negative aspects of the nation's largest city help to shape the nature of this program. The inherent demands and challenges are both grueling and exhilarating.

Strong long-term commitment to teaching in the urban environment of NYC is required. Teaching areas include: deaf/hard of hearing, learning disabled, mentally retarded, blind/visually impaired, and TESOL.

*Benefits:* Scholarships covering one-third to one-half tuition costs; starting teacher's salary of ±$31,000, full health coverage under Teacher's Union contract.

Daniel Fergus Tamulonis, Coordinator
Peace Corps Fellows Program, Box 90
Teachers College/Columbia University
New York, NY 10027

212. 678.4080
dft5@columbia.edu

## UNIVERSITY OF NEW MEXICO

Fellows teach full-time while pursuing a Master's degree and New Mexico Teacher Certification. Most schools in the program are located within or adjacent to the Navajo Nation. During the academic year, teacher education classes are offered at branch campuses, 150 miles west of the UNM main campus, to support the Fellows. Summer classes, as well as a spring-summer pre-service preparation, occur at the main campus in Albuquerque. These include classroom and in-the-field experiential learning opportunities focusing on Native American, Hispanic, and Anglo history, culture in the Southwest, and multicultural pedagogical methods relevant to teaching in NM.

*Benefits:* 30% of tuition costs.

Dr. Paul Miko, Program Coordinator
UNM/COE Peace Corps Fellows/USA Program
UNM Johnson Center, Room 112C
Albuquerque, NM 87131-1251

Initial inquiries by mail only please

## UNIVERSITY OF TEXAS AT EL PASO

University of Texas at El Paso offers Fellows an opportunity to teach in urban or rural schools along the U.S.-Mexico border while earning a Teaching Certificate and a Master's degree. Fellows serve as teachers-of-record and receive regular teachers' salaries based on degree and experience. Fellows share costs of program.

*Benefits:* $1,000 relocation allowance; tuition equivalent to 9 semester hours; possibility of additional tuition assistance; low in-state tuition for remainder of program.

Dr. Thomas Wood, Associate Dean

*or* Ms. Jane Enright, Ass't. Project Coord.
College of Education, Room 414
The University of Texas at El Paso
El Paso, TX 79968-0569

915. 747.5186
twood@utep.edu
915. 747.5572
800. 687.5598
jane@utep.edu

# · RESOURCES ·

**Campus Ecology — A Guide To Assessing Environmental Quality & Creating Strategies For Change** A guidebook from the country's leading student environmental organization for learning practical environmental management skills and greening your campus. April Smith and Student Environmental Action Coalition. Living Planet Press, 1993

**Center for Campus Organizing** publishes *Infusion, The National Magazine for Progressive Campus Activists*, which documents on-going campus organizing for a more democratic and egalitarian society, disseminates information useful to student and faculty activists, and provides a forum for debate and thoughtful analysis. CCO 165 Friend St. #1, Boston, MA 02114 (617) 725-2886  cco@igc.org  www.cco.org

**Colleges That Change Lives - 40 Schools You Should Know About Even if You're Not A Straight A Student** Worth reading. Many of the same colleges as in this guide, many different. A critical look at standard thinking about colleges. Loren Pope, Penguin, 1996

**Community-Campus Partnerships for Health — A Guide for Developing Community-Responsive Models in Health Professions Education** An excellent source of newly emergent models of health education. Profiles programs in medicine, dentistry, nursing. Sarena Seifer and Kara Connors, UCSF Center for the Health Professions 1997 (415) 476-8181

**ECO — The Environmental Careers Organization** a non-profit organization offering paid, short-term environmental positions for undergraduates and other entry-level environmental job seekers. They sponsor environmental career conferences, workshops, and advising through their Environmental Career Services. They publish *The New Complete Guide to Environmental Careers* Island Press, an important resource for environmental job hunting.

**Earth In Mind — On Education, Environment, and the Human Prospect** A collection of insightful essays from Oberlin Professor David Orr on the implications of typical current higher education practices, and thought provoking suggestions on better ways to go. Highly recommended for parents!!! Island Press, 1994

**EarthSave** Non-profit organization founded by John Robbins, author of *Diet for A New America*. EarthSave educates the public about the relationship between how they eat and environmental and health impacts. Santa Cruz, CA  (831) 423-4069

**Ecodemia — Campus Environmental Stewardship at the Turn of the 21st Century, Lessons in Smart Management from Administrators, Staff, and Students** Innovative green management practices at universities across the country. Much information can be easily extrapolated. Julian Keniry, National Wildlife Federation, 1995  (800) 432-6564

**Education For an Ecologically Sustainable Culture — Rethinking Moral Education, Creativity, Intelligence, and Other Modern Orthodoxies** Deep reading. Bowers, C.A. State University of New York Press, 1995

**Educational and Career Opportunities in Alternative Medicine — All You Need to Find Your Calling in the Healing Professions.** Rosemary Jones, Prima Publishing, 1998

**Green Corps, Field School for Environmental Organizing** Trains college students who have an interest in organizing as a career. Training includes advocacy organizing, case studies of organizing problems, skills and training clinics, working case study, campaign trainings and lectures. 29 Temple Pl. Boston, MA 02111 (617) 426-8506

**Guide to Graduate Education in Public Affairs and Public Administration, NASPAA Directory of Programs** Craig Donovan, National Association of Schools of Public Affairs and Administration, 1997 (202) 628-8965  naspaa@naspaa.org

**Guide to Graduate Environmental Programs** Over 150 green graduate programs — long on data, short on information about the actual studies. Student Conservation Association Island Press, 1997

**The International Partnership for Service-Learning** The original experts in international service-learning — vital programs all across the world. IPSL, 815 Second Avenue, Suite 315, New York, NY 10017-4594  (212) 986-0989  www.ipsl.org

**Making a Difference While Making a Living** Excellent book for those seeking "right livelihood". Wide range of sectors from business to government to non-profits. Melissa Everett, New Society Publishers

**National School for Strategic Organizing** A six-month organizer training program. The Labor/Community Strategy Center, a multi-racial "think/act tank" that organizes the School, addresses all aspects of urban life: class-conscious labor organizing, fighting for environmental justice, immigrant rights and more. Strategy Center   (213) 387-2800 www.thestrategycenter.com

**Student Conservation Association** Helps college students find volunteer positions as professional assistants in national and state parks, nat'l forest and wildlife refuges. Work for 3-4 months and gain valuable training and field experience. Provides funds to cover travel and food expenses plus free housing. Publishes *Earth Work*, a monthly magazine for folks seeking conservation employment. PO Box 550, Charlestown, NH 03603   (603) 826-4301

**Student Environmental Action Coalition** SEAC is a student and youth run national network of progressive organizations and individuals whose aim is to uproot environmental injustices through action and education. We define the environment to include the physical, economical, political and cultural conditions in which we live. SEAC works to create progressive social change on both the local and global levels. Great activist alerts via email. SEAC, PO Box 31909, Philadelphia, PA 19104  (215) 222-4711   seac@seac.org www.seac.org

**Student Pugwash** Provides college and select high school students with programs to better understand the social and ethical implications of science and technology. Chapters at over 25 colleges. They publish *Jobs You Can Live With*, have alternative job fairs, and promote mentor relationships with concerned professionals. 1638 R St. NW, Suite 32, Washington, D.C. 20009   (800) WOW-A-PUG

**Volunteers for Peace International** Publishes the *International Work Camp Directory*, the ultimate for 900 inexpensive (under $200) international work camps primarily in Europe. Restore medieval villages, work with refugee children, learn bio-dynamic gardening, help at music festivals — A great prelude to college.  (802) 259-2759  vfp@vfp.org   www.vfp.org.

# UNDERGRADUATE COLLEGE INDEX - ALPHABETICAL

# STATE-BY-STATE UNDERGRADUATE INDEX

# GRADUATE PROGRAM INDEX

# PEACE CORPS MASTER'S INTERNATIONALIST PROGRAMS

# RETURNED PEACE CORPS FELLOWS PROGRAM

## ABOUT THE AUTHOR

Miriam Weinstein lives with a fluctuating number of her four children and a very fluffy cat in San Anselmo, California. She has an avid interest in education and has studied many philosophies of education from the elementary level through college. Active in environmental and social causes since her early teens, Ms. Weinstein was founder and director of the Eco Design & Builders Guild of the San Francisco Bay Area, one of the first "green building" networks in the country. An award-winning photographer, Miriam describes herself as an educated tree-hugging vegetarian who recycles conscientiously. She is a graduate of New College of California.

Ms. Weinstein's SageWorks Press formerly published both *Making A Difference College & Graduate Guide*, and *Making A Difference Scholarships for a Better World*. The current editions are available directly from her by calling (800) 218-4242 or online at www.making-a-difference.com. Ms. Weinstein can be reached at sageworks@igc.org.

Both guides — along with many other excellent books for making a better world — are also available directly from New Society Publishers at (800) 567-6772 or www.newsociety.com.

If you have enjoyed *Making A Difference College & Graduate Guide*,
you might also enjoy other

## BOOKS TO BUILD A NEW SOCIETY

New Society Publishers' mission is to publish books that
contribute in fundamental ways to building an ecologically sustainable
and just society, and to do so with the least possible impact on the
environment, in a manner that models this vision.

Our books provide positive solutions for people
who want to make a difference.
We specialize in:

**Sustainable Living**

**Ecological Design and Planning**

**Environment and Justice**

**New Forestry**

**Conscientious Commerce**

**Resistance and Community**

**Nonviolence**

**The Feminist Transformation**

**Progressive Leadership**

**Educational and Parenting Resources**

For a full list of NSP's titles, please call 1-800-567-6772
or check out our web site at:
**www.newsociety.com**

## NEW SOCIETY PUBLISHERS